HONDA ACCORD/ 1984-95 REPAIR MANUAL

Covers all U.S. and Canadian models of Honda Accord and Prelude

by **Will Kessler,** A.S.E., S.A.E.

CHILTON *Automotive Books*

PUBLISHED BY **HAYNES NORTH AMERICA.** Inc.

Manufactured in USA
© 1995 Haynes North America, Inc.
ISBN 0-8019-8680-X
Library of Congress Catalog Card No. 92-069435
12 13 14 15 16 9876543210

Haynes Publishing Group
Sparkford Nr Yeovil
Somerset BA22 7JJ England

Haynes North America, Inc
861 Lawrence Drive
Newbury Park
California 91320 USA

ABCDE
FGHI

2

8E1

Contents

Contents

DRIVE TRAIN   **7**

SUSPENSION AND STEERING   **8**

BRAKES   **9**

BODY AND TRIM   **10**

GLOSSARY

MASTER INDEX

SAFETY NOTICE

Proper service and repair procedures are vital to the safe, reliable operation of all motor vehicles, as well as the personal safety of those performing repairs. This manual outlines procedures for servicing and repairing vehicles using safe, effective methods. The procedures contain many NOTES, CAUTIONS and WARNINGS which should be followed, along with standard procedures to eliminate the possibility of personal injury or improper service which could damage the vehicle or compromise its safety.

It is important to note that repair procedures and techniques, tools and parts for servicing motor vehicles, as well as the skill and experience of the individual performing the work vary widely. It is not possible to anticipate all of the conceivable ways or conditions under which vehicles may be serviced, or to provide cautions as to all possible hazards that may result. Standard and accepted safety precautions and equipment should be used when handling toxic or flammable fluids, and safety goggles or other protection should be used during cutting, grinding, chiseling, prying, or any other process that can cause material removal or projectiles.

Some procedures require the use of tools specially designed for a specific purpose. Before substituting another tool or procedure, you must be completely satisfied that neither your personal safety, nor the performance of the vehicle will be endangered.

Although information in this manual is based on industry sources and is complete as possible at the time of publication, the possibility exists that some car manufacturers made later changes which could not be included here. While striving for total accuracy, the authors or publishers cannot assume responsibility for any errors, changes or omissions that may occur in the compilation of this data.

PART NUMBERS

Part numbers listed in this reference are not recommendations by Haynes North America, Inc. for any product brand name. They are references that can be used with interchange manuals and aftermarket supplier catalogs to locate each brand supplier's discrete part number.

SPECIAL TOOLS

Special tools are recommended by the vehicle manufacturer to perform their specific job. Use has been kept to a minimum, but where absolutely necessary, they are referred to in the text by the part number of the tool manufacturer. These tools can be purchased, under the appropriate part number, from your local dealer or regional distributor, or an equivalent tool can be purchased locally from a tool supplier or parts outlet. Before substituting any tool for the one recommended, read the SAFETY NOTICE at the top of this page.

ACKNOWLEDGMENTS

The publisher expresses appreciation to Honda Motor Company for their generous assistance.

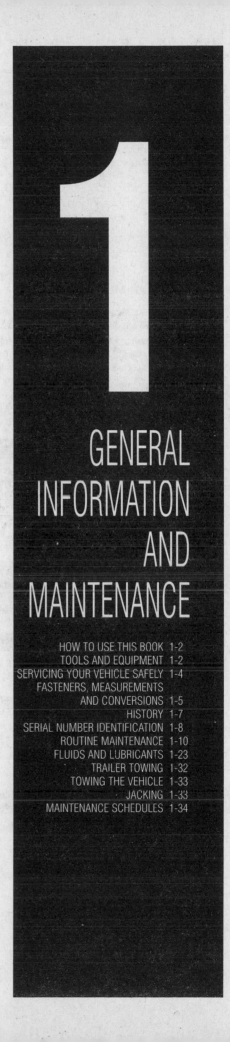

1

GENERAL INFORMATION AND MAINTENANCE

HOW TO USE THIS BOOK

This Chilton's Total Car Care manual for the 1984–95 Accord and Prelude is intended to help you learn more about the inner workings of your vehicle while saving you money on its upkeep and operation.

The beginning of the book will likely be referred to the most, since that is where you will find information for maintenance and tune-up. The other sections deal with the more complex systems of your vehicle. Systems (from engine through brakes) are covered to the extent that the average do-it-yourselfer can attempt. This book will not explain such things as rebuilding a differential because the expertise required and the special tools necessary make this uneconomical. It will, however, give you detailed instructions to help you change your own brake pads and shoes, replace spark plugs, and perform many more jobs that can save you money and help avoid expensive problems.

A secondary purpose of this book is a reference for owners who want to understand their vehicle and/or their mechanics better.

Where to Begin

Before removing any bolts, read through the entire procedure. This will give you the overall view of what tools and supplies will be required. So read ahead and plan ahead. Each operation should be approached logically and all procedures thoroughly understood before attempting any work.

If repair of a component is not considered practical, we tell you how to remove the part and then how to install the new or rebuilt replacement. In this way, you at least save labor costs.

Avoiding Trouble

Many procedures in this book require you to "label and disconnect . . ." a group of lines, hoses or wires. Don't be think you can remember where everything goes—you won't. If you hook up vacuum or fuel lines incorrectly, the vehicle may run poorly, if at all. If you hook up electrical wiring incorrectly, you may instantly learn a very expensive lesson.

You don't need to know the proper name for each hose or line. A piece of masking tape on the hose and a piece on its fitting will allow you to assign your own label. As long as you remember your own code, the lines can be reconnected by matching your tags. Remember that tape will dissolve in gasoline or solvents; if a part is to be washed or cleaned, use another method of identification. A permanent felt-tipped marker or a metal scribe can be very handy for marking metal parts. Remove any tape or paper labels after assembly.

Maintenance or Repair?

Maintenance includes routine inspections, adjustments, and replacement of parts which show signs of normal wear. Maintenance compensates for wear or deterioration. Repair implies that something has broken or is not working. A need for a repair is often caused by lack of maintenance. for example: draining and refilling automatic transmission fluid is maintenance recommended at specific intervals. Failure to do this can shorten the life of the transmission/transaxle, requiring very expensive repairs. While no maintenance program can prevent items from eventually breaking or wearing out, a general rule is true: MAINTENANCE IS CHEAPER THAN REPAIR.

Two basic mechanic's rules should be mentioned here. First, whenever the left side of the vehicle or engine is referred to, it means the driver's side. Conversely, the right side of the vehicle means the passenger's side. Second, screws and bolts are removed by turning counterclockwise, and tightened by turning clockwise unless specifically noted.

Safety is always the most important rule. Constantly be aware of the dangers involved in working on an automobile and take the proper precautions. Please refer to the information in this section regarding SERVICING YOUR VEHICLE SAFELY and the SAFETY NOTICE on the acknowledgment page.

Avoiding the Most Common Mistakes

Pay attention to the instructions provided. There are 3 common mistakes in mechanical work:

1. Incorrect order of assembly, disassembly or adjustment. When taking something apart or putting it together, performing steps in the wrong order usually just costs you extra time; however, it CAN break something. Read the entire procedure before beginning. Perform everything in the order in which the instructions say you should, even if you can't see a reason for it. When you're taking apart something that is very intricate, you might want to draw a picture of how it looks when assembled in order to make sure you get everything back in its proper position. When making adjustments, perform them in the proper order. One adjustment possibly will affect another.

2. Overtorquing (or undertorquing). While it is more common for overtorquing to cause damage, undertorquing may allow a fastener to vibrate loose causing serious damage. Especially when dealing with aluminum parts, pay attention to torque specifications and utilize a torque wrench in assembly. If a torque figure is not available, remember that if you are using the right tool to perform the job, you will probably not have to strain yourself to get a fastener tight enough. The pitch of most threads is so slight that the tension you put on the wrench will be multiplied many times in actual force on what you are tightening.

There are many commercial products available for ensuring that fasteners won't come loose, even if they are not torqued just right (a very common brand is Loctite®). If you're worried about getting something together tight enough to hold, but loose enough to avoid mechanical damage during assembly, one of these products might offer substantial insurance. Before choosing a threadlocking compound, read the label on the package and make sure the product is compatible with the materials, fluids, etc. involved.

3. Crossthreading. This occurs when a part such as a bolt is screwed into a nut or casting at the wrong angle and forced. Crossthreading is more likely to occur if access is difficult. It helps to clean and lubricate fasteners, then to start threading the bolt, spark plug, etc. with your fingers. If you encounter resistance, unscrew the part and start over again at a different angle until it can be inserted and turned several times without much effort. Keep in mind that many parts have tapered threads, so that gentle turning will automatically bring the part you're threading to the proper angle. Don't put a wrench on the part until it's been tightened a couple of turns by hand. If you suddenly encounter resistance, and the part has not seated fully, don't force it. Pull it back out to make sure it's clean and threading properly.

Be sure to take your time and be patient, and always plan ahead. Allow yourself ample time to perform repairs and maintenance.

TOOLS AND EQUIPMENT

▶ **See Figures 1 thru 15**

Without the proper tools and equipment it is impossible to properly service your vehicle. It would be virtually impossible to catalog every tool that you would need to perform all of the operations in this book. It would be unwise for the amateur to rush out and buy an expensive set of tools on the theory that he/she may need one or more of them at some time.

The best approach is to proceed slowly, gathering a good quality set of those tools that are used most frequently. Don't be misled by the low cost of bargain tools. It is far better to spend a little more for better quality. Forged wrenches, 6 or 12-point sockets and fine tooth ratchets are by far preferable to their less expensive counterparts. As any good mechanic can tell you, there are few worse experiences than trying to work on a vehicle with bad tools. Your monetary savings will be far outweighed by frustration and mangled knuckles.

Begin accumulating those tools that are used most frequently: those associated with routine maintenance and tune-up. In addition to the normal assortment of screwdrivers and pliers, you should have the following tools:

• Wrenches/sockets and combination open end/box end wrenches in sizes ⅛–¾ in. and/or 3mm–19mm ¹³⁄₁₆ in. or ⅝ in. spark plug socket (depending on plug type).

➡**If possible, buy various length socket drive extensions. Universal-joint and wobble extensions can be extremely useful, but be careful when using them, as they can change the amount of torque applied to the socket.**

• Jackstands for support.
• Oil filter wrench.

• Spout or funnel for pouring fluids.
• Grease gun for chassis lubrication (unless your vehicle is not equipped with any grease fittings)
• Hydrometer for checking the battery (unless equipped with a sealed, maintenance-free battery).
• A container for draining oil and other fluids.
• Rags for wiping up the inevitable mess.

In addition to the above items there are several others that are not absolutely necessary, but handy to have around. These include an equivalent oil absorbent gravel, like cat litter, and the usual supply of lubricants, antifreeze and fluids. This is a basic list for routine maintenance, but only your personal needs and desire can accurately determine your list of tools.

After performing a few projects on the vehicle, you'll be amazed at the other tools and non-tools on your workbench. Some useful household items are: a large turkey baster or siphon, empty coffee cans and ice trays (to store parts), a ball of twine, electrical tape for wiring, small rolls of colored tape for tagging lines or hoses, markers and pens, a note pad, golf tees (for plugging vacuum lines), metal coat hangers or a roll of mechanic's wire (to hold things out of the way), dental pick or similar long, pointed probe, a strong magnet, and a small mirror (to see into recesses and under manifolds).

A more advanced set of tools, suitable for tune-up work, can be drawn up easily. While the tools are slightly more sophisticated, they need not be outrageously expensive. There are several inexpensive tach/dwell meters on the market that are every bit as good for the average mechanic as a professional model. Just be sure that it goes to a least 1200–1500 rpm on the tach scale and that it works on 4, 6 and 8-cylinder engines. The key to these purchases is to make them with an eye towards adaptability and wide range. A basic list of tune-up tools could include:
• Tach/dwell meter.
• Spark plug wrench and gapping tool.
• Feeler gauges for valve adjustment.
• Timing light.

The choice of a timing light should be made carefully. A light which works on the DC current supplied by the vehicle's battery is the best choice; it should

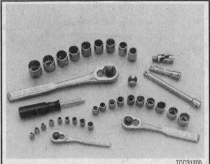

Fig. 1 All but the most basic procedures will require an assortment of ratchets and sockets

Fig. 2 In addition to ratchets, a good set of wrenches and hex keys will be necessary

Fig. 3 A hydraulic floor jack and a set of jackstands are essential for lifting and supporting the vehicle

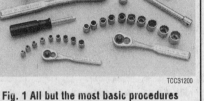

Fig. 4 An assortment of pliers, grippers and cutters will be handy for old rusted parts and stripped bolt heads

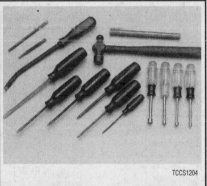

Fig. 5 Various drivers, chisels and prybars are great tools to have in your toolbox

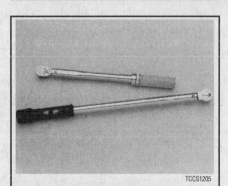

Fig. 6 Many repairs will require the use of a torque wrench to assure the components are properly fastened

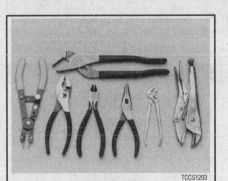

Fig. 7 Although not always necessary, using specialized brake tools will save time

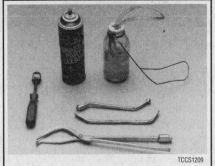

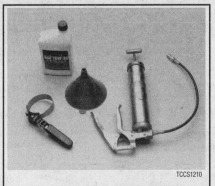

Fig. 8 A few inexpensive lubrication tools will make maintenance easier

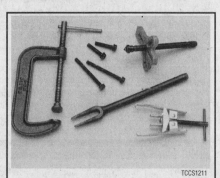

Fig. 9 Various pullers, clamps and separator tools are needed for many larger, more complicated repairs

Fig. 10 A variety of tools and gauges should be used for spark plug gapping and installation

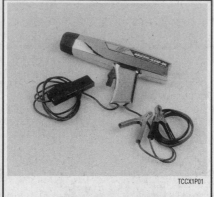

Fig. 11 Inductive type timing light

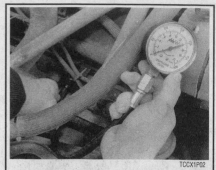

Fig. 12 A screw-in type compression gauge is recommended for compression testing

Fig. 13 A vacuum/pressure tester is necessary for many testing procedures

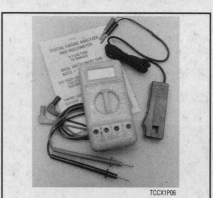

Fig. 14 Most modern automotive multimeters incorporate many helpful features

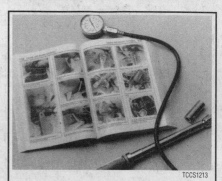

Fig. 15 Proper information is vital, so always have a Chilton Total Car Care manual handy

have a xenon tube for brightness. On any vehicle with an electronic ignition system, a timing light with an inductive pickup that clamps around the No. 1 spark plug cable is preferred.

In addition to these basic tools, there are several other tools and gauges you may find useful. These include:

• Compression gauge. The screw-in type is slower to use, but eliminates the possibility of a faulty reading due to escaping pressure.

• Manifold vacuum gauge.

• 12V test light.

• A combination volt/ohmmeter

• Induction Ammeter. This is used for determining whether or not there is current in a wire. These are handy for use if a wire is broken somewhere in a wiring harness.

As a final note, you will probably find a torque wrench necessary for all but the most basic work. The beam type models are perfectly adequate, although the newer click types (breakaway) are easier to use. The click type torque wrenches tend to be more expensive. Also keep in mind that all types of torque wrenches should be periodically checked and/or recalibrated. You will have to decide for yourself which better fits your pocketbook, and purpose.

Special Tools

Normally, the use of special factory tools is avoided for repair procedures, since these are not readily available for the do-it-yourself mechanic. When it is possible to perform the job with more commonly available tools, it will be pointed out, but occasionally, a special tool was designed to perform a specific function and should be used. Before substituting another tool, you should be convinced that neither your safety nor the performance of the vehicle will be compromised.

Special tools can usually be purchased from an automotive parts store or from your dealer. In some cases special tools may be available directly from the tool manufacturer.

SERVICING YOUR VEHICLE SAFELY

▶ See Figures 16, 17 and 18

It is virtually impossible to anticipate all of the hazards involved with automotive maintenance and service, but care and common sense will prevent most accidents.

The rules of safety for mechanics range from "don't smoke around gasoline," to "use the proper tool(s) for the job." The trick to avoiding injuries is to develop safe work habits and to take every possible precaution.

Do's

• Do keep a fire extinguisher and first aid kit handy.

• Do wear safety glasses or goggles when cutting, drilling, grinding or prying, even if you have 20–20 vision. If you wear glasses for the sake of vision, wear safety goggles over your regular glasses.

• Do shield your eyes whenever you work around the battery. Batteries contain sulfuric acid. In case of contact with, flush the area with water or a mixture of water and baking soda, then seek immediate medical attention.

• Do use safety stands (jackstands) for any undervehicle service. Jacks are for raising vehicles; jackstands are for making sure the vehicle stays raised until you want it to come down.

• Do use adequate ventilation when working with any chemicals or hazardous materials. Like carbon monoxide, the asbestos dust resulting from some brake lining wear can be hazardous in sufficient quantities.

• Do disconnect the negative battery cable when working on the electrical system. The secondary ignition system contains EXTREMELY HIGH VOLTAGE. In some cases it can even exceed 50,000 volts.

• Do follow manufacturer's directions whenever working with potentially hazardous materials. Most chemicals and fluids are poisonous.

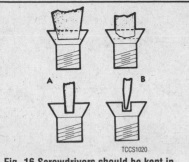

Fig. 16 Screwdrivers should be kept in good condition to prevent injury or damage which could result if the blade slips from the screw

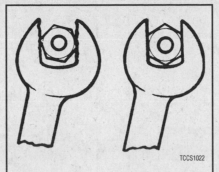

Fig. 17 Using the correct size wrench will help prevent the possibility of rounding off a nut

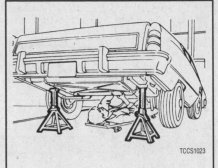

Fig. 18 NEVER work under a vehicle unless it is supported using safety stands (jackstands)

• Do properly maintain your tools. Loose hammerheads, mushroomed punches and chisels, frayed or poorly grounded electrical cords, excessively worn screwdrivers, spread wrenches (open end), cracked sockets, slipping ratchets, or faulty droplight sockets can cause accidents.

• Likewise, keep your tools clean; a greasy wrench can slip off a bolt head, ruining the bolt and often harming your knuckles in the process.

• Do use the proper size and type of tool for the job at hand. Do select a wrench or socket that fits the nut or bolt. The wrench or socket should sit straight, not cocked.

• Do, when possible, pull on a wrench handle rather than push on it, and adjust your stance to prevent a fall.

• Do be sure that adjustable wrenches are tightly closed on the nut or bolt and pulled so that the force is on the side of the fixed jaw.

• Do strike squarely with a hammer; avoid glancing blows.

• Do set the parking brake and block the drive wheels if the work requires a running engine.

Don'ts

• Don't run the engine in a garage or anywhere else without proper ventilation—EVER! Carbon monoxide is poisonous; it takes a long time to leave the human body and you can build up a deadly supply of it in your system by simply breathing in a little at a time. You may not realize you are slowly poisoning yourself. Always use power vents, windows, fans and/or open the garage door.

• Don't work around moving parts while wearing loose clothing. Short sleeves are much safer than long, loose sleeves. Hard-toed shoes with neoprene soles protect your toes and give a better grip on slippery surfaces. Watches and jewelry is not safe working around a vehicle. Long hair should be tied back under a hat or cap.

• Don't use pockets for toolboxes. A fall or bump can drive a screwdriver deep into your body. Even a rag hanging from your back pocket can wrap around a spinning shaft or fan.

• Don't smoke when working around gasoline, cleaning solvent or other flammable material.

• Don't smoke when working around the battery. When the battery is being charged, it gives off explosive hydrogen gas.

• Don't use gasoline to wash your hands; there are excellent soaps available. Gasoline contains dangerous additives which can enter the body through a cut or through your pores. Gasoline also removes all the natural oils from the skin so that bone dry hands will suck up oil and grease.

• Don't service the air conditioning system unless you are equipped with the necessary tools and training. When liquid or compressed gas refrigerant is released to atmospheric pressure it will absorb heat from whatever it contacts. This will chill or freeze anything it touches.

• Don't use screwdrivers for anything other than driving screws! A screwdriver used as a prying tool can snap when you least expect it, causing injuries. At the very least, you'll ruin a good screwdriver.

• Don't use an emergency jack (that little ratchet, scissors, or pantograph jack supplied with the vehicle) for anything other than changing a flat! These jacks are only intended for emergency use out on the road; they are NOT designed as a maintenance tool. If you are serious about maintaining your vehicle yourself, invest in a hydraulic floor jack of at least a 1½ ton capacity, and at least two sturdy jackstands.

FASTENERS, MEASUREMENTS AND CONVERSIONS

Bolts, Nuts and Other Threaded Retainers

▶ **See Figures 19 and 20**

Although there are a great variety of fasteners found in the modern car or truck, the most commonly used retainer is the threaded fastener (nuts, bolts, screws, studs, etc.). Most threaded retainers may be reused, provided that they are not damaged in use or during the repair. Some retainers (such as stretch bolts or torque prevailing nuts) are designed to deform when tightened or in use and should not be reinstalled.

Whenever possible, we will note any special retainers which should be replaced during a procedure. But you should always inspect the condition of a retainer when it is removed and replace any that show signs of damage. Check all threads for rust or corrosion which can increase the torque necessary to achieve the desired clamp load for which that fastener was originally selected. Additionally, be sure that the driver surface of the fastener has not been compromised by rounding or other damage. In some cases a driver surface may become only partially rounded, allowing the driver to catch in only one direction. In many of these occurrences, a fastener may be installed and tightened, but the driver would not be able to grip and loosen the fastener again.

If you must replace a fastener, whether due to design or damage, you must ALWAYS be sure to use the proper replacement. In all cases, a retainer of the

Fig. 19 There are many different types of threaded retainers found on vehicles

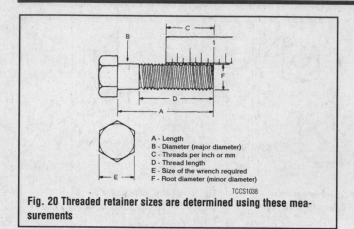

A - Length
B - Diameter (major diameter)
C - Threads per inch or mm
D - Thread length
E - Size of the wrench required
F - Root diameter (minor diameter)

TCCS1038

Fig. 20 Threaded retainer sizes are determined using these measurements

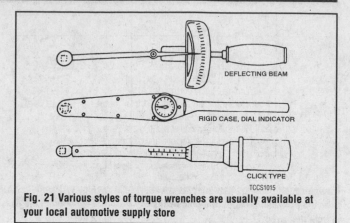

DEFLECTING BEAM

RIGID CASE, DIAL INDICATOR

CLICK TYPE

TCCS1015

Fig. 21 Various styles of torque wrenches are usually available at your local automotive supply store

same design, material and strength should be used. Markings on the heads of most bolts will help determine the proper strength of the fastener. The same material, thread and pitch must be selected to assure proper installation and safe operation of the vehicle afterwards.

Thread gauges are available to help measure a bolt or stud's thread. Most automotive and hardware stores keep gauges available to help you select the proper size. In a pinch, you can use another nut or bolt for a thread gauge. If the bolt you are replacing is not too badly damaged, you can select a match by finding another bolt which will thread in its place. If you find a nut which threads properly onto the damaged bolt, then use that nut to help select the replacement bolt.

❋❋ WARNING

Be aware that when you find a bolt with damaged threads, you may also find the nut or drilled hole it was threaded into has also been damaged. If this is the case, you may have to drill and tap the hole, replace the nut or otherwise repair the threads. NEVER try to force a replacement bolt to fit into the damaged threads.

Torque

Torque is defined as the measurement of resistance to turning or rotating. It tends to twist a body about an axis of rotation. A common example of this would be tightening a threaded retainer such as a nut, bolt or screw. Measuring torque is one of the most common ways to help assure that a threaded retainer has been properly fastened.

When tightening a threaded fastener, torque is applied in three distinct areas, the head, the bearing surface and the clamp load. About 50 percent of the measured torque is used in overcoming bearing friction. This is the friction between the bearing surface of the bolt head, screw head or nut face and the base material or washer (the surface on which the fastener is rotating). Approximately 40 percent of the applied torque is used in overcoming thread friction. This leaves only about 10 percent of the applied torque to develop a useful clamp load (the force which holds a joint together). This means that friction can account for as much as 90 percent of the applied torque on a fastener.

TORQUE WRENCHES

♦ See Figure 21

In most applications, a torque wrench can be used to assure proper installation of a fastener. Torque wrenches come in various designs and most automotive supply stores will carry a variety to suit your needs. A torque wrench should be used any time we supply a specific torque value for a fastener. Again, the general rule of "if you are using the right tool for the job, you should not have to strain to tighten a fastener" applies here.

Beam Type

The beam type torque wrench is one of the most popular types. It consists of a pointer attached to the head that runs the length of the flexible beam (shaft) to a scale located near the handle. As the wrench is pulled, the beam bends and the pointer indicates the torque using the scale.

Click (Breakaway) Type

Another popular design of torque wrench is the click type. To use the click type wrench you pre-adjust it to a torque setting. Once the torque is reached, the wrench has a reflex signaling feature that causes a momentary breakaway of the torque wrench body, sending an impulse to the operator's hand.

Pivot Head Type

♦ See Figure 22

Some torque wrenches (usually of the click type) may be equipped with a pivot head which can allow it to be used in areas of limited access. BUT, it must be used properly. To hold a pivot head wrench, grasp the handle lightly, and as you pull on the handle, it should be floated on the pivot point. If the handle comes in contact with the yoke extension during the process of pulling, there is a very good chance the torque readings will be inaccurate because this could alter the wrench loading point. The design of the handle is usually such as to make it inconvenient to deliberately misuse the wrench.

➡ It should be mentioned that the use of any U-joint, wobble or extension will have an effect on the torque readings, no matter what type of wrench you are using. For the most accurate readings, install the socket directly on the wrench driver. If necessary, straight extensions (which hold a socket directly under the wrench driver) will have the least effect on the torque reading. Avoid any extension that alters the length of the wrench from the handle to the head/driving point (such as a crow's foot). U-joint or wobble extensions can greatly affect the readings; avoid their use at all times.

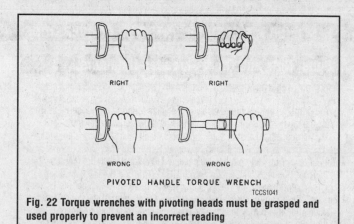

RIGHT

RIGHT

WRONG

WRONG

PIVOTED HANDLE TORQUE WRENCH

TCCS1041

Fig. 22 Torque wrenches with pivoting heads must be grasped and used properly to prevent an incorrect reading

Rigid Case (Direct Reading)

A rigid case or direct reading torque wrench is equipped with a dial indicator to show torque values. One advantage of these wrenches is that they can be held at any position on the wrench without affecting accuracy. These wrenches are often preferred because they tend to be compact, easy to read and have a great degree of accuracy.

TORQUE ANGLE METERS

Because the frictional characteristics of each fastener or threaded hole will vary, clamp loads which are based strictly on torque will vary as well. In most applications, this variance is not significant enough to cause worry. But, in certain applications, a manufacturer's engineers may determine that more precise clamp loads are necessary (such is the case with many aluminum cylinder heads). In these cases, a torque angle method of installation would be specified. When installing fasteners which are torque angle tightened, a predetermined seating torque and standard torque wrench are usually used first to remove any compliance from the joint. The fastener is then tightened the specified additional portion of a turn measured in degrees. A torque angle gauge (mechanical protractor) is used for these applications.

Standard and Metric Measurements

▶ **See Figure 23**

Throughout this manual, specifications are given to help you determine the condition of various components on your vehicle, or to assist you in their installation. Some of the most common measurements include length (in. or cm/mm), torque (ft. lbs., inch lbs. or Nm) and pressure (psi, in. Hg, kPa or mm Hg). In most cases, we strive to provide the proper measurement as determined by the manufacturer's engineers.

Though, in some cases, that value may not be conveniently measured with what is available in your toolbox. Luckily, many of the measuring devices which are available today will have two scales so the Standard or Metric measurements may easily be taken. If any of the various measuring tools which are available to you do not contain the same scale as listed in the specifications, use the accompanying conversion factors to determine the proper value.

The conversion factor chart is used by taking the given specification and multiplying it by the necessary conversion factor. For instance, looking at the first line, if you have a measurement in inches such as "free-play should be 2 in." but your ruler reads only in millimeters, multiply 2 in. by the conversion factor of 25.4 to get the metric equivalent of 50.8mm. Likewise, if the specification was given only in a Metric measurement, for example in Newton Meters (Nm), then look at the center column first. If the measurement is 100 Nm, multiply it by the conversion factor of 0.738 to get 73.8 ft. lbs.

CONVERSION FACTORS

LENGTH-DISTANCE

Inches (in.)	x 25.4	= Millimeters (mm)	x .0394	= Inches
Feet (ft.)	x .305	= Meters (m)	x 3.281	= Feet
Miles	x 1.609	= Kilometers (km)	x .0621	= Miles

VOLUME

Cubic Inches (in3)	x 16.387	= Cubic Centimeters	x .061	= in3
IMP Pints (IMP pt.)	x .568	= Liters (L)	x 1.76	= IMP pt.
IMP Quarts (IMP qt.)	x 1.137	= Liters (L)	x .88	= IMP qt.
IMP Gallons (IMP gal.)	x 4.546	= Liters (L)	x .22	= IMP gal.
IMP Quarts (IMP qt.)	x 1.201	= US Quarts (US qt.)	x .833	= IMP qt.
IMP Gallons (IMP gal.)	x 1.201	= US Gallons (US gal.)	x .833	= IMP gal.
Fl. Ounces	x 29.573	= Milliliters	x .034	= Ounces
US Pints (US pt.)	x .473	= Liters (L)	x 2.113	= Pints
US Quarts (US qt.)	x .946	= Liters (L)	x 1.057	= Quarts
US Gallons (US gal.)	x 3.785	= Liters (L)	x .264	= Gallons

MASS-WEIGHT

Ounces (oz.)	x 28.35	= Grams (g)	x .035	= Ounces
Pounds (lb.)	x .454	= Kilograms (kg)	x 2.205	= Pounds

PRESSURE

Pounds Per Sq. In. (psi)	x 6.895	= Kilopascals (kPa)	x .145	= psi
Inches of Mercury (Hg)	x .4912	= psi	x 2.036	= Hg
Inches of Mercury (Hg)	x 3.377	= Kilopascals (kPa)	x .2961	= Hg
Inches of Water (H₂O)	x .07355	= Inches of Mercury	x 13.783	= H₂O
Inches of Water (H₂O)	x .03613	= psi	x 27.684	= H₂O
Inches of Water (H₂O)	x .248	= Kilopascals (kPa)	x 4.026	= H₂O

TORQUE

Pounds-Force Inches (in-lb)	x .113	= Newton Meters (N·m)	x 8.85	= in-lb
Pounds-Force Feet (ft-lb)	x 1.356	= Newton Meters (N·m)	x .738	= ft-lb

VELOCITY

Miles Per Hour (MPH)	x 1.609	= Kilometers Per Hour (KPH)	x .621	= MPH

POWER

Horsepower (Hp)	x .745	= Kilowatts	x 1.34	= Horsepower

FUEL CONSUMPTION*

Miles Per Gallon IMP (MPG)	x .354	= Kilometers Per Liter (Km/L)	
Kilometers Per Liter (Km/L)	x 2.352	= IMP MPG	
Miles Per Gallon US (MPG)	x .425	= Kilometers Per Liter (Km/L)	
Kilometers Per Liter (Km/L)	x 2.352	= US MPG	

*It is common to covert from miles per gallon (mpg) to liters/100 kilometers (1/100 km), where mpg (IMP) x 1/100 km = 282 and mpg (US) x 1/100 km = 235.

TEMPERATURE

Degree Fahrenheit (°F)	= (°C x 1.8) + 32
Degree Celsius (°C)	= (°F − 32) x .56

TCCS1044

Fig. 23 Standard and metric conversion factors chart

HISTORY

In 1946, after the close of World War II, Soichiro Honda established his Technical Research Institute in Hamamatsu, Japan, to develop auxiliary gasoline engines for bicycles. The young company successfully marketed gasoline-engined bicycles and primitive motorcycles. Within 5 years, the company established a production record within the Japanese motorcycle industry by producing 130 units per day at its new Tokyo plant.

Through the 1950's and into the next decade, the company grew steadily, pioneering and refining many phases of motorcycle engineering and production, leading to the opening of a separate research and development center. Honda furthered its reputation by participating in many domestic and international motorcycle racing events. Additionally, the company adapted its small engine technology to non-road vehicle use by introducing engines for farm equipment, generators and marine use. Manufacturing and support facilities were established throughout Japan, Asia and Europe.

By August, 1963, Honda had produced a small utility truck powered by a 360cc engine. This was closely followed by a series of passenger coupes and sedans, all powered by engines well below 1 liter. As an adjunct to the automobile program, a Honda-powered Formula One (Grand Prix) car competed in the 1964–1968 seasons.

The 15 millionth motorcycle was produced in March, 1971. The CVCC engine was perfected in the same year and hailed as the first engine to meet the 1975 U.S Clean Air Act specifications. Honda won many awards for design, engineering and manufacturing as well as industrial pollution control and community betterment. Mr. Honda retired as president of the company in 1973 but remained as supreme advisor.

The first Honda passenger cars began appearing in North America in the early 1970's, lead by the 600 family and followed closely by the Civic, Honda's first water cooled vehicle. The year 1976 saw the introduction of the Accord, a larger, 5 passenger vehicle with the CVCC engine. The Accord was an immediate hit in North America. The company's success was bolstered by the begin-

ning of motorcycle manufacture in Marysville, Ohio in September, 1979. By 1980, Honda had produced 4,000,000 power products (generators, lawn mowers, etc.), 2 million Civics, and over 30 million motorcycles. The Prelude appeared as "an advanced engineering platform" in 1979.

Through the 1980's, Honda Motor Co. continued to grow and introduce new models and body styles. The year 1983 marked the beginning of automobile manufacture at the expanded Marysville plant. By August of the same year, the plant was producing 300 cars per day. Honda re-entered international Formula One racing, winning many events and manufacturer's championships with both Team Williams and Team McLaren. Engine manufacture was begun at Marysville in September of 1986.

Within 45 years of inception, Honda Motor Co. had established itself as a major manufacturer in the world market. The automotive products have been praised by owners, media, and competitors alike. By 1990, the Accord had established itself as the best selling car in the United States for several consecutive quarters.

Soichiro Honda died August 5th, 1991 at the age of 82. His company now has motorcycle or automobile manufacturing facilities in over 30 countries. The first Accord produced at the Ohio plant is on display at the Henry Ford Museum in Dearborn, Michigan.

This repair manual for Hondas covers the various model changes from 1984 through 1995. While the model names Accord and Prelude are familiar to almost everyone, several families exist within each model. The vehicles encompass carbureted and fuel injected engines as well as hatchback, coupe, sedan and wagon body styles. Trim and equipment levels further divide the families into subgroups such as DX, LX, Si, LXi, EX and Si4WS.

The Accord and Prelude have endured through several generations or body styles.

- Accord 1st generation: 1976–81
- Accord 2nd generation: 1982–85
- Accord 3rd generation: 1986–89

- Accord 4th generation: 1990–93
- Accord 5th generation: 1994–95
- Prelude 1st generation: 1979–82

- Prelude 2nd generation: 1983–87
- Prelude 3rd generation: 1988–91
- Prelude 4th generation: 1992–95

SERIAL NUMBER IDENTIFICATION

Vehicle Identification Number

▶ See Figures 24 and 25

All 1984–95 Honda vehicles have the Vehicle Identification Number (VIN) stamped on a plate mounted to the left side of the instrument panel. The plate is visible by looking through the windshield from the outside. The number is also stamped into the firewall at the rear of the engine compartment. Additionally, the vehicle identification number appears on a label, attached to the left front or rear (on 4-door models) door jamb.

Engine Number

▶ See Figure 24

The engine serial number is stamped into the right front side of the engine block. This number identifies the engine family, application and build sequence of the engine. The engine number should be used any time engine parts are purchased; many parts within engine families are unique to the family and not interchangeable with other engines.

For example, the engine number ES3–2900001 for a 1985 Accord, breaks down as follows:

- ES3: Engine family, fuel injected
- 2: Model year (1985)
- 9: Emission group, 49 state and high-altitude
- 00001: Serial number or production number

Meanings of numbers change from model to model and year to year. It isn't necessary to know what each digit means as long as the complete number is

Fig. 25 The VIN plate is visible through the windshield

available when buying parts. From 1987 on, engines use a 5 character family designation, such as B21A1 or A20A3.

In this book, when specific engines must be identified, we will use the family designation (all the characters before the dash in the engine number). In more general cases, we'll use the more everyday designations such as displacement and/or fuel and emission system. An example would refer to all fuel injected 2.0L engines or all 1.8L engines except California vehicles.

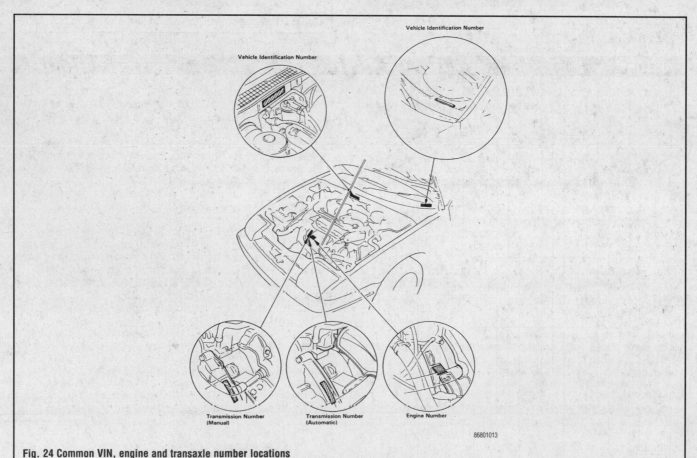

Fig. 24 Common VIN, engine and transaxle number locations

ENGINE IDENTIFICATION

Year	Model	Engine Displacement Liters (cc)	Engine Series (ID/VIN)	Fuel System	No. of Cylinders	Engine Type
1984	Accord	1.8 (1829)	ES2	3 bbl	4	SOHC 12-valve
	Prelude	1.8 (1829)	ES1	Dual Sidedraft	4	SOHC 12-valve
1985	Accord	1.8 (1829)	ES2	2 bbl	4	SOHC 12-valve
	Accord SE-i	1.8 (1829)	ES3	EFI	4	SOHC 12-valve
	Prelude	1.8 (1829)	ET2	Dual Sidedraft	4	SOHC 12-valve
1986	Accord	2.0 (1955)	BS	2 bbl	4	SOHC 12-valve
	Accord LXi	2.0 (1955)	BT	EFI	4	SOHC 12-valve
	Prelude	1.8 (1829)	ET2	Dual Sidedraft	4	SOHC 12-valve
1987	Accord	2.0 (1955)	A20A1	2 bbl	4	SOHC 12-valve
	Accord LX-i	2.0 (1955)	A20A3	EFI	4	SOHC 12-valve
	Prelude	1.8 (1829)	A18A1	Dual Sidedraft	4	SOHC 12-valve
1988	Accord, DX/LX	2.0 (1955)	A20A1	2 bbl	4	SOHC 12-valve
	Accord LX-i	2.0 (1955)	A20A3	EFI	4	SOHC 12-valve
	Prelude	2.0 (1955)	B20A3	Dual Sidedraft	4	SOHC 12-valve
	Prelude Si	2.0 (1955)	B20A5	MPFI	4	DOHC 16-valve
1989	Accord DX/LX	2.0 (1955)	A20A1	2 bbl	4	SOHC 12-valve
	Accord LX-i	2.0 (1955)	A20A3	EFI	4	SOHC 12-valve
	Prelude	2.0 (1955)	B20A3	Dual Sidedraft	4	SOHC 12-valve
	Prelude Si	2.0 (1955)	B20A5	MPFI	4	DOHC 16-valve
1990	Accord, DX/LX	2.2 (2156)	F22A1 [1]	MPFI	4	SOHC 16-valve
	Accord EX	2.2 (2156)	F22A4 [2]	MPFI	4	SOHC 16-valve
	Prelude S	2.0 (1955)	B20A3	Dual Sidedraft	4	SOHC 12-valve
	Prelude Si	2.1 (2056)	B21A1	MPFI	4	DOHC 16-valve
1991	Accord, DX/LX	2.2 (2156)	F22A1 [1]	MPFI	4	SOHC 16-valve
	Accord EX	2.2 (2156)	F22A4 [2]	MPFI	4	SOHC 16-valve
	Accord SE	2.2 (2156)	F22A6 [3]	MPFI	4	SOHC 16-valve
	Prelude Si	2.0 (1955)	B20A5	MPFI	4	DOHC 16-valve
	Prelude Si	2.1 (2056)	B21A1	MPFI	4	DOHC 16-valve
1992	Accord, DX/LX	2.2 (2156)	F22A1 [1]	MPFI	4	SOHC 16-valve
	Accord EX	2.2 (2156)	F22A4 [2]	MPFI	4	SOHC 16-valve
	Accord EX-R	2.2 (2156)	F22A6 [3]	MPFI	4	SOHC 16-valve
	Prelude S	2.2 (2156)	F22A1	MPFI	4	SOHC 16-valve
	Prelude Si	2.3 (2259)	H23A1	MPFI	4	DOHC 16-valve
1993	Accord DX/LX [4]	2.2 (2156)	F22A1	MPFI	4	SOHC 16-valve
	Accord EX/SE [5]	2.2 (2156)	F22A6	MPFI	4	SOHC 16-valve
	Prelude S	2.2 (2156)	F22A1	MPFI	4	SOHC 16-valve
	Prelude Si VTEC	2.2 (2157)	H22A1	MPFI	4	DOHC 16-valve
	Prelude Si [6]	2.3 (2259)	H23A1	MPFI	4	DOHC 16-valve

86801300

ENGINE IDENTIFICATION

Year	Model	Engine Displacement Liters (cc)	Engine Series (ID/VIN)	Fuel System	No. of Cylinders	Engine Type
1994	Accord EX [7]	2.2 (2156)	F22B1	MPFI	4	SOHC 16-valve
	Accord DX/LX [4]	2.2 (2156)	F22B2	MPFI	4	SOHC 16-valve
	Prelude S	2.2 (2156)	F22A1	MPFI	4	SOHC 16-valve
	Prelude Si VTEC	2.2 (2157)	H22A1	MPFI	4	DOHC 16-valve
	Prelude Si [6]	2.3 (2259)	H23A1	MPFI	4	DOHC 16-valve
1995	Accord EX [7]	2.2 (2156)	F22B1	MPFI	4	SOHC 16-valve
	Accord DX/LX [4]	2.2 (2156)	F22B2	MPFI	4	SOHC 16-valve
	Accord V-6	2.7 (2675)	C27A4	MPFI	6	SOHC 24-valve
	Prelude S	2.2 (2156)	F22A1	MPFI	4	SOHC 16-valve
	Prelude Si VTEC	2.2 (2157)	H22A1	MPFI	4	DOHC 16-valve
	Prelude Si [6]	2.3 (2259)	H23A1	MPFI	4	DOHC 16-valve

EFI- Electronic Fuel Injection
MPFI- Multi-port Fuel Injection
SOHC- Single Overhead Cam
DOHC- Dual Overhead Cam
1- Single exhaust manifold
2- Dual exhaust manifold
3- Dual intake manifold
4- Canadian models: LX/EX
5- Canadian models: EX-R/SE
6- Including 4WS
7- Canadian models: EX-R

86801301

Transaxle Serial Number

▶ See Figure 24

The transaxle serial number is located on the top of the transaxle/clutch case. As with the engine numbers, this number uniquely identifies the unit and its application. Besides the obvious difference of 4 and 5-speed manual transaxles and 3 or 4-speed automatics, the transaxles differ internally with regard to gear and final drive ratios as well as the presence of electronic controls.

ROUTINE MAINTENANCE

Air Cleaner

REMOVAL & INSTALLATION

▶ See Figures 26 thru 35

The air cleaner element must be replaced every 2 years or 30,000 miles (48,000 km), whichever occurs first. This is a maximum interval; the filter should be checked periodically and replaced when dirty or obstructed. The air filter element is one of the cheapest forms of insurance for the engine. Never operate the engine with the filter element removed or the filter housing lid removed.

When buying replacement parts in the aftermarket, compare the replacement unit to the old one. Check that the diameter and height are identical. Cheap, poorly made filters will not seal properly, allowing dust and road grit into the engine.

1. Unplug any electrical or vacuum connections on the air cleaner cover.
2. On 1994–95 4-cylinder Accords, remove the air cleaner duct by pulling it straight out. Now, loosen the screws from the battery set plate and push it away from the air cleaner.
3. Release the wing nut(s), bolts and/or spring clips from the air cleaner cover. Some Preludes use a canister type filter; the lid is retained with bolts.
4. Remove the air cleaner cover and the air cleaner element.
5. Using a damp, clean rag, wipe the inside of the air cleaner housing.

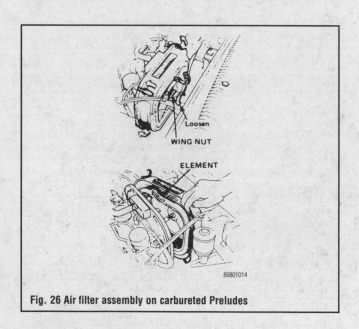

Fig. 26 Air filter assembly on carbureted Preludes

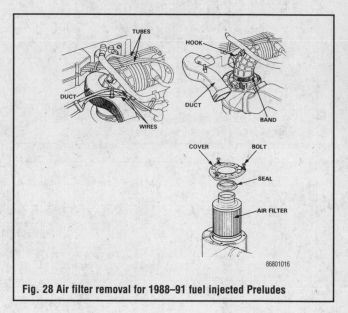

Fig. 28 Air filter removal for 1988–91 fuel injected Preludes

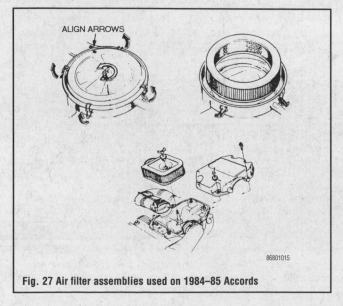

Fig. 27 Air filter assemblies used on 1984–85 Accords

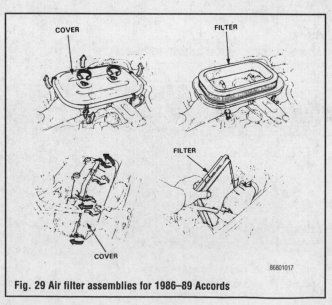

Fig. 29 Air filter assemblies for 1986–89 Accords

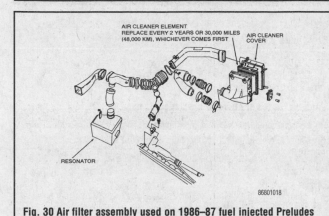

Fig. 30 Air filter assembly used on 1986–87 fuel injected Preludes

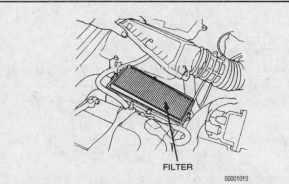

Fig. 31 Air filter removal for 1990–95 Accords. On 1994–95 4-cylinder models, it will be necessary to remove the air duct first

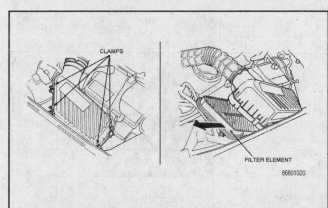

Fig. 32 Air filter removal for 1992–95 Preludes

To install:

6. Install a new air cleaner element. Make absolutely certain the air filter element is properly seated; the lid will mate to the filter, sealing the housing and forcing all intake air through the filter.

➥**Air cleaner elements are not interchangeable, although they may appear to be. Make sure you have the proper element for the year and model.**

7. Fit the lid or cover onto the housing. Many round housings have arrows stamped into the metal; align the arrows before attempting to install the lid. Correct alignment insures a tight seal.

8. Install the nuts/bolts or engage the spring clips. On 1994–95 4-cylinder Accords, install the battery set plate and air duct.

9. Connect any electrical or vacuum connections as necessary.

Fuel Filter

All vehicles use disposable type fuel filter(s) which cannot be disassembled for cleaning. On Accords through 1994 and all Prelude models, the filter must be replaced every 4 years or 60,000 miles (96,000 km), whichever occurs first. Earlier replacement is necessary whenever restricted fuel flow is suspected. On 1995 Accords, the filter is replaced when fuel pressure is below specification, or if fuel system contamination is suspected.

Honda also recommends that all fuel hoses and lines be inspected at 60,000 mile (96,000 km) intervals. Replace any hoses which may be hard, cracking, brittle or swollen. Replace any lines with signs of corrosion or damage.

✻✻ CAUTION

Fuel injected systems operate at high fuel pressures and maintain the pressure in the lines when the engine is OFF. The pressure must be safely released before any work is performed on fuel lines or fuel system components. Failure to relieve the fuel pressure may result in fire, personal injury and/or property damage. Carbureted vehicles may also hold some residual pressure in the tank and lines. Always remove the filler cap before performing any work on the fuel lines or fuel system components. Always release pressure slowly and contain spillage. Observe "no smoking/no open flame" precautions. Have a Class B-C (dry powder) fire extinguisher within arm's reach at all times.

RELIEVING FUEL PRESSURE

Carbureted Vehicles

On carbureted vehicles, it is recommended that the fuel filler cap be removed to vent any excess pressure in the system. Make sure the ignition key is in the **OFF** position, as these vehicles utilize an electric fuel pump which is energized when the ignition is **ON**. Remember to install the fuel filler cap after the necessary service procedures have been performed.

Fig. 33 The air cleaner cover is usually secured by wing nuts . . .

Fig. 34 . . . and a series of clamps

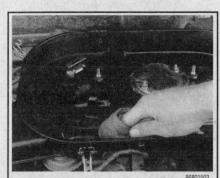

Fig. 35 After removing the air cleaner element, wipe the inside of the housing with a rag

Fuel Injected Vehicles

▶ See Figure 36

1. Disconnect the negative battery cable.
2. Remove the fuel filler cap.
3. On Accords through 1989, Preludes through 1991 and the 1995 V-6 Accord, the pressure release point is at the top of the fuel filter. On other models, the pressure release point is on the fuel rail. Look at the banjo bolt on the fuel filter or rail, as applicable. On top of this bolt is a smaller bolt; this is called the service bolt. Use an open end wrench to hold the banjo bolt and fit a 6mm closed (box end) wrench to the service bolt.

➡ **On some models, the service bolt may be covered by a plastic cap, remove this first.**

4. Place a cloth over the service bolt. Slowly loosen the service bolt one full turn. Fuel will escape the system into the cloth, releasing the system pressure. The cloth is now a flammable item; treat it carefully and dispose of it properly.
5. When the service procedures have been completed, tighten the service bolt to 9 ft. lbs. (12 Nm). Be sure to replace the washers.

➡ **Although the system pressure is now much below normal, always wrap fuel line connections in a cloth before disconnecting them; some pressure differential may still remain in the system.**

REMOVAL & INSTALLATION

Carbureted Engines

These vehicles use two replaceable fuel filters. A small one is in the fuel line under the hood; a larger one is located at the rear, just inboard of the left rear wheel.

Whenever the filter(s) are replaced, take great care to avoid the entry of dirt into the lines. Also, pay attention to the correct installation position. It is possible to install the filter backwards.

FRONT

▶ See Figure 37

1. If applicable, disengage the filter or hose from its retaining clip.
2. Using two fuel line clamps, pinch off both fuel lines. Take care not to crush the lines; just clamp them shut.

➡ **If the fuel hoses are hard or cracked, it is necessary to replace them.**

3. Loosen the fuel line clamps and slide them back.
4. Using a twisting motion, remove the fuel lines from the filter.
5. To install, use a new fuel filter and reverse the removal procedures. Start the engine and check for leaks. Correct any leaks immediately.

REAR

▶ See Figures 38, 39, 40 and 41

1. Raise and safely support the rear of the vehicle. Remove the left rear wheel.
2. Remove the bolts securing the filter and its basket to the fuel tank.
3. Push the fuel filter retaining tab and release it from the basket.
4. Using two fuel line clamps, pinch off both fuel lines. Take care not to crush the lines; just clamp them shut.

➡ **If the fuel hoses are hard or cracked, it is necessary to replace them.**

5. Loosen the fuel line clamps and slide them back.
6. Using a twisting motion, pull the fuel lines from the fuel filter; remove the filter.

To install:

7. Use a new filter and reverse the removal procedures.
8. Make certain the retaining tabs are engaged when the filter is installed in the holder. Tighten the bolts until snug.
9. Install the left rear wheel. Lower the car to the ground.
10. Start the engine and check for leaks. Correct any leaks immediately.

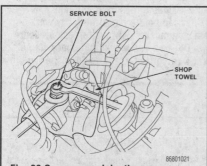

Fig. 36 On some models, the pressure release point is on the fuel rail (shown). On others, it is threaded into the banjo bolt on top of the fuel filter

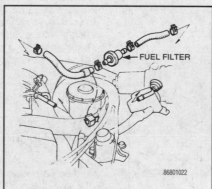

Fig. 37 Front fuel filter used on carbureted engines

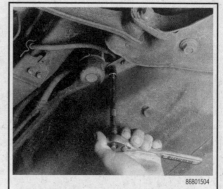

Fig. 38 Remove the bolts securing the filter and its basket to the fuel tank . . .

Fig. 39 . . . then release the basket from the filter

Fig. 40 Clamp the fuel lines shut. If the lines are hard, cracked or brittle, they must be replaced

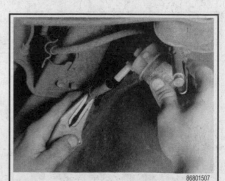

Fig. 41 After sliding the retaining clamps back, the filter can be removed from the lines

Fuel Injected Engines

▶ **See Figures 42 thru 47**

The canister fuel filter is located in the engine compartment. When buying the new filter, also buy new washers for the banjo bolts and the service bolt.

Failure to replace these washers invites high-pressure fuel leaks. Replacing the washers is required, not recommended.

1. Disconnect the negative battery terminal.
2. The fuel system is under pressure. Release pressure slowly and contain spillage. Observe "no smoking/no open flame" precautions. Have a Class B-C (dry powder) fire extinguisher within arm's reach at all times.

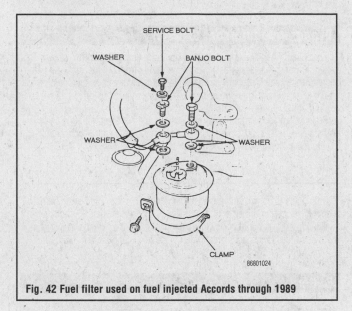

Fig. 42 Fuel filter used on fuel injected Accords through 1989

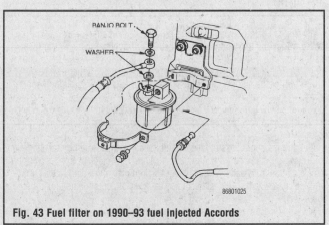

Fig. 43 Fuel filter on 1990–93 fuel injected Accords

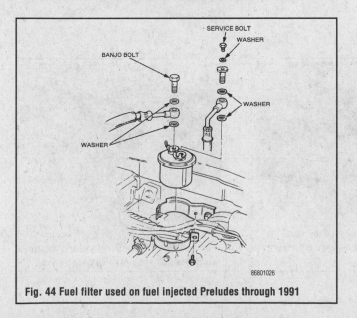

Fig. 44 Fuel filter used on fuel injected Preludes through 1991

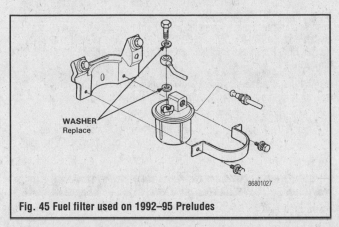

Fig. 45 Fuel filter used on 1992–95 Preludes

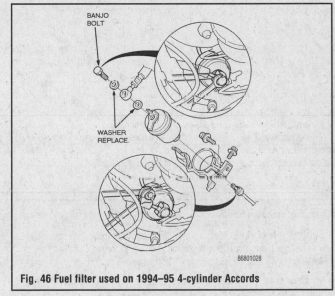

Fig. 46 Fuel filter used on 1994–95 4-cylinder Accords

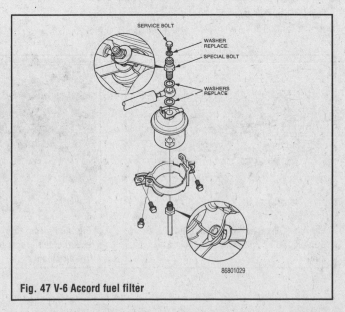

Fig. 47 V-6 Accord fuel filter

3. Disconnect the banjo bolts and/or threaded fuel line fitting from the fuel filter. Use of a flare nut or line wrench is recommended for disconnecting and attaching this fitting.

4. Loosen the fuel filter clamp bolt, then remove the filter.

To install:

5. Install the new filter and secure the clamp bolt.

6. The upper and lower washers on each banjo bolt and the washer on the service bolt MUST be replaced whenever the bolts are loosened. Install the washers and banjo bolts. Tighten the banjo bolts to 16 ft. lbs. (22 Nm) on all models except 1992–95 Preludes. On these models, tighten the bolt to 20 ft. lbs. (28 Nm). If applicable, tighten the threaded fuel line fitting to 27 ft. lbs. (37 Nm).

➡It will be necessary to use a crow's foot attachment on a torque wrench to properly tighten the threaded fuel line fitting.

7. Tighten the service bolt to 9 ft. lbs. (12 Nm).

8. Start the engine and check for leaks. The engine may crank longer than normal until full fuel pressure is developed. Correct any leaks immediately.

Positive Crankcase Ventilation (PCV) Valve

♦ **See Figure 48**

The engine is equipped with a Positive Crankcase Ventilation (PCV) system in which blow-by gas is returned to the combustion chamber through the intake manifold and/or the air cleaner. Blow-by gas is the portion of the normal combustion gasses that get by the piston rings and pressurize the lower part of the engine. If not vented, these gasses will eventually force their way through gaskets at the top or bottom of the engine, causing improper running and/or fluid leaks.

The PCV system captures these gasses and routes them back into the engine where they can be reburned. The PCV valve controls the flow into the engine. If the valve sticks closed, excess pressure can build in the engine. If it sticks open, too much gas may be admitted to the engine, causing a rich mixture, black exhaust smoke and generally poor driveability.

The function of the PCV valve should be checked every 60,000 miles (96,000 km) or whenever an emission-related problem is being diagnosed. As long as the valve is functioning properly, it does not need replacement.

TESTING

♦ **See Figures 49 and 50**

Inspect the hoses for cracks, leaks or clogging. With the engine running at warm idle, use fingers or pliers to gently pinch the PCV hose running to the valve. You shoud hear the valve click when the hose is pinched.

➡On some models, it will be necessary to remove the air cleaner support brace to access the PCV valve.

If no clicking is heard, inspect the rubber grommet around the valve for cracks or damage. If the grommet is good, replace the valve.

REMOVAL & INSTALLATION

To remove the valve, disconnect the hose and pull the valve from the grommet. Install the new valve and connect the hose. Attempting to clean the valve is not recommended; always replace it. Install the new valve firmly into the grommet. Connect and secure the hose.

Evaporative Charcoal Canister

The charcoal canister is part of the evaporative emission control system. This system prevents the escape of raw gasoline vapors from the fuel tank and carburetor. The activated charcoal element within the canister acts as a storage device for the fuel vapors at times when engine operating conditions do not allow burning of the vapors.

Periodic replacement of the canister is not required, however, if the charcoal element is saturated (possibly from engine flooding), the entire canister will require replacement.

SERVICING

On models through 1992, the hoses should be inspected and a careful operational check be performed at 60,000 miles (96,000 km). On 1993 and later models, there is no maintenance interval recommended by Honda. However, it is still a good idea to inspect the condition of the hoses at 60,000 mile (96,000 km) intervals. See Section 4 for testing procedures.

Battery

PRECAUTIONS

Always use caution when working on or near the battery. Never allow a tool to bridge the gap between the negative and positive battery terminals. Also, be careful not to allow a tool to provide a ground between the positive cable/terminal and any metal component on the vehicle. Either of these conditions will cause a short circuit, leading to sparks and possible personal injury.

Do not smoke or all open flames/sparks near a battery; the gases contained in the battery are very explosive and, if ignited, could cause severe injury or death.

All batteries, regardless of type, should be carefully secured by a battery hold-down device. If not, the terminals or casing may crack from stress during vehicle operation. A battery which is not secured may allow acid to leak, making it discharge faster. The acid can also eat away at components under the hood.

Always inspect the battery case for cracks, leakage and corrosion. A white corrosive substance on the battery case or on nearby components would indicate a leaking or cracked battery. If the battery is cracked, it should be replaced immediately.

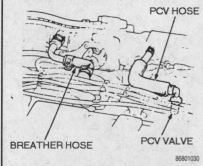

Fig. 48 PCV valve and breather hose location on 1989 Preludes. All models are similar

Fig. 49 If necessary, remove the nuts securing the brace, then remove it from the air cleaner

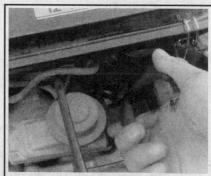

Fig. 50 Using your fingers or pliers, gently pinch the PCV hose running to the valve

GENERAL MAINTENANCE

Always keep the battery cables and terminals free of corrosion. Check and clean these components about once a year.

Keep the top of the battery clean, as a film of dirt can help discharge a battery that is not used for long periods. A solution of baking soda and water may be used for cleaning, but be careful to flush this off with clear water. DO NOT let any of the solution into the filler holes. Baking soda neutralizes battery acid and will de-activate a battery cell.

Batteries in vehicles which are not operated on a regular basis can fall victim to parasitic loads (small current drains which are constantly drawing current from the battery). Normal parasitic loads may drain a battery on a vehicle that is in storage and not used for 6–8 weeks. Vehicles that have additional accessories such as a phone or an alarm system may discharge a battery sooner. If the vehicle is to be stored for longer periods in a secure area and the alarm system is not necessary, the negative battery cable should be disconnected to protect the battery.

Remember that constantly deep cycling a battery (completely discharging and recharging it) will shorten battery life.

BATTERY FLUID

♦ See Figure 51

Check the battery electrolyte level at least once a month, or more often in hot weather or during periods of extended vehicle operation. On non-sealed batteries, the level can be checked either through the case (if translucent) or by removing the cell caps. The electrolyte level in each cell should be kept filled to the split ring inside each cell, or the line marked on the outside of the case.

If the level is low, add only distilled water through the opening until the level is correct. Each cell must be checked and filled individually. Distilled water should be used, because the chemicals and minerals found in most drinking water are harmful to the battery and could significantly shorten its life.

If water is added in freezing weather, the vehicle should be driven several miles to allow the water to mix with the electrolyte. Otherwise, the battery could freeze.

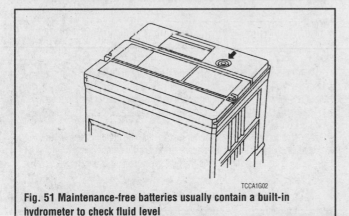

TCCA1G02

Fig. 51 Maintenance-free batteries usually contain a built-in hydrometer to check fluid level

Although some maintenance-free batteries have removable cell caps, the electrolyte condition and level on all sealed maintenance-free batteries must be checked using the built-in hydrometer "eye." The exact type of eye will vary. But, most battery manufacturers, apply a sticker to the battery itself explaining the readings.

➡**Although the readings from built-in hydrometers will vary, a green eye usually indicates a properly charged battery with sufficient fluid level. A dark eye is normally an indicator of a battery with sufficient fluid, but which is low in charge. A light or yellow eye usually indicates that electrolyte has dropped below the necessary level. In this last case, sealed batteries with an insufficient electrolyte must usually be discarded.**

Checking the Specific Gravity

♦ See Figures 52, 53 and 54

A hydrometer is required to check the specific gravity on all batteries that are not maintenance-free. On batteries that are maintenance-free, the specific gravity is checked by observing the built-in hydrometer "eye" on the top of the battery case.

✳✳ CAUTION

Battery electrolyte contains sulfuric acid. If you should splash any on your skin or in your eyes, flush the affected area with plenty of clear water. If it lands in your eyes, get medical help immediately.

The fluid (sulfuric acid solution) contained in the battery cells will tell you many things about the condition of the battery. Because the cell plates must be kept submerged below the fluid level in order to operate, the fluid level is extremely important. And, because the specific gravity of the acid is an indication of electrical charge, testing the fluid can be an aid in determining if the battery must be replaced. A battery in a vehicle with a properly operating charging system should require little maintenance, but careful, periodic inspection should reveal problems before they leave you stranded.

At least once a year, check the specific gravity of the battery. It should be between 1.20 and 1.26 on the gravity scale. Most auto stores carry a variety of inexpensive battery hydrometers. These can be used on any non-sealed battery to test the specific gravity in each cell.

The battery testing hydrometer has a squeeze bulb at one end and a nozzle at the other. Battery electrolyte is sucked into the hydrometer until the float is lifted from its seat. The specific gravity is then read by noting the position of the float. If gravity is low in one or more cells, the battery should be slowly charged and checked again to see if the gravity has come up. Generally, if after charging, the specific gravity between any two cells varies more than 50 points (0.50), the battery should be replaced, as it can no longer produce sufficient voltage to guarantee proper operation.

CABLES

♦ See Figures 55, 56, 57 and 58

Once a year (or as necessary), the battery terminals and the cable clamps should be cleaned. Loosen the clamps and remove the cables, negative cable

TCCA1P07

Fig. 52 On non-sealed batteries, the fluid level can be checked by removing the cell caps

TCCA1P08

Fig. 53 If the fluid level is low, add only distilled water until the level is correct

TCCA1P09

Fig. 54 Check the specific gravity of the battery's electrolyte with a hydrometer

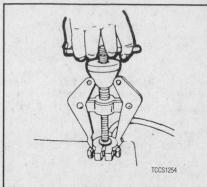

Fig. 55 A special tool is available to pull the clamp from the post

Fig. 56 The underside of this special battery tool has a wire brush to clean post terminals

Fig. 57 Place the tool over the battery posts and twist to clean until the metal is shiny

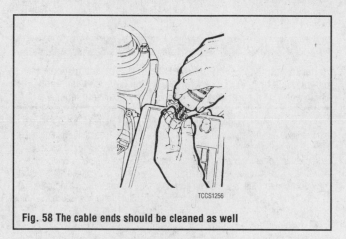

Fig. 58 The cable ends should be cleaned as well

first. On top post batteries, the use of a puller specially made for this purpose is recommended. These are inexpensive and available in most parts stores. Side terminal battery cables are secured with a small bolt.

Clean the cable clamps and the battery terminal with a wire brush, until all corrosion, grease, etc., is removed and the metal is shiny. It is especially important to clean the inside of the clamp thoroughly (an old knife is useful here), since a small deposit of oxidation there will prevent a sound connection and inhibit starting or charging. Special tools are available for cleaning these parts, one type for conventional top post batteries and another type for side terminal batteries. It is also a good idea to apply some dielectric grease to the terminal, as this will aid in the prevention of corrosion.

After the clamps and terminals are clean, reinstall the cables, negative cable last; DO NOT hammer the clamps onto battery posts. Tighten the clamps securely, but do not distort them. Give the clamps and terminals a thin external coating of grease after installation, to retard corrosion.

Check the cables at the same time that the terminals are cleaned. If the cable insulation is cracked or broken, or if the ends are frayed, the cable should be replaced with a new cable of the same length and gauge.

CHARGING

✳✳ CAUTION

The chemical reaction which takes place in all batteries generates explosive hydrogen gas. A spark can cause the battery to explode and splash acid. To avoid personal injury, be sure there is proper ventilation and take appropriate fire safety precautions when working with or near a battery.

A battery should be charged at a slow rate to keep the plates inside from getting too hot. However, if some maintenance-free batteries are allowed to discharge until they are almost "dead," they may have to be charged at a high rate to bring them back to "life." Always follow the charger manufacturer's instructions on charging the battery.

REPLACEMENT

When it becomes necessary to replace the battery, select one with an amperage rating equal to or greater than the battery originally installed. Deterioration and just plain aging of the battery cables, starter motor, and associated wires makes the battery's job harder in successive years. This makes it prudent to install a new battery with a greater capacity than the old.

Belts

INSPECTION

▶ **See Figures 59, 60, 61, 62 and 63**

On Accord and Prelude models, inspect the drive belt(s) every at least every 2 years or 30,000 miles (48,000 km). Determine the belt tension at a point

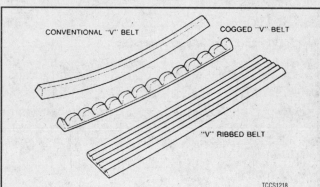

Fig. 59 There are typically 3 types of accessory drive belts found on vehicles today

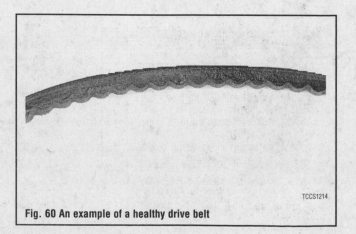

Fig. 60 An example of a healthy drive belt

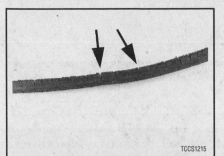

Fig. 61 Deep cracks in this belt will cause flex, building up heat that will eventually lead to belt failure

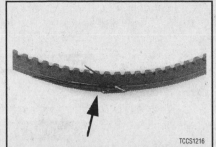

Fig. 62 The cover of this belt is worn, exposing the critical reinforcing cords to excessive wear

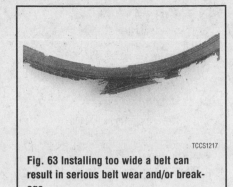

Fig. 63 Installing too wide a belt can result in serious belt wear and/or breakage

halfway between the pulleys by pressing on the belt with moderate thumb pressure. The belt should deflect about ¼ in. (6mm) over a 7–10 in. (178mm) span or ½ in. (13mm) over a 13–16 in. (330–406mm) span. If the deflection is found too much or too little, perform the tension adjustments.

Before adjusting, inspect the belt to see that it is not cracked or worn. Be sure that its surfaces are free of grease and oil. A glazed belt will be perfectly smooth and shiny from slippage; a belt in good condition will have a slight texture of fabric visible on the faces. Cracks will generally start at the inner edge of the belt and run outward. Replace the belt at the first sign of cracking or if the glazing is severe.

➡When adjusting the belt, do not attempt the tightest possible adjustment by levering the component until the belt is rigid. The extreme tension of the belt will cause premature wear on the driven component. A belt adjusted to the correct amount of deflection will be loose enough to drive the component without noisy operation.

ADJUSTING TENSION

♦ See Figure 64

Alternator

1984–85 ACCORD AND 1984–87 PRELUDE

1. Loosen the alternator adjusting bolt and mounting nut.
2. Carefully pry on the alternator until the proper belt tension is reached, then tighten the bolt and nut. Recheck the tension and readjust as required.
3. Tighten the adjusting bolt to 17 ft. lbs. (24 Nm) and the mounting nut to 33 ft. lbs. (45 Nm).
4. Start the engine and allow it to run for several minutes. Recheck the belt tension and readjust as required.

1986–89 ACCORD

1. Loosen the alternator adjusting nut, mounting nut and bolt.
2. Turn the adjusting nut until the proper belt tension is reached. Recheck the tension and readjust as required.
3. Tighten the mounting bolt to 18 ft. lbs. (26 Nm) and the mounting nut to 33 ft. lbs. (45 Nm).
4. Start the engine and allow it to run for several minutes. Recheck the belt tension and readjust as required.

1990–93 ACCORD AND 1988–91 PRELUDE

1. Loosen the alternator mounting nut/bolt and through-bolts.
2. Turn the adjusting nut until the proper belt tension is reached. Recheck the tension and readjust as required.
3. Tighten the mounting nut/bolt to 18 ft. lbs. (26 Nm) and the through-bolts to 33 ft. lbs. (45 Nm).
4. Start the engine and allow it to run for several minutes. Recheck the belt tension and readjust as required.

1994–95 ACCORD AND 1992–95 PRELUDE

1. Loosen the adjustment bolt locknut and the through-bolt(s). On the Accord, also loosen the mounting nut.

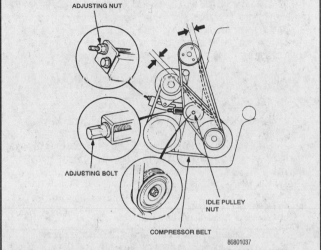

Fig. 64 Examples of adjusting nuts and bolts. A 1989 Prelude is shown, others are similar although location may vary

2. Turn the adjusting bolt until the proper belt tension is reached. Recheck the tension and readjust as required.
3. Tighten the adjustment bolt locknut to 16 ft. lbs. (22 Nm) and the through-bolt(s) to 33 ft. lbs. (45 Nm). On the Accord, tighten the mounting nut to 18 ft. lbs. (26 Nm).
4. Start the engine and allow it to run for several minutes. Recheck the belt tension and readjust as required.

Power Steering

1984–89 ACCORD AND 1984–87 PRELUDE

1. Loosen the pump pivot bolt and adjusting nut.
2. Carefully pry on the power steering pump until the proper belt tension is reached, then tighten the adjusting nut. Recheck the tension and readjust as required.
3. On 1984–85 Accord and Prelude, tighten the pivot bolt to 32 ft. lbs. (45 Nm) and the adjusting nut to 20 ft. lbs. (27 Nm). On 1986–89 Accord, tighten the pivot bolt to 28 ft. lbs. (39 Nm) and the adjusting nut to 16 ft. lbs. (22 Nm). On 1986–87 Prelude, tighten both the pivot bolt and the adjusting nut to 28 ft. lbs. (39 Nm).
4. Start the engine and turn the wheel lock-to-lock several times. Recheck the belt tension and readjust as required.

1990–93 ACCORD

1. Loosen the pump through-bolt and nut.
2. Turn the adjusting bolt until the desired tension is reached.
3. Tighten the through-bolt to 33 ft. lbs. (45 Nm) and the nut to 16 ft. lbs. (22 Nm).
4. Start the engine and turn the wheel lock-to-lock several times. Recheck the belt tension and readjust as required.

1988–91 PRELUDE

1. Loosen the pump idler pulley bolt.
2. Turn the adjusting bolt until the desired tension is reached.
3. Tighten the pulley bolt to 35 ft. lbs. (49 Nm).
4. Start the engine and turn the wheel lock-to-lock several times. Recheck the belt tension and readjust as required.

1994–95 ACCORD

1. Loosen the pump mounting nuts.
2. Turn the adjusting bolt until the desired tension is reached.
3. Tighten the mounting nuts to 17 ft. lbs. (24 Nm).
4. Start the engine and turn the wheel lock-to-lock several times. Recheck the belt tension and readjust as required.

1992–95 PRELUDE

1. Loosen the pump mounting nuts, bolt and adjusting bolt locknut.
2. Turn the adjusting bolt until the desired tension is reached. Tighten the locknut to 11 ft. lbs. (15 Nm).
3. Tighten the mounting nuts and bolt to 16 ft. lbs. (22 Nm).
4. Start the engine and turn the wheel lock-to-lock several times. Recheck the belt tension and readjust as required.

Air Conditioning

1984–85 ACCORD AND 1984–87 PRELUDE

1. On Honda/Keihin type compressors, adjust as follows:
    a. Loosen the pump pivot bolt and adjusting bolt.
    b. Carefully pry on the A/C compressor until the proper belt tension is reached, then tighten the adjusting bolt. Recheck the tension and readjust as required.
    c. Tighten the pivot bolts to 34 ft. lbs. (47 Nm) and the adjusting bolt to 31 ft. lbs. (43 Nm).
2. On Nippodenso type compressors:
    a. Loosen the pivot bolts and the adjustment lockbolt.
    b. Turn the adjusting bolt until the desired tension is reached. Tighten the lockbolt and pivot bolts to 34 ft. lbs. (47 Nm).
3. Start the engine and allow it to run for several minutes. Recheck the belt tension and readjust as required.

1986–89 ACCORD

1. On some models, loosen the adjustment nut locknut.
2. Turn the adjusting nut until the desired tension is reached. Tighten the locknut until snug.
3. Start the engine and allow it to run for several minutes. Recheck the belt tension and readjust as required.

1990–95 ACCORD AND 1988–95 PRELUDE

On these models, the air conditioning compressor is driven by the same belt as the alternator. Refer the alternator belt tensioning procedures.

REMOVAL & INSTALLATION

When buying replacement belts, remember that the fit is critical according to the length of the belt (diameter), the width of the belt, the depth of the belt and the angle or profile of the V-shape. The belt shape should exactly match the shape of the pulley; belts that are not an exact match can cause noise, slippage and premature failure.

If a belt must be replaced, first loosen the adjuster if one is present. The driven unit may also need to be loosened or moved towards the engine to allow removal of the belt. After removing the old belt, check the pulleys for dirt or built-up material which could affect belt contact. Carefully install the new belt, remembering that it is new and unused—it may appear to be just a little too small to fit over the pulley flanges.

Fit the belt over the largest pulley (usually the crankshaft pulley at the bottom center of the engine) first, then work on the smaller one(s). Gentle pressure in the direction of rotation is helpful. some belts run around a third or idler pulley, which acts as an additional pivot. Depending on which belt(s) you are replacing, it may be necessary to loosen or remove other interfering belts to get at the one you want.

After the new belt is installed, be sure the belt is at the correct tension. A new belt can be expected to stretch a bit after installation. Be prepared to check, and if necessary, readjust the belt(s) within the first 5 minutes of use.

Timing Belts

INSPECTION

✴✴ WARNING

Severe engine damage will occur if the timing belt should break. Honda uses an "interference" engine design. If the timing belt breaks, the valves will contact the pistons and likely become damaged.

On models through 1989, Honda does not specify a recommended inspection or replacement interval. However, since these engines utilize an interference design, it is highly recommended to at least inspect the timing belt at 60,000 mile (96,000 km) intervals. It is an even better idea to replace the belt at these intervals. On 1990–94 models, Honda recommends the timing belt to be replaced at 90,000 mile (144,000 km) intervals. On 1995 models, the recommended interval is 60,000 miles (96,000 km).

Replacing the timing belt before its recommended interval is a wise choice. It is far less expensive to replace the belt than to repair the engine damage which results from the belt breaking.

When checking the belt, inspect for cracks, missing teeth and wear on any of the surfaces. Inspect the sprockets for grease and other deposits. If any of these conditions exist, the belt should be replaced. Please refer to Section 3 for procedures on timing belt removal and installation.

Hoses

▶ **See Figures 65, 66, 67 and 68**

✴✴ CAUTION

Always disconnect the negative battery cable, or fan motor wiring harness connector before replacing any radiator/heater hose. Under certain circumstances, the fan may come on even though the ignition is OFF!

Inspect the condition of the radiator and heater hoses periodically. Early spring and at the beginning of the fall or winter, when you are performing other maintenance, are good times. Make sure the engine and cooling system are cold. Visually inspect for cracking, rotting or collapsed hoses, replace as necessary. Run your hand along the length of the hose. If a weak or swollen spot is noted when squeezing the hose wall, replace the hose.

Don't overlook the smaller hoses conducting coolant around the outside of the engine block, carburetor or throttle body. Honda recommends that all hoses be thoroughly inspected every 30,000 miles (48,000 km).

TCCS1219

Fig. 65 The cracks developing along this hose are a result of age-related hardening

Fig. 66 A hose clamp that is too tight can cause older hoses to separate and tear on either side of the clamp

Fig. 67 A soft spongy hose (identifiable by the swollen section) will eventually burst and should be replaced

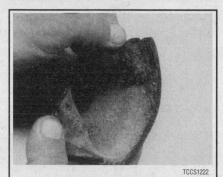

Fig. 68 Hoses are likely to deteriorate from the inside if the cooling system is not periodically flushed

REPLACEMENT

Replacing hoses requires draining the cooling system. This potentially messy job involves working under the car and handling antifreeze, a slippery, smelly, stain-making chemical. Have a large drain pan or bucket available along with healthy supply of rags. Be prepared to deal with fluid spills immediately. See the list of Do's and Don'ts in the beginning of this section for other hints.

✳✳ CAUTION

When draining coolant, keep in mind that cats and dogs are attracted by ethylene glycol antifreeze, and are quite likely to drink any that is left in an uncovered container or in puddles on the ground. This will prove fatal in sufficient quantity. Always drain the coolant into a sealable container.

1. Drain the cooling system. This is always done with the engine cold. Attempting to drain hot coolant is very foolish; you can be badly scalded. Honda engines and radiators may be drained by opening the drain cock at the base of the radiator. If the coolant is drained in this fashion, remember to close the draincock before adding coolant again.
2. An alternative method is:
   a. Remove the radiator cap.
   b. Position the drain pan under the point where the lower radiator hose hooks to the radiator. Loosen the clamp on the hose and slide it back so it's out of the way.
   c. Gently break the grip of the hose on its fitting by twisting or prying with a suitable tool. Do not exert too much force or you will damage the radiator fitting. As the hose loosens, you can expect a gush of fluid—be ready.
   d. Remove the hose end from the radiator and direct the hose into the drain pan. You now have fluid running from both the hose and the radiator. When the system stops draining, proceed with replacement of the damaged hose.
3. Loosen the hose clamps on the damaged hose with a screwdriver and slide the clamps either off the hose altogether or in toward center.
4. Break the grip of the hose at both ends by prying it free with a suitable tool or by twisting it with your hand.
5. Remove the hose.
6. Install a new hose. A small amount of soapy water or window cleaner on the inside of the hose end will ease installation.

➡**Radiator hoses should be routed with no kinks and, when installed, should be in the same position as the original. If other than specified hose is used, make sure it does not rub against either the engine or any other component while the engine is running, as this may wear a hole in the hose. Contact points may be insulated with a piece of sponge or foam; plastic wire ties are particularly handy for this job.**

7. Slide the hose clamps back into position and re-tighten. When tightening the clamps, tighten them enough to seal in the coolant but not so much that the clamp cuts into the hose or causes it internal damage. If a clamp shows signs of any damage (bent, too loose, hard to tighten, etc.) now is the time to replace it. A good rule of thumb is that a new hose is always worth new clamps.
8. Reinstall the lower radiator hose and secure its clamp.

9. Fill the system with coolant. Honda strongly recommends that the coolant mixture be a 50/50 mix of antifreeze and water. This mixture gives best combination of anti-freeze and anti-boil characteristics for year-round driving.

➡**Cold weather anti-freezing protection is best at the 50/50 mixture. If the mixture contains 40 percent water or less, engine cooling is impaired. Do not use additional rust inhibitors or other such products. The cooling system may be damaged by incompatible fluids.**

10. When adding coolant to the radiator and or the coolant reservoir (jug), take great care to prevent spillage onto the fuse and relay panel under the hood. Should spillage occur, wipe it off immediately.
11. Loosen the bleeder bolt. This is usually located on the thermostat housing.
12. Replace and tighten the radiator cap. Start the engine and check visually for leaks. Allow the engine to warm up fully and continue to check your work for signs of leakage. A very small leak may not be noticed until the system develops internal pressure. Leaks at hose ends are generally clamp related and can be cured by snugging the clamp. Larger leaks may require removing the hose again. To do this, you must wait until the engine has cooled down, generally a period of hours. NEVER UNCAP A HOT RADIATOR! The bleeder bolt may be tightened after a steady stream of coolant comes out with no bubbles. After all leaks are repaired, check the coolant level in the radiator (with the engine cold) and top up as necessary.

CV-Boots

INSPECTION

▶ **See Figures 69 and 70**

The Constant Velocity (CV) boots should should be checked for damage every 7,500 miles (12,000 km) and anytime the vehicle is raised for service. These boots keep water, grime, dirt and other damaging matter from entering the CV-joints. Any of these can cause early CV-joint failure which can be expensive to repair. Heavy grease thrown around the inside of the front wheel(s) and on the brake caliper can be an indication of a torn boot. Thoroughly check the boots for missing clamps and tears. If the boot is damaged, it should be replaced immediately. Please refer to Section 7 for procedures.

Fig. 69 CV-boots must be inspected periodically for damage

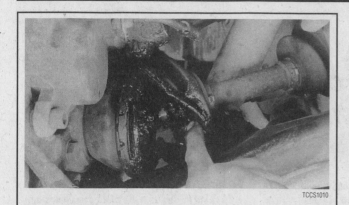

TCCS1010

Fig. 70 A torn boot should be replaced immediately

Air Conditioning System

SYSTEM SERVICE & REPAIR

➡**It is recommended that the A/C system be serviced by an EPA Section 609 certified automotive technician utilizing a refrigerant recovery/recycling machine.**

The do-it-yourselfer should not service his/her own vehicle's A/C system for many reasons, including legal concerns, personal injury, environmental damage and cost.

According to the U.S. Clean Air Act, it is a federal crime to service or repair (involving the refrigerant) a Motor Vehicle Air Conditioning (MVAC) system for money without being EPA certified. It is also illegal to vent R-12 and R-134a refrigerants into the atmosphere. State and/or local laws may be more strict than the federal regulations, so be sure to check with your state and/or local authorities for further information.

➡**Federal law dictates that a fine of up to $25,000 may be levied on people convicted of venting refrigerant into the atmosphere.**

When servicing an A/C system you run the risk of handling or coming in contact with refrigerant, which may result in skin or eye irritation or frostbite. Although low in toxicity (due to chemical stability), inhalation of concentrated refrigerant fumes is dangerous and can result in death; cases of fatal cardiac arrhythmia have been reported in people accidentally subjected to high levels of refrigerant. Some early symptoms include loss of concentration and drowsiness.

➡**Generally, the limit for exposure is lower for R-134a than it is for R-12. Exceptional care must be practiced when handling R-134a.**

Also, some refrigerants can decompose at high temperatures (near gas heaters or open flame), which may result in hydrofluoric acid, hydrochloric acid and phosgene (a fatal nerve gas).

It is usually more economically feasible to have a certified MVAC automotive technician perform A/C system service on your vehicle.

R-12 Refrigerant Conversion

If your vehicle still uses R-12 refrigerant, one way to save A/C system costs down the road is to investigate the possibility of having your system converted to R-134a. The older R-12 systems can be easily converted to R-134a refrigerant by a certified automotive technician by installing a few new components and changing the system oil.

The cost of R-12 is steadily rising and will continue to increase, because it is no longer imported or manufactured in the United States. Therefore, it is often possible to have an R-12 system converted to R-134a and recharged for less than it would cost to just charge the system with R-12.

If you are interested in having your system converted, contact local automotive service stations for more details and information.

PREVENTIVE MAINTENANCE

Although the A/C system should not be serviced by the do-it-yourselfer, preventive maintenance should be practiced to help maintain the efficiency of the vehicle's A/C system. Be sure to perform the following:

• The easiest and most important preventive maintenance for your A/C system is to be sure that it is used on a regular basis. Running the system for five minutes each month (no matter what the season) will help ensure that the seals and all internal components remain lubricated.

➡**Some vehicles automatically operate the A/C system compressor whenever the windshield defroster is activated. Therefore, the A/C system would not need to be operated each month if the defroster was used.**

• In order to prevent heater core freeze-up during A/C operation, it is necessary to maintain proper antifreeze protection. Be sure to properly maintain the engine cooling system.

• Any obstruction of or damage to the condenser configuration will restrict air flow which is essential to its efficient operation. Keep this unit clean and in proper physical shape.

➡**Bug screens which are mounted in front of the condenser (unless they are original equipment) are regarded as obstructions.**

• The condensation drain tube expels any water which accumulates on the bottom of the evaporator housing into the engine compartment. If this tube is obstructed, the air conditioning performance can be restricted and condensation buildup can spill over onto the vehicle's floor.

SYSTEM INSPECTION

Although the A/C system should not be serviced by the do-it-yourselfer, system inspections should be performed to help maintain the efficiency of the vehicle's A/C system. Be sure to perform the following:

The easiest and often most important check for the air conditioning system consists of a visual inspection of the system components. Visually inspect the system for refrigerant leaks, damaged compressor clutch, abnormal compressor drive belt tension and/or condition, plugged evaporator drain tube, blocked condenser fins, disconnected or broken wires, blown fuses, corroded connections and poor insulation.

A refrigerant leak will usually appear as an oily residue at the leakage point in the system. The oily residue soon picks up dust or dirt particles from the surrounding air and appears greasy. Through time, this will build up and appear to be a heavy dirt impregnated grease.

For a thorough visual and operational inspection, check the following:

• Check the surface of the radiator and condenser for dirt, leaves or other material which might block air flow.

• Check for kinks in hoses and lines. Check the system for leaks.

• Make sure the drive belt is properly tensioned. During operation, make sure the belt is free of noise or slippage.

• Make sure the blower motor operates at all appropriate positions, then check for distribution of the air from all outlets.

➡**Remember that in high humidity, air discharged from the vents may not feel as cold as expected, even if the system is working properly. This is because moisture in humid air retains heat more effectively than dry air, thereby making humid air more difficult to cool.**

Windshield Wipers

ELEMENT (REFILL) CARE & REPLACEMENT

▶ **See Figures 71, 72 and 73**

For maximum effectiveness and longest element life, the windshield and wiper blades should be kept clean. Dirt, tree sap, road tar and so on will cause streaking, smearing and blade deterioration if left on the glass. It is advisable to wash the windshield carefully with a commercial glass cleaner at least once a

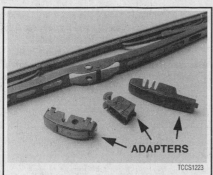

Fig. 71 Most aftermarket blades are available with multiple adapters to fit different vehicles

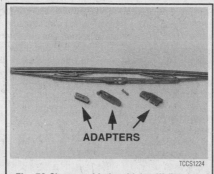

Fig. 72 Choose a blade which will fit your vehicle, and that will be readily available next time you need blades

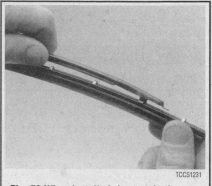

Fig. 73 When installed, be certain the blade is fully inserted into the backing

month. Wipe off the rubber blades with the wet rag afterwards. Do not attempt to move wipers across the windshield by hand; damage to the motor and drive mechanism will result.

To inspect and/or replace the wiper blade elements, place the wiper switch in the **LOW** speed position and the ignition switch in the **ACC** position. When the wiper blades are approximately vertical on the windshield, turn the ignition switch to **OFF**.

Examine the wiper blade elements. If they are found to be cracked, broken or torn, they should be replaced immediately. Replacement intervals will vary with usage, although ozone deterioration usually limits element life to about one year. If the wiper pattern is smeared or streaked, or if the blade chatters across the glass, the elements should be replaced. It is easiest and most sensible to replace the elements in pairs.

If your vehicle is equipped with aftermarket blades, there are several different types of refills and your vehicle might have any kind. Aftermarket blades and arms rarely use the exact same type blade or refill as the original equipment.

Regardless of the type of refill used, be sure to follow the part manufacturer's instructions closely. Make sure that all of the frame jaws are engaged as the refill is pushed into place and locked. If the metal blade holder and frame are allowed to touch the glass during wiper operation, the glass will be scratched.

Tires and Wheels

Common sense and good driving habits will afford maximum tire life. Make sure that you don't overload the vehicle or run with incorrect pressure in the tires. Either of these will increase tread wear. Fast starts, sudden stops and sharp cornering are hard on tires and will shorten their useful life span.

➡**For optimum tire life, keep the tires properly inflated, rotate them often and have the wheel alignment checked periodically.**

Inspect your tires frequently. Be especially careful to watch for bubbles in the tread or sidewall, deep cuts or underinflation. Replace any tires with bubbles in the sidewall. If cuts are so deep that they penetrate to the cords, discard the tire. Any cut in the sidewall of a radial tire renders it unsafe. Also look for uneven tread wear patterns that may indicate the front end is out of alignment or that the tires are out of balance.

TIRE ROTATION

▶ **See Figure 74**

Tires must be rotated periodically to equalize wear patterns that vary with a tire's position on the vehicle. Tires will also wear in an uneven way as the front steering/suspension system wears to the point where the alignment should be reset.

Rotating the tires will ensure maximum life for the tires as a set, so you will not have to discard a tire early due to wear on only part of the tread. Regular rotation is required to equalize wear.

When rotating "unidirectional tires," make sure that they always roll in the same direction. This means that a tire used on the left side of the vehicle must not be switched to the right side and vice-versa. Such tires should only be rotated front-to-rear or rear-to-front, while always remaining on the same side of the vehicle. These tires are marked on the sidewall as to the direction of rotation; observe the marks when reinstalling the tire(s).

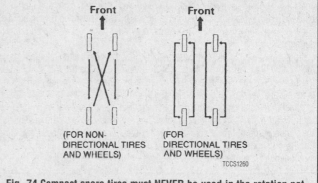

Fig. 74 Compact spare tires must NEVER be used in the rotation pattern

Some styled or "mag" wheels may have different offsets front to rear. In these cases, the rear wheels must not be used up front and vice-versa. Furthermore, if these wheels are equipped with unidirectional tires, they cannot be rotated unless the tire is remounted for the proper direction of rotation.

➡**The compact or space-saver spare is strictly for emergency use. It must never be included in the tire rotation or placed on the vehicle for everyday use.**

TIRE DESIGN

▶ **See Figure 75**

For maximum satisfaction, tires should be used in sets of four. Mixing of different brands or types (radial, bias-belted, fiberglass belted) should be avoided. In most cases, the vehicle manufacturer has designated a type of tire on which the vehicle will perform best. Your first choice when replacing tires should be to use the same type of tire that the manufacturer recommends.

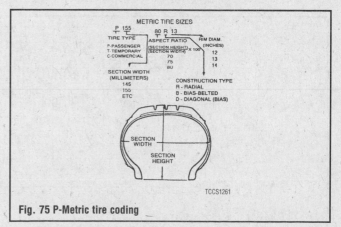

Fig. 75 P-Metric tire coding

When radial tires are used, tire sizes and wheel diameters should be selected to maintain ground clearance and tire load capacity equivalent to the original specified tire. Radial tires should always be used in sets of four.

❊❊❊ CAUTION

Radial tires should never be used on only the front axle.

When selecting tires, pay attention to the original size as marked on the tire. Most tires are described using an industry size code sometimes referred to as P-Metric. This allows the exact identification of the tire specifications, regardless of the manufacturer. If selecting a different tire size or brand, remember to check the installed tire for any sign of interference with the body or suspension while the vehicle is stopping, turning sharply or heavily loaded.

Snow Tires

Good radial tires can produce a big advantage in slippery weather, but in snow, a street radial tire does not have sufficient tread to provide traction and control. The small grooves of a street tire quickly pack with snow and the tire behaves like a billiard ball on a marble floor. The more open, chunky tread of a snow tire will self-clean as the tire turns, providing much better grip on snowy surfaces.

To satisfy municipalities requiring snow tires during weather emergencies, most snow tires carry either an M + S designation after the tire size stamped on the sidewall, or the designation "all-season." In general, no change in tire size is necessary when buying snow tires.

Most manufacturers strongly recommend the use of 4 snow tires on their vehicles for reasons of stability. If snow tires are fitted only to the drive wheels, the opposite end of the vehicle may become very unstable when braking or turning on slippery surfaces. This instability can lead to unpleasant endings if the driver can't counteract the slide in time.

Note that snow tires, whether 2 or 4, will affect vehicle handling in all non-snow situations. The stiffer, heavier snow tires will noticeably change the turning and braking characteristics of the vehicle. Once the snow tires are installed, you must re-learn the behavior of the vehicle and drive accordingly.

➥Consider buying extra wheels on which to mount the snow tires. Once done, the "snow wheels" can be installed and removed as needed. This eliminates the potential damage to tires or wheels from seasonal removal and installation. Even if your vehicle has styled wheels, see if inexpensive steel wheels are available. Although the look of the vehicle will change, the expensive wheels will be protected from salt, curb hits and pothole damage.

TIRE STORAGE

If they are mounted on wheels, store the tires at proper inflation pressure. All tires should be kept in a cool, dry place. If they are stored in the garage or basement, do not let them stand on a concrete floor; set them on strips of wood, a mat or a large stack of newspaper. Keeping them away from direct moisture is of paramount importance. Tires should not be stored upright, but in a flat position.

INFLATION & INSPECTION

▶ See Figures 76 thru 81

The importance of proper tire inflation cannot be overemphasized. A tire employs air as part of its structure. It is designed around the supporting strength of the air at a specified pressure. For this reason, improper inflation drastically reduces the tire's ability to perform as intended. A tire will lose some air in day-to-day use; having to add a few pounds of air periodically is not necessarily a sign of a leaking tire.

Two items should be a permanent fixture in every glove compartment: an accurate tire pressure gauge and a tread depth gauge. Check the tire pressure (including the spare) regularly with a pocket type gauge. Too often, the gauge on the end of the air hose at your corner garage is not accurate because it suffers too much abuse. Always check tire pressure when the tires are cold, as pressure increases with temperature. If you must move the vehicle to check the tire inflation, do not drive more than a mile before checking. A cold tire is generally one that has not been driven for more than three hours.

Fig. 76 Tires with deep cuts, or cuts which bulge, should be replaced immediately

TCCS1095

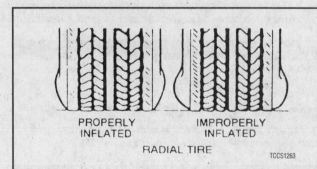

PROPERLY INFLATED   IMPROPERLY INFLATED

RADIAL TIRE

TCCS1263

Fig. 77 Radial tires have a characteristic sidewall bulge; don't try to measure pressure by looking at the tire. Use a quality air pressure gauge

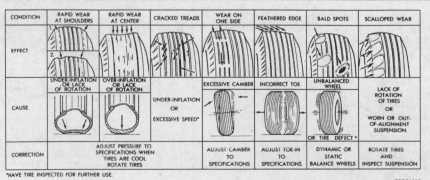

Fig. 78 Common tire wear patterns and causes

A plate or sticker is normally provided somewhere in the vehicle (door post, hood, tailgate or trunk lid) which shows the proper pressure for the tires. Never counteract excessive pressure build-up by bleeding off air pressure (letting some air out). This will cause the tire to run hotter and wear quicker.

✳✳ CAUTION

Never exceed the maximum tire pressure embossed on the tire! This is the pressure to be used when the tire is at maximum loading, but it is rarely the correct pressure for everyday driving. Consult the owner's manual or the tire pressure sticker for the correct tire pressure.

Once you've maintained the correct tire pressures for several weeks, you'll be familiar with the vehicle's braking and handling personality. Slight adjustments in tire pressures can fine-tune these characteristics, but never change the cold pressure specification by more than 2 psi. A slightly softer tire pressure will give a softer ride but also yield lower fuel mileage. A slightly harder tire will give crisper dry road handling but can cause skidding on wet surfaces. Unless you're fully attuned to the vehicle, stick to the recommended inflation pressures.

All automotive tires have built-in tread wear indicator bars that show up as ½ in. (13mm) wide smooth bands across the tire when ¹⁄₁₆ in. (1.5mm) of tread remains. The appearance of tread wear indicators means that the tires should be replaced. In fact, many states have laws prohibiting the use of tires with less than this amount of tread.

You can check your own tread depth with an inexpensive gauge or by using a Lincoln head penny. Slip the Lincoln penny (with Lincoln's head upside-down) into several tread grooves. If you can see the top of Lincoln's head in 2 adjacent grooves, the tire has less than ¹⁄₁₆ in. (1.5mm) tread left and should be replaced. You can measure snow tires in the same manner by using the "tails" side of the Lincoln penny. If you can see the top of the Lincoln memorial, it's time to replace the snow tire(s).

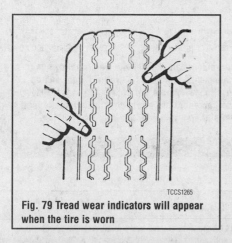

Fig. 79 Tread wear indicators will appear when the tire is worn

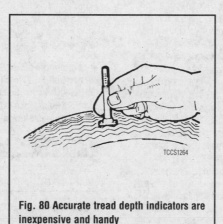

Fig. 80 Accurate tread depth indicators are inexpensive and handy

Fig. 81 A penny works well for a quick check of tread depth

FLUIDS AND LUBRICANTS

Fluid Disposal

Used fluids such as engine oil, transmission/transaxle fluid, antifreeze and brake fluid are hazardous wastes and must be disposed of properly. Before draining any fluids, consult with local authorities; in many cases, waste oil, etc., is accepted in recycling programs. A number of service stations and auto parts stores are also accepting waste fluids for recycling.

Be sure of the recycling center's policies before draining the fluids, as many will not accept mixed fluids such as oil and antifreeze.

Engine Oil and Fuel Recommendations

OIL

♦ See Figure 82

The Society of Automotive Engineers (SAE) grade number indicates the viscosity of the engine oil (its resistance to flow at a given temperature). The lower the SAE grade number, the lighter the oil. For example, the mono-grade oils begin with SAE 5 weight, which is a thin, light oil, and continue in viscosity up to SAE 80 or 90 weight, which are heavy gear lubricants. These oils are also known as "straight weight," meaning they are of a single viscosity, and do not vary with engine temperature.

Multi-viscosity oils offer the important advantage of being adaptable to temperature extremes. These oils have designations such as 10W-40, 20W-50, etc. For example, 10W-40 means that in winter (the "W" in the designation) the oil acts like a thin, 10 weight oil, allowing the engine to spin easily when cold and offering rapid lubrication. Once the engine has warmed up, however, the oil acts like a straight 40 weight, maintaining good lubrication and protection for the engine's internal components. A 20W-50 oil would therefore be slightly heavier and not as ideal in cold weather as the 10W-40, but would offer better protection at higher rpm and temperatures because, when warm, it acts like a 50 weight oil. Whichever oil viscosity you choose when changing the oil, make sure you are anticipating the temperatures your engine will be operating in until the oil is changed again. Refer to the oil viscosity chart for oil recommendations according to temperature.

➡Honda does not recommend the use of any oil additive or supplement in the engine. A normal engine does not need them. If the engine is worn or damaged, it's usually too late for any benefit.

The American Petroleum Institute (API) designation indicates the classification of engine oil used under certain given operating conditions. Only oils designated for use "Service SG or SH" should be used. Oils of the SG/SH type perform a variety of functions inside the engine in addition to the basic function as a lubricant. An SG/SH rated oil may be substituted for SF or SE oils in older

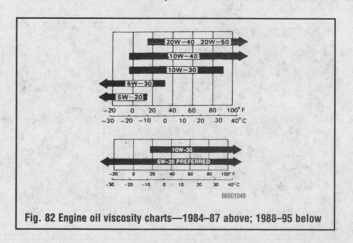

Fig. 82 Engine oil viscosity charts—1984–87 above; 1988–95 below

vehicles. A new vehicle requiring SG/SH oil may be damaged by using oil with a lesser rating. API labels may also carry other letter ratings such as CD or CC; these oils are acceptable for use as long as the designation SG/SH is also present.

Through a balanced system of metallic detergents and polymeric dispersants, the oil prevents the formation of high and low temperature deposits and also keeps sludge and particles of dirt in suspension. Acids, particularly sulfuric acid, as well as other by-products of combustion, are neutralized. Both the SAE grade number and the API designation can be found on the label of the oil bottle. For recommended oil viscosities, refer to the accompanying chart.

Synthetic Oil

There are many excellent synthetic oils currently available that can provide better gas mileage, longer service life, and in some cases better engine protection. These benefits do not come without a few hitches, however. The main drawback is the price of synthetic oils, which is three or four times the price per quart of conventional oil.

Synthetic oil is not for every car and every type of driving, so you should consider your engine's condition and your driving situation. Also, check your vehicle's warranty conditions regarding the use of synthetic oils.

Both brand new engines and older, high mileage engines are usually the wrong candidates for synthetic oil. The synthetic oils are so slippery that they may prevent the proper break-in of new engines; most oil manufacturers recommend that you wait until the engine is properly broken in (at least 3000 miles) before using synthetic oil. Older engines with wear have a different problem with synthetics. The slippery synthetic oils get past these worn parts easily. If your engine is leaking conventional oil, it will use synthetics much faster. Also, if your car is leaking oil past old seals you'll have a much greater leak problem with synthetics.

Consider your type of driving. If most of your accumulated mileage is high speed, highway type driving, the more expensive synthetic oils may be a benefit. Extended highway driving gives the engine a chance to warm up, accumulating less acids in the oil and putting less stress on the engine over the long run. Cars with synthetic oils may show increased fuel economy in highway driving, due to less internal friction.

If synthetic oil is used, it should still be replaced at regular intervals as stated in the maintenance schedule. While the oil itself will last much longer than regular oil, pollutants such as soot, water and unburned fuel still accumulate within the oil. These are the damaging elements within a engine and must be drained regularly to prevent damage

FUEL

It is important to use fuel of the proper octane rating in your Honda. Octane rating is based on the quantity of anti-knock compounds added to the fuel and it determines the speed at which the gas will burn. The lower the octane rating, the faster it burns. The higher the octane, the slower the fuel will burn and a greater percentage of compounds in the fuel prevent spark ping (knock), detonation and pre-ignition (dieseling).

As the temperature of the engine increases, the air/fuel mixture exhibits a tendency to ignite before the spark plug is fired. If fuel of an octane rating too low for the engine is used, this will allow combustion to occur before the piston has completed its compression stroke, thereby creating a very high pressure very rapidly.

Fuel of the proper octane rating will slow the combustion process sufficiently to allow the spark plug enough time to ignite the mixture completely and smoothly. The use of super-premium fuel is no substitution for a properly tuned and maintained engine. Chances are that if your engine exhibits any signs of spark ping, detonation or pre-ignition when using regular fuel, the ignition timing should be checked against specifications or the cylinder head should be removed for decarbonizing.

All Accords and Preludes covered by this book are equipped with catalytic converters and must use UNLEADED GASOLINE only. Use of leaded fuel shortens the life of spark plugs, exhaust systems and EGR valves. It can also damage the catalytic converter. These engines are designed to operate quite efficiently using unleaded gasoline with a minimum rating of 91 octane. Use of unleaded gas with octane ratings lower than 91 can cause persistent spark knock which could lead to engine damage.

Some light spark knock may be noticed when accelerating or driving up hills, particularly with a carbureted engine. The slight knocking may be considered normal (with 91 octane) because the maximum fuel economy is obtained under conditions of minimal knock. Gasoline with an octane rating higher than 91 may be used, but it is not necessary for proper operation of a properly tuned engine.

➡ **Your engine's fuel requirement can change with time, mainly due to carbon buildup, which changes the compression ratio. If your engine pings, knocks or runs on, first switch to a different brand of fuel, not a higher grade. Each refiner incorporates certain chemicals into the fuel; some engines show a definite preference for one brand or another.**

Engine

OIL LEVEL CHECK

▶ **See Figures 83, 84, 85 and 86**

Checking the oil level is one of the simplest and most important checks. It should be performed frequently since low oil level can lead to engine overheating and eventual starvation of the oil pump. This can mean inadequate lubrication and immediate, severe engine damage. Because oil consumption patterns of an engine can change quickly and unexpectedly due to leakage or internal causes, check the oil every time you stop for fuel.

➡ **If the engine has been running, allow it to rest for a few minutes until the oil accumulates in the sump, before checking the oil level.**

1. With the car parked on a level surface, raise the hood, pull the oil dipstick from the engine and wipe it clean.
2. Reinsert the dipstick into the engine until it is fully seated, then, remove it and check the reading.

➡ **The oil level on all Hondas should register within the crosshatch design on the dipstick or between the two lines or dots, depending on the type of stick.**

3. Oil is added through the capped opening of the rocker arm cover. Do not add oil if the level is significantly above the lower mark on the dipstick. If the

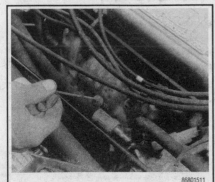

Fig. 83 Pull the dipstick from the engine . . .

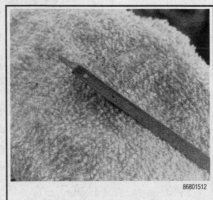

Fig. 84 . . . then wipe it clean

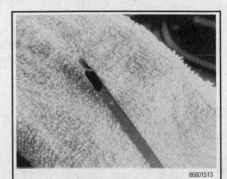

Fig. 85 Reinsert the dipstick into the engine until it is fully seated, then, remove it and check the reading

Fig. 86 Oil is added through the capped opening in the rocker arm (valve) cover

level is near or below the lower line, ADD oil but do not overfill. The length covered by the area on the dipstick is roughly equivalent to one quart of oil.

4. If oil has been added, install the dipstick and recheck the level. It is important to avoid overfilling the crankcase. Doing so will cause the oil to foam with the motion of the crankshaft; this affects lubrication and may also force oil by the seals.

OIL & FILTER CHANGE

▶ See Figures 87 thru 92

The oil and filter should be changed at least every 7,500 miles (12,000 km), although circumstances often dictate more frequent changes. The type of engine used in the Accord and Prelude (overhead camshaft) is particularly sensitive to proper lubrication with clean oil. Don't risk an expensive repair or diminished performance by neglecting the easiest maintenance item on the car. Change the oil and filter regularly. The filter must be changed every time the oil is changed.

The oil drain plug is located on the bottom, rear of the oil pan (bottom of the engine, underneath the car). The oil plug has a washer on it to seal it to the oil pan. The washer should always be replaced when the oil is drained. Purchase a new washer at the same time you get the filter; if the store tells you they don't have the washer or the washer isn't required, take your business elsewhere or find another source for the washer.

On 4-cylinder models, the oil filter is located on the side of the engine, between the block and the firewall. On 6-cylinder models, the filter is located on the bottom of the engine block, near the oil drain plug. When purchasing an oil filter, spend the extra dollar or two for a quality part. It must be a Honda filter or its equivalent. Keep in mind that not all aftermarket filters meet this specification.

➡The oil filter cannot be reached or changed without working from below. The car must be elevated, safely supported and the filter removed by reaching up between the block and firewall. Additionally, the space available makes removing the filter with a standard band wrench very difficult. Use of a cap or filter-end wrench is recommended; the tool is inexpensive and available in most automotive retail stores.

The mileage figures given are the Honda recommended intervals assuming normal driving and conditions. Normal driving requires that the vehicle be driven far enough to warm up the oil; usually this is about 10 miles or so. If your everyday use is shorter than this (one way), your use qualifies as severe duty.

Severe duty also includes dusty, polluted or off-road conditions, as well as stop-and-go short haul uses. Regularly towing a trailer also puts the car in this category, as does constant operation with a near capacity load. Change the oil and filter at ½ the normal interval (3,750 miles or 6,000 km).

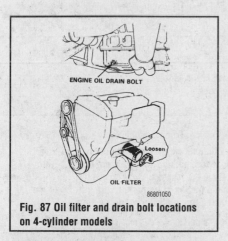
Fig. 87 Oil filter and drain bolt locations on 4-cylinder models

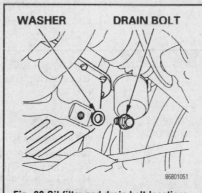
Fig. 88 Oil filter and drain bolt locations on 6-cylinder models

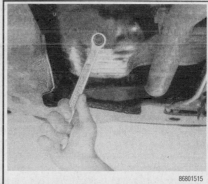
Fig. 89 Loosen the drain plug with a wrench

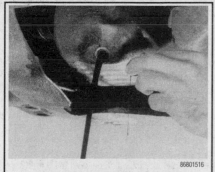
Fig. 90 Keep an inward pressure while unthreading the plug, then quickly pull it away to avoid burning yourself with hot oil

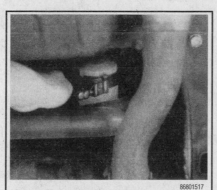
Fig. 91 An inexpensive strap wrench is very useful for loosening the filter

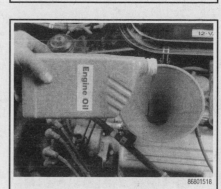
Fig. 92 Refill the engine with fresh oil. A funnel will help keep oil from spilling over the engine

Always drain the oil after the engine has been running long enough to bring it to normal operating temperature. Hot oil will flow easier and more contaminants will be removed along with the oil than if it were drained cold. To change the oil and filter:

1. Run the engine until it reaches normal operating temperature, then shut it **OFF**.
2. Jack up the front of the car and support it on safety stands.
3. Slide a drain pan of at least 6 quarts capacity under the oil pan.

✳ CAUTION

The oil and the engine components will be hot. Take precautions to avoid burns.

4. Loosen the drain plug with a wrench. Turn the plug out by hand. By keeping an inward pressure on the plug as you unscrew it, oil won't escape past the threads. When the last thread is released, whisk the plug out of the way and the hot oil will flow into the pan.
5. Allow the oil to drain completely, then install the drain plug. Tighten it to 32 ft. lbs. (44 Nm). Don't overtighten the plug, or you'll be buying a new pan or a replacement plug for stripped threads.
6. Using a filter wrench, remove the oil filter. Keep in mind that it's holding almost a quart of dirty, hot oil. Make certain the old gasket comes off with the filter and is not stuck to the block mating surface.
7. Empty the old filter into the drain pan. Place the filter in a plastic sandwich bag. The filter should be disposed at a recycling center or your local gas station.
8. Using a clean rag, wipe off the filter adapter on the engine block. Be sure that the rag doesn't leave any lint which could clog an oil passage.
9. Coat the rubber gasket on the filter with fresh oil. Spin it onto the engine by hand; when the gasket touches the adapter surface give it another ½–¾ turn. No more, or you'll squash the gasket and it may leak.
10. Double check the drain plug; is it in place and snug? Refill the engine with the correct amount of fresh oil. See the capacities chart in this section.
11. Double check everything: Filler cap on? Dipstick in place? Oil drain pan and tools out from under the car? Lower the car to the ground.
12. Check the oil level on the dipstick. It is normal for the level to be a little bit above the full mark since the filter is still empty. Start the engine without using the accelerator and allow it to idle for a few minutes.

✳ CAUTION

Do not run the engine above idle speed until it has developed oil pressure, indicated when the oil light goes out.

13. Shut off the engine, allow the oil to drain for a minute, and check the oil level. Check around the filter and drain plug for any leaks, and correct as necessary.
So it's all done; either your first oil change or just another oil change. You now have about 5 quarts of dirty oil in a pan and one rather nasty oil filter in a bag. Use a funnel and an empty gallon milk jug to store the oil. Wipe out the drain pan and discard the rags.
Inquire by phone or in person at your gas station, parts supplier or municipal office about a place to deliver the oil for recycling. Most gas stations are willing to accept small amounts of used oil from regular customers. You can further this relationship by giving the station your business when buying the oil and/or filter. Many local governments have established oil drop-off points within the township or county. Used engine oil is a toxic waste; you are responsible for the proper disposal of your oil.

Manual Transaxles

FLUID RECOMMENDATIONS

▶ See Figure 93

All manual transaxles use engine oil, not gear oil, as a lubricant. The oil should meet SG oil standards (preferred), however, SF is acceptable. For Accords through 1993 and Preludes through 1991, refer to the illustration to determine the proper viscosity. On other models, use 10W-30 or 10W-40 oil.

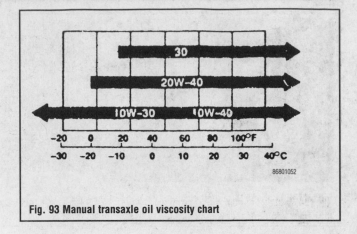

Fig. 93 Manual transaxle oil viscosity chart

Under normal conditions, the transaxle oil must be changed every 24 months or 30,000 miles (48,000 km), whichever comes first. For severe conditions, this interval should be halved. The level should be inspected routinely once a year or more frequently if leakage is noticed.

LEVEL CHECK

There's no dipstick on the manual transaxle. Fluid must be checked by removing the oil filler bolt on the side of the transaxle. The bolt is located by the right axle at approximately 9 o'clock when viewed over the right fender.
The vehicle must be level. If you're agile enough, the bolt may be removed with the car on the ground by working from the top. Some prefer to check the level from below. If this is the case, not only must the car be elevated and safely supported, it must be elevated and level, possibly requiring the installation of 4 jackstands. Just lifting the front yields an improper reading.
Once level, remove the bolt. The fluid level should be just to the bottom of the hole and may be felt with a finger. In the unlikely event that the fluid is low, oil should be added through the inspection hole. Adding oil is tricky since it must be conducted into a horizontal opening. Creative use of funnels and tubing is encouraged. Also, a common kitchen turkey baster may provide some help with this. When the oil is up to the correct level, reinstall the bolt and tighten it to 33 ft. lbs. (45 Nm). Do not overtighten the nut; the penalty could be a very expensive transaxle case.

DRAIN & REFILL

▶ See Figures 94, 95 and 96

➡ **If you have determined that checking and filling the transaxle will require the use of 4 jackstands, be sure to have them handy before starting this procedure. Once the transaxle is drained, it is too late to decide that you don't have a means of properly refilling it. Read the information on level checking found earlier in this section.**

The oil drain plug for the manual transaxle is located by and below the right axle. The drain bolt is easily recognized by the round head with a square recess; it does not look like all the other bolts in the transaxle case. Like the engine oil drain bolt, this one also has a washer on it which must be replaced at each change.

1. The car should be at operating temperature before beginning. If possible, drive several miles to warm the transaxle oil before draining.
2. With the engine **OFF**, raise and support the front of the vehicle. Agility and long arms may allow the job to be done with the car on the ground but it's much easier with the car raised and safely supported.
3. Place a fluid catch pan under the transaxle.
4. Remove the lower drain plug by using a ratchet in the square recess; don't hurt yourself by trying to grab a round bolt with a pair of pliers. Drain the fluid. Loosening or removing the upper (inspection) bolt will make draining easier.
5. Using a new washer, install the bottom plug and tighten it to 29 ft. lbs. (40 Nm).
6. Refill the transaxle through the inspection hole until the oil just runs out the hole. Reinstall the bolt and tighten it just finger-tight.

Fig. 94 A ratchet can be used to remove the drain and fill/inspection plugs

Fig. 95 Quickly pull the plug away from the transaxle and allow the fluid to drain completely

Fig. 96 Use a long-neck funnel to refill the transaxle

7. Lower the car to the ground and check that it sits level. Remove the filler bolt and double check the level, topping up if necessary. Reinstall the bolt, tightening it to 33 ft. lbs. (45 Nm).

Automatic Transaxles

FLUID RECOMMENDATIONS

All Honda automatics use Dexron®II Automatic Transmission/Transaxle Fluid (ATF) or its superceding fluid type.

LEVEL CHECK

▶ **See Figures 97 and 98**

The transaxle fluid should be checked about once a month and replaced every 2 years or 30,000 miles (48,000 km), whichever comes first. Shorten this to every 12 months or 15,000 miles (24,000 km) under severe driving conditions. The vehicle should be driven several miles to fully warm the oil before checking. Before checking the fluid level, make certain the car is parked level with the engine **OFF**.

The dipstick is located on the right front of the transaxle housing, near or beneath the battery. The dipstick is either a threaded fit (unscrew it) or a small dipstick similar to the engine oil dipstick (pull it out). To check the fluid level, remove the dipstick, wipe it clean and reinsert it.

➡ **The threaded dipstick must NOT be rethreaded into the case to check the fluid level. The first part of the threads should just sit on the case. Rethreading the dipstick will yield a false reading.**

Remove the dipstick. The fluid level should be within the cross-hatch marks on the stick, between the upper and lower marks. If the addition of fluid is necessary, add the ATF through the dipstick hole. Add only the amount necessary to bring the fluid level to the correct point on the dipstick. Overfilling can damage the transaxle. The space between the upper and lower marks on the dipstick is less than 1 qt. When reinstalling the dipstick, thread the screw-in type and tighten it just finger-tight; never use a wrench. Make certain the push-in type is fully seated.

DRAIN & REFILL

▶ **See Figure 99**

1. The car should be at operating temperature before beginning. If possible, drive several miles to warm the transaxle oil before draining.
2. With the engine **OFF**, raise and support the front of the vehicle. Agility and long arms may allow the job to be done with the car on the ground but it's much easier with the car raised and safely supported.
3. Place a fluid catch pan under the transaxle.
4. Remove the lower drain plug by using a ratchet in the square recess; don't hurt yourself by trying to grab a round bolt with a pair of pliers. Drain the fluid.
5. Using a new washer, install the bottom plug and tighten it to 29 ft. lbs. (40 Nm) on Accords through 1989 and Preludes through 1991. On other models, tighten the plug to 36 ft. lbs. (50 Nm).
6. Lower the car to the ground and check that it sits level.
7. Refill the transaxle through the dipstick hole until the level is between the upper and lower marks. A narrow funnel may be required on later models with the pull-out type dipstick. On Accords with 6-cylinder engines, the transaxle can be filled either through the dipstick or a filler bolt hole on top of the transaxle. Tighten the bolt to 58 ft. lbs. (78 Nm). Check the level frequently with the dipstick. Do not overfill.
8. Start the engine and move the shift lever slowly through all the gear positions. Allow the engine to reach normal operating temperature. This will allow the fluid in the transaxle to warm and provide for a more accurate level check.
9. Turn the ignition **OFF**. Remove the dipstick and double check the level, topping up if necessary. Reinstall the dipstick securely.

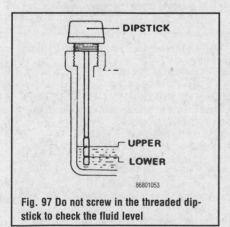

Fig. 97 Do not screw in the threaded dipstick to check the fluid level

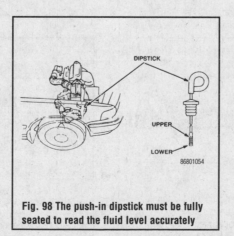

Fig. 98 The push-in dipstick must be fully seated to read the fluid level accurately

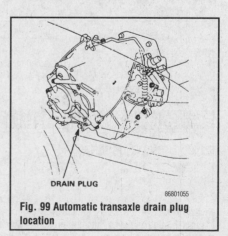

Fig. 99 Automatic transaxle drain plug location

Cooling System

FLUID RECOMMENDATIONS

Use a quality, ethylene-glycol based engine coolant specifically recommended for use with vehicles utilizing aluminum engine parts that are in contact with the coolant. Note that some coolants, although labeled for use in such vehicles, actually may fail to provide effective corrosion protection. If necessary, consult your dealer or a professional mechanic. Honda's engine warranty does not cover damage caused by the use of improper coolant.

It is best to buy a top-quality product that is known to work effectively under such conditions. Always add coolant mixed with the proper amount of clean water. Never add either water or coolant alone. Mix the coolant at a 50/50 ratio in the amount needed. Consult the chart on the antifreeze container and utilize the proportions recommended for the lowest expected temperatures in your area.

LEVEL CHECK

▶ See Figures 100, 101 and 102

❋❋ WARNING

Keep hands and clothing away from the radiator fans. On some vehicles, the fans may start automatically up to 15 minutes after the engine is shut OFF!

The coolant level should be checked with the engine at normal operating temperature. To check the coolant level, simply see if the coolant is up to the FULL line on the expansion tank. On some models, the expansion tank is buried in the front fender well. Lift the lid of the tank, then remove the plastic dipstick. Wipe the dipstick, then check the coolant level as you would check the engine oil. The radiator cap should be removed only for the purpose of cleaning or draining the system.

Add coolant to the expansion tank if the level is low, being sure to mix it with clean water. Never add cold water or coolant to a hot engine as damage to both the cooling system and the engine could result. If any coolant mixture should spill or splash onto painted surfaces, rinse it off immediately with plenty of clean water. The coolant will damage the paint.

❋❋ CAUTION

The cooling system is under pressure when hot. Removing the radiator cap when the engine is warm or overheated will cause coolant to spill or spray out, possibly causing serious burns! The system should be allowed to cool for a period of hours before attempting removal of the radiator cap or hoses.

DRAIN & REFILL

▶ See Figures 103, 104, 105, 106 and 107

❋❋ CAUTION

When draining coolant, keep in mind that cat and dogs are attracted by ethylene glycol antifreeze, and are quite likely to drink any that is left in an uncovered container or in puddles on the ground. This will prove fatal in sufficient quantity. Always drain the coolant into a sealable container.

The radiator coolant should be changed at 36 month or 45,000 mile (72,000 km) intervals whichever comes first. Perform this maintenance only on a cold engine; overnight cold is best to avoid scalds.

1. Remove the radiator cap. Just turn it, don't press down.
2. Slide a fluid catch pan under the radiator. Loosen the draincock at the base of the radiator and allow the coolant to drain. Honda engines are equipped with a drain bolt in the block as well, but these can be difficult to access. The drain is either under the exhaust manifold or above the oil filter. In either case, getting it loose almost always requires working from under the

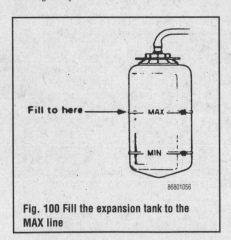

Fig. 100 Fill the expansion tank to the MAX line

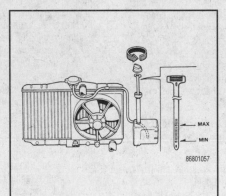

Fig. 101 Some coolant tanks have their own dipsticks

Fig. 102 Add coolant to the expansion tank if the level is low

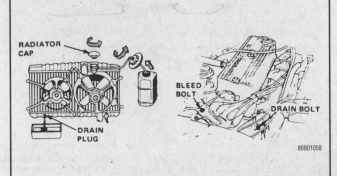

Fig. 103 Cooling system drain and bleed bolt locations; 1984–89 Accord and 1984–91 Prelude

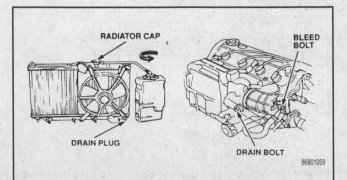

Fig. 104 Cooling system drain and bleed bolt locations; 1990–95 4-cylinder Accord and 1992–95 Prelude

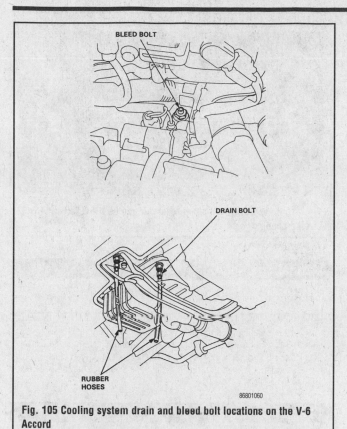

BLEED BOLT

DRAIN BOLT

RUBBER HOSES

86801060

Fig. 105 Cooling system drain and bleed bolt locations on the V-6 Accord

engine. An alternate method is to disconnect the lower radiator hose from the radiator.

3. Drain the coolant in the reservoir tank by unclipping and disconnecting the hose. If the tank is buried in the fender well, use a mechanical siphon or suction tool such as a turkey baster to draw out the fluid.

4. Mix a solution of 50 percent ethylene glycol (designed for use in aluminum engines) and 50 percent clean water. Use a stronger solution, only as specified on the antifreeze container (if the climate in your area demands it). Tighten the drain bolt(s) and double check them. Reinstall the lower radiator hose if it was disconnected.

5. Loosen the cooling system bleed bolt on the top of the thermostat housing. Fill the radiator with the coolant mixture. When coolant flows out of the bleed port in a steady stream without air bubbles, close the bolt and refill the radiator with coolant up to the base of the neck.

6. To purge any air trapped in other parts of the cooling system, leave the radiator cap off and set the heater control to Hot. Start the engine and allow it to reach normal operating temperature; this means that the temperature gauge is in the normal range and the radiator fan has cycled on at least twice.

7. When the engine reaches normal operating temperatures, top off the radiator and keep checking until the level stabilizes. Refill the coolant reservoir to the FULL mark and make sure that the radiator cap is properly tightened.

➡ Fresh antifreeze has a cleansing effect in the passages. If the coolant has not been changed on schedule, the new coolant may dislodge sludge within the system. If the discoloration is extreme, the system may need to be drained a second time.

FLUSHING & CLEANING THE SYSTEM

1. Refer to the thermostat removal and installation procedures in Section 3 and remove the thermostat from the engine.
2. Using a water hose, force fresh water into the thermostat housing opening, allowing the water to back-flush into the engine, heater and radiator. Flush the system until the water flowing from the radiator hose is clear.
3. After cleaning, reverse the removal procedures. Refill the cooling system with fresh coolant.

Brake and Clutch Master Cylinders

FLUID RECOMMENDATIONS

Use only DOT 3 or DOT 4 specification brake fluid from a tightly sealed container. If you are unsure of the condition of the fluid (whether or not it has been tightly sealed), use new fluid rather than taking a chance of introducing moisture into the system. It is critically important that the fluid meet the specification so the heat generated by modern disc brakes will not cause it to boil and reduce braking performance. Fluid must be moisture-free for the same reason.

LEVEL CHECK

Brake Master Cylinder

▸ **See Figures 108 and 109**

The brake master cylinder fluid level should be checked every few weeks for indication of leaks or low fluid level. A sudden drop in fluid level may indicate a fluid leak in the system. The reservoir is located at the left rear of the engine compartment at the firewall. The reservoir is made of translucent plastic; the fluid level may be checked from the outside.

➡ The normal wear of the brake pads and shoes will cause a gradual drop in the fluid level. The fluid is not missing; it is just relocated within the system. If the fluid has been dropping gradually, check the front brakes before refilling the fluid. If the system is refilled before new brakes are installed, the reservoir will overflow.

On all Hondas there is a MAX and MIN line on the brake fluid reservoir. The brake fluid should always be maintained at the MAX line, but not above it. The reservoir cap has an arrow on it which must always point to the front of the car when installed. When adding brake fluid, the following precautions should be observed:

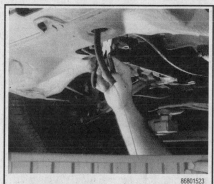

86801523

Fig. 106 A pair of pliers can be helpful for loosening the draincock on the radiator

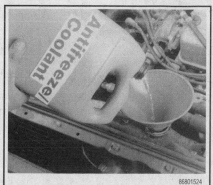

86801524

Fig. 107 Refill the system through the opening in the radiator

86801525

Fig. 108 The master cylinder reservoir is equipped with lower and upper level lines

Fig. 109 The reservoir can be filled after removing the capped opening

Fig. 110 If necessary, the pump reservoir can be filled through the capped opening

• Use only recommended brake fluid: DOT 3 or DOT 4; SAE J 1703b HD type.
• Never reuse brake fluid and never use fluid that is dirty, cloudy or has air bubbles.
• Store brake fluid in a clean dry place in the original container. Cap tightly and do not puncture a breather hole in the container.
• Carefully remove any dirt from around the master cylinder reservoir cap before opening.
• Take special care not to spill the fluid. The painted surface of the vehicle will be damaged by brake fluid.

Clutch Master Cylinder

Manual transaxles in 1990–95 Accords and 1988–95 Preludes use a hydraulic clutch actuation system. When the clutch pedal is pushed to the floor, fluid is compressed and the clutch is activated. Other vehicles use a cable-actuated clutch.

The clutch fluid reservoir is located in the same area as the brake master cylinder reservoir. The clutch reservoir may not be as easily seen as it is smaller and sometimes lower on the firewall. The system uses brake fluid and is checked or filled in the same fashion as the brake fluid reservoir. Always wipe off the cover of the reservoir before removing it. The clutch reservoir may require periodic topping off to compensate for clutch wear.

Power Steering Pump

FLUID RECOMMENDATIONS

Only genuine Honda power steering fluid may be used when adding fluid. Honda states that ATF or fluids manufactured for use in other brands of vehicles are not compatible with the Honda power steering system. The use of any other fluid will cause the seals to swell and create leaks. Honda's proprietary fluid is not generally available in retail outlets; purchase a can of fluid at your dealer and keep it stored until needed.

RESERVOIR LEVEL CHECK

▶ **See Figure 110**

The fluid in the power steering reservoir should be checked every few weeks for indications of leaks or low fluid level. The fluid is not routinely changed. If necessary to drain the fluid during repairs, it may be reused if it is not contaminated by system failure or a dirty container.

The power steering fluid reservoir is located at either the left or right front of the engine compartment, just behind the headlight area. Check the fluid with the engine cold and the vehicle parked on a level spot. View the level through the side of the reservoir. The level should be between the upper and lower marks. Fluid need not be added right away unless it has dropped almost to the lower mark. Do not overfill the reservoir.

Manual Steering Gear

INSPECTION

The manual steering used on Hondas is of the rack and pinion design. This unit is packed with grease and therefore does not require a periodic fluid level check. However, inspect the box and associated rubber boot-type seals for obvious grease leaks or torn boots. This is easily done whenever the car is elevated for other maintenance.

Chassis Greasing

All the suspension fittings on the Hondas covered by this guide are permanently lubricated. However, at the time when the steering box is inspected for grease leakage, inspect the suspension and steering joints for grease leakage and/or for torn rubber boots, then make repairs as necessary.

Body Lubrication

Lubricate all locks and hinges with multi-purpose grease every 6 months or 6,000 miles (9,600 km). Pay particular attention to the hinges and latches which don't get a lot of use. They are the ones that will bind with age.

Rear Wheel Bearings

To check the wheel bearings for basic problems, jack up each wheel to clear the ground. Hold the wheel and shake it to check the bearings for any play. Also rotate the wheel to check for any roughness. If any play is felt or there is noticeable roughness, the bearing may have to be replaced.

➡**Over tightening the spindle nuts will cause excessive bearing friction. This will result in rough wheel rotation and eventual bearing failure. Therefore, follow the procedures given in Section 8 exactly, using the proper procedures and tools.**

CLEANING & REPACKING

Only the 1984–85 Accord and 1984–87 Prelude use rear wheel bearings which can be serviced. All other rear bearings, and all front wheel bearings, are sealed. The sealed bearings are considered life-of-the-car components and are replaced only in the event of mechanical failure. Procedures for replacing the pressed-in bearings are found in Section 8.

❈❈❈ CAUTION

Servicing the wheel bearings exposes the brake shoes or pads. Brake pads and shoes may contain asbestos, which has been determined to be a cancer causing agent. Never clean the brake surfaces with compressed air. Avoid inhaling any dust from brake surfaces. When cleaning brakes, use commercially available brake cleaning fluids.

1984–87 Prelude

▶ See Figures 111 and 112

➡A torque wrench is REQUIRED for this procedure.

1. Loosen the rear wheel lug nuts slightly. Raise and support the rear of the vehicle.
2. Release the parking brake. Remove the rear wheel assembly.
3. If equipped, remove the caliper shield. Disconnect the parking brake cable from the caliper. Remove the caliper-to-bracket bolts and suspend the caliper on a wire; do not disconnect the brake hose.
4. Remove the caliper bracket mounting bolts and the bracket.
5. Remove the grease cap, the cotter pin, the castle nut, the spindle nut, the thrust washer and the outer bearing. Pull the rear disc assembly from the spindle.
6. Using a hammer and a drift punch, drive the outer bearing race from the hub of the disc.

➡When removing the bearing races, use a crisscross pattern to avoid cocking the race in the hub bore.

7. Turn the hub over and drive the inner bearing race and grease seal from the hub; discard the grease seal.

To install:

8. Using solvent, clean the bearings, races and the hub. Allow the components to air dry; never use compressed air to dry the bearing.
9. Using a bearing driver tool of the correct size, such as Honda tool 07749–0010000 and driver attachment tool 07946–6920100 or their equivalents, drive the bearing races evenly into the hub until they seat against the shoulders.
10. Using wheel bearing grease, pack the wheel hub and the wheel bearings. The bearings must be completely and thoroughly packed. Lightly coat the lips of the grease seal. Install the inner bearing into the hub.

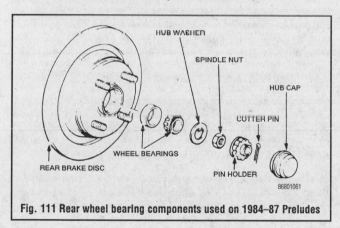

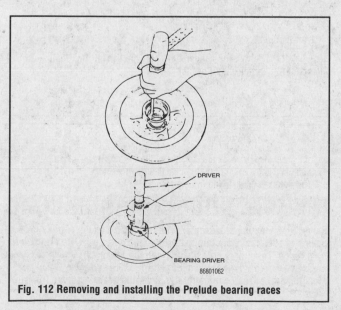

Fig. 111 Rear wheel bearing components used on 1984–87 Preludes

Fig. 112 Removing and installing the Prelude bearing races

11. Using a mallet, tap a new grease seal (using a crisscross method) into the rear of the hub until it is flush with it.
12. To install the hub, fit the outer bearing into the disc. Holding the bearing loosely in place with a thumb, reinstall the disc and bearings onto the hub.
13. Assemble and install the bearing washer and the spindle nut. Tighten the spindle nut just finger-tight.
14. Using the torque wrench, adjust the spindle nut as follows:
   a. Tighten the spindle nut to 18 ft. lbs. (25 Nm). Rotate the brake disc two or three rotations. Retighten the spindle nut. Continue this rotating and tightening process until the spindle nut stays at 18 ft. lbs. (25 Nm) after the disc is rotated.
   b. Loosen the spindle nut. The nut should just break free, but not be turned more than needed.
   c. Tighten the nut to 48 inch lbs. (5.5 Nm).
   d. Install the castle nut and align a slot with the hole in the spindle.

➡If the cotter pin holes do not align, try removing the castle nut and reinstalling it after a slight rotation. If the holes still don't align, tighten the spindle nut slightly until they do.

   e. Using a new cotter pin, install it through the holes in the castle nut and axle.
15. To complete the installation, fill the grease cap with wheel bearing grease and install it on the disc. Make certain it is firmly and evenly seated.
16. Install the caliper bracket mounting bolts and the bracket. Tighten the caliper bracket mounting bolts to 28 ft. lbs. (38 Nm).
17. Install the caliper and brake pads. Tighten the caliper-to-bracket bolts to 17 ft. lbs. (23 Nm).
18. Reconnect the parking brake cable to the caliper.
19. Install the caliper shield if it was removed.
20. Install the wheel and tighten the lug nuts evenly.

1984–87 Accord

▶ See Figures 113 and 114

➡A torque wrench is REQUIRED for this procedure.

1. Slightly loosen the rear wheel lug nuts. Raise and support the rear of the vehicle.
2. Release the parking brake. Remove the rear wheel assembly.
3. Remove the grease cap, the cotter pin, the castle nut, the spindle nut, the thrust washer and the outer bearing. Pull the rear drum assembly from the spindle.
4. Remove the inner grease seal, then remove the inner bearing.
5. Using a hammer and a drift punch, drive the outer bearing race from the drum.

➡When removing the bearing races, use a crisscross pattern to avoid cocking the race in the hub bore.

6. Turn the drum over and drive the inner bearing race and from the hub; discard the grease seal.

To install:

7. Using solvent, clean the bearings, races and the inner or hub area of the drum. Allow the components to air dry; never use compressed air to dry the bearing.
8. Using a bearing driver tool of the correct size, such as Honda tool 07749–0010000 and driver attachment tool 07947–67101000 or their equivalents, drive the bearing races evenly into the hub until they seat against the shoulders.

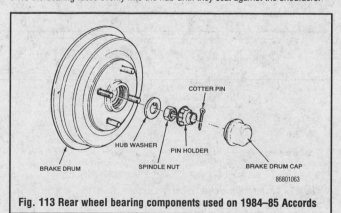

Fig. 113 Rear wheel bearing components used on 1984–85 Accords

9. Using wheel bearing grease, pack the wheel hub and the wheel bearings. The bearings must be completely and thoroughly packed. Lightly coat the lips of the grease seal. Install the inner bearing into the hub.

10. Using a mallet, tap a new grease seal (using a crisscross method) into the rear of the hub until it is flush with it.

11. To install the hub, fit the outer bearing into the drum. Holding the bearing loosely in place with a thumb, reinstall the drum and bearings onto the hub.

12. Assemble and install the bearing washer and the spindle nut. Tighten the spindle nut just finger-tight.

13. Using the torque wrench, adjust the spindle nut as follows:

a. Tighten the spindle nut to 18 ft. lbs. (25 Nm). Rotate the brake drum two or three rotations.

b. Loosen the spindle nut. The nut should just break free, but not be turned more than needed.

c. Tighten the nut to 48 inch lbs. (5.5 Nm)

d. Install the castle nut and align a slot with the hole in the spindle.

➡**If the cotter pin holes do not align, try removing the castle nut and reinstalling it after a slight rotation. If the holes still don't align, tighten the spindle nut slightly until they do.**

e. Using a new cotter pin, install it through the holes in the castle nut and axle.

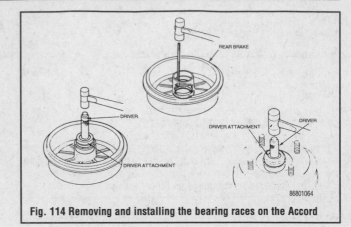

Fig. 114 Removing and installing the bearing races on the Accord

14. To complete the installation, fill the grease cap with wheel bearing grease and install it on the disc. Make certain it is firmly and evenly seated.

15. Install the wheel. Hand-tighten the lug nuts.

16. Lower the car to the ground and tighten the lug nuts evenly.

TRAILER TOWING

General Recommendations

♦ **See Figure 115**

Honda does not recommend that 1984–88 vehicles tow any type of trailer. Your car was primarily designed to carry passengers and cargo. Towing a trailer will place additional loads on your vehicle's engine, drive train, steering, braking and other systems.

The 1989–95 Accord and Prelude models may tow trailers subject to the following rules. All rules must be met for safe towing:

• Do not tow a trailer during the 600 mile break-in period.

• The weight of the trailer and its cargo cannot exceed 1000 lbs. (450 kg).

• The Gross Vehicle Weight must not exceed the Gross Vehicle Weight Rating (GVWR) shown on the certification label inside the left door. The gross weight of the vehicle is the grand total of vehicle, passengers, luggage and loaded trailer.

• The maximum trailer tongue load or weight is 100 lbs. (45 kg). If a smaller trailer is being used, tongue weight should be approximately 10 percent of trailer weight. This is usually achieved by loading the trailer with about 60 percent of the weight forward of the trailer axle.

• The total weight supported by each axle must not exceed the Gross Axle Weight Rating (GAWR) shown on the certification label. This requires that the load (passengers, cargo and trailer) be evenly distributed within the car.

• Electric trailer brakes are recommended for all but the smallest trailers. Never tap into the car's hydraulic brake system for trailer brakes. Consult a reputable recreational vehicle dealer for information on electric brake controllers.

• All trailers must be secured to the tow vehicle by safety chains as well as the hitch.

Local laws may require specific equipment such as fender mounted mirrors. Check your state or provincial laws.

Trailer Hitches

The hitch should be appropriate for the type of trailer being towed. The most common is the familiar ball hitch although receiver hitches are sometimes found on Honda vehicles. Honda does not provide hitches at the time of purchase; they must be purchased and installed separately. The hitch mounts must be securely attached to the body of the car. Never use a hitch attached only to the bumper and never use a hitch designed for temporary use.

When you've determined the hitch that you'll need, follow the manufacturer's installation instructions exactly, especially when it comes to fastener torques. The hitch will subjected to a lot of stress and good hitches come with hardened bolts. Never substitute an inferior bolt for a hardened bolt.

Trailer Lighting

♦ **See Figures 116 and 117**

Trailer lighting ranges from primitive to sophisticated depending on the unit. The smallest trailers still require stop and turn lighting; a modern camping trailer may have side markers, reverse lights and separate turn signals.

The trailer wiring connections must be made by a competent automotive electrician. A poor or incorrect job can damage the lighting system or render it inoperative. Remember that when properly connected, the trailer lamps add electrical load to the car's lighting circuits; fuse ratings may need to be checked.

➡**The 1991–95 Accord comes equipped with a pre-wired trailer connector. Look for it behind the access panel for the left tail light bulbs or in the spare tire compartment of the wagon.**

Most trailers use combined stop, tail and turn signals (all red, one bulb). An electrical converter or adapter will be required to make the car lighting control

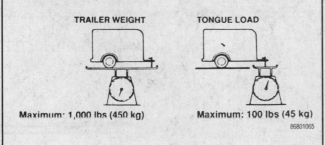

Fig. 115 Total trailer weight must not exceed 1000 lbs.; tongue weight must not exceed 100 lbs.

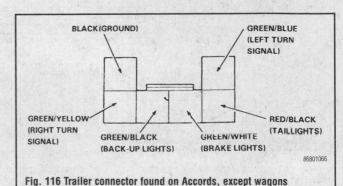

Fig. 116 Trailer connector found on Accords, except wagons

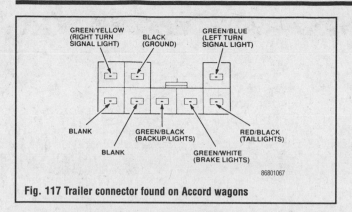

Fig. 117 Trailer connector found on Accord wagons

the trailer lighting. These units are readily available at trailer or camping outlets. Install the unit according to the manufacturer's instructions.

Handling A Trailer

Towing a trailer with ease and safety requires a certain amount of experience. It's a good idea to learn the feel of a trailer by practicing turning, stopping and backing in an open area such as an empty parking lot. Observe these rules:

- After hitching the trailer to the car, check that the car sits approximately level. If the car is severely nose-up, redistribute the trailer cargo and/or the cargo in the vehicle.
- Always check the function of trailer lights before departing.
- The weight of the trailer may lighten the load on the front tires. This will affect vehicle handling and stopping, particularly on wet or slippery roads.
- Allow for much greater stopping distances when towing.
- Drive smoothly. Jerky starts and hard stops increase wear and may cause handling problems.
- Avoid any sudden or sharp maneuvers. Allow for wider turning radius.
- Crosswinds and turbulence from larger vehicles will cause your car and trailer to become unstable. Be prepared.
- Maintain vehicle and trailer tire pressures at the proper inflation at all times.
- Any problems or changes in vehicle feel while towing will be magnified greatly in foul weather. Slow down.
- Passing requires considerable time and distance due to the length and weight of the trailer. Plan ahead.
- Backing up accurately with a trailer must be learned. Practice with the trailer in a remote area before the skill is needed.
- Use the mirrors frequently to check oncoming traffic as well as status of the trailer.
- If the trailer begins to sway, DON'T make any sudden changes in speed. Depending on traffic, very gradual acceleration or deceleration will bring the trailer into line. A sudden change may cause the trailer to jackknife.

TOWING THE VEHICLE

If an Accord or Prelude must be towed, use of a flat-bed or rollback is the first choice. This type of truck transports the car completely off the ground, so the risk of damage is greatly reduced. If this is not available, a wheel-lift truck which can lift the car by the front tires (not the axles) is recommended. The classic tow truck with boom and winch can be used, but great care must be taken to prevent damage to drive axles and front body panels.

If your Honda's rear wheels are operable, you can tow your vehicle with the rear wheels on the ground. Due to its front wheel drive, the Honda is a relatively easy vehicle to tow with the front wheels up. Before doing so, you should release the parking brake.

If the rear axle is defective, the vehicle must then be transported on a flat bed. Towing the vehicle with the front wheels on the ground may cause damage to the driveline and/or transaxle. A vehicle with an automatic transaxle must NEVER be towed with the front wheels on the ground.

JACKING

♦ **See Figures 118, 119 and 120**

Your Honda comes equipped with a scissors jack. This jack is fine for changing a flat tire or other operations not requiring you to go beneath the vehicle. There are four lifting points where this jack may be used: one behind each front wheel well and one in front of each rear wheel well in reinforced sheet metal brackets beneath the rocker panels.

A more convenient way of jacking is the use of a garage or floor jack. You may use the floor jack beneath any of the four scissors jacking points or you can raise the entire front of the vehicle using the front crossmember. The rear of the vehicle may be jacked beneath the center of the rear axle beam or reinforced lift point.

Never place the jack under the radiator, engine or transmission components. Severe and expensive damage will result when the jack is raised. Additionally, never jack under the floorpan or bodywork; the metal will deform.

The following safety points cannot be overemphasized:
- Always block the opposite wheel or wheels to keep the vehicle from rolling off the jack.
- When raising the front of the vehicle, firmly apply the parking brake.
- Always use jack stands to support the vehicle when you are working underneath. Place the stands beneath the scissors jacking brackets. Before climbing underneath, rock the vehicle a bit to make sure it is firmly supported.

If you are going to have your Honda serviced on a garage hoist, make sure the four hoist platform pads are placed beneath the scissors jacking brackets. These brackets are reinforced and will support the weight of the entire vehicle.

Fig. 118 The front of the vehicle can be raised using the front crossmember

Fig. 119 The rear of the vehicle can be raised from the rear axle beam or from the reinforced lift point

Fig. 120 Jackstands may be placed between the notches on the rocker panels

MAINTENANCE SCHEDULES

Fig. 122 1984-87 Prelude maintenance schedule

Service at the interval listed x 1,000 miles (or km) or after that number of months, whichever occurs first.

R—Replace
C—Clean
I—Inspect
After inspection, clean, adjust, repair or replace if necessary.

*1 Tension adjustment only
*2 Thereafter, replace every 2 years or 30,000 miles (48,000 km), whichever comes first.
*3 Recommended by manufacturer only for cars sold in California.

	x 1,000 miles	15	30	45	60	75
	x 1,000 km	24	48	72	96	120
	months	12	24	36	48	60
Idle speed and idle CO						
Valve clearance			I*1			
Alternator drive belt						
Engine oil and filter		Replace every 7,500 miles (12,000 km) or 6 months				
Transmission oil	Manual					
	Automatic					
Radiator coolant		R		R*2		R
Cooling system hoses and connections						
E.G.R. system						
Secondary air supply system						
Air cleaner element			R		R	
Fuel filter and hoses (Inc. aux. filter)					R	
Intake air temp. control system						
Fuel line connections						
Throttle control unit						
Choke mechanism			C			
Choke opener operation						
Evaporative emission control system						
Ignition timing and control system						
Spark plugs		R		R		R
Distributor cap and rotor			R		R	
Ignition wiring						
Crankcase emission control system			I*3			
Brake hoses, lines			R		R	
Brake fluid						
Brake discs and calipers						
Brake pads		Inspect every 7,500 miles (12,000 km) or 6 months				
Parking brake						
Clutch release arm travel						
Exhaust pipe and muffler						
Suspension mounting bolts						
Front wheel alignment						
Steering operation, tie rod ends, steering gear box and boots						
Rear wheel bearing grease				R		R
Power steering system						
Power steering pump belt			I*1			
Catalytic converter heat shield						

CAUTION: The following items must be serviced more frequently on cars normally used under severe driving conditions. Refer to the chart below for the appropriate maintenance intervals.

Severe driving conditions include:
A: Repeated short distance driving
B: Driving in dusty conditions
C: Driving in severe cold weather
D: Driving in areas using road salt or other corrosive materials
E: Driving on rough and/or muddy roads

Condition	Maintenance item	Maintenance operation	Interval
A, B ...	Engine oil and oil filter	R	Every 3,000 miles (5,000 km) or 3 months
A, B · D · E	Brake discs and calipers and pads	I	Every 7,500 miles (12,000 km) or 6 months
A, B, C · E	Clutch release-arm travel	I	Every 7,500 miles (12,000 km) or 6 months
B, C · E	Power steering system	I	Every 7,500 miles (12,000 km) or 6 months

Fig. 121 1984-85 Accord maintenance schedule

Service at the interval listed x 1,000 miles (or km) or after that number of months, whichever occurs first.

R—Replace,
C—Clean
I—Inspect
After inspection, clean, adjust, repair or replace if necessary.

*Tension adjustment only
**Thereafter, replace every 2 years or 30,000 miles (48,000 km), whichever comes first.
***Recommended by manufacturer only for cars sold in California.

	miles/months	7.5	15	22.5	30	37.5	45	52.5	60	67.5	75
	km	12	24	36	48	60	72	84	96	108	120
Idle speed and idle CO											
Valve clearance			I		I		I		I		I
Alternator drive belt					I*						
Engine oil		R	R	R	R	R	R	R	R	R	R
Engine oil filter		R	R	R	R	R	R	R	R	R	R
Transmission oil	Manual										
	Automatic										
Radiator coolant			R				R**				R
Cooling system hoses and connections					I						
E.G.R. system											
Secondary air supply system											
Air cleaner element					R				R		
Fuel filter and hoses (Inc. aux. filter)					R				R		
Intake air temp. control system											
Fuel line connections											
Throttle control unit											
Choke mechanism					C						
Choke opener operation											
Evaporative emission control system											
Ignition timing and control system											
Spark plugs			R		R		R		R		R
Distributor cap and rotor											
Ignition wiring											
Crankcase emission control system					I***						
Brake hoses, lines					R				R		
Brake fluid					R				R		
Rear brakes											
Front brake pads, discs and calipers											
Parking brake											
Clutch release-arm travel											
Exhaust pipe and muffler, suspension mounting bolts											
Front wheel alignment											
Steering operation, tie rod ends, steering gear box and boots											
Rear wheel bearing grease									R		
Power steering system											
Power steering pump belt					I*						
Catalytic converter heat shield											

CAUTION:
- If you use the car for a lot of short distance driving, or you drive it in severe cold or heavy dust, change the engine oil and filter every 3,000 miles (5,000 km) or 3 months, whichever occurs first.
- Disc brakes should be serviced every 7.5 months or 7,500 miles (12,000 km), however, in areas using a high concentration of road salt or other corrosive materials, more frequent servicing may be required.

Fig. 123 1986–89 Accord maintenance schedule

R—Replace
C—Clean
I—Inspect
After inspection, clean, adjust, repair or replace if necessary.

*1 Tension adjustment only.
*2 Thereafter, replace every 2 years or 30,000 miles (48,000 km), whichever comes first.
*3 For cars sold in California, this service is recommended; for all other areas, it is required.
*4 LX only
*5 LX only

Service at the interval listed x 1,000 miles (or km) or after that number of months, whichever comes first.	15 / 24 / 12	30 / 48 / 24	45 / 72 / 36	60 / 96 / 48	75 / 120 / 60
Idle speed and idle CO		I*1		I	
Valve clearance		I		I	
Alternator drive belt		I*1		I	
▪ Engine oil and oil filter (◊)	Replace every 7,500 miles (12,000 km) or 6 months				
Transmission oil (◊)		R		R	R*2
▪ Radiator coolant					R*2
Cooling system hoses and connections				I*4	
E.G.R. system					I*4
Secondary air supply system		R		R	R*5
Air cleaner element				R	R*4
Fuel filter and hoses (including aux. filter)				I*4	
Fuel line connections		I*3*5		I*4	
Intake air temp. control system				I*4	
Throttle control system				I*4	
Choke mechanism		C*4		I*4	
Choke opener operation				I*4	
Evaporative emission control system					I
Ignition timing and control system					I
Spark plugs		R		R	
Distributor cap and rotor					I
Ignition wiring					I
Positive crankcase ventilation valve					I
Blow-by filter		I*3*4		I*4	
Brake hoses and lines		I		I	
Brake fluid		R		R	
Front brake discs and calipers (◊)	Inspect every 7,500 miles (12,000 km) or 6 months				
Front brake pads	Inspect every 7,500 miles (12,000 km) or 6 months				
Rear brake drums, wheel cylinders and linings		I		I	
Parking brake		I		I	
Clutch release arm travel (◊)		I		I	
Exhaust pipe and muffler		I		I	
Suspension mounting bolts		I		I	
Front wheel alignment		I		I	
Steering operation, tie rod ends, steering gear box and boots		I		I	
Power steering system (◊)		I		I	
Power steering pump belt		I*1		I	
Catalytic converter heat shield					I

▪ Remark: Check oil and coolant level at each fuel stop.
(◊) Remark: Service more frequently on cars normally used under severe driving conditions.

CAUTION: The following items must be serviced more frequently on cars normally used under severe driving conditions. Refer to the chart below for the appropriate maintenance intervals.

Severe driving conditions include:
A: Repeated short distance driving
B: Driving in dusty conditions
C: Driving in severe cold weather
D: Driving in areas using road salt or other corrosive materials
E: Driving on rough and/or muddy roads
F: Towing a trailer

Condition	Maintenance item	Maintenance operation	Interval
A B · · · F	Engine oil and oil filter	R	Every 3,000 miles (5,000 km) or 3 months
· · · · · F	Transmission oil	R	Every 15,000 miles (24,000 km) or 12 months
A B · D E F	Front brake discs and calipers		Every 7,500 miles (12,000 km) or 6 months
A B C · E F	Clutch release arm travel		Every 3,000 miles (5,000 km) or 3 months
· B C · E ·	Power steering system		Every 7,500 miles (12,000 km) or 6 months

86901202

Fig. 124 1988–91 Prelude maintenance schedule

R—Replace
C—Clean
I—Inspect
After inspection, clean, adjust, repair or replace if necessary.

*1 Tension adjustment only.
*2 Thereafter, replace every 2 years or 30,000 miles (48,000 km), whichever comes first.
*3 For cars sold in California, this service is recommended; for other areas, it is required.
*4 S
*5 S except California S model
*6 Si

Service at the interval listed x 1,000 miles (or km) or after that number of months, whichever comes first.	15 / 24 / 12	30 / 48 / 24	45 / 72 / 36	60 / 96 / 48	75 / 120 / 60
Idle speed and idle CO		I		I	
Valve clearance		I*1		I	
Alternator drive belt		I*1		I	
▪ Engine oil and oil filter (◊)	Replace every 7,500 miles (12,000 km) or 6 months				
Transmission oil (◊)		R		R	R*2
▪ Radiator coolant					R*2
Cooling system hoses and connections				I*4	
E.G.R. system					I*5
Secondary air supply system				R	I*4
Air cleaner element		R		R	
Fuel filter and hoses (inc. aux. filter)		R*5		R	
Fuel line connections		I*3*6		I*4	
Intake air temp. control system				I*4	
Throttle control unit				I*4	
Choke mechanism		C*4		I*4	
Choke opener operation				I*4	
Evaporative emission control system					I
Ignition timing and control system					I
Spark plugs		R		R	
Distributor cap and rotor					I
Ignition wiring					I
Positive crankcase ventilation valve					I
Blow-by filter		I*3*4		I*4	
Brake hoses and lines		I		I	
Brake fluid		R		R	
Front brake discs and calipers (◊)	Inspect every 7,500 miles (12,000 km) or 6 months				
Front brake pads	Inspect every 7,500 miles (12,000 km) or 6 months				
Rear brake discs, calipers and pads (◊)	Inspect every 7,500 miles (12,000 km) or 6 months				
Parking brake		I		I	
Exhaust pipe and muffler		I		I	
Suspension mounting bolts		I		I	
Front and rear wheel alignment (except 4WS models)		I		I	
Front and rear wheel alignment (4WS models)		I		I	
Steering operation, tie rod ends, steering gear box and boots (including center shaft for 4WS models)		I		I	
Power steering system (◊)		I		I	
Power steering pump belt		I*1		I	
Catalytic converter heat shield					I

▪ Remark: Check oil and coolant level at each fuel stop.
(◊) Remark: Service more frequently on cars normally used under severe driving conditions.

CAUTION: The following items must be serviced more frequently on cars normally used under severe driving conditions. Refer to the chart below for the appropriate maintenance intervals.

Severe driving conditions include:
A: Repeated short distance driving
B: Driving in dusty conditions
C: Driving in severe cold weather
D: Driving in areas using road salt or other corrosive materials
E: Driving on rough and/or muddy roads
F: Towing a trailer

Condition	Maintenance item	Maintenance operation	Interval
A B · · · F	Engine oil and oil filter	R	Every 3,000 miles (5,000 km) or 3 months
· · · · · F	Transmission oil	R	Every 15,000 miles (24,000 km) or 6 months
A B · D E F	Brake discs, calipers and rear brake pads		Every 7,500 miles (12,000 km) or 6 months
· B C · E ·	Power steering system		Every 7,500 miles (12,000 km) or 6 months

86901203

Fig. 126 1992–93 Prelude maintenance schedule

R – Replace   I – Inspect   After inspection, clean, adjust, repair or replace if necessary.

Emission Related	x 1,000 km	12	24	36	48	60	72	84	96	108	120	132	144
Service at the interval listed x 1,000 miles (or miles) or after that number of months, whichever comes first.	x 1,000 miles	7.5	15	22.5	30	37.5	45	52.5	60	67.5	75	82.5	90
	months	6	12	18	24	30	36	42	48	54	60	66	72
☐ Air cleaner element													R
Idle speed and idle CO							I						
E.G.R. System													
Evaporative emission control system									I				
Ignition timing													
Positive crankcase ventilation valve													
Valve clearance					R								R
Fuel filter									R				
Fuel line and connections					I**			I					I
Spark plugs					R			R					R
Distributor cap and rotor								R					
Ignition wiring													
● Engine oil and oil filter		R	R	R	R	R	R	R	R	R	R	R	R
● Power steering pump belt					I**								
Cooling system hoses and connections							I						
● Radiator coolant										R*³			
● Transmission oil				R		R			R			R	
Engine (Non-Emission Related)													
Timing belt and timing balancer belt													R
Water pump													
Catalytic converter heat shield													
Exhaust pipe and muffler					I			I					I

● : Check oil and coolant level at each fuel stop.
☐ : Under severe driving conditions, service these items more often.
*1 : For cars sold in California, this service is recommended only; other areas, it is required.
*2 : Tension adjustment only.
*3 : Thereafter, replace every 2 years or 48,000 km (30,000 miles), whichever comes first.
*4 : For cars with Anti-lock brake system. (US, Si 4WS, Canada: SR, SR 4WS)

Brakes (Non-Emission Related)	x 1,000 km	12	24	36	48	60	72	84	96	108	120	132	144
Service at the interval listed x 1,000 km (or miles) or after that number of months, whichever comes first.	x 1,000 miles	7.5	15	22.5	30	37.5	45	52.5	60	67.5	75	82.5	90
	months	6	12	18	24	30	36	42	48	54	60	66	72
Front brake pads		I	☐	I	☐	I	☐	I	☐	I	☐	I	☐
Front brake discs and calipers			☐		☐		☐		☐		☐		☐
Rear brake discs, calipers and pads			☐		☐		☐		☐		☐		☐
Brake hoses and lines (including Anti-lock brake system*¹)					I			I					I
Parking brake					I			I					I
Brake fluid (including Anti-lock brake system*¹)			R		R		R		R		R		R
Anti-lock brake system operation**					R			R					R
Anti-lock brake system high pressure hose**								R					
Steering and suspension (Non-Emission Related)													
Front wheel alignment (Except 4WS model)			I		I		I		I		I		I
Front and rear wheel alignment (For 4WS model)			I		I		I		I		I		I
Steering operation, tie rod ends, steering gear box and boots			I		I		I		I		I		I
Suspension mounting bolts	Except 4WS model												
(including rear actuator for 4WS model)	For 4WS model												
☐ Power steering system													
Suspension mounting bolts					I			I					I

The services are:
– Clean the air cleaner element every 24,000 km (15,000 miles) or 12 months and replace every 48,000 km (30,000 miles) or 24 months under condition B or E.
– Replace engine oil and oil filter every 6,000 km (3,750 miles) or 3 months under condition A, B or F.
– Replace transmission oil every 24,000 km (15,000 miles) or 12 months under condition F.
– Inspect front brake discs and calipers, and rear brake discs, calipers and pads every 12,000 km (7,500 miles) or 6 months under condition A, B, D, E or F.
– Inspect the power steering system every 12,000 km (7,500 miles) or 6 months under condition B, C or E.

The conditions are:
A. Repeated short distance driving.
B. Dusty conditions.
C. Severe cold weather.
D. Areas with road salt or other corrosive materials.
E. Rough or muddy roads.
F. Towing a trailer.

Severe Driving Conditions
Items with an ☒ or ☐ in the chart will need service more often, if you drive in some service conditions.

86801205

Fig. 125 1990–93 Accord maintenance schedule

R – Replace   C – Clean   I – Inspect   After inspection, clean, adjust, repair or replace if necessary.

Service at the interval listed x 1,000 miles (or km) or after that number of months, whichever comes first.		*1 Tension adjustment only.				
		*4 US: EX, Canada: EX-R				
	x 1,000 miles	15	30	45	60	75	90
	x 1,000 km	24	48	72	96	120	144
	months	12	24	36	48	60	72
Idle speed and idle CO		I	I	I	I	I	I
Valve clearance							
Alternator drive belt		I*¹		I*¹		I*¹	
Timing belt and timing balancer belt					R		
Water pump							
● Engine oil and oil filter ●	Replace every 7,500 miles (12,000 km) or 6 months	R	R	R	R	R	R
● Transmission oil			R		R		R*²
Radiator coolant ●					R		
Cooling system hoses and connections					I		
E.G.R. system							
● Air cleaner element			R		R		R
Fuel filter					R		
Fuel line and connections					I		
Evaporative emission control system					I*³		
Ignition timing							
Spark plugs			R		R		R
Distributor cap and rotor							
Ignition wiring							
Positive crankcase ventilation valve							
Brake hoses and lines (including ABS) *⁴					I		
Brake fluid (including ABS) *⁴	Inspect every 7,500 miles (12,000 km) or 6 months	R		R		R	
Front brake discs, calipers and calipers *⁴							
Front brake pads							
Rear brake drums, wheel cylinders and linings							
Parking brake							
Exhaust pipe and muffler					I		
Suspension mounting bolts							
Front wheel alignment							
Steering operation, tie rod ends, steering gear box and boots					R		
ABS high pressure hose *⁴					R		
● ABS operation *⁴							
● Power steering system							
Power steering pump belt		I*¹		I*¹		I*¹	
Catalytic converter heat shield							

● Check oil and coolant level at each fuel stop.
● Under severe driving conditions, service these items more often.

*2 Thereafter, replace every 2 years or 30,000 miles (48,000 km), whichever comes first.
*3 For cars sold in California, this service is recommended only; other areas, it is required.

Severe Driving Conditions
CAUTION:
The following items must be serviced more frequently on cars normally used under severe driving conditions. Refer to the chart below for the appropriate maintenance intervals.

Severe driving conditions include:
A: Repeated short distance driving
B: Driving in dusty conditions
C: Driving in severe cold weather
D: Driving in areas using road salt or other corrosive materials
E: Driving on rough and/or muddy roads
F: Towing a trailer

Condition	Maintenance item	Maintenance operation	Interval
● B ● ● ● E	Air cleaner element	● R	Every 15,000 miles (24,000 km) or 12 months
A B ● ● ● F	Engine oil and oil filter	R	Every 3,750 miles (6,000 km) or 3 months
● ● ● ● ● F	Transmission oil	R	Every 15,000 miles (24,000 km) or 12 months
A B ● D E F	Front brake discs and calipers, and rear brake discs, calipers and pads	I	Every 7,500 miles (12,000 km) or 6 months
● B ● C ● E	Power steering system	I	Every 7,500 miles (12,000 km) or 6 months

86801204

Fig. 128 1994–95 Accord severe maintenance schedule

Service at the indicated distance or time — whichever comes first.	km x 1,000	24	48	72	96	120	144	168
	miles x 1,000	15	30	45	60	75	90	105
	months	12	24	36	48	60	72	84
Replace engine oil and oil filter		Replace every 6,000 km (3,750 miles) or 3 months						
Check engine oil and coolant		Check oil and coolant at each fuel stop						
Clean (O) or replace (●) air cleaner element		O				O		O
Inspect valve clearance			●		●		●	
Replace spark plugs			●				●	
Inspect distributor cap, rotor, and ignition wires					●		●	
Replace timing belt, timing balancer belt, and inspect water pump		Replace every 96,000 km (60,000 miles)						
Inspect and adjust drive belts			●		●		●	
Inspect idle speed					●			
Inspect PCV valve					●			
Replace engine coolant		●		●		●		●
Replace transmission fluid		Inspect every 12,000 km (7,500 miles) or 6 months						
Inspect front and rear brakes		●	●	●	●	●	●	●
Replace brake fluid (including ABS)			●			●		
Check parking brake adjustment		●		●		●		●
Rotate tires (Check tire inflation and condition at least once per month)		Rotate tires every 12,000 km (7,500 miles)						
Visually inspect the following items:								
Tie rod ends, steering gear box, and boots							●	
Suspension components		Every 12,000 km (7,500 miles) or 6 months						
Driveshaft boots								
Brake hoses and lines								
All fluid levels								
Cooling system hoses and connections		●		●		●		●
Exhaust system								
Fuel pipes, hoses, and connections								
Inspect supplemental restraint system		10 years after production						

8680 1207

Fig. 127 1994–95 Accord normal maintenance schedule

Service at the indicated distance or time — whichever comes first.	km x 1,000	24	48	72	96	120	144	168
	miles x 1,000	15	30	45	60	75	90	105
	months	12	24	36	48	60	72	84
Replace engine oil and oil filter		Replace every 12,000 km (7,500 miles) or 6 months						
Check engine oil and coolant		Check oil and coolant at each fuel stop						
Replace air cleaner element			●			●		
Inspect valve clearance			●		●		●	
Replace spark plugs					●			●
Inspect distributor cap, rotor, and ignition wires					●		●	
Replace timing belt, timing balancer belt, and inspect water pump							●	
Inspect and adjust drive belts			●		●		●	
Inspect idle speed					●			
Inspect PCV valve					●			
Replace engine coolant			●		●		●	●
Replace transmission fluid				●			●	
Inspect front and rear brakes		●	●	●	●	●	●	●
Replace brake fluid (including ABS)			●			●		
Check parking brake adjustment		●	●	●	●	●	●	●
Rotate tires (Check tire inflation and condition at least once per month)		Rotate tires every 12,000 km (7,500 miles)						
Visually inspect the following items:								
Brake hoses and lines								
All fluid levels								
Tie rod ends, steering gear box, and boots								
Suspension components								
Driveshaft boots								
Cooling system hoses and connections		●	●	●	●	●	●	●
Exhaust system								
Fuel pipes, hoses, and connections								
Inspect supplemental restraint system		10 years after production						

8680 206

Service at the indicated distance or time – whichever comes first.		km x 1,000	24	48	72	96	120	144	168
		miles x 1,000	15	30	45	60	75	90	105
		months	12	24	36	48	60	72	84
Replace engine oil and oil filter		Replace every 12,000 km (7,500 miles) or 6 months							
Check engine oil and coolant		Check oil and coolant at each fuel stop							
Replace air cleaner element			●		●		●		
Inspect valve clearance	US: S, Si, Canada: S, SR, SR 4WS		●		●		●		
	US: VTEC, Canada: SR-V	●	●	●	●	●	●	●	
Replace spark plugs	non platinum US: S, Si, Canada: S, SR, SR 4WS		●		●		●		
	platinum type US: VTEC, Canada: SR-V	Replace every 96,000 km (60,000 miles) or 72 months							
Inspect distributor cap , rotor , and ignition wires					●				
Replace timing belt , timing balancer belt, and inspect water pump							●		
Inspect and adjust drive belts			●		●		●		
Replace fuel filter					●				
Inspect idle speed					●				
Inspect PCV valve					●				
Replace engine coolant				●		●		●	
Replace transmission fluid			●		●		●		
Inspect front and rear brakes		●	●	●	●	●	●	●	
Replace brake fluid (including ABS)			●		●		●		
Replace ABS high pressure hose					●				
Check parking brake adjustment		●	●	●	●	●	●	●	
Rotate tires (Check tire inflation and condition at least once per month)		Rotate tires every 12,000 km (7,500 miles)							
Visually inspect the following items:									
Brake hoses and lines/ All fluid levels/Tie rod ends, steering gear box, and boots (including 4WS rear actuator)/Suspension components/Driveshaft boots/ Cooling system hoses and connections/Exhaust system / Fuel pipes, hoses, and connections		●	●	●	●	●	●	●	
Inspect Supplemental Restraint System		10 years after production							

86801208

Fig. 129 1994–95 Prelude normal maintenance schedule

Service at the indicated distance or time – whichever comes first.		km x 1,000	24	48	72	96	120	144	168
		miles x 1,000	15	30	45	60	75	90	105
		months	12	24	36	48	60	72	84
Replace engine oil and oil filter		Replace every 6,000 km (3,750 miles) or 3 months							
Check engine oil and coolant		Check oil and coolant at each fuel stop							
Clean (O) or replace (●) air cleaner element			O	●	O	●	O	●	O
Inspect valve clearance	US: S, Si, Canada: S, SR, SR 4WS			●		●		●	
	US: VTEC, Canada: SR-V		●	●	●	●	●	●	●
Replace spark plugs	non platinum US: S, Si, Canada: S, SR, SR 4WS			●		●		●	
	platinum type US: VTEC, Canada: SR-V	Replace every 96,000 km (60,000 miles) or 72 months							
Inspect distributor cap , rotor , and ignition wires						●			
Replace timing belt , timing balancer belt, and inspect water pump		Replace every 96,000 km (60,000 miles)							
Inspect and adjust drive belts				●		●		●	
Replace fuel filter						●			
Inspect idle speed						●			
Inspect PCV valve						●			
Replace engine coolant					●		●		●
Replace transmission fluid			●	●	●	●	●	●	●
Inspect front and rear brakes		Inspect every 12,000 km (7,500 miles) or 6 months							
Replace brake fluid (including ABS)				●		●		●	
Replace ABS high pressure hose						●			
Check parking brake adjustment			●	●	●	●	●	●	●
Rotate tires (Check tire inflation and condition at least once per month)		Rotate tires every 12,000 km (7,500 miles)							
Visually inspect the following items:									
Tie rod ends, steering gear box, and boots (including 4WS rear actuator)/Suspension components/Driveshaft boots		Every 12,000 km (7,500 miles) or 6 months							
Brake hoses and lines/All fluid levels/Cooling system hoses and connections/Exhaust system /Fuel pipes, hoses, and connections			●	●	●	●	●	●	●
Inspect Supplemental Restraint System		10 years after production							

86801209

Fig. 130 1994–95 Prelude severe maintenance schedule

CAPACITIES

Year	Model	Engine ID/VIN	Engine Displacement Liters (cc)	Engine Oil with Filter	Transmission (pts.)			Transfer Case (pts.)	Drive Axle		Fuel Tank (gal.)	Cooling System (qts.)
					4-Spd	5-Spd	Auto.		Front (pts.)	Rear (pts.)		
1984	Accord	ES2, ES3	1.8 (1829)	3.7	-	5.0	6.0	-	-	-	15.8	6.4
	Prelude	ET2	1.8 (1829)	3.7	-	5.0	5.8	-	-	-	15.9	6.3 [1]
1985	Accord	ES2, ES3	1.8 (1829)	3.7	-	5.0	6.0	-	-	-	15.8	6.4
	Prelude	ET2	1.8 (1829)	3.7	-	5.0	5.8	-	-	-	15.9	6.3 [1]
1986	Accord	BS	2.0 (1955)	3.7	-	5.0	5.2	-	-	-	15.9	5.2
	Prelude	ET2	1.8 (1829)	3.7	-	5.0	5.8	-	-	-	15.9	6.3
	Prelude	BT	2.0 (1955)	3.7	-	5.0	5.8	-	-	-	15.9	6.3
1987	Accord	A20A1	2.0 (1955)	3.7	-	5.0	5.2	-	-	-	15.9	5.2 [2]
	Prelude	A18A1	1.8 (1829)	3.7	-	5.0	5.8	-	-	-	15.9	6.3 [3]
	Prelude Si	A20A3	2.0 (1955)	3.7	-	5.0	5.8	-	-	-	15.9	6.3 [3]
1988	Accord	A20A1	2.0 (1955)	3.7	-	5.0	6.0	-	-	-	15.9	5.8
	Prelude	B20A3	2.0 (1955)	4.1	4.0	4.0	6.0	-	-	-	15.9	8.2
1989	Accord	A20A1	2.0 (1955)	3.7	-	4.8	6.4	-	-	-	15.9	[4]
	Prelude	B20A3	2.0 (1955)	4.1	4.0	4.0	6.0	-	-	-	15.9	[5]
1990	Accord, DX/LX	F22A1	2.2 (2156)	4.0	-	4.0	5.0	-	-	-	17.0	[6]
	Accord EX	F22A4	2.2 (2156)	4.0	-	4.0	5.0	-	-	-	17.0	[6]
	Prelude S	B20A3	2.0 (1955)	4.0	-	4.4	6.0	-	-	-	15.9	[7]
	Prelude Si	B20A5	2.0 (1955)	4.0	-	4.4	6.0	-	-	-	15.9	[7]
	Prelude Si	B21A1	2.1 (2056)	4.0	-	4.4	6.0	-	-	-	15.9	8.2
1991	Accord, DX/LX	F22A1	2.2 (2156)	4.0	-	4.0 [1]	5.0	-	-	-	17.0	[6]
	Accord EX	F22A4	2.2 (2156)	4.0	-	4.0	5.0	-	-	-	17.0	[6]
	Accord SE	F22A6	2.2 (2156)	4.0	-	4.0	5.0	-	-	-	17.0	[6]
	Prelude Si	B20A5	2.0 (1955)	4.0	-	4.4	6.0	-	-	-	15.9	[7]
	Prelude Si	B21A1	2.1 (2056)	4.0	-	4.4	6.0	-	-	-	15.9	8.2
1992	Accord, DX/LX	F22A1	2.2 (2156)	4.0	-	4.0	5.0	-	-	-	17.0	[8]
	Accord EX	F22A4	2.2 (2156)	4.0	-	4.0	5.0	-	-	-	17.0	[8]
	Accord EX-R	F22A6	2.2 (2156)	4.0	-	4.0	5.0	-	-	-	17.0	[8]
	Prelude S	F22A1	2.2 (2156)	4.0	-	4.0	5.6	-	-	-	15.9	[9]
	Prelude Si	H23A1	2.3 (2259)	4.5	-	4.0	5.6	-	-	-	15.9	[10]
1993	Accord DX/LX [11]	F22A1	2.2 (2156)	4.0	-	4.0	5.0	-	-	-	17.0	[13]
	Accord EX/SE [12]	F22A6	2.2 (2156)	4.0	-	4.0	5.0	-	-	-	17.0	[13]
	Prelude S	F22A1	2.2 (2156)	4.0	-	4.0	5.0	-	-	-	15.9	[14]
	Prelude VTEC	H22A1	2.2 (2157)	5.1	-	4.0	-	-	-	-	15.9	4.4
	Prelude Si	H23A1	2.3 (2259)	4.5	-	4.0	5.0	-	-	-	15.9	[15]
1994	Accord EX [16]	F22B1	2.2 (2156)	4.0	-	4.0	5.0	-	-	-	17.0	[18]
	Accord DX/LX [17]	F22B2	2.2 (2156)	4.0	-	4.0	5.0	-	-	-	17.0	[18]
	Prelude S	F22A1	2.2 (2156)	4.0	-	4.0	5.0	-	-	-	15.9	[19]
	Prelude VTEC	H22A1	2.2 (2157)	5.1	-	4.0	-	-	-	-	15.9	4.6
	Prelude Si	H23A1	2.3 (2259)	4.5	-	4.0	5.0	-	-	-	15.9	[15]
1995	Accord EX [16]	F22B1	2.2 (2156)	4.5	-	4.0	5.0	-	-	-	17.0	[18]
	Accord DX/LX [17]	F22B2	2.2 (2156)	4.0	-	4.0	5.0	-	-	-	17.0	[18]
	Accord V-6	C27A4	2.7 (2675)	4.6	-	-	6.2	-	-	-	17.0	7.2
	Prelude S	F22A1	2.2 (2156)	4.0	-	4.0	5.0	-	-	-	15.9	[19]
	Prelude VTEC	H22A1	2.2 (2157)	5.1	-	4.0	-	-	-	-	15.9	4.6
	Prelude Si	H23A1	2.3 (2259)	4.5	-	4.0	5.0	-	-	-	15.9	[15]

NOTE: Capacities given are service, not overhaul capacities

1- Automatic transaxle: 7.1
2- Automatic transaxle: 5.8
3- Automatic transaxle: 7.1
4- Manual transaxle: 6.9
   Automatic transaxle: 7.2
5- Fuel Injection: 8.2
   Carbureted with M/T: 7.2
   Carbureted with A/T: 7.9

6- Manual transaxle: 7.0
   Automatic transaxle: 7.5
7- Prelude 2.0 S
   Manual transaxle: 7.2
   Automatic transaxle: 7.9
8- Automatic transaxle: 7.3
   Manual transaxle: 7.4
9- Automatic transaxle: 7.4
   Manual transaxle: 7.5

10- Automatic transaxle: 7.7
   Manual transaxle: 7.8
11- Canadian models: LX/EX
12- Canadian models: EX-R/SE
13- Automatic transaxle: 3.7
   Manual transaxle: 3.2
14- Automatic transaxle: 3.6
   Manual transaxle: 3.8

15- Automatic transaxle: 3.9
   Manual transaxle: 4.0
16- Canadian models: EX-R
17- Canadian models: LX/FX
18- Automatic transaxle: 5.6
   Manual transaxle: 5.7
19- Automatic transaxle: 3.6
   Manual transaxle: 3.7

86801302

ENGLISH TO METRIC CONVERSION: MASS (WEIGHT)

Current mass measurement is expressed in pounds and ounces (lbs. & ozs.). The metric unit of mass (or weight) is the kilogram (kg). Even although this table does not show conversion of masses (weights) larger than 15 lbs, it is easy to calculate larger units by following the data immediately below.

To convert ounces (oz.) to grams (g): multiply th number of ozs. by 28
To convert grams (g) to ounces (oz.): multiply the number of grams by .035

To convert pounds (lbs.) to kilograms (kg): multiply the number of lbs. by .45
To convert kilograms (kg) to pounds (lbs.): multiply the number of kilograms by 2.2

lbs	kg	lbs	kg	oz	kg	oz	kg
0.1	0.04	0.9	0.41	0.1	0.003	0.9	0.024
0.2	0.09	1	0.4	0.2	0.005	1	0.03
0.3	0.14	2	0.9	0.3	0.008	2	0.06
0.4	0.18	3	1.4	0.4	0.011	3	0.08
0.5	0.23	4	1.8	0.5	0.014	4	0.11
0.6	0.27	5	2.3	0.6	0.017	5	0.14
0.7	0.32	10	4.5	0.7	0.020	10	0.28
0.8	0.36	15	6.8	0.8	0.023	15	0.42

ENGLISH TO METRIC CONVERSION: TEMPERATURE

To convert Fahrenheit (°F) to Celsius (°C): take number of °F and subtract 32; multiply result by 5; divide result by 9

To convert Celsius (°C) to Fahrenheit (°F): take number of °C and multiply by 9; divide result by 5; add 32 to total

Fahrenheit (F)		Celsius (C)		Fahrenheit (F)		Celsius (C)		Fahrenheit (F)		Celsius (C)	
°F	°C	°C	°F	°F	°C	°C	°F	°F	°C	°C	°F
−40	−40	−38	−36.4	80	26.7	18	64.4	215	101.7	80	176
−35	−37.2	−36	−32.8	85	29.4	20	68	220	104.4	85	185
−30	−34.4	−34	−29.2	90	32.2	22	71.6	225	107.2	90	194
−25	−31.7	−32	−25.6	95	35.0	24	75.2	230	110.0	95	202
−20	−28.9	−30	−22	100	37.8	26	78.8	235	112.8	100	212
−15	−26.1	−28	−18.4	105	40.6	28	82.4	240	115.6	105	221
−10	−23.3	−26	−14.8	110	43.3	30	86	245	118.3	110	230
−5	−20.6	−24	−11.2	115	46.1	32	89.6	250	121.1	115	239
0	−17.8	−22	−7.6	120	48.9	34	93.2	255	123.9	120	248
1	−17.2	−20	−4	125	51.7	36	96.8	260	126.6	125	257
2	−16.7	−18	−0.4	130	54.4	38	100.4	265	129.4	130	266
3	−16.1	−16	3.2	135	57.2	40	104	270	132.2	135	275
4	−15.6	−14	6.8	140	60.0	42	107.6	275	135.0	140	284
5	−15.0	−12	10.4	145	62.8	44	112.2	280	137.8	145	293
10	−12.2	−10	14	150	65.6	46	114.8	285	140.6	150	302
15	−9.4	−8	17.6	155	68.3	48	118.4	290	143.3	155	311
20	−6.7	−6	21.2	160	71.1	50	122	295	146.1	160	320
25	−3.9	−4	24.8	165	73.9	52	125.6	300	148.9	165	329
30	−1.1	−2	28.4	170	76.7	54	129.2	305	151.7	170	338
35	1.7	0	32	175	79.4	56	132.8	310	154.4	175	347
40	4.4	2	35.6	180	82.2	58	136.4	315	157.2	180	356
45	7.2	4	39.2	185	85.0	60	140	320	160.0	185	365
50	10.0	6	42.8	190	87.8	62	143.6	325	162.8	190	374
55	12.8	8	46.4	195	90.6	64	147.2	330	165.6	195	383
60	15.6	10	50	200	93.3	66	150.8	335	168.3	200	392
65	18.3	12	53.6	205	96.1	68	154.4	340	171.1	205	401
70	21.1	14	57.2	210	98.9	70	158	345	173.9	210	410
75	23.9	16	60.8	212	100.0	75	167	350	176.7	215	414

TCCS1C01

ENGLISH TO METRIC CONVERSION: LENGTH

To convert inches (ins.) to millimeters (mm): multiply number of inches by 25.4

To convert millimeters (mm) to inches (ins.): multiply number of millimeters by .04

Inches	Decimals	Milli-meters	Inches to millimeters inches	mm	Inches	Decimals	Milli-meters	Inches to millimeters inches	mm
1/64	0.051625	0.3969	0.0001	0.00254	33/64	0.515625	13.0969	0.6	15.24
1/32	0.03125	0.7937	0.0002	0.00508	17/32	0.53125	13.4937	0.7	17.78
3/64	0.046875	1.1906	0.0003	0.00762	35/64	0.546875	13.8906	0.8	20.32
1/16	0.0625	1.5875	0.0004	0.01016	9/16	0.5625	14.2875	0.9	22.86
5/64	0.078125	1.9844	0.0005	0.01270	37/64	0.578125	14.6844	1	25.4
3/32	0.09375	2.3812	0.0006	0.01524	19/32	0.59375	15.0812	2	50.8
7/64	0.109375	2.7781	0.0007	0.01778	39/64	0.609375	15.4781	3	76.2
1/8	0.125	3.1750	0.0008	0.02032	5/8	0.625	15.8750	4	101.6
9/64	0.140625	3.5719	0.0009	0.02286	41/64	0.640625	16.2719	5	127.0
5/32	0.15625	3.9687	0.001	0.0254	21/32	0.65625	16.6687	6	152.4
11/64	0.171875	4.3656	0.002	0.0508	43/64	0.671875	17.0656	7	177.8
3/16	0.1875	4.7625	0.003	0.0762	11/16	0.6875	17.4625	8	203.2
13/64	0.203125	5.1594	0.004	0.1016	45/64	0.703125	17.8594	9	228.6
7/32	0.21875	5.5562	0.005	0.1270	23/32	0.71875	18.2562	10	254.0
15/64	0.234375	5.9531	0.006	0.1524	47/64	0.734375	18.6531	11	279.4
1/4	0.25	6.3500	0.007	0.1778	3/4	0.75	19.0500	12	304.8
17/64	0.265625	6.7469	0.008	0.2032	49/64	0.765625	19.4469	13	330.2
9/32	0.28125	7.1437	0.009	0.2286	25/32	0.78125	19.8437	14	355.6
19/64	0.296875	7.5406	0.01	0.254	51/64	0.796875	20.2406	15	381.0
5/16	0.3125	7.9375	0.02	0.508	13/16	0.8125	20.6375	16	406.4
21/64	0.328125	8.3344	0.03	0.762	53/64	0.828125	21.0344	17	431.8
11/32	0.34375	8.7312	0.04	1.016	27/32	0.84375	21.4312	18	457.2
23/64	0.359375	9.1281	0.05	1.270	55/64	0.859375	21.8281	19	482.6
3/8	0.375	9.5250	0.06	1.524	7/8	0.875	22.2250	20	508.0
25/64	0.390625	9.9219	0.07	1.778	57/64	0.890625	22.6219	21	533.4
13/32	0.40625	10.3187	0.08	2.032	29/32	0.90625	23.0187	22	558.8
27/64	0.421875	10.7156	0.09	2.286	59/64	0.921875	23.4156	23	584.2
7/16	0.4375	11.1125	0.1	2.54	15/16	0.9375	23.8125	24	609.6
29/64	0.453125	11.5094	0.2	5.08	61/64	0.953125	24.2094	25	635.0
15/32	0.46875	11.9062	0.3	7.62	31/32	0.96875	24.6062	26	660.4
31/64	0.484375	12.3031	0.4	10.16	63/64	0.984375	25.0031	27	690.6
1/2	0.5	12.7000	0.5	12.70					

ENGLISH TO METRIC CONVERSION: TORQUE

To convert foot-pounds (ft. lbs.) to Newton-meters: multiply the number of ft. lbs. by 1.3

To convert inch-pounds (in. lbs.) to Newton-meters: multiply the number of in. lbs. by .11

in lbs	N-m	in lbs	N-m	in lbs	N-m	in lbs	N-m	in lbs	N-m
0.1	0.01	1	0.11	10	1.13	19	2.15	28	3.16
0.2	0.02	2	0.23	11	1.24	20	2.26	29	3.28
0.3	0.03	3	0.34	12	1.36	21	2.37	30	3.39
0.4	0.04	4	0.45	13	1.47	22	2.49	31	3.50
0.5	0.06	5	0.56	14	1.58	23	2.60	32	3.62
0.6	0.07	6	0.68	15	1.70	24	2.71	33	3.73
0.7	0.08	7	0.78	16	1.81	25	2.82	34	3.84
0.8	0.09	8	0.90	17	1.92	26	2.94	35	3.95
0.9	0.10	9	1.02	18	2.03	27	3.05	36	4.0

ENGLISH TO METRIC CONVERSION: TORQUE

Torque is now expressed as either foot-pounds (ft./lbs.) or inch-pounds (in./lbs.). The metric measurement unit for torque is the Newton-meter (Nm). This unit—the Nm—will be used for all SI metric torque references, both the present ft./lbs. and in./lbs.

ft lbs	N-m	ft lbs	N-m	ft lbs	N-m	ft lbs	N-m
0.1	0.1	33	44.7	74	100.3	115	155.9
0.2	0.3	34	46.1	75	101.7	116	157.3
0.3	0.4	35	47.4	76	103.0	117	158.6
0.4	0.5	36	48.8	77	104.4	118	160.0
0.5	0.7	37	50.7	78	105.8	119	161.3
0.6	0.8	38	51.5	79	107.1	120	162.7
0.7	1.0	39	52.9	80	108.5	121	164.0
0.8	1.1	40	54.2	81	109.8	122	165.4
0.9	1.2	41	55.6	82	111.2	123	166.8
1	1.3	42	56.9	83	112.5	124	168.1
2	2.7	43	58.3	84	113.9	125	169.5
3	4.1	44	59.7	85	115.2	126	170.8
4	5.4	45	61.0	86	116.6	127	172.2
5	6.8	46	62.4	87	118.0	128	173.5
6	8.1	47	63.7	88	119.3	129	174.9
7	9.5	48	65.1	89	120.7	130	176.2
8	10.8	49	66.4	90	122.0	131	177.6
9	12.2	50	67.8	91	123.4	132	179.0
10	13.6	51	69.2	92	124.7	133	180.3
11	14.9	52	70.5	93	126.1	134	181.7
12	16.3	53	71.9	94	127.4	135	183.0
13	17.6	54	73.2	95	128.8	136	184.4
14	18.9	55	74.6	96	130.2	137	185.7
15	20.3	56	75.9	97	131.5	138	187.1
16	21.7	57	77.3	98	132.9	139	188.5
17	23.0	58	78.6	99	134.2	140	189.8
18	24.4	59	80.0	100	135.6	141	191.2
19	25.8	60	81.4	101	136.9	142	192.5
20	27.1	61	82.7	102	138.3	143	193.9
21	28.5	62	84.1	103	139.6	144	195.2
22	29.8	63	85.4	104	141.0	145	196.6
23	31.2	64	86.8	105	142.4	146	198.0
24	32.5	65	88.1	106	143.7	147	199.3
25	33.9	66	89.5	107	145.1	148	200.7
26	35.2	67	90.8	108	146.4	149	202.0
27	36.6	68	92.2	109	147.8	150	203.4
28	38.0	69	93.6	110	149.1	151	204.7
29	39.3	70	94.9	111	150.5	152	206.1
30	40.7	71	96.3	112	151.8	153	207.4
31	42.0	72	97.6	113	153.2	154	208.8
32	43.4	73	99.0	114	154.6	155	210.2

TCCS1C03

ENGLISH TO METRIC CONVERSION: FORCE

Force is presently measured in pounds (lbs.). This type of measurement is used to measure spring pressure, specifically how many pounds it takes to compress a spring. Our present force unit (the pound) will be replaced in SI metric measurements by the Newton (N). This term will eventually see use in specifications for electric motor brush spring pressures, valve spring pressures, etc.

To convert pounds (lbs.) to Newton (N): multiply the number of lbs. by 4.45

lbs	N	lbs	N	lbs	N	oz	N
0.01	0.04	21	93.4	59	262.4	1	0.3
0.02	0.09	22	97.9	60	266.9	2	0.6
0.03	0.13	23	102.3	61	271.3	3	0.8
0.04	0.18	24	106.8	62	275.8	4	1.1
0.05	0.22	25	111.2	63	280.2	5	1.4
0.06	0.27	26	115.6	64	284.6	6	1.7
0.07	0.31	27	120.1	65	289.1	7	2.0
0.08	0.36	28	124.6	66	293.6	8	2.2
0.09	0.40	29	129.0	67	298.0	9	2.5
0.1	0.4	30	133.4	68	302.5	10	2.8
0.2	0.9	31	137.9	69	306.9	11	3.1
0.3	1.3	32	142.3	70	311.4	12	3.3
0.4	1.8	33	146.8	71	315.8	13	3.6
0.5	2.2	34	151.2	72	320.3	14	3.9
0.6	2.7	35	155.7	73	324.7	15	4.2
0.7	3.1	36	160.1	74	329.2	16	4.4
0.8	3.6	37	164.6	75	333.6	17	4.7
0.9	4.0	38	169.0	76	338.1	18	5.0
1	4.4	39	173.5	77	342.5	19	5.3
2	8.9	40	177.9	78	347.0	20	5.6
3	13.4	41	182.4	79	351.4	21	5.8
4	17.8	42	186.8	80	355.9	22	6.1
5	22.2	43	191.3	81	360.3	23	6.4
6	26.7	44	195.7	82	364.8	24	6.7
7	31.1	45	200.2	83	369.2	25	7.0
8	35.6	46	204.6	84	373.6	26	7.2
9	40.0	47	209.1	85	378.1	27	7.5
10	44.5	48	213.5	86	382.6	28	7.8
11	48.9	49	218.0	87	387.0	29	8.1
12	53.4	50	224.4	88	391.4	30	8.3
13	57.8	51	226.9	89	395.9	31	8.6
14	62.3	52	231.3	90	400.3	32	8.9
15	66.7	53	235.8	91	404.8	33	9.2
16	71.2	54	240.2	92	409.2	34	9.4
17	75.6	55	244.6	93	413.7	35	9.7
18	80.1	56	249.1	94	418.1	36	10.0
19	84.5	57	253.6	95	422.6	37	10.3
20	89.0	58	258.0	96	427.0	38	10.6

TCCS1CC04

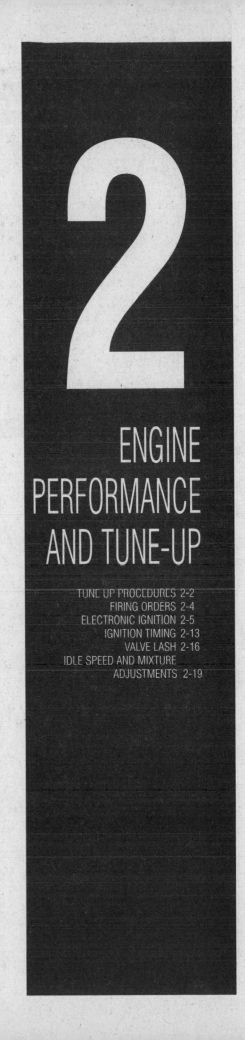

2

ENGINE PERFORMANCE AND TUNE-UP

TUNE UP PROCEDURES

In order to extract the best performance and economy from your engine, it is essential that it be properly tuned at regular intervals. Although computerized engine controls and more durable components have reduced ignition maintenance, a regular tune-up will keep your Honda's engine running smoothly and will prevent the annoying minor breakdowns and poor performance associated with an untuned engine.

Federal law now requires manufacturers to certify that their vehicle's spark plugs will meet emission rules for 30,000 miles (48,300 km). The maintenance schedules reflect this, showing a mandatory replacement at this mileage. This is a minimum specification; but for many vehicles, 30,000 miles (48,300 km) is too long. Plan on at least checking spark plugs and other ignition components at least once per year. Check them anytime a deterioration of engine performance is noted. Replaceable tune-up components are relatively inexpensive compared to the inconveniences of a poorly running vehicle or one that will not start.

This inspection interval should be halved if the car is operated under severe conditions, such as trailer towing, prolonged idling, continual stop and start driving, or if starting or running problems are noticed. It is assumed that the routine maintenance described in Section 1 has been kept up, as this will have a profound effect on the results of a tune-up. All of the applicable steps of a tune-up should be followed in order, as the result is a cumulative one.

If the specifications on the tune-up or emission label in the engine compartment of your Honda disagree with the tune-up specifications chart in this section, the figures on the sticker must be used. The sticker often reflects changes made during the production run.

Spark Plugs

Spark plugs ignite the air and fuel mixture in the cylinder as the piston reaches the top of the compression stroke. The controlled explosion that results forces the piston down, turning the crankshaft and the rest of the drive train.

The average life of a spark plug is dependent on a number of factors: the mechanical condition of the engine, the type of fuel, the driving conditions and the driver. Although the standard factory plugs will last a considerable period of time, extended life may be gained in some engines by using platinum-tipped plugs. You must decide if the benefits outweigh the extra cost.

When you remove the spark plugs, check their condition. They are a good indicator of the condition of the engine. A small deposit of light tan or gray material (or rusty red with some fuels) on a spark plug that has been used for any period of time is to be considered normal. Any other color, or abnormal amounts of deposit, indicates that there is something amiss in the engine.

The gap between the center electrode and the side or ground electrode can be expected to increase very slightly under normal conditions.

When a spark plug is functioning normally or, more accurately, when the plug is installed in an engine that is functioning properly, the plugs can be taken out, cleaned, regapped, and reinstalled in the engine without doing the engine any harm. This is acceptable as an improvement or emergency measure, but new plugs are always recommended.

When, and if, a plug fouls and begins to misfire, you will have to investigate, correct the cause of the fouling, and either clean or replace the plug. Replacement is always recommended if possible.

Spark plugs suitable for use in your engine are offered in different heat ranges. The amount of heat which the plug absorbs is determined by the length of the lower insulator. The longer the insulator the hotter the plug will operate; the shorter the insulator, the cooler it will operate. A spark plug that absorbs little heat and remains too cool will accumulate deposits of lead, oil, and carbon, because it is not hot enough to burn them off. This leads to fouling and consequent misfiring.

A spark plug that absorbs too much heat will have no deposits, but the electrodes will burn away quickly and, in some cases, preignition may result. Preignition occurs when the spark plug tips get so hot, they ignite the air/fuel mixture before the actual spark fires. This premature ignition will usually cause a pinging sound under conditions of low speed and heavy load. In severe cases, the heat may become high enough to start the air/fuel mixture burning throughout the combustion chamber rather than just to the front of the plug. In this case, the resultant explosion will be strong enough to damage pistons, rings, and valves.

In most cases the factory recommended heat range is correct; it is chosen to perform well under a wide range of operating conditions. However, if most of your driving is long distance, high speed travel, you may want to install a spark plug one step colder than standard. If most of your driving is of the short trip variety, when the engine may not always reach operating temperature, a hotter plug may help burn off the deposits normally accumulated under those conditions.

REMOVAL

▶ See Figures 1, 2 and 3

✳✳ CAUTION

Keep hands, clothing and tools away from the radiator fan(s). On certain vehicles, the fans may start automatically up to 15 minutes after the engine is switched off.

1. Tag and number the spark plug wires so that you won't cross them during installation.
2. Remove the wire from the end of the spark plug by grasping the wire on the rubber boot. If the boot sticks to the plug, remove it by twisting and pulling at the same time. Do not pull wire itself or you will damage the core. On Dual Overhead Cam (DOHC) engines, the plugs are deeply recessed between the cams. The wires have long, solid tubes running through the tunnels to the plugs; use great care in removing the wires and tubes.
3. Use a spark plug socket to loosen all of the plugs about two turns. Depending on location of the plug, a short extension on the wrench can be very handy. Make certain to keep the line of the wrench exactly on the line of the plug; if the wrench is cocked to one side, the plug may break off.

➡ **The cylinder head is cast from aluminum alloy. Remove the spark plugs when the engine is cold, if possible, to prevent damage to the threads. If removal of the plugs is difficult, apply a few drops of penetrating oil or silicone spray to the area around the base of the plug, and allow it some time to work.**

4. If compressed air is available, apply it to the area around the spark plug holes. Otherwise, use a rag or a brush to clean the area. Be careful not to allow any foreign material to drop into the spark plug holes.

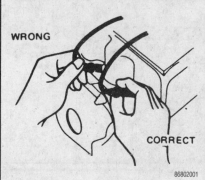

Fig. 1 Never pull on the wire; always grasp the boot of the spark plug wire

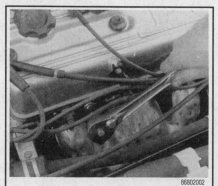

Fig. 2 An extension is useful for reaching the spark plugs

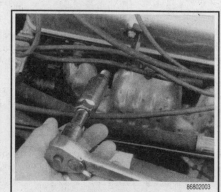

Fig. 3 Carefully withdraw the spark plug from the cylinder head after unscrewing it

5. Remove the plugs by unscrewing them the rest of the way from the engine. If the plug can be reached by hand, remove the plug manually. On DOHC engines, the plug must be unscrewed and lifted out with the plug wrench.

INSPECTION

▶ See Figures 4, 5, 6 and 7

Check the plugs for deposits and wear. If they are not going to be replaced, clean the plugs thoroughly. This may be done with very fine sandpaper or a small flat file. Do not use a wire brush. Remember that any kind of deposit will decrease the efficiency of the plug. Plugs can be cleaned on a spark plug cleaning machine, which can sometimes be found in service stations. If the plugs are cleaned, the electrodes must be filed flat. Use an ignition point file, not an emery board or the like, which will leave deposits. The electrodes must be filed perfectly flat with sharp edges; rounded edges reduce the spark plug voltage by as much as 50 percent.

Check the spark plug gap before installation. The ground electrode (the L-shaped one connected to the body of the plug) must be parallel to the center electrode and the specified-size wire gauge must fit in the gap with slight resistance. Correct gap for all Accords and Preludes covered by this book is 0.039–0.043 in. (1.0–1.1mm).

➡**NEVER adjust the gap on a platinum-tipped spark plug.**

Always check the gap on new plugs too. NEVER rely on so-called "pregapped plugs." Do not use a flat feeler gauge when measuring the gap; the reading will be inaccurate. Wire-type plug gapping tools usually have a bending tool attached. Use that to adjust the side electrode until the proper distance is obtained. Absolutely never bend the center electrode. Also, be careful not to bend the side electrode too far or too often. It may weaken and break off within the engine, requiring removal of the cylinder head to retrieve it.

INSTALLATION

▶ See Figure 8

➡**On some 1990 and later models, a new type of plug with an extended tip and shorter terminal is used. When replacing these plugs, make certain the identical type of spark plug is used. Vehicles using this type of plug have small reminder emblems sealed onto the air cleaner cover.**

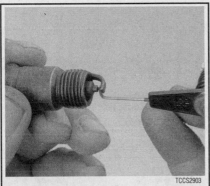

Fig. 4 Checking the spark plug gap with a feeler gauge

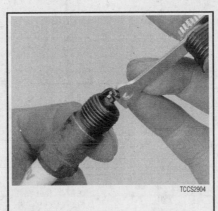

Fig. 5 Adjusting the spark plug gap

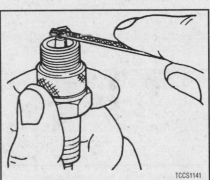

Fig. 6 If the standard plug is in good condition, the electrode may be filed flat— WARNING: do not file platinum plugs

A **normally worn** spark plug should have light tan or gray deposits on the firing tip.

A **physically damaged** spark plug may be evidence of severe detonation in that cylinder. Watch that cylinder carefully between services, as a continued detonation will not only damage the plug, but could also damage the engine.

An **oil fouled** spark plug indicates an engine with worn poston rings and/or bad valve seals allowing excessive oil to enter the chamber.

This spark plug has been **left in the engine too long**, as evidenced by the extreme gap- Plugs with such an extreme gap can cause misfiring and stumbling accompanied by a noticeable lack of power.

A **carbon fouled** plug, identified by soft, sooty, black deposits, may indicate an improperly tuned vehicle. Check the air cleaner, ignition components and engine control system.

A **bridged or almost bridged** spark plug, identified by a build-up between the electrodes caused by excessive carbon or oil build-up on the plug.

Fig. 7 Inspect the spark plug to determine engine running conditions

1. Lubricate the threads of the spark plugs with a drop of oil or anti-seize compound. Install the plugs by hand and tighten them just finger-tight. Never attempt to perform the initial installation with a wrench; take care not to cross-thread them. For DOHC engines, detach the ratchet driver; use your hand to turn the socket and extension very gently until the plug threads seat and the plug turns in.

2. Tighten the spark plugs with the socket (approximately a ½ turn). Do not apply the same amount of force you would use for a bolt; just snug them in. If a torque wrench is available, tighten them to 13 ft. lbs. (18 Nm).

3. Install the wires on their respective plugs. Make sure the wires are firmly connected. You will be able to feel them click into place. Additionally, make certain each wire is replaced into any clip or holder on its path. These wiring clips keep the spark plug wires from creating electrical interference in each other and also keep the engine looking neat.

Spark Plug Wires

TESTING & REPLACEMENT

◗ **See Figures 9 and 10**

At every tune-up, visually inspect the spark plug cables for burns, cuts, or breaks in the insulation. Check the boots and the nipples on the distributor cap and coil. Replace any damaged wiring. Always replace spark plug wiring in sets, with a coil wire as well. Length is important; get the correct set for your vehicle.

Every 36,000 miles (58,000 km) or so, the resistance of the wires should be checked with an ohmmeter. Wires with excessive resistance will cause misfiring, and may make the engine difficult to start in damp weather. Generally, the useful life of the cables is 36,000–50,000 miles (58,000–80,000 km).

To check resistance, remove the wire from the plug and the distributor cap. Look at each contact inside the wire for any sign of cracking or burning. A small amount of discoloration is normal but there should be no heavy burn marks. Connect one lead of an ohmmeter to each end of the cable. Replace any wire which shows a resistance over 25,000 ohms.

Test the high tension lead from the coil in the same fashion. If resistance is more than 25,000 ohms, replace the cable. It should be remembered that resistance is also a function of length; the longer the cable, the greater the resistance. Thus, if the cables on your car are longer than the factory originals, resistance will be higher, quite possibly outside these limits. Honda recommends the 25,000 ohm limit be observed in all cases.

When installing new cables, replace them one at a time to avoid mixups. Start by replacing the longest one first. Install the boot firmly over the spark plug. Route the wire over the same path as the original. Insert the nipple firmly into the tower on the cap or the coil. Make certain each cable is replaced in any holding or retaining clips along the route.

Fig. 8 These marks indicate the use of a new design spark plug. Do not use conventional plugs in engines equipped with this type of spark plug

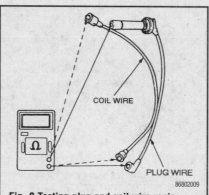

Fig. 9 Testing plug and coil wire resistance

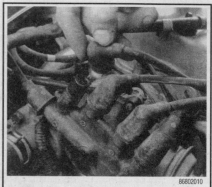

Fig. 10 Note the cylinder number markings on the wire and distributor cap

FIRING ORDERS

◗ **See Figures 11, 12, 13, 14 and 15**

➥**To avoid confusion, remove and tag the spark plug wires one at a time, for replacement.**

If a distributor is not keyed for installation with only one orientation, it could have been removed previously and rewired. The resultant wiring would hold the correct firing order, but could change the relative placement of the plug towers in relation to the engine. For this reason it is imperative that you label all wires before disconnecting any of them. Also, before removal, compare the current wiring with the accompanying illustrations. If the current wiring does not match, make notes in your book to reflect how your engine is wired.

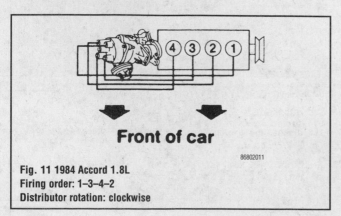

Fig. 11 1984 Accord 1.8L
Firing order: 1–3–4–2
Distributor rotation: clockwise

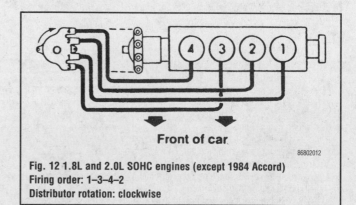

Fig. 12 1.8L and 2.0L SOHC engines (except 1984 Accord)
Firing order: 1–3–4–2
Distributor rotation: clockwise

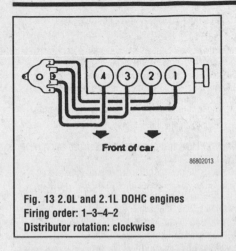

Fig. 13 2.0L and 2.1L DOHC engines
Firing order: 1–3–4–2
Distributor rotation: clockwise

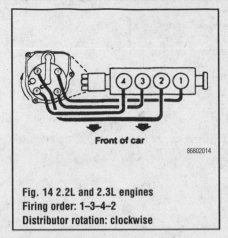

Fig. 14 2.2L and 2.3L engines
Firing order: 1–3–4–2
Distributor rotation: clockwise

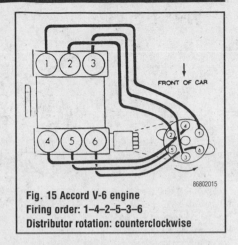

Fig. 15 Accord V-6 engine
Firing order: 1–4–2–5–3–6
Distributor rotation: counterclockwise

ELECTRONIC IGNITION

Description and Operation

All vehicles covered in this manual are equipped with an electronic ignition system. This system eliminates the points and condenser. With fewer moving parts, it requires less periodic maintenance.

The electronic ignition system used on 1984–89 Accords and 1984–90 carbureted Preludes employ a magnetic pulse/igniter distributor and a conventional ignition coil. The distributor cap, rotor, advance mechanism (vacuum and centrifugal) and secondary ignition wires are also of standard design. The distributor contains the stator, reluctor and pulse generator (pick-up coil) and igniter assembly.

During operation, when the teeth of the reluctor align with the stator, a signal is generated by the pulse generator (pick-up coil) and sent to the igniter (module). The module, upon receiving the signal, opens the primary windings of the ignition coil. As the primary magnetic field collapses, a high voltage surge is developed in the secondary windings of the coil. This high voltage surge travels from the coil to the distributor cap and rotor through the secondary ignition wires to the spark plugs.

The system used on 1990–95 Accords and 1989–95 fuel injected Preludes uses the distributor components to signal the engine computer. The ECU triggers the spark through the igniter unit and coil. This spark timing is controlled by the computer as an integrated function of the fuel management system. The distributor contains a crankshaft angle sensor and a No. 1 Cylinder Top Dead Center (TDC) sensor. Using these and other electrical inputs, the computer controls spark timing electrically. This system eliminates the need for mechanical and/or vacuum advance mechanisms within the distributor.

Diagnosis and Testing

➡The electronic ignition system on your Honda requires special handling. Unlike conventional ignition systems, it is very sensitive to abrupt changes in voltage or voltage applied in the wrong direction. Observe the following precautions listed to prevent expensive system damage.

• Always disconnect the battery cables before doing repair work on the electronic ignition system
• Always double check the markings on the battery and the routing of the cables before making connections, especially if the battery has been removed and might have been reinstalled in the opposite position. Hooking the battery connections up backwards will cause current to flow through the electronic ignition system in an improper way. Immediate damage may result
• Do not allow the wires connected to the pulse generator to touch other ignition wiring connections
• Abnormal voltage pulses may damage the system. Be sure to either disconnect the battery or switch the ignition OFF before performing any work on the vehicle that is of an electrical nature
• Connect tachometers to the negative terminal of the ignition coil; not to any other connection on the ignition coil
• Always double check any connection involving the ignition system before reconnecting the battery and putting the system into operation
• When cranking the engine for compression testing or similar purposes, disable the ignition system. This can be accomplished by unplugging the connectors on the primary side of the coil. Make sure the ignition key is in the OFF position first

SERVICE PROCEDURES

Spark Test

The spark test is used to see if the ignition system is delivering electricity through the coil wire to the distributor. Use this test as a preliminary test if the engine cranks but won't start. It's a simple test, but can give a nasty shock if not performed correctly.

1. Disconnect the end of the coil wire at the distributor.
2. Use a well-insulated tool (such as ignition wire pliers) to hold the exposed end of the wire about ½ in. (13 mm) from the metal of the engine block.

❊❊ CAUTION

Do not attempt to hold the wire with your bare hand. Use as much insulation as possible between the wire and the tool holding it. Do not stand on wet concrete while testing. Do not lean on the bodywork of the car while testing. The electrical charge will pass through the easiest path to ground; make certain it's not you. Make certain the metal ground point nearest the cable end is safe; don't choose components that might contain fluids or wires.

3. Have an assistant crank the engine by turning the ignition switch to the START position, but only for 1 or 2 seconds. Keep clear of moving parts under the hood, and keep clothing and hair well out of the way. If the cable end is the correct distance from solid metal, a distinct, blue-white spark should jump to the metal as the engine cranks.
4. The engine may be cranked in 1–2 second bursts. Longer cranking will cause the fuel injectors to deliver fuel into the cylinders, flooding the engine or at least fouling the spark plugs.
5. If no spark is present, turn the ignition switch OFF and proceed to check the resistance of the coil wire, the voltage supply to the coil (12 volts with ignition ON), the coil resistance, and if applicable, the air gap within the distributor.

Reluctor Gap Inspection and Adjustment

▸ See Figure 16

➡This procedure is applicable only to 1984–89 Accords and 1984–90 carbureted Preludes.

1. Remove the distributor cap and the rotor.
2. Turn the crankshaft to align the reluctor points with the stator ends.
3. Using a non-metallic feeler gauge, check the reluctor-to-stator air gaps; they must be equal.
4. If necessary, loosen the stator-to-distributor screws, then adjust the stator-to-reluctor air gaps and tighten the screws.
5. Recheck the air gaps.

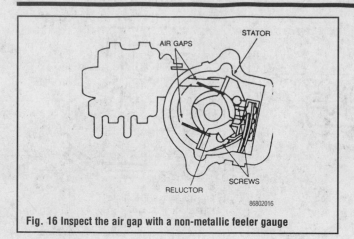

Fig. 16 Inspect the air gap with a non-metallic feeler gauge

Igniter Unit Test

1984–89 ACCORD AND PRELUDE WITH HITACHI DISTRIBUTOR

♦ See Figure 17

➡ This procedure is not applicable to 1988–89 fuel injected Preludes.

1. Remove the distributor cap.
2. Disconnect the lead wires from the igniter unit.
3. Using a voltmeter with the ignition switch **ON**, check the voltage between the blue wire and body ground, then the black/yellow wire to body ground. There should be battery voltage present.
4. If no voltage is present, check the wiring to the igniter unit.
5. Turn the ignition **OFF**. Using an ohmmeter, check the continuity of the igniter at the terminals:
    a. Place the positive probe on the black/yellow wire terminal and negative probe on the blue wire terminal; continuity should be read on ohmmeter.
    b. Place the positive probe on the blue wire terminal and negative probe on the black/yellow wire terminal; no continuity should be read on the ohmmeter.
6. If ohmmeter readings are not as specified, replace the igniter unit.

1984–85 ACCORD AND PRELUDE WITH TOYO DENSO DISTRIBUTOR

♦ See Figure 18

1. Remove the igniter unit.
2. Using a voltmeter with the ignition switch **ON**, check the voltage between the blue wire and ground, then the black/yellow wire to ground. There should be battery voltage.

3. If no voltage is present, check the wiring to igniter unit.
4. Turn the ignition switch **OFF**.
5. Connect a jumper wire between the green and blue terminals. Using an ohmmeter, check the continuity of the igniter at the terminals:
    a. Place the positive probe on the black/yellow wire terminal and negative probe on the blue wire terminal; continuity should be read on ohmmeter.
    b. Place the positive probe on the blue wire terminal and negative probe on the black/yellow wire terminal; no continuity should be read on the ohmmeter.
6. If ohmmeter readings are not as specified, replace igniter unit.

1986–89 ACCORD AND PRELUDE WITH TOYO DENSO DISTRIBUTOR

♦ See Figures 19 and 20

➡ This procedure is not applicable to 1988–89 fuel injected Preludes.

1. Remove the distributor cap, rotor and shield. Remove the distributor hold-down bolts and remove the distributor for access. Leave the distributor wiring harness connected.
2. Remove the igniter unit from the distributor housing.
3. With the ignition switch **ON**, use a voltmeter to check for the presence of battery voltage at the black/yellow wire terminal, then at the terminal for the "BLU 1" wire. Battery voltage should be present in both cases.
4. Turn the ignition switch **OFF**.
5. Measure the resistance between the "BLU 2" and the adjacent green wire terminals. It should be approximately 750 ohms.

➡ The following steps do not pertain to 1989 models.

6. Check the continuity in both directions between terminals A and B of the igniter unit. There should be continuity in only one direction.
7. Connect the ohmmeter positive probe to terminal D of the igniter and the negative probe to ground. The resistance should be approximately 50,000 ohms.
8. If ohmmeter readings are not as specified, replace igniter unit.

1990–91 ACCORD

♦ See Figure 21

1. Remove the distributor cap, rotor and shield.
2. Label and disconnect the 4 wires from the igniter unit.
3. Switch the ignition **ON**. Use a voltmeter to check for voltage between the black/yellow wire and ground. Battery voltage should be present. If the voltage is not present, check the black/yellow wire between the igniter and the ignition switch.
4. Check for voltage between the white/blue wire and ground. Battery voltage should be present with the ignition **ON**. If voltage is not present, check the white/blue wire from the igniter to the coil an test the ignition coil.
5. Turn the ignition **OFF**. Check for continuity in the yellow/green wire between the igniter and the ECU.

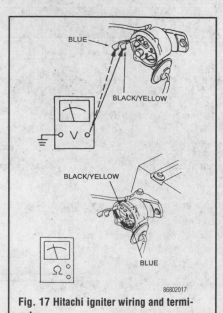

Fig. 17 Hitachi igniter wiring and terminals

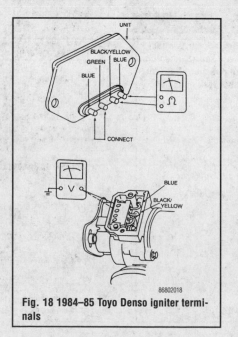

Fig. 18 1984–85 Toyo Denso igniter terminals

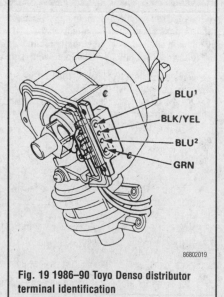

Fig. 19 1986–90 Toyo Denso distributor terminal identification

6. Check the blue wire for continuity between the tachometer and the igniter.

7. Check the resistance between the terminals which connect to the blue and white/yellow wires. It should be between 1,100–3,300 ohms. If not, the igniter must be replaced.

1992–93 ACCORD

▶ **See Figure 22**

1. Remove the distributor cap, rotor and the inner cover.

2. Disconnect the black/yellow, light green, yellow/green and blue wires from the igniter.

3. Check for voltage between the black/yellow wire and ground. Battery voltage should be present with the ignition **ON**. If voltage is not present, check the black/yellow wire between the ignition switch and the igniter.

4. Check for voltage between the light green wire and ground. Battery voltage should be present with the ignition **ON**. If voltage is not present, check the ignition coil and the light green (black/white) wire between the ignition coil and the igniter.

5. Turn the ignition switch **OFF**.

6. Check the yellow/green wire between the engine control module and the igniter for continuity. Also check the blue wire between the tachometer and the igniter for continuity.

7. Check the resistance between the terminals which connect to the blue and light green wires. It should be between 1,100–3,300 ohms. If not, the igniter must be replaced.

1994–95 ACCORD EXCEPT V-6

▶ **See Figures 23 and 24**

1. Remove the distributor cap, rotor and the inner cover.

2. Disconnect the wires from the igniter.

3. Check for voltage between the black/yellow wire and ground. Battery voltage should be present with the ignition **ON**. If voltage is not present, check the black/yellow wire between the ignition switch and the igniter.

4. Check for voltage between the green wire ("BLU 2" on VTEC) and ground. Battery voltage should be present with the ignition **ON**. If voltage is not present, check the ignition coil and the green ("BLU 2" on VTEC) wire between the ignition coil and the igniter.

5. Turn the ignition switch **OFF**.

6. Check the yellow/green wire between the engine control module and the igniter for continuity. Then check the BLU 1 wire between the tachometer and the igniter for continuity.

7. If the wiring is OK and a problem still exists, the igniter is probably at fault.

1995 ACCORD V-6

▶ **See Figure 25**

1. Remove the distributor cap, rotor and the inner cover.

2. Disconnect the wires from the igniter.

3. Check for voltage between the yellow wire and ground. Battery voltage should be present with the ignition **ON**. If voltage is not present, check the ignition coil and the yellow wire between the ignition coil and the igniter.

4. Check for voltage between the green wire and ground. Battery voltage should be present with the ignition **ON**. If voltage is not present, check the ignition coil and the green wire between the ignition coil and the igniter.

5. Turn the ignition switch **OFF**.

6. Check the yellow/green wire between the engine control module and the igniter for continuity.

7. If the wiring is OK and a problem still exists, the igniter is probably at fault.

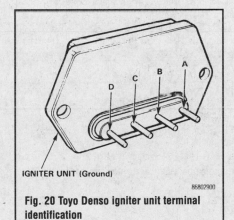

Fig. 20 Toyo Denso igniter unit terminal identification

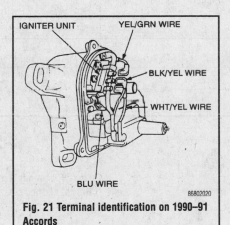

Fig. 21 Terminal identification on 1990–91 Accords

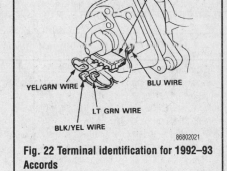

Fig. 22 Terminal identification for 1992–93 Accords

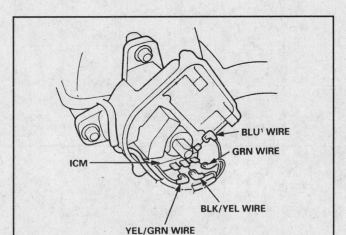

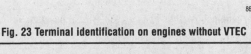

Fig. 23 Terminal identification on engines without VTEC

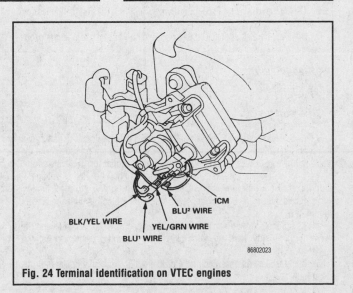

Fig. 24 Terminal identification on VTEC engines

1990 CARBURETED PRELUDE WITH TOYO DENSO DISTRIBUTOR

▶ See Figure 19

1. Remove the distributor cap, rotor and shield. Remove the distributor hold-down bolts and remove the distributor for access. Leave the distributor wiring harness connected.
2. Remove the igniter.
3. Switch the ignition **ON** and test for battery voltage between terminal "BLU 1" (the outermost blue wire) and ground.
4. Check for battery voltage between the black/yellow terminal and ground.
5. If voltage is not present in either one or both tests, switch the ignition **OFF**. Check the "BLU 1" wire between the igniter and the ignition coil for continuity. Check the black/yellow wire between the igniter, the ignition switch and the coil for continuity. Also, test the coil.
6. If all wiring tests OK and a problem still exists, replace the igniter.
7. Reinstall the shield, rotor and cap. Install the distributor.

1990 CARBURETED PRELUDE WITH HITACHI DISTRIBUTOR

▶ See Figure 26

1. Remove the distributor cap.
2. Label and disconnect the wires from the igniter.
3. Switch the ignition **ON**. Check for voltage between the blue wire and ground. Battery voltage should be present.
4. Check for voltage between the black/yellow wire and ground. Battery voltage should be present.
5. If voltage is not present in either one or both tests, switch the ignition **OFF**. Check for continuity in the blue wire between the ignition coil and the igniter. Check for continuity in the black/yellow wire between the ignition switch, coil and igniter.
6. Using an ohmmeter, check for continuity between the pins of the igniter. Continuity should exist only in one direction.
7. If all tests are as specified and a problem still exists, the igniter must be replaced.
8. Reinstall the distributor cap.

1988–91 FUEL INJECTED PRELUDE

▶ See Figure 27

1. The igniter is located on the right front shock tower. With the ignition **OFF**, unplug the wiring connector from the igniter.
2. Switch the ignition **ON**. Check for voltage between the blue wire (white/blue on some models) and ground. Battery voltage should be present.
3. Check for voltage between the black/yellow wire and ground. Battery voltage should be present.
4. If voltage is not present in either test, switch the ignition **OFF**. Check for continuity in the blue wire between the ignition coil and the igniter. Check for continuity in the black/yellow wire between the ignition switch, coil and igniter.
5. Check the white wire for continuity between the ECU and the igniter connector.
6. If all tests are as specified and a problem still exists, the igniter is probably at fault.

1992–95 PRELUDE

▶ See Figure 28

1. Remove the distributor cap, rotor and the inner cover.
2. Disconnect the wires from the igniter.
3. Check for voltage between the black/yellow wire and ground. Battery voltage should be present with the ignition **ON**. If voltage is not present, check the black/yellow wire between the ignition coil and the igniter for continuity.
4. Check for voltage between the green wire and ground. Battery voltage should be present with the ignition **ON**. If voltage is not present, check the ignition coil and the green (blue) wire between the ignition coil and the igniter for continuity.
5. Check the yellow/green wire between the engine control module and the igniter for continuity. Then check the blue wire between the tachometer and the igniter for continuity.
6. If all tests are as specified and a problem still exists, the igniter is probably at fault.

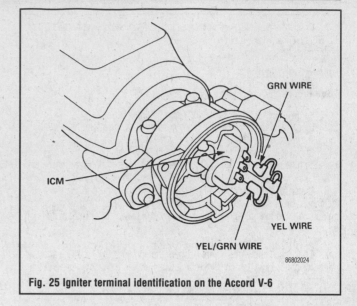

Fig. 25 Igniter terminal identification on the Accord V-6

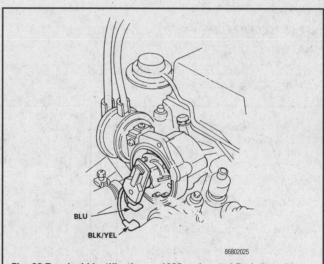

Fig. 26 Terminal identification on 1990 carbureted Preludes with Hitachi distributors

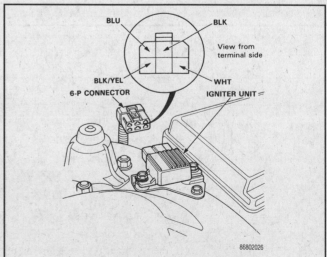

Fig. 27 Igniter terminal identification on 1988–91 fuel injected Preludes

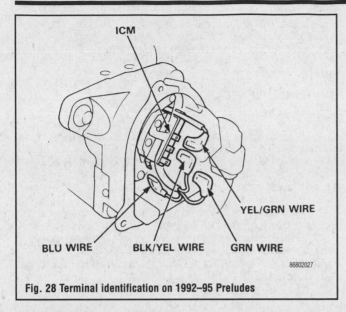

Fig. 28 Terminal identification on 1992–95 Preludes

Ignition Coil Test

➡ **All test resistance values are given for a coil temperature of 70°F (21°C). Resistance will vary slightly with temperature. Use common sense and good judgment when interpreting readings.**

1984–85 ACCORD AND 1984–86 PRELUDE

▶ **See Figure 29**

1. Label and disconnect the wiring from the coil. The small external primary winding terminals are marked on the coil case. The large coil terminal (from which the coil wire runs to the distributor) is the secondary winding terminal.
2. With the ignition **OFF**, measure the resistance across the primary terminals. Resistance should be 1.06–1.24 ohms.
3. Measure the resistance between the secondary terminal and the primary positive terminal; resistance should be 7,400–11,000 ohms.
4. If the coil circuit resistances are outside the test specifications, the coil must be replaced.

1986–89 ACCORD AND 1987–91 PRELUDE

▶ **See Figure 30**

1. These vehicles use a 4-pin primary wiring configuration. With the ignition **OFF**, unplug the primary and secondary wiring connectors from the coil.
2. Measure resistance between terminals A and D. On 1986-89 Accords and 1987-89 Preludes, the resistance on the primary side should be 1.2-1.5 ohms. On 1990-91 Preludes, it should be 0.3-0.4 ohms.
3. Measure the resistance between terminal A and the secondary terminal. On 1986-89 Accords and 1987 Preludes, the resistance should be

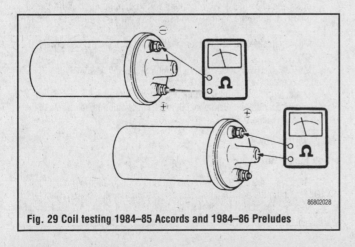

Fig. 29 Coil testing 1984–85 Accords and 1984–86 Preludes

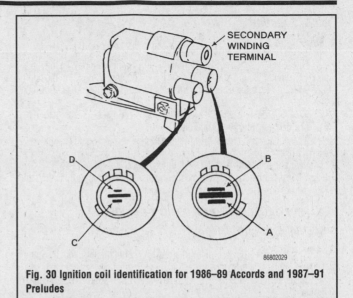

Fig. 30 Ignition coil identification for 1986–89 Accords and 1987–91 Preludes

11,074-11,526 ohms. On 1988-91 Preludes, it should be 9,040-13,560 ohms.
4. Check the resistance between terminals B and D. It should be approximately 2,100-2,300 ohms for all vehicles.
5. On carbureted engines, test at terminals A and C. Continuity must be present.

➡ **Fuel injected engines do not use terminal C.**

6. All test conditions must be met. If any test condition is not satisfied, the coil must be replaced.

1990–91 ACCORD

▶ **See Figure 31**

1. The ignition coil is contained within the distributor. With the ignition **OFF**, remove the distributor cap.
2. Remove the screws securing the black/yellow wire and white/blue wires from the terminals. The black/yellow wire is connected to the primary positive terminal and the white/blue wire is connected to the primary negative terminal.
3. Measure resistance between the terminals. Resistance should be between 0.6-0.8 ohms.
4. Measure the resistance between the primary positive terminal and the secondary terminal. Resistance should be 12,800–19,200 ohms.
5. All test conditions must be met. If any test condition is not satisfied, the coil must be replaced.

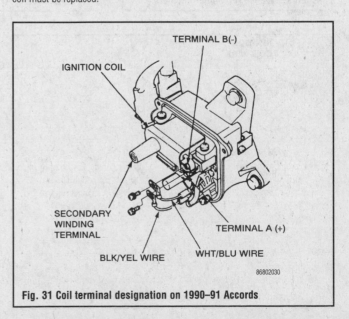

Fig. 31 Coil terminal designation on 1990–91 Accords

1992–93 ACCORD

▶ **See Figure 32**

1. These vehicles use a 4-pin primary wiring configuration. With the ignition **OFF**, unplug the primary and secondary wiring connectors from the coil.

2. Measure resistance between terminals A and C. It should be between 0.6–0.8 ohms.

3. Measure the resistance between terminal A and the secondary terminal. It should be between 14,000–22,000 ohms.

4. Check the resistance between terminals B and D. It should be approximately 2,090–2,310 ohms.

5. Test at terminals A and B. Continuity must be present.

6. All test conditions must be met. If any test condition is not satisfied, the coil must be replaced.

1994–95 ACCORD EXCEPT VTEC AND V-6 MODELS

▶ **See Figure 32**

1. These vehicles use a 4-pin primary wiring configuration. With the ignition **OFF**, unplug the primary and secondary wiring connectors from the coil.

2. Measure resistance between terminals A and B. It should be between 0.6–0.8 ohms.

3. Measure the resistance between terminal A and the secondary terminal. It should be between 14,000–22,000 ohms.

4. Test at terminals A and C. Continuity must be present.

5. All test conditions must be met. If any test condition is not satisfied, the coil must be replaced.

1994–95 ACCORD VTEC

▶ **See Figure 33**

1. The ignition coil is contained within the distributor. With the ignition **OFF**, remove the distributor cap.

2. Remove the screws holding the black/yellow wire and blue wire from the terminals. The black/yellow wire is connected to the primary positive terminal and the blue wire is connected to the primary negative terminal.

3. Measure resistance between the primary positive and negative terminals. Resistance should be between 0.4-0.6 ohms.

4. Measure the resistance between the primary positive terminal and the secondary terminal. Resistance should be 22,000–34,000 ohms.

5. All test conditions must be met. If any test condition is not satisfied, the coil must be replaced.

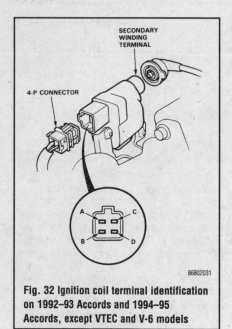

Fig. 32 Ignition coil terminal identification on 1992–93 Accords and 1994–95 Accords, except VTEC and V-6 models

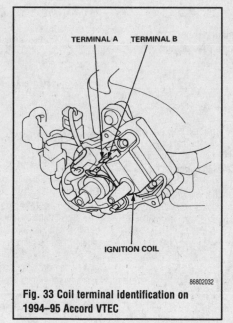

Fig. 33 Coil terminal identification on 1994–95 Accord VTEC

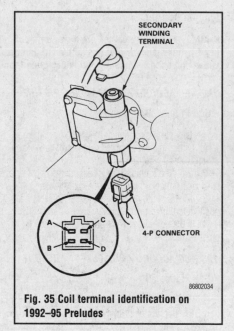

Fig. 35 Coil terminal identification on 1992–95 Preludes

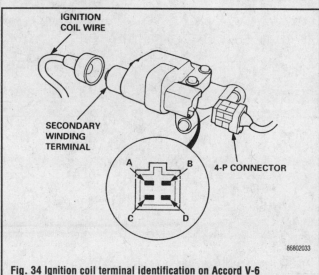

Fig. 34 Ignition coil terminal identification on Accord V-6

ACCORD V-6

▶ **See Figure 34**

1. These vehicles use a 4-pin primary wiring configuration. With the ignition **OFF**, unplug the primary and secondary wiring connectors from the coil.

2. Measure resistance between terminals A and C. It should be between 0.3-0.4 ohms.

3. Measure the resistance between terminal A and the secondary terminal. It should be between 14,000–22,000 ohms.

4. Test at terminals A and B. Continuity must be present.

5. All test conditions must be met. If any test condition is not satisfied, the coil must be replaced.

1992–95 PRELUDE

▶ **See Figure 35**

1. These vehicles use a 4-pin primary wiring configuration. With the ignition **OFF**, unplug the primary and secondary wiring connectors from the coil.

2. Measure resistance between terminals A and B. It should be between 0.6-0.8 ohms.

3. Measure the resistance between terminal A and the secondary terminal. It should be between 14,000–22,000 ohms.

4. Test at terminals A and C. Continuity must be present.

5. All test conditions must be met. If any test condition is not satisfied, the coil must be replaced.

Parts Replacement

→On 1990–95 Accords and 1988–95 fuel injected Preludes, the distributor cap, rotor and igniter are the only serviceable parts in the distributor. If the reluctor(s) or pickup coil(s) are found to be defective on these models, it will be necessary to replace the entire distributor housing.

REMOVAL & INSTALLATION

Distributor Cap and Rotor

▶ See Figures 36, 37 and 38

The distributor cap is retained by screws to the distributor housing. With the ignition **OFF**, loosen or remove the screws, then remove the cap. Inspect the inside of the cap for cracking, burning or heavy wear on the wire terminals. Replace the cap if there is any sign of anything abnormal. Slight wear on the terminals is normal.

Some models use a set screw to secure the rotor to the shaft; loosen or remove (but don't lose) the screw before attempting to remove the rotor. Remove the ignition rotor by lifting it straight off the shaft. Inspect the rotor for any sign of wear; dressing or refiling the rotor is not recommended except in emergency circumstances.

Before installing, align the rotor and shaft; both have a flat side to insure correct placement. Press the rotor onto the shaft. Install and tighten the set screw if applicable. Install the cap and any seal or gasket carefully onto the distributor; tighten the screws just snug.

Reluctor

▶ See Figure 39

1. Turn the ignition switch **OFF**.
2. Disconnect the negative battery terminal.
3. Remove the distributor cap and rotor.
4. Use two small or medium sized flat tools to pry the reluctor smoothly and evenly from the shaft. Protect the case of the distributor with rags or cloth. Use great care not to damage the stator or other components.

→Be careful not to lose the roll pin!

To install:

5. Position the reluctor with the manufacturer's number facing up. Install the reluctor by pushing it firmly onto the distributor shaft.

6. Install the roll pin with the slot of the roll pin facing away from the distributor shaft.

Pickup Coil

▶ See Figure 40

→This procedure applies only to Toyo Denso distributors. On Hitachi distributors, the pickup coil and igniter unit are integral with each other. Refer to the igniter removal and installation procedure for these units.

Fig. 36 Remove the screws securing the cap to the distributor . . .

Fig. 37 . . . then pull the cap out from the distributor

Fig. 38 On most models, the rotor can simply be pulled from the distributor shaft

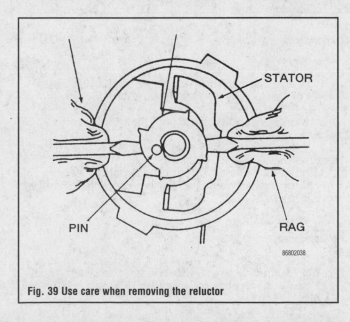
Fig. 39 Use care when removing the reluctor

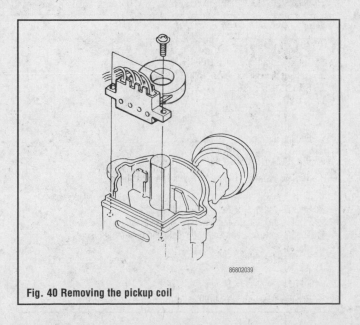
Fig. 40 Removing the pickup coil

1. Turn the ignition switch **OFF**.
2. Remove the distributor cap, rotor and reluctor.
3. Unplug the electrical connector from the pickup coil.
4. Remove the retaining screws securing the pickup coil, then remove the coil assembly.

To install:

5. Position the pickup coil in the distributor, then tighten the retaining screws until snug.
6. Engage the electrical connection.
7. Install the reluctor, then check the air gap.
8. Install the rotor and distributor cap.

Igniter

TOYO DENSO

▶ **See Figure 41**

➡ **The igniter on these models is externally mounted on the side of the distributor and plugs directly into the distributor case.**

1. Turn the ignition switch **OFF**.
2. Remove the two screws securing the igniter unit assembly and the harness clip.
3. Carefully pull the igniter from the distributor. Use care not to damage the igniter and the mating terminals.

To install:

4. Before installation, coat the igniter pins and the connector housing with silicone grease.
5. Carefully push the igniter into its mating terminals.
6. Install the screws securing the igniter assembly and harness clip. Tighten until snug.

HITACHI

▶ **See Figure 42**

➡ **The igniter is internally mounted in the distributor.**

1. Turn the ignition switch **OFF**.
2. Remove the distributor cap, rotor and reluctor.
3. Unplug the electrical connections.
4. The igniter may be removed by removing the retaining screws. Note the position of the retaining screws; one is diamagnetic and must be reinstalled in the original location.

To install:

5. Position the igniter in the distributor, then tighten the retaining screws until snug. Make sure the diamagnetic screw is installed in its original location.
6. Engage the electrical connections.
7. Install the reluctor, then check the air gap.
8. Install the rotor and distributor cap.

1988–91 FUEL INJECTED PRELUDE

➡ **The igniter is located on the passenger side strut tower.**

1. Turn the ignition switch **OFF**.
2. Unplug the electrical connector from the igniter unit.
3. Remove the bolts securing the igniter, then remove the unit from the vehicle.

To install:

4. Secure the igniter to the strut tower with its retaining bolts. Tighten them until snug.
5. Engage the electrical connection.

1990–95 ACCORD AND 1992–95 PRELUDE

➡ **The igniter is internally mounted in the distributor.**

1. Turn the ignition switch **OFF**.
2. Remove the distributor cap and rotor.
3. Unplug the electrical connections from the igniter.
4. The igniter may be removed by removing its retaining screws.

To install:

5. Position the igniter in the distributor, then tighten the retaining screws until snug.
6. Engage the electrical connections.
7. Install the rotor and distributor cap.

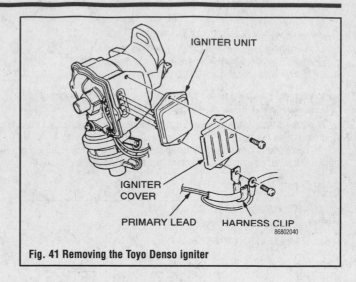

Fig. 41 Removing the Toyo Denso igniter

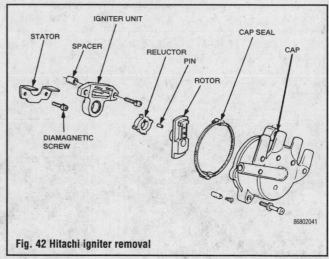

Fig. 42 Hitachi igniter removal

Advance Diaphragm

▶ **See Figures 43 and 44**

1. Remove the distributor cap, rotor and dust cover.
2. Label and disconnect the vacuum hoses from the diaphragm.

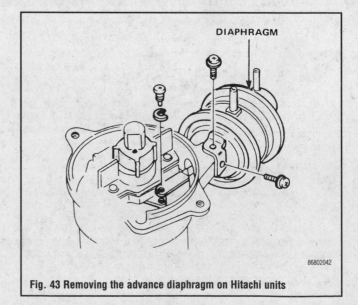

Fig. 43 Removing the advance diaphragm on Hitachi units

3. Remove the diaphragm mounting screws.

4. On Hitachi units, remove the screw and washer securing the diaphragm arm to the breaker plate. On Toyo Denso types, carefully remove the E-clip securing the diaphragm arm to the pin screw on the breaker plate.

5. Pull the advance diaphragm out from the distributor unit. Discard the old O-ring.

To install:

6. Install the advance diaphragm with a new O-ring.

7. Connect the advance diaphragm arm to the breaker plate. On Toyo Denso units, use a new clip.

8. Tighten the advance diaphragm mounting screws until snug.

9. Install the remaining components in the reverse order of removal.

Ignition Coil

EXTERNALLY MOUNTED

1. Turn the ignition switch **OFF**.

2. Unplug the primary and the secondary wiring connectors from the ignition coil.

3. Remove the ignition coil-to-mount screws/bolts and the coil from the vehicle.

4. To install, reverse the removal procedures.

DISTRIBUTOR MOUNTED

♦ **See Figure 45**

1. Turn the ignition switch **OFF**.

2. Remove the distributor cap, rotor, cap seal. Remove the shield or leak cover from the coil.

3. Label and disconnect the two wires running to the coil terminals. These wires must be reinstalled correctly.

4. Remove the two screws securing the coil unit. Slide the coil out of the distributor housing.

To install

5. Carefully position the coil and slide it into the distributor housing.

6. Install the retaining screws.

7. Connect the wires to the terminals (be sure they are connected to the correct terminals.)

8. Install the leak cover and cap seal. Make certain these seals align properly with their mounts.

9. Install the rotor and cap.

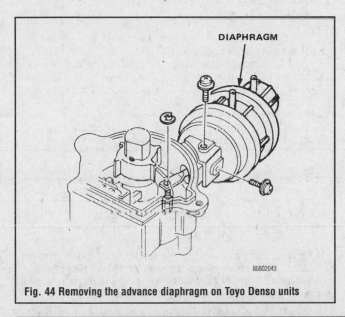

Fig. 44 Removing the advance diaphragm on Toyo Denso units

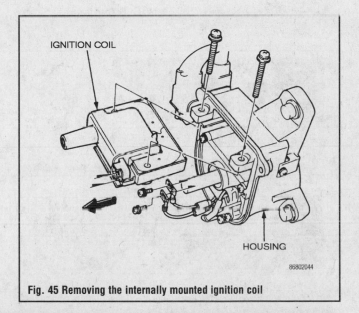

Fig. 45 Removing the internally mounted ignition coil

IGNITION TIMING

General Information

Ignition timing is the measurement, in degrees of crankshaft rotation, of the instant the spark plugs in the cylinders fire in relation to the location of the piston.

Ideally, the air/fuel mixture in the cylinder will be ignited and just beginning its rapid expansion as the piston passes Top Dead Center (TDC). If this happens, the piston will be beginning the power stroke just as the compressed and ignited air/fuel mixture starts to expand. The expansion of the air/fuel mixture will force the piston down on the power stroke and turn the crankshaft.

Due to the time it takes for the spark from the plug to completely ignite the mixture in the cylinder, the plug must fire before the piston reaches TDC so the mixture is completely ignited as the piston passes TDC. This measurement is given in degrees of crankshaft rotation before the piston reaches top dead center (BTDC). If the ignition timing setting is 6 degrees BTDC, this means that the spark plug must fire at a time when the piston for that cylinder is 6 degrees BTDC of its compression stroke. However, this only holds true while the engine is at idle.

As you accelerate from idle, the speed of your engine increases. This increase in engine speed means that the pistons are now traveling up and down much faster. Because of this, the spark plugs will have to fire even sooner if the mixture is to be completely ignited as the piston passes TDC. To accomplish this, the system incorporates a means to advance the timing of the spark as engine speed increases.

The mechanical distributor has two means of advancing the ignition timing. One is centrifugal advance and is actuated by weights in the distributor. The other is vacuum advance and is controlled in that large circular "can" on the side of the distributor. Fully electronic systems use the Engine Control Unit (ECU) to control the trigger signal to the coil. The computer can provide for much more accurate spark control than mechanical units.

In addition, some Honda distributors have a vacuum retard mechanism which is contained in the same housing on the side of the distributor as the vacuum advance. Models having two hoses going to the distributor vacuum housing have both vacuum advance and retard. The function of this mechanism is to regulate the timing of the ignition spark under certain engine conditions. This causes more complete burning of the air/fuel mixture in the cylinder and consequently lowers exhaust emissions.

If ignition timing is set too far advanced (BTDC), the ignition and burning of the air/fuel mixture in the cylinder will try to oppose the motion of the piston in the cylinder while it is still traveling upward. This causes engine ping, a sound similar to marbles in a coffee can. If the ignition timing is too far retarded (after, or ATDC), the piston will have already started down on the power stroke when the air/fuel mixture ignites. This will cause the piston to be forced down with much less power. This will result in rough engine performance, lack of power and poor gas mileage.

CHECKING & ADJUSTING

▶ See Figures 46, 47 and 48

> **❄❄ CAUTION**
>
> **DO NOT grasp the top of the distributor cap while the engine is running, as you might receive a nasty shock. Instead, grab the distributor housing to rotate.**

1984–85 Accord and Prelude

The timing marks are located on the flywheel (manual transaxle) or torque converter drive plate (automatic transaxle), with a pointer on the rear of the cylinder block. All are visible from the front right side of the engine compartment after removing a special rubber access plug in the timing mark window. In all cases, the timing is checked with the engine warmed to operating temperature and at idle.

1. Following the manufacturer's instructions, connect a timing light to the engine. The positive and negative leads connect to their corresponding battery terminals and the spark plug lead to No. 1 spark plug wire.
2. Make sure that all wires are clear of the cooling fan and hot exhaust manifolds.
3. Set the parking brake and block the front wheels. Start the engine. Check that the idle speed is set to specifications.

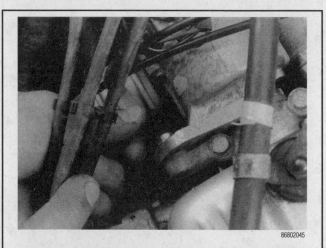

Fig. 46 On some engines, the distributor hold-down bolt is covered with a cap

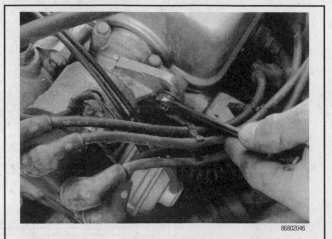

Fig. 47 If necessary, loosen the hold-down bolt, then turn the distributor to adjust the timing

4. Point the timing light at the timing marks. When the engine is idling, the red mark must align with the pointer. Some timing marks are indicated by 3 lines; the center one must be aligned with the pointer.
5. If necessary to adjust the timing, loosen the distributor hold-down bolt(s) and/or nut and slowly rotate the distributor in the required direction while observing the timing marks.
6. To complete the adjustment operation, tighten the hold-down bolt, taking care not to disturb the adjustment.
7. Switch the ignition **OFF**. Reinstall the rubber plug in the timing window and remove the timing light.

1986–89 Accord, 1986–87 Prelude and 1988–90 Carbureted Prelude

The timing marks are located on the flywheel (manual transaxle) or torque converter drive plate (automatic transaxle), with a pointer on the rear of the cylinder block. All are visible from the front right side of the engine compartment after removing a special rubber access plug in the timing mark window. In all cases, the timing is checked with the engine warmed to operating temperature and at idle.

1. Disconnect the vacuum hoses from the vacuum advance diaphragm, then plug them.
2. Following the manufacturer's instructions, connect a timing light to the engine. The positive and negative leads connect to their corresponding battery terminals and the spark plug lead to No. 1 spark plug wire.
3. Make sure that all wires are clear of the cooling fan and hot exhaust manifolds.
4. Set the parking brake and block the front wheels. Start the engine. Check that the idle speed is set to specifications.
5. Point the timing light at the timing marks. When the engine is idling, the white mark must align with the pointer.
6. If necessary to adjust the timing, loosen the distributor hold-down bolt(s) and/or nut and slowly rotate the distributor in the required direction while observing the timing marks.
7. Unplug, then connect the vacuum hoses to the advance diaphragm.
8. Point the timing light at the timing marks. The red mark must now align with the pointer. If not, the vacuum advance diaphragm and mechanism should be checked.
9. Switch the ignition **OFF**. Reinstall the rubber plug in the timing window and remove the timing light.

1988–95 Fuel Injected Prelude and 1990–95 Accord

▶ See Figures 49, 50, 51, 52 and 53

➡ **The ignition timing on these cars is controlled by the engine computer. It should not be necessary to routinely reset the timing during other maintenance work. On the Accord V-6, the timing is not adjustable. However, ignition timing can be checked using this procedure.**

1. Remove the rubber cap from the timing window on the engine (except on 1994–95 Accords).
2. Start the engine and allow it to warm up. The engine is fully warmed when the cooling fans come on at least once. Switch the ignition **OFF**.
3. Locate the service check connector and, if applicable, remove the cap. On 1988–91 Preludes, the cap is yellow and the connector is located next to the vacuum control box in the engine compartment. On 1992–95 Preludes, the service

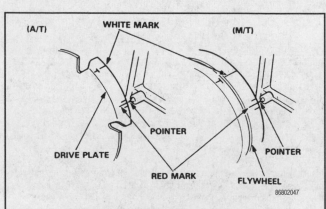

Fig. 48 Examples of timing marks used on Accords and Preludes

connector is located under the middle of the dash. On 1990–93 Accords, the connector is blue and is located behind the right front kick panel, under the dashboard. On 1994–95 Accords, the service connector is located behind the glove box. Use a jumper wire to connect the two terminals of the service connector.

4. Following the manufacturers instructions, connect a timing light to the engine. The positive and negative leads connect to their corresponding battery terminals and the spark plug lead to No. 1 spark plug wire.

5. Make sure that all wires are clear of the cooling fan and hot exhaust manifolds.

6. Set the parking brake and block the front wheels. Start the engine. Check that the idle speed is set to specifications.

7. Point the timing light at the timing marks. On all models except 1994–95 Accords, the marks are on the flywheel. On the 1994–95 Accords, the timing marks are on the crankshaft pulley. When the engine is idling, the red mark must align with the pointer. Some timing marks are indicated by 3 lines; the center one must be aligned with the pointer.

8. If necessary to adjust the timing, loosen the distributor hold-down bolt(s) and/or nut and slowly rotate the distributor in the required direction while observing the timing marks.

9. To complete the adjustment operation, tighten the hold-down bolt, taking care not to disturb the adjustment.

10. Switch the engine **OFF**. Reinstall the rubber plug in the timing window and remove the timing light. Remove the jumper wire.

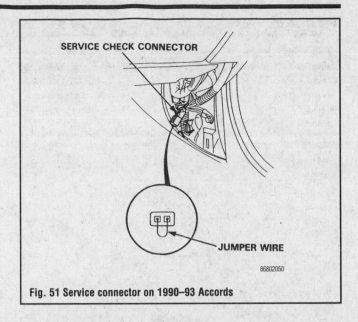

Fig. 51 Service connector on 1990–93 Accords

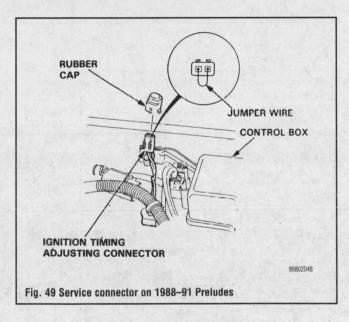

Fig. 49 Service connector on 1988–91 Preludes

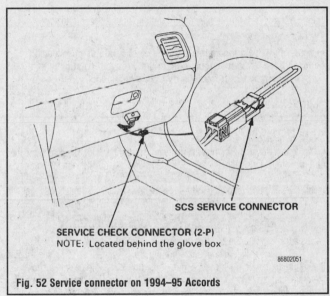

Fig. 52 Service connector on 1994–95 Accords

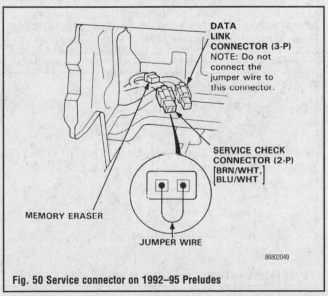

Fig. 50 Service connector on 1992–95 Preludes

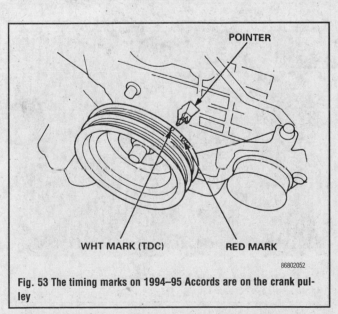

Fig. 53 The timing marks on 1994–95 Accords are on the crank pulley

VALVE LASH

General Information

➡ Periodic valve lash adjustment is not necessary on the Accord V-6. These engines are equipped with hydraulic tappets which automatically take up valve clearance during engine temperature changes and component wear. The adjusting nuts and screws on the exhaust rocker arms are provided for initial adjustment of the pushrods after cylinder head service. Please refer to Section 3 for procedures.

As part of every major tune-up or service interval, the valve clearance should be checked and adjusted if necessary.

If the valve clearance is too large, part of the lift of the camshaft will be used up in removing the excessive clearance, thus the valves will not be opened far enough. This condition makes the valve train noisy as they take up the excessive clearance. The engine will perform poorly, since a smaller amount of air/fuel mixture will be admitted to the cylinders. The exhaust valves will not open far enough to vent the cylinder completely; retained pressure (back pressure) will restrict the entry of the next air/fuel charge.

If the valve clearance is too small, the intake and exhaust valves will not fully seat on the cylinder head when they close. This causes internal cylinder leakage and prevents the hot valve from transferring some heat to the head and cooling off. Therefore, the engine will run poorly (due to gases escaping from the combustion chamber), and the valves will overheat and burn (since they cannot transfer heat unless they are firmly touching the seat in the cylinder head).

➡ While all valve adjustments must be as accurate as possible, it is better to have the valve adjustment slightly loose than slightly tight, as burnt valves may result from overly tight adjustments.

ADJUSTMENT

▶ **See Figures 54 and 55**

Valve lash must always be adjusted with the engine cold. The head temperature must be below 100°F (38°C). Generally, this means allowing the engine to cool for at least 3 hours after driving. Overnight cold is best. If the valve adjustment is being performed as part of a routine maintenance or mileage service regimen, do it before the engine is warmed up to check timing or idle.

Valve location will vary with the type of engine. As a guide, the intake valves always are aligned with the ports or runners of the intake manifold. The exhaust valves align with the tubes of the exhaust manifold.

Adjusting the valves requires positioning No. 1 cylinder at TDC, then rotating the engine to certain other precise positions. Rotate the engine with a socket on the crankshaft pulley. (The crank pulley is the lowest pulley on the engine.) This engine rotation is much easier if the spark plugs are removed before hand, elim-

Fig. 55 Turn the adjusting screw to obtain the proper clearance, then tighten the locknut to its proper specification

inating the compression from the cylinders. Always rotate the engine in a counterclockwise direction as viewed from the pulley end.

If you miss a mark during the rotation, keep going in the same direction until it comes around again. Turning the engine backwards may cause the timing belt to jump a tooth or slacken, risking engine damage when restarted. Remember that cylinder No. 1 is the one closest to the pulley end of the engine.

The engine is at TDC No. 1 if ALL of the following are true:
- The TDC mark on the flywheel or flexplate is aligned with the pointer in the timing inspection window at the rear of the engine. The TDC mark is generally white; it is never red
- The distributor rotor is pointing at cap terminal or plug wire No. 1. Mark the cap with the corresponding wire numbers, then lift the cap check the rotor position
- The alignment marks on the camshaft pulley are positioned as indicated in the individual procedure
- The rocker arms for at least one of the valves on cylinder No. 1 is loose; the points or lobes of the cam are not putting pressure on the rocker arms

1984–89 Accord, 1984–87 Prelude and 1988–90 SOHC Prelude

▶ **See Figures 56, 57, 58 and 59**

All engines in these vehicles use a Single Overhead Camshaft (SOHC) that operates the valves. The engines used in 1984-85 Accords use 2 intake valves, 1 exhaust and 1 auxiliary intake valve per cylinder. The auxiliary valves are located on the exhaust side and are smaller than the other valves. The other vehicles use the same arrangement without the auxiliary intake valve.

Fig. 54 If the feeler gauge passes with no drag or cannot be inserted, hold the adjusting screw with a screwdriver, then loosen the locknut

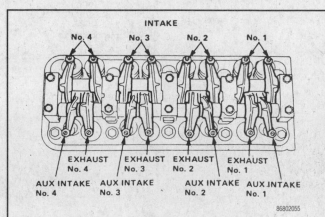

Fig. 56 Valve placement on 1984–85 Accords

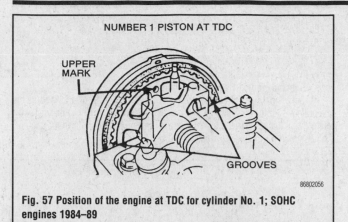

Fig. 57 Position of the engine at TDC for cylinder No. 1; SOHC engines 1984–89

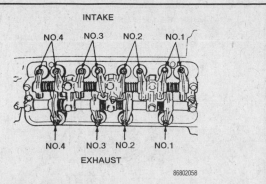

Fig. 59 Valve placement on 1986–89 Accord and SOHC Prelude to 1990

Clearances for the valves are:
• Intake, including auxiliary valve on 1984–85 Accord: 0.005–0.007 in. (0.12–0.17mm)
• Exhaust: 0.010–0.012 in. (0.25–0.30mm)
1. With the ignition **OFF**, remove the valve cover.
2. Set the engine to TDC No. 1 cylinder. The UP mark or dot on the camshaft pulley should be at the top of the pulley. The two grooves on the back (valve) side of the pulley should both be visible and aligned with the surface of the cylinder head. The distributor rotor points to No. 1 terminal or wire.
3. Check the clearance on all the valves for cylinder No. 1 with a flat feeler gauge inserted between the tip of the valve and the contact surface of the rocker. The gauge should pass the gap with slight drag.
4. If the gauge passes with no drag or cannot be inserted, adjust as follows:
   a. Loosen the adjusting screw locknut.
   b. Turn the adjusting screw to obtain the proper clearance.
   c. Hold the adjusting screw in position and tighten the locknut. Correct locknut torque is 14 ft. lbs. (20 Nm), except on auxiliary valves which are 10 ft. lbs. (14 Nm). After the locknut is tightened, recheck the clearance and readjust as necessary.

5. Rotate the crankshaft 180 degrees (the camshaft will turn 90 degrees). One of the grooves in the pulley is now vertical and aligned with the indented mark on the timing belt cover. The UP mark or dot is not visible and the distributor rotor points to terminal or wire No. 3.
6. Check all the valves for cylinder No. 3, repeating the adjusting steps previously described as necessary.
7. Rotate the crankshaft 180 degrees. Both grooves on the cam pulley are visible and aligned with the head surfaces. The distributor rotor points to terminal or wire No. 4.
8. Check all the valves for cylinder No. 4, repeating the adjusting steps previously described as necessary.
9. Rotate the crankshaft 180 degrees. One groove on the pulley is again vertical, aligned with the indentation on the timing belt cover. The UP mark or dot is visible, but is not at the top. The distributor rotor points to terminal or wire No. 2.
10. Check all the valves for cylinder No. 2, repeating the adjusting steps previously described as necessary.
11. Reinstall the valve cover.

1990–95 Accord and 1992–95 SOHC Prelude

▶ **See Figures 60 and 61**

The engines in these cars use 2 intake valves and 2 exhaust valves per cylinder. Valve clearances for the valves are:
• Intake: 0.009–0.011 in. (0.24–0.28mm)—0.10 in. (0.26mm) preferred
• Exhaust: 0.011–0.013 in. (0.28–0.32mm)—0.012 in. (0.30mm) preferred.
1. With the ignition **OFF**, remove the valve cover.
2. Set the engine to TDC No. 1 cylinder. The UP mark on the camshaft pulley should be at the top of the pulley. The two grooves on the side of the pulley

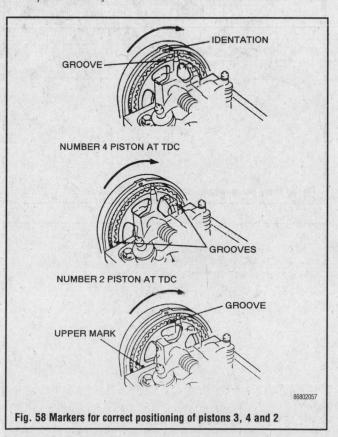

Fig. 58 Markers for correct positioning of pistons 3, 4 and 2

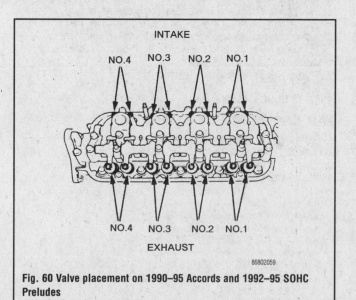

Fig. 60 Valve placement on 1990–95 Accords and 1992–95 SOHC Preludes

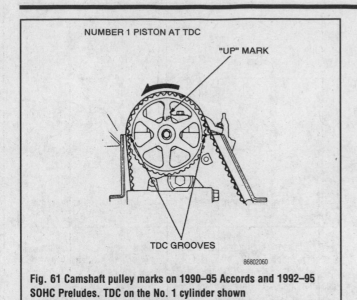

Fig. 61 Camshaft pulley marks on 1990–95 Accords and 1992–95 SOHC Preludes. TDC on the No. 1 cylinder shown

should both be visible and aligned with the surface of the cylinder head. The distributor rotor points to No. 1 terminal or wire.

3. Check the clearance on all the valves for cylinder No. 1 with a flat feeler gauge inserted between the tip of the valve and the contact surface of the rocker. The gauge should pass the gap with slight drag.

4. If the gauge passes with no drag or cannot be inserted, adjust as follows:

   a. Loosen the adjusting screw locknut.

   b. Turn the adjusting screw to obtain the proper clearance.

   c. Hold the adjusting screw in position and tighten the locknut. Correct locknut torque is 14 ft. lbs. (20 Nm). After the locknut is tightened, recheck the clearance and readjust as necessary.

5. Rotate the crankshaft 180 degrees (the camshaft will turn 90 degrees). One of the grooves in the pulley is now vertical and aligned with the indented mark on the timing belt cover. The UP mark is now at the exhaust side and the distributor rotor points to terminal or wire No. 3.

6. Check all the valves for cylinder No. 3, repeating the adjusting steps previously described as necessary.

7. Rotate the crankshaft 180 degrees. Both grooves on the cam pulley are visible and aligned with the head surfaces. The distributor rotor points to terminal or wire No. 4. The UP mark is upside down or at the bottom of the cam pulley.

8. Check all the valves for cylinder No. 4, repeating the adjusting steps previously described as necessary.

9. Rotate the crankshaft 180 degrees. One groove on the pulley is again vertical, aligned with the indentation on the timing belt cover. The UP mark is at the intake side. The distributor rotor points to terminal or wire No. 2.

10. Check all the valves for cylinder No. 2, repeating the adjusting steps previously described as necessary.

11. Reinstall the valve cover.

1988–95 DOHC Prelude

▶ **See Figures 62, 63, 64, 65 and 66**

These engines employ Dual Overhead Camshafts (DOHC) and use 4 valves per cylinder (2 intake and 2 exhaust). The intake valves are operated by one cam and the exhaust valves by the other. Valve adjustment on these engines is similar to other engines. Each camshaft pulley has UP or arrow marks and grooves; when the engine is rotated during the adjustment, the marks must be aligned both with the cylinder head and with each other.

Valve clearances for 1988–91 Preludes are:
- Intake: 0.003–0.005 in. (0.08–0.12mm)
- Exhaust: 0.006–0.008 in. (0.16–0.20mm)

Valve clearances for 1992 Preludes are:
- Intake: 0.004–0.005 in. (0.09–0.13mm)
- Exhaust: 0.006–0.007 in. (0.15–0.19mm)

Valve clearances for 1993–95 Preludes without VTEC are:

- Intake: 0.003–0.004 in. (0.07–0.11mm)
- Exhaust: 0.006–0.007 in. (0.15–0.19mm)

Valve clearances for 1993–95 Preludes with VTEC are:
- Intake: 0.006–0.007 in. (0.15–0.19mm)
- Exhaust: 0.007–0.008 in. (0.17–0.21mm)

1. With the ignition **OFF**, remove the valve cover.

2. Set the No. 1 piston at top dead center (TDC). The UP or arrow marks on the pulleys should be at the top, and the TDC grooves on the edge or side of the pulley should align with the cylinder head surface. The distributor rotor should be pointing towards the No. 1 spark plug wire.

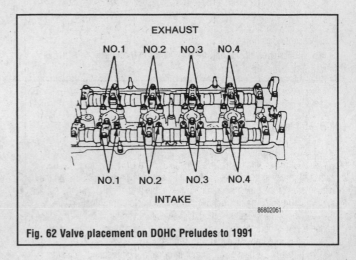

Fig. 62 Valve placement on DOHC Preludes to 1991

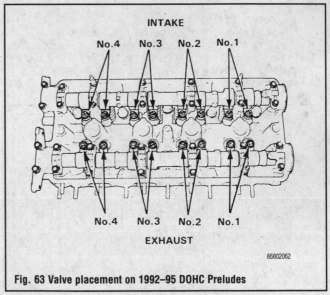

Fig. 63 Valve placement on 1992–95 DOHC Preludes

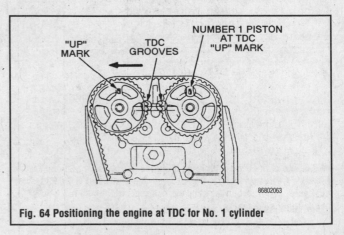

Fig. 64 Positioning the engine at TDC for No. 1 cylinder

3. Check the clearance on all the valves for cylinder No. 1 with a feeler gauge. The gauge should pass the gap with slight drag.

4. If the gauge passes with no drag or cannot be inserted, adjust as follows:

   a. Loosen the adjusting screw locknut.

   b. Turn the adjusting screw to obtain the proper clearance.

   c. Hold the adjusting screw in position and tighten the locknut. Correct locknut torque is 20 ft. lbs. (27 Nm) on models without VTEC and 14 ft. lbs. (20 Nm) on models with VTEC. After the locknut is tightened, recheck the clearance and readjust as necessary.

5. Rotate the crankshaft 180 degrees counterclockwise (the cam pulley will turn 90 degrees). The UP or arrow marks should be at the exhaust side. The distributor rotor should point to the number three spark plug wire. At this point the valves on No. 3 cylinder can be checked. Repeat the adjusting steps previously described as necessary.

6. Rotate the crankshaft 180 degrees counterclockwise to bring the No. 4 piston up to TDC. Both UP or arrow marks should be at the bottom and the distributor rotor should point to the number four spark plug wire. The grooves on the pulley align with the cylinder head surface and with each other. Check the valves for cylinder No. 4. Repeat the adjusting steps previously described as necessary.

7. Rotate the crankshaft 180 degrees counterclockwise to bring the No. 2 cylinder up to TDC. The UP or arrow marks should be at the intake side. The distributor rotor should point at the number two spark plug wire. Check all the valves for cylinder No. 2, repeating the adjusting steps previously described as necessary.

8. Once all the valves have been adjusted and rechecked, reinstall the valve cover on the engine. Reinstall the distributor cap. Start the engine and check for oil leaks.

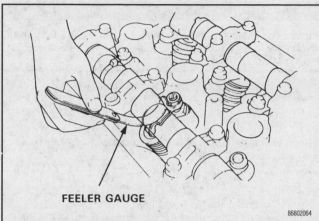

FEELER GAUGE

Fig. 65 On DOHC engines, pass the feeler gauge under the cam lobe to check the valve clearance

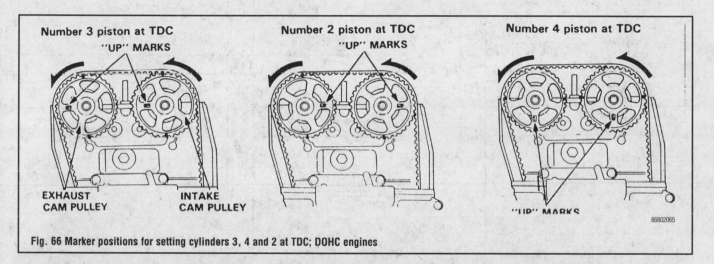

Fig. 66 Marker positions for setting cylinders 3, 4 and 2 at TDC; DOHC engines

IDLE SPEED AND MIXTURE ADJUSTMENTS

Air/Fuel Mixture

Fuel injected vehicles do not allow the manual adjustment of the air/fuel mixture. The engine control unit or ECU is in charge of that and controls the function of the fuel injectors according to the electric signals sent to it by a host of sensors and monitors. If a fuel injected engine suffers an emission related problem, the sensors and computer-controlled output components must be tested and repaired.

On carbureted engines, this procedure is used to adjust the base idle after carburetor disassembly or repair. In general, the mixture is preset at the factory and should not be altered or adjusted casually. Federal law requires the manufacturer to insert tamper-proof plugs or other devices to keep the uninformed out of the carburetor. These procedures require a fair amount of disassembly, including the removal of the carburetor in some cases. If you are anticipating performing a mixture adjustment solely as part of a maintenance program, don't. The risk of creating more problems outweighs a slight adjustment on an otherwise properly running engine.

➡ **The use of the correct tools, in this case a propane enrichment kit, is required for this procedure. Do not begin the procedure if the kit is not available. Make certain the propane bottle is sufficiently full before beginning the procedure.**

The mixture may also be determined through the use of an exhaust gas analyzer or emissions tester, but this equipment is rarely available to the home mechanic. If this method is used, you must still gain access to the mixture adjusting screw(s) to perform the adjustments.

ADJUSTMENT

1984–85 Accord and 1986–89 Accord with Manual Transaxles

♦ **See Figures 67 thru 73**

➡ **A Keihin 2-barrel carburetor is used on these models.**

1. Place the vehicle in the Park or Neutral. Apply the emergency brake and block the drive wheels. Start the engine and allow it to reach normal operating temperature. The cooling fan(s) should come on at least once.

2. Remove the vacuum hose from the intake air control diaphragm and clamp or plug the hose end.

3. Connect a suitable tachometer to the engine following the manufacturers instructions.

4. Check the idle speed with all the accessories turned OFF. If necessary, adjust the idle speed by turning the throttle stop screw.

5. Disconnect the air cleaner intake tube from the air duct on the radiator bulkhead.

6. Insert the hose from the propane kit into the intake tube approximately 4 inches (10 cm).

※※ CAUTION

Propane is a flammable gas. Observe "no smoking/no open flame" precautions. Have a Class B-C (dry powder) fire extinguisher within arm's reach at all times.

7. With the engine idling, depress the lock button on top of the propane device, then slowly open the propane control valve to obtain the maximum engine speed. The engine speed should increase as the percentage of propane injected goes up.

➡**Open the propane control valve slowly; a sudden burst of propane may cause the engine to stall.**

8. The engine idle speed should increase as follows:
- 1984–85 Accord w/MT—75–125 rpm
- 1984–85 Accord w/AT—30–70 rpm
- 1986 Accord w/MT—15–55 rpm
- 1987–89 Accord w/MT—30–70 rpm

9. If the engine speed increases according to specifications, remove the propane kit, all test equipment and reconnect all disconnected vacuum hoses. If the engine speed fails to increase as specified, continue with the following steps. Switch the ignition **OFF**.

10. Disconnect the vacuum hose to the fast idle unloader. Pull the throttle cable out of the bracket.

11. Remove the carburetor nuts, washers and bolts securing the steel tubing vacuum manifold. Lift the carburetor clear of the studs, then tilt it backward to obtain the access to the throttle controller bracket screws.

12. Remove the throttle controller bracket. Remove the mixture adjusting screw hole cap from the throttle controller bracket, then reinstall the bracket. With the plug removed, the adjusting screw can now be reached from the outside of the carburetor body with the carburetor in place.

13. Reinstall the carburetor, reconnect the vacuum hose to the fast idle unloader. Reinstall the air cleaner.

14. Start the engine and let it warm up again to normal operating temperature.

15. Remove the vacuum hose from the intake air control diaphragm and clamp or plug the hose end. Reinstall the propane enrichment kit and recheck the maximum propane enrichment rpm.

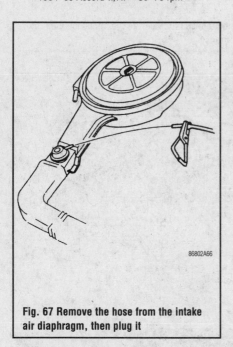

Fig. 67 Remove the hose from the intake air diaphragm, then plug it

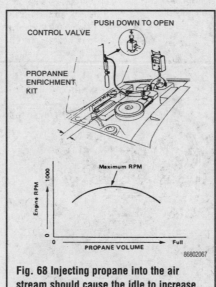

Fig. 68 Injecting propane into the air stream should cause the idle to increase, then decrease. Adjust the flow to hold maximum idle speed

Fig. 69 Remove the screw securing the throttle control bracket; 1984 Accord shown

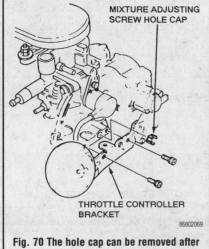

Fig. 70 The hole cap can be removed after the bracket is removed; 1984–85 Accord shown

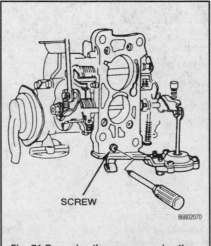

Fig. 71 Removing the screw securing the throttle control bracket; 1987 Accord shown

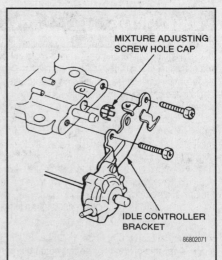

Fig. 72 The hole cap can be removed after the bracket is removed

16. If the propane enriched speed is too low, the mixture is rich. Turn the mixture screw a ¼ turn clockwise and recheck.

17. If the propane enriched speed is too high, the mixture is lean. Turn the mixture screw a ¼ turn counterclockwise and recheck.

18. Close the propane control valve and recheck the idle speed. Be sure to run the engine at 2500 rpm for 10 seconds to stabilize the idle condition.

19. If the engine speed is set to specifications, remove the propane enrichment kit, all test equipment and reconnect all vacuum hoses and the air cleaner intake tube.

20. If the engine speed is not set to specifications, adjust by turning the throttle stop screw. Now repeat the propane enriched speed checks. Once again, check the idle speed and adjust if necessary, by turning the idle control screw.

21. If equipped with air conditioning, make a second check with the air conditioning engaged. Adjust the speed if necessary by turning the adjusting screw on the idle boost diaphragm.

➡**Some 1984 Accord models may develop a stalling problem at idle. The probable cause of this stalling is a sticking slow mixture cut-off solenoid. If this is the case, the solenoid should be removed and replaced with the updated type of solenoid. Additionally, various cold starting and driveability problems on these cars were cured through the addition of assorted "cold-start" kits from Honda. Consult your dealer's service department for details.**

1986–89 Accord with Automatic Transaxles

▶ **See Figures 74 thru 79**

➡**A Keihin 2-barrel carburetor is used on these models.**

1. Place the vehicle in Park or Neutral, then apply the emergency brake and block the drive wheels. Start the engine and allow it to reach normal operating temperature. The cooling fan(s) should come on at least once.

2. Remove vacuum hose from the intake air control diaphragm and clamp or plug the hose end.

3. Connect a suitable tachometer to the engine following the manufacturer's instructions.

4. Remove air filter from frequency solenoid valve "C", then plug the opening in solenoid valve.

5. With no engine load, lower the idle speed as much as possible by turning the throttle stop screw.

6. Adjust the idle speed to 550–650 rpm (580–680 rpm on 1987–89 models) by turning the idle control screw.

7. With headlights on, rear defroster on and the heater blower set to maximum, adjust the idle speed by turning adjusting screw "A." Idle should be 550–650 rpm on 1986 models and 650–750 rpm on 1987–89 models.

8. If equipped with air conditioning, adjust the idle speed to 650–750 rpm by turning adjusting screw "B" with air conditioning on.

9. With no engine load, remove the inside vacuum hose from the idle boost throttle controller, then plug the hose.

10. Adjust the idle speed to 650–750 rpm (600–700 rpm at high altitude) by turning throttle stop screw.

11. Disconnect the hose from frequency solenoid valve "A" and connect to air control valve "A."

12. Disconnect the air cleaner intake tube from the air duct on the radiator bulkhead.

13. Insert the hose from the propane kit into the intake tube approximately 4 inches (10 cm).

Fig. 73 With the air conditioning operating, adjust the idle at screw B

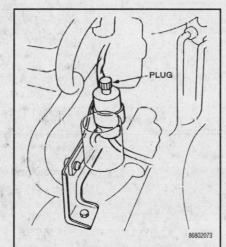

Fig. 74 For vehicles with automatic transaxles, plug the opening in the frequency solenoid valve after the filter is removed

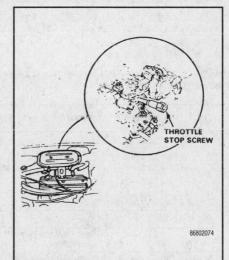

Fig. 75 Throttle stop screw for mechanical idle adjustment

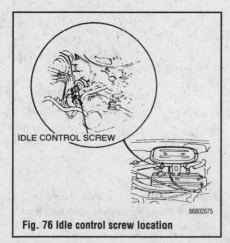

Fig. 76 Idle control screw location

Fig. 77 Location of adjusting screw A

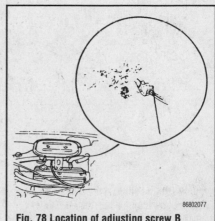

Fig. 78 Location of adjusting screw B

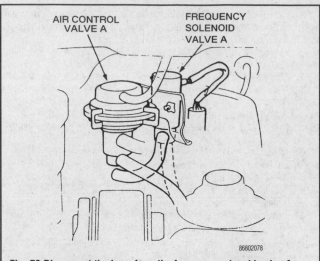

Fig. 79 Disconnect the hose from the frequency solenoid valve A, then connect it to the control valve

✳✳✳ CAUTION

Propane is a flammable gas. Observe "no smoking/no open flame" precautions. Have a Class B-C (dry powder) fire extinguisher within arm's reach at all times.

14. With the engine idling, depress the lock button on top of the propane device, then slowly open the propane control valve to obtain the maximum engine speed. The engine speed should increase as the percentage of propane injected goes up.

➡**Open the propane control valve slowly; a sudden burst of propane may cause the engine to stall.**

15. The engine idle speed should increase 100–170 rpm.

16. If the engine speed increases according to specifications, remove the propane kit, all test equipment and reconnect all disconnected vacuum hoses. If the engine speed fails to increase as specified, continue with the following steps. Switch the ignition **OFF**.

17. Disconnect the vacuum hose to the fast idle unloader. Pull the throttle cable out of the bracket.

18. Remove the carburetor nuts, washers and bolts securing the steel tubing vacuum manifold. Lift the carburetor clear of the studs, then tilt it backward to obtain the access to the throttle controller bracket screws.

19. Remove the throttle controller bracket. Remove the mixture adjusting screw hole cap from the throttle controller bracket, then reinstall the bracket. With the plug removed, the adjusting screw can now be reached from the outside of the carburetor body with the carburetor in place.

20. Reinstall the carburetor, reconnect the vacuum hose to the fast idle unloader. Reinstall the air cleaner.

21. Start the engine and let it warm up again to normal operating temperature.

22. Remove the vacuum hose from the intake air control diaphragm and clamp or plug the hose end. Reinstall the propane enrichment kit and recheck the maximum propane enrichment rpm.

23. If the propane enriched speed is too low, the mixture is rich. Turn the mixture screw a ¼ turn clockwise and recheck.

24. If the propane enriched speed is too high, the mixture is lean. Turn the mixture screw a ¼ turn counterclockwise and recheck.

25. Close the propane control valve and recheck the idle speed. Be sure to run the engine at 2500 rpm for 10 seconds to stabilize the idle condition.

26. If the engine speed is set to specifications, remove the propane enrichment kit, all test equipment and reconnect all vacuum hoses and the air cleaner intake tube.

27. If the engine speed is not set to specifications, adjust by turning the throttle stop screw. Now repeat the propane enriched speed checks.

28. Stop the engine. Close the propane control valve, remove all plugs and reconnect all the hoses.

29. Restart the engine and recheck idle speed.

➡**Raise the engine speed to 2500 rpm 2 or 3 times in 10 seconds, and then check idle speed. Idle speed should be 650–750 rpm on 1986 models and 680–780 rpm on 1987–89 models.**

30. Recheck the idle speed with headlights, heater blower and rear window defroster ON. Idle speed should be 650–750 rpm.

31. Recheck the idle speed with automatic transmission lever in gear. Idle speed should be 650–750 rpm.

32. Recheck the idle speed with air conditioning ON and with the shift lever in Park or Neutral position. Idle speed should be 650–750 rpm.

33. Recheck idle speed with air conditioning ON and in gear. Idle should be 700–800 rpm.

34. If the idle does not reach the specified idle speeds, inspect the idle control system.

Keihin Dual Sidedraft Carburetors 1984–90 Prelude

◆ **See Figures 80 thru 89**

➡**Check that the carburetors are synchronized properly before making idle speed and mixture inspection (see Section 5.) It will also be necessary to remove the ECU fuse from the fuse box for at least 10 seconds to reset the control unit after this procedure is complete.**

1. Start engine and warm up to normal operating temperature. The cooling fans should come on at least once.

2. Remove the vacuum hose from intake air control diaphragm and clamp or plug the hose end.

➡**All wires and hoses should be labeled at the time of removal. The amount of time saved during reassembly makes the extra effort well worthwhile.**

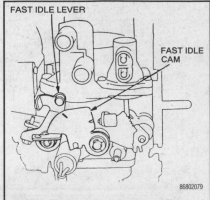

Fig. 80 The fast idle cam must not be engaged during propane enrichment testing

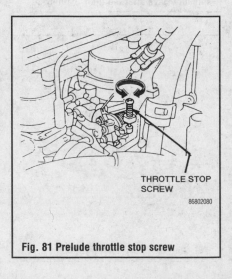

Fig. 81 Prelude throttle stop screw

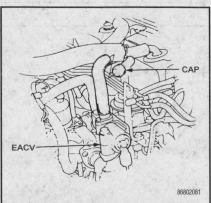

Fig. 82 On 1988–90 Preludes, disconnect the hose from the manifold, then plug the end

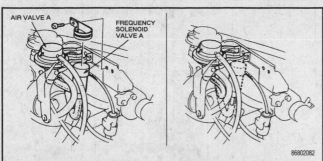

Fig. 83 On 1984–86 automatic transaxle vehicles, disconnect the hoses and connect the lower hose to air control valve A

3. Connect a tachometer. Check that the fast idle lever is not seated against the fast idle cam. If the fast idle lever is seated against the fast idle cam, it may be necessary to replace the left carburetor.

4. Check the idle speed with all accessories turned OFF. Idle speed should be 750–850 rpm (700–750 rpm on automatic transaxles in gear). Adjust the idle speed, if necessary, by turning the throttle stop screw.

➡ **If the idle speed is excessively high, check the throttle control.**

5. On 1987 automatic transmission cars only, unplug the wiring connector from frequency solenoid valve "A" and use jumper wires to connect the valve to

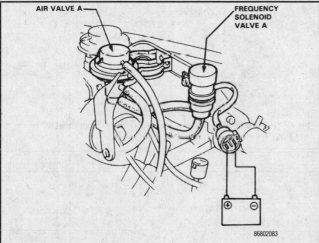

Fig. 84 Automatic 1987 Preludes require the frequency valve to be jumpered to 12 volts

12 volts. On all other vehicles, unplug the two prong connector from the Electronic Air Control Valve (EACV), disconnect the hose from the vacuum hose manifold and cap the hose end.

6. Unplug the vacuum tubes and connect the lower hose to air control valve "A." Disconnect the vacuum hose from the air conditioning idle boost throttle controller. Disconnect the air cleaner intake tube from the air intake duct.

7. Insert propane enrichment hose into the opening of intake tube about 4 inches (10 cm).

❄❄ **CAUTION**

Propane is a flammable gas. Observe "no smoking/no open flame" precautions. Have a Class B-C (dry powder) fire extinguisher within arm's reach at all times.

8. With the engine idling, depress the lock button on top of the propane device, then slowly open propane control valve to obtain maximum engine speed. Engine speed should increase as percentage of propane injected goes up.

➡ **Open the propane control valve slowly. A sudden burst of propane may stall the engine.**

9. Propane enrichment maximum rpm:
- 1984–86 w/MT—20–70 rpm.
- 1984–86 w/AT—85–135 rpm (In D3 or D4).
- 1987 w/MT—45–85 rpm.
- 1987 w/AT—105–155 rpm (in D3 or D4).
- 1988–90 w/MT—150–190 rpm.
- 1988–90 w/AT—40–60 rpm.

10. If the engine speed change is proper, the procedure is complete. Disconnect the test equipment and reassemble the disconnected lines and hoses. If engine speed does not increase per specification, the mixture must be adjusted. On 1984–87 Preludes, remove the carburetors. On later cars, the plugs may be removed without removing the carburetors.

a. Place a drill stop on a drill bit so that only ⅛ in. (3mm) of the bit is exposed. Drill through the center of each mixture screw hole plug.

➡ **If drilled deeper than this measurement, damage to mixture adjusting screw may result from the bit.**

b. Screw a 5mm sheet metal screw into hole plugs.
c. Grab the screw head with a pair of pliers and remove the hole plugs.
d. If applicable, reinstall the carburetors.

11. Start engine and warm up to normal operating temperature. The cooling fan(s) must come on at least once.

12. Recheck maximum propane enriched rpm. If mixture is rich (engine speed too slow), turn both mixture screws ¼ turn counterclockwise. If mixture is lean (engine speed too high), turn both mixture screws ¼ turn clockwise.

13. Close the propane control valve.

14. Run engine at 2,500 rpm for 10 seconds to stabilize mixture conditions, then check idle speed. Adjust the idle speed, if necessary.

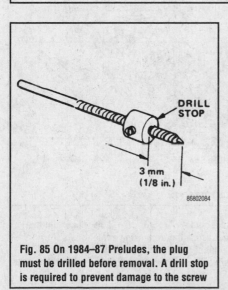

Fig. 85 On 1984–87 Preludes, the plug must be drilled before removal. A drill stop is required to prevent damage to the screw

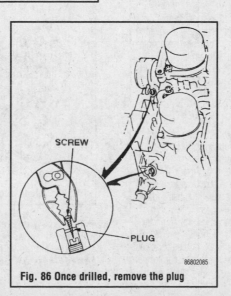

Fig. 86 Once drilled, remove the plug

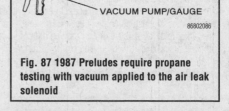

Fig. 87 1987 Preludes require propane testing with vacuum applied to the air leak solenoid

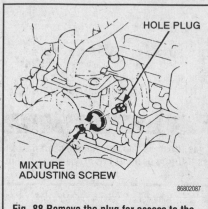

Fig. 88 Remove the plug for access to the adjusting screw on 1988–90 Preludes

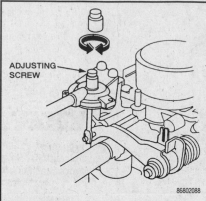

Fig. 89 Adjusting screw for idle with air conditioning engaged; 1988–90 Preludes

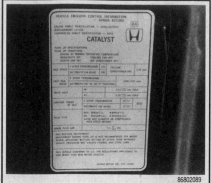

Fig. 90 Tune-up specifications can be found listed on the underhood emissions label

15. On 1984–86 models, remove propane enrichment kit and reconnect the intake air control diaphragm hose. Install new plugs into idle mixture screw holes.

16. On 1987–89 models, disconnect the number "5" vacuum hose from the air suction valve, then plug the hose.

17. On 1987 Preludes, disconnect the upper number "22" vacuum hose from the air leak solenoid valve at the air jet controller support, then plug the end of hose. Connect a vacuum gauge to the solenoid valve.

18. With the engine idling, depress the lock button on top of the propane device, then slowly open the propane control valve and check vacuum. Vacuum should be available.

19. If no vacuum is present, inspect the air leak solenoid valve and thermovalve "C."

20. Remove the propane enrichment kit and engage the connector.

➡Some 1984–85 Prelude models may experience hesitation on acceleration before the engine has reached normal operating temperature. This can be corrected by installing a cold driveability kit from the manufacturer. This kit holds full vacuum advance to the distributor when the engine is cold.

21. On 1988–90 vehicles equipped with air conditioning, check the idle with the A/C running at the end of the procedure. If adjustment is necessary, remove the small cap from the adjusting screw and make necessary adjustments.

Idle Speed

ADJUSTMENT

▶ See Figure 90

Minor adjustments of warm idle speed may be needed as a result of an ignition tune-up or other maintenance procedures. In general, engine idle speed adjustment does not change by itself; if the idle is too low or a stalling problem is present, search out the real cause instead of hiding it with a higher idle speed.

Carbureted Engines

▶ See Figures 91 and 92

On carbureted engines, the idle should be checked with the engine at normal operating temperature and the fast idle system fully disengaged. Connect a tachometer to the vehicle following the manufacturers instructions.

Adjustments are made at the throttle stop screw on the carburetor. This is a mechanical adjustment which simply opens or closes the throttle plate a small amount, thus altering the idle speed. On Accords, the throttle stop has a knurled plastic knob to make adjustment easier. The knob, however, is located on the firewall side of the carburetor and may be difficult to reach. The spring on the adjuster also makes the knob a bit stiff to turn.

Preludes, with their dual-carb arrangement, use a vertically placed screw acting on the throttle linkage. The screw is located between the two carburetors on the linkage.

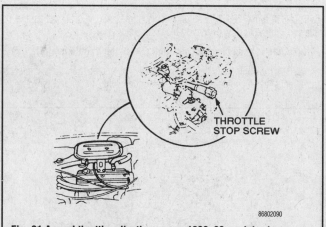

Fig. 91 Accord throttle adjusting screw; 1986–89 models shown, 1984–85 models are similar

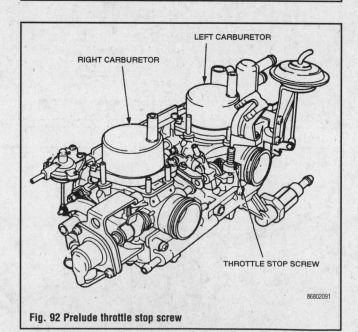

Fig. 92 Prelude throttle stop screw

➡ Particularly on Preludes, but on Accords also, be very certain that you have found the proper screw before making adjustments. Any linkage screw sealed with a dot of paint (usually yellow) is NOT to be altered. These are factory set and, in some cases, are not resettable in the field.

Fuel Injected Engines

1985 ACCORD

▶ **See Figure 93**

1. Start the engine and allow it to reach normal operating temperature. The cooling fan must come on at least once.
2. Connect a suitable tachometer using the manufacturer's instructions.
3. Check idle speed with all accessories OFF.

➡ **To prevent the idle control system from operating, pinch off vacuum hose number "27."**

4. Idle speed should be 700–800 rpm (in neutral). Adjust the idle speed, if necessary, by turning idle adjusting screw.
5. Check the idle controller boosted speed with the air conditioning ON. Idle speed should be 750–850 rpm (in neutral).
6. Adjust idle speed, if necessary, by turning the air conditioning idle adjusting screw.

1986–95 ACCORD AND PRELUDE

▶ **See Figures 94, 95 and 96**

1. Start engine and warm up to normal operating temperature; cooling fan will come on twice.
2. Connect a tachometer following the tool manufacturer's instructions.
3. On 1986–87 Accords and 1984–87 Preludes, disconnect the upper vacuum hose to the idle control solenoid valve (between the valve and intake manifold) from the intake manifold. Cap the end of the hose and intake manifold.
4. On 1988–95 vehicles, unplug the Electronic Air Control Valve (EACV) connector.
5. With all accessories OFF, check the idle speed. Compare the idle speed to the specification found on the underhood sticker or to the tune-up specifications chart (in this section). If necessary, adjust by turning the idle adjusting screw.
6. Turn the ignition switch OFF.
7. Engage the EACV connector, then remove either the CLOCK or BACK UP fuse in the underhood fuse box for at least 10 seconds; this resets the ECU.
8. Check the idle speed with heater fan switch on HI and the air conditioning ON. Idle speed should be 700–800 rpm (in neutral). Adjust the idle speed, if necessary, by turning the adjusting bolt on the air conditioning idle boost valve.
9. After adjustment, connect the idle control solenoid valve vacuum hose.
10. After adjusting the idle speed on automatic transaxle models, check that it remains within specified limit when shifted in gear.
11. Check the idle speed with all accessories ON and the air conditioning OFF. Idle should remain at 700–800 rpm.

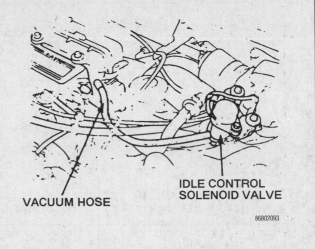

Fig. 94 On 1986–87 Accords and 1984–87 Preludes, disconnect the upper vacuum hose to the idle control solenoid valve

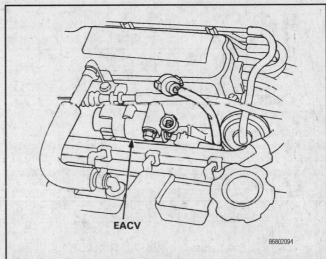

Fig. 95 On 1988–95 vehicles, unplug the Electronic Air Control Valve (EACV) connector

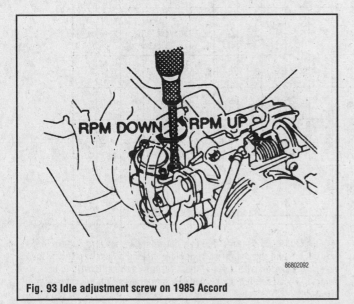

Fig. 93 Idle adjustment screw on 1985 Accord

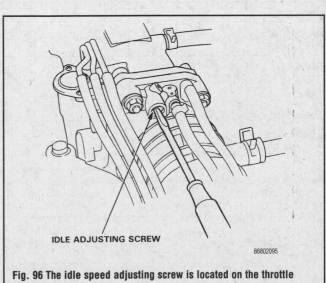

Fig. 96 The idle speed adjusting screw is located on the throttle body

GASOLINE ENGINE TUNE-UP SPECIFICATIONS

Year	Engine ID/VIN	Engine Displacement Liters (cc)	Spark Plugs Gap (in.)	Ignition Timing (deg.) MT	Ignition Timing (deg.) AT	Fuel Pump (psi)	Idle Speed (rpm) MT	Idle Speed (rpm) AT	Valve Clearance In.	Valve Clearance Ex.
1991	F22A1	2.2 (2156)	0.039-0.043	15B	15B	36	700-800	700-800	0.009-0.011	0.011-0.013
	F22A4	2.2 (2156)	0.039-0.043	15B	15B	36	700-800	700-800	0.009-0.011	0.011-0.013
	F22A6	2.2 (2156)	0.039-0.043	15B	15B	36	700-800	700-800	0.009-0.011	0.011-0.013
	B20A5	2.0 (1958)	0.039-0.043	15B	15B	36	700-800	700-800	0.003-0.005	0.006-0.008
	B21A1	2.1 (2056)	0.039-0.043	15B	15B	36	700-800	700-800	0.003-0.005	0.006-0.008
1992	F22A1	2.2 (2156)	0.039-0.043	15B	15B	36	650-750	650-750	0.009-0.011	0.011-0.013
	F22A4	2.2 (2156)	0.039-0.043	15B	15B	40	650-750	650-750	0.009-0.011	0.011-0.013
	F22A6	2.2 (2156)	0.039-0.043	15B	15B	40	650-750	650-750	0.009-0.011	0.011-0.013
	H23A1	2.3 (2259)	0.039-0.043	15B	15B	36	650-750	650-750	0.003-0.004	0.006-0.007
1993	F22A1	2.2 (2156)	0.039-0.043	15B	15B	30-38	650-750	650-750	0.009-0.011	0.011-0.013
	F22A6	2.2 (2156)	0.039-0.043	15B	15B	30-38	650-750	650-750	0.009-0.011	0.011-0.013
	H22A1	2.2 (2157)	0.039-0.043	15B	-	24-31	650-750	-	0.006-0.007	0.007-0.008
	H23A1	2.3 (2259)	0.039-0.043	15B	15B	28-35	650-750	650-750	0.003-0.004	0.006-0.007
1994	F22B1	2.2 (2156)	0.039-0.043	15B	15B	30-37	650-750	650-750	0.009-0.011	0.011-0.013
	F22B2	2.2 (2156)	0.039-0.043	15B	15B	30-37	650-750	650-750	0.009-0.011	0.011-0.013
	F22A1	2.2 (2156)	0.039-0.043	15B	15B	28-35	650-750	650-750	0.009-0.011	0.011-0.013
	H22A1	2.2 (2157)	0.039-0.043	15B	-	24-31	650-750	-	0.006-0.007	0.007-0.008
	H23A1	2.3 (2259)	0.039-0.043	15B	15B	28-35	650-750	650-750	0.003-0.004	0.006-0.007
1995	F22B1	2.2 (2156)	0.039-0.043	15B	15B	30-37	650-750	650-750	0.009-0.011	0.011-0.013
	F22B2	2.2 (2156)	0.039-0.043	15B	15B	30-37	650-750	650-750	0.009-0.011	0.011-0.013
	F22A1	2.2 (2156)	0.039-0.043	15B	15B	28-35	650-750	650-750	0.009-0.011	0.011-0.013
	H22A1	2.2 (2157)	0.039-0.043	15B	-	24-31	650-750	-	0.006-0.007	0.007-0.008
	H23A1	2.3 (2259)	0.039-0.043	15B	15B	28-35	650-750	650-750	0.003-0.004	0.006-0.007
	C27A4	2.7 (2675)	0.039-0.043	-	15B	30-37	650-750	750	Hyd.	Hyd.

NOTE: The Vehicle Emission Control Information label often reflects specification changes made during production. The label figures must be used if they differ from those in this chart.

86802C02

GASOLINE ENGINE TUNE-UP SPECIFICATIONS

Year	Engine ID/VIN	Engine Displacement Liters (cc)	Spark Plugs Gap (in.)	Ignition Timing (deg.) MT	Ignition Timing (deg.) AT	Fuel Pump (psi)	Idle Speed (rpm) MT	Idle Speed (rpm) AT	Valve Clearance In.	Valve Clearance Ex.
1984	ES2	1.8 (1829)	0.039-0.043	22B	18B	2.5	700-800	650-750	0.005-0.007	0.010-0.012
	ES1	1.8 (1829)	0.039-0.043	20B	12B	2.5	750-850	750-850	0.005-0.007	0.010-0.012
1985	ES2	1.8 (1829)	0.039-0.043	22B	18B	2.5	700-800	650-750	0.005-0.007	0.010-0.012
	ES3	1.8 (1829)	0.039-0.043	18B	18B	35	700-800	700-800	0.005-0.007	0.010-0.012
	ET2	1.8 (1829)	0.039-0.043	20B	12B	2.5	750-850	750-850	0.005-0.007	0.010-0.012
1986	BS	2.0 (1955)	0.039-0.043	24B	15B	3.0	700-800	750-850	0.005-0.007	0.010-0.012
	ET	2.0 (1955)	0.039-0.043	15B	15B	35	700-800	700-800	0.005-0.007	0.010-0.012
	ET2	1.8 (1829)	0.039-0.043	20B	12B	2.5	700-800	750-850	0.005-0.007	0.010-0.012
1987	A20A1	2.0 (1955)	0.039-0.043	24B	15B	3.0	700-800	650-750	0.005-0.007	0.010-0.012
	A20A3	2.0 (1955)	0.039-0.043	15B	15B	35	750-850	750-850	0.005-0.007	0.010-0.012
	A18A1	1.8 (1829)	0.039-0.043	20B	12B	2.5	700-800	700-800	0.005-0.007	0.010-0.012
1988	A20A1	2.0 (1955)	0.039-0.043	24B	15B	3.0	700-800	650-750	0.005-0.007	0.010-0.012
	A20A3	2.0 (1955)	0.039-0.043	15B	15B	35	750-850	750-850	0.005-0.007	0.010-0.012
	B20A3	2.0 (1955)	0.039-0.043	20B	12B	2.5	700-800	700-800	0.005-0.007	0.010-0.012
	B20A5	2.0 (1955)	0.039-0.043	20B	15B	35	800-850	750-850	0.005-0.007	0.010-0.012
1989	A20A1	2.0 (1955)	0.039-0.043	24B	15B	2.5	750-850	750-850	0.005-0.007	0.010-0.012
	A20A3	2.0 (1955)	0.039-0.043	15B	15B	35	800-850	700-800	0.005-0.007	0.010-0.012
	B20A3	2.0 (1955)	0.039-0.043	20B	12B	2.6-3.3	750-850	750-800	0.005-0.007	0.010-0.012
	B20A5	2.0 (1955)	0.039-0.043	20B	15B	33-39	800-800	680-790	0.005-0.007	0.010-0.012
1990	F22A1	2.2 (2156)	0.039-0.043	15B	15B	2.5	750-850	700-800	0.005-0.007	0.010-0.012
	F22A4	2.2 (2156)	0.039-0.043	15B	15B	1.3-2.1	650-750	650-750	0.009-0.011	0.011-0.013
	B2CA3	2.0 (1955)	0.039-0.043	20B	15B	36	650-750	650-750	0.009 0.011	0.011 0.013
	B2CA5	2.0 (1955)	0.039-0.043	15B	15B	1.3-2.1	700-800	700-800	0.003-0.005	0.006-0.008
	B21A1	2.1 (2056)	0.039-0.043	15B	15B	36	700-800	700-800	0.003-0.005	0.006-0.008

86802C01

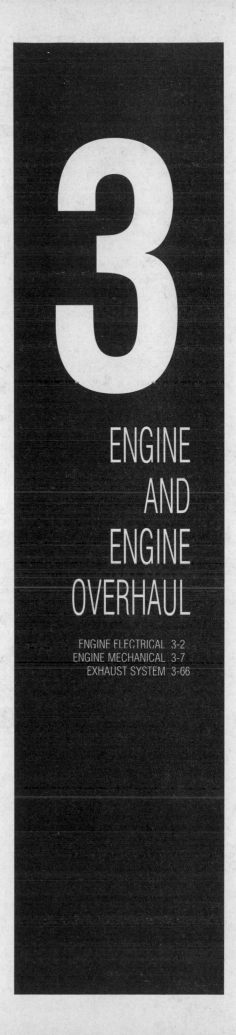

3

ENGINE AND ENGINE OVERHAUL

ENGINE ELECTRICAL

Distributor

The distributor is the device responsible for sending the spark to the correct plug. It is essentially a rotating switch, turning the current on and off to each terminal. For the vehicles covered in this book, all distributors are driven directly by a camshaft and are mounted at the end of the head. Some distributors employ some combination of mechanical and vacuum advance system. These systems cause the spark timing to change in proportion to the speed and load of the engine. Some engines also employ vacuum retard. On the 1990–95 Accord and 1988–95 fuel injected Prelude, the system is fully electronic, with all timing control handled by the Program Fuel Injection computer. No mechanical or vacuum advance is used.

A visual inspection of the distributor will reveal its type of advance; if only one vacuum hose is present, running to a round diaphragm housing on the side of the distributor, the system uses vacuum advance only. Two hoses indicate an advance and retard system. No hoses indicates a fully electronic system.

REMOVAL & INSTALLATION

1. Using masking tape, remove the spark plug wires from the cap and number them for installation as they are removed. Factory distributor caps will have a mark indicating cylinder No. 1.
2. Label and disconnect the vacuum hoses, the primary wire and the high tension wire. Some early models require disconnection of these wires at the coil. Label and disconnect any external wiring connectors at the distributor.
3. Remove the hold-down bolt(s) and remove the distributor from the head.
4. Remove and discard the O-ring from the distributor shaft.
   To install
5. Using a new O-ring, install it on the distributor shaft. Coat it lightly with clean engine oil.
6. The drive lugs in the end of the distributor shaft are slightly offset to match the offset in the end of the camshaft. Position the distributor shaft for an approximate match, then fit the distributor in place.

➡**The distributor will only engage the cam in the correct matching position. This enlightened design allows the distributor to be installed correctly regardless of engine position, even if the engine was turned with the distributor removed.**

7. Make certain the drive lugs are correctly engaged and the O-ring is in place. Install the retaining bolts centered in the mounts and just snug enough to hold the distributor in place.
8. Reconnect the external wiring and install the spark plug wires. Double check their placement.
9. Start the engine and set the timing. Tighten the distributor bolts.

Alternator

The alternator converts the mechanical energy which is supplied by the drive belt into electrical energy by electromagnetic induction. When the ignition switch is turned **ON**, current flows from the battery, through the charging system light, to the voltage regulator and finally to the alternator.

When the engine is started, the drive belt turns the rotating field (rotor) in the stationary windings (stator), inducing alternating current. This alternating current is converted into usable direct current by the diode rectifier. Most of this current is used to charge the battery and power the electrical components of the vehicle. A small part is returned to the field windings of the alternator enabling it to increase its power output. When the current in the field windings reaches a predetermined control voltage, the voltage regulator grounds the circuit, preventing any further increase. The cycle is continued so that the voltage remains constant.

All present day Hondas use a nominal 12 volt alternator. (Exact output should be higher, generally 13.5–15.1 volts.) Amperage ratings may vary according to year, model and accessories. All use either a transistorized, non-adjustable voltage regulator or control the alternator output through the engine computer (ECU) used for the fuel injection. The 1984–87 Preludes use an external regulator mounted on the right shock tower; all others are contained within the alternator case.

PRECAUTIONS

To prevent damage to the alternator, regulator and ECU, the following precautionary measures must be taken when working with the electrical system.

1. Never reverse the battery connections. Always check the battery polarity visually. This is to be done before any connections are made to ensure that all of the connections correspond to the battery ground polarity of the vehicle.
2. Booster batteries must be connected properly. Make sure the positive cable of the booster battery is connected to the positive terminal of the battery which is getting the boost.
3. Disconnect the battery cables before using a fast charger; the charger has a tendency to force current through the diodes in the opposite direction. This causes damage.
4. Never use a fast charger as a booster for starting the car.
5. Never disconnect the alternator or regulator connectors while the engine is running.
6. Do not ground the alternator output terminal.
7. Do not operate the alternator on an open circuit with the field energized.
8. Do not attempt to polarize the alternator.
9. Disconnect the battery cables and remove the alternator before using an electric arc welder on the vehicle.
10. Protect the alternator from excessive moisture. If the engine is to be steam cleaned, cover or remove the alternator.

TESTING

Honda recommends the use of the Sun VAT-40 (or an equivalent charging system tester) for testing of the charging system. Follow the instructions supplied by the test equipment manufacturer.

REMOVAL & INSTALLATION

The alternator is generally mounted low on the engine on the firewall side. This makes access very awkward. The work must be done both over-the-fender and from below, depending on your agility and reach. Whenever the work is to be performed from below, the vehicle must be safely supported on jackstands. If only the front is supported, the parking brake must be applied and the rear wheels firmly blocked. Once elevated, the gravel or splash shield must be removed from under the engine.

1984–85 Accord
▶ **See Figure 1**

1. With the ignition **OFF**, disconnect the negative battery cable.
2. Unplug the alternator wire harness connector and remove the terminal nut.

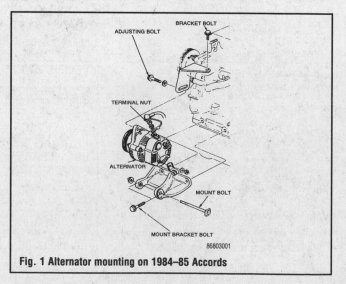

Fig. 1 Alternator mounting on 1984–85 Accords

3. Remove the alternator adjusting bolt; loosen the nut on the mount bolt.

4. Swing the alternator towards the engine; remove the belt.

5. Remove the bolts holding the alternator bracket to the engine and remove the alternator with the bracket.

To install:

6. Install the alternator and bracket. Once in position with the bolts finger-tight, install the belt. Tighten the mounting bracket bolts and the alternator mount (pivot) bolt to 33 ft. lbs. (45 Nm).

7. Install the adjusting bolt, adjust the belt and tighten the nut to 16 ft. lbs. (22 Nm).

8. Install the wire harness connector and secure the terminal nut.

9. Reconnect the negative battery cable.

10. If the vehicle was elevated, reinstall the splash shield. Lower the vehicle to the ground.

1986–89 Accord

▶ **See Figure 2**

1. Disconnect the negative battery cable.
2. Elevate and safely support the vehicle.
3. Remove the splash shield from under the vehicle.
4. Disconnect the left driveshaft from the steering knuckle. Refer to Section 7 for procoduro.
5. Unplug the multi-pin connector from the back of the alternator. Remove the clip from the harness bracket.
6. Remove the terminal nut and disconnect the white wire from the B terminal.
7. Remove the alternator pivot or upper bolt and nut, then remove the belt from the alternator pulley.
8. Support the alternator; remove the through-bolt and remove the alternator.
9. The alternator mount or bracket may be removed if desired.

To install:

10. Fit the alternator into its mount; install the through-bolt finger-tight. Fit the belt onto the pulley.

11. Install the upper alternator bolt. Make certain it goes through the eye of the adjusting bolt.

12. Adjust the belt tension. Tighten the nut on the through-bolt to 33 ft. lbs. (45 Nm) and tighten the upper bolt to 17 ft. lbs. (24 Nm).

13. Install the white wire on the B terminal and tighten the nut.

14. Install the multi-pin harness to the alternator and secure the harness clip(s).

15. Reinstall the left driveshaft to the steering knuckle.

16. Install the splash shield. Lower the car to the ground.

17. Connect the negative battery cable.

1990–93 Accord

▶ **See Figure 3**

1. With the ignition **OFF**, disconnect the negative battery cable.
2. Remove the power steering pump. Refer to Section 8 for the complete procedure.

3. Remove the cruise control actuator but do not disconnect the actuator cable; simply move the unit out of the way with the cable attached.

4. Unplug the multi-pin electrical connector.

5. Remove the terminal nut and remove the wire from the terminal.

6. Loosen the adjusting bolt; remove the alternator nut.

7. Remove the belt from the alternator pulley.

8. Remove the adjusting bolt, the lower through-bolt and the small support stay.

9. Support the alternator. Remove the upper through-bolt and remove the alternator.

10. If desired, remove the alternator mounting brackets.

To install:

11. If the alternator brackets were removed, reinstall them. Coat the bolts with a thread sealer or liquid thread lock. Install the bracket bolts and tighten them to 36 ft. lbs. (50 Nm).

12. Fit the alternator into place. Install the upper through-bolt and tighten it to 33 ft. lbs. (45 Nm).

13. Install the small stay, the lower through-bolt and the adjusting bolt. Make certain the adjusting bolt is properly installed.

14. Install the belt. Install the alternator nut. Adjust the belt tension. Tighten the alternator nut to 19 ft. lbs. (26 Nm).

15. Connect the wire to the terminal and tighten the nut.

16. Engage the multi-pin connector to the alternator.

17. Install the cruise control actuator.

18. Install the power steering pump.

19. Connect the negative battery cable.

1994–95 Accord

▶ **See Figure 4**

EXCEPT V-6 MODELS

1. Disconnect the negative battery cable, then the positive cable.
2. Remove the power steering pump. Refer to Section 8 for procedures.
3. Unplug the multi-connector from the back of the alternator.
4. Remove the terminal nut and remove the wire from the terminal.
5. Loosen the through-bolt, adjustment locknut, and the adjusting bolt.
6. Remove the belt from the alternator.
7. Remove the adjustment nut and bolt.
8. Remove the through-bolt and the alternator.

To install:

9. Fit the alternator into place. Install the through-bolt and tighten it to 33 ft. lbs. (45 Nm).

10. Install the adjustment bolt and nut.

11. Install the belt and adjust the tension. Tighten the locknut to 16 ft. lbs. (22 Nm).

12. Connect the wire to the terminal and tighten the nut.

13. Engage the multi-pin connector to the alternator.

14. Install the power steering pump.

15. Connect the positive battery cable, then the negative cable.

V-6 MODELS

1. Disconnect the negative battery cable, then the positive cable.
2. Unplug the multi-connector from the back of the alternator.

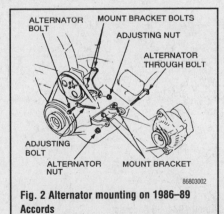

Fig. 2 Alternator mounting on 1986–89 Accords

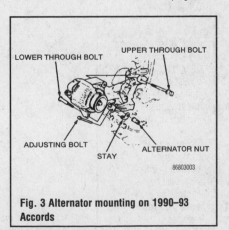

Fig. 3 Alternator mounting on 1990–93 Accords

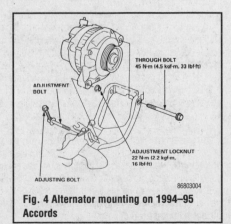

Fig. 4 Alternator mounting on 1994–95 Accords

3. Remove the terminal nut and remove the wire from the terminal.
4. Loosen the through-bolt, adjustment locknut, and the adjusting bolt.
5. Remove the belt from the alternator.
6. Remove the adjustment bolt/adjusting bolt assembly and the locknut.
7. Remove the through-bolt and the alternator.

To install:

8. Fit the alternator into place. Install the through-bolt and tighten it to 33 ft. lbs. (45 Nm).
9. Install the adjustment bolt/adjusting bolt assembly and the locknut.
10. Install the belt and adjust the tension. Tighten the locknut to 16 ft. lbs. (22 Nm).
11. Connect the wire to the terminal and tighten the nut.
12. Engage the multi-pin connector to the alternator.
13. Connect the positive battery cable, then the negative cable.

1984–87 Prelude

▶ **See Figures 5 and 6**

1. Disconnect the negative battery cable.
2. Remove the air cleaner assembly.
3. On carbureted engines, disconnect the engine wiring harness. The connector uses locking tabs on the top and bottom; lift both tabs at the same time before pulling the connector loose.
4. On fuel injected engines, Unplug the connector from the alternator and remove the clip at the harness bracket.
5. Remove the terminal nut; remove the wiring.
6. On carbureted engines, remove the alternator adjusting bolt and nut, then remove the belt from the pulley. On fuel injected engines, remove the alternator bolt and nut and remove the belt from the pulley.
7. Remove the alternator through-bolt (lower bolt) and remove the alternator.
8. The mounting brackets may be removed if desired.

To install:

9. Install the mounting brackets if they were removed. Tighten the bolts to 33 ft. lbs. (45 Nm).
10. Fit the alternator into position and install the through-bolt.

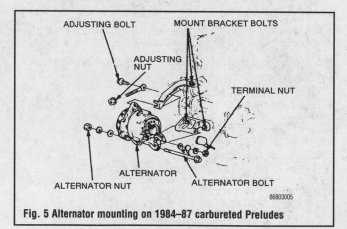

Fig. 5 Alternator mounting on 1984–87 carbureted Preludes

11. Install the belt. Install the adjusting or upper alternator bolt. Make certain the adjuster is correctly positioned.
12. Adjust the belt. Tighten the lower alternator nut or bolt to 33 ft. lbs. (45 Nm). Tighten the upper alternator or adjusting nut to 17 ft. lbs. (24 Nm).
13. Install the wiring on the terminal stud and tighten the terminal nut.
14. Engage the wiring harness connector to the alternator.
15. Install the air cleaner housing.
16. Connect the negative battery cable.

1988–91 Prelude

▶ **See Figure 7**

1. Disconnect the negative battery cable.
2. Unplug the alternator connector from the alternator; remove the wire harness clip from the bracket.
3. Remove the terminal nut; remove the wiring from the terminal.
4. Loosen the through-bolt and the adjusting nut.
5. Remove the alternator bolt, then remove the belt.
6. Remove the through-bolt and remove the alternator.

To install:

7. Install the alternator in position and fit the through-bolt.
8. Install the belt on the pulley, then install the alternator bolt. Make certain the alternator bolt engages the adjuster.
9. Adjust the belt. Tighten the through-bolt to 33 ft. lbs. (45 Nm) and the alternator bolt to 18 ft. lbs. (25 Nm).
10. Install the wiring on the terminal and secure the nut.
11. Secure the wiring harness connector to the alternator.
12. Connect the negative battery cable.

1992–95 Prelude

▶ **See Figure 8**

1. With the ignition **OFF**, disconnect the negative battery cable.
2. Remove the power steering pump. Refer to Section 8 for complete procedure.
3. Remove the cruise control actuator but do not disconnect the actuator cable; simply move the unit out of the way with the cable attached.
4. Unplug the multi-pin electrical connector.
5. Remove the terminal nut and remove the wire from the terminal.
6. Loosen the through-bolt, then loosen the adjustment locknut and bolt.
7. Remove the belt from the alternator.
8. Remove the adjustment bolt and nut.
9. Remove the through-bolt, then remove the alternator.

To install:

10. Fit the alternator into place. Install the upper through-bolt finger-tight.
11. Install the adjustment bolt and nut.
12. Install the belt and adjust the tension. Tighten the through-bolt to 33 ft. lbs. (45 Nm) and the adjustment locknut to 16 ft. lbs. (22 Nm).
13. Connect the wire to the terminal and tighten the nut.
14. Engage the multi-pin connector to the alternator.
15. Install the cruise control actuator.
16. Install the power steering pump.
17. Connect the negative battery cable.

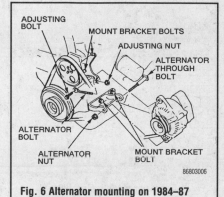

Fig. 6 Alternator mounting on 1984–87 fuel injected Preludes

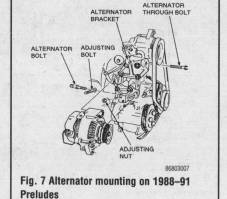

Fig. 7 Alternator mounting on 1988–91 Preludes

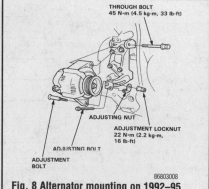

Fig. 8 Alternator mounting on 1992–95 Preludes

Voltage Regulator

The regulator controls the output of the alternator. If the regulator did not limit the voltage output of the alternator, the excessive output could damage components of the electrical system, as well as the alternator or battery.

REMOVAL & INSTALLATION

Carbureted 1984–87 Prelude

▶ See Figure 9

1. The external voltage regulator is located on the right front shock tower.
2. With the ignition **OFF**, disconnect the wiring harness and ground connection bolt.
3. Unbolt and remove the regulator.
4. Reassemble in reverse order.

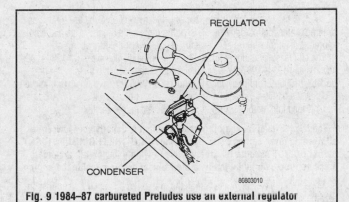

Fig. 9 1984–87 carbureted Preludes use an external regulator

Except Accord V-6 and 1984–87 Carbureted Prelude

▶ See Figure 10

➡ This procedure does not apply to the Accord V-6. If the regulator fails on these models, replace the entire alternator assembly.

1. Remove the alternator.
2. At the back or non-pulley end, remove the nuts, then remove the end cover.

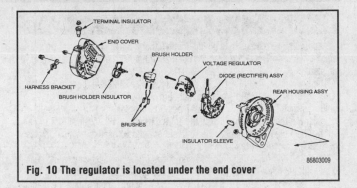

Fig. 10 The regulator is located under the end cover

3. Remove the insulator from the brush holder.
4. Remove the screws securing the brush holder, then remove the holder.
5. Remove the bolts holding the regulator and remove the regulator.

To install:

6. Install the regulator with the retaining screws.
7. Install the brush holder.
8. Reassemble and reinstall the alternator.

Battery

Please refer to Section 1 for battery maintenance and care.

REMOVAL & INSTALLATION

The battery is located in the engine compartment on all models.

1. Make sure the ignition switch is turned **OFF**.
2. Disconnect the negative battery cable first, then the positive cable from the battery.
3. Remove the battery hold-down clamp nuts, the clamp and the battery from the vehicle.
4. To install, reverse the removal procedures; be sure the battery is seated correctly on the battery tray. Make certain the battery retainer is securely fastened.

➡ Before re-installing an old battery, cleaning the battery posts and the terminal connectors is highly recommended.

5. Connect the positive battery cable first, then the negative battery cable. Coat the battery terminals with a non-metallic grease; this will keep the terminals from oxidizing.

ALTERNATOR SPECIFICATIONS

Year	Model	Alternator Output (amps)	Regulated Volts
1984	Accord	65A	14V
	Prelude	60A	14V
1985	Accord	65A	14V
	Prelude	60A	14V
1986	Accord	65A	14V
	Prelude-Carbureted	60A	14V
	Prelude-Fuel Injected	65A	14V
1987	Accord	65A	14V
	Prelude-Carbureted	60A	14V
	Prelude-Fuel Injected	65A	14V
1988	Accord	65A	14V
	Prelude	70A	13.5V
1989	Accord	65A	14V
	Prelude	70A	13.5V
1990	Accord	80A	13.5V
	Prelude	70A	13.5V
1991	Accord	80A	13.5V
	Prelude	70A	13.5V
1992	Accord	80A	13.5V
	Prelude	80A [1]	13.5V
1993	Accord	80A	13.5V
	Prelude	80A [1]	13.5V
1994	Accord	80A [2]	13.5V
	Prelude	80A [1]	13.5V
1995	Accord	80A [2]	13.5V
	Prelude	80A [1]	13.5V

[1] 90 and 95 amp also used on some models; check the alternator label
[2] 90 amp also used on some models; check the alternator label

86803900

Starter

Accords and Preludes may be fitted with either a direct-drive starter or a gear reduction starter. The differences are internal and depend on the manufacturer of the starter.

The two units are similar in operation and service. Both starters are 4-pole, series wound, DC units to which an outboard solenoid is mounted. When the ignition switch is turned to the **START** position, the solenoid armature is drawn in, engaging the starter pinion with the engine flywheel. When the starter pinion and flywheel are fully engaged, the solenoid armature closes the main contacts for the starter, causing the starter to crank the engine.

When the engine starts, the increased speed of the flywheel causes the gear to overrun the starter clutch and rotor. The gear continues in full mesh until the ignition is released from the **START** to the **ON** position, interrupting the starter current. A spring then returns the gear to its neutral position.

REMOVAL & INSTALLATION

▶ See Figures 11 and 12

1. Disconnect both battery terminals, negative first.
2. Disconnect the large cable from the starter motor; label and disconnect the wiring to the starter solenoid. Certain engine/transmission combinations have an engine harness secured in a clip on the starter or transaxle. Remove the harness from the clip and position it out of the way.
3. Remove the starter motor by loosening the attaching bolts.

To install:

4. To install, reverse the removal procedures. Tighten the starter-to-engine bolts to 47 ft. lbs. (64 Nm) on the Accord V-6 and 32 ft. lbs. (45 Nm) on other models.
5. Connect the wiring to the starter securely.
6. Connect the battery cables, positive cable first.

STARTER SOLENOID REPLACEMENT

1. Remove the starter from the vehicle.
2. Remove the screws securing the solenoid to the starter housing.
3. Pull out the solenoid. On the Nippodenso type, there is a spring on the shaft and a steel ball at the end of the shaft, be sure not to lose them. On the Mitsuba type, move the solenoid away from the plane of the armature to disengage it from the solenoid lever.

To install:

4. Install the solenoid with a new gasket (if equipped). On the Mitsuba type, make certain the lever is correctly installed to, and engaged with, the lever. On the Nippodenso unit, make certain the steel ball and spring are correctly placed. All the sliding surfaces of the solenoid should be lightly greased before installation.
5. Tighten the retaining screws until snug.
6. Install the starter.

Sending Units and Sensors

➡This heading covers only engine sensors not related to computer engine controls for either carbureted or fuel injected vehicles. Engine control sensors are covered in Section 4.

REMOVAL & INSTALLATION

Oil Pressure Sender

▶ See Figure 13

The oil pressure sending switch is an on-off switch controlled by the oil pressure in the lubrication system. Under normal conditions, the switch is held open by strong oil pressure. Should the oil pressure drop below acceptable levels, the switch will close, turning on the oil pressure warning lamp on the instrument panel. In many cases, this circuit communicates with either the engine ECU or the Integrated Control Unit. When a low oil pressure message is received, either of these units may cause protective action to be taken such as shutting off the fuel pump relay. By shutting the engine off, the system attempts to protect itself from more severe damage due to lack of lubrication.

The oil pressure sender is located on or near the oil filter base. On 1984–1989 Accords and 1984–1987 Preludes, the sender is threaded into the oil filter base. On 1990–1995 Accords (except V-6) and 1988–1995 Preludes, look for it above or below the oil filter, threaded into the side of the engine block. On V-6 Accords, it is threaded into the block above the oil filter next to the crank pulley.

➡The trigger level for the oil pressure switch is usually very low; if the oil warning lamp comes on while driving, SHUT THE ENGINE OFF RIGHT AWAY! DO NOT assume that the vehicle is simply low on oil; a sudden pressure drop usually indicates a mechanical problem inside the engine.

To remove the sensor, make certain the ignition switch is **OFF**, then disconnect the sensor wiring. Using a wrench of the proper size, unscrew the sensor. The threads are coated with sealant; it may be stiff to turn. Use care not to damage surrounding components.

When installing the sensor, coat the threads with a non-hardening oil-proof sealant or compound. Install the sensor, tightening it to 13 ft. lbs. (18 Nm). Connect the wire to the sender or harness. Double check the oil level on the dipstick if there was any leakage or spillage during repair.

➡If it is ever necessary to perform an oil pressure test on the engine, the pressure gauge should be connected into the oil pressure sensor port after the sensor is removed.

Coolant Temperature Gauge Sender

The coolant temperature sender is a variable resistor. Changes in coolant temperature affect the ground path for the temperature gauge on the instrument panel. This sending unit or sensor is not to be confused with other temperature senders or sensors related to engine or fuel system control through the com-

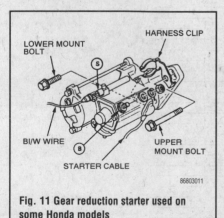

Fig. 11 Gear reduction starter used on some Honda models

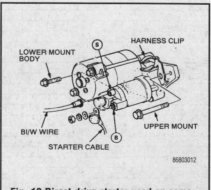

Fig. 12 Direct-drive starter used on some Honda models

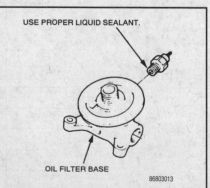

Fig. 13 On some models, the oil pressure sender is threaded into the oil filter base

puter or sensors used for air conditioning control. Some models have as many as six sensors and switches reacting to coolant temperature.

On 1984–1989 carbureted Accords, the sensor is found in the bottom of the intake manifold. It is usually in company with several other sensors and hoses and may be recognized by the fact that it feeds only a wire; it's the one without the vacuum hoses. On 1990–1995 Accords (except V-6), the gauge sender is located at the rear of the cylinder head; it is the smaller of the two sensors found there. On V-6 Accords, it is located on the coolant crossover pipe on the transaxle side of the engine. It is the smaller of the two sensors next to the bleed bolt.

On 1984–1987 carbureted Preludes, the gauge sender is located low on the intake manifold below the EGR valve. For carbureted 1988–1990 Preludes and fuel injected Preludes to 1991, the sensor is located on the thermostat housing on the rear of the cylinder head. The sensor is recognizable by the single wire running to it and the lack of vacuum hoses. On 1992–1995 Preludes, it is the small sensor next to the thermostat housing.

1. With the ignition **OFF** and the engine cold, drain the coolant to a level at least below the level of the sensor.
2. Unplug the wire or harness connector from the sensor.
3. Remove the sensor using a wrench of the correct size. Contain coolant spillage.
4. Install the new sensor, tightening it to 7 ft. lbs. (10 Nm).
5. Connect the wiring.
6. Refill the coolant to the proper level.

Radiator Fan Switch

This switch is the primary controller of the operation of the radiator fan(s) used for cooling. When the coolant in the system reaches a pre-determined temperature, the fan switch closes and completes a circuit. The fans will be brought on. Generally, the switch communicates with the fan relay, although the later PGM-FI cars send the signal through one of the many solid-state controllers first. Do not assume that the switch is the only component in the radiator fan circuit which controls its operation. There are many other components whose failure may prevent the radiator fan from operating. If the fans are not working when the engine is very warm, check the fuses first.

On all vehicles except 1990–95 Accords and 1992–95 Preludes, the fan switch is located in the bottom of the radiator. On 1990–95 Accords (except V-6) and 1992–95 Preludes, the switch is located in the housing at the rear end of the coolant connecting pipe. This is the pipe running along the outside of the engine, just above the oil filter. The switch the only electrical component in the housing. On the Accord V-6, it threaded into the side of the coolant crossover pipe (not next to the bleed bolt) on the transaxle side of the engine.

1. With the ignition **OFF** and the engine cold, drain the radiator to a level at least below the sensor. On some models, this means the radiator must be empty. Use a catch pan of sufficient capacity.
2. Disconnect the wiring for the sensor.
3. Remove the sensor by unscrewing it. On radiator mounted units, use extreme care not to damage the sensor mount or the radiator.
4. Install the new sensor. Tighten radiator mounted units to 17 ft. lbs. (23 Nm). On 1990–93 Accords and 1992–95 Preludes, tighten the switch in the housing to 20 ft. lbs. (28 Nm). On 1994–95 Accords, tighten it to 17 ft. lbs. (24 Nm).
5. Connect the wiring to the sensor.
6. Refill the coolant.

Low Fuel Sender

The sender or switch controlling the low fuel light on the instrument panel is integral with the fuel level sender controlling the fuel gauge. Both are located within the fuel tank. For tank and sender removal, please refer to Section 5 of this manual.

Brake Fluid Level Sensor

If the fluid level in the brake fluid reservoir drops to an unsafe level, the BRAKE warning lamp on the dashboard will illuminate. This simple circuit is controlled by the brake fluid level sensor, located in the cap of the reservoir on the master cylinder.

Wipe the cap and reservoir with a clean cloth, removing all dust and road grit. Unscrew the cap about ¼ turn and lift it up. Under the cap you'll see a shaft with a circular float on it. The bottom of the shaft contains a reed switch; the float contains a magnet. As long as the fluid level keeps the float near the top of the shaft, the reed switch is open. When the fluid level drops, the float drops down to the reed switch causing the switch to close. The circuit is completed and the warning lamp comes on.

Since the sensor and float are integral with the cap, the only repair for a failed switch is a new reservoir cap. Disconnect the wiring connector(s) and replace the cap.

ENGINE MECHANICAL

Understanding the Engine

The piston engine is a metal block containing a series of round chambers or cylinders. These chambers may be arranged in line or in a V; hence, the description of an engine as an "inline 4 or 6" or a "V6 or V8". The engines used in the Honda Accord and Prelude are water cooled, overhead cam, transversely mounted powerplants. The upper part of the engine block is usually an iron or aluminum-alloy casting. The casting forms outer walls around the cylinders with hollow areas in between, through which coolant circulates. The lower block provides a number of rigid mounting points for the crankshaft and its bearings. The lower block is referred to as the crankcase.

The crankshaft is a long, steel shaft mounted at the bottom of the engine and free to turn in its mounts. The mounting points (generally four to seven) and the bearings for the crankshaft are called main bearings. The crankshaft is the shaft which is made to turn through the function of the engine; this motion is then passed into the transmission/transaxle and on to the drive wheels.

Attached to the crankshaft are the connecting rods which run up to the pistons within the cylinders. As the air/fuel mixture explodes within the tightly sealed cylinder, the piston is forced downward. This motion is transferred through the connecting rod to the crankshaft and the shaft turns. As one piston finishes its power stroke, its next upward journey forces the burnt gasses out of the cylinder through the now-open exhaust valve. By the top of the stroke, the exhaust valve has closed and the intake valve has begun to open, allowing the fresh air/fuel charge to be sucked into the cylinder by the downward stroke of the piston. The intake valve closes, the piston once again comes back up and compresses the charge in the closed cylinder. At the top (approximately) of this stroke the spark plug fires, the charge explodes and another power stroke takes place. If you count the piston motions between power strokes, you'll see why automotive engines are called four-stroke or four-cycle engines.

While one cylinder is performing this cycle, all the others are also contributing in different timing. Obviously, all the cylinders cannot fire at once or the power flow would not be steady. As any one cylinder is on its power stroke, another is on its exhaust stroke, another on intake and another on compression. These constant power pulses keep the crank turning; a large round flywheel attached to the end of the crankshaft provides a stable mass to smooth out the rotation.

At the top of the engine, the cylinder head(s) provide tight covers for the cylinders. They contain machined chambers into which the fuel charge is forced as the piston reaches the top of its travel. These combustion chambers contain at least one intake and one exhaust valve which are opened and closed through the action of the camshaft. The spark plugs are screwed into the cylinder head so that the tips of the plugs protrude into the chamber.

Since the timing of the valve action (opening and closing) is critical to the combustion process, the camshaft is driven by a belt or chain. The valves are operated either by pushrods (called overhead valves—the valves are above the cam) or by the direct action of the cam pushing on the valves (overhead cam). All Accord and Prelude engines use Overhead Cam (OHC) engines. Some vehicles use two cams; thus the designation Dual Overhead Cam (DOHC).

Lubricating oil is stored in a pan or sump at the bottom of the engine. It is force fed to all the parts of the engine by the oil pump which may be driven by either the crank or the camshaft. The oil lubricates the entire engine by travelling through passages in the block and head. Additionally, the circulation of the oil provides 25–40 percent of the engine cooling.

If all this seems very complicated, keep in mind that the sole purpose of any motor—gas, diesel, electric, solar—is to turn a shaft. The motion of the shaft is then harnessed to perform a task such as pumping water, moving the vehicle, etc. Due to the constantly changing operating conditions found in a motor vehicle, accomplishing this shaft-turning in an automotive engine requires many supporting systems such as fuel delivery, exhaust handling, lubrication, cooling, starting, etc. Operation of these systems involve principles of mechanics, vacuum, electronics, etc. Being able to identify a problem by what system is involved will allow you to begin accurate diagnosis of the symptoms and causes.

Engine Overhaul Tips

Most engine overhaul procedures are fairly standard. In addition to specific parts replacement procedures and complete specifications for your individual engine, this section also is a guide to accepted rebuilding procedures. Examples of standard rebuilding practice are shown and should be used along with specific details concerning your particular engine.

Competent and accurate machine shop services will ensure maximum performance, reliability and engine life.

In most instances it is more profitable for the do-it-yourself mechanic to remove, clean and inspect the component, buy the necessary parts and deliver these to a shop for actual machine work.

On the other hand, much of the rebuilding work (crankshaft, block, bearings, piston rods, and other replaceable components) is usually within the scope of the do-it-yourself mechanic. Patience, proper tools, and common sense coupled with a basic understanding of the engine can yield satisfying and economical results.

TOOLS

The tools required for an engine overhaul or parts replacement will depend on the depth of your involvement. With a few exceptions, they will be the tools found in a mechanic's tool kit (see Section 1). More in-depth work will require any or all of the following:

• A dial indicator (reading in thousandths of an inch or metric equivalent) mounted on a universal base. The base may or may not come with a new unit.
• Micrometers and telescope gauges
• Jaw and screw-type pullers
• Gasket scrapers; the best are wood or plastic
• Valve spring compressor
• Ring groove cleaner
• Piston ring expander and compressor
• Ridge reamer
• Cylinder hone or glaze breaker
• Plastigage®
• Engine stand. This single tool may be the most expensive piece of equipment in your garage but is well worth the cost. The engine can be bolted to it and then rotated into any position for work on the upper or lower end.
• Engine hoist or crane. Generally not worth the high cost of purchase unless you plan to remove engines on a regular basis, these units can be rented from many supply houses. Engine hoists are superior to overhead chain lifts because the castered lift can be repositioned instead of moving the vehicle.

The use of most of these tools is illustrated in this section. Many can be rented for a one-time use from a local parts jobber or tool supply house specializing in automotive work.

Occasionally, the use of special tools is called for. See the information on Special Tools and the Safety Notice in the front of this book before substituting another tool.

INSPECTION TECHNIQUES

Procedures and specifications are given in this Section for inspecting, cleaning and assessing the wear limits of most major components. Other procedures such as MagnaFlux® and Zyglo® can be used to locate material flaws and stress cracks. MagnaFlux® is a magnetic process applicable only to ferrous (iron and steel) materials. The Zyglo® process coats the material with a fluorescent dye penetrant and can be used on any material. Checks for suspected surface cracks can be more readily made using spot check dye. The dye is sprayed onto the suspected area, wiped off and the area sprayed with a developer. Cracks will show up brightly.

OVERHAUL TIPS

Aluminum has become extremely popular for use in engines, due to its low weight. Observe the following precautions when handling aluminum parts:
• Never hot tank aluminum parts (the caustic hot tank solution will eat the aluminum.)
• Remove all aluminum parts (identification tag, etc.) from engine parts prior to the tanking.
• Always coat threads lightly with engine oil or anti-seize compounds before installation to prevent seizure.
• Never overtighten bolts or spark plugs especially in aluminum threads.
Stripped threads in any component can be repaired using any of several commercial repair kits (Heli-Coil®, Microdot®, Keenserts®, etc.).

When assembling the engine, any parts that will be in frictional contact must be pre-lubed to provide lubrication at initial start-up. Any product specifically formulated for this purpose can be used. Engine oil is NOT recommended as a pre-lube.

When semi-permanent (locked, but removable) installation of bolts or nuts is desired, threads should be cleaned and coated with Loctite® or other similar, commercial non-hardening sealant.

REPAIRING DAMAGED THREADS

▶ **See Figures 14, 15, 16, 17 and 18**

Several methods of repairing damaged threads are available. Heli-Coil® (shown here), Keenserts® and Microdot® are among the most widely used. All involve basically the same principle—drilling out stripped threads, tapping the hole and installing a prewound insert—making welding, plugging and oversize fasteners unnecessary.

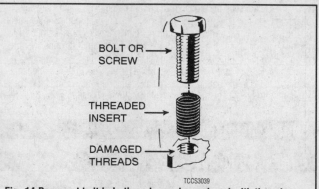

TCCS3039

Fig. 14 Damaged bolt hole threads can be replaced with thread repair inserts

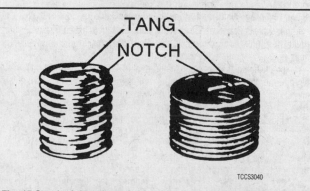

TCCS3040

Fig. 15 Standard thread repair insert (left), and spark plug thread insert

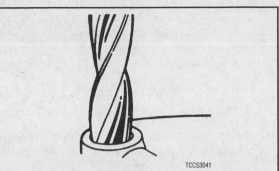

Fig. 16 Drill out the damaged threads with the specified drill. Be sure to drill completely through the hole or to the bottom of a blind hole

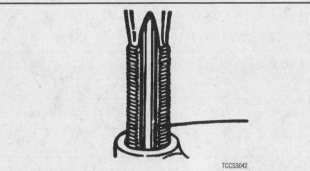

Fig. 17 Using the kit, tap the hole in order to receive the thread insert. Keep the tap well oiled and back it out frequently to avoid clogging the threads

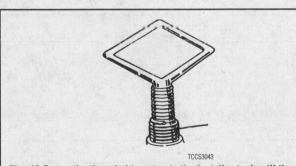

Fig. 18 Screw the threaded insert onto the installer tool until the tang engages the slot. Thread the insert into the hole until it is ¼ or ½ turn below the top surface, then remove the tool and break off the tang using a punch

Two types of thread repair inserts are usually supplied: a standard type for most inch coarse, inch fine, metric course and metric fine thread sizes and a spark lug type to fit most spark plug port sizes. Consult the individual manufacturer's catalog to determine exact applications. Typical thread repair kits will contain a selection of prewound threaded inserts, a tap (corresponding to the outside diameter threads of the insert) and an installation tool. Spark plug inserts usually differ because they require a tap equipped with pilot threads and a combined reamer/tap section. Most manufacturers also supply blister-packed thread repair inserts separately in addition to a master kit containing a variety of taps and inserts plus installation tools.

Before attempting to repair a threaded hole, remove any snapped, broken or damaged bolts or studs. Penetrating oil can be used to free frozen threads. The offending item can be removed with locking pliers or using a screw/stud extractor. After the hole is clear, the thread can be repaired, as shown in the series of accompanying illustrations and in the kit manufacturer's instructions.

Checking Engine Compression

A noticeable lack of engine power, excessive oil consumption and/or poor fuel mileage measured over an extended period are all indicators of internal engine wear. Worn piston rings, scored or worn cylinder bores, leaking head gaskets, sticking or burnt valves and worn valve seats are all possible culprits here. A check of each cylinder's compression will help you locate the problems.

As mentioned in the Tools and Equipment part of Section 1, a screw-in type compression gauge is more accurate that the type you simply hold against the spark plug hole, although it takes slightly longer to use. It's worth it to obtain a more accurate reading. Follow the procedures below.

1. With the engine cold, carefully remove the spark plugs and coat the threads with an anti-sieze compound.
2. Install the spark plugs.
3. Warm up the engine to normal operating temperature.
4. Shut the engine off, then carefully remove all the spark plugs.
5. Unplug the primary side electrical connectors from the ignition coil.
6. Screw the compression gauge into the No. 1 spark plug hole until the fitting is snug.

✳✳ WARNING

Be careful not to crossthread the plug hole. On aluminum cylinder heads use extra care, as the threads in these heads are easily ruined.

7. Ask an assistant to depress the accelerator pedal fully on both carbureted and fuel injected vehicles.
8. While you read the compression gauge, ask the assistant to crank the engine two or three times in short bursts using the ignition switch.
9. Read the compression gauge at the end of each series of cranks, and record the highest of these readings. Repeat this procedure for each of the engine's cylinders. As a general rule, new motors will have compression on the order of 150–170 pounds per square inch (psi). This number will decrease with age and wear. The number of pounds of pressure that your test shows is not as important as the evenness between all the cylinders. Many engines run very well with all cylinders at 105 psi (723 kPa). The lower number simply shows a general deterioration internally. This motor probably burns a little oil and may be a bit harder to start, but, based on these numbers, doesn't warrant an engine tear-down yet. Compare the highest reading of all the cylinders. Any variation of more than 10 percent should be considered a sign of potential trouble. For example, on a 4-cylinder engine, if your compression readings for cylinders 1 through 4 were: 135 psi, 125 psi, 90 psi and 125 psi, it would be fair to say that cylinder number three is not working efficiently and is almost certainly the cause of your oil burning, rough idle or poor fuel mileage.
10. If a cylinder is unusually low, pour a tablespoon of clean engine oil into the cylinder through the spark plug hole and repeat the compression test. If the compression comes up after adding the oil, it appears that the cylinder's piston rings or bore are damaged or worn. (The oil sealed some of the leakage.) If the pressure remains low, the valves may not be seating properly (a valve job is needed), or the head gasket may be blown near that cylinder. If compression in any two adjacent cylinders is low, and if the addition of oil doesn't help the compression, there is leakage past the head gasket. Oil and coolant in the combustion chamber can result from this problem. There may also be evidence of water droplets on the engine oil dipstick when a head gasket has failed.

GENERAL ENGINE SPECIFICATIONS

Year	Engine ID/VIN	Engine Displacement Liters (cc)	Fuel System Type	Net Horsepower @ rpm	Net Torque @ rpm (ft. lbs.)	Bore x Stroke (in.)	Compression Ratio	Oil Pressure @ rpm
1994	F22B1	2.2 (2156)	MPFI	145@5500	147@4500	3.35x3.74	8.8:1	50@3000
	F22B2	2.2 (2156)	MPFI	130@5300	139@4200	3.35x3.74	8.8:1	50@3000
	F22A1	2.2 (2156)	MPFI	135@5200	142@4000	3.35x3.74	8.8:1	50@3000
	H22A1	2.2 (2157)	MPFI	190@6800	158@5500	3.43x3.57	10.0:1	50@3000
	H23A1	2.3 (2259)	MPFI	160@5800	156@4500	3.43x3.74	9.8:1	50@3000
1995	F22B1	2.2 (2156)	MPFI	145@5500	147@4500	3.35x3.74	8.8:1	50@3000
	F22B2	2.2 (2156)	MPFI	130@5300	139@4200	3.35x3.74	8.8:1	50@3000
	F22B6	2.2 (2156)	MPFI	140@5600	145@4600	3.35x3.74	8.8:1	50@3000
	F22A1	2.2 (2156)	MPFI	135@5200	142@4000	3.35x3.74	8.8:1	50@3000
	H22A1	2.2 (2157)	MPFI	190@6800	158@5500	3.43x3.57	10.0:1	50@3000
	H23A1	2.3 (2259)	MPFI	160@5800	156@4500	3.43x3.74	9.8:1	50@3000
	C27A4	2.7 (2675)	MPFI	170@5600	165@4500	3.43x2.95	9.0:1	63@3000

EFI- Electronic Fuel Injection
MPFI- Multi Point Fuel Injection

86803902

GENERAL ENGINE SPECIFICATIONS

Year	Engine ID/VIN	Engine Displacement Liters (cc)	Fuel System Type	Net Horsepower @ rpm	Net Torque @ rpm (ft. lbs.)	Bore x Stroke (in.)	Compression Ratio	Oil Pressure @ rpm
1984	ES2	1.8 (1829)	3 bbl	86 @ 5800	99 @ 3500	3.15 x 3.58	9.0:1	50 @ 2000
	ES1	1.8 (1829)	Dual Sidedraft	100 @ 5500	104 @ 4000	3.15 x 3.58	9.1:1	55 @ 2000
1985	ES2	1.8 (1829)	2 bbl	86 @ 5800	99 @ 3500	3.15 x 3.58	9.0:1	50 @ 2000
	ES3	1.8 (1829)	EFI	101 @ 5800	108 @ 2500	3.15 x 3.58	8.8:1	50 @ 2000
	ET2	1.8 (1829)	Dual Sidedraft	100 @ 5500	104 @ 4000	3.15 x 3.58	9.1:1	55 @ 2000
1986	BS	2.0 (1955)	2 bbl	98 @ 5500	110 @ 3500	3.25 x 3.58	9.1:1	55 @ 2000
	BT	2.0 (1955)	EFI	110 @ 5500	114 @ 4500	3.25 x 3.58	8.8:1	55 @ 2000
	ET2	1.8 (1829)	Dual Sidedraft	100 @ 5500	107 @ 4000	3.15 x 3.58	9.1:1	50 @ 2000
1987	A20A3	2.0 (1955)	2 bbl	98 @ 5500	109 @ 3500	3.25 x 3.58	9.1:1	55 @ 2000
	A20A3	2.0 (1955)	EFI	110 @ 5500	114 @ 4500	3.25 x 3.58	8.8:1	55 @ 2000
	A18A1	1.8 (1829)	Dual Sidedraft	100 @ 5500	107 @ 4000	3.15 x 3.58	9.1:1	50 @ 2000
1988	A20A1	2.0 (1955)	2 bbl	98 @ 5500	109 @ 3500	3.25 x 3.58	9.1:1	55 @ 2000
	A20A3	2.0 (1955)	EFI	110 @ 5500	114 @ 4500	3.25 x 3.58	9.3:1	55 @ 2000
	B20A3	2.0 (1955)	Dual Sidedraft	100 @ 5500	107 @ 4000	3.19 x 3.74	9.1:1	50 @ 2000
1989	B20A5	2.0 (1955)	MPFI	110 @ 5500	114 @ 4500	3.18 x 3.74	9.0:1	50 @ 2000
	A20A1	2.0 (1955)	2 bbl	98 @ 5500	109 @ 3500	3.26 x 3.58	9.1:1	55-65 @ 3000
	A20A3	2.0 (1955)	EFI	120 @ 5800	122 @ 4000	3.26 x 3.58	9.3:1	55-65 @ 3000
	B20A3	2.0 (1955)	Dual Sidedraft	100 @ 5500	111 @ 4800	3.19 x 3.74	9.1:1	75-87 @ 3000
1990	B20A5	2.0 (1955)	MPFI	135 @ 6200	127 @ 4500	3.19 x 3.74	9.0:1	75-87 @ 3000
	F22A1	2.2 (2156)	MPFI	125 @ 5200	137 @ 4000	3.35 x 3.74	8.8:1	50 @ 3000
	F22A4	2.2 (2156)	MPFI	130 @ 5200	142 @ 4000	3.35 x 3.74	8.8:1	50 @ 3000
	B20A3	2.0 (1955)	Dual Sidedraft	100 @ 5500	111 @ 4000	3.19 x 3.74	9.1:1	50 @ 3000
1991	B20A5	2.0 (1955)	MPFI	135 @ 6200	127 @ 4000	3.19 x 3.74	9.0:1	50 @ 3000
	F22A1	2.1 (2056)	MPFI	140 @ 5800	135 @ 5000	3.27 x 3.74	9.4:1	50 @ 3000
	F22A1	2.2 (2156)	MPFI	125 @ 5200	137 @ 4000	3.35 x 3.74	8.8:1	50 @ 3000
	F22A4	2.2 (2156)	MPFI	130 @ 5600	142 @ 4000	3.35 x 3.74	8.8:1	50 @ 3000
	F22A6	2.2 (2156)	MPFI	140 @ 5600	142 @ 4500	3.35 x 3.74	8.8:1	50 @ 3000
1992	B20A5	2.0 (1958)	MPFI	135 @ 6200	127 @ 4000	3.19 x 3.74	9.0:1	50 @ 3000
	B21A1	2.1 (2056)	MPFI	140 @ 5800	135 @ 5000	3.27 x 3.74	9.4:1	50 @ 3000
	F22A1	2.2 (2156)	MPFI	125 @ 5200	137 @ 4000	3.35 x 3.74	8.8:1	50 @ 3000
	F22A4	2.2 (2156)	MPFI	130 @ 5200	142 @ 4000	3.35 x 3.74	8.8:1	50 @ 3000
	F22A6	2.2 (2156)	MPFI	140 @ 5600	142 @ 4000	3.35 x 3.74	8.8:1	50 @ 3000
	H23A1	2.3 (2259)	MPFI	160 @ 5800	156 @ 4500	3.43 x 3.74	9.8:1	50 @ 3000
1993	F22A1	2.2 (2156)	MPFI	125 @ 6200	137 @ 4000-	3.35 x 3.74	8.8:1	50 @ 3000
	F22A6	2.2 (2156)	MPFI	140 @ 5600	142 @ 4000	3.35 x 3.74	8.8:1	50 @ 3000
	H22A1	2.2 (2157)	MPFI	190 @ 6800	158 @ 5300	3.43 x 3.57	10.0:1	50 @ 3000
	H23A1	2.3 (2259)	MPFI	160 @ 5800	156 @ 4500	3.43 x 3.74	9.8:1	50 @ 3000

86803901

VALVE SPECIFICATIONS (1993–1995)

Year	Engine ID/VIN	Engine Displacement Liters (cc)	Seat Angle (deg.)	Face Angle (deg.)	Spring Test Pressure (lbs. @ in.)	Spring Installed Height (in.)	Stem-to-Guide Clearance (in.) Intake	Stem-to-Guide Clearance (in.) Exhaust	Stem Diameter (in.) Intake	Stem Diameter (in.) Exhaust
1993	F22A1, A6	2.2 (2156)	45	45	NA	NA	0.0008-0.0030	0.0022-0.0050	0.2148-0.2163	0.2134-0.2150
	H22A1	2.2 (2157)	45	45	NA	NA	0.0010-0.0030	0.0020-0.0040	0.2144-0.2159	0.2144-0.2159
	H23A1	2.3 (2259)	45	45	NA	NA	0.0010-0.0030	0.0020-0.0040	0.2580-0.2594	0.2570-0.2583
1994	F22B1	2.2 (2156)	45	45	NA	NA	0.0008-0.0030	0.0022-0.0050	0.2148-0.2163	0.2134-0.2150
	F22B2	2.2 (2156)	45	45	NA	NA	0.0008-0.0018	0.0022-0.0031	0.2159-0.2163	0.2146-0.2150
	F22A1	2.2 (2156)	45	45	NA	NA	0.0008-0.0030	0.0022-0.0050	0.2148-0.2163	0.2134-0.2150
	H22A1	2.2 (2157)	45	45	NA	NA	0.0010-0.0030	0.0020-0.0040	0.2144-0.2159	0.2144-0.2159
	H23A1	2.3 (2259)	45	45	NA	NA	0.0010-0.0030	0.0020-0.0040	0.2580-0.2594	0.2570-0.2583
1995	F22B1	2.2 (2156)	45	45	NA	NA	0.0008-0.0030	0.0022-0.0050	0.2148-0.2163	0.2134-0.2150
	F22B2	2.2 (2156)	45	45	NA	NA	0.0008-0.0030	0.0022-0.0050	0.2148-0.2163	0.2134-0.2150
	F22B6	2.2 (2156)	45	45	NA	NA	0.0008-0.0030	0.0022-0.0050	0.2148-0.2163	0.2134-0.2150
	F22A1	2.2 (2156)	45	45	NA	NA	0.0008-0.0030	0.0022-0.0050	0.2148-0.2163	0.2134-0.2150
	H22A1	2.2 (2157)	45	45	NA	NA	0.0010-0.0030	0.0020-0.0040	0.2459	0.2459
	H23A1	2.3 (2259)	45	45	NA	NA	0.0010-0.0030	0.0020-0.0040	0.2580-0.2594	0.2570-0.2583
	C27A4	2.7 (2675)	45	45	NA	NA	0.0008-0.0030	0.0020-0.0040	0.2580-0.2594	0.2570-0.2583

N/A - Not Available

VALVE SPECIFICATIONS (1984–1992)

Year	Engine ID/VIN	Engine Displacement Liters (cc)	Seat Angle (deg.)	Face Angle (deg.)	Spring Test Pressure (lbs. @ in.)	Spring Installed Height (in.)	Stem-to-Guide Clearance (in.) Intake	Stem-to-Guide Clearance (in.) Exhaust	Stem Diameter (in.) Intake	Stem Diameter (in.) Exhaust
1984	ES2, ES1	1.8 (1829)	45	45	NA	NA	0.001-0.0020	0.002-0.0040	0.2591-0.2594	0.2532-0.2536
1985	ES2, ES3, ET2	1.8 (1829)	45	45	NA	NA	0.001-0.0020	0.002-0.0040	0.2591-0.2594	0.2532-0.2536
1986	ET2	1.8 (1829)	45	45	NA	NA	0.001-0.0020	0.002-0.0040	0.2591-0.2594	0.2579-0.2936
	BS, BT	2.0 (1955)	45	45	NA	NA	0.001-0.0020	0.002-0.0040	0.2591-0.2594	0.2532-0.2536
1987	A18A1	1.8 (1829)	45	45	NA	NA	0.001-0.0020	0.002-0.0040	0.2591-0.2594	0.2532-0.2536
	A20A1, A20A3	2.0 (1955)	45	45	NA	NA	0.001-0.0020	0.002-0.0040	0.2591-0.2594	0.2532-0.2536
1988	A20A1, A20A3	2.0 (1955)	45	45	NA	NA	0.001-0.0020	0.002-0.0040	0.2591-0.2594	0.2532-0.2536
	B20A3	2.0 (1955)	45	45	NA	NA	0.001-0.0020	0.002-0.0040	0.2591-0.2594	0.2532-0.2536
	B20A5	2.0 (1955)	45	45	NA	NA	0.001-0.0020	0.002-0.0030	0.2591-0.2594	0.2583
1989	A20A1, A20A3	2.0 (1955)	45	45	NA	NA	0.001-0.0020	0.002-0.0040	0.2591-0.2594	0.2532-0.2536
	B20A3	2.0 (1955)	45	45	NA	NA	0.001-0.0020	0.002-0.0040	0.2591-0.2594	0.2532-0.2536
	B20A5	2.0 (1955)	45	45	NA	NA	0.001-0.0020	0.002-0.0030	0.2591-0.2594	0.2583
1990	F22A1, A4	2.2 (2156)	45	45	NA	NA	0.001-0.0020	0.002-0.0030	0.2146-0.2150	0.2146-0.2150
	B20A3	2.0 (1955)	45	45	NA	NA	0.001-0.0020	0.002-0.0040	0.2591-0.2594	0.2532-0.2536
	B20A5	2.0 (1955)	45	45	NA	NA	0.001-0.0020	0.002-0.0040	0.2591-0.2594	0.2532-0.2536
	B21A1	2.1 (2056)	45	45	NA	NA	0.001-0.0020	0.002-0.0030	0.2591-0.2594	0.2579-0.2583
1991	F22A1, A4, A6	2.2 (2156)	45	45	NA	NA	0.0009-0.0019	0.002-0.0030	0.2157-0.2161	0.2146-0.2150
	B20A5	2.0 (1955)	45	45	NA	NA	0.001-0.0020	0.002-0.0030	0.2591-0.2594	0.2532-0.2583
	B21A1	2.1 (2056)	45	45	NA	NA	0.001-0.0020	0.002-0.0030	0.2591-0.2594	0.2579-0.2583
1992	F22A1, A4, A6	2.2 (2156)	45	45	NA	NA	0.0008-0.0020	0.0021-0.0031	0.2159-0.2163	0.2145-0.2149
	H23A1	2.3 (2259)	45	45	NA	NA	0.001-0.0020	0.002-0.0030	0.2591-0.2594	0.2579-0.2583

CAMSHAFT SPECIFICATIONS
All measurements given in inches.

Year	Engine ID/VIN	Engine Displacement Liters (cc)	Journal Diameter 1	2	3	4	5	Elevation In.	Ex.	Bearing Clearance	Camshaft End-Play
1984	ES2	1.8 (1829)	NA	NA	NA	NA	NA	[1]	1.4870	0.006 [11]	0.002-0.020
	ES1	1.8 (1829)	NA	NA	NA	NA	NA	[3]	[4]	0.006 [11]	0.002-0.020
1985	ES2	1.8 (1829)	NA	NA	NA	NA	NA	[1]	1.4870	0.006 [11]	0.002-0.020
	ES3	1.8 (1829)	NA	NA	NA	NA	NA	[2]	1.5274	0.006 [11]	0.002-0.020
1986	ET2	1.8 (1829)	NA	NA	NA	NA	NA	[3]	[4]	0.006 [11]	0.002-0.020
	ET2	1.8 (1829)	NA	NA	NA	NA	NA	[3]	[4]	0.006 [11]	0.002-0.020
	BS	2.0 (1955)	NA	NA	NA	NA	NA	[5]	[6]	0.006 [11]	0.002-0.020
	BT	2.0 (1955)	NA	NA	NA	NA	NA	[7]	1.5274	0.006 [11]	0.002-0.020
1987	A18A1	1.8 (1829)	NA	NA	NA	NA	NA	1.3274	[5]	0.006 [11]	0.002-0.020
	A20A1	2.0 (1955)	NA	NA	NA	NA	NA	[7]	1.5274	0.006 [11]	0.002-0.020
1988	A20A3	2.0 (1955)	NA	NA	NA	NA	NA	[5]	1.5274	0.006 [11]	0.002-0.020
	A20A1	2.0 (1955)	NA	NA	NA	NA	NA	[7]	1.5274	0.006 [11]	0.002-0.020
	A20A3	2.0 (1955)	NA	NA	NA	NA	NA	[5]	1.3359	0.006 [11]	0.002-0.020
	B20A3	2.0 (1955)	NA	NA	NA	NA	NA	1.3274	1.3359	0.006 [11]	0.002-0.020
	B20A5	2.0 (1955)	NA	NA	NA	NA	NA	1.3274	1.3359	0.006 [11]	0.002-0.020
1989	A20A1	2.0 (1955)	NA	NA	NA	NA	NA	[7]	1.5274	0.006 [11]	0.002-0.020
	A20A3	2.0 (1955)	NA	NA	NA	NA	NA	[5]	[6]	0.006 [11]	0.002-0.020
	B20A3	2.0 (1955)	NA	NA	NA	NA	NA	1.3072	1.3200	0.006 [11]	0.002-0.020
	B20A5	2.0 (1955)	NA	NA	NA	NA	NA	1.3072	1.3200	0.006 [11]	0.002-0.020
1990	B20A3	2.0 (1955)	NA	NA	NA	NA	NA	1.3072	1.3200	0.006	0.002-0.020
	B20A5	2.0 (1955)	NA	NA	NA	NA	NA	1.3072	1.3200	0.006	0.002-0.020
	B21A1	2.1 (2056)	NA	NA	NA	NA	NA	1.3072	1.3300	0.006	0.002-0.020

86803905

CAMSHAFT SPECIFICATIONS
All measurements given in inches.

Year	Engine ID/VIN	Engine Displacement Liters (cc)	Journal Diameter 1	2	3	4	5	Elevation In.	Ex.	Bearing Clearance	Camshaft End-Play
1990	F22A1	2.2 (2156)	NA	NA	NA	NA	NA	1.5167	1.5266	0.006	0.002-0.020
	F22A4	2.2 (2156)	NA	NA	NA	NA	NA	1.5167	1.5266	0.006	0.002-0.020
1991	B20A5	2.0 (1955)	NA	NA	NA	NA	NA	1.3072	1.3200	0.006	0.002-0.020
	B21A1	2.1 (2056)	NA	NA	NA	NA	NA	1.3072	1.3300	0.006	0.002-0.020
	F22A1	2.2 (2156)	NA	NA	NA	NA	NA	1.5167	1.5266	0.006	0.002-0.020
	F22A4	2.2 (2156)	NA	NA	NA	NA	NA	1.5167	1.5266	0.006	0.002-0.020
1992	F22A6	2.2 (2156)	NA	NA	NA	NA	NA	1.5252	1.5343	0.006	0.002-0.006
	F22A1	2.2 (2156)	NA	NA	NA	NA	NA	1.5167	1.5266	0.006	0.002-0.006
	F22A6	2.2 (2156)	NA	NA	NA	NA	NA	1.5252	1.5343	0.006 [12]	0.002-0.006
	H23A1	2.3 (2259)	NA	NA	NA	NA	NA	1.3252	1.3278	0.006	0.002-0.006
1993	F22A1	2.2 (2156)	NA	NA	NA	NA	NA	1.5167	1.5266	0.006	0.0020-0.0060
	F22A6	2.2 (2156)	NA	NA	NA	NA	NA	1.5252	1.5343	0.006	0.0020-0.0060
	H22A1	2.2 (2157)	NA	NA	NA	NA	NA	[8]	[9]	0.006	0.0020-0.0060
	H23A1	2.3 (2259)	NA	NA	NA	NA	NA	1.3252	1.3278	0.006 [12]	0.0020-0.0060
1994	F22B1	2.2 (2156)	NA	NA	NA	NA	NA	[10]	1.5105	0.006	0.0020-0.0060
	F22B2	2.2 (2156)	NA	NA	NA	NA	NA	1.5168	1.5267	0.006	0.0020-0.0060
	F22A1	2.2 (2156)	NA	NA	NA	NA	NA	1.5168	1.5267	0.006	0.0020-0.0060
	H22A1	2.2 (2157)	NA	NA	NA	NA	NA	[8]	[9]	0.006	0.0020-0.0060
	H23A1	2.3 (2259)	NA	NA	NA	NA	NA	1.3252	1.3278	0.006 [12]	0.0020-0.0060
1995	F22B1	2.2 (2156)	NA	NA	NA	NA	NA	[10]	1.5105	0.006	0.0020-0.0060
	F22B2	2.2 (2156)	NA	NA	NA	NA	NA	1.5168	1.5267	0.006	0.0020-0.0060
	F22B6	2.2 (2156)	NA	NA	NA	NA	NA	1.5252	1.5343	0.006	0.0020-0.0060

86803906

CRANKSHAFT AND CONNECTING ROD SPECIFICATIONS
All measurements are given in inches.

Year	Engine ID/VIN	Engine Displacement Liters (cc)	Main Brg. Journal Dia.	Crankshaft Main Brg. Oil Clearance	Shaft End-play	Thrust on No.	Connecting Rod Journal Diameter	Oil Clearance	Side Clearance
1984	ES1, ES2	1.8 (1829)	1.9673-1.9683	0.0010-0.0022	0.004-0.014	3	1.7707-1.7717	0.0006-0.0015	0.006-0.0120
1985	ES2, ES3, ET2	1.8 (1829)	1.9673-1.9683	0.0010-0.0022	0.004-0.014	3	1.7707-1.7717	0.0006-0.0015	0.006-0.0120
1986	ET2	1.8 (1829)	1.9673-1.9683	0.0010-0.0022	0.0040-0.0140	3	1.7707-1.7717	0.0008-0.0015	0.006-0.012
	BS, BT	2.0 (1955)	1.9673-1.9683	0.0010-0.0022	0.0040-0.0140	3	1.7707-1.7717	0.0008-0.0015	0.006-0.012
1987	A18A1	1.8 (1829)	1.9673-1.9683	0.0010-0.0022	0.004-0.014	3	1.7707-1.7717	0.0006-0.0015	0.006-0.012
	A20A1, A20A3	2.0 (1955)	1.9673[2]-1.9683	0.0010-0.0022[1]	0.004-0.014	3	1.7707-1.7717	0.0006-0.0015	0.006-0.012
1988	A20A1, A20A3	2.0 (1955)	[2]-1.9683	0.0010-0.0022[1]	0.004-0.0140	3	1.7707-1.7717[4]	0.0008-0.0015	0.006-0.012
	B20A3, B20A5	2.0 (1955)	2.1644-2.1654	0.0010-0.0017[3]	0.004-0.0140	3	1.7717	0.0010-0.0017	0.006-0.012
1989	A20A1, A20A3	2.0 (1955)	[2]-1.9683	0.0010-0.0022[1]	0.004-0.0140	3	1.7707-1.7717[4]	0.0008-0.0015	0.006-0.012
	B20A3, B20A5	2.0 (1955)	2.1644-2.1654	0.0010-0.0017[3]	0.004-0.0140	3	1.7717	0.0010-0.0017	0.006-0.012
1990	F22A1, F22A4	2.2 (2156)	2.1644-2.1654	0.0017[4]	0.004-0.014	4	1.7710-1.7717	0.0008-0.0017	0.006-0.012
	B20A5	2.0 (1955)	2.1644-2.1654	[7]	0.004-0.014	3	1.7707-1.7717	0.0008-0.0010	0.006-0.012
	B21A1	2.1 (2056)	2.1644-2.1654	[7]	0.004-0.014	3	1.8888-1.8900	0.0010-0.0017	0.006-0.012
1991	F22A1, A4, A6	2.2 (2156)	[6]	[4]	0.004-0.014	4	1.7710-1.7717	0.0008-0.0017	0.006-0.012
	B20A5	2.0 (1955)	2.1644-2.1654	[9]	0.004-0.014	3	1.7707-1.7717	0.0008-0.0015	0.006-0.012
	B21A1	2.1 (2056)	2.1644-2.1654	[7]	0.004-0.0180	3	1.8888-1.8898	0.0010-0.0024	0.006-0.012
1992	F22A1, A6	2.2 (2156)	[6]	[4]	0.0040-0.0180	4	1.8888-1.8900	0.0008-0.0017	0.0060-0.0160
	H22A1	2.2 (2157)	[8]	[9]	0.0040-0.0180	4	1.8888-1.8898	0.0011-0.0021	0.0060-0.0160
	H23A1	2.3 (2259)	[8]	[9]	0.0040-0.0180	4	1.8888-1.8898	0.0011-0.0024	0.0060-0.0160
1993	F22A1, A6	2.2 (2156)	[6]	[4]	0.0040-0.0180	4	1.8888-1.8900	0.0008-0.0017	0.0060-0.0160
	H22A1	2.2 (2157)	[8]	[9]	0.0040-0.0180	4	1.8888-1.8898	0.0011-0.0021	0.0060-0.0160
	H23A1	2.3 (2259)	[8]	[9]	0.0040-0.0180	4	1.8888-1.8898	0.0011-0.0024	0.0060-0.0160

86803908

CAMSHAFT SPECIFICATIONS
All measurements given in inches.

Year	Engine ID/VIN	Engine Displacement Liters (cc)	Journal Diameter 1	2	3	4	5	Elevation In.	Ex.	Bearing Clearance	Camshaft End-Play
1995	F22A1	2.2 (2156)	NA	NA	NA	NA	NA	1.5163	1.5267	0.006	0.0020-0.0060
	H22A1	2.2 (2157)	NA	NA	NA	NA	NA	[8]	[9]	0.006	0.0020-0.0060
	H23A1	2.3 (2259)	NA	NA	NA	NA	NA	1.3252	1.3278	0.006[12]	0.0020-0.0060
	C27A4	2.7 (2675)	NA	NA	NA	NA	NA	1.5537	1.5515	0.004	0.0020-0.0060

NA - Not Available
1 Manual transmission:
auxiliary: 1.7447
main: 1.5894; Civic HF: 1.5845
Automatic transmission:
auxiliary: 1.7447
main: 1.5894
2 Intake A: 1.5297
Intake B: 1.5200
3 Manual transmission:
Intake A: 1.5300
Intake B: 1.5120
Automatic transmission:
Intake A: 1.5220
Intake B: 1.5050
4 Manual transmission:1.5320
Automatic transmission:1.5130
5 Manual transmission:1.5148
Automatic transmission:1.5174
6 Automatic transmission: 1.5218
Automatic transmission: 1.5200
7 Intake A: 1.5296
Intake B: 1.5198
8 Primary: 1.3402
Mid: 1.4510
9 Secondary: 1.3768
Primary: 1.3285
10 Mid: 1.4300
Secondary: 1.3655
Primary: 1.4872
Mid: 1.5640
11 Secondary: 1.3575
Journals 2-4: 0.009
12 Journal 5: 0.008

86803907

PISTON AND RING SPECIFICATIONS
All measurements are given in inches.

Year	Engine ID/VIN	Engine Displacement Liters (cc)	Piston Clearance	Ring Gap Top Compression	Ring Gap Bottom Compression	Ring Gap Oil Control	Ring Side Clearance Top Compression	Ring Side Clearance Bottom Compression	Ring Side Clearance Oil Control
1984	ES2, ES1	1.8 (1829)	0.0008-0.0016	0.008-0.0140	0.008-0.0140	0.008-0.0350	0.0008-0.0018	0.0008-0.0018	Snug
1985	ES2, ES3, ET2	1.8 (1829)	0.0008-0.0016	0.008-0.0140	0.008-0.0140	0.008-0.0350	0.0008-0.0018	0.0008-0.0018	Snug
1986	ET2	1.8 (1829)	0.0008-0.0016	0.008-0.0140	0.008-0.0140	0.008-0.0350	0.0008-0.0018	0.0008-0.0018	Snug
	BS, BT	2.0 (1955)	0.0008-0.0016	0.008-0.0140	0.010-0.0150	0.008-0.0200	0.0012-0.0220	0.0012-0.0022	Snug
1987	A18A1	1.8 (1829)	0.0008-0.0016	0.008-0.0140	0.008-0.0140	0.008-0.0350	0.0008-0.0018	0.0008-0.0018	Snug
	A20A1, A20A3	2.0 (1955)	0.0008-0.0016	0.008-0.0140	0.008-0.0140	0.008-0.0200	0.0012-0.0024	0.0012-0.0024	Snug
1988	A20A1, A20A3	2.0 (1955)	0.0008-0.0016	0.008-0.0140	0.008-0.0220	0.008-0.0280	0.0012-0.0024	0.0012-0.0024	Snug
	B20A3, B20A5	2.0 (1955)	0.0008-0.0016	0.008-0.0140	0.016-0.0220	0.008-0.0200	0.0022	0.0022	Snug
1989	A20A1, A20A3	2.0 (1955)	0.0008-0.0016	0.008-0.0140	0.016-0.0220	0.008-0.0280	0.0012-0.0024	0.0012-0.0024	Snug
	B20A3, B20A5	2.0 (1955)	0.0008-0.0016	0.008-0.0140	0.016-0.0220	0.008-0.0200	0.0012-0.0022	0.0012-0.0022	Snug
1990	F22A1	2.2 (2156)	0.0008-0.0016	0.008-0.0140	0.016-0.0220	0.007-0.0270	0.0014-0.0024	0.0011-0.0022	Snug
	B20A3	2.0 (1955)	0.0008-0.0016	0.008-0.0140	0.016-0.0220	0.008-0.0200	0.0012-0.0024	0.0012-0.0022	Snug
1991	B21A1	2.1 (2056)	0.0004-0.0013	0.010-0.0140	0.018-0.0220	0.008-0.0200	0.0022	0.0022	Snug
	F22A1	2.2 (2156)	0.0008-0.0016	0.008-0.0140	0.016-0.0220	0.008-0.0200	0.0026	0.0024	Snug
	B20A5	2.0 (1955)	0.0008-0.0016	0.008-0.0140	0.016-0.0220	0.007-0.0270	0.0014-0.0024	0.0011-0.0022	Snug
1992	B21A1	2.1 (2056)	0.0004-0.0013	0.010-0.0140	0.018-0.0220	0.008-0.0200	0.0022	0.0022	Snug
	F22A1	2.2 (2156)	0.0008-0.0016	0.008-0.0140	0.016-0.0220	0.008-0.0200	0.0026	0.0024	Snug
	H23A1	2.3 (2259)	0.0008-0.0016	0.008-0.0140	0.016-0.0220	0.008-0.0280	0.0014-0.0024	0.0011-0.0022	Snug
1993	F22A1	2.2 (2156)	0.0008-0.0020	0.0080-0.0240	0.0160-0.0280	0.0080-0.0310	0.0014-0.0050	0.0012-0.0050	Snug
	F22A6	2.2 (2156)	0.0008-0.0020	0.0080-0.0240	0.0160-0.0280	0.0080-0.0310	0.0014-0.0050	0.0012-0.0050	Snug
	H22A1	2.2 (2157)	0.0003-0.0020	0.0100-0.0240	0.0240-0.0350	[1]	0.0050	0.0050	Snug
	H23A1	2.3 (2259)	0.0003-0.0020	0.0100-0.0240	0.0240-0.0350	[1]	0.0014-0.0050	0.0012-0.0050	Snug

86803910

CRANKSHAFT AND CONNECTING ROD SPECIFICATIONS
All measurements are given in inches.

Year	Engine ID/VIN	Engine Displacement Liters (cc)	Crankshaft Main Brg. Journal Dia.	Crankshaft Main Brg. Oil Clearance	Crankshaft Shaft End-play	Crankshaft Thrust on No.	Connecting Rod Journal Diameter	Connecting Rod Oil Clearance	Connecting Rod Side Clearance
1994	F22B1, B2	2.2 (2156)	[10]	[11]	0.0040-0.0180	4	1.8888-1.8898	0.0008-0.0024	0.0060-0.0160
	F22A1	2.2 (2156)	[10]	[11]	0.0040-0.0180	4	1.8888-1.8898	0.0008-0.0022	0.0060-0.0160
	H22A1	2.2 (2157)	[8]	[9]	0.0040-0.0180	4	1.8888-1.8898	0.0011-0.0024	0.0060-0.0160
	H23A1	2.3 (2259)	[10]	[11]	0.0040-0.0180	4	1.8888-1.8898	0.0008-0.0022	0.0060-0.0160
1995	F22B1, B2	2.2 (2156)	[10]	[11]	0.0040-0.0180	4	1.8888-1.8898	0.0008-0.0024	0.0060-0.0160
	F22A1	2.2 (2156)	[10]	[11]	0.0040-0.0180	4	1.8888-1.8898	0.0008-0.0022	0.0060-0.0160
	H22A1	2.2 (2157)	[8]	[9]	0.0040-0.0180	4	1.8888-1.8898	0.0011-0.0024	0.0060-0.0160
	H23A1	2.3 (2259)	[10]	[11]	0.0040-0.0180	4	1.8888-1.8898	0.0008-0.0022	0.0060-0.0160
	C27A4	2.7 (2675)	2.5187-2.5197	0.0009-0.0020	0.0040-0.0180	3	2.0463-2.0472	0.0010-0.0020	0.0060-0.0120

86803909

1- No. 3: 0.0013-0.0024
2- Accord; No. 1: 1.9676-1.9685, No. 3: 1.9671-1.9680, No. 2, 4, 5: 1.9673-1.9683
3- No. 3: 0.0012-0.0019
4- Prelude S: 1.8888-1.8900
5- No. 1, 5: C:0.0010-0.0014, No. 2, 4: C:0.0010-0.0017, No. 3: 0.0012-0.0019
6- No. 1, 2: 1.9676-1.9685, No. 3: 1.9674-1.9665, No. 4, 5: 1.9655-1.9668
7- No. 1, 2: C:0.0009-0.0018, No. 3: 0.0014-0.0017
8- No. 1, 2: 1.9676-1.9685, No. 3: 1.9674-1.9683, No. 4: 1.9679-1.9688, No. 5: 1.9680-1.9690
9- No. 1-2: 0.0008-0.0020, No. 3: 0.0010-0.0021, No. 4: 0.0005-0.0020, No. 5: 0.0004-0.0020
10- No. 1, 4: 1.9679-1.9688, No. 2: 1.9676-1.9685, No. 3: 1.9674-1.9683, No. 5: 1.9680-1.9690
11- No. 1, 4: C:0.0005-0.0020, No. 2: 0.0009-0.0020, No. 3: 0.0010-0.0022, No. 5: 0.0004-0.0016

TORQUE SPECIFICATIONS
All readings in ft. lbs.

Year	Engine ID/VIN	Engine Displacement Liters (cc)	Cylinder Head Bolts	Main Bearing Bolts	Rod Bearing Bolts	Crankshaft Damper Bolts	Flywheel Bolts	Manifold Intake	Manifold Exhaust	Spark Plugs	Lug Nut
1984	ES1, ES2	1.8 (1829)	49 [1]	48 [1]	23 [1]	83	76 [3]	16	23	13	80
1985	ES2, ES3	1.8 (1829)	49 [1]	48 [1]	23 [1]	83	76 [3]	16	23	13	80
	ET2	1.8 (1829)	49 [1]	48 [1]	23 [1]	83	76 [3]	16	23	13	80
1986	BS, BT	2.0 (1955)	49 [1]	48 [1]	23 [1]	83	76 [3]	16	23	13	80
1987	A18A1	1.8 (1829)	49 [1]	48 [1]	23 [1]	83	76 [3]	16	23	13	80
	A20A1	2.0 (1955)	49 [1]	48 [1]	23 [1]	83	76 [3]	16	23	13	80
	A20A3	2.0 (1955)	49 [1]	48 [1]	23 [1]	83	76 [3]	16	23	13	80
1988	A20A1	2.0 (1955)	49 [1]	48 [1]	23 [1]	83	76 [3]	16	23	13	80
	A20A3	2.0 (1955)	49 [1]	48 [1]	23 [1]	83	76 [3]	16	23	13	80
	B20A3	2.0 (1955)	49 [1]	48 [1]	23 [1]	83 [2]	76 [3]	16	23	13	80
	B20A5	2.0 (1955)	49 [1]	48 [1]	23 [1]	83 [2]	76 [3]	16	23	13	80
1989	A20A1	2.0 (1955)	49 [1]	48 [1]	23 [1]	108	76 [3]	16	23	13	80
	A20A3	2.0 (1955)	49 [1]	48 [1]	23 [1]	108	76 [3]	16	23	13	80
	B20A3	2.0 (1955)	49 [1]	48 [1]	23 [1]	83 [2]	76 [3]	16	23	13	80
	B20A5	2.0 (1955)	49 [1]	48 [1]	23 [1]	83 [2]	76 [3]	16	23	13	80
1990	F22A1	2.2 (2156)	78 [1]	52 [1]	34 [1]	166	76 [3]	16	23	13	80
	F22A4	2.2 (2156)	78 [1]	52 [1]	34 [1]	166	76 [3]	16	23	13	80
	B20A3	2.0 (1955)	49 [1]	48 [1]	23 [1]	83 [2]	76 [3]	16	23	13	80
	B20A5	2.0 (1955)	49 [1]	48 [1]	23 [1]	83 [2]	76 [3]	16	23	13	80
1991	B21A1	2.1 (2056)	49 [1]	48 [1]	23 [1]	108	76 [3]	16	23	13	80
	F22A1	2.2 (2156)	78 [1]	52 [1]	34 [1]	159	76 [3]	16	23	13	80
	F22A4	2.2 (2156)	78 [1]	52 [1]	34 [1]	159	76 [3]	16	23	13	80
	F22A6	2.2 (2156)	78 [1]	52 [1]	34 [1]	159	76 [3]	16	23	13	80
	B20A5	2.0 (1955)	49 [1]	48 [1]	23 [1]	108	76 [3]	16	23	13	80
1992	B21A1	2.1 (2056)	49 [1]	48 [1]	23 [1]	108	76 [3]	16	23	13	80
	F22A1	2.2 (2156)	78 [1]	52 [1]	34 [1]	159	76 [3]	16	23	13	80
	F22A4	2.2 (2156)	78 [1]	52 [1]	34 [1]	159	76 [3]	16	23	13	80
	F22A6	2.2 (2156)	78 [1]	52 [1]	34 [1]	159	76 [3]	16	23	13	80
	H23A1	2.3 (2259)	72 [1]	52 [1]	34 [1]	159	76 [3]	16	23	13	80
1993	F22A1	2.2 (2156)	78 [1]	52 [1]	34 [1]	159	76 [3]	16	23	13	80
	F22A6	2.2 (2156)	78 [1]	52 [1]	34 [1]	159	76 [3]	16	23	13	80
	H22A1	2.2 (2157)	72 [1]	52 [1]	34 [1]	159	76 [3]	16	23	13	80
	H23A1	2.3 (2259)	72 [1]	52 [1]	34 [1]	159	76 [3]	16	23	13	80
1994	F22B1	2.2 (2156)	72 [1]	52 [1]	34 [1]	181	76 [3]	16	23	13	80
	F22B2	2.2 (2156)	72 [1]	52 [1]	34 [1]	181	76 [3]	16	23	13	80
	H22A1	2.2 (2157)	72 [1]	52 [1]	34 [1]	181	76 [3]	16	23	13	80
	H23A1	2.3 (2259)	72 [1]	52 [1]	34 [1]	181	76 [3]	16	23	13	80
1995	F22B1	2.2 (2156)	72 [1]	52 [1]	34 [1]	181	76 [3]	16	23	13	80
	F22B2	2.2 (2156)	72 [1]	52 [1]	34 [1]	181	76 [3]	16	23	13	80
	F22B6	2.2 (2156)	72 [1]	52 [1]	34 [1]	181	76 [3]	16	23	13	80
	F22A1	2.2 (2156)	72 [1]	52 [1]	34 [1]	181	76 [3]	16	23	13	80

86803912

PISTON AND RING SPECIFICATIONS
All measurements are given in inches.

Year	Engine ID/VIN	Engine Displacement Liters (cc)	Piston Clearance	Ring Gap Top Compression	Ring Gap Bottom Compression	Ring Gap Oil Control	Ring Side Clearance Top Compression	Ring Side Clearance Bottom Compression	Ring Side Clearance Oil Control
1994	F22B1	2.2 (2156)	0.0008-0.0020	0.0080-0.0240	0.0160-0.0280	0.0060-0.0310	0.0014-0.0050	0.0012-0.0050	Snug
	F22B2	2.2 (2156)	0.0008-0.0020	0.0080-0.0240	0.0160-0.0280	0.0060-0.0310	0.0014-0.0050	0.0012-0.0050	Snug
	F22A1	2.2 (2156)	0.0008-0.0020	0.0080-0.0240	0.0160-0.0280	0.0060-0.0310	0.0014-0.0050	0.0012-0.0050	Snug
	H22A1	2.2 (2157)	0.0003-0.0020	0.0100-0.0240	0.0240-0.0350	0.03-0 [1]	0.0018-0.0050	0.0016-0.0050	Snug
	H23A1	2.3 (2259)	0.0003-0.0020	0.0100-0.0240	0.0240-0.0350	0.03-0 [1]	0.0018-0.0050	0.0016-0.0050	Snug
1995	F22B1	2.2 (2156)	0.0008-0.0020	0.0080-0.0240	0.0160-0.0280	0.0080-0.0310	0.0014-0.0050	0.0012-0.0050	Snug
	F22B2	2.2 (2156)	0.0008-0.0020	0.0080-0.0240	0.0160-0.0280	0.0080-0.0310	0.0014-0.0050	0.0012-0.0050	Snug
	F22B6	2.2 (2156)	0.0008-0.0020	0.0080-0.0240	0.0160-0.0280	0.0080-0.0310	0.0014-0.0050	0.0012-0.0050	Snug
	F22A1	2.2 (2156)	0.0008-0.0020	0.0080-0.0240	0.0160-0.0280	0.0080-0.0310	0.0014-0.0050	0.0012-0.0050	Snug
	H22A1	2.2 (2157)	0.0003-0.0020	0.0100-0.0240	0.0240-0.0350	0.03-0 [1]	0.0018-0.0050	0.0016-0.0050	Snug
	H23A1	2.3 (2259)	0.0003-0.0020	0.0100-0.0240	0.0240-0.0350	0.03-0 [1]	0.0018-0.0024	0.0016-0.0050	Snug
	C27A4	2.7 (2675)	0.0008-0.0030	0.0080-0.0240	0.0140-0.0280	0.0310	0.0257	0.0063	Snug

1 TEIKOKU manufactured piston ring: 0.0080-0.0240
RIKEN manufactured piston ring: 0.0080-0.0310

86803911

TORQUE SPECIFICATIONS
All readings in ft. lbs.

Year	Engine ID/VIN	Engine Displacement Liters (cc)	Cylinder Head Bolts	Main Bearing Bolts	Rod Bearing Bolts	Crankshaft Damper Bolts	Flywheel Bolts	Manifold Intake	Manifold Exhaust	Spark Plugs	Lug Nut
1995	H22A1	2.2 (2157)	72 ①	52 ①	34 ①	181	76 ③	16	23	13	80
	H23A1	2.3 (2259)	72 ①	52 ①	34 ①	181	76 ③	16	23	13	80
	C27A4	2.7 (2675)	72 ①	52 ①	34 ①	181	54 ③	16	23	13	80

1: Final torque listed. For sequence, refer to the text.
2: Fuel Injection 108
3: Automatic transaxle 54

86803913

Engine

REMOVAL & INSTALLATION

✳✳ CAUTION

If any repair operation requires the removal of a component of the air conditioning system (on vehicles so equipped), do not disconnect the refrigerant lines. If it is impossible to move the component out of the way with the lines attached, have the air conditioning system evacuated by a trained service professional. The air conditioning system contains refrigerant under pressure. This gas can be very dangerous. When draining the coolant, keep in mind that cats and dogs are attracted by ethylene glycol antifreeze, and are quite likely to drink any that is left in an uncovered container or in puddles on the ground. This will prove fatal in sufficient quantity. Always drain the coolant into a sealable container. The EPA warns that prolonged contact with used engine oil may cause a number of skin disorders, including cancer! You should make every effort to minimize your exposure to used engine oil. Protective gloves should be worn when changing the oil. Wash your hands and any other exposed skin areas as soon as possible after exposure to used engine oil. Soap and water, or waterless hand cleaner should be used.

1984–85 Accord and 1984–87 Prelude

▶ **See Figures 19 and 20**

➡**All wires and hoses should be labeled at the time of removal. The amount of time saved during reassembly makes the extra effort well worthwhile.**

1. Apply the parking brake and place blocks behind the rear wheels. Raise and support the front of the vehicle on jackstands.
2. Disconnect the negative battery cable, then the positive battery cable. Remove the battery and the battery tray from the engine compartment.
3. Double check the security of the jackstands and supports under the car.
4. Remove the splash guard under the engine. Using a felt tip marker, mark the hood hinge outline on the hood; remove the hood bolts and the hood.

➡**For Prelude, remove the caps on the headlight motor manual control knobs. Raise the headlights to the UP position. Remove the 5 screws holding the grille and remove the grille.**

5. Drain the engine oil.

➡**When installing the drain plug be sure to use a new washer.**

6. Remove the radiator cap. Open the radiator drain petcock and drain the coolant from the radiator.
7. Remove the transaxle filler plug; remove the drain plug and drain the transaxle.
8. If equipped with a carburetor, perform the following procedures:
   a. Label and remove the coil wires and the engine secondary ground cable located on the valve cover.
   b. Remove the air cleaner cover and filter.

c. Remove the air intake ducts, the air cleaner nuts/bolts, the air control valve and the air cleaner.
   d. Loosen the throttle cable locknut and adjusting nut. Slip the cable end from the carburetor linkage.

➡**Be careful not to bend or kink the throttle cable. Always replace a damaged cable.**

e. Disconnect the No. 1 control box connector. Remove the control box from its bracket; support it with stiff wire and allow it hang next to the engine.
   f. Disconnect the fuel line from the fuel filter and the solenoid vacuum hose from the charcoal canister.
   g. For California or High Altitude models, remove the air jet controller.
9. If equipped with fuel injection, perform the following procedures:
   a. Remove the air intake duct. Disconnect the cruise control vacuum hose from the air intake duct and remove the resonator tube.
   b. Remove the secondary ground cable from the top of the engine.
   c. Disconnect the air box connecting tube. Unscrew the tube clamp bolt and disconnect the emission tubes.
   d. Remove the air cleaner mounting nuts and remove the air cleaner case assembly.
   e. Loosen the throttle cable locknut and adjusting nut. Slip the cable end from the bracket and linkage.
   f. Disconnect the vacuum hose from the brake booster.
   g. Disconnect the fuel return hose from the pressure regulator. Remove the banjo nut, then the fuel hose.

➡**Be careful not to bend or kink the throttle cable. Always replace a damaged cable.**

h. Disconnect the following wires:
   • The ground cable from the fuse box.
   • The engine compartment sub harness connector and clamp.
   • The high tension wire and ignition primary leaks from the coil.
   • The radio condenser connector from the coil.
10. To relieve the fuel pressure, perform the following procedures:
   • Using a shop rag, place it over the fuel filter to absorb any gasoline which may be sprayed on the engine.
   • Slowly loosen the service bolt approximately one full turn; this will relieve any pressure in the system.
   • Using a new sealing washer, retighten the service bolt.
11. Label and disconnect the radiator and heater hoses from the engine.
12. If equipped with an automatic transaxle, disconnect the oil cooler hoses from the transaxle and drain the fluid. Support the hoses near the radiator without kinking them.
13. If equipped with a manual transaxle, loosen the clutch cable adjusting nut and remove the clutch cable from the release arm.
14. Disconnect the battery cable from the transaxle and the starter cable from the starter motor terminal.
15. Unplug both electrical harness connectors from the engine.
16. Remove the speedometer cable clip. Pull the cable from the holder.

➡**DO NOT remove the holder as the speedometer gear may drop into the transaxle.**

17. If equipped with power steering perform the following procedures:
   a. Remove the speed sensor-to-transaxle bolt and the sensor complete with the hoses.

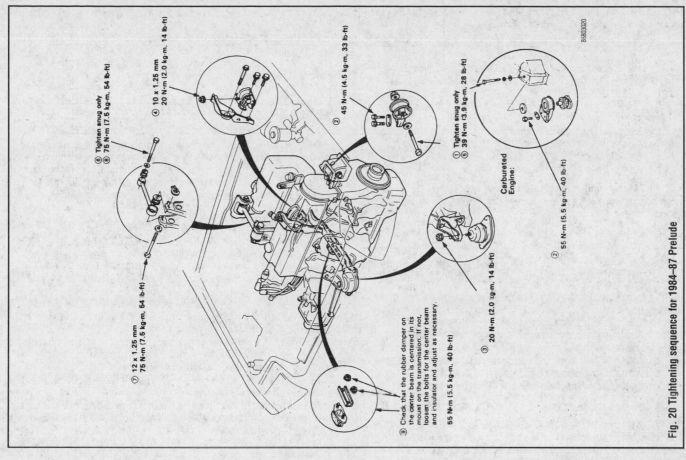

Fig. 20 Tightening sequence for 1984–87 Prelude

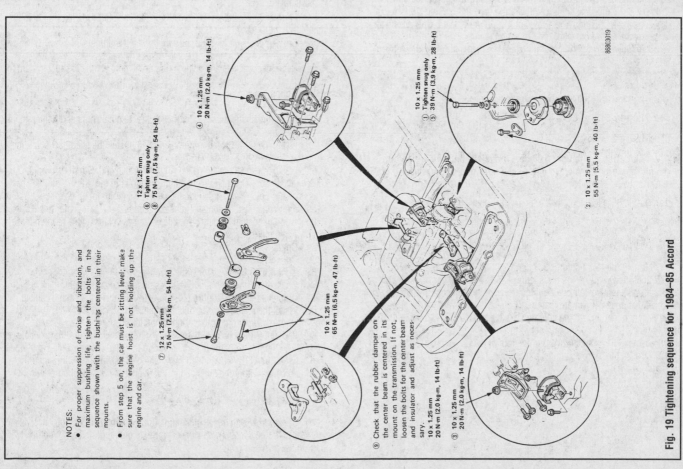

Fig. 19 Tightening sequence for 1984–85 Accord

NOTES:

- For proper suppression of noise and vibration, and maximum bushing life, tighten the bolts in the sequence shown with the bushings centered in their mounts.

- From step 5 on, the car must be sitting level; make sure that the engine hoist is not holding up the engine and car.

⑨ Check that the rubber damper on the center beam is centered in its mount on the transmission. If not, loosen the bolts for the center beam and insulator and adjust as necessary.

➡**Do not disconnect the hoses from the speed sensor; simply move the sensor out of the way with the hoses attached.**

b. Remove the power steering pump adjusting bolt, mounting bolt and the V-belt.

c. Without disconnecting the hoses, pull the pump away from its mounting bracket and position it out of the way. Support it with stiff wire—DO NOT allow it to hang by the hoses.

d. Remove the power steering hose bracket from the cylinder head.

18. Remove the center beam beneath the engine. Loosen the radius rod nuts to aid in the later removal of the halfshafts.

19. If equipped with air conditioning, perform the following procedures:

a. Remove the compressor clutch lead wire.

b. Loosen the belt adjusting bolt and the drive belt.

➡**DO NOT loosen or disconnect the air conditioner hoses. The air conditioner compressor can be moved without discharging the air conditioner system.**

c. Remove the compressor mounting bolts and lift the compressor out of the bracket, with the hoses attached. Support it on the front bulkhead with a piece of strong wire. Never hang the compressor by its hoses.

20. If equipped with a manual transaxle, remove the shift rod yoke attaching bolt and disconnect the shift lever torque rod from the clutch housing.

21. If equipped with an automatic transaxle, perform the following procedures:

a. Remove the center console.

b. Place the shift lever in Reverse. Remove the lock pin from the end of the shift cable.

c. Remove the shift cable mounting bolts and the shift cable holder.

d. Remove the throttle cable from the throttle lever. Loosen the lower locknut and remove the cable from the bracket.

➡**DO NOT loosen the upper locknut as it will change the transaxle shift points.**

22. Disconnect the right and left lower ball joints and the tie rod ends.

23. To remove the halfshafts, perform the following procedures:

a. Remove the jackstands and lower the vehicle. Using a 32mm socket, loosen the spindle nuts. Again raise and support the vehicle on jackstands.

b. Remove the front wheel and the spindle nut.

c. Remove the ball joint bolt and separate the ball joint from the front hub.

d. Disconnect the tie rods from the steering knuckles.

e. Remove the sway bar bolts.

f. Pull the front hub outward and off the halfshafts.

g. Using a small pry bar, pry out the inboard CV-joint approximately ½ inch to release the spring clip from the differential. Pull the halfshaft from the transaxle case.

➡**When installing the halfshaft, insert the shaft until the spring clip clicks into the groove. Always use a new spring clip when installing halfshafts.**

24. On fuel injected models, disconnect the sub-engine harness connectors and clamp.

25. Remove the exhaust header pipe.

26. Attach a chain hoist to the engine and raise it slightly to remove the slack.

27. Unplug the No. 2 control box connector, lift the control box off of its bracket and allow it hang next to the engine.

28. If equipped with air conditioning, remove the idle control solenoid valve.

29. If equipped with an air chamber (Calif. and High Altitude), remove it.

30. From under the air chamber, remove the three engine mount bolts. Push the engine mount into the engine mount tower.

31. Remove the front and rear engine mount nuts.

32. Loosen the alternator bolts and remove the drive belt. Disconnect the alternator wire harness and remove the alternator.

33. At the engine, remove the bolt from the rear torque rod; loosen the bolt in the frame mount, swing the rod up and out of the way.

34. Carefully raise the engine from the vehicle, checking that all wires and hoses have been removed from the engine/transaxle. Remove it from the vehicle.

35. Remove the transaxle.

36. If manual transaxle, remove the clutch cover (pressure plate) and clutch disc.

37. Mount the engine on an engine stand, making sure the mounting bolts are tight. If an engine stand is not available, support the engine in an upright position with blocks. Never leave an engine hanging from a lift or hoist.

To install:

38. The transaxle assembly should be installed to the engine before reinstallation. The engine should be completely assembled with oil pan, valve cover, etc. in place, even if they are to be removed later.

39. Lower the engine into the vehicle.

➡**When installing the engine mounts and vibration dampers in the following steps, the bolts running through the large rubber bushings should only be set snug or finger-tight until all are in place. They must be tightened to the correct tension in the correct order if they are to dampen vibration properly.**

40. Install the rear torque rod to the engine.

41. Install the front and rear engine mount nuts.

42. Install the alternator brackets, alternator and belt.

43. Install the rear engine mount bracket.

44. Install the rear engine mount nut. Tighten it to 14 ft. lbs. (20 Nm).

45. Install the front engine mount nut, tightening the bolt to 14 ft. lbs. (20 Nm).

46. Retrieve the engine mount from inside the tower; install the bolts and tighten the solo bolt (on top) to 28 ft. lbs. (39 Nm). Tighten the adjacent pair of bolts to 40 ft. lbs. (55 Nm).

47. Slacken the chain in the engine hoist. Proceed to each bushing and motor mount bolt, tightening them in order to the correct torque.

48. Install the cruise control vacuum hoses.

49. Install the drive shafts. Use a new circlip and make certain the shaft is locked into the transaxle.

50. For automatic transmission vehicles, connect the throttle control cable to the bracket, tighten the locknut and attach the cable to the throttle lever on the transaxle. Install the shift cable and cable clamps; tighten the cable mounting bolts at the transaxle only to 7 ft. lbs. (10 Nm). Reconnect the shift cable at the shifter inside the vehicle and install the center console.

51. For manual transmission vehicles, install the shift rod yoke and bolt; tighten it to 16 ft. lbs. (22 Nm).

52. Connect the shift lever torque rod; tighten the bolt to 7 ft. lbs. (10 Nm).

53. Install the air conditioning compressor and belt.

54. Using new gaskets and self-locking bolts, connect the exhaust system to the engine. Tighten the nuts to 40 ft. lbs. (55 Nm). Install and tighten the 2 bolts for the support bracket.

55. Tighten the radius rod nuts to 32 ft. lbs. (44 Nm).

56. Install the center beam under the engine. Use new nuts and tighten them to 35 ft. lbs. (50 Nm).

57. Install the power steering pump and belt. Install the speed sensor, tightening the bolt only to 7 ft. lbs. (10 Nm).

58. Install the speedometer cable. Align the cable end with the slot in the holder. Install the locking clip so that the bent leg is in the groove. double check this installation by pulling gently on the cable; it should not come loose.

59. If equipped with automatic transaxle, connect the ATF cooler lines.

60. If equipped with manual transaxle, install the clutch cable to the release arm. Adjust the clutch free-play.

61. Connect the transaxle ground cable.

62. Connect the radiator and heater hoses.

63. Connect the fuel hose(s) at the fuel filter.

64. On Calif. and High Altitude vehicles, install the air jet controller.

65. Connect the purge control solenoid valve vacuum hose at the canister.

66. Install the control box onto its bracket.

67. Connect the throttle cable. Tighten the locknut.

68. Reconnect the electrical harnesses including the coil, idle control solenoid valve, engine wire harness connector and the secondary ground cable running between the bodywork and the valve cover. Check all the wiring, insuring that it is retained within the clips and not in danger of contact with hot or moving parts.

69. Install the air cleaner and air intake tubes. Make certain the vacuum hoses are correctly installed.

70. Double check all installation items, paying particular attention to loose hoses or hanging wires, untightened nuts, poor routing of hoses and wires (too tight or rubbing) and tools left in the engine area.

71. Refill the transmission fluid to the proper level.

72. Refill the cooling system.

73. Refill the engine oil.

74. Install the hood. On Prelude, reinstall the grille and crank the headlamps to the DOWN position.

75. Connect the battery cables, positive first.

76. Disconnect the coil wire from the distributor. Insulate or protect the end of the cable so it does not arc to the engine or surrounding metal. Without touching the accelerator, turn the ignition switch to the START position and crank the engine for about 5–10 seconds; this will develop some oil pressure within the motor. Do not exceed 10 seconds cranking.

77. Switch the ignition OFF and reconnect the coil.

78. Start the engine, allowing it to idle. Check the hoses and lines carefully for any sign of leakage.

79. Bleed the air from the cooling system; check the timing and idle speed.

80. After the engine has warmed up fully and the fan(s) have come on at least once, recheck the engine for fluid leaks. Shut the engine off.

81. Adjust the belts, clutch and throttle cable as necessary.

1986–89 Accord

▶ See Figure 21

1. Elevate and safely support the vehicle on jackstands. Double check the security of the supports.

2. Disconnect the negative battery cable, then the positive cable.

3. Use a felt-tip marker to outline the hood hinges on the inside of the hood. Disconnect the washer fluid hose and remove the hood.

4. Remove the splash shield from below the engine. Drain the engine oil. Install a new washer on the drain plug and tighten it properly. This prevents embarrassment after the engine is reinstalled.

5. With the engine cold, drain the coolant into a container.

6. Drain the transaxle. Reinstall the drain plug with a new washer and tighten properly.

7. Remove the air intake duct. Remove the retaining bolts holding the air filter housing and remove the housing assembly.

8. On fuel injected vehicles, relieve the fuel pressure using the correct procedure.

✳✳✳ CAUTION

The fuel system is under pressure. Release pressure slowly and contain spillage. Observe "no smoking/no open flame" precautions. Have a Class B-C (dry powder) fire extinguisher within arm's reach at all times.

9. All wires and hoses should be labeled at the time of removal. The amount of time saved during reassembly makes the extra effort well worthwhile. Whenever possible, disconnect a vacuum hose from a component on the firewall or fender, not at the engine. The engine will be removed with the lines and hoses attached.

10. On fuel injected vehicles, disconnect or remove the following items:

a. At the fusebox: ground cables (remove the plastic caps for access), condenser, coil wires and ignition leads.

b. Hoses from the charcoal canister.

c. Fuel line and return line at the pressure regulator. Plug the hoses and ports to prevent fuel spillage or the entry of dirt.

d. Control box on right side firewall. It will come out with the engine.

e. Electrical connectors near the control box.

f. Clamp bolt holding the power steering hose at the front of the engine.

g. Ground cable running from the valve cover to the radiator support.

h. Engine harness connectors at the left side of the engine.

i. Remove the battery and battery tray, then disconnect the harness connectors found below the tray. Remove the bracket holding the engine harness.

j. Disconnect the vacuum hose(s) from the cruise control actuator. Remove the two bolts holding the actuator and move the assembly well out of the way. Do not disconnect or kink the cable.

k. Disconnect the large vacuum hose running to the brake booster.

l. Disconnect the throttle cable by loosening the lock and adjusting nuts; slip the cable out of the bracket and linkage. Do not kink the cable; do not use pliers to remove the cable from the linkage.

11. On carbureted engines, disconnect or remove the following items:

a. The battery and battery tray. Unplug the wiring harness connectors found below the tray. Remove the clips holding the engine side of the wiring harnesses

b. Disconnect the retaining screws holding the vacuum valves next to the battery tray. Move the bracket and assembly onto the engine.

c. Vacuum hoses from the charcoal canister.

d. Mounting bolts holding the air jet controller, next to the canister. Remove the clamp bolt holding the large hose below the air jet controller.

e. Control box on right side firewall. Lift the box off its bracket, support it with wire and allow it to hang next to the engine. It will come out with the engine.

f. Vacuum hoses in front of the brake master cylinder. Also disconnect the large vacuum hose running to the brake booster.

g. Fuel line at the inline fuel filter near the firewall. Plug the lines to prevent fuel leakage or entry of dirt.

h. Ground cable running from the valve cover to the radiator support. Also remove the hose clamp bolt at the front right of the engine.

i. Disconnect the throttle cable by loosening the lock and adjusting nuts; slip the cable out of the bracket and linkage. Do not kink the cable; do not use pliers to remove the cable from the linkage.

12. On all vehicles, disconnect the heater and radiator hoses from the engine. Be prepared to contain spillage of the remaining coolant.

13. On automatic transaxles, disconnect the oil cooler lines from the transaxle case. Plug the lines immediately to eliminate oil spillage.

14. Remove the retaining bolt holding the speed sensor; remove the sensor from the transaxle case. Do not disconnect the hoses from the sensor.

15. For automatic transaxle vehicles:

a. Remove the center console.

b. Place the shift lever in Reverse. Remove the lock pin from the end of the shift cable.

c. Remove the bolts holding the shift cable and remove the cable bracket. Separate the shift cable from the shifter.

d. At the transaxle, loosen the lower bolt (A) on the throttle control cable and disconnect the cable from the transaxle. Do not loosen or change the upper bolt (B); the shift points of the transaxle will be affected.

16. On manual transaxle vehicles, disconnect the clutch cable at the transaxle.

17. Disconnect the transaxle ground strap at the case.

18. Disconnect the shift rod yoke and shift lever torque rod at the transaxle.

19. Disconnect the exhaust pipe at the manifold. Discard the self-locking nuts—they are not reusable.

20. Disconnect the exhaust pipe at the joint just behind the flexible section and remove the pipe.

21. Remove the cotter pin and castle nut from the left and right lower ball joints. Carefully separate the joint using a puller.

22. Disconnect the driveshafts from the transaxle. Remove the circlip from the each shaft and discard them—they must be replaced at installation. Wrap the splined end of each shaft in a plastic bag and secure the wrapping. The machined splines must be protected from dirt and damage.

23. Remove the power steering pump adjusting bolt and remove the belt. Remove the pump from its mount and move it out of the way with the hoses attached. Support it out of the work area with stiff wire.

24. Disconnect the wiring to the air conditioning compressor. Loosen the mounting bolts and remove the belt. Remove the compressor from its mounts and suspend it out of the work area with stiff wire. DO NOT disconnect or loosen any A/C hoses.

25. Disconnect the alternator wire harness connectors. Remove the belt after loosening the adjusting bolt. Remove the alternator from its mount.

26. Remove the center beam under the engine.

27. Install the engine hoisting equipment. Attach one chain to the eyehook on the left end of the engine, near the timing belt. Secure the other to the eyehook at the transaxle. Adjust the chain and hoist to remove the slack from all chains.

28. Carefully inspect the area surrounding the engine and transaxle, making sure that there are no hoses, vacuum lines or wiring running between the bodywork and engine/trans assembly. At this point, the only items connecting the engine/trans to the bodywork should be the various engine mounts and anti-torque rods.

29. Remove the bolt from the anti-torque rod at the rear of the engine. Loosen the bolt in the body mount; pivot the rod up and out of the way.

30. Double check the hoist installation. Take up any slack in the chains; the hoist should be under minimal tension, just holding the engine without lifting the car.

31. Remove the rear engine mount nut. Remove the three bolts from the rear engine mount bracket. Label or diagram the bolt placement, as one is longer than the others and must be replaced correctly. Remove the bracket.

32. Remove the front engine mount bolt.

33. Remove the side engine mount and bolts.

34. Slowly raise the hoist, checking frequently for items still connected. Raise the engine just enough to allow the engine mounting brackets to clear the studs. Lower the engine again onto the mounts. Shorten the chain to the timing belt side by ½ its length and resecure it to the eyehook.

35. Elevate the engine slowly; the shortened chain will cause the engine to tilt up on the pulley end. Raise the engine above the bodywork and remove it.

36. Remove the transmission.

37. On manual transaxles, remove the clutch cover (pressure plate) and clutch disc.

38. Mount the engine on an engine stand, making sure the mounting bolts are tight. If an engine stand is not available, support the engine in an upright position with blocks. Never leave an engine hanging from a lift or hoist.

To install:

39. Assemble the clutch disc and pressure plate to the flywheel for manual transaxle vehicles.

40. Install the transaxle.

41. Lift the engine into position and lower it into the car, aligning the mounts and bushings.

➥**When installing the engine mounts and vibration dampers in the following steps, the bolts running through the large rubber bushings should only be set snug or finger-tight until all are in place. They must be tightened to the correct tension in the correct order if they are to dampen vibration properly.**

42. Install the through-bolt for the left engine mount. Install the two smaller bolts, tightening them to 33 ft. lbs. (45 Nm).

43. Install the nut on the front motor mount, tightening it to 14 ft. lbs. (20 Nm). Install the three bolts holding the rear engine mount bracket to the engine. Tighten them to 28 ft. lbs. (39 Nm). Tighten the nut to 14 ft. lbs. (20 Nm).

44. Install the anti-torque rod at the rear of the engine. Make certain the washers are correctly placed.

45. Install the center beam under the engine. Check that the rubber damper on the beam is centered in its mount on the transmission. If not centered, loosen the bolts for the beam and/or damper and adjust as needed. Tighten the beam retaining bolts to 37 ft. lbs. (50 Nm) and the damper bolts to 40 ft. lbs. (55 Nm).

46. At this point the engine is loosely mounted in the vehicle. Slacken the hoist chains, allowing the engine to settle into place. The vehicle must be sitting level during the next step.

47. With the vehicle sitting level, tighten the mounting bolts/nuts in the order given to the proper torque. Both the order and tightness are important; the bushings play a great role in damping engine vibration.

48. Disconnect and remove the hoist equipment from the engine. If the car was lowered to the ground for the previous step, re-elevate it and support it safely on jackstands.

49. Install the alternator, belt and connect the wiring harness.

50. Install the compressor, belt and connect the wiring.

51. Install the power steering pump and belt.

52. Replace the circlip on each drive shaft. Install the shafts, making sure each clip is heard to click into place.

53. Reassemble the lower ball joints and install the nuts. Install a new cotter pin.

54. Using new nuts and gaskets, install the exhaust header pipe. Tighten the nuts at the manifold to 40 ft. lbs. (55 Nm).

55. Install the shift rod anti-torque rod, tightening the through-bolt to 9 ft. lbs. (12 Nm).

56. On manual transmissions, attach the shift rod to the transmission and tighten the bolt to 16 ft. lbs. (22 Nm).

57. Install the transaxle ground strap at the case.

58. Install the clutch cable, if so equipped.

59. For automatic transaxle vehicles, install or connect:

a. The throttle control cable to the lever. Do not adjust or tighten the top bolt; tighten the lower locknut.

b. Shifter and shifter cable inside the car. Install the lock pin onto the cable, secure the cable bracket or guide, and install the retaining bolts holding the cable assembly to the shifter housing. Reinstall the console.

60. Install the speed sensor assembly, tightening the bolt only to 9 ft. lbs. (12 Nm).

61. Connect the automatic transaxle oil cooler lines, if so equipped.

62. Connect the heater and radiator hoses.

63. For carbureted vehicles, install or connect:

a. The throttle cable.

b. Ground cable to the valve cover.

c. Fuel line at the filter near the firewall.

d. Vacuum hose to the brake booster.

e. Emission vacuum hoses near the brake booster.

f. Control box to its mounts on the firewall.

g. Air jet controller if it was removed.

h. Vacuum hoses to the charcoal canister.

i. Vacuum valves next to the battery tray.

j. Wiring connectors under the battery tray.

k. Battery tray and battery.

64. On fuel injected engines, connect or install the following:

a. Throttle cable.

b. Brake booster vacuum hose.

c. Cruise control actuator and vacuum hose.

d. Harness connectors under the battery tray.

e. Harness connectors at the left side of the engine.

f. Ground cable to the valve cover and clamp bolt holding hose to the front of the engine.

g. Harness connectors near the control box.

h. Control box to its mount on the right firewall.

i. Fuel lines at the pressure regulator.

j. Vacuum hoses to the charcoal canister.

k. Ground, ignition and coil wires at the right side of the engine compartment.

l. Battery tray and battery.

65. Install the air cleaner housing. Install the intake ductwork.

66. Double check the drain plug on the transaxle, tightening it if needed. Fill the transaxle with correct amount of fluid.

67. Double check the draincock on the radiator. Refill the cooling system.

68. Double check the engine oil drain bolt. Install the correct amount of engine oil.

69. Double check all installation items, paying particular attention to loose hoses or hanging wires, untightened nuts, poor routing of hoses and wires (too tight or rubbing) and tools left in the engine area.

70. Install the hood.

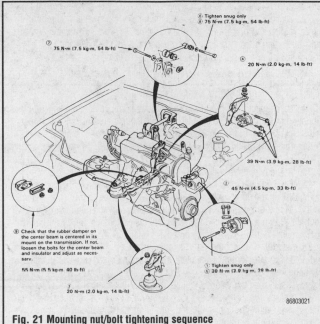

Fig. 21 Mounting nut/bolt tightening sequence

71. Connect the battery cables, positive first.

72. Disconnect the coil wire from the distributor. Insulate or protect the end of the cable so it does not arc to the engine or surrounding metal. Without touching the accelerator, turn the ignition switch to the **START** position and crank the engine for about 5–10 seconds; this will develop some oil pressure within the motor. Do not exceed 10 seconds cranking.

73. Switch the ignition **OFF** and reconnect the coil.

74. Start the engine, allowing it to idle. Check the hoses and lines carefully for any sign of leakage.

75. Bleed the air from the cooling system; check the timing and idle speed.

76. After the engine has warmed up fully and the fan(s) have come on at least once, recheck the engine for fluid leaks. Shut the engine **OFF**.

77. Adjust the belts, clutch and throttle cable as necessary.

1990–93 Accord

▶ See Figure 22

1. Disconnect the battery cables, negative first. Remove the battery and battery case.

2. Raise and safely support the vehicle. Double check the security and placement of the stands.

3. Place the hood in a vertical position and safely support it in place. Do not remove the hood.

4. Remove the engine splash shield. Drain the engine oil, coolant and transaxle fluid.

5. Remove the air intake duct and the air cleaner case.

6. Relieve the fuel system pressure using the correct procedure.

7. Remove the fuel feed hose from the fuel pipe and the return hose from the pressure control valve.

8. Remove the control box from the firewall.

➡ **Do not disconnect the vacuum hoses.**

9. Disconnect the vacuum hose from the charcoal canister and the charcoal canister hose from the throttle body.

10. Remove the ground cable from the transaxle.

11. Remove the throttle cable by loosening the locknut, then slip the cable end out of the throttle bracket and accelerator linkage.

➡ **Be careful not to bend the cable when removing. Do not use pliers to remove the cable from the linkage. Always replace a kinked cable with a new one.**

12. Unplug the connector and the vacuum hose, then remove the cruise control actuator.

13. Remove the brake booster vacuum hose and mount; remove the vacuum hose from the intake manifold.

14. Unplug the three engine harness connectors from the main wire harness at the right side of the engine compartment. Remove the engine wire harness terminal and the starter cable terminal from the underhood relay box and clamps. Then remove the transaxle ground terminal.

15. Unplug the two engine wire harness connectors from the main harness and the resistor at the left side of the engine compartment.

16. Remove the engine ground wire from the valve cover. Remove the power steering pump bracket.

17. Remove the mounting bolts and the power steering belt from the power steering pump, then, without disconnecting the hoses, pull the pump away from its mounting bracket. Support the pump out of the way.

18. Remove the mounting bolts and belt from the air conditioning compressor. Without disconnecting the hoses, pull the compressor away from it's mounting bracket. Support the compressor with stiff wire out of the way.

19. Disconnect the heater hoses. Disconnect the radiator hoses, automatic transaxle cooler hoses and the cooling fan connectors. Remove the radiator/cooling fan assembly.

20. Remove the speed sensor without disconnecting the hoses or connector.

21. Remove the center beam.

22. Remove the exhaust pipe nuts and bracket mounting bolts.

23. Remove the halfshafts as follows:

   a. Remove the front wheels.

   b. Raise the locking tab on the spindle nut and remove it.

   c. Remove the damper fork nut, damper pinch bolt and remove the damper fork.

   d. Remove the cotter pin and castle nut from the lower ball joint.

   e. Using a suitable puller, separate the lower control arm from the knuckle.

   f. Pull the knuckle outward and remove the halfshaft outboard CV-joint from the knuckle using a suitable plastic hammer.

   g. Using a suitable pry bar, pry the halfshaft out to force the set ring at the end of the halfshaft past the groove.

   h. Pull the inboard CV-joint and remove the halfshaft and CV-joint out of the differential case or intermediate shaft as an assembly.

➡ **Do not pull on the halfshaft, as the CV-joint may come apart. Tie plastic bags over the halfshaft ends to protect them.**

24. On manual transaxle equipped vehicles, remove the clutch release hose from the clutch damper on the transaxle housing. Remove the shift cable and the select cable with the cable bracket from the transaxle.

➡ **Be careful not to bend the cable when removing. Do not use pliers to remove the cable. Always replace a kinked cable with a new one.**

25. On automatic transaxle equipped vehicles, remove the engine stiffener, then remove the torque converter cover. Remove the cable holder, then remove the shift control lever bolt and shift control cable.

26. Attach a suitable lifting device to the engine. Raise the engine to unload the engine mounts.

27. Remove the front and rear engine mounting bolts.

28. Remove the engine side mount and mounting bolt. Remove the side transaxle mount and mounting bolt.

29. Make sure the engine/transaxle assembly is completely free of vacuum hoses, fuel and coolant hoses and electrical wires.

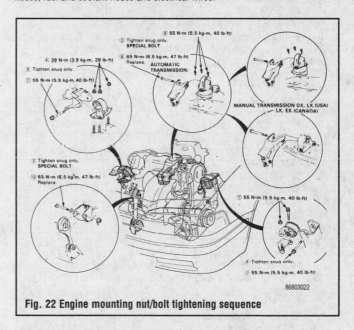

Fig. 22 Engine mounting nut/bolt tightening sequence

30. Slowly raise the engine approximately 6 in. (152mm). Check again that all hoses and wires have been disconnected from the engine/transaxle assembly.

31. Raise the engine/transaxle assembly all the way and remove it from the vehicle.

32. Remove the transaxle.

33. On manual transaxles, remove the clutch cover (pressure plate) and clutch disc.

34. Mount the engine on an engine stand, making sure the mounting bolts are tight. If an engine stand is not available, support the engine in an upright position with blocks. Never leave an engine hanging from a lift or hoist.

To install:

35. Assemble the clutch disc and pressure plate to the flywheel for manual transaxle vehicles.

36. Install the transaxle.

37. Lift the engine into position and lower it into the car, aligning the mounts and bushings.

➡**When installing the engine mounts and vibration dampers in the following steps, the bolts running through the large rubber bushings should only be set snug or finger-tight until all are in place. They must be tightened to the correct tension in the correct order if they are to dampen vibration properly.**

38. Install the side engine mount and mounting bolt. Install the through-bolt.

39. Install the side transmission mount and bolt.

40. Install the front and rear engine mounting bolts.

41. At this point the engine is loosely mounted in the vehicle. Slacken the hoist chains, allowing the engine to settle into place. The vehicle must be sitting level during the next step.

42. With the vehicle sitting level, tighten the mounting nuts/bolts in the order given to the proper torque. Both the order and tightness are important; the bushings play a great role in damping engine vibration.

43. Remove the hoist equipment from the engine. If the car was lowered for the previous step, re-elevate it and support it safely.

44. For automatic transaxles, install the shift control cable and cable holder. Install the torque converter cover and the engine stiffener.

45. For manual transaxles, connect the shift cable and shift select cable. Install the clutch release hose.

46. Install the driveshafts. Use a new circlip on each; install the shaft until a positive click is heard as the axle locks into place.

47. Install the ball joints to the lower arms and tie rods. Tighten the lower arm nuts to 40 ft. lbs. (55 Nm) and the tie rod nuts to 32 ft. lbs. (44 Nm). Install new cotter pins.

48. Install the exhaust pipe. Use new nuts; tighten the pipe-to-manifold nuts to 40 ft. lbs. (55 Nm).

49. Install the center beam. Tighten the bolts to 28 ft. lbs. (39 Nm).

50. Install the speed sensor. Tighten the retaining bolt to 7 ft. lbs. (10 Nm).

51. Install the radiator; connect the coolant and transmission oil cooler lines. Engage the cooling fan connectors.

52. Connect the heater inlet and outlet hoses to the cylinder head and connecting pipe, respectively.

53. Install the A/C compressor and belt, tightening the mounting bolts to 16 ft. lbs. (22 Nm).

54. Install the power steering pump and belt. Tighten the bolt to 33 ft. lbs. (45 Nm) and the nut to 16 ft. lbs. (22 Nm).

55. Connect the engine ground wire to the valve cover and the power steering pump bracket.

56. Connect the transaxle ground strap. Connect the starter cable terminal and install the engine wire harness terminal. Connect the three connectors for the main wire harness at the right side of the engine compartment.

57. Connect the brake booster vacuum hose to the manifold and to the brake booster.

58. Connect the throttle cable and secure the locknut.

59. Connect the ground cable to the transaxle.

60. Install the control box on the firewall and engage the wiring connectors.

61. Using new washers, connect the fuel line and return hose to the pressure control valve.

62. Install the air cleaner and the intake ductwork.

63. Refill the transaxle fluid.

64. Refill the cooling system.

65. Refill the engine oil.

66. Install the battery base and battery.

67. Double check all installation items, paying particular attention to loose hoses or hanging wires, untightened nuts, poor routing of hoses and wires (too tight or rubbing) and tools left in the engine area.

68. Connect the battery cables, positive first.

69. Disconnect the coil wire from the distributor. Insulate or protect the end of the cable so it does not arc to the engine or surrounding metal. Without touching the accelerator, turn the ignition switch to the **START** position and crank the engine for about 5–10 seconds; this will develop some oil pressure within the motor. Do not exceed 10 seconds cranking.

70. Switch the ignition **OFF** and reconnect the coil.

71. Start the engine, allowing it to idle. Check the hoses and lines carefully for any sign of leakage.

72. Bleed the air from the cooling system; check the timing and idle speed.

73. After the engine has warmed up fully and the fan(s) have come on at least once, recheck the engine for fluid leaks. Shut the engine off.

74. Adjust the belts, clutch and throttle cable as necessary.

75. Install the front wheels. Lower the hood.

1994–95 Accord 2.2L Engines

◆ **See Figure 23**

1. Disconnect the battery cables, negative first. Remove the battery and battery case.

2. Raise and safely support the vehicle. Double check the security and placement of the stands.

3. Place the hood in a vertical position and safely support it in place. Do not remove the hood.

4. Remove the engine splash shield. Drain the engine oil; coolant and transaxle fluid.

5. Remove the throttle and cruise control cables by loosening the locknuts, then slip the cable end out of the throttle linkage. Do not loosen the adjusting nut and take care not to bend the cable when removing it.

6. Remove the air intake duct and the air cleaner case.

7. Unplug the intake air resonator control solenoid valve connector, then remove the vacuum hose and resonator.

8. Remove the battery cables from the underhood fuse/relay boxes.

9. Unplug the engine wire harness connectors on the right side of the engine compartment.

10. Disconnect the brake booster vacuum hose. Also, label and disconnect the three vacuum hoses adjacent to it.

11. Relieve the fuel system pressure using the correct procedure.

12. Disconnect the fuel feed and return hose.

13. Unplug the engine wire harness connectors, terminal and clamps on the left side of the engine compartment.

14. Unplug the injector resistor connector on the left side of the engine compartment.

15. Remove the power steering hose clamp. Also, label and disconnect the two vacuum hoses adjacent to it.

16. Remove the power steering belt and pump.

17. Remove the alternator belt.

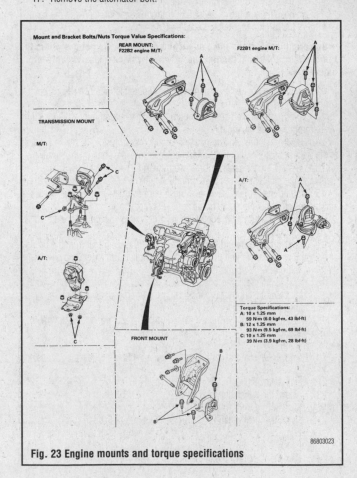

Fig. 23 Engine mounts and torque specifications

18. On cars with manual transaxles:
   a. Remove the shift and select cables from the transaxle.
   b. Unplug the back-up light switch connectors and disconnect the starter motor cable.
   c. Remove the clutch slave cylinder from the transaxle. Do not disconnect the pipe/hose assembly and do not operate the clutch pedal once the cylinder is removed.
19. Unplug the vehicle speed sensor connector.
20. Remove the front wheels.
21. Disconnect the radiator hoses and the transaxle cooler hoses (if equipped). Remove the radiator.
22. Remove the air conditioning compressor but DO NOT disconnect any hoses from it. Move the compressor out of the work area and support it with stiff wire; do not let it hang by the hoses.
23. From under the car, remove the center beam and front exhaust pipe.
24. On automatic transaxles cars, disconnect the shift cable from the transaxle.
25. Remove the forks securing the struts to the lower suspension arms. Disconnect the lower suspension arms from the ball joints.
26. Remove the driveshafts. Coat the splines and machined surfaces with clean engine oil, then tie plastic bags over the ends.
27. Attach a suitable lifting device to the engine. Raise the engine to unload the engine mounts.
28. Remove the front and rear engine mounting bolts and brackets.
29. Remove the engine side mount and mounting bolt. Remove the side transaxle mount and mounting bolt.
30. Make sure the engine/transaxle assembly is completely free of vacuum hoses, fuel and coolant hoses and electrical wires.
31. Slowly raise the engine approximately 6 in. (152mm). Check again that all hoses and wires have been disconnected from the engine/transaxle assembly.
32. Raise the engine/transaxle assembly all the way and remove it from the vehicle.
33. Remove the transaxle.
34. On manual transaxles, remove the clutch cover (pressure plate) and clutch disc.
35. Mount the engine on an engine stand, making sure the mounting bolts are tight. If an engine stand is not available, support the engine in an upright position with blocks. Never leave an engine hanging from a lift or hoist.

To install:
36. Assemble the clutch disc and pressure plate to the flywheel for manual transaxle vehicles.
37. Install the transaxle.
38. Lift the engine into position and lower it into the car, aligning the mounts and bushings.

➡**When installing the engine mounts and vibration dampers in the following steps, they must be tightened to the correct tension in the correct order if they are to dampen vibration properly.**

39. Install the side engine mount and mounting bolt. Install the through-bolt and tighten to 47 ft. lbs. (64 Nm). Remove the smaller bolt under the through-bolt. Do not tighten the bolt/nut on the engine side.
40. Install the side transaxle mount and bolt. Tighten the through-bolt to 47 ft. lbs. (64 Nm), then remove the smaller bolt next to it. Do not tighten the nuts on the transaxle side.
41. Install the rear mount bracket using new bolts. Tighten the four bolts to 40 ft. lbs. (54 Nm) first, then tighten the single through-bolt to 47 ft. lbs. (64 Nm).
42. Install the front mount using a new through-bolt and tighten to 47 ft. lbs. (64 Nm). Do not tighten the bolts on the engine side.
43. Tighten the side engine mount bolts to 40 ft. lbs. (54 Nm). Tighten the nuts/bolts on the transaxle mount and front mount to 28 ft. lbs. (38 Nm).
44. Remove the hoist equipment from the engine.
45. For automatic transaxles, install the shift control cable.
46. For manual transaxles, connect the shift cable and shift select cable. Install the clutch slave cylinder. Tighten the bolts to 16 ft. lbs. (22 Nm).
47. Install the driveshafts. Use a new circlip on each; install the shaft until a positive click is heard as the axle locks into place.
48. Install the ball joints to the lower arms. Tighten the lower arm nuts to 40 ft. lbs. (55 Nm). Install new cotter pins.

49. Install the exhaust pipe. Use new nuts; tighten the pipe-to-manifold nuts to 40 ft. lbs. (55 Nm).
50. Install the center beam. Tighten the bolts to 37 ft. lbs. (50 Nm).
51. Install the radiator; connect the coolant and transmission oil cooler lines. Engage the cooling fan connectors.
52. Connect the heater inlet and outlet hoses to the cylinder head and connecting pipe.
53. Install the A/C compressor and belt, tightening the mounting bolts to 16 ft. lbs. (22 Nm).
54. Install the power steering pump and belt. Tighten the nuts to 16 ft. lbs. (22 Nm).
55. Engage the injector resistor and vehicle speed sensor connectors.
56. Connect the starter cable terminal and install the engine wire harness terminal. Engage the connectors for the main wire harness at the right side of the engine compartment.
57. Connect the brake booster vacuum hose and the adjacent vacuum hoses.
58. Connect the throttle cable and secure the locknut.
59. Install the control box on the firewall and engage the wiring connectors.
60. Using new washers, connect the fuel line and return hose to the pressure control valve.
61. Install the air cleaner and the intake ductwork.
62. Refill the transaxle fluid.
63. Refill the cooling system.
64. Refill the engine oil.
65. Install the battery base and battery.
66. Double check all installation items, paying particular attention to loose hoses or hanging wires, untightened nuts, poor routing of hoses and wires (too tight or rubbing) and tools left in the engine area.
67. Connect the battery cables, positive first.
68. Disconnect the coil wire from the distributor. Insulate or protect the end of the cable so it does not arc to the engine or surrounding metal. Without touching the accelerator, turn the ignition switch to the **START** position and crank the engine for about 5–10 seconds; this will develop some oil pressure within the motor. Do not exceed 10 seconds cranking.
69. Switch the ignition **OFF** and reconnect the coil.
70. Start the engine, allowing it to idle. Check the hoses and lines carefully for any sign of leakage.
71. Bleed the air from the cooling system; check the timing and idle speed.
72. After the engine has warmed up fully and the fan(s) have come on at least once, recheck the engine for fluid leaks. Shut the engine off.
73. Adjust the belts, clutch and throttle cable as necessary.
74. Install the front wheels. Lower the hood.

1995 Accord V-6

1. Disconnect the battery cables, negative first. Remove the battery and battery case.
2. Raise and safely support the vehicle. Double check the security and placement of the stands.
3. Remove the support struts, then place the hood in a vertical position and safely secure it in place. Do not remove the hood.
4. Remove the intake air duct.
5. Remove the throttle cable and cruise control cable by loosening the locknut, then slip the cable end out of the accelerator linkage.
6. Detach the starter cable from the strut tower brace. Remove the strut tower brace.
7. Unplug the engine wire harness connectors and injector resistor connector on the left side of the engine compartment.
8. Relieve the fuel system pressure, then disconnect the feed hose from the fuel filter.
9. Label and disconnect the brake booster, evaporative emissions canister, and fuel return hoses.
10. Disconnect the battery cables from the underhood fuse/relay boxes.
11. Unplug the engine harness connectors from the right side of the engine compartment.
12. Remove the side engine mount.
13. Remove the A/C compressor, alternator and power steering pump belts. Remove the bolt securing the ground cable in the front of the engine compartment.

14. Disconnect the inlet hose from the power steering pump, then plug the hose and pump. Remove the mounting nuts/bolts, then remove the power steering pump and position it aside.

15. Remove the radiator cap and front splash shield. Drain the coolant.

16. Drain the transmission fluid and engine oil. Reinstall the drain plugs using new washers.

17. Remove the center beam.

18. Unplug the oxygen sensor connector, then remove the front exhaust pipe.

19. Remove the crankshaft pulley (refer to the procedure later in this section). Disconnect the oil pressure switch. Remove the oil filter base attaching bolts, then remove the base.

20. Remove the shift cable.

21. Remove the forks securing the struts to the lower suspension arms. Disconnect the lower suspension arms from the ball joints.

22. Remove the driveshafts. Coat the splines and machined surfaces with clean engine oil, then tie plastic bags over the ends.

23. Remove the radiator. Remove the bolts securing the A/C compressor, then position the compressor aside. Do not disconnect the hoses.

24. Attach a suitable lifting device to the engine. Raise the engine to unload the engine mounts.

25. Remove the transaxle mount and the front mount.

26. Disconnect the vacuum hose from the rear mount, then remove the mount.

27. Make sure the engine/transaxle assembly is completely free of vacuum hoses, fuel and coolant hoses and electrical wires.

28. Slowly raise the engine approximately 6 in. (15 cm). Check again that all hoses and wires have been disconnected from the engine/transaxle assembly.

29. Raise the engine/transaxle assembly all the way and remove it from the vehicle.

30. Remove the transaxle.

31. Mount the engine on an engine stand, making sure the mounting bolts are tight. If an engine stand is not available, support the engine in an upright position with blocks. Never leave an engine hanging from a lift or hoist.

To install:

32. Install the transaxle.

33. Lift the engine into position and lower it into the car, aligning the mounts and bushings.

➡**When installing the engine mounts and vibration dampers in the following steps, they must be tightened to the correct tension in the correct order if they are to dampen vibration properly.**

34. Install the rear mount, then tighten the bolts to 43 ft. lbs. (59 Nm). Connect the vacuum hose.

35. Install the front mount and tighten the bolts to 43 ft. lbs. (59 Nm).

36. Install the side engine mount with new bolts. Tighten the engine side bolts to 40 ft. lbs. (54 Nm). Do not tighten the through-bolt.

37. Install the transaxle mount and tighten the nuts to 28 ft. lbs. (38 Nm). Do not tighten the through-bolt.

38. Tighten the through-bolt on the side mount to 47 ft. lbs. (64 Nm), then tighten the through-bolt on the transaxle mount to the same specification.

39. Remove the hoist equipment from the engine.

40. Install the A/C compressor, tightening the mounting bolts to 16 ft. lbs. (22 Nm).

41. Install the radiator; connect the coolant and transmission oil cooler lines. Engage the cooling fan connectors.

42. Install the shift control cable.

43. Install the driveshafts. Use a new circlip on each; install the shaft until a positive click is heard as the axle locks into place.

44. Install the ball joints to the lower arms. Tighten the lower arm nuts to 40 ft. lbs. (55 Nm). Install new cotter pins. Install the strut forks.

45. Install the oil filter base with new O-rings. Tighten the bolts to 16 ft. lbs. (22 Nm). Connect the oil pressure switch.

46. Install the crank pulley. Refer to the procedure later in this section.

47. Install the exhaust pipe. Use new nuts; tighten the pipe-to-manifold nuts to 40 ft. lbs. (55 Nm).

48. Install the center beam. Tighten the bolts to 37 ft. lbs. (50 Nm).

49. Install the power steering pump. Tighten the nuts/bolts to 16 ft. lbs. (22 Nm).

50. Install the belts. Connect the ground cable to the front of the engine compartment.

51. Connect the battery cables to the underhood fuse/relay panels.

52. Engage the injector resistor and left side engine harness connectors.

53. Install the strut tower brace and attach the starter cable. Tighten the bolts to 16 ft. lbs. (22 Nm).

54. Connect the starter cable terminal and install the engine wire harness terminal. Engage the connectors for the main wire harness at the right side of the engine compartment.

55. Connect the brake booster, evaporative emissions and fuel return hoses.

56. Connect the cruise control and throttle cable. Secure the locknut.

57. Using new washers, connect the fuel line to the filter.

58. Install the air cleaner and the intake ductwork.

59. Refill the transaxle fluid.

60. Refill the cooling system.

61. Refill the engine oil.

62. Install the battery base and battery.

63. Adjust the throttle and shift cables.

64. Double check all installation items, paying particular attention to loose hoses or hanging wires, untightened nuts, poor routing of hoses and wires (too tight or rubbing) and tools left in the engine area.

65. Connect the battery cables, positive first.

66. Disconnect the coil wire from the distributor. Insulate or protect the end of the cable so it does not arc to the engine or surrounding metal. Without touching the accelerator, turn the ignition switch to the **START** position and crank the engine for about 5–10 seconds; this will develop some oil pressure within the motor. Do not exceed 10 seconds cranking.

67. Switch the ignition **OFF** and reconnect the coil.

68. Start the engine, allowing it to idle. Check the hoses and lines carefully for any sign of leakage.

69. Bleed the air from the cooling system; check the idle speed.

70. After the engine has warmed up fully and the fan(s) have come on at least once, recheck the engine for fluid leaks. Shut the engine off.

71. Install the splash shield. Connect the support struts to the hood.

1988–91 Prelude

➡ **See Figure 24**

1. Elevate and safely support the vehicle. Double check the placement and stability of the stands.

2. Disconnect the negative battery terminal, then the positive cable.

3. Disconnect the washer hose at the hood. Outline the hood hinges on the inner surface of the hood; remove the bolts and remove the hood.

4. Drain the engine oil. Replace the washer on the drain plug and reinstall the plug.

5. Drain the transaxle fluid. Reinstall the drain plug and tighten it.

6. Drain the coolant from the radiator and engine.

7. For carbureted vehicles:

  a. Remove the battery and battery base.

  b. Remove the air intake duct and air filter housing.

  c. Disconnect the fuel hose at the fuel filter. Plug the line to prevent spillage.

  d. Disconnect the brake booster vacuum hose at the one-way valve.

  e. Remove the air jet controller, but do not disconnect the vacuum hoses.

8. For fuel injected vehicles:

  a. Remove the battery and base.

  b. Remove the air intake hose, air cleaner and resonator assembly.

  c. Disconnect the battery wires from the relay box.

  d. Relieve the fuel pressure using the proper procedure.

  e. Disconnect the fuel feed and fuel return hoses.

9. Disconnect the vacuum hose to the charcoal canister at the throttle valve.

10. Disconnect the throttle cable, either at the carburetor or throttle body.

11. On carbureted engines, disconnect the coil wire, condenser and ignition primary wires.

12. Remove the distributor.

13. Disconnect the heater inlet and outlet hoses.

14. For automatic transaxles, disconnect and plug the oil cooler lines.

15. Disconnect the vacuum hose to the cruise control actuator, remove the actuator.

16. For fuel injected engines, unplug the wire harness connectors at the right side of the engine compartment.

17. Remove the control box from its mount. Remove the vacuum tank.

18. Disconnect the brake booster vacuum hose.
19. Loosen the power steering pump and the alternator; remove the belts.
20. Cover the alternator with a thick rag or cloth. Disconnect the power steering inlet hose. Fluid will flow out—protect the alternator. Remove the power steering pump.
21. Remove the alternator.
22. Remove the condenser fan shroud if equipped with air conditioning.
23. Remove the air conditioning compressor but DO NOT disconnect any hoses from it. Move the compressor out of the work area and support it with stiff wire; do not let it hang by the hoses.
24. For manual transaxles, disconnect the shift and select cables from the transaxle and remove the cable bracket.
25. For automatic transaxles, disconnect the shift cable.
26. Disconnect the transmission ground wire.
27. Remove the left and right axles or half-shafts.
28. Remove the clutch slave cylinder but do not disconnect the hose.
29. Remove the speed sensor and speedometer cable. Take great care not to bend the cable. Do not use pliers to remove the cable.
30. Install the hoisting equipment. Attach the chains to the eyehooks at the pulley and transaxle ends of the engine. The chain to the pulley-end eyehook should be shorter than the other to tilt the pulley end up on removal. Take the slack out of the chains but do not put lift the engine.
31. Remove the rear engine mount bolt, then remove the mount bracket.
32. Remove the front engine mount bolt.
33. Remove the side engine mount bolts.
34. Remove the transmission mount bolt.
35. Lift the engine about 4–6 in. (10–15 cm); inspect the area for any remaining wires, vacuum lines or hoses.
36. Tilt the engine, pulley end up, and remove the engine/transaxle from the vehicle.
37. Remove the transaxle.
38. On manual transaxles, remove the clutch cover (pressure plate) and clutch disc.
39. Mount the engine on an engine stand, making sure the mounting bolts are tight. If an engine stand is not available, support the engine in an upright position with blocks. Never leave an engine hanging from a lift or hoist.

To install:
40. Assemble the clutch disc and pressure plate to the flywheel for manual transaxle vehicles.
41. Install the transaxle.
42. Lift the engine into position and lower it into the car, aligning the mounts and bushings.

➡ **When installing the engine mounts and vibration dampers in the following steps, the bolts running through the large rubber bushings should only be set snug or finger-tight until all are in place. They must be tightened to the correct tension in the correct order if they are to dampen vibration properly.**

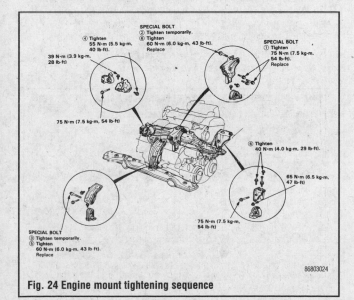

Fig. 24 Engine mount tightening sequence

43. Install the transmission mount bolt.
44. Install the side engine mount bracket bolts. Install the through-bolt.
45. Install the front engine mount bolt.
46. Install the rear engine mount bolts.
47. At this point the engine is loosely mounted in the vehicle. Slacken the hoist chains, allowing the engine to settle into place.
48. With the vehicle sitting approximately level, tighten the mounts in the order given to the proper torque. Both the order and tightness are important; the bushings play a great role in damping engine vibration.
49. Install the speed sensor and speedometer cable. Tighten the retaining bolt only to 9 ft. lbs. (12 Nm).
50. Install the clutch slave cylinder.
51. Install the left and right axles. Use new circlips; make certain each axle is heard to click into place as the clip engages the groove.
52. Install the transaxle ground wire.
53. Connect the shift cable to the automatic transaxle or connect the shift and select cables to the manual transaxle. Secure the cable bracket.
54. Install the A/C compressor and belt. Tighten the mounting bolts to 18 ft. lbs. (25 Nm).
55. Install the alternator, tightening the mounting bolts to 33 ft. lbs. (45 Nm).
56. Install the power steering pump. Tighten the mounting bolts to 20 ft. lbs. (27 Nm) and connect the inlet hose.
57. Install the drive belts for the power steering pump and alternator.
58. Connect the brake booster hose.
59. Install the vacuum tank and control box back on the firewall. Engage the wiring connectors.
60. Reinstall the cruise control actuator and connect the vacuum hose.
61. Connect the automatic transaxle oil cooler lines if they were removed.
62. Connect the heater inlet and outlet hoses.
63. Connect the upper and lower radiator hoses.
64. Install the distributor. For carbureted engines, connect the ignition wiring, condenser and primary wires.
65. Connect the throttle cable.
66. For fuel injected engines, reconnect the fuel supply and return hoses. Use new washers on the banjo fitting. Tighten the banjo bolt to 16 ft. lbs. (22 Nm).
67. For fuel injected engines, connect the battery wires to the relay box. Install the air cleaner assembly with the intake hose and resonator.
68. For carbureted engines, install the air jet controller; check that the vacuum lines are not crimped or twisted.
69. For carbureted engines, connect the fuel line at the filter. Install the air cleaner housing and air intake ducts.
70. Install the battery tray and battery.
71. Refill the engine coolant.
72. Refill the engine oil.
73. Refill the transaxle fluid.
74. Double check all installation items, paying particular attention to loose hoses or hanging wires, untightened nuts, poor routing of hoses and wires (too tight or rubbing) and tools left in the engine area.
75. Connect the battery cables, positive first.
76. Disconnect the coil wire from the distributor. Insulate or protect the end of the cable so it does not arc to the engine or surrounding metal. Without touching the accelerator, turn the ignition switch to the **START** position and crank the engine for about 5–10 seconds; this will develop some oil pressure within the motor. Do not exceed 10 seconds cranking.
77. Switch the ignition **OFF** and reconnect the coil.
78. Start the engine, allowing it to idle. Check the hoses and lines carefully for any sign of leakage.
79. Bleed the air from the cooling system; check the timing and idle speed.
80. After the engine has warmed up fully and the fan(s) have come on at least once, recheck the engine for fluid leaks. Shut the engine off.
81. Adjust the belts, clutch and throttle cable as necessary.

1992–95 Prelude

◆ **See Figure 25**

1. Disconnect the battery cables and remove the battery and battery case.
2. Raise and safely support the vehicle.
3. Place the hood in a vertical position and safely support it in place. Remove the radiator cap.

4. Remove the front wheels and remove the engine splash shield. Drain the engine oil, coolant and transaxle fluid.

5. Remove the air intake duct and the air cleaner case.

6. Relieve the fuel system pressure by slowly loosening the service bolt on the fuel pipe about 1 turn.

7. Remove the fuel feed hose from the fuel pipe.

8. Disconnect the resistor connector from the resistor on the left side of the engine compartment.

9. Disconnect the throttle cable by loosening the locknut and slipping the cable end out of the accelerator linkage.

➡**Be careful not to bend or kink the cable when removing it. If cable is kinked it must be replaced.**

10. Remove the engine wire harness connectors, terminal and clamps from the right side of the engine.

11. Disconnect the power cable from the under hood fuse/relay box.

12. Disconnect the brake booster vacuum hose and emission control vacuum tubes from the intake manifold.

13. Disconnect the vacuum tube and electrical connector from the cruise control actuator and remove the actuator.

14. Remove the engine ground cable from the cylinder head.

15. Remove the power steering belt and pump. Do not disconnect the power steering hoses.

16. Remove the air conditioner condenser fan and shroud and place a shield in front of the radiator.

17. Remove the air conditioning compressor drive belt and compressor. Do not remove the air conditioning lines. Position the compressor aside.

18. Remove the upper and lower radiator hoses and the heater hoses.

19. On automatic transaxle, remove the shift cable, transaxle ground cable and the cooler lines.

20. On manual transaxle, remove the shift cable and select cable. Remove the clutch slave cylinder and pipe/hose assembly.

21. Remove the clutch damper assembly and the speed sensor assembly.

22. Remove the exhaust pipe and stay.

23. Remove the fork securing the strut to the lower arm. Using a puller, disconnect the suspension lower arm ball joint.

24. Remove the driveshaft and swing it out of the way, under the fender.

25. Attach an engine lifting device to the engine.

26. Remove the rear mounting bracket. Remove the front mounting bracket.

27. Remove the left side engine mount and remove the transaxle mount and mounting bracket.

28. Raise the engine and check that all necessary disconnections were made.

29. Remove the engine from the vehicle.

To install:

30. Installation is the reverse of the removal procedure. Attention to the following steps will aid installation.

31. Tighten the engine mounting bolts in the following sequence:

   a. Tighten the rear engine mount-to-frame bolts snug only.

   b. Replace the rear engine mount through-bolt with a new one and tighten snug only.

   c. Replace the rear engine mount through-bolt with a new one and tighten snug only.

   d. Tighten the side transaxle mount through-bolt snug only.

   e. Tighten the engine side mount through-bolt snug only.

   f. Tighten the side transaxle mount-to-block nuts to 28 ft. lbs. (39 Nm).

   g. Tighten the engine side mount-to-block bolt and nut to 40 ft. lbs. (55 Nm).

   h. Tighten the rear engine mount through-bolt to 47 ft. lbs. (65 Nm).

   i. Tighten the rear engine mount-to-frame bolts to 40 ft. lbs. (55 Nm).

   j. Tighten the front engine mount through-bolt to 47 ft. lbs. (65 Nm).

   k. Tighten the side transaxle mount through-bolt to 40 ft. lbs. (55 Nm).

   l. Tighten the engine side mount through-bolt to 40 ft. lbs. (55 Nm).

➡**Failure to tighten the bolts in the proper sequence can cause excessive noise and vibration and reduce bushing life. Check that the bushings are not twisted or offset.**

32. Make sure the spring clip on the end of each halfshaft clicks into place. Use new clips when installing.

33. Bleed the air from the cooling system at the bleed bolt with the heater valve open.

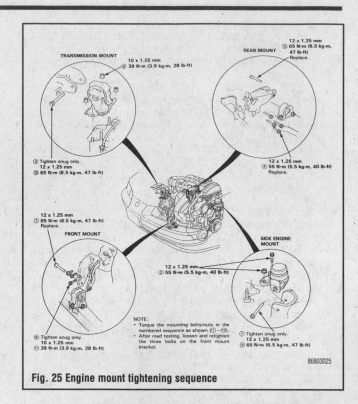

Fig. 25 Engine mount tightening sequence

34. Adjust the throttle cable tension and check the clutch pedal free-play.

35. Check that the transaxle shifts into gear smoothly.

36. Adjust the tension of the accessory drive belts.

37. After installing all fuel system components, pressurize the fuel system by cycling the ignition switch **ON** and then **OFF**. Do not operate the starter. Repeat 2–3 times and check for fuel leakage.

38. Check the ignition timing.

Valve Cover/Rocker Arm Cover

REMOVAL & INSTALLATION

▶ **See Figures 26, 27, 28, 29 and 30**

1. On some models, it will be necessary to remove the air cleaner assembly.

2. Remove the ground cable, the spark plug wires (if necessary) and the throttle cable (if necessary) from the rocker arm cover.

3. If equipped, disconnect the PCV hose from the rocker arm cover.

4. Remove the rocker arm cover-to-cylinder head nuts/bolts, the washer/grommet assemblies and the rocker arm cover.

➡**If the cover is difficult to remove, use a plastic mallet to bump it loose. Never use a metal object to strike the cover.**

Fig. 26 Remove any components which are secured to the valve cover

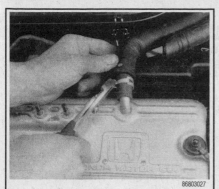

Fig. 27 If equipped, remove the PCV hose connected to the valve cover

Fig. 28 Remove the cover from the cylinder head. Be careful not to lose any washer/grommets

Fig. 29 Remember to the install the ground wire, if equipped

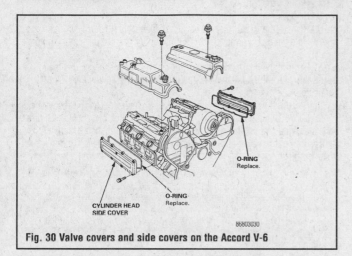

Fig. 30 Valve covers and side covers on the Accord V-6

5. Clean the gasket mounting surfaces and check the gasket for deformation.

To install:

6. Generally, the rubber gasket may be reused if in good condition. Fit it into the flange in the cover, making sure it is not twisted.

7. Install the cover and gasket onto the head. Install the insulators.

8. Install the ground wire, then install the nuts. Tighten the rocker arm cover-to-cylinder head nuts/bolts to 11 ft. lbs. (15 Nm) on the Accord V-6 or 7 ft. lbs. (10 Nm) on other models.

9. Reinstall the air cleaner, spark plug wires or other components removed for access.

Side Covers

REMOVAL & INSTALLATION

▶ **See Figure 30**

➡ **This procedure is applicable to the Accord V-6 only.**

1. Disconnect the negative battery cable.
2. Remove any components necessary to access the covers.
3. Remove the bolts securing the side covers to the cylinder heads.
4. If the cover is difficult to remove, use a plastic mallet to bump it loose. Never use a metal object to strike the cover.
5. Clean the gasket mounting surfaces and discard the old gasket.

To install:

6. Install the side covers using new gaskets. Tighten the bolts to 9 ft. lbs. (12 Nm).

7. Install any components removed earlier.
8. Connect the negative battery cable.

Rocker Arms/Shafts

REMOVAL & INSTALLATION

SOHC 4-Cylinder Engines

▶ **See Figures 31, 32, 33 and 34**

1. Disconnect the negative battery cable.
2. Remove the valve cover and bring the No. 1 cylinder to TDC on the compression stroke.
3. Loosen the adjusting screws on the rocker arms.
4. Relieve the tension on the timing belt.
5. Remove the rocker arm assembly retaining bolts. Unscrew the bolts 2 turns at a time, in a crisscross pattern, to prevent damaging the valves or rocker assembly. The tension must be released evenly and constantly.

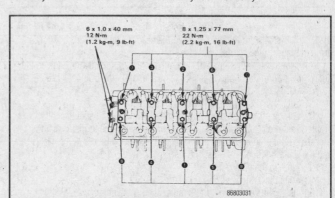

Fig. 31 Rocker shaft bolt tightening sequence—1984–91 Prelude and 1984–89 Accord

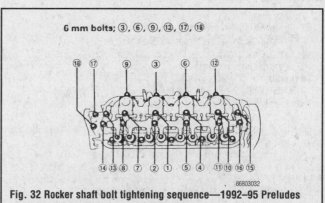

Fig. 32 Rocker shaft bolt tightening sequence—1992–95 Preludes and 1990–95 Accords without VTEC

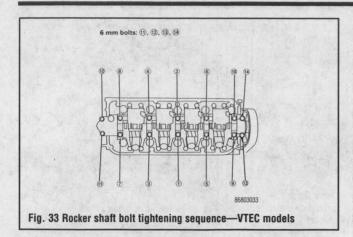

Fig. 33 Rocker shaft bolt tightening sequence—VTEC models

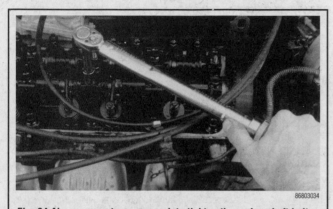

Fig. 34 Always use a torque wrench to tighten the rocker shaft bolts

6. Remove the rocker arm/shaft assemblies. Leave the rocker arm bolts in place as the shafts are removed to keep the bearing caps, springs and rocker arms in place on the shafts.

7. If the rocker arms or shafts are to be replaced, identify the parts as they are removed from the shafts to insure reinstallation in the original location.

To install:

8. Lubricate the camshaft journals and lobes.

9. Set the rocker arm assembly in place and loosely install the bolts. Tighten each bolt 2 turns at a time in the proper sequence to insure that the rockers do not bind on the valves. Tighten the 6mm bolts to 9 ft. lbs. (12 Nm) and the 8mm bolts to 16 ft. lbs. (22 Nm).

10. Tension the timing belt.

11. Adjust the valve lash.

12. Install the valve cover and connect the negative battery cable.

DOHC Engines

EXCEPT VTEC

1. Disconnect the negative battery cable.

2. Remove the valve cover and bring the No. 1 cylinder to TDC.

3. Remove the timing belt cover and the timing belt.

4. Remove the camshaft bearing caps and remove the camshafts.

5. Remove the rocker arms.

To install:

6. Make certain the keyways on the camshafts are facing up. Valve locknuts should be loosened and the adjusting screws backed off before installation.

7. Place the rocker arms on the pivot bolts and valve stems.

8. Install the camshafts and seals. The seals should be installed with the open or spring side facing inward.

9. Note that the cam retainers are marked I (intake) or E (exhaust) and consecutively numbered to indicate correct placement. Do not apply oil to the surfaces of the holders which mate with the seals. Apply a liquid gasket or sealer to the head mating surfaces for the No. 1 and No. 6 camshaft holders.

10. Install the camshaft holders.

11. Tighten the camshaft holders temporarily. Make sure the rocker arms are properly positioned on the valve stems.

12. Use a seal driver of the correct size to install the camshaft oil seals.

13. Tighten the bolts two turns at a time, using the correct sequence. Bring each bolt to the correct tension. Please refer to the camshaft procedures in this section.

14. Install the timing belt and covers.

15. Adjust the valve lash.

16. Reinstall the valve cover.

VTEC

▶ See Figures 35 and 36

1. Disconnect the negative battery cable.

2. Remove the valve cover.

3. Remove the timing belt.

4. Remove the camshafts.

5. Remove the cylinder head from the vehicle.

6. Remove the VTEC solenoid valve and filter from the head.

7. Hold the rocker arms together with a rubber band to prevent them from separating.

8. Remove the intake and exhaust rocker shaft orifices. Note that their shapes are different. Mark the parts as they are removed to ensure correct installation later.

9. Remove the sealing bolts from the end of the head. Discard the washers.

10. Screw 12mm bolts into the rocker arm shafts. Remove each rocker arm while slowly pulling out the intake and exhaust rocker arm shafts. Mark the parts as they are removed to ensure reinstallation in the proper locations.

To install:

11. Clean all parts in solvent, dry them and apply lubricant to any contact points.

12. The rocker locknuts should be loosened and the adjusting screws backed off before installation.

13. Install the rocker arms in their original locations while passing the rocker arm shaft through the cylinder head. Remove the rubber bands after installing the rockers.

14. Using new O-rings, install the rocker shaft orifices in their correct locations. After installing the orifices, try to turn the shaft to make sure the orifice has been inserted in the hole of the rocker shaft correctly. If the orifice is in place, it should not turn.

15. Install the sealing bolts with new washers. Tighten them to 43 ft. lbs. (60 Nm).

16. Install the VTEC solenoid valve with a new filter. Tighten the bolts to 9 ft. lbs. (12 Nm).

17. Install the cylinder head on the engine, then install the camshafts.

18. Install the timing belt.

19. Adjust the valve lash.

20. Install the rocker cover and connect the negative battery cable.

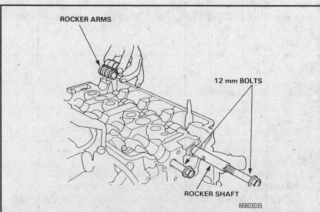

Fig. 35 Removing the rocker arms from the engine. Note the rubber band holding the rocker arm assembly together

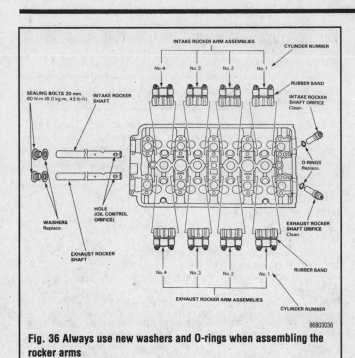

Fig. 36 Always use new washers and O-rings when assembling the rocker arms

Accord V-6

INNER ROCKER ARMS

▶ See Figure 37

1. Disconnect the negative battery cable.
2. Remove the rocker arm and side covers.
3. Remove the camshafts. Refer to the procedure outlined in this section.
4. Remove the intake rocker arms, inner exhaust rocker arms and pushrods. Identify the parts as they are removed to ensure reinstallation in the proper locations.
5. If necessary, remove the rocker arm guides by removing the bolts securing them to the head. The bolts are of different lengths; be sure to mark them for correct installation later.

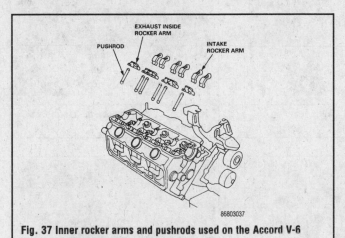

Fig. 37 Inner rocker arms and pushrods used on the Accord V-6

To install:

6. If necessary, install the rocker arm guides. Tighten the bolts to 9 ft. lbs. (12 Nm). Be sure the bolts are installed in their correct locations.
7. Clean all parts in solvent, dry them and apply lubricant to any contact points.
8. If the hydraulic tappets were removed, bleed them using the procedure found later in this section.
9. Position the rocker arms and pushrods in their correct locations.
10. Install the camshafts. Refer to the procedure outlined in this section.

11. Adjust the exhaust rocker arms as described in the shaft-mounted arm procedure.
12. Install the rocker arm and side covers. Connect the negative battery cable.

SHAFT-MOUNTED ARMS

▶ See Figure 38

1. Disconnect the negative battery cable.
2. Remove the cylinder head(s) from the engine.

➡Identify the parts as they are removed to ensure reinstallation in the proper locations.

3. Remove the 22mm sealing bolt from the end of the head. Discard the washer.
4. Remove the rocker shaft using a 12x1.25mm bolt. Remove the rockers and wave washers as the shaft is extracted from the head.

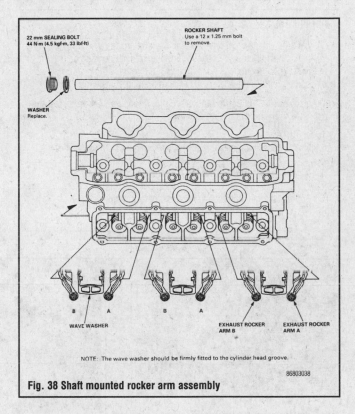

Fig. 38 Shaft mounted rocker arm assembly

To install:

5. Clean all parts in solvent, dry them and apply lubricant to any contact points.
6. If the hydraulic tappets were removed, bleed them using the procedure found later in this section.
7. Position the rocker arms and wave washers in their correct locations. Make sure the wave washers are firmly fitted to the cylinder head groove.
8. Carefully install the shaft into the cylinder head. Be careful not to damage the rockers or shaft when installing. Make sure the wave washers are still properly installed. Install the sealing bolt with a new washer and tighten to 36 ft. lbs. (49 Nm).
9. Install the cylinder head(s) and the timing belt. Do not install the side and rocker covers at this time.
10. Adjust the exhaust rocker arms as follows:
   a. Position the No. 1 piston at TDC on the compression stroke.
   b. Loosen the locknuts on the exhaust rockers.
   c. Tighten the adjusting screws for the No. 1, 2 and 4 cylinders. When you feel the screw contact the valve, tighten the screw 1⅛ turn. Tighten the locknut to 14 ft. lbs. (20 Nm).
   d. Rotate the crankshaft one turn clockwise, then tighten the adjusting screws for cylinders No. 3, 5 and 6. When you feel the screw contact the

valve, tighten the screw 1 ⅛ turn. Tighten the locknut to 14 ft. lbs. (20 Nm).

11. Install the side and rocker covers. Connect the negative battery cable.

Thermostat

❊❊ CAUTION

When draining the coolant, keep in mind that cats and dogs are attracted by ethylene glycol antifreeze, and are quite likely to drink any that is left in an uncovered container or in puddles on the ground. This will prove fatal in sufficient quantity. Always drain the coolant into a sealable container.

REMOVAL & INSTALLATION

◆ **See Figures 39, 40, 41 and 42**

1. With the engine cold, drain the cooling system.
2. Disconnect the radiator hose from the thermostat housing outlet.
3. Remove the thermostat housing outlet and remove the thermostat.
4. Using a putty knife, clean the gasket mounting surfaces.

➡**If the thermostat is equipped with a pin valve, be sure to install the thermostat with the pin facing upward.**

To install:

5. Install a new thermostat the gasket, O-ring or sealant (as applicable). Always install the spring end of the thermostat facing the engine.
6. Tighten the thermostat cover-to-thermostat housing bolts to 9 ft. lbs. (12 Nm).
7. Connect the radiator hose to the thermostat housing.
8. Fill, then bleed the cooling system. Check for leaks.

Intake Manifold

REMOVAL & INSTALLATION

❊❊ CAUTION

When draining the coolant, keep in mind that cats and dogs are attracted by ethylene glycol antifreeze, and are quite likely to drink any that is left in an uncovered container or in puddles on the ground. This will prove fatal in sufficient quantity. Always drain the coolant into a sealable container.

Carbureted Models

◆ **See Figures 43 thru 49**

1. Position a clean drain pan under the radiator, remove the drain plug and drain the cooling system.
2. Remove the air cleaner and housing from the carburetor(s).
3. Remove the air valve, the Exhaust Gas Recirculation (EGR) valve, the Air Suction (AS) valve and the air chamber (if equipped).

➡**On some models, it may be necessary to remove the air suction pipe and EGR crossover pipe to remove the intake manifold.**

4. Label and unplug any electrical connectors from the carburetor(s) and intake manifold.
5. Disconnect the fuel line(s) from the carburetor. Disconnect the throttle cable from the carburetor.
6. Remove the carburetor(s) from the intake manifold.
7. Remove the nuts/bolts securing the manifold to any support brackets. On some models, it may be necessary to remove these nuts/bolts from under the car; safely raise and support the vehicle.

Fig. 39 Use a pair of pliers to compress the spring clamp, then slide it up the hose and disconnect the hose from the housing

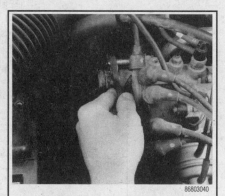

Fig. 40 Remove the nuts/bolts securing the thermostat housing . . .

Fig. 41 . . . then remove the thermostat housing

Fig. 42 Once the housing is removed, the thermostat can be removed from the engine

Fig. 43 To remove the air suction valve, first disconnect the pipe from the valve assembly . . .

Fig. 44 . . . then remove the retaining bolts and remove the assembly from the engine. The carburetor is removed for clarity

Fig. 45 The EGR crossover pipe will have to be removed on some models as well

Fig. 46 An extension is helpful for reaching some intake manifold nuts

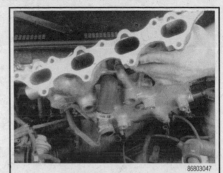

Fig. 47 Once everything is disconnected from the manifold, it can be removed from the engine

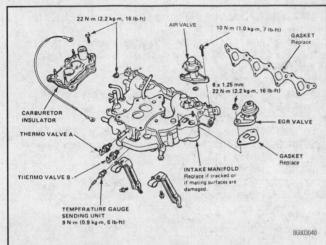

Fig. 48 Intake manifold used on 1984–85 carbureted Accords

8. Remove the intake manifold-to-cylinder head nuts (using a crisscross pattern), beginning from the center and moving out to both ends; then remove the manifold.

9. Using a putty knife or piece of stiff plastic, clean the gasket mounting surfaces on the head. Do not use razor scrapers; the machined surfaces may be damaged, resulting in a leak.

10. If the intake manifold is to be replaced, transfer all the necessary components to the new manifold.

To install:

11. Use new gaskets and position the gasket and manifold on the head. Hand-tighten the nuts snug. Starting with the inner or center nuts, tighten the nuts in a crisscross pattern to the correct torque. The tension must be even across the entire face of the manifold if leaks are to be prevented. Correct torque is:

- 1984–89 Accord: 16 ft. lbs. (22 Nm)
- 1984–87 Prelude: 23 ft. lbs. (32 Nm)
- 1988–90 Prelude: 17 ft. lbs. (24 Nm)

12. If applicable, secure the manifold to the support brackets. Tighten the nuts/bolts to 16 ft. lbs. (22 Nm).

13. Install the carburetor(s), making sure the insulator or base gasket is not damaged and is properly seated.

14. Connect the fuel lines and the throttle cable. Adjust the cable if necessary.

15. Engage the electrical and vacuum connections to the carburetor and manifold.

16. Install the emissions and air-control equipment removed for access. Always use a new gasket for the EGR valve; use care when handling and installing the air control valve, chamber and piping.

17. Install the air cleaner and housing.

18. Refill the coolant.

19. Start the engine, checking carefully for any leaks of fuel, coolant or vacuum. Check the manifold gasket area carefully for any leakage of vacuum.

Fuel Injected Models

EXCEPT ACCORD V-6

▶ See Figures 50 and 51

1. Position a clean catch pan under the radiator, remove the radiator drain plug and drain the cooling system to a level below the intake manifold. Disconnect the cooling hoses from the intake manifold.

2. Label and unplug the vacuum hoses and electrical connectors on the manifold and throttle body. Disconnect the cable(s) from the throttle body. Unplug the connector from the Exhaust Gas Recirculation (EGR) valve.

3. Relieve the fuel pressure using the correct procedure.

4. Remove the fuel rail/injector assembly.

5. If equipped, remove the EGR crossover pipe.

6. On some models, it may be necessary to remove the upper intake manifold plenum/throttle body assembly in order to access the nuts securing the manifold to the head. On dual stage intake models, remove the intake air bypass actuator first. Remove the nuts/bolts securing the plenum/throttle body assembly to the manifold, then remove it.

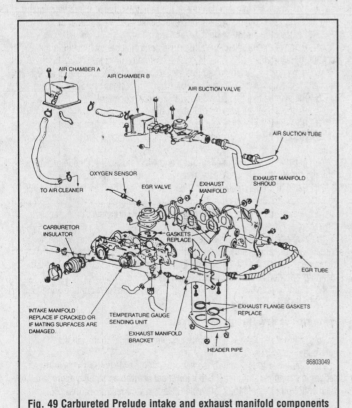

Fig. 49 Carbureted Prelude intake and exhaust manifold components

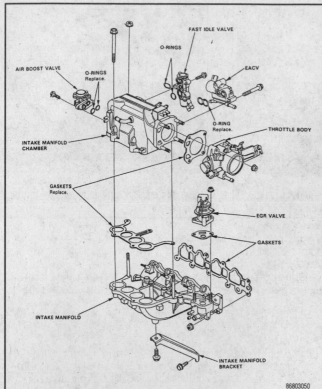

Fig. 50 Single stage intake manifold used on 1990–95 Accords and 1988–95 Preludes

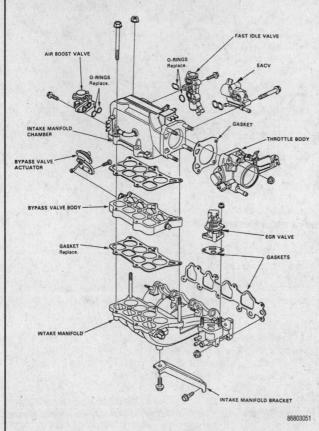

Fig. 51 A dual stage intake manifold is also used on some models

7. Remove the intake manifold support bracket bolts and the bracket(s). It may be necessary to access these from under the car; raise and support the vehicle safely.

8. While supporting the intake manifold, remove the intake manifold-to-cylinder head nuts; remove the manifold and the gasket from the cylinder head.

9. Using a putty knife or similar tool, clean the gasket mounting surfaces. Using a straight edge, check the surfaces for warpage; replace any warped parts.

➡ **If the cylinder head/manifold mating surface is warped, it must be machined or replaced.**

To install:

10. Using a new gasket, place the manifold into position and support it. Install the nuts snug on the studs.

11. Install the support bracket(s) below the manifold. Tighten the bolts holding the brackets to the manifold to 16 ft. lbs. (22 Nm).

12. Starting with the inner or center nuts, tighten the nuts in a crisscross pattern to the correct torque. The tension must be even across the entire face of the manifold if leaks are to be prevented. Correct torque is 16 ft. lbs. (22 Nm) for all models.

13. If applicable, install the EGR crossover pipe. Use new gaskets and tighten the nuts to 9 ft. lbs. (12 Nm).

14. Using a new gasket, install the plenum/throttle body assembly if it was removed as a separate unit. Tighten the nuts and bolts holding the chamber to 16 ft. lbs: (22 Nm).

15. Connect the throttle body cable(s).

16. Install the fuel rail/injector assembly. Connect the fuel lines. Always use new washers at the banjo fittings.

17. Engage the electrical and vacuum connections.

18. Double check all installation items, paying particular attention to loose hoses or hanging wires, untightened nuts, poor routing of hoses and wires (too tight or rubbing) and tools left in the work area.

19. Refill the engine coolant.

20. Start the engine, checking carefully for any leaks of fuel, coolant or vacuum. Check the manifold gasket areas carefully for any leakage of vacuum.

ACCORD V-6

♦ **See Figure 52**

1. Disconnect the negative battery cable.

2. Position a clean catch pan under the radiator, remove the radiator drain plug and drain the cooling system to a level below the intake manifold.

3. Remove the air intake duct.

4. Remove the throttle cable and cruise control cable by loosening the locknut, then slip the cable end out of the accelerator linkage.

5. It may be necessary to remove the strut tower brace for ease of access. If so, detach the starter cable from the strut tower brace, then remove the brace.

6. Relieve the fuel pressure using the correct procedure.

7. Remove the feed hose from the fuel filter.

8. Remove the brake booster, evaporative canister, and fuel return hoses.

9. Remove the intake manifold cover. It is secured by a series of small bolts.

10. Label and disconnect all vacuum and water hoses from the intake manifold and throttle body. If necessary, remove the vacuum pipe assembly.

11. Label and unplug all electrical connections on the manifold and throttle body. Remove the harness covers from the intake manifold.

12. Remove the Exhaust Gas Recirculation (EGR) crossover pipe. Discard the gasket.

13. Remove the bolts/nuts securing the intake manifold to the engine. Make sure all vacuum and electrical connections are unplugged. Remove any other components which may interfere with intake manifold removal. Carefully lift the manifold from the engine. Discard the gaskets.

14. Using a putty knife or similar tool, clean the gasket mounting surfaces.

To install:

➡ **Always use new O-rings and gaskets.**

15. Using new gaskets, place the manifold into position. Install the nuts/bolts until just snug.

16. Starting with the inner or center nuts, tighten the nuts in a crisscross pattern to the correct torque. The tension must be even across the entire face of the manifold if leaks are to be prevented. Correct torque is 16 ft. lbs. (22 Nm)

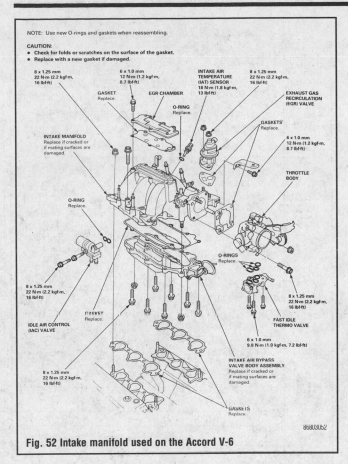

NOTE: Use new O-rings and gaskets when reassembling.

CAUTION:
● Check for folds or scratches on the surface of the gasket.
● Replace with a new gasket if damaged.

8 x 1.25 mm
22 N·m (2.2 kgf·m,
16 lbf·ft)

6 x 1.0 mm
12 N·m (1.2 kgf·m,
8.7 lbf·ft)

INTAKE AIR
TEMPERATURE
(IAT) SENSOR
18 N·m (1.8 kgf·m,
13 lbf·ft)

8 x 1.25 mm
22 N·m (2.2 kgf·m,
16 lbf·ft)

GASKET
Replace.

EGR CHAMBER

O-RING
Replace.

EXHAUST GAS
RECIRCULATION
(EGR) VALVE

GASKETS
Replace.

INTAKE MANIFOLD
Replace if cracked or
if mating surfaces are
damaged.

6 x 1.0 mm
12 N·m (1.2 kgf·m,
8.7 lbf·ft)

THROTTLE
BODY

O-RING
Replace.

O-RINGS
Replace.

8 x 1.25 mm
22 N·m (2.2 kgf·m,
16 lbf·ft)

8 x 1.25 mm
22 N·m (2.2 kgf·m,
16 lbf·ft)

GASKET
Replace.

IDLE AIR CONTROL
(IAC) VALVE

FAST IDLE
THERMO VALVE

6 x 1.0 mm
9.8 N·m (1.0 kgf·m, 7.2 lbf·ft)

INTAKE AIR BYPASS
VALVE BODY ASSEMBLY
Replace if cracked or
if mating surfaces are
damaged.

8 x 1.25 mm
22 N·m (2.2 kgf·m,
16 lbf·ft)

GASKETS
Replace.

86803052

Fig. 52 Intake manifold used on the Accord V-6

17. Install the EGR crossover pipe using a new gasket. Tighten the nuts (to the intake manifold) to 9 ft. lbs. (12 Nm) and the pipe (to the exhaust manifold) to 43 ft. lbs. (59 Nm).

18. Install the harness covers on the intake manifold. Tighten the bolts to 9 ft. lbs. (12 Nm).

19. If applicable, install the vacuum pipe assembly. Tighten the bolts to 9 ft. lbs. (12 Nm).

20. Engage all electrical and vacuum connections on the throttle body and manifold. Install the intake manifold cover. Tighten the bolts to 9 ft. lbs. (12 Nm).

21. Connect the brake booster, evaporative canister, and fuel return hoses.

22. Connect the feed hose to the fuel filter with new gaskets. Tighten the union bolt to 16 ft. lbs. (22 Nm) and the service (pressure release) bolt to 9 ft. lbs. (12 Nm).

23. If applicable, install the strut tower brace. Tighten the bolts to 16 ft. lbs. (22 Nm). Attach the starter cable.

24. Install the throttle and cruise control cables. Install the air intake duct.

25. Double check all installation items, paying

particular attention to loose hoses or hanging wires, untightened nuts, poor routing of hoses and wires (too tight or rubbing) and tools left in the work area.

26. Refill the engine coolant. Connect the negative battery cable.

27. Start the engine, checking carefully for any leaks of fuel, coolant or vacuum. Check the manifold gasket areas carefully for any leakage of vacuum.

Exhaust Manifold

REMOVAL & INSTALLATION

❊❊ WARNING

Do not perform this operation on a warm or hot engine.

Except Accord V-6

▶ **See Figures 53, 54, 55, 56 and 57**

➡Breaking loose exhaust manifold bolts is one of the nastiest jobs around. They are usually rusted solid; a generous application of penetrating oil several hours before beginning the job will make it easier.

1. Elevate and safely support the car.

2. Remove the header pipe-to-manifold nuts and separate the pipe from the manifold. Support the pipe with wire; do not allow it to hang by itself.

3. If necessary, disconnect and remove the oxygen sensor(s).

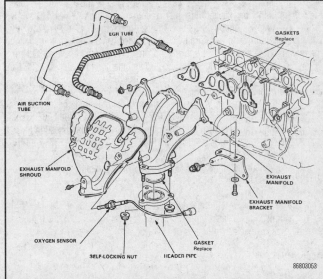

EGR TUBE

GASKETS
Replace

AIR SUCTION
TUBE

EXHAUST MANIFOLD
SHROUD

EXHAUST
MANIFOLD

EXHAUST MANIFOLD
BRACKET

OXYGEN SENSOR

SELF-LOCKING NUT

HEADER PIPE

GASKET
Replace

86803053

Fig. 53 On some models, it will be necessary to remove the air suction and EGR crossover pipes

86803054

Fig. 54 The heat shield is usually secured by three bolts

86803055

Fig. 55 Use a crisscross pattern when loosening the exhaust manifold nuts

86803056

Fig. 56 After the nuts are removed, the manifold can be removed from the engine

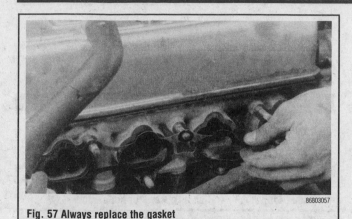

Fig. 57 Always replace the gasket

86803057

4. If equipped, remove the Air Suction (AS) and Exhaust Gas Recirculation (EGR) crossover pipes.

5. Remove the exhaust manifold heat shield.

6. If applicable, remove the exhaust manifold bracket bolts.

7. Using a crisscross pattern (starting from the center), remove the exhaust manifold-to-cylinder head nuts, the manifold and the gaskets (discard them).

8. Using a putty knife or similar tool, clean the gasket mounting surfaces. Inspect the mating faces with a straightedge, checking that they are not warped.

To install:

9. Using a new gasket and nuts, place the manifold into position and support it. Install the nuts snug on the studs.

10. If applicable, install the support bracket(s) below the manifold. Tighten the bolts holding the bracket(s) to the manifold to 17 ft. lbs. (24 Nm).

11. Starting with the inner or center nuts, tighten the nuts in a crisscross pattern to the correct torque. The tension must be even across the entire face of the manifold if leaks are to be prevented. Correct torque is 23 ft. lbs. (32 Nm).

12. Install the heat shield or shroud. Tighten the bolts to 16 ft. lbs. (22 Nm).

13. Connect the AS pipe. Tighten the connections to 50 ft. lbs. (70 Nm).

14. Connect the EGR pipe.

a. On carbureted engines, tighten the exhaust manifold connection to 43 ft. lbs. (60 Nm) on all models except the 1987 Prelude. On the 1987 Prelude, tighten to 36 ft. lbs. (50 Nm). Tighten the intake manifold connection to 36 ft. lbs. (50 Nm) on Accords to 1989 and Preludes to 1987. On 1988–1990 Preludes, tighten it to 43 ft. lbs. (60 Nm).

b. On fuel injected engines, tighten the exhaust manifold connection to 43 ft. lbs. (60 Nm) and the nuts at the intake manifold to 9 ft. lbs. (12 Nm). Use a new gasket.

15. If applicable, install the oxygen sensors. Tighten to 33 ft. lbs. (45 Nm).

16. Connect the exhaust pipe, using new gaskets and nuts. Tighten the exhaust pipe-to-manifold nuts to 40 ft. lbs. (55 Nm).

Accord V-6

▶ See Figure 58

➡ **Breaking loose exhaust manifold bolts is one of the nastiest jobs around. They are usually rusted solid; a generous application of penetrating oil several hours before beginning the job will make it easier.**

1. Disconnect the negative battery cable.

2. Position a clean drain pan under the radiator and remove the radiator cap. Drain the cooling system.

3. Remove the radiator.

4. Detach the starter cable from the strut tower brace. Remove the brace.

5. If necessary for additional clearance, remove the vacuum control box on the firewall. Position it aside with the vacuum hoses attached.

6. Raise and safely support the vehicle.

7. Remove the front wheels, then remove the splash shield from under the engine.

8. Remove the center beam.

9. Disconnect the exhaust pipe from the exhaust manifolds and the catalytic converter. Remove it from the vehicle.

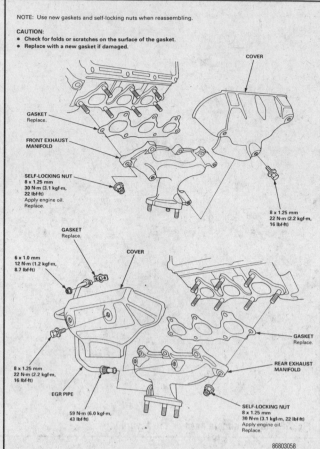

NOTE: Use new gaskets and self-locking nuts when reassembling.

CAUTION:
● Check for folds or scratches on the surface of the gasket.
● Replace with a new gasket if damaged.

COVER

GASKET
Replace.

FRONT EXHAUST
MANIFOLD

SELF-LOCKING NUT
8 x 1.25 mm
30 N·m (3.1 kgf·m,
22 lbf·ft)
Apply engine oil.
Replace.

8 x 1.25 mm
22 N·m (2.2 kgf·m,
16 lbf·ft)

GASKET
Replace.

6 x 1.0 mm
12 N·m (1.2 kgf·m,
8.7 lbf·ft)

COVER

GASKET
Replace.

REAR EXHAUST
MANIFOLD

8 x 1.25 mm
22 N·m (2.2 kgf·m,
16 lbf·ft)

EGR PIPE

59 N·m (6.0 kgf·m,
43 lbf·ft)

SELF-LOCKING NUT
8 x 1.25 mm
30 N·m (3.1 kgf·m, 22 lbf·ft)
Apply engine oil.
Replace.

86803058

Fig. 58 Exploded view of the exhaust manifolds used on the Accord V-6

10. Remove the bolts securing the heat shields on the exhaust manifolds. It will be necessary to work from above and below the engine.

11. Remove the EGR crossover pipe from the engine.

12. Remove the nuts securing the manifolds to the cylinder heads. Once again, it will be necessary to work from above and below the engine. Remove the manifolds and gaskets from the engine.

To install:

13. Using new gaskets and nuts, place the manifolds into position. Lightly oil the threads, then install the nuts snug on the studs.

14. Starting with the inner or center nuts, tighten the nuts in a crisscross pattern to the correct torque. The tension must be even across the entire face of the manifold if leaks are to be prevented. Correct torque is 22 ft. lbs. (30 Nm).

15. Install the EGR crossover pipe with a new gasket. Tighten the nuts to 9 ft. lbs. (12 Nm) and the exhaust manifold connection to 43 ft. lbs. (59 Nm).

16. Install the heat shields on the manifolds. Tighten the bolts to 16 ft. lbs. (22 Nm).

17. Install the exhaust pipe with new nuts and gaskets. Tighten the exhaust manifold connections to 40 ft. lbs. (54 Nm) and the catalytic converter to 25 ft. lbs. (33 Nm).

18. Install the center beam. Tighten the bolts to 37 ft. lbs. (50 Nm).

19. Install the splash shield and front wheels.

20. Install the vacuum control box and the radiator.

21. Install the strut tower brace and secure the starter cable. Tighten the bolts to 16 ft. lbs. (22 Nm).

22. Fill the cooling system.

23. Start the engine and allow it to reach normal operating temperature. Check for leaks.

Radiator

❄❄ CAUTION

DO NOT attempt to open the cooling system when the engine is hot; the system will be under pressure and scalding may occur. Wait until the radiator and hoses are cool to the touch; generally a period of hours after the engine was operated.

REMOVAL & INSTALLATION

▶ **See Figures 59, 60, 61 and 62**

1. Position a clean drain pan under the radiator and remove the radiator cap. Drain the cooling system.
2. Unplug the electrical connectors from the thermo-switch and the cooling fan motor.
3. Disconnect the coolant hoses from the radiator.
4. On cars with automatic transaxles, disconnect and plug the transaxle fluid cooler lines.
5. If necessary for additional clearance, remove the radiator fans.
6. Remove the retaining bolts and remove the radiator.

➡ **When removing the radiator, take care not to damage the core and fins. Take note of the rubber mounts or bushings; they must be replaced in their exact original positions.**

7. If not already done so, the fan can now be easily unbolted from the radiator.
8. Inspect the hoses for damage, leaks and/or deterioration; if necessary, replace them. If the radiator fins are clogged, wash off any insects or dirt with low pressure water. Fins may be straightened using a blunt, non-metallic tool such as an ice cream stick.

To install:

9. When installing, fit the radiator into place, making certain the rubber bushings or grommets are in place at the bottom and/or sides of the mounts.
10. Install the retaining bolts, tightening them to 7 ft. lbs. (10 Nm).
11. On automatic transaxles, connect the cooler hoses to the radiator using new clamps.
12. Connect the coolant hoses to their ports; use new hose clamps.
13. If applicable, install the fans.
14. Engage the electrical connections.
15. Double check the drain plug on the radiator, making sure it is closed. Refill the coolant.
16. On cars with automatic transaxles, check the transaxle fluid level. Add if necessary.
17. Start the engine and allow it to reach normal operating temperature. Check for leaks. Recheck the fluid levels.

Engine Fans

REMOVAL & INSTALLATION

▶ **See Figures 63 and 64**

1. Disconnect the negative battery cable.
2. On some models, it may be necessary to disconnect the coolant hoses from the radiator to allow clearance for removing the fans. If so, drain the cooling system, then disconnect the hoses.
3. Unplug the fan electrical connections.
4. Remove the mounting bolts holding the fan shroud and remove the shroud with the fan. Once removed, the fan blade may be unbolted from the shaft and the fan motor removed from the shroud.

To Install:

5. Position the fan on the radiator and install the mounting bolts. Tighten them to 5 ft. lbs. (7 Nm).

Fig. 59 Disconnect the reservoir tank hose from the filler neck . . .

Fig. 60 . . . as well as the other coolant hoses from the radiator

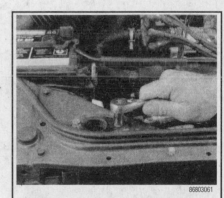

Fig. 61 Remove the bolts securing the radiator to the vehicle

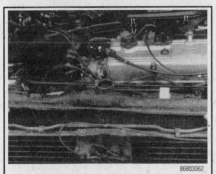

Fig. 62 Be careful not to damage the core and fins when removing the radiator from the vehicle

Fig. 63 The fan shrouds are secured to the radiator with a series of small bolts

Fig. 64 When removing the fan shroud, be careful not to damage the radiator cooling fins

6. Engage the electrical connections.
7. If applicable, refill the cooling system.
8. Start the engine and allow it run until it reaches normal operating temperature. Check that the fan(s) turn on. Check for leaks.

Water Pump

REMOVAL & INSTALLATION

➡These operations require removal of many individual components. Some are more easily performed from either above or below, depending on your arm length and agility. Whenever you must elevate the car, it MUST be safely supported on jackstands. Never work under a car supported only by a jack.

1984–89 Accord and 1984–87 Prelude

▶ See Figure 65

1. Disconnect the negative battery cable.
2. Place a clean drain pan under the radiator and drain the cooling system.
3. Break loose (do not remove) the water pump pulley bolts.
4. Loosen and remove the water pump drive belt.
5. Remove the pulley bolts and remove the pulley.
6. Remove the water pump retaining bolts and the O-ring. Discard the O-ring.
7. Clean the mounting surfaces.

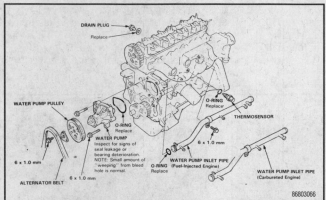

Fig. 65 The water pump on early model Accords and Preludes is driven by an accessory belt

To install:

8. Use a new O-ring and install the pump to the block. Make certain the O-ring does not deform or move.
9. Install the retaining bolts, tightening them to 9 ft. lbs. (12 Nm).
10. Install the pulley and pulley bolts; tighten the pulley bolts to 9 ft. lbs. (12 Nm).
11. Install the belt and adjust it to the proper tension; do not overtighten the belt.
12. Refill the engine coolant.
13. Start the engine and check for leaks.

1990–95 Accord and 1988–95 Prelude

▶ See Figures 66 and 67

➡This operation requires removal of the timing belt. Do not attempt to replace the water pump if you are not familiar with timing belt procedures.

1. Disconnect the negative battery cable.
2. Turn the engine to align the timing marks and set cylinder No. 1 to TDC on the compression stroke. Once in this position, the engine must NOT be turned or disturbed.
3. Drain the engine coolant. Use a clean container and cap it when full. Wipe up spillage immediately.

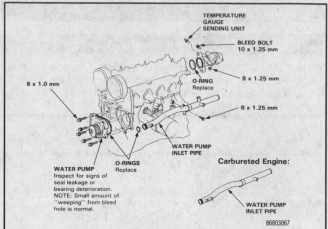

Fig. 66 On later model Accords and Preludes, the water pump is driven by the timing belt

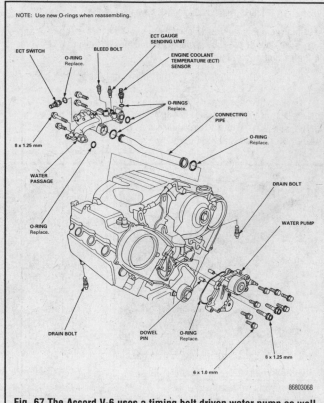

Fig. 67 The Accord V-6 uses a timing belt driven water pump as well

4. Remove the timing belt.
5. Remove the bolts holding the water pump; pay attention to the locations of any bigger or longer bolts.
6. Remove the water pump and the O-ring.
To install:
7. Replace the O-ring and install the water pump. Make certain the O-ring does not deform or come out of place. Tighten the mounting bolts to 9 ft. lbs. (12 Nm). On the Accord V-6, tighten the 8mm bolts to 16 ft. lbs. (22 Nm) and the 6mm bolts to 9 ft. lbs. (12 Nm).
8. Install the timing belt.
9. Refill the engine coolant.
10. Connect the negative battery cable.
11. Start the engine, allowing it to idle. Check the work area carefully for any sign of fluid leakage or any indication of the belt rubbing or slapping the covers. Bleed the cooling system.
12. Shut the engine off. Reinstall the splash shield.

Cylinder Head

REMOVAL & INSTALLATION

Except Accord V-6

♦ See Figures 68 thru 78

➡The cylinder head temperature must be below 100°F (38°C); allow the engine to cool several hours if the car has been recently driven. Turn the crankshaft pulley so that the number one piston is at Top Dead Center (TDC) of the compression stroke.

1. Disconnect the battery ground cable.
2. Drain the cooling system.
3. Remove the air cleaner and intake duct assembly.

4. Label and remove the brake booster, PCV and charcoal canister vacuum hoses from the intake manifold.
5. Remove the engine ground cable from the cylinder head or valve cover.
6. Relieve the fuel pressure using the proper procedure. Disconnect the fuel lines.
7. Disconnect the accelerator cable at the throttle body or carburetor. On automatic transaxle vehicles, also disconnect the throttle control cable.
8. Disconnect and tag all the wire harnesses and vacuum hoses from the cylinder head, intake manifold and throttle body/carburetor. Disconnect the spark plug wires, then position them aside.
9. Disconnect the upper radiator hose. Remove the heater hoses from the cylinder head.
10. If equipped, remove the cruise control actuator. Do not disconnect the cable; move the actuator out of the work area with the cable attached.
11. Remove accessory drive belts.
12. Disconnect the inlet hose from the power steering pump and plug the

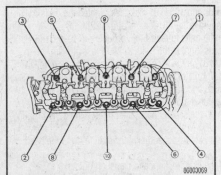

Fig. 68 Bolt loosening sequence on 1990–93 Accords and 1992–95 Preludes with 2.2L engines

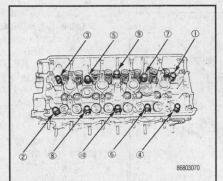

Fig. 69 Bolt loosening sequence on 1992–95 Preludes with 2.3L engines

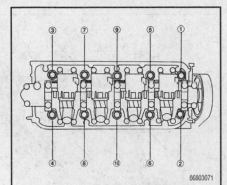

Fig. 70 Bolt loosening sequence on 1994–95 Accords

Fig. 71 A breaker bar is helpful for loosening the cylinder head bolts

Fig. 72 Have an assistant help lift the cylinder head assembly off the engine

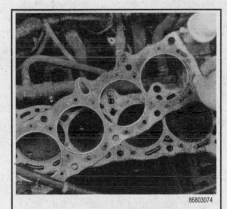

Fig. 73 Never reuse the old gasket

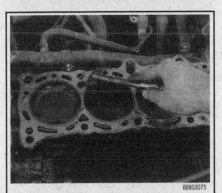

Fig. 74 Carefully use a scraper to remove any remaining gasket material

Fig. 75 Always tighten the bolts with a torque wrench

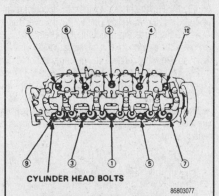

CYLINDER HEAD BOLTS

Fig. 76 Cylinder head bolt torque sequence A

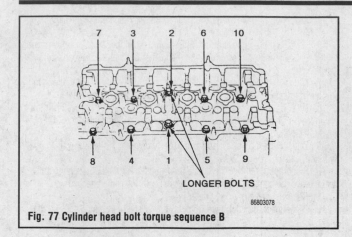

Fig. 77 Cylinder head bolt torque sequence B

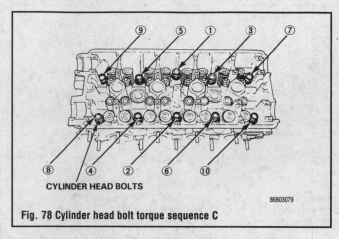

Fig. 78 Cylinder head bolt torque sequence C

hose immediately to prevent fluid leakage. Remove the power steering pump from the cylinder head and position it aside.

➡**When the power steering hose is disconnected, the fluid will flow out. Cover the alternator with a shop towel to prevent the fluid from leaking into it.**

13. If the alternator is mounted to the cylinder head, remove it.

14. Remove the power steering and alternator brackets if they are mounted on the cylinder head.

15. Remove the distributor. Be sure to scribe a line relating the position of the distributor to the engine for easy installation.

16. If equipped, remove the cylinder sensor next to the distributor.

17. Remove the valve cover.

18. Remove the timing belt.

➡**Do not crimp or bend the timing belt.**

19. Remove the exhaust header pipe nuts and the header pipe bracket (if equipped). Pull the pipe away from the exhaust manifold.

20. If equipped, remove the EGR crossover and air suction pipes.

21. On Accords through 1989 and Preludes through 1991, the cylinder head can be removed with the intake and exhaust manifolds either still attached or removed. On other models, the manifolds should be removed first.

22. On some engines, it will be necessary to remove the camshaft holders, camshafts and rocker arms to access the cylinder head bolts. If so, refer to the proper procedures in this section.

23. Remove the cylinder head bolts in sequence (take notice of any bolt holes occupied by longer bolts). Failure to follow this procedure may cause the head to warp.

  a. On 1984–89 Accords and 1984–91 Preludes, work from the ends toward the center. Loosen each bolt about ½ turn each time and make several passes to release the tension evenly.

  b. On 1990–95 Accords and 1992–95 Preludes, follow the loosening sequence shown in the illustrations. Loosen each bolt about ⅓ turn each time. Repeat the sequence until all bolts are loosened.

24. Remove the cylinder head. The head may resist removal, even with the bolts out. Tap the edge of the head with a plastic or rubber mallet; lift the head straight up to remove it.

25. Remove the cylinder head gasket and clean the mating surfaces.

26. If applicable, remove the intake and exhaust manifolds from the cylinder head.

To install:

27. Install a new head gasket on the engine, making certain it is positioned correctly. The cylinder head dowel pins and the oil jet must be in place. Refer to the illustrations if necessary.

28. Install the head. Lower it straight down onto the block, aligning it correctly.

29. Apply clean engine oil to the bolt threads and the contact face of the bolt head. Install the head bolts finger-tight.

30. On all models except 1988–89 DOHC Prelude and 1992–95 Preludes with 2.3L and VTEC engines, tighten the head bolts following sequence A. On 1988–89 DOHC Preludes, use sequence B. Use sequence C on 1992–95 Preludes with 2.3L and VTEC engines.

  a. On 1984–89 Accords and 1984–91 Preludes, tighten the bolts in two passes. The first pass should bring the bolts to about 22 ft. lbs. (30 Nm). On the second pass, tighten the bolts to their final torque of 49 ft. lbs. (68 Nm).

  b. On 1990–93 Accords, tighten the bolts to 29 ft. lbs. (40 Nm) on the first pass, 51 ft. lbs. (70 Nm) on the second pass, then tighten the bolts to their final torque of 78 ft. lbs. (108 Nm).

  c. On 1994–95 Accords and 1992–95 Preludes, the bolts are also tightened in three passes. Tighten the bolts to 29 ft. lbs. (40 Nm) on the first pass, 51 ft. lbs. (70 Nm) on the second pass, then tighten the bolts to their final torque of 72 ft. lbs. (100 Nm).

31. If applicable, assemble the intake and exhaust manifolds to the head. Use new gaskets.

32. If applicable, install the cam, rockers and camshaft holders.

33. If equipped, install the EGR crossover and air suction pipes.

34. Connect the exhaust pipe to the manifold using new nuts.

35. Install the timing belt.

36. Install the valve cover.

37. Install the cylinder sensor (if equipped) and the distributor.

38. If applicable, install the alternator.

39. Install the power steering pump, then connect the inlet hose to the pump.

40. Install the accessory drive belts. Adjust the belt tensions.

41. Install the heater hoses.

42. Install the cruise control actuator if it was removed.

43. Connect the spark plug wires. Connect all the wire harnesses and vacuum hoses to the cylinder head, intake manifold and throttle body/carburetor.

44. Connect the throttle control cable and/or accelerator cable at the throttle body.

45. Connect the fuel lines.

46. Install the brake booster, PCV and charcoal canister vacuum hoses.

47. Install the air cleaner and intake duct.

48. Refill the engine coolant. It is recommended that the engine oil be changed whenever a cylinder head is removed.

49. Connect the negative battery cable.

50. Start the engine, allowing it to idle. Bleed the cooling system. Check the work area carefully for any signs of fluid leakage or any indication of the timing belt rubbing or slapping the covers.

Accord V-6

▶ **See Figures 79 thru 84**

➡**The cylinder head temperature must be below 100°F (38°C); allow the engine to cool several hours if the car has been recently driven. Turn the crankshaft pulley so that the number one piston is at Top Dead Center (TDC) of the compression stroke.**

1. Disconnect the battery ground cable.

2. Drain the cooling system.

3. Remove the air intake duct.

4. Disconnect the accelerator and cruise control cables from the throttle body. Loosen the locknuts, then slip the cable ends out of the linkage.

5. Detach the starter cable from the strut tower brace, then remove the brace.

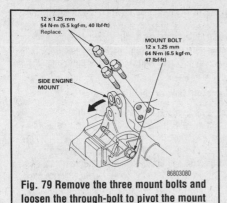

Fig. 79 Remove the three mount bolts and loosen the through-bolt to pivot the mount out of the way

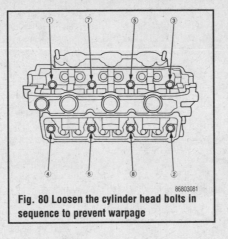

Fig. 80 Loosen the cylinder head bolts in sequence to prevent warpage

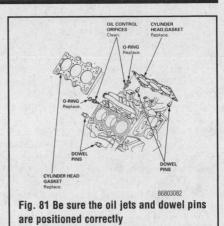

Fig. 81 Be sure the oil jets and dowel pins are positioned correctly

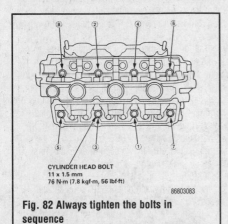

Fig. 82 Always tighten the bolts in sequence

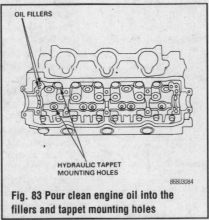

Fig. 83 Pour clean engine oil into the fillers and tappet mounting holes

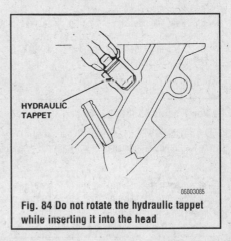

Fig. 84 Do not rotate the hydraulic tappet while inserting it into the head

6. Relieve the fuel pressure by loosening the service bolt on the top of the fuel filter about a turn. Disconnect the fuel feed hose from the filter. Remove the fuel return hose.

7. Label and disconnect all vacuum hoses from the throttle body, intake manifold and cylinder head.

8. Disconnect the water bypass hose from the throttle body.

9. Remove the accessory drive belts.

10. Disconnect the engine ground cable.

11. Remove the vacuum pipe assembly.

12. Support the engine with a floor jack on the oil pan (use a cushion between the jack and pan). Tension the jack so that it is just supporting the engine but not lifting it.

13. Remove the three mount bolts, then loosen the through-bolt. Pivot the side engine mount out of the way.

14. Disconnect the inlet hose from the power steering pump, then plug the hose and pump. Remove the power steering pump.

15. Remove the harness cover and ground cable from the water passage.

16. Label and disconnect all wiring harnesses from the cylinder head, intake manifold and throttle body.

17. Disconnect the spark plug wires from the cylinder head, then remove the distributor.

18. Remove the upper and lower radiator hoses, then the heater hoses.

19. Remove the Intake Air Bypass (IAB) vacuum tank.

20. Remove the water passage. Discard the O-rings.

21. Remove the harness covers from the intake manifold.

22. Remove the EGR crossover pipe.

23. Remove the intake manifold.

24. Remove the exhaust manifolds.

25. Remove the valve covers and side covers.

26. Remove the timing belt.

27. Remove the camshaft pulleys and back covers.

28. Remove the camshaft holder plates, camshaft holders and camshafts.

29. Remove the rocker arms, exhaust inner rocker arms and pushrods.

30. Remove the cylinder head bolts using the sequence shown in the illustration. Loosen each bolt about ⅓ turn each time. Repeat the sequence until all

bolts are loosened. Failure to follow this procedure may result in cylinder head warpage.

31. Clean the gasket mounting surfaces.

To install:

32. Install new head gaskets on the engine, making certain they are positioned correctly. The cylinder head dowel pins and the oil jets must be in place. Refer to the illustrations if necessary.

33. Install the head. Lower it straight down onto the block, aligning it correctly.

34. Apply clean engine oil to the cylinder head bolts and washers.

35. Torque the cylinder head bolts (following the sequence in the illustration) in two progressive steps. First to 29 ft. lbs. (39 Nm), then to 56 ft. lbs. (76 Nm).

36. Pour clean engine oil into the cylinder head hydraulic tappet mounting holes, up to the level of the oil path. Also, pour clean engine oil into the fillers on the cylinder head (refer to the illustration).

37. Install the hydraulic tappets into the cylinder head. Do not rotate the hydraulic tappet while inserting it into the head.

38. Install the pushrods and rocker arms. Be sure to install each part in its original position. Loosen the rocker arm adjusting screws and locknuts before installation.

39. Install the camshafts and camshaft oil seals. Install the camshaft holders and plates (refer to the procedures in this section).

40. Install the back covers and camshaft pulleys. Tighten the back cover bolts to 9 ft. lbs. (12 Nm) and the pulley bolts to 23 ft. lbs. (31 Nm).

41. Install the timing belt.

42. Adjust the exhaust rocker arms. Refer to the Rocker Arm procedures in this section.

43. Install the side covers and valve covers.

44. Install the intake manifold.

45. Install the exhaust manifold.

46. Install the EGR crossover pipe.

47. Install the water passage with new O-rings. Tighten the bolts to 16 ft. lbs. (22 Nm).

48. Install the IAB vacuum tank. Tighten the bolts to 9 ft. lbs. (12 Nm).

49. Install the heater hoses, then the upper and lower radiator hoses.

50. Install the distributor. Connect the spark plug wires.

51. Connect the wiring harnesses to the intake manifold, cylinder head and throttle body as applicable.

52. Install the ground cable and harness cover at the water passage.

53. Install the power steering pump and connect the inlet hose.

54. Install the side mount (refer to the engine removal and installation procedure). Remove the jack supporting the engine.

55. Install the vacuum pipe assembly. Tighten the bolts to 9 ft. lbs. (12 Nm).

56. Install the engine ground cable.

57. Install, then tension the accessory drive belts.

58. Connect the water bypass hose to the throttle body.

59. Connect the vacuum hoses to the intake manifold, cylinder head and throttle body as applicable.

60. Connect the fuel lines. Use new gaskets.

61. Install the strut tower brace and attach the starter cable. Tighten the bolts to 16 ft. lbs. (22 Nm).

62. Connect the cruise control and accelerator cables to the linkage to the throttle body.

63. Install the air intake duct.

64. Refill the cooling system. It is recommended that the engine oil be changed whenever a cylinder head is removed.

65. Reconnect the battery ground cable. Start the engine and bleed the cooling system. Check for leaks.

CLEANING AND INSPECTION

♦ See Figures 85, 86, 87, 88 and 89

1. Using a wire brush chucked into an electric drill, remove all the carbon from the combustion chambers in the head. Be careful not to scratch the valve seats.

2. Use a gasket scraper and remove all material from the manifold and head surfaces, again being careful not to scratch the surface.

3. Refer to the valve removal and installation procedures in this section and remove the valves from the cylinder head.

TCCS3802

Fig. 85 Using a wire brush chucked into an electric drill, remove all the carbon from the combustion chambers in the head

4. Use a valve guide brush or a fine-bristled rifle bore brush with solvent to clean the valve guides.

5. Use a clean cloth and a stiff bristle brush with solvent to thoroughly clean the head assembly. Make sure that no material is washed into the bolt holes or passages. If possible, dry the head with compressed air to remove fluid and solid matter from all the passages.

➡**Do not clean the head in a hot tank or chemical bath.**

6. Measure the valve stem clearance as follows:

   a. Mount a dial indicator on one side of the cylinder head rocker arm cover gasket rail.

   b. Locate the indicator so movement of the valve stem from side-to-side (crosswise to the head) will cause a direct movement of the indicator stem. The indicator stem must contact the side of the valve stem just above the valve guide.

   c. Install the valve (without the springs) and prop the valve head about 0.39 in. (10mm) off the valve seat.

   d. Move the stem of the valve from side-to-side using light pressure to obtain a clearance reading. If the clearance exceeds specification (refer to the valve specifications chart), it will be necessary to knurl or replace the valve guides.

7. Check the camshaft journal oil clearance. If the clearance is greater than specified, check the total run-out and the journal diameters of the camshaft. If they are within specification, the cylinder head must be replaced. If they are out of specification, replace the camshaft, then recheck the oil clearances. If the oil clearances are still out of specification, the cylinder head must also be replaced.

8. With the head clean and dry, use a precision straightedge and a feeler gauge to measure the head for warpage. If it is less than 0.002 in. (0.05mm), resurfacing is not required. If warpage is between 0.002–0.008 in. (0.05–0.2mm), the head must be resurfaced. Any warpage in excess of this requires replacement of the head.

9. If all is well with the head to this point, it is highly recommended that it be taken to a professional facility such as a machine shop for sophisticated crack testing. The various procedures are much more reliable than simple examination by eye. The cost is reasonable and the peace of mind is well worth the cost. If any cracks are found, the head must be replaced.

10. While the head is being checked, carefully scrape the carbon from the tops of the pistons. Don't scratch the metal of the piston tops and don't damage the cylinder walls. Remove all the carbon and fluid from the cylinder.

11. If repairs are needed to the valves, camshaft or other components, follow the appropriate procedures outlined in this section.

RESURFACING

The Honda cylinder heads for all engines may be resurfaced by a reputable machine shop. Resurfacing is recommended if the engine suffered a massive overheating, such as from a failed head gasket.

The heads are manufactured to be as light as possible; consequently, there is not much excess metal on the face. Any machining must be minimal. If too much metal is removed, the head becomes unusable. A head which exceeds the maximum warpage specification CANNOT be resurfaced. The machine shop will have a list of minimum head thicknesses; at no time may this minimum be exceeded.

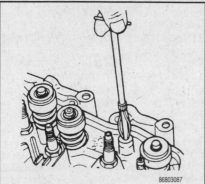

86803087

Fig. 86 Use a guide brush to clean the valve guides

86803088

Fig. 87 A dial indicator can be used to check the valve stem clearance

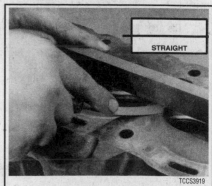

STRAIGHT

TCCS3919

Fig. 88 Check for warpage across the head surface . . .

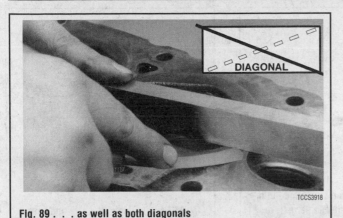

Fig. 89 . . . as well as both diagonals

Valves

REMOVAL & INSTALLATION

▶ **See Figures 90, 91, 92 and 93**

➥This procedure requires the use of a valve spring compressor. This common tool is available at most auto supply stores. It may also be possible to rent one from a tool supplier. It is absolutely essential that all components be kept in order after removal. Old ice trays make excellent holders for small parts. The containers should be labeled so that the parts may be reinstalled in their original location. Keep the valves in numbered order in a holder such as an egg carton or an inverted box with holes punched in it. Label the container so that each valve may be replaced in its exact position. (Example: Exhaust No. 1, No. 2, etc.)

1. Following the procedures outlined in this section, remove the head from the engine then remove the rocker arms and camshaft.

2. Compress the valve spring (using a valve spring compressor) and remove the keepers at the top of the valve.

3. Slowly release the tension on the compressor and remove it. Remove the spring retainer (upper cap), the valve spring, the valve stem oil seal and the lower spring seat. Keep the springs in their correct orientation; they must be reinstalled exactly as they were, not upside down.

4. The valve is then removed from the bottom of the head.

5. Repeat for each valve in the head, keeping them labeled and in order.

6. Thoroughly clean and decarbon each valve. Inspect each valve and spring as outlined later in this section.

To install:

7. Lubricate the the valve stem and guide with clean engine oil. Install the valve in the cylinder head and position the lower spring seat.

8. Lubricate the new valve stem seal with clean engine oil and install it.

9. Install the valve spring and the upper seat, compress the spring and install the two keepers. Relax tension on the compressor and make sure everything is properly placed. Tap the spring retainer of the installed valve with a plastic mallet to ensure proper locking of the retainers.

10. Complete the reassembly of the head by installing the camshafts and rocker arms. Refer to the procedures in this section.

INSPECTION AND LAPPING

▶ **See Figures 94, 95, 96, 97 and 98**

➥Accurate measuring equipment capable of reading to 0.0001 (ten thousandths) inch is necessary for this procedure.

Inspect the valve faces and seats for pits, burned spots, and other evidence of poor seating. The valve can be refaced to remove pits and carbon. If the valve is in such poor shape that refacing it will reduce the margin thickness out of specification, discard the valve. Never try to straighten and reuse a bent valve. It is recommended that any seat resurfacing or valve refacing be done by a reputable machine shop.

Fig. 90 Be careful not to lose the valve keepers

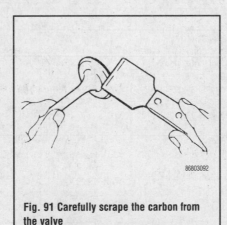

Fig. 91 Carefully scrape the carbon from the valve

Fig. 92 Always use new valve stem seals

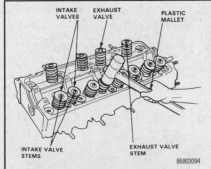

Fig. 93 Lightly tap the spring retainer of the installed valve with a plastic mallet to ensure proper locking of the retainers

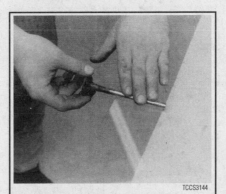

Fig. 94 Valve stems may be rolled on a flat surface to check for bends

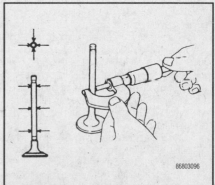

Fig. 95 Measure the valve stem at these points with a micrometer

Fig. 96 If the margin thickness is less than specified, replace the valve

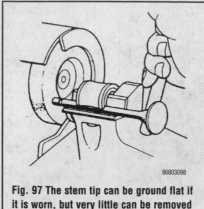

Fig. 97 The stem tip can be ground flat if it is worn, but very little can be removed

Fig. 98 Hand lapping the valve and seat

Check the valve stem for scoring and/or burned spots. If the stem and head are in acceptable condition, clean the valve thoroughly with solvent to remove all gum and varnish.

Use the micrometer to measure the diameter of the valve stem. Compare the reading to the Valve Specifications Chart. If not within specification, replace the valve.

The valve head margin thickness should be checked both before and after refacing. If at any time it is below the minimum thickness specification, it must be replaced. The specifications are as follows:

- Accords through 1989 and Preludes through 1991—Intake: 0.045 in. (1.15mm) Exhaust: 0.057 in. (1.45mm)
- 1990–95 four cylinder Accords—Intake: 0.026 in. (0.65mm) Exhaust: 0.037 in. (0.95mm)
- Accord V-6—Intake: 0.045 in. (1.15mm) Exhaust: 0.057 in. (1.45mm)
- 1992–95 Preludes with SOHC engines—Intake: 0.026 in. (0.65mm) Exhaust: 0.037 in. (0.95mm)
- 1992–95 Preludes with DOHC engines (except VTEC)—Intake: 0.026 in. (0.65mm) Exhaust: 0.033 in. (0.85mm)
- 1992–95 Preludes with DOHC VTEC engines—Intake: 0.033 in. (0.85mm) Exhaust: 0.057 in. (1.45mm)

Check the top of each valve stem for pitting, mushrooming and unusual wear due to improper rocker adjustment, etc. The stem tip can be ground flat if it is worn, but very little can be removed. If more than just a touch of grinding is needed to make the tip flat and square, the valve must be replaced. If the valve stem tips are ground, make sure you fix the valve securely into a jig designed for this purpose. The tip must contact the grinding wheel squarely at exactly 90 degrees. Most machine shops that handle automotive work are equipped for this job.

The valves should also be checked for proper seat contact.

1. Apply a thin coat of prussian blue (or white lead) to the valve face and place the valve in the head.

2. Apply light pressure to the valve, but do not rotate it.

3. Carefully remove the valve from the head then check the valve and seat. If blue appears 360 degrees around the valve seat, the seat and valve are concentric.

4. Check that the seat contact is in the middle of the valve face.

5. If the valve and seat are not concentric or the seat contact is not in the middle of the valve face, you should consult a reputable machine shop for proper refacing.

6. After machine work has been performed on valves/seats, it may be necessary to lap the valves to assure proper contact. For this, you should first consult your machine shop to determine if lapping is necessary. Some machine shops will perform this for you as part of the service, but the precision machining which is available today often makes lapping unnecessary. Additionally, the hardened valves/seats used in modern automobiles may make lapping difficult or impossible. If your machine shop recommends that you lap the valves proceed as follows:

a. Coat the valve face and seat with a light coat of valve grinding compound. Attach the suction cup end of the valve grinding tool to the head of the valve (it helps to moisten it first).

b. Rotate the tool between the palms, changing position and and lifting the tool often to prevent grooving. Lap in the valve until a smooth, evenly polished surface is evident on both the seat and face.

c. Remove the valve from the head. Wipe away all traces of grinding compound from the surfaces. Clean out the valve guide with a solvent-soaked rag. Make sure there are NO traces of compound in or on the head.

d. Proceed through the remaining valves, lapping them one at a time to their seats. Clean the area after each valve is done.

e. When all the valves have been lapped, thoroughly clean or wash the head with solvent. There must be NO trace of grinding compound present.

REFACING

Due to the skill involved and the high cost of purchasing the proper equipment, it is recommended that valve refacing be handled by a reputable machine shop.

Valve Stem Seals

▶ **See Figure 99**

REPLACEMENT

Cylinder Head Installed

▶ **See Figure 100**

1. Disconnect the negative battery cable.

2. Remove the valve cover, camshaft and rockers using the procedures outlined in this section.

3. Remove the spark plugs.

4. Attach a fixture at the flywheel to prevent the engine from rotating. Make sure the fixture will not damage any components in case of movement.

5. Thread an adaptor into the spark plug hole that can be hooked up to an air compressor hose.

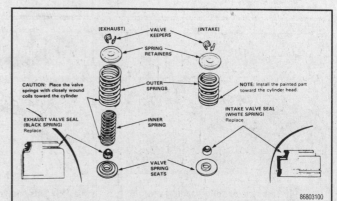

Fig. 99 Valve spring and seal components commonly used on most Honda engines. Note that some models do not use double springs

6. Apply 90 psi (620 kPa) of compressed air to the adaptor hose. This is done to keep the valves from dropping down into the cylinder when the valve springs are removed.

✳✳ CAUTION

To avoid personal injury, wear eye and ear protection. Keep hands and clothing away from engine parts that move in case air pressure does cause rotation.

7. With the cylinder under pressure, remove the valve spring retainer and the spring using a spring compressor tool. Hitting the spring retainer lightly with a soft hammer may help loosen the valve keepers if the retainer will not move downwards exposing the keepers.

✳✳ WARNING

DO NOT push the valve downwards into the cylinder when the spring is removed. Doing so will only introduce the potential of the valve dropping into the cylinder, possibly causing valve, piston, and cylinder wall damage. Head removal would be required to retrieve it.

8. Release tension on the spring compressor and lift it clear of the valve. Remove the retainer and the valve spring(s). Keep the springs in their correct orientation; they must be reinstalled exactly as they were, not upside down.

9. Remove the valve seal, either with your fingers or with a valve seal removal tool.

To install:

10. Install the new valve seal. Make certain the seal is firmly placed against the spring seat.

11. Install the valve spring, retainer and keepers. Follow procedures described earlier.

12. Release the air pressure from the cylinder.

13. Install the rockers, camshaft, and valve cover as described in this section. Adjust the valves as necessary.

14. Install the spark plugs.

15. Connect the negative battery cable.

Cylinder Head Removed

▶ See Figure 101

1. Remove the cylinder head. Use the procedures outlined earlier in this section

2. Remove the camshaft, rockers, valve springs and retainers using the appropriate procedures. Keep the springs in their correct orientation; they must be reinstalled exactly as they were, not upside down.

3. Remove the valve seal, either with your fingers or with a valve seal removal tool.

To install:

4. Install the new valve seal. Make certain the seal is firmly placed against the spring seat.

5. Install the valve spring, retainer and keepers. Follow procedures described earlier.

6. Install the rockers and camshaft as described in this section. Install the cylinder head.

7. Adjust the valves as necessary.

Valve Springs

REMOVAL & INSTALLATION

Valve spring removal and installation is part of the valve removal and installation procedure covered earlier in this section.

INSPECTION

▶ See Figure 102

Valve springs should be checked while the valve train is disassembled. Place each valve spring on a flat surface next to a steel square. Measure the length of the spring, and rotate it against the edge of the square to measure distortion. If spring length varies (by comparison) by more than 0.039 in. (1mm) or if distortion exceeds 0.039 in. (1mm), replace the spring.

Honda does not offer a specification for spring tension. Springs will loose tension over time and may even break. This loss of tension will have a direct effect on engine performance. In addition, if a valve spring were to break, engine damage could result. Because of this, it is a good idea to replace the springs if the head is being rebuilt. They are usually a fairly inexpensive item and a worthwhile investment.

Valve Seats

The valve seats in the engines covered in this guide are all non-replaceable and must be recut when service is required. Seat recutting requires special tools and experience, and should be handled at a reputable machine shop. Seat concentricity should also be checked by a machinist.

Valve Guides

REMOVAL & INSTALLATION

Replacing the valve guides involves heating the head to high temperatures and driving the old guide out with the use of special tools. The head may have to be machined for an oversize guide if the bushing bore dimension is over the standard specifications. The new guide is then reamed for the proper valve stem-to-guide clearance. This repair requires a high level of mechanical skill and should only be performed by a reputable machine shop.

Valve guides which are not excessively worn or distorted may, in some cases, be knurled rather than replaced. Knurling is a process in which metal inside the valve guide bore is displaced and raised, thereby reducing clearance. The possibility of knurling rather than replacing the guides should be discussed with a machinist.

Fig. 100 This type of spring compressor can be used to remove the springs with the head still installed

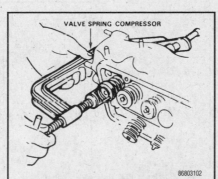

Fig. 101 This compressor, which resembles a C-clamp, can be used to compress the springs with the cylinder head removed

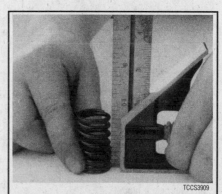

Fig. 102 Measure the length of the spring and check for squareness

Hydraulic Valve Lifters/Tappets

➡This procedure applies only to the Accord V-6.

REMOVAL & INSTALLATION

♦ See Figures 83 and 84

1. Disconnect the negative battery cable.
2. Remove the valve and side covers.
3. Remove the camshafts.
4. Remove the inner rockers arms and pushrods. Be sure to mark them for correct installation later.
5. Pull the tappets from their bores in the cylinder head. The lifters must be installed in their original bores. Be sure to mark them for correct installation later.
6. Inspect the tappets.

To install:

7. Pour clean engine oil into the tappet bores, up to the level of the oil path. Also, pour clean engine oil into the fillers on the cylinder head (refer to the illustration).
8. Install the hydraulic tappets into the cylinder head. Do not rotate the hydraulic tappet while inserting it into the head.
9. Install the pushrods and rocker arms. Be sure to install each part in its original position. Loosen the outer rocker arm adjusting screws and locknuts before installation.
10. Install the camshafts.
11. Adjust the exhaust rocker arms. Refer to the Rocker Arm procedures in this section.
12. Install the side and valve covers.
13. Start the engine and check for leaks.

INSPECTION

♦ See Figures 103 and 104

➡Never attempt to disassemble the tappets.

1. Check the tappets for wear, damage and clogged oil holes. Replace any tappets as necessary.
2. Insert a 0.078 in. (2mm) thick brass rod into the tappet. Do not substitute anything else for this rod, as damage to the tappet may result.
3. Submerge the tappet in a container filled with clean 10W-30 engine oil.
4. Slowly push, then release the rod until there are no more air bubbles coming out of the tappet.

➡Keep the tappet upright and below the surface of the oil while you push and release the rod.

5. Mount a dial indicator onto a surface plate, then position the tappet under the plunger of the indicator. Set the plunger with approximately 0.118 in. (3mm) of preload, then zero the dial indicator.

6. Quickly compress the plunger of the tappet by hand. Record the compression stroke as measured by the dial indicator. The stroke should be 0.0004–0.003 in. (0.01–0.008mm). If it is not within specfication, replace the tappet.

Oil Pan

REMOVAL & INSTALLATION

♦ See Figures 105 thru 111

❋❋ CAUTION

The EPA warns that prolonged contact with used engine oil may cause a number of skin disorders, including cancer! You should make every effort to minimize your exposure to used engine oil. Protective gloves should be worn when changing the oil. Wash your hands and any other exposed skin areas as soon as possible after exposure to used engine oil. Soap and water, or waterless hand cleaner should be used.

1. Disconnect the negative battery cable.
2. Firmly apply the parking brake and block the rear wheels.
3. Raise and support the front of the vehicle on jackstands.
4. Drain the engine oil.
5. If necessary for additional clearance, remove the center beam.
6. Disconnect the exhaust pipe from the exhaust manifold(s), then position it aside or remove it from the vehicle.
7. If equipped with flywheel dust shield, it may be necessary to remove it for access.
8. If equipped, disconnect the breather hose from the oil pan.
9. Remove the oil pan nuts/bolts (in a crisscross pattern) and the oil pan. If necessary, use a mallet to tap the corners of the oil pan. DO NOT pry on the pan to get it loose.
10. Remove and discard the old gasket.

To install:

11. Use a new gasket. Apply sealant at the inner corners of the pan, where it matches to the crank seals.
12. Install the pan. Tighten the nuts/bolts to 10 ft. lbs. (14 Nm). Use an alternating or crisscross pattern to tighten the nuts and bolts.
13. If applicable, connect the breather hoses to the oil pan.
14. Install and/or connect the exhaust pipe to the manifold.
15. Install the flywheel dust cover, center beam and lower mount if they were removed.
16. Lower the vehicle to the ground. Install clean, fresh oil.
17. Start the engine, allowing it to idle. Check for leaks.

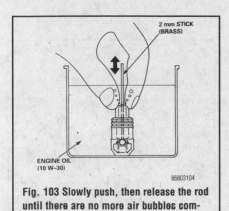

Fig. 103 Slowly push, then release the rod until there are no more air bubbles coming out of the tappet

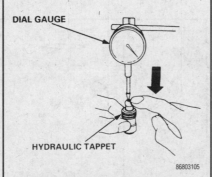

Fig. 104 Use a dial indicator to check the compression stroke of the tappet

Fig. 105 On most models, it will be necessary to remove the center beam to access the oil pan

Fig. 106 After disconnecting the exhaust pipe from the manifold, the bracket securing the pipe to the engine block should be removed

Fig. 107 The dust shield is secured by several small bolts

Fig. 108 The dust shield may require some maneuvering to remove. Be careful not to damage it

Fig. 109 If equipped, the breather hose must be disconnected from the oil pan

Fig. 110 After its attaching bolts are removed, the oil pan can be removed from the engine. Never pry on the pan to get it loose

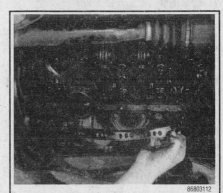

Fig. 111 The gasket must always be replaced

Oil Pump

REMOVAL & INSTALLATION

1984–87 Prelude and 1984–89 Accord

▶ See Figure 112

1. Disconnect the negative battery cable.
2. Remove the timing belt.
3. On 1984–85 Accord and 1984 Prelude, remove the oil pump drive pulley by unbolting it. Use caution; this nut has LEFT-HAND threads. On later models, the pulley is secured to the shaft by other means and comes off with the front pump cover.
4. Remove the oil pump retaining bolts/nuts; remove the oil pump.
5. Clean the gasket mounting surfaces.

Fig. 112 On early model Accords and Preludes, the oil pump is driven by the timing belt

6. Remove the pump cover-to-pump housing bolts and the cover.
7. Inspect the pump for wear and/or damage; replace the parts, if necessary.
8. Reassemble the pump assembly and torque the pump cover-to-pump housing bolts to 5 ft. lbs. (7 Nm).

To install:

9. Using a new O-rings, install the pump. Tighten the oil pump mounting nut and bolts to 9 ft. lbs. (12 Nm).
10. Install the oil pump drive pulley if it was removed. Apply thread sealant before the nut is installed. Remember that the nut is left-hand threaded. Tighten the nut to 22 ft. lbs. (30 Nm).
11. Reinstall the timing belt and set the tension correctly.
12. Start the engine and check for leaks.

1990–95 Four Cylinder Accords and 1988–95 Preludes

▶ See Figures 113 and 114

1. Disconnect the negative battery cable.
2. Raise and safely support the vehicle.
3. Drain the engine oil.
4. Bring the No. 1 cylinder to TDC.
5. Remove the valve cover and upper timing belt cover.
6. Remove the power steering pump belt and the alternator belt and the air conditioning belt if so equipped.
7. Remove the crankshaft pulley and the lower timing belt cover.
8. On Accords and 1992–95 Preludes, remove the following:
   a. Timing balancer belt.
   b. Timing belt.
   c. Timing belt tensioner.
   d. Timing balancer belt tensioner.
   e. Timing belt drive pulley.
   f. Timing balancer belt driven pulley. Insert a suitable tool into the maintenance hole in the front balancer shaft in order to hold the shaft in place and remove the front balancer driven pulley.
   g. Balancer drive gear case

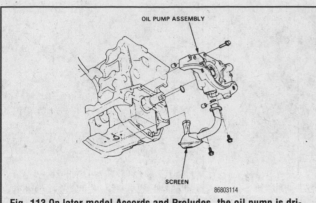

Fig. 113 On later model Accords and Preludes, the oil pump is driven directly by the crankshaft

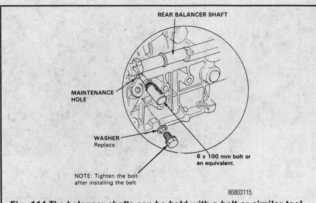

Fig. 114 The balancer shafts can be held with a bolt or similar tool through the maintenance holes

h. Balancer driven gear. Remove the maintenance hole bolt from the cylinder block next to the rear balancer shaft. Insert a 6x100mm bolt or equivalent, to a depth of 3 in. (74mm) through the maintenance hole and into the rear balancer shaft. Remove the balancer shaft driven gear.

9. On 1988–91 Preludes, remove the following:
   a. Timing belt tensioner.
   b. Timing belt.
   c. Timing belt drive pulley.

10. Remove the oil pan and oil screen.

11. Remove the oil pump mount bolts and the oil pump assembly.

To install:

12. Make sure all gasket mating surfaces are clean prior to installation.

13. Inspect the crankshaft oil seal and replace as necessary prior to installing the oil pump.

14. Apply liquid gasket to the cylinder block mating surface of the block. Apply a light coat of oil to the crankshaft seal lip. Install a new O-ring on the cylinder block and install the oil pump. Apply liquid gasket to the threads of the oil pump mounting bolts and tighten them to 9 ft. lbs. (12 Nm).

➡ Once the sealant is applied, do not wait longer than 15 minutes to install the parts; the sealant will become ineffective. After final assembly, wait at least 30 minutes before adding oil to the engine, giving the sealant time to set.

15. Install the oil screen.

16. On Accords and 1992–95 Preludes, perform the following procedure:
   a. Apply molybdenum disulfide grease to the thrust surfaces of the balancer gears, before installing the balancer driven gear and the balancer drive gear case.
   b. Hold the rear balancer shaft with the 6x100mm bolt or equivalent, then install the balancer driven gear and the balancer drive belt pulley. Tighten the retaining bolt to 18 ft. lbs. (25 Nm).
   c. Hold the front balancer shaft with a suitable tool, then install the tim-

ing balancer belt driven pulley. Tighten the retaining bolt to 22 ft. lbs. (30 Nm).
   d. Install the balancer gear case to the oil pump. Align the groove on the pulley edge to the pointer on the gear case when holding the rear balancer shaft with the 6x100mm bolt or equivalent, then install the gear case. Tighten the balancer gear case bolts to 18 ft. lbs. (25 Nm).
   e. Remove the 6x100mm bolt and install the maintenance hole bolt.

17. Install the oil pan and the remainder of the components. Be sure to properly tension the timing belt after installation. Tighten the crankshaft pulley bolt to specification.

18. Start the engine and check for leaks.

Accord V-6

▶ **See Figures 115 and 116**

1. Disconnect the negative battery cable.
2. Raise and safely support the vehicle.
3. Drain the engine oil.
4. Bring the No. 1 cylinder to TDC.
5. Remove the splash shield from under the vehicle.
6. Remove the timing belt.
7. Unplug the crankshaft position sensor. Loosen the bolts securing it to the engine, then remove it from the vehicle.
8. Remove the timing belt tensioner.
9. Remove the stopper plate next to the timing belt drive pulley.
10. Remove the oil filter. Disconnect the oil pressure switch terminal and remove the bolts from the filter base. Remove the oil filter base from the engine.
11. Remove bolts securing the oil screen, baffle plate, oil pass pipe and oil pump. Remove components from the engine.

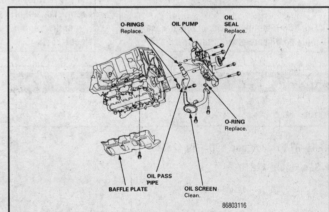

Fig. 115 The oil pump used on the Accord V-6 is driven directly by the crankshaft

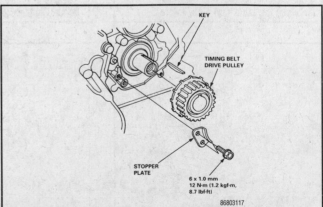

Fig. 116 The stopper plate is positioned next to the timing belt drive pulley

To install:

12. Make sure all gasket mating surfaces are clean prior to installation.

13. Inspect the oil seal and replace as necessary prior to installing the oil pump.

14. Apply liquid gasket to the pump housing, then apply a coat of grease to the seal lip. Install the oil pump. Apply liquid gasket to the threads of the oil pump mounting bolts. Tighten the 6mm bolts to 9 ft. lbs. (12 Nm) and the 8mm bolts to 16 ft. lbs. (22 Nm).

➡ **Once the sealant is applied, do not wait longer than 15 minutes to install the parts; the sealant will become ineffective. After final assembly, wait at least 30 minutes before adding oil to the engine, giving the sealant time to set.**

15. Install the oil pass pipe, baffle plate and oil screen. Use new O-rings. Tighten the bolts to 9 ft. lbs. (12 Nm).

16. Apply liquid gasket to the areas shown in the illustration. Install the oil pan with a new gasket.

17. Install the remainder of the components. Be sure to properly tension the timing belt after installation. Tighten the crankshaft pulley bolt to specification.

18. Start the engine and check for leaks.

INSPECTION & OVERHAUL

➡ **These procedures are performed with the oil pump removed from the engine.**

1984–87 Prelude and 1984–89 Accord

▶ **See Figures 117, 118 and 119**

1. Check the radial clearance between the inner and outer rotors. Maximum clearance is 0.008 in. (0.20mm).

2. Check the axial clearance between the housing cover and the outer rotor. The limit is 0.006 in. (0.15mm).

3. Remove the pump housing cover.

4. Check the housing-to-outer rotor radial clearance. Maximum allowable clearance is 0.008 in. (0.20mm).

5. Inspect the rotors for scoring or other damage.

6. If the rotors require replacement, install the inner and outer rotors with the punch marks aligned adjacent to one another.

7. Install new seals and O-rings in the case halves. If applicable, use a seal driver of the correct diameter to install the shaft seal. Gently drive the seal in until the driver contacts the cover.

8. Reassemble the pump. Use threadlocking compound on the small pump case screws. Tighten them to 5 ft. lbs. (7 Nm).

9. Make sure the pump turns without any binding or locking.

1988–95 Prelude and 1990–95 Accord

▶ **See Figures 120, 121 and 122**

1. With the oil pump removed, separate the housing and cover by removing the bolts.

2. Check the radial clearance between the inner and outer pump rotors. The wear limit is 0.008 in. (0.20mm).

3. Check the axial clearance between the pump housing and the outer rotor. Use a precision straightedge across the housing. Maximum clearance is 0.005 in. (0.12mm).

4. Inspect the radial clearance between the housing and the outer rotor. The wear limit is 0.008 in. (0.20mm).

5. Visually check both rotors for cracking or scoring. Replace them as needed.

6. Remove the oil seal and O-rings. Install a new one with the proper diameter seal driver. Gently tap the seal into place until the driver contacts the housing.

7. Reassemble the pump. Apply thread locking compound to the bolts and tighten them to 5 ft. lbs. (7 Nm). Check that the oil pump turns freely without any binding or locking.

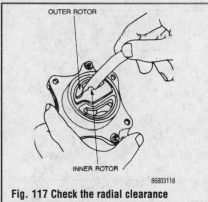

Fig. 117 Check the radial clearance between the inner and outer rotors

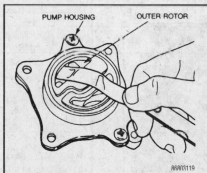

Fig. 118 The axial clearance between the housing cover and outer rotor must also be checked

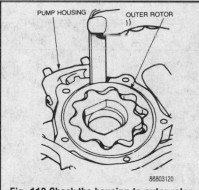

Fig. 119 Check the housing-to-outer rotor radial clearance as well

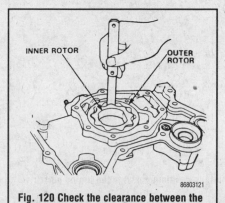

Fig. 120 Check the clearance between the inner and outer rotors

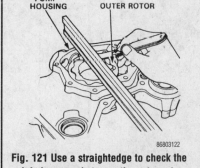

Fig. 121 Use a straightedge to check the axial clearance between the outer rotor and housing

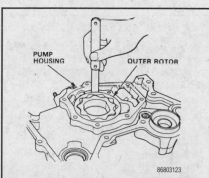

Fig. 122 The radial clearance between the outer rotor and housing must also be checked

Crankshaft Pulley

REMOVAL & INSTALLATION

▶ See Figures 123, 124 and 125

1. Disconnect the negative battery cable.
2. Remove the accessory drive belts.
3. If necessary, secure the crankshaft with a flywheel holding tool.

➡**For some engines, a special pulley holder tool is available to secure the pulley while removing and installing the bolt (refer to the illustration).**

4. Remove the crankshaft pulley bolt.

➡**This bolt can be difficult to remove. Spray the bolt with penetrating oil and allow it to soak overnight.**

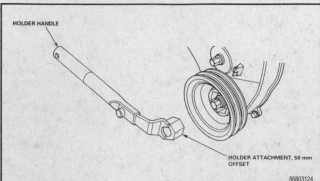

Fig. 123 On some engines, a special holding tool is available to secure the pulley

Fig. 124 After the bolt is removed, the pulley can be removed from the crankshaft

Fig. 125 Always tighten the bolt with a torque wrench

5. Carefully remove the pulley from the crankshaft. Do not pry it off.
6. Remove the key from the crankshaft sprocket. Be sure not to lose it.
7. If necessary, remove the tool holding the crankshaft.

To install:

8. Install the key on the crankshaft sprocket, then slide the pulley onto the crank.
9. Apply clean engine oil to the threads of the crank pulley bolt, but not to the contact surfaces of the washer.
10. Secure the crankshaft either with a flywheel holding tool, or if applicable, the pulley holder tool.
11. Tighten the pulley bolt as follows:

- 1984–89 Accord and 1984–87 Prelude—83 ft. lbs. (115 Nm)
- 1988–90 carbureted Prelude—83 ft. lbs. (115 Nm)
- 1988–91 fuel injected Prelude—108 ft. lbs. (150 Nm)
- 1990 Accord—166 ft. lbs. (230 Nm)
- 1991–93 Accord and 1992–93 Prelude—159 ft. lbs. (220 Nm)
- 1994–95 Accord and Prelude—181 ft. lbs. (245 Nm)

12. Install the accessory drive belts.

Timing Belts and Covers

REMOVAL & INSTALLATION

1984–89 Accord and 1984–87 Prelude

▶ See Figures 126 thru 131

1. Rotate the crankshaft to align the flywheel pointer to Top Dead Center (TDC) of the No. 1 cylinder's compression stroke.
2. Remove the valve cover and upper timing belt cover bolts and the covers.
3. Loosen the alternator and remove the pulley belt(s).
4. On all vehicles with externally driven water pumps, remove the water pump pulley bolts, the belt and the pulley.
5. Remove the crankshaft pulley.

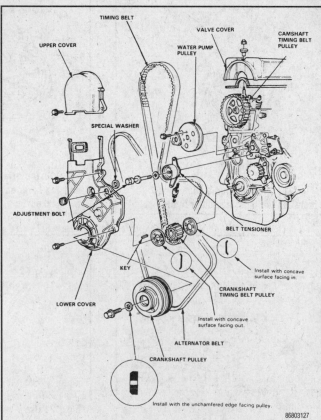

Fig. 126 Timing belt and components used on 1984–89 Accord and 1984–87 Prelude

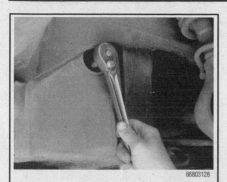

Fig. 127 The crankshaft can be rotated through the access hole in the splash shield

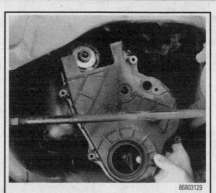

Fig. 128 The lower timing belt cover can be removed from under the vehicle

Fig. 129 Be sure the engine is properly positioned. Note the UP mark on the cam pulley

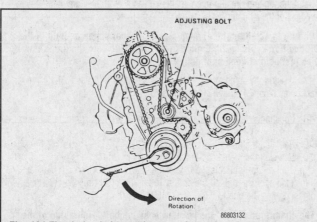

Fig. 130 Don't forget to install the timing belt guides

Fig. 131 The timing belt must be properly tensioned to prevent early belt failure

➡Expect this bolt to be very tight. Make certain the vehicle is securely supported before applying force to the bolt; the amount of force required may cause the car to become unstable on the jackstands.

6. Remove the timing belt cover retaining bolts and the timing belt covers.

7. Loosen but do not remove the belt adjuster locking bolt. Move the adjuster (against the spring tension) to relax the belt and secure the adjusting bolt to hold the adjuster in the loosened position.

8. Use a piece of chalk or a marker to place an identifying arrow on the timing belt. The arrow can identify the direction of rotation or the outer edge of the belt. The belt must be reinstalled so it moves in the same direction. Carefully remove the belt from the pulleys without crimping it. Protect the belt from oil, coolant, etc. It's an even better idea to replace the belt at this point.

9. Inspect the teeth of the pulleys and sprockets, making sure the faces are clean and square.

To install:

10. Double check the position of the engine. The timing pointer must be aligned with the white mark on the flywheel; the cam pulley must be set so the small dot or the word UP is vertical and the marks on the edges of the pulley are aligned with the surface of the head.

11. Fit the belt to the engine and slide it onto the cam pulley.

12. Loosen the adjusting bolt slowly, allowing the adjuster to move against the belt. Tighten the adjuster bolt temporarily.

13. Install the lower timing belt cover.

14. Install the crankshaft pulley and key.

15. Adjust the timing belt tension. Loosen the adjusting bolt. Rotate the crankshaft counterclockwise until the camshaft pulley has moved 3 teeth. Tighten the adjusting bolt to 31 ft. lbs. (43 Nm).

16. Install the water pump belt and pulley. Tighten the pulley bolts to 9 ft. lbs. (12 Nm).

17. Install the drive belts, tension them properly and secure the alternator.

18. Install the upper timing belt cover and the valve cover.

19. Start the engine, allowing it to idle. Listen carefully for any indication of the belt rubbing or slapping the covers.

1988–91 Prelude

▸ See Figures 132, 133 and 134

1. Disconnect the negative battery cable.

2. Turn the engine to align the timing marks and set cylinder No. 1 to TDC on the compression stroke. Once in this position, the engine must NOT be turned or disturbed.

3. Drain the engine coolant. Use a clean container and cap it when full. Wipe up spillage immediately.

4. Support the engine with a floor jack on the oil pan (use a cushion between the jack and pan). Tension the jack so that it is just supporting the engine but not lifting it.

5. Remove the side engine support bolts and nuts, then remove the side mount. Remove the cruise control actuator if so equipped; move the actuator out of the way without disconnecting or kinking the cable.

6. Remove the splash shield from below the engine.

7. Loosen the adjusting nut for the power steering belt and remove the belt. Remove the adjusting pulley and the power steering pump. Move the pump out of the way with the hoses attached.

8. Disconnect the wiring at the alternator. Remove the alternator through-bolt; remove the mounting and adjusting bolts and remove the alternator and belt.

9. On cars with air conditioning, remove the compressor mounting bolts. Remove the compressor and belt. Do not disconnect the lines from the compressor. Position the compressor out of the way and support it with stiff wire.

10. On fuel injected vehicles, remove the ignition wires from the valve cover and remove the harness protector from the cylinder head.

11. Remove the valve cover.

12. Unfasten the crankshaft bolt and remove the crankshaft pulley.

➡This bolt is one of the tightest on the entire car. The pulley must be held in place while the bolt is loosened. One trick is to wrap an old drive belt around the pulley to hold it steady—don't try this with a belt that is to go back on the car; it will be stretched or damaged.

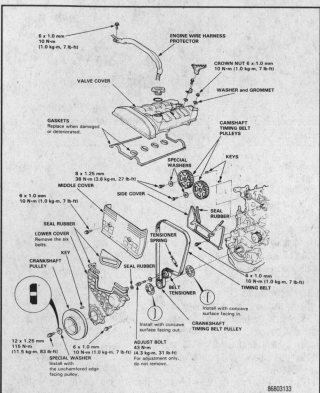

Fig. 132 Timing belt and components used on DOHC Prelude engines

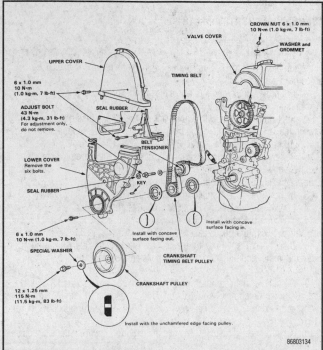

Fig. 133 Timing belt and components used on SOHC Prelude engines

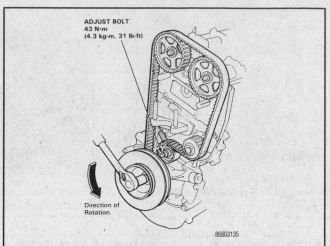

Fig. 134 Rotate the crankshaft counterclockwise until the camshaft pulley has moved 3 teeth, then tighten the adjuster bolt to the specified torque

13. Remove the timing belt covers.

14. Loosen, but do not remove, the adjusting bolt on the timing belt tensioner. Move the tensioner off the belt and retighten the bolt.

15. Use a piece of chalk or a marker to place an identifying arrow on the timing belt. The arrow can identify the direction of rotation or the outer edge of the belt. The belt must be reinstalled so it moves in the same direction. Carefully remove the belt from the pulleys without crimping it. Protect the belt from oil, coolant, etc. It's an even better idea to replace the belt at this point.

To install:

16. Double check the engine position; it must be at TDC for No. 1 cylinder. All of the following conditions must be met: The timing pointer is aligned with the white mark on the flywheel or flexplate, the UP mark on each camshaft pulley is at the top and the alignment marks on each cam pulley are aligned with the edges of the cylinder head.

➡On fuel injected engines, each of the camshafts may be held in the TDC position by inserting 5mm diameter punches into the alignment holes just behind each cam pulley.

17. If using the same timing belt, install it so that it rotates in the same direction as before. Remove the punches holding the cams if they were installed.

18. Loosen the tensioner adjusting bolt, and allow it to apply pressure to the belt.

19. Reinstall the lower belt cover.

20. Reinstall the crankshaft pulley and key. Coat the threads of the bolt with light oil, but do not lubricate the face of the bolt which contacts the washer. On fuel injected engines, tighten the bolt to 108 ft. lbs. (150 Nm); on carbureted engines, tighten the bolt to 83 ft. lbs. (115 Nm).

➡The chamfered side of the washer faces the bolt. Tightening of the bolt is best accomplished with the wheels blocked, the parking brake applied and the transmission in gear (manual) or in Park (automatic).

21. Loosen the timing belt adjuster bolt. Rotate the crankshaft counterclockwise until the camshaft pulley has moved 3 teeth to create tension on the belt. Tighten the adjuster bolt to 31 ft. lbs. (43 Nm).

22. Install the valve cover and the upper belt covers. On fuel injected vehicles, reinstall the ignition wires and the harness protector.

23. Reinstall the A/C compressor and belt. Tighten the mounting bolts to 18 ft. lbs. (25 Nm).

24. Reinstall the alternator and belt.

25. Install the power steering pump and belt, tightening the bolts to 20 ft. lbs. (27 Nm).

26. Adjust the accessory belt tensions.

27. Install the side engine mount and the cruise control actuator if it was removed. Tighten the engine mount bolts to 29 ft. lbs. (40 Nm) and the nuts to 47 ft. lbs. (65 Nm).

28. Refill the engine coolant.
29. Connect the negative battery cable.
30. Start the engine, allowing it to idle. Check the work area carefully for any sign of fluid leakage or any indication of the belt rubbing or slapping the covers. Bleed the cooling system.
31. Shut the engine off. Reinstall the splash shield.

1990–95 4-Cylinder Accord and 1992–95 Prelude

▶ See Figures 135, 136, 137 and 138

1. Disconnect the negative battery cable.
2. Turn the engine to align the timing marks and set cylinder No. 1 to TDC on the compression stroke. Once in this position, the engine must NOT be turned or disturbed. On DOHC Preludes without VTEC, hold each of the camshafts in the TDC position by inserting 5mm diameter punches into the alignment holes just behind each cam pulley.
3. Remove the splash shield from below the engine.
4. Drain the engine coolant. Use a clean container; cap or cover the container and wipe up spillage.
5. Unplug the electrical connector at the cruise control actuator, then remove the actuator. Don't disconnect the cable; simply move the actuator out of the work area.
6. Remove the belt from the power steering pump. Remove the mounting bolts for the pump. Without disconnecting the hoses, move the pump out of the way.
7. Unplug the alternator wiring and connectors; remove the engine wiring harness from the valve cover.
8. Loosen the adjusting and mounting bolts for the alternator and/or compressor. Remove the drive belt(s).
9. Remove the valve cover.
10. Remove the side engine mount support bracket, if equipped.
11. Remove the upper timing belt cover.
12. Support the engine with a floor jack on the oil pan (use a cushion between the jack and pan). Tension the jack so that it is just supporting the engine but not lifting it.
13. Remove the side engine mount.
14. Remove the dipstick and dipstick tube.
15. Remove the crankshaft pulley bolt and remove the crankshaft pulley.

➡ **This bolt is one of the tightest on the entire car. The pulley must be held in place while the bolt is loosened. One trick is to wrap an old drive belt around the pulley to hold it steady—don't try this with a belt that is to go back on the car; it will be stretched or damaged.**

16. If necessary for additional clearance to remove the lower timing belt cover, remove the two rear bolts from the center beam. Slowly lower the jack and the engine until the clearance is gained.
17. Remove the rubber seal from around the belt tension adjusting nut (do not loosen the nut). Remove the lower timing belt cover.

18. On all models except Prelude with VTEC, lock the timing belt adjuster arm in place using one of the lower cover (6 x 1mm) mounting bolts.

➡ **There are two belts in this system; the one running to the camshaft pulley is the timing belt. The other, shorter one drives the balance shaft and is referred to as the balancer belt or timing balancer belt. Use a piece of chalk or a marker to place an identifying arrow on the belts. The arrow can identify the direction of rotation or the outer edge of the belts. The belts must be reinstalled so it moves in the same direction. Protect the belts from oil, coolant, etc. It's an even better idea to replace the belts at this point.**

19. Loosen the timing belt adjustment nut. Push on the tensioner to relieve tension from the balancer belt, then tighten the nut. Remove the balancer belt.
20. On all models except Prelude with VTEC, loosen the lockbolt installed earlier and the adjusting nut. Push on the tensioner to release the timing belt, then tighten the nut. Carefully remove the timing belt. On Prelude VTEC models, remove the timing belt from the pulleys, then remove the bolts securing the auto-tensioner. Remove the auto-tensioner from the engine.

To install:

21. Check the position of the timing marks. The timing pointer must be perfectly aligned with the TDC (white mark) on the flywheel or flex-plate; the camshaft pulley must be aligned so that the word UP is at the top of the pulley and the marks on the edge of the pulley are aligned with the surfaces of the head. Additionally, the face of the front timing balancer pulley has a mark which must be aligned with the notch on the oil pump body. This pulley is the one to the left crank when viewed from the pulley end.
22. Fit the timing belt over the pulleys and tensioner. On DOHC engines without VTEC, remove the 5mm pin punches from behind the cam pulleys.
23. Except Prelude VTEC models:
  a. Temporarily install the crank pulley and bolt.
  b. Loosen the tensioner adjusting nut 1 turn, then tighten it. Rotate the crankshaft counterclockwise until the camshaft pulley has moved 3 teeth to create tension on the belt. Loosen the nut again, then tighten it to 33 ft. lbs. (45 Nm).

➡ **Always rotate the crankshaft counterclockwise when viewed from the pulley end. Rotating it clockwise will cause improper adjustment and possible damage.**

  c. Tighten the lockbolt installed earlier to lock the timing belt adjuster arm. Remove the crank pulley.
24. On Prelude VTEC models:
  a. Hold the auto-tensioner with the maintenance bolt facing up. Loosen and remove the bolt.

➡ **Handle the tensioner carefully so the oil inside does not spill or leak. Replenish with clean engine oil if any does leak. Total capacity is ¼ fl. oz. (8 ml).**

  b. Clamp the mounting flange of the tensioner in a vise using a cloth or blocks of wood to protect it. Insert a flat blade screwdriver into the maintenance hole. Place the stopper (tool number 14540-P13-003) or an equivalent clamp on the tensioner, then turn the screwdriver clockwise to compress the bottom. Be careful not to damage the threads or the gasket contact surface.
  c. Install the maintenance bolt on the tensioner with a new gasket. Tighten to 6 ft. lbs. (8 Nm).

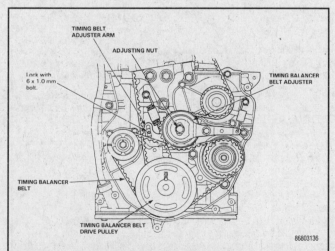

Fig. 135 On all engines except VTEC, the belt adjuster arm must be locked in place using one of the lower cover mounting bolts

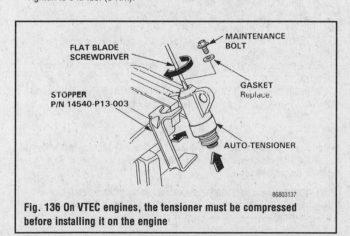

Fig. 136 On VTEC engines, the tensioner must be compressed before installing it on the engine

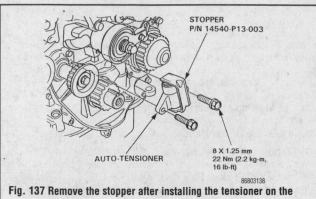

Fig. 137 Remove the stopper after installing the tensioner on the engine

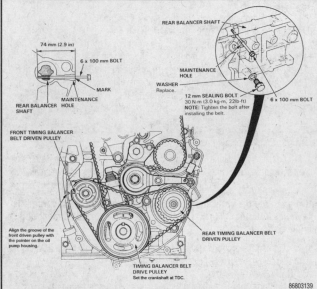

Fig. 138 The balancer shaft must be held in position during timing belt installation

d. Make sure no oil is leaking from around the maintenance bolt, then install the tensioner on the engine. Make sure the stopper stays in place and tighten the bolts to 16 ft. lbs. (22 Nm).

e. Remove the stopper.

25. Make sure all timing marks are positioned correctly (as described earlier).

26. Align the rear timing balancer pulley (to the right of the crank pulley) using a 6x100mm bolt or rod. Mark the bolt or rod at a point 2.913 in. (74mm) from the end. Remove the bolt from the maintenance hole on the side of the block; insert the rod into the hole. Align the 74mm mark with the face of the hole. This pin will hold the shaft in place during installation.

27. Loosen the tensioner adjusting nut and verify that the timing balancer belt adjuster moves freely.

28. Fit the balancer belt over the pulleys. Remove the bolt or rod from the maintenance hole.

29. Temporarily install the crank pulley. Rotate the engine one turn counter-clockwise, then tighten the tensioner adjusting nut to 33 ft. lbs. (45 Nm). Double check the positions of the timing marks and make sure they still line up. If not remove the belts and repeat the procedures.

➥ Both belt adjusters are spring-loaded to properly tension the belts. Do not apply any additional pressure to the pulleys or tensioners while performing the adjustment.

30. Remove the crank pulley. Remove the lockbolt installed earlier on the timing belt adjuster arm. Install the maintenance bolt with a new washer. Tighten it to 22 ft. lbs. (30 Nm).

31. Install the lower cover, making certain the rubber seals are in place and correctly located. Tighten the retaining bolts to 9 ft. lbs. (12 Nm).

32. If applicable, raise the lower beam and engine into place. Install the rear bolts for the lower beam. Tighten them to 28 ft. lbs. (39 Nm) on 1990–91 Accords, 37 ft. lbs. (50 Nm) on 1992–95 Accords and 43 ft. lbs. (60 Nm) on 1992–95 Preludes.

33. Install the key on the crankshaft and install the crankshaft pulley. Apply oil to the bolt threads and tighten it to the following:

- 1990 Accord: 166 ft. lbs. (230 Nm)
- 1991–93 Accord: 159 ft. lbs. (220 Nm)
- 1992–93 Prelude: 159 ft. lbs. (220 Nm)
- 1994–95 Accord and Prelude: 181 ft. lbs. (245 Nm)

34. Install the dipstick tube and dipstick.

35. Install the side engine mount (refer to engine removal and installation for procedures). Remove the jack from under the engine.

36. Install the upper belt cover.

37. Install the side engine mount support bracket if it was removed.

38. Install the valve cover.

39. Install the compressor and/or alternator drive belt; adjust the tension.

40. Route the wiring harness over the valve cover and connect the wiring to the alternator.

41. Install the power steering pump and install the belt.

42. Reinstall the cruise control actuator. Connect the vacuum hose and the electrical connector.

43. Double check all installation items, paying particular attention to loose hoses or hanging wires, untightened nuts, poor routing of hoses and wires (too tight or rubbing) and tools left in the engine area.

44. Refill the engine coolant.

45. Install the splash shield under the engine.

46. Connect the negative battery cable.

47. Start the engine, allowing it to idle. Check for any signs of leakage or any sound of the belts rubbing or binding.

Accord V-6

▶ See Figures 139 and 140

1. Disconnect the negative battery cable.

2. Turn the engine to align the timing marks and set cylinder No. 1 to TDC on the compression stroke. Once in this position, the engine must NOT be turned or disturbed.

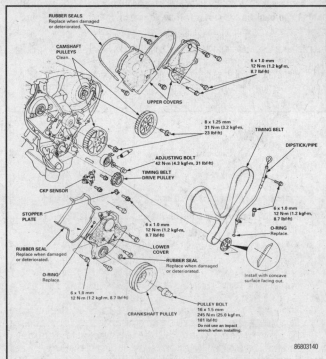

Fig. 139 Timing belt and components used on the Accord V-6

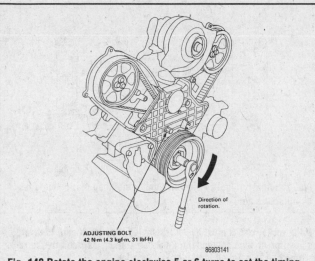

Fig. 140 Rotate the engine clockwise 5 or 6 turns to set the timing belt

3. Raise and safely support the vehicle. Remove the front wheels and the splash shield from below the engine.

4. Drain the engine coolant. Use a clean container; cap or cover the container and wipe up spillage.

5. Support the engine with a floor jack on the oil pan (use a cushion between the jack and pan). Tension the jack so that it is just supporting the engine but not lifting it.

6. Remove the side engine mount.

7. Remove the belt from the power steering pump.

8. Loosen the adjusting and mounting bolts for the alternator and compressor. Remove the drive belt(s).

9. Remove the dipstick and tube.

10. Remove the crankshaft pulley bolt and remove the crankshaft pulley.

➡This bolt is one of the tightest on the entire car. The pulley must be held in place while the bolt is loosened. One trick is to wrap an old drive belt around the pulley to hold It steady—don't try this with a belt that is to go back on the car; It will be stretched or damaged.

11. Remove the upper and lower timing belt covers.

12. Loosen the timing belt adjustment bolt. Push on the tensioner to relieve tension from the belt, then tighten the bolt. Remove the timing belt.

To install:

13. Check the position of the timing marks. The pointer on the oil pump must be perfectly aligned with the TDC mark (keyway) on the timing belt drive pulley; the camshaft pulleys must be aligned so that the marks on the edge of the pulleys are aligned with the notches on the back covers.

14. Fit the timing belt over the pulleys and tensioner in the following sequence.

　a. Timing belt drive pulley (crankshaft).

　b. Tensioner.

　c. Front camshaft pulley (front side of the engine compartment).

　d. Water pump pulley.

　e. Rear camshaft pulley (firewall side of the engine compartment).

➡Make sure the timing belt drive pulley and the camshaft pulleys are still at TDC.

15. Loosen the tensioner adjusting bolt to tension the belt, then tighten it.

16. Install the lower and upper covers, making certain the rubber seals are in place and correctly located. Tighten the retaining bolts to 9 ft. lbs. (12 Nm).

17. Install the crankshaft pulley. Apply oil to the bolt threads and tighten it to 181 ft. lbs. (245 Nm).

18. Rotate the engine clockwise 5 or 6 turns to set the timing belt. Loosen the tensioner adjusting bolt 180 degrees, then tighten it to 31 ft. lbs. (42 Nm).

19. Double check the positions of the TDC timing marks on the crankshaft and camshaft pulleys and make sure they still line up. If not remove the belt and repeat the procedures.

20. Install the dipstick tube and dipstick.

21. Install the side engine mount (refer to engine removal and installation for procedures). Remove the jack from under the engine.

22. Install the compressor and alternator drive belts; adjust the tension.

23. Install the power steering pump belt. Adjust the tension.

24. Double check all installation items, paying particular attention to loose hoses or hanging wires, untightened nuts, poor routing of hoses and wires (too tight or rubbing) and tools left in the engine area.

25. Refill the engine coolant.

26. Install the splash shield under the engine and the front wheels.

27. Connect the negative battery cable.

28. Start the engine, allowing it to idle. Check for any signs of leakage or any sound of the belt rubbing or binding.

Camshaft Sprockets

REMOVAL & INSTALLATION

▶ **See Figures 141 and 142**

1. Disconnect the negative battery cable.

2. Remove the valve cover(s).

3. Loosen the camshaft sprocket bolt. Have an assistant hold the crankshaft pulley center bolt with an appropriate sized wrench to prevent the engine from turning.

4. Turn the crankshaft pulley until cylinder No. 1 is at Top Dead Center of the compression stroke.

5. Remove the timing belt.

6. Remove the center bolt from the sprocket, then carefully remove it from the camshaft. The sprocket is aligned to the shaft with a Woodruff key; don't lose it.

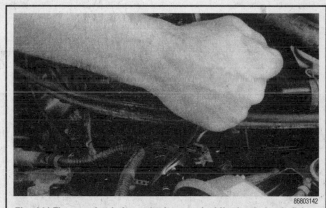

Fig. 141 The sprocket bolt can be loosened while the timing belt is still installed

Fig. 142 Once the timing belt is removed, the sprocket can be pulled from the camshaft

To install:

7. Make certain the groove in the end of the camshaft is facing up. If necessary, the cam(s) may be turned at the faceted casting of the camshaft (do not use the lobes).

8. Install the key, then install the pulley. Make certain the original washer is reinstalled with the retaining bolt. Tighten the retaining bolt to the following:

- Except Prelude with VTEC and Accord V-6—27 ft. lbs. (38 Nm)
- Prelude with VTEC—37 ft. lbs. (51 Nm)
- Accord V-6—23 ft. lbs. (31 Nm)

9. Install the timing belt.

10. Install the valve cover(s).

11. Start the engine. Check the work area carefully for any sign of fluid leakage or any indication of the belt rubbing or slapping the covers.

Camshafts

REMOVAL & INSTALLATION

Four Cylinder Engines

SOHC ENGINES

▶ See Figures 143, 144 and 145

➡Engine temperature must be below 100°F (38°C). To facilitate the installation, make sure that No. 1 piston is at Top Dead Center before removing the camshaft.

1. Disconnect the negative battery cable.
2. Remove the valve cover.
3. Remove the distributor and the camshaft position sensor (if equipped).
4. Remove the timing belt. If necessary, remove the camshaft sprocket.
5. Remove the rocker arms, shafts and holders as an assembly (refer to the rocker arm removal and installation procedure in this section). To keep the assembly together, do not remove the cam holder bolts from the holes.

Fig. 143 After the rocker shaft assembly has been removed, the camshaft can be removed from the cylinder head

Fig. 144 Always discard the old oil seal

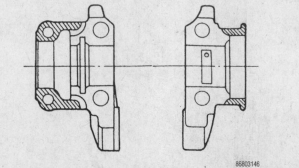

Fig. 145 Apply a liquid gasket sealant to the head mating surfaces of the outer cam holders

➡If the rocker shafts must be disassembled, use great care to catalog the position of each component. Each component, particularly the rockers, must be reinstalled in its original location.

6. Remove the camshaft from the cylinder head.
7. Inspect the camshaft, measuring the lobes and checking for any signs of wear or scoring. Check the journals as well as the lobes carefully.

To install:

8. Wipe the camshaft and the mounting surfaces. Lubricate the cam journals and mounting surfaces with a thin coat of assembly grease.
9. Fit the camshaft to the head with the keyway on the sprocket end facing upward.
10. Install a new camshaft oil seal with the spring end facing inward (towards the valves).
11. Lightly lubricate the cam lobes with clean engine oil.
12. Loosen the locknut and back off the adjusting screw for each rocker arm. Check the integrity of rocker assembly if it was disassembled. If the camshaft was replaced, it is strongly recommended that the rockers be replaced as well.
13. On 1986–95 Accords and 1985–95 Preludes, apply a liquid gasket sealant to the head mating surfaces of the outer cam holders.
14. Set the rocker arm assembly in place and install the bolts finger-tight.
15. Use a seal driver of the proper diameter and reach to seat the camshaft oil seal.
16. Tighten the bolts in the correct pattern two turns at a time (refer to the rocker arm procedures in this section). Keep a close watch to prevent the rockers from binding on the valves. Bring the bolts to final torque evenly and smoothly.
17. Install the camshaft sprocket if it was removed. Install the timing belt.
18. Install the distributor and the camshaft position sensor (if equipped).
19. Adjust the valve clearance. Reinstall the valve cover.

DOHC ENGINES

▶ See Figures 146, 147, 148 and 149

➡Engine temperature must be below 100°F. (38°C). To facilitate the installation, make sure that No. 1 piston is at Top Dead Center before removing the camshaft.

1. Disconnect the negative battery cable.
2. Remove the valve cover.
3. Remove the distributor and the camshaft position sensor (if equipped).
4. Remove the timing belt. If necessary, remove the camshaft sprockets.
5. Loosen the rocker arm adjusting screws.
6. Unscrew the camshaft holder bolts two turns at a time using a crisscross pattern on non-VTEC engines. On VTEC engines, follow the loosening sequence in the illustration. Remove the holders from the cylinder head. Note the positioning of the holders (they are marked) so they may be installed in the same locations.
7. Remove the camshafts from the cylinder head.
8. Inspect the camshaft, measuring the lobes and checking for any signs of wear or scoring. Check the journals as well as the lobes carefully.

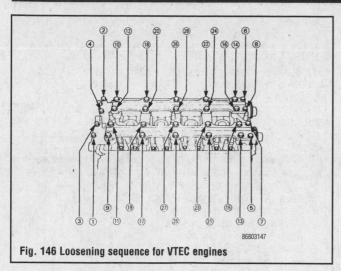

Fig. 146 Loosening sequence for VTEC engines

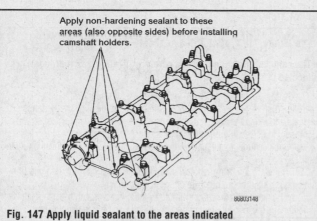

Apply non-hardening sealant to these areas (also opposite sides) before installing camshaft holders.

Fig. 147 Apply liquid sealant to the areas indicated

Specified torque:
Except Intake ⑤, ⑦. Exhaust ⑥, ⑧:
  10 N·m (1.0 kg-m, 7 lb-ft)
Intake ⑤, ⑦. Exhaust ⑥, ⑧:
  12 N·m (1.2 kg-m, 9 lb-ft)

TIGHTENING SEQUENCE

INTAKE

EXHAUST

Fig. 148 Tightening sequence and torque specifications for DOHC engines except VTEC

Specified torque:
①—⑳ 8 x 1.25 mm
  26 N·m (2.6 kg-m, 19 lb-ft)
㉑—㉘ 6 x 1.0 mm
  12 N·m (1.2 kg-m, 9 lb-ft)

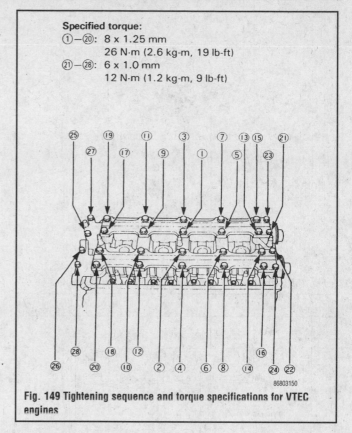

Fig. 149 Tightening sequence and torque specifications for VTEC engines

To install:

9. After cleaning the camshafts and journal surfaces, lubricate both surfaces with the assembly grease.

10. Position the camshafts in the cylinder head so the keyways are facing up (number one cylinder at TDC).

11. Install new camshaft seals with the open (spring) side facing in.

12. Apply liquid gasket to the head mating surfaces of the outer camshaft holders. Install the cam holders with the bolts finger-tight.

➡When installing the cam holders, note that each is lettered, numbered and marked with an arrow. Each holder MUST be put in the correct location.

13. Make sure the oil seals are fully seated in the holders.

14. Tighten the holder bolts two turns at a time using the proper sequence. Refer to the illustration for the proper torque specification.

15. Install the camshaft sprockets and the timing belt.

16. Reinstall the distributor and the cam position sensor (if equipped).

17. Adjust the valves.

18. Install the valve cover.

Accord V-6

▶ See Figures 150, 151 and 152

➡Engine temperature must be below 100°F (38°C). To facilitate the installation, make sure that No. 1 piston is at Top Dead Center before removing the camshaft.

1. Disconnect the negative battery cable.

2. Remove the distributor.

3. Remove the side and valve covers.

4. Remove the timing belt. If necessary, remove the camshaft sprockets.

5. Unscrew the bolts securing the camshaft holders two turns at a time using a crisscross pattern, then remove them from the cylinder head. Note the locations of the different sized bolts.

6. Remove the camshafts from the cylinder head.

7. Loosen the exhaust rocker arms adjusting screws.

8. Inspect the camshafts, measuring the lobes and checking for any signs of wear or scoring. Check the journals as well as the lobes carefully.

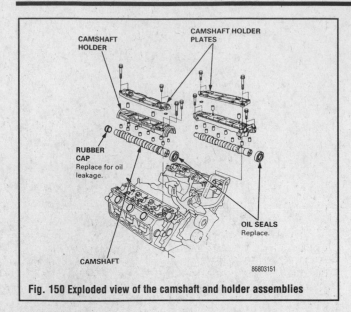

Fig. 150 Exploded view of the camshaft and holder assemblies

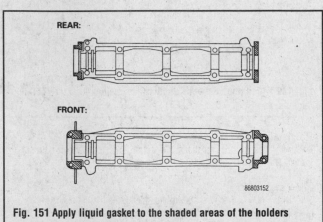

Fig. 151 Apply liquid gasket to the shaded areas of the holders

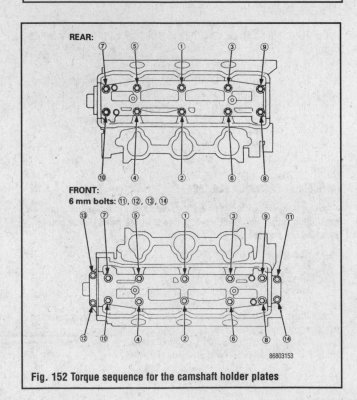

Fig. 152 Torque sequence for the camshaft holder plates

To install:

9. Make sure the rocker arms are properly positioned on the valve stems.

10. Advance the crankshaft 30 degrees from TDC to prevent interference between the pistons and valves.

11. Install new oil seals and rubber caps on the camshafts. Apply liquid gasket around the rubber caps.

12. Lightly lubricate the cam lobes with clean engine oil.

13. Position the camshafts on the cylinder heads. Position the rear camshaft on the cylinder head so that the cam is not pushing on a valve.

14. Apply liquid gasket to the endcaps of the camshaft holders. Install the camshaft holders and plates on the cylinder heads.

15. Apply clean engine oil to the threads of the bolts. Install the bolts and tighten them using the correct sequence. The 6mm bolts should be tightened to 9 ft. lbs. (12 Nm) and the 8mm bolts to 20 ft. lbs. (27 Nm).

16. If applicable, install the camshaft sprockets.

17. Set the camshafts and crankshaft to TDC.

18. Install the timing belt.

19. Adjust the exhaust rocker arms.

20. Install the side and valve covers.

21. Install the distributor.

INSPECTION

▶ **See Figures 153, 154, 155 and 156**

➡**The camshaft must be handled carefully; it will break if dropped or subjected to sharp impact.**

Overhead camshaft engines are very sensitive to proper lubrication with clean, fresh oil. A worn cam may be your report card for poor maintenance intervals and late oil changes. If a new cam is required, order new rockers to accompany it so that there are two new surfaces in contact.

1. Degrease the camshaft using solvent. Clean all the oil grooves and passages.

2. The end-play or thrust clearance of the camshaft is measured with the camshaft installed in the head. To check the end-play:

a. Position the camshaft(s) in the cylinder head. Install the camshaft holders or rocker arm shaft/camshaft holder assembly (as applicable). Be sure the rocker arm adjusting screws are fully loosened.

b. Seat the camshaft(s) by prying it toward the distributor end of the head.

c. Set a dial indicator on the end of the camshaft. Zero the dial indicator against the end of the distributor drive, then pry the camshaft back and forth. Read the end-play; the service limit is 0.020 in. (0.5mm). On DOHC and V-6 engines, perform this for both camshafts. If the end-play is excessive, replace the camshaft, then remeasure. If it is still excessive, the head must be replaced.

3. Remove the camshaft(s) from the cylinder head.

4. Using a micrometer or caliper, measure the height of all the lobes. Record the readings and compare them to the Camshaft Specifications Chart in this section. Any measurement beyond the stated limits indicates wear and the camshaft must be replaced.

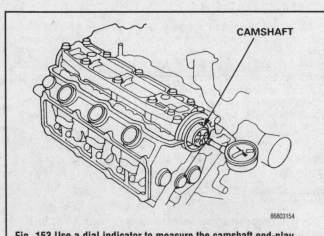

Fig. 153 Use a dial indicator to measure the camshaft end-play

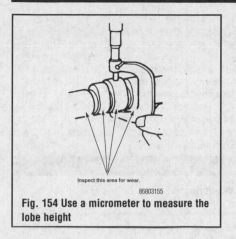

Fig. 154 Use a micrometer to measure the lobe height

Fig. 155 A dial indicator can also be used to measure run-out

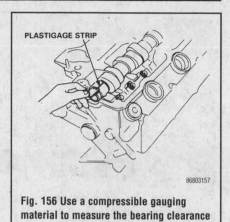

Fig. 156 Use a compressible gauging material to measure the bearing clearance

5. Mount the cam in V-blocks and set the dial indicator up on the round center journal. Zero the dial and rotate the camshaft. The run-out must not exceed the following:
- 1984–89 Accord and 1984–91 Prelude—0.0023 in. (0.06mm)
- 1990–95 4-cylinder Accord and 1992–95 Prelude—0.0015 in. (0.04mm)
- Accord V-6—0.0011 in. (0.03mm)

6. If the run-out is excessive, replace the camshaft.

7. The clearance between the camshaft and its journals must also be checked. Clean the camshaft, the journals and the bearing caps of any remaining oil and place the camshaft in position on the head. Lay a piece of compressible gauging material (Plastigage® or similar) on top of each journal on the cam.

8. Install the camshaft holders or rocker arm shaft/camshaft holder assembly (as applicable). Be sure the rocker arm adjusting screws are fully loosened.

➥Do not turn the camshaft with the gauging material installed.

9. Remove the bearing caps (in the correct order) and measure the gauging material at its widest point by comparing it to the scale provided with the package. The clearance should not exceed the following:
- 1984–89 Accord and 1984–90 SOHC Prelude—Journals 1,3 and 5 are 0.006 in. (0.15mm), journals 2 and 4 are 0.009 in. (0.23mm)
- 1990–95 4-cylinder Accord, 1988–91 DOHC Prelude, 1992–95 DOHC Prelude with VTEC and 1992–95 SOHC Prelude—0.006 in. (0.15mm)
- 1992–95 DOHC Prelude without VTEC—No. 5 exhaust journal is 0.008 in. (0.20mm), other journals are 0.006 in. (0.15mm)
- Accord V-6—0.004 in. (0.10mm)

10. If the clearance is excessive, replace the camshaft, then remeasure. If it is still excessive, the head must be replaced.

Pistons and Connecting Rods

REMOVAL

▶ See Figures 157, 158, 159, 160 and 161

➥This procedure requires removal of the head and oil pan. It is much easier to perform this work with the engine removed from the vehicle and mounted on a stand. These procedures require certain hand tools which may not be in your tool box. A cylinder ridge reamer, a numbered punch set, piston ring expander, snapring pliers and piston installation tool (ring compressor) are all necessary for proper piston and rod repair. These tools are commonly available from retail tool suppliers; you may be able to rent them from larger automotive supply houses.

1. If the pistons and rods are being removed as part of a complete teardown, follow the procedures described in Crankshaft and Main Bearings in this section. If you are removing the pistons and connecting rods without removing the crankshaft and main bearings, proceed from this point.

2. Remove the cylinder head(s), following the procedures given in this section.

3. Remove the oil pan.

4. On engines so equipped, it will be necessary to remove the main bearing cap bridge assembly. This is secured by a series of bolts. Loosen the bolts using the correct sequence (refer to the crankshaft procedures in this section).

Fig. 157 Remove the nuts securing the cap . . .

Fig. 158 . . . then remove the cap from the engine

Fig. 159 Remove the ridge at the top of the bore with a ridge cutter

Fig. 160 Place lengths of rubber hose over the connecting rod studs in order to protect the crankshaft and cylinders from damage

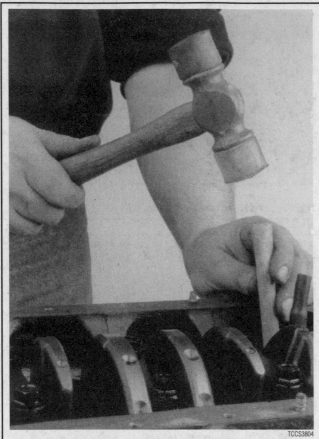

Fig. 161 Carefully tap the piston out of the bore using a wooden dowel or hammer handle

5. The connecting rods are marked to indicate which surface faces front, but the bearing caps should be matchmarked before disassembly. Use a number punch set and a small hammer to mark the number (of the cylinder) over the seam so that each piece will be reused in its original location. Note that the rods and bearing caps may already have numbers stamped on them; these are indicators of original bearing thickness, not of location or sequence.

6. Remove the connecting rod cap nuts, pull the caps off the rods and place them on a bench in order.

7. Inspect the upper portions of the cylinder (near the head) for a ridge formed by ring wear. If there is a ridge, it must be removed by first shifting the piston down in the cylinder and then covering the piston top completely with a rag soaked with clean engine oil. Use a ridge reamer to remove metal at the lip until the cylinder is smooth. If this is not done, the pistons may be damaged during removal. Remove the rag and all the metal chips; use a magnet if necessary.

8. Place pieces of rubber hose over the bolts to keep the ends from scoring the cylinder and journals. Use a piece of wood or a hammer handle under the piston to tap it upward. If you're working on an engine with the crankshaft still in place, turn the crankshaft until the crankpin for each cylinder is in a convenient position. Be careful not to subject the piston and/or rod to heavy impact and do not allow the piston rod to damage the cylinder walls on the way out. The slightest nick in the metal can cause problems after reassembly.

9. Clean the pistons, rings, and rods in parts solvent with a soft bristle brush. Do not use a wire brush even to remove heavy carbon. The metal may become damaged. Use a ring groove cleaner or a piece of a broken piston ring to clean the lands (grooves) in the piston.

✳✳ CAUTION

Wear goggles and gloves during cleaning. Do not spatter solvent onto painted surfaces.

CONNECTING ROD BEARING REPLACEMENT

▶ **See Figures 162 and 163**

Connecting rod bearings on all Honda engines consist of two halves or shells which are not interchangeable in the rod and cap. When the shells are in position, the ends extend slightly beyond the rod and cap surfaces so that when the bolts are tightened, the shells will be clamped tightly in place. This insures positive seating and prevents turning. A small tang holds the shells in place within the cap and rod housings.

➡ **The ends of the bearing shells must never be filed flush with the mating surface of the rod or cap.**

If a rod becomes noisy or is worn so that its clearance on the crankshaft is sloppy, a new bearing of the correct undersize must be selected and installed. There is no provision for adjustment. Under no circumstances should the rod end or cap be filed to compensate for wear, nor should shims of any type be used.

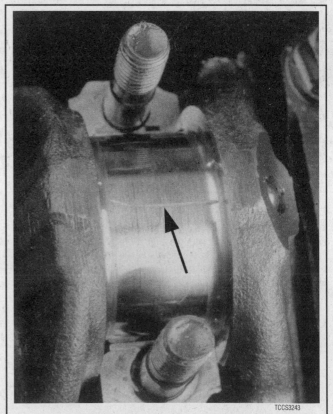

Fig. 162 Place a piece of the measuring material across the crank journal, then install and torque the cap

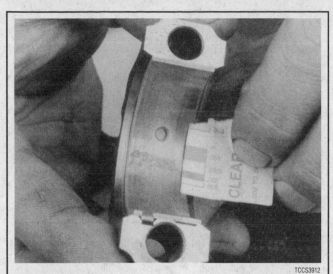

Fig. 163 After the bearing cap has been removed, use the gauge supplied with the material to check the clearance

Inspect the rod bearings while the rods are out of the engine. If the shells are scored or show flaking they should be replaced. ANY scoring or ridge on the crankshaft means the crankshaft must be replaced. Because of the metallurgy in the crankshaft, welding and/or regrinding the crankshaft is not recommended.

Replacement bearings are available in standard sizes, usually marked either on the bearing shell or possibly on the rod cap. Do not confuse the mark on the bearing cap with the cylinder number. For example, it is quite possible that the No. 3 piston rod contains a number 1 size bearing. The rod cap may have a "1" marked on it (stamped at the factory indicating the bearing size). You should have stamped a "3" or other identifying code on both halves of the rod during disassembly to indicate the cylinder number.

Measuring the clearance between the connecting rod bearings and the crankshaft (oil clearance) is done with a plastic measuring material such as Plastigage® or similar product.

1. Remove the rod cap with the bearing shell. Completely clean the cap, bearing shells and the journal on the crankshaft. Blow any oil from the oil hole in the crank. The plastic measuring material is soluble in oil and will begin to dissolve if the area is not totally free of oil.

2. Place a piece of the measuring material across the crank journal. Install the cap and shell and tighten the bolts in three passes to the correct torque.

➡Do not turn the crankshaft with the measuring material installed.

3. Remove the bearing cap with the shell. The flattened plastic material will be found sticking to either the bearing shell or the crank journal. DO NOT remove it yet.

4. Use the scale printed on the packaging for the measuring material to measure the flattened plastic at its widest point. The number within the scale which is closest to the width of the plastic indicates the bearing clearance in thousandths of an inch. Note this measurement, then remove the gauging material.

5. Check the specifications chart in this section for the proper clearance. If there is any measurement approaching the maximum acceptable value, replace the bearing.

6. When the correct bearing is obtained, oil the bearing thoroughly on its working face and install it in the cap. Install the other half of the bearing into the rod end and attach the cap to the rod. Tighten the nuts evenly, in three passes to the proper value.

7. With the proper bearing installed and the nuts properly tightened, it should be possible to move the connecting rod back and forth a bit on the crankshaft. If the rod cannot be moved, either the bearing is too small or the rod is misaligned. Check the connecting rod side-play (refer to the crankshaft and main bearing procedures in this section).

INSPECTION

◗ See Figures 164 thru 171

1. Measure the bore of the cylinder at three levels and in two dimensions (fore-and-aft and side-to-side). That's six measurements for each cylinder. By comparing the 3 vertical readings, the taper of the cylinder can be determined and by comparing the front-rear and left-right readings the out-of-round can be determined. The block should be measured: at the level of the top piston ring at the top of piston travel; in the center of the cylinder; and at the bottom. Compare your readings with the specifications in the chart.

2. If the cylinder bore is within specifications for taper and out-of-round and the wall is not scored or scuffed, boring of the cylinder is not needed. If not

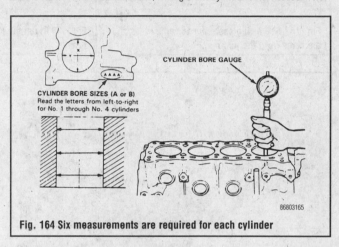

Fig. 164 Six measurements are required for each cylinder

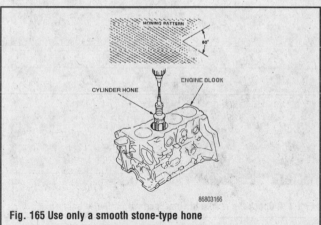

Fig. 165 Use only a smooth stone-type hone

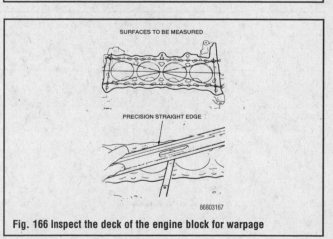

Fig. 166 Inspect the deck of the engine block for warpage

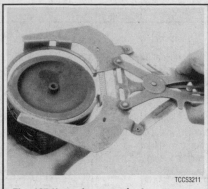

Fig. 167 Use a ring expander to remove the rings from the pistons

Fig. 168 Clean the grooves using a ring groove cleaner

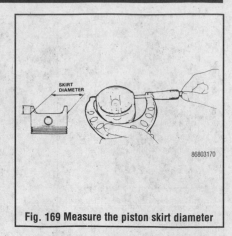

Fig. 169 Measure the piston skirt diameter

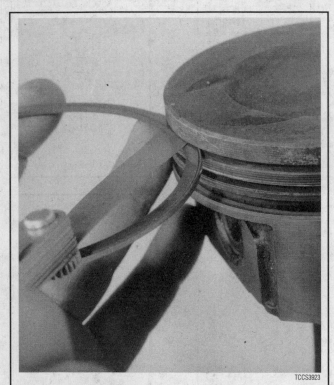

Fig. 170 Check the ring side clearance with a feeler gauge

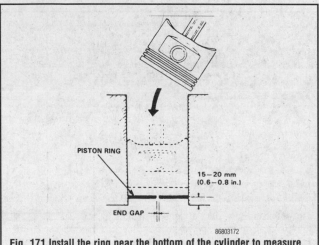

Fig. 171 Install the ring near the bottom of the cylinder to measure the end gap

within specifications. it should be bored oversize, as necessary, to insure elimination of out-of-round and taper. Under these circumstances, the block should be taken to a machine shop for proper boring by a qualified machinist using specialized equipment.

➡ **If the cylinder is bored, oversize pistons and rings must be installed. Since all pistons must be the same size, all cylinders must be rebored if any one is out of specification.**

3. Even if the cylinders do not require boring, they must be fine-honed for proper break-in. A deglazing tool may be used in a power drill to remove the glossy finish on the cylinder walls. Use only the smooth stone-type hone, not the beaded or "bottle brush" type.

4. The cylinder head top deck (gasket surface) should be inspected for warpage. Run a straightedge along all four edges of the block, across the center and diagonally. If you can pass a feeler gauge of 0.004 in (0.1mm) under the straightedge, the top surface of the block should be machined or trued.

5. The rings must be removed from the pistons with a ring expander. Keep all rings in order and with the piston from which they were removed. The rings and piston ring grooves should be cleaned thoroughly as deposits will alter readings of ring wear.

6. Before any measurements are begun, visually examine the piston (a magnifying glass is helpful) for any signs of cracks, particularly in the skirt area. Anything other than light surface scoring disqualifies the piston from further use. The metal will become unevenly heated and the piston may break apart during use.

7. Piston diameter should be measured at the skirt, at right angles to the piston pin. Compare the measurement either with the specified piston diameter or subtract the diameter from the cylinder bore dimension to get clearance. If clearance is excessive, the piston should be replace. If a new piston still does not produce piston-to-wall clearance within specifications, select an oversize piston and have the cylinders bored accordingly.

8. Compression ring side clearance should be measured by using a ring expander to put cleaned rings back in their original positions on the pistons. Measure side clearance on one side by attempting to slide a feeler gauge of the thickness specified between the ring and the edge of the ring groove. If the gauge will not pass into the groove, the ring may be re-used although new rings are always recommended. If the gauge will pass, but a gauge of slightly greater thickness representing the wear limit will not, the piston may be reused, but new rings must be installed.

9. Ring end gap must be measured for all three rings in the cylinder by using a piston to (upside down) to press the ring squarely into the cylinder. The rings must be between 0.6–0.8 in. (15–20mm) from the bottom of the cylinder. Use a feeler gauge to measure the end-gap and compare it with specifications. If the gap is too great, the ring should be checked with a gauge representing the wear limit. If cylinder bore wear is very slight, you may use new rings to bring the end-gap to specification without boring the cylinder. Measure the gap with the ring located near the minimum dimension at the bottom of the cylinder, not near the top where wear is greatest.

10. The connecting rods must be free from wear, cracking and bending. Visually examine the rod, particularly at its upper and lower ends. Look for any sign of metal stretching or wear. The piston pin should fit cleanly and tightly through the upper end, allowing no sideplay or wobble. The bottom end should also be an exact ½ circle with no deformity of shape. The bolts must be firmly

mounted and parallel. The rods may be taken to a machine shop for exact measurement of twist or bend. This is generally cheaper and easier than purchasing a seldom-used rod alignment tool.

PISTON PIN REPLACEMENT

The piston pins or wrist pins are press fitted into place. Special tools including an adjustable pin driver, pilot collar, and spring loaded piston pin assembly jig are required as well as access to a hydraulic press. The piston pins cannot be removed by any common method in the average garage. If the pins must be removed, take the pistons to a reputable machine shop.

INSTALLATION

▶ **See Figures 172, 173, 174 and 175**

1. Remember that if you are installing oversize pistons, you must also use new rings of the correct oversize.

2. Install the rings on the piston, lowest ring first. This requires the use of a ring expander. There is a high risk of ring breakage or piston damage if the rings are installed without the expander. The correct spacing of the ring end gaps is critical to oil control. No two gaps should align; they should be evenly spaced around the piston with the gap in the oil ring expander facing the front of the piston (aligned with the mark on the top of the piston). Once the rings are installed, the pistons must be handled carefully and protected from dirt and impact.

3. Install the number two compression ring next and then the top compression ring using the ring expander. Note that these rings have the same thickness but different cross-sections or profiles; they must be installed in the proper locations. Make sure all markings face upward and that the gaps are all stag-

Fig. 174 A ring compressor must be used to install the piston in the block

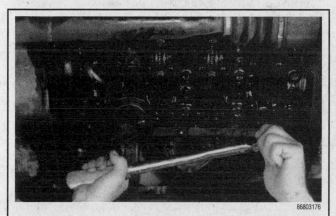
Fig. 175 Always use a torque wrench to tighten the bearing cap nuts

gered. Gaps must also not be in line with either the piston pin or thrust faces of the piston.

4. All the pistons, rods, and caps must be reinstalled in the correct cylinder. Make certain that all labels and stamped numbers are present and legible. Double check the piston rings; make certain that the gaps do NOT line up and are properly spaced around the piston (refer to the illustration). Double check the bearing insert at the bottom of the rod for proper mounting. Reinstall the protective pieces of rubber hose on the rod bolts.

5. Liberally coat the cylinder wall and the crankshaft journals with clean, fresh motor oil. Also apply oil to the bearing surfaces on the connecting rod and the cap.

6. Identify the FRONT mark on each piston and rod. Position the piston and rod assembly loosely in each cylinder with the marks facing the front or timing belt end of the engine. Make certain the number stamped on each piston corresponds to the number of the cylinder.

❊❊ WARNING

Failure to observe the marking and its correct placement can lead to sudden and catastrophic engine failure.

7. Install the ring compressor around one piston and tighten it gently until the rings are compressed almost completely.

8. Gently press down on the piston top with a wooden hammer handle or similar soft faced tool; drive the piston into the cylinder bore. Once all three rings are in the bore, the piston will move with some ease.

❊❊ WARNING

If any resistance or binding is encountered during the installation, DO NOT apply force. Tighten or adjust the ring compressor and/or reposition the piston. Brute force will break the ring(s) or damage the piston.

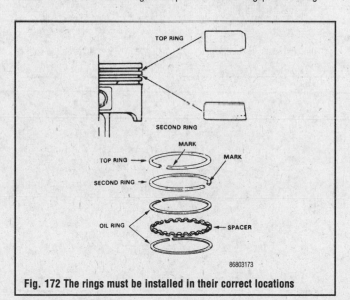
Fig. 172 The rings must be installed in their correct locations

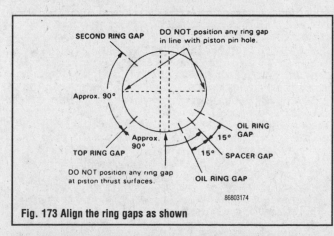
Fig. 173 Align the ring gaps as shown

9. From underneath, pull the connecting rod into place on the crankshaft. Remove the rubber hoses from the bolts. Check the rod cap to confirm that the bearing is present and correctly mounted, then install the rod cap (observing the correct number and position and its nuts. Leaving the nuts finger-tight will make installation of the remaining pistons easier.

10. With all the pistons installed and the bearing caps secured finger-tight, the retaining nuts may be tightened to their final setting. Refer to the torque specifications chart in this section. For each pair of nuts, make 3 passes alternating between the two nuts on any given rod cap. The three tightening steps should be about one third of the final torque; for example, if the final torque is 36 ft. lbs., draw the nuts tight in steps to 12, 24 and then 36 ft. lbs. The intent is to draw each cap up to the crank straight and under even pressure.

11. Turn the crankshaft through several rotations, making sure everything moves smoothly and there is no binding. With the piston rods connected, the crank may be stiff to turn. Try to turn it in a smooth continuous motion so that any stiff spots may be felt.

12. If equipped with a main bearing cap bridge, loosen the main bearing cap bolts, then tighten the cap and bridge bolts using the proper sequence (refer to the crankshaft procedures in this section).

13. Reinstall the oil pan. Even if the engine is to remain apart for other repairs, install the pan to protect the bottom end. Install all the pan bolts and tighten them to the correct tightness; this eliminates one easily overlooked item during future reassembly.

14. If the engine is to remain apart for other repairs, pack the cylinders with crumpled newspaper or clean rags to keep out dust and grit; cover the top of the cylinders with a large rag. If the engine is on a stand, the entire block can be covered with a large trash bag.

15. If no further work is to be performed, continue reassembly by installing the head, timing belt, etc.

16. When the engine is restarted after assembly, the exhaust will be very smoky as the oil within the cylinders burns off. This is normal; the smoke should clear quickly during warm up. Depending on the state of the spark plugs, it may be wise to check for any oil fouling on the spark plugs after the engine is shut off.

17. A reminder: once the engine is assembled and driveable, remember that you are breaking in an essentially new engine—follow the break-in interval as you would for a new car.

Freeze Plugs

REMOVAL & INSTALLATION

▶ **See Figures 176 and 177**

The freeze plugs can be loosened and removed using a punch and a hammer. Or, drill a small hole in the middle of the freeze plug, then thread a large sheet metal screw into the hole. Remove the plug with a slide hammer. When installing, coat the freeze plugs with sealer. Tap into position using a piece of pipe, slightly smaller than the plug, as a driver.

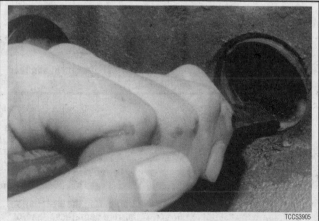
TCCS3905
Fig. 176 The freeze plug can be loosened in the block with a punch and hammer

TCCS3906
Fig. 177 Once the freeze plug has been loosened, it can be removed from the block

Crankshaft Main Seals

REMOVAL & INSTALLATION

1984–89 Accord and 1984–87 Prelude

▶ **See Figures 178 and 179**

1. Disconnect the negative battery cable.
2. The front and rear main or crankshaft seals are held by the crankshaft endcaps; they are removed with the crankshaft. When reassembling, apply non-hardening sealant along the seams where the cap joins the block before installing the seals. The crank and caps should be in place, although the bolts

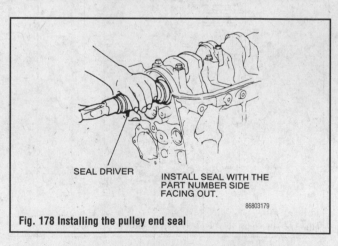
SEAL DRIVER
INSTALL SEAL WITH THE PART NUMBER SIDE FACING OUT.
86803179
Fig. 178 Installing the pulley end seal

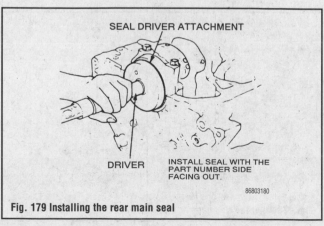
SEAL DRIVER ATTACHMENT
DRIVER
INSTALL SEAL WITH THE PART NUMBER SIDE FACING OUT.
86803180
Fig. 179 Installing the rear main seal

for the crank endcaps should not be fully tightened until after the seals are installed.

3. Apply a light coat of grease to the sealing surfaces of both seals. Pack the back of each seal with grease to hold the spring in place during installation.

4. Using a seal driver of the correct diameter and reach, install the pulley-end seal until the driver bottoms out against the snout of the crankshaft. The seal should be installed with the part number facing the outside.

5. Using a seal driver of the correct size and reach, install the rear or flywheel-end seal. Align the hole in the driver to fit over the pin on the crankshaft. Drive the seal in until the driver bottoms on the block.

6. Tighten the remaining crank bearing caps to specification.

1990–95 Accord and 1988–95 Prelude

▶ **See Figure 180**

1. Disconnect the negative battery cable.
2. Raise and safely support the vehicle.
3. Remove the transaxle assembly.
4. Remove the flywheel.
5. Remove the oil pan.
6. Remove the bolts securing the seal housing, then remove it from the engine. Remove the rear main seal.

To install:

7. Installation is the reverse of the removal procedure. Lubricate the lip of the seal prior to installation. Pack the inner spring pocket of the seal with grease to prevent the spring from dislodging during installation.

8. Install the rear main seal in the seal housing using a suitable installation tool. Install the seal with the part number side towards the installation tool. Apply liquid gasket to the block mating surface and the seal housing retainer bolts. Install the seal housing on the block. Tighten the bolts to 9 ft. lbs. (12 Nm).

9. Install the remainder of the components.

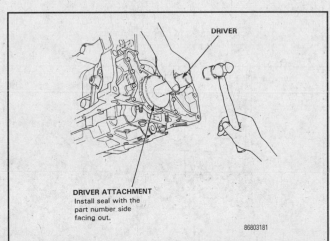

Fig. 180 Drive the main seal until the tool bottoms against the block

Crankshaft and Main Bearings

REMOVAL & INSTALLATION

1984–89 Accord and 1984–91 Prelude

▶ **See Figure 181**

1. Remove the engine from the vehicle and place it on a work stand.
2. Remove the crankshaft pulley attaching bolts and washer.
3. Remove the front cover and the air conditioning idler pulley assembly, if so equipped. Remove the cover assembly.
4. Remove the timing belt and sprockets.
5. Invert the engine on a work stand. Remove the flywheel and the rear seal cover. Remove the oil pan and gasket. Remove the oil pump inlet and the oil pump assembly.

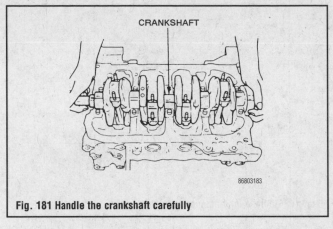

Fig. 181 Handle the crankshaft carefully

6. Insure all bearing caps (main and connecting rod) are marked so they can be installed in their original positions.

7. Remove the main bearing caps (and bridge assembly, if equipped). Use a crisscross pattern making three passes to loosen the bolts.

8. Turn the crankshaft until the connecting rod from which the cap is to be removed is up. Remove the connecting rod cap. Push the connecting rod and piston assembly up in the cylinder. Repeat the procedure for the remaining connecting rod assemblies.

9. Carefully lift crankshaft out of the block so the upper thrust bearing surfaces are not damaged. If the bearings are to be reused, they should be identified to insure that they are installed in their original position.

❋❋ WARNING

Handle the crankshaft with care to avoid damage, fracture or scratching of the finished surfaces.

To install:

10. Inspect all the machined surfaces on the crankshaft for nicks, scratches or scores which could cause premature bearing wear. Inspect the bearing clearances.

11. If necessary for replacement, remove the main and connecting rod bearing inserts. Refer to the applicable bearing replacement procedures in this section.

12. Install a new rear oil seal in the seal cover.

13. Apply a thin coat of grease to the rear crankshaft surface. Do not apply sealer to the area forward of oil sealer groove.

14. Apply a light coat of assembly grease to the journals and bearings. Carefully lower the crankshaft into place.

15. Turn the crankshaft throw to the bottom of the stroke. Push the piston until the rod bearing seats on the crankshaft journal.

16. Install the connecting rod cap with the nuts finger-tight. Repeat this for the remaining pistons, then tighten them to the proper specification.

17. Install the main bearing caps (and bridge assembly, if equipped). Tighten the bolts to specification (refer to the torque specification chart in this section). Use a crisscross pattern making three passes to tighten the bolts.

18. Check the crankshaft end-play.

19. If the end-play exceeds specification, replace the thrust bearing. If the end-play is less than the specification, inspect the thrust bearing faces for damage, dirt or improper alignment. Install the thrust bearing and align the faces. Recheck the end-play.

20. After the piston and connecting rod assemblies have been installed, check the connecting rod side-play.

21. Install the remaining components in the reverse order of removal.

1990–95 Accord and 1992–95 Prelude

▶ **See Figures 182 thru 188**

➡**Steps are given for crankshaft removal with the pistons in place in the block.**

1. With the engine removed from the car and the flywheel removed from the engine, unbolt the rear or right side cover from the engine.
2. Remove the balancer drive case.

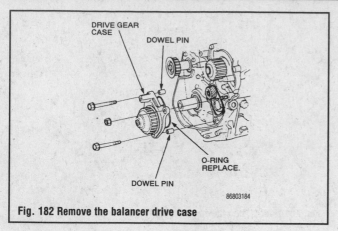

Fig. 182 Remove the balancer drive case

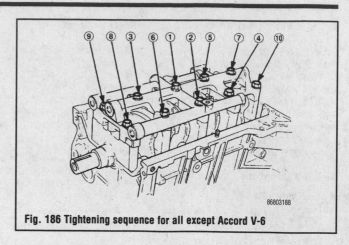

Fig. 186 Tightening sequence for all except Accord V-6

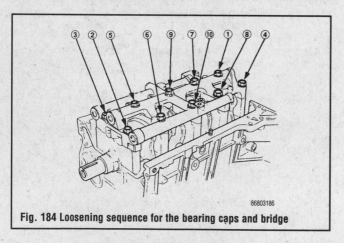

Fig. 183 Hold the balancer shaft with a bolt or similar tool through the maintenance hole

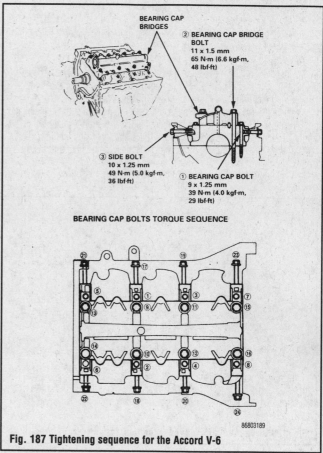

Fig. 187 Tightening sequence for the Accord V-6

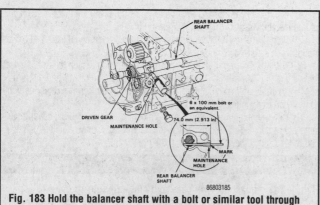

Fig. 184 Loosening sequence for the bearing caps and bridge

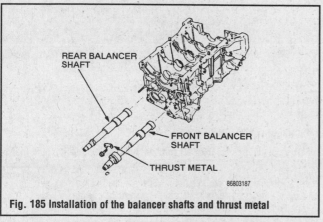

Fig. 185 Installation of the balancer shafts and thrust metal

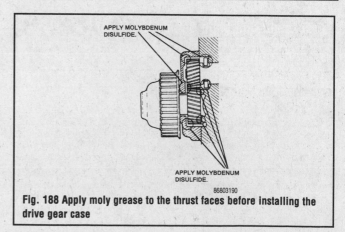

Fig. 188 Apply moly grease to the thrust faces before installing the drive gear case

3. Insert a metal dowel or similar tool in the maintenance hole of the front balancer shaft to hold it in place. Unbolt the belt sprocket and remove it.

4. Remove the bolt from the maintenance hole for the rear balancer shaft. Align the bolt hole and the balancer shaft hole. Insert a 6x100mm dowel or bolt to engage and hold the shaft; remove the sprocket or drive gear.

5. Remove the oil screen and the oil pump. Remove the baffle plate.

6. Remove the bolts securing the bearing caps (and bridge, if equipped), then remove the bearing caps. Release the tension by turning each bolt about ⅓ of a turn at a time, beginning at one corner, then moving to the diagonally opposite corner. On all except Accord V-6, follow the sequence shown in the illustration.

7. Turn the crankshaft so that the No. 2 and 3 crankpins are at the bottom. Remove the rod caps and bearings, keeping them in order.

8. Lift the crankshaft out of the engine, being careful not to damage the journals.

9. Remove the bolts securing the retainer, then remove the front and rear balancer shafts.

To install:

10. Insert the bearing halves into the block and piston rods.

11. Hold the crankshaft so that the journals for pistons No. 2 and 3 are straight down; lower the crankshaft into the block. Make certain the crank journals seat into piston rods 2 and 3.

12. Install the rod caps and nuts finger-tight.

13. Rotate the crankshaft clockwise and seat the journals into connecting rods 1 and 4. Install the rod caps and nuts finger-tight.

14. Check the rod bearing clearance using Plastigage® or similar compressible measuring media.

15. Coat the thrust washer and bolt threads with a light coat of clean oil. Install the thrust washers, main bearing caps and bearing cap bridge. Check the bearing clearance using Plastigage® or similar compressible measuring media.

16. Tighten the bolts in two passes: On the first pass, in the correct sequence, bring each bolt to approximately 22 ft. lbs. (30 Nm). On the second pass, in the correct sequence, bring each bolt to its final torque of 52 ft. lbs. (72 Nm).

17. Insert the balancer shafts into the block, then install the thrust metal to the front balancer shaft and block. Tighten the retaining bolt to 9 ft. lbs. (12 Nm).

18. Make certain the mating surfaces of the right side cover and the block are absolutely clean and dry. Apply a liquid gasket sealant to the contact face of the cover, then install it on the block. Tighten the retaining bolts to 9 ft. lbs. (12 Nm).

19. Make certain the mating surfaces of the oil pump and engine block are absolutely clean and dry. Apply a liquid gasket sealant to the contact surface of the oil pump. Apply grease to the lips of the oil pump seal and the balancer seal. Install the oil pump and tighten the bolts to 9 ft. lbs. (12 Nm). Wipe the excess grease from the crank and balancer shafts; check that the oil seals did not distort during installation.

20. Install the baffle plate, then install the oil screen.

21. Apply molybdenum disulfide grease to the thrust surfaces of the balance gears before installation of the driven gear and the drive gear case.

22. Use the 6x100mm tool to hold the rear balancer shaft in place. Install the balancer pulley and gear. Tighten the bolt to 18 ft. lbs. (25 Nm).

23. Pin the front balancer shaft in place and install its pulley; tighten the bolt to 22 ft. lbs. (30 Nm).

24. On the balancer gear case, align the groove on the pulley edge to the pointer on the gear case.

25. Hold the rear balancer shaft in place and install the gear case. Tighten the nut and bolts to 18 ft. lbs. (25 Nm).

CLEANING AND INSPECTION

♦ **See Figure 189**

With the crankshaft removed from the engine, clean the crank, bearings and block areas thoroughly. Visually inspect each crankshaft section for any sign of wear or damage, paying close attention to the main bearing journals. ANY scoring or ridge on the crankshaft means the crankshaft must be replaced. Because of the crankshaft metallurgy, welding and/or regrinding the crankshaft is not recommended. The bearing faces of the crank may not be restored to their original condition which would cause the risk of premature bearing wear and possible failure.

Using a micrometer, measure the diameter of each journal on the crankshaft

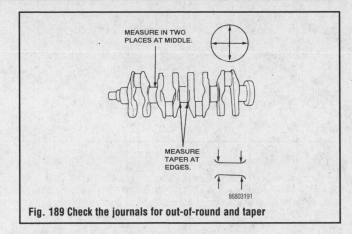

Fig. 189 Check the journals for out-of-round and taper

and record the measurements. The acceptable specifications for both connecting rod and main journals are found in the Crankshaft and Connecting Rod specifications chart in this section. If ANY journal is beyond the acceptable range, the crank must be replaced.

Additionally, each journal must be measured at both outer edges. When one measurement is subtracted from the other, the difference is the measurement of journal taper. Any taper beyond 0.0031 in. (0.08mm) is a sign of excess wear on the journal; the crankshaft must be replaced.

BEARING REPLACEMENT

1. With the engine out of the car and inverted on a stand, remove the main bearing caps following the procedures given in this section.

2. Once the bearing caps are removed, the lower bearing shell may be inspected. Check closely for scoring or abrasion of the bearing surface. If this lower bearing is worn or damaged, both the upper and lower half should be replaced.

➡**Always replace bearing shells in complete pairs.**

3. If the lower bearing half is in good condition, the upper shell usually may also be considered usable.

4. The bearing shells, the crank throws and the flat surface of the engine block (on the oil pan face) are stamped with a code indicating the standard bearing size. This size is determined during the initial manufacturing and assembly process; replacement bearings must be of the same code (thickness) if the correct clearances are to be maintained. If the code on the bearing shell is unreadable, use the code on the block and/or the crank throw to determine the bearing size. A well equipped machine shop or parts outlet should be able to help you find the correct bearing size for that position.

5. Lift the crankshaft from the engine block and remove the upper bearing shells. Clean the area thoroughly (including the crankshaft journals) and allow the surfaces to air dry.

6. Install the upper bearing shells, then carefully place the crankshaft in position. Install the lower bearing shells into clean, dry caps. Do not oil the upper/lower bearing shells or the crankshaft journals at this time.

7. Place a piece of plastic gauging material (such as Plastigage® or similar) lengthwise (fore-and-aft) across the full width of each of the crankshaft main bearing journals. Remember that the measuring material is dissolved by oil. Keep the crankshaft and bearings clean and dry.

8. Install the bearing caps with their bearing shells in their correct location.

9. Install the bearing cap bolts (and bridge assembly, if equipped) and tighten them using the correct sequence to the proper specification. Follow the procedures outlined in this section.

➡**Do not rotate the crankshaft with the measuring plastic installed.**

10. Observing the correct removal sequence, gradually loosen and remove the bearing cap bolts. Carefully remove the bearing caps (and bridge assembly, if equipped). The gauging material will be stuck to either the inside of the bearing shell or the face of the crankshaft.

11. Using the scale provided with the package of the gauging material, measure the material at its widest point. This measurement represents the main bearing oil clearance and should be checked against the Crankshaft and Connecting Rod Specifications chart in this section.

12. Remove every piece of the plastic gauging material from the crank and bearing caps. Remove the crankshaft, then coat the journals and bearings with clean motor oil.

13. If the bearing insert and journal appear intact, and are within tolerances, no further main bearing service is required. If it is out of specification, determine if the journals are worn. If so, replace the crank. If the journals are within specification, replace the bearings.

14. Assemble the engine using the procedures in this section.

CRANKSHAFT END-PLAY/CONNECTING ROD SIDE-PLAY

▶ **See Figure 190**

Place a small pry bar between a main bearing cap and crankshaft casting, taking care not to damage any journals. Pry backward and forward; measure the distance between the thrust bearing and crankshaft with a feeler gauge or dial indicator. Compare the reading with specifications. If too great a clearance is determined, a main bearing with a larger thrust surface or crank replacement may be required. Check with an automotive machine shop for their advice.

Connecting rod clearance between the rod and crankthrow casting can be checked with a feeler gauge. Pry the rod carefully on one side as far as possible and measure the distance on the other side of the rod. Compare the reading with specifications.

TCCS3805

Fig. 190 A dial indicator can be used to check crankshaft end-play

Flywheel and Ring Gear

REMOVAL & INSTALLATION

▶ **See Figure 191**

1. Disconnect the negative battery cable.
2. Remove the transaxle.
3. For cars equipped with automatic transaxles:
   a. Matchmark the driveplate and the crankshaft.
   b. Loosen the retaining bolts a little at a time in a crisscross pattern. Support the driveplate as the last bolts are removed and then lift the driveplate away from the engine.

EXHAUST SYSTEM

Safety Precautions

For a number of reasons, exhaust system work can be the most dangerous type of work you can do on your car. Always observe the following precautions:

• Support the car extra securely. Not only will you often be working directly under it, but you'll frequently be using a lot of force to dislodge rusted parts. This can cause a car that's improperly supported to shift and possibly fall.

• Wear goggles. Exhaust system parts are always rusty. Metal chips can be

86803193

Fig. 191 Note that the locating dowel on the crankshaft must engage in the small hole on the flywheel

4. For manual transaxle cars:
   a. Remove the clutch/pressure plate assembly.
   b. Matchmark the flywheel and crankshaft. Loosen the retaining bolts evenly in a crisscross pattern. Support the flywheel during removal of the last bolts and remove the flywheel.

5. Carefully inspect the teeth on the flywheel or driveplate for any signs of wearing or chipping. If anything beyond minimal contact wear is found, replace the unit.

➡ **Since the flywheel is driven by the starter gear, you would be wise to inspect the starter drive should any wear be found on the flywheel teeth. A worn starter can cause damage to the flywheel.**

To install:

6. When reassembling, place the flywheel or driveplate in position on the crankshaft and make sure the matchmarks align. Install the retaining bolts finger-tight.

➡ **All major rotating components including the flywheel are individually balanced. Engine assembly balancing is not required. Balance weights should NOT be installed on new flywheels.**

7. Tighten the attaching bolts to the correct torque using a cross-tightening sequence. For all manual transaxles, tighten the flywheel bolts to 76 ft. lbs. (105 Nm). For all automatic transaxles, tighten the bolts to 54 ft. lbs. (75 Nm).

8. Install the clutch/pressure plate assembly on manual transaxle vehicles. Refer to the appropriate procedures in this manual.

➡ **If the clutch appears worn or cracked in any way, replace it with a new disc, pressure plate and release bearing. The slight extra cost of the parts will prevent having to remove the transaxle again later.**

9. Reinstall the transaxle assembly.

RING GEAR REPLACEMENT

If the ring gear teeth on the driveplate or flywheel are damaged, the assembly must be replaced. The ring gear cannot be separated or reinstalled individually.

If a flywheel is replaced on a manual transmission car, the installation of a new clutch disc, pressure plate and release bearing is highly recommended.

dislodged, even when you're only turning rusted bolts. Attempting to pry pipes apart with a metal tool makes the chips fly even more frequently.

• If you're using any source of heat, keep it a great distance from either the fuel tank or lines. Stop what you're doing and feel the temperature of the fuel lines on the tank frequently. Even slight heat can expand and/or vaporize fuel, resulting in accumulated vapor, or even a liquid leak.

• Watch where your hammer blows fall and make sure you hit squarely. You could easily tap a brake or fuel line when you hit an exhaust system part with a glancing blow. Inspect all lines and hoses in the area where you've been working.

✳✳ CAUTION

Be very careful when working on or near the catalytic converter. External temperatures can reach well over 500°F (260°C), causing severe burns. Removal or installation should be performed only on a cold exhaust system.

• It is quite helpful to use solvents designed to loosen rusted bolts or flanges. Soaking rusted parts the night before you do the job can speed the work of freeing rusted parts considerably. Remember that these solvents are often flammable. Apply only to parts after they are cool!.

The exhaust system of Accord and Prelude vehicles consists of several pieces. Thankfully, the pieces are attached by nuts and bolts rather than being welded. Each bolted joint contains a gasket which must be replaced whenever repairs are made.

The first section of pipe connects the exhaust manifold to the catalytic converter. The catalytic converter is a sealed, non-serviceable unit which can be easily unbolted from the system and replaced if necessary.

The exhaust system is attached to the body by several welded hooks and flexible rubber hangers; these hangers absorb exhaust vibrations and isolate the system from the body of the car. The hangers MUST be in place and correctly mounted to avoid vibration and body-contact. A series of metal heat shields runs along the exhaust piping, protecting the underbody from excess heat. The heat shields must always be reinstalled when a pipe or component is replaced.

➡**The heat shields can be a source of several irritating sounds including buzzes or rattles related to engine speed. Make certain the shields are tightly attached and free of gravel.**

The system terminates in the muffler and tailpipe at the rear of the car. The entry pipe, muffler and tailpipe are one-piece and should be replaced as a unit.

When inspecting or replacing exhaust system parts, make sure there is adequate clearance from all points on the body to avoid possible overheating of the floorpan. Check the complete system for broken damaged, missing or poorly positioned parts. Rattles and vibrations in the exhaust system are usually caused by misalignment of parts. When aligning the system, leave all the nuts and bolts loose until everything is in its proper place, then tighten the hardware working from the front to the rear. Remember that what appears to be proper clearance during repair may change as the car moves down the road. The motion of the engine, body and suspension must be considered when replacing parts.

REMOVAL & INSTALLATION

▶ **See Figures 192 thru 203**

✳✳ CAUTION

DO NOT perform exhaust repairs with the engine or exhaust hot. Allow the system to cool completely before attempting any work. Exhaust systems are noted for sharp edges, flaking metal and rusted bolts. Gloves and eye protection are required. A supply of penetrating oil and rags is highly recommended.

➡**ALWAYS use a new gasket at each pipe joint whenever the joint is disassembled. Use new nuts and bolts to hold the joint properly. These two low-cost items will serve to prevent future leaks as the system ages.**

Front Pipe

1. Raise and safely support the car.
2. Remove the heat shield(s), if present.
3. Remove the nuts securing the pipe to the exhaust manifold.
4. Remove the nuts/bolts securing the front pipe to the converter or mid-pipe (if equipped).
5. If applicable, remove the nuts/bolts securing the pipe to the support bracket.
6. Remove the front pipe and gaskets.
7. Using new gaskets and nuts/bolts, install the front pipe. Tighten the bolts to the specification shown in the appropriate illustration.

Mid-Pipe

1. Raise and safely support the car.
2. Remove the heat shield(s), if present.
3. If applicable, unplug the oxygen sensor connector.
4. Remove the bolts securing the mid-pipe to the converter and front pipe.
5. Using new gaskets and nuts/bolts, install the mid-pipe. Tighten the bolts to the specification shown in the appropriate illustration.
6. If applicable, engage the oxygen sensor connector.

Catalytic Converter

1. Raise and safely support the car.
2. Remove the heat shield(s).
3. Remove the three bolts at the front and rear of the converter.

➡**Always support the pipe running to the manifold, either by the normal clamps/hangers or by using string, stiff wire, etc. If left loose, the pipe can develop enough leverage to crack the manifold.**

4. Remove the converter and gaskets.
5. Using new gaskets, connect the converter to the exhaust pipes. Tighten the bolts to the specification shown in the appropriate illustration.

Muffler/Tail Pipe

The muffler and tail pipe on all Hondas is one piece and should be replaced as a unit. The chromed tailpipe extension is a separate part and does not come with replacement units; if yours is still in good shape, remove it by loosening the set screw on the bottom of the extension. To remove the muffler and tailpipe:

1. Elevate and firmly support the rear of the vehicle.
2. Disconnect the nuts holding the muffler and/or tailpipe to the adjacent pipes.
3. Remove or disconnect the clamps and supports holding the pipe at either end. Leave the supports closest to the center in place until last.
4. Remove the last supports or hangers and lower the unit to the ground. At no time should the muffler be allowed to hang partially supported; the leverage can break the next component in line.

➡**If the muffler or tailpipe is being replaced due to rust or corrosion, adjacent pipes should be checked for the same condition.**

5. Lift the new unit into place and loosely attach the hangers or supports to hold it in place. Allow some play to adjust the muffler.
6. Using new gaskets, connect each end to the adjoining pipe. Tighten the joint bolts and nuts to the specification shown in the appropriate illustration.
7. Tighten the supports and hangers. Make certain the rubber hangers are securely attached to their mounts.

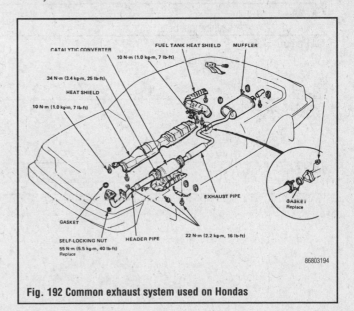

Fig. 192 Common exhaust system used on Hondas

TORQUE SPECIFICATIONS

Component			US	Metric
Alternator				
	Pivot bolt		33 ft. lbs.	45 Nm
	Adjusting nut		16 ft. lbs.	22 Nm
	Bracket bolts		36 ft. lbs.	50 Nm
Starter				
	Accord V-6		47 ft. lbs.	64 Nm
	Others		32 ft. lbs.	45 Nm
Rocker Arm/Valve Cover				
	Accord V-6		11 ft. lbs.	15 Nm
	Others		7 ft. lbs.	10 Nm
Side Covers				
	Retaining bolts		9 ft. lbs.	12 Nm
Rocker Arms/Shafts				
	4-Cylinder SOHC			
		6mm bolts	9 ft. lbs.	12 Nm
		8mm bolts	16 ft. lbs.	22 Nm
	DOHC			
		sealing bolts	43 ft. lbs.	60 Nm
		solenoid	9 ft. lbs.	12 Nm
	Accord V-6	rocker arm guides	9 ft. lbs.	12 Nm
		sealing bolts	36 ft. lbs.	49 Nm
Thermostat				
	Housing bolts		9 ft. lbs.	12 Nm
Radiator				
	Mounting bolts		7 ft. lbs.	10 Nm
Oil Cooler				
	Center bolt		54 ft. lbs.	75 Nm
Engine Fans				
	Mounting bolts		5 ft. lbs	7 Nm
Water Pump				
	Retaining bolts			
		6mm	9 ft. lbs.	12 Nm
		8mm	16 ft. lbs.	22 Nm
	Pulley bolts		9 ft. lbs.	12 Nm
Oil Pan				
	Retaining nut/bolts		10 ft. lbs.	14 Nm
Oil Pump				
	Mounting nut/bolts			
		6mm	9 ft. lbs.	12 Nm
		8mm	16 ft. lbs.	22 Nm
Camshaft Sprocket				
	Accord V-6		23 ft. lbs.	31 Nm
	VTEC Prelude		37 ft. lbs.	51 Nm
	Others		27 ft. lbs.	38 Nm
Main Seal Housing				
	Mounting nuts/bolts		9 ft. lbs.	12 Nm

86803950

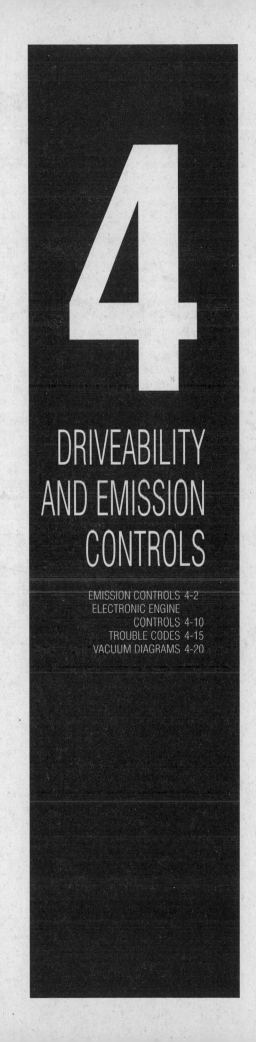

4

DRIVEABILITY AND EMISSION CONTROLS

EMISSION CONTROLS

Component location and vacuum routing diagrams are located at the end of this section. Please refer to them before beginning any disassembly or testing. Wiring diagrams are located at the end of Section 6.

Specific emission control equipment packages have been devised to conform to varying state, federal, and provincial regulations. The U.S. emission equipment is generally divided into two categories: California and 49 State (federal). In this section, the terms "California," "Calif." or "Cal" applies to vehicles originally built to be in compliance with the current California emissions regulations in affect at the time of the vehicle's production. California emissions equipment normally includes the federal equipment as well as other items required by California's more stringent regulations. Models built to be sold in Canada may also have specific emissions equipment. Although in most years, federal and Canadian equipment is the same.

Terms Used In This Section

- CO—Carbon monoxide, a federally regulated exhaust emission
- CVC Valve—Constant Volume Control valve
- EACV—Engine Air Control Valve
- ECU—Electronic Control Unit
- HC—Unburnt hydrocarbon, a federally regulated exhaust or fuel system emission
- MAP Sensor—Manifold Absolute Pressure sensor
- PA Sensor—Atmospheric pressure sensor
- TA Sensor—Intake air temperature sensor
- TDC—Top Dead Center
- TW Sensor—Engine coolant temperature sensor

Positive Crankcase Ventilation (PCV) System

OPERATION

▶ See Figures 1, 2 and 3

All Honda vehicles covered by this manual utilize a closed positive crankcase ventilation system. This system cycles unburned fuel vapors (which work their way past the piston rings) back into the intake manifold for reburning with the

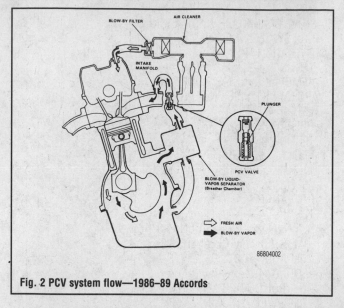

Fig. 2 PCV system flow—1986–89 Accords

air/fuel mixture. The oil filler cap is sealed; the air is drawn from the top of the crankcase into the intake manifold through a valve with a variable orifice. This valve is commonly known as the PCV valve.

The recirculation system relies on the integrity of the engine seals. Any air leak around a valve cover, head gasket, oil pan, dipstick, oil filler cap air intake ducts or vacuum hoses can introduce excess air into the air/fuel mixture, causing rough running or reduced efficiency. Likewise, a plugged hose or passage can cause sludging, stalling and/or oil leaks.

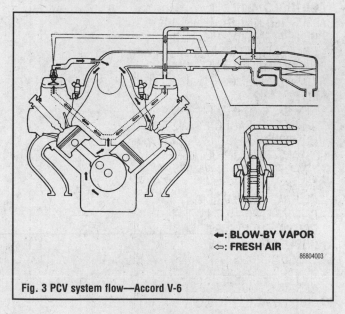

◄: BLOW-BY VAPOR
⇦: FRESH AIR

Fig. 3 PCV system flow—Accord V-6

TESTING

▶ See Figure 4

The PCV valve is easily checked with the engine running at normal idle speed (warmed up). Gently pinch the hose shut, then release it; the valve should click.

If there is no click, check for plugged hoses or ports. If these are open, the valve is faulty. With the engine **OFF**, remove the valve from the engine. Shake it, listening for the rattle of the plunger inside the valve. If no rattle is heard, the

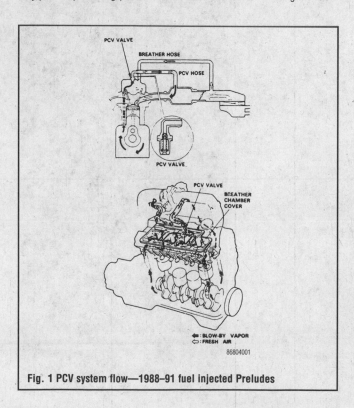

Fig. 1 PCV system flow—1988–91 fuel injected Preludes

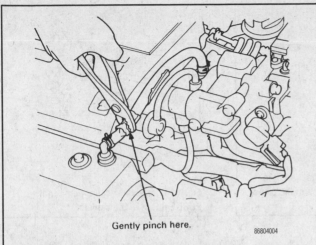

Fig. 4 Gently pinch the hose leading to the PCV valve shut, then release it; the valve should click—Accord V-6 shown

plungor is jammed (probably with oil sludge) and should be replaced. Never operate the engine without the PCV valve or with the hose blocked.

➡**Don't blow directly into the valve in an effort to free the plunger; petroleum vapors and deposits within the valve are harmful.**

REMOVAL & INSTALLATION

▶ **See Figures 5, 6, 7 and 8**

Remove the PCV valve from the valve cover or intake manifold. Remove the hose from the valve. Take note of which end of the valve was in the manifold

Fig. 5 Pliers can be helpful for removing the PCV valve, but be careful not to damage the valve casing

This one-way valve must be reinstalled correctly or it will not function properly.

While the valve is removed, the hoses should be checked for splits, kinks and blockages. Some models, are equipped with a breather port and filter on the side of the air cleaner which should also be inspected at this time. Replace the filter if it is dirty or saturated with oil.

➡**Remember that the correct function of the PCV system is based on a sealed engine. An air leak at the oil filler cap and/or around the oil pan can defeat the design of the system.**

Evaporative Emission Control System

OPERATION

This type of system prevents gasoline vapors from escaping into the atmosphere from the fuel tank and carburetor (if equipped). The actual systems used on these cars will vary between vehicle families, based on year and equipment. Purge control (the admission of fresh air into the canister), may be accomplished either by mechanical means (temperature and vacuum operated controls) or electronically by the Engine Control Unit (ECU). Note that the use of computers is not limited solely to fuel injected vehicles.

The system works by storing fuel vapor in the fuel tank expansion chamber and in the vapor line. When system pressure becomes higher than the set value of the one-way valve, the valve opens and allows vapor into the charcoal canister. While the engine is stopped or idling, the idle cut-off valve or purge control system is closed and the vapor is absorbed by the charcoal.

At partially opened throttle, the idle cut-off valve is opened by manifold vacuum. The vapor that was stored in the charcoal canister and in the vapor line is purged into the intake manifold. Any excessive pressure or vacuum which might build up in the fuel tank is relieved by the two-way valve in the filler cap or fuel line.

TESTING

Carbureted 1984–85 Accord and Prelude

THERMOVALVE

▶ **See Figure 9**

1. Disconnect the upper hose (purge control diaphragm valve) from the evaporative canister. Connect the hose to a hand vacuum pump or vacuum gauge.

➡**Coolant temperature must be below the thermovalve set temperature. To check this, use an ohmmeter to test for continuity across the thermovalve terminals. If it is below the set temperature, continuity should be present. If continuity is not present, the thermovalve may either be defective or the engine has not cooled sufficiently.**

2. Start the engine and allow it to idle; there should be no vacuum indicated on the gauge.
3. If there is vacuum, replace thermovalve A on Accords, or thermovalve B

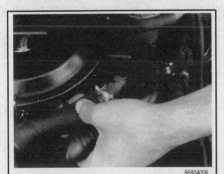

Fig. 6 Remove the PCV system hoses and inspect them for splits, kinks and blockages

Fig. 7 If equipped, remove the screws securing the breather port to the air cleaner . . .

Fig. 8 . . . then remove and inspect the filter. If it is dirty (like this one), it must be replaced

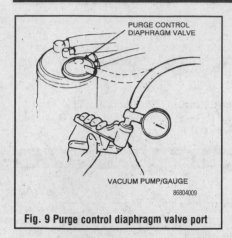

Fig. 9 Purge control diaphragm valve port

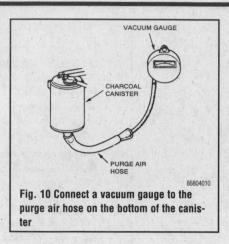

Fig. 10 Connect a vacuum gauge to the purge air hose on the bottom of the canister

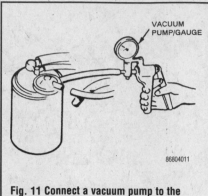

Fig. 11 Connect a vacuum pump to the PURGE fitting of the canister

on Preludes, then retest. To locate the thermovalve, trace the vacuum line leading from the charcoal canister to the air cleaner.

➡**The engine must at normal operating temperature for the following steps. The cooling fan(s) must cycle on and off at least once.**

4. Allow the engine to idle; there should be vacuum indicated on the gauge.
5. If there is no vacuum, inspect thermovalve A on Accords or B on Preludes by pinching its hose leading to the air cleaner. If vacuum is now available to the canister, replace the thermovalve. If vacuum is still not available, inspect hose No. 19 to the intake manifold for leaks or blockage (refer to the vacuum diagrams in this section.)

CHARCOAL CANISTER

▶ **See Figures 10, 11 and 12**

➡**The engine must at normal operating temperature for the following steps. The cooling fan(s) must cycle on and off at least once.**

1. Connect a tachometer to the engine.
2. Remove the fuel filler cap.
3. Disconnect the purge air hose from under the canister and connect a vacuum gauge to it.
4. Start the engine.
5. Raise the engine speed to 3500 rpm; vacuum should appear on the gauge in 1 minute. If vacuum appears, proceed to the last test step.
6. If no vacuum appears:
   a. Stop the engine.
   b. Disconnect the vacuum gauge and reinstall the fuel filler cap.
   c. Remove the charcoal canister and check for signs of damage or defects.
   d. If necessary, replace the canister.
7. Disconnect the PCV hose from the charcoal canister.
8. Connect a vacuum pump to the PURGE fitting on the canister and apply vacuum. If the vacuum remains steady, proceed with the next step; if the vacuum drops, replace the canister and retest.

9. Reconnect the PCV hose and start the engine. The purge vacuum should drop to zero. If the vacuum does not drop to zero, replace the canister and retest.
10. If purge vacuum does drop to zero, connect the vacuum pump to the canister PCV fitting and draw vacuum; it should remain steady. If vacuum remains steady, disconnect the pump and recheck the operation of the thermovalve. If vacuum drops, replace the canister and retest.
11. Connect a hand vacuum pump to the TANK fitting on the canister and draw vacuum. No vacuum should be held. If there is no vacuum present, reinstall the fuel filler cap; the test is complete. If vacuum is held, replace the canister and retest.

Fuel Injected 1985 Accord

CHARCOAL CANISTER

▶ **See Figures 10, 13, 14 and 15**

1. Connect a tachometer to the engine.
2. Remove the fuel filler cap.
3. Disconnect the purge air hose from under the canister and connect a vacuum gauge to it.
4. Start the engine and allow it to reach normal operating temperature; the cooling fan should cycle on and off at least once.
5. Raise the engine speed to 3500 rpm; vacuum should appear on the gauge in 1 minute. If vacuum appears, proceed to the last test step.
6. If no vacuum appears:
   a. Disconnect the vacuum gauge and reinstall the fuel filler cap.
   b. Remove the charcoal canister and check for signs of damage or defects.
   c. If necessary, replace the canister.
7. Connect the vacuum pump to the canister PURGE fitting and apply vacuum; which should then remain steady once applied. If the vacuum drops, replace the canister and retest.
8. Using a 2nd vacuum pump, draw a vacuum from the canister PCV fit-

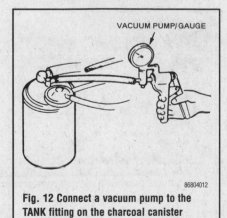

Fig. 12 Connect a vacuum pump to the TANK fitting on the charcoal canister

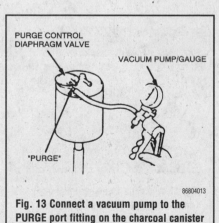

Fig. 13 Connect a vacuum pump to the PURGE port fitting on the charcoal canister

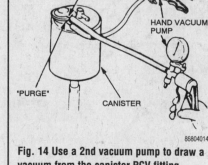

Fig. 14 Use a 2nd vacuum pump to draw a vacuum from the canister PCV fitting

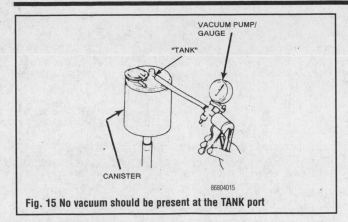

Fig. 15 No vacuum should be present at the TANK port

ting. Purge side vacuum should drop to zero. If vacuum does not drop, replace the canister and retest.

9. Disconnect the vacuum pump from the PURGE port. Draw vacuum at the PCV port; steady vacuum should be held. If vacuum drops, replace the canister.

10. Connect the vacuum pump to the TANK port and draw vacuum. If no vacuum is present, reinstall the filler cap; the test is complete. If vacuum is present, replace the canister and retest.

TWO-WAY VALVE

▶ See Figure 16

1. Remove the fuel filler cap.
2. Elevate and safely support the vehicle.
3. Remove the vapor line from the liquid/vapor separator pipe at the side of

the fuel tank. Connect a T-fitting for both a vacuum gauge and vacuum pump to the hose running into the tank.

4. Slowly draw a vacuum while watching the gauge. Vacuum should stabilize as the two-way valve opens between 0.2–0.6 in. Hg (5–15 mm Hg). If the valve opens too early or too late, replace the two-way valve and retest.

5. Move the vacuum pump hose from the vacuum to the pressure fitting on the pump.

6. Slowly pressurize the vapor line while watching the gauge. Pressure should stabilize between 1.0–2.2 in. Hg. (25–55 mm Hg). If this is true, the valve is OK. If the pressure stabilizes too early or too late, replace the valve.

Carbureted 1986–89 Accords and 1986–90 Preludes

THERMOVALVE

▶ See Figures 17, 18 and 19

➡The engine coolant temperature must be below 131°F (55°C) on Accords or 104°F (40°C) on Preludes.

1. Disconnect the vacuum hose at the purge control diaphragm valve on the top of the canister. Connect a vacuum pump to the hose.

2. Start the engine, allowing it to idle. Vacuum should not be available. If vacuum is present, replace the thermovalve and retest.

3. Allow the engine to reach normal operating temperature. Vacuum should be present. If no vacuum is present, disconnect the vacuum hose at thermovalve and check for vacuum. If vacuum is now present, replace the thermovalve.

4. Shut the engine OFF.

5. Disconnect the vacuum pump, then reconnect the hose.

6. Remove the fuel filler cap.

7. Remove the purge air hose from under the canister, then connect a vacuum gauge to it.

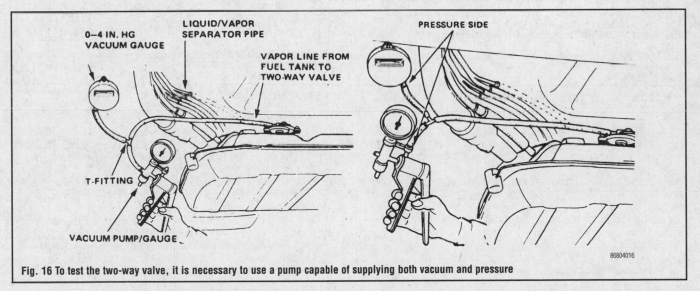

Fig. 16 To test the two-way valve, it is necessary to use a pump capable of supplying both vacuum and pressure

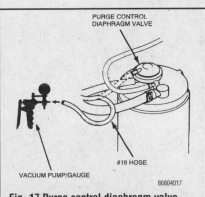

Fig. 17 Purge control diaphragm valve vacuum hose fitting location

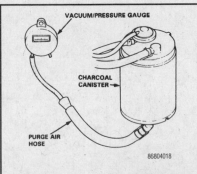

Fig. 18 Connect a vacuum gauge to the canister purge air hose from under the canister or on the frame (as applicable)

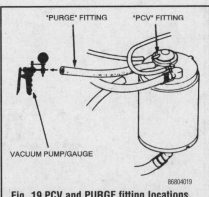

Fig. 19 PCV and PURGE fitting locations on the canister

8. Start the engine, then raise the speed to 3500 rpm. Allow the engine to run for 1 minute. Vacuum should appear on the gauge. If no vacuum is present, remove the charcoal canister and inspect for physical damage. Replace it if necessary. If vacuum is present, proceed to the next step.

9. Disconnect the hose from the canister PCV fitting. Connect a vacuum pump to the PURGE fitting and apply vacuum, which should remain steady. If vacuum drops, replace the canister.

10. Connect the PCV hose to the fitting, then restart the engine. Vacuum at the purge port should drop to 0. If not, replace the canister. If it does, continue with the next step.

11. Connect a vacuum pump to the canister PCV fitting and apply vacuum, which should hold steady. If the vacuum does not hold, replace the canister and retest.

12. Connect the vacuum pump to the TANK fitting on the canister and apply vacuum, which should NOT be held.

If vacuum is present, replace the canister.

CARBURETOR THERMOVALVE

▶ See Figure 20

➡ This test procedure applies to the Accord only.

1. Begin the test on a cold engine; the coolant temperature must be below 86°F (30°C).

2. Disconnect the hose at the carburetor thermovalve, then connect a hand vacuum pump to the valve. Draw a vacuum of 8 in. Hg (200 mm Hg) to the valve; the vacuum should remain steady. If the vacuum cannot be held, replace the thermovalve.

3. Reconnect the vacuum hose to the carburetor thermovalve. Start the engine, allowing it to warm up to normal operating temperature. Coolant temperature must be above 104°F (40°C).

4. Repeat the test. No vacuum should be held. If vacuum is held, replace the carburetor thermovalve.

Fuel Injected 1986–89 Accords and 1986–91 Preludes

SYSTEM TEST

▶ See Figure 18

➡ Begin the test on a cold engine. Coolant temperature must be below 131°F (55°C).

1. Inspect the vacuum lines for cracks, blockages and proper connections.

2. Disconnect the No. 3 vacuum hose (refer to the vacuum diagrams later in this section) from the purge control diaphragm valve and connect a vacuum gauge to the hose.

3. Start the engine and allow it to idle. While the engine is cold, vacuum should not be available. If vacuum is present, replace the thermovalve and retest.

4. Allow the engine to warm up to normal operating temperature. Vacuum should become available as the engine coolant passes 131°F (55°C). If vacuum is not present, replace the thermovalve.

5. Turn the engine **OFF**.

6. Disconnect the vacuum gauge and reconnect the hose.

7. Remove the fuel filler cap.

8. Remove the canister purge air hose from the frame and connect the hose to a vacuum gauge.

9. Start the engine, then raise the speed to 3500 rpm. Allow the engine to run for 1 minute. Vacuum should appear on the gauge. If no vacuum is present, remove the charcoal canister and inspect for physical damage. Replace it if necessary. If vacuum is present, proceed to the next step.

10. Disconnect the hose from the canister PCV fitting. Connect a vacuum pump to the PURGE fitting and apply vacuum, which should remain steady. If vacuum drops, replace the canister.

11. Connect the PCV hose to the fitting, then restart the engine. Vacuum at the purge port should drop to 0. If not, replace the canister. If it does, continue with the next step.

12. Connect a vacuum pump to the canister PCV fitting and apply vacuum. Steady vacuum should be held. If not, replace the canister and retest.

13. Connect the vacuum pump to the TANK fitting on the canister and draw vacuum. No vacuum should be held; if vacuum is present, replace the canister.

TWO-WAY VALVE

▶ See Figure 21

1. Remove the fuel filler cap.
2. Elevate and safely support the vehicle.
3. Remove the vapor line from the liquid/vapor separator pipe at the side of the fuel tank. Connect a T-fitting for both a vacuum gauge and vacuum pump to the hose running into the tank.
4. Slowly draw a vacuum while watching the gauge. The vacuum should stabilize as the two-way valve opens at between 0.2–0.6 in. Hg (5–15 mm Hg). If the valve opens too early or too late, replace the two-way valve and retest.
5. Move the vacuum pump hose from the vacuum to the pressure fitting on the pump. If necessary, move the gauge hose to the pressure side.
6. Slowly pressurize the vapor line while watching the gauge. Pressure should stabilize between 1.0–2.2 in Hg. (25–55 mm Hg). If this is true, the valve is OK. If the pressure stabilizes too early or too late, replace the valve.

1990–95 Accord and 1992–95 Prelude

TWO-WAY VALVE

▶ See Figure 22

1. Remove the fuel filler cap.
2. Elevate and safely support the vehicle.
3. Remove the vapor line from the liquid/vapor separator pipe at the side of the fuel tank. Connect a T-fitting for both a vacuum gauge and vacuum pump to the hose running into the tank.
4. Slowly draw a vacuum while watching the gauge. Vacuum should stabilize as the two-way valve opens between 0.2–0.6 in. Hg (5–15 mm Hg). If the valve opens too early or too late, replace the two-way valve and retest.
5. Move the vacuum pump hose from the vacuum to the pressure fitting on the pump. If necessary, move the gauge hose to the pressure side.
6. Slowly pressurize the vapor line while watching the gauge. Pressure should stabilize between 1.0–2.2 in Hg. (25–55 mm Hg). If this is true, the valve is OK. If the pressure stabilizes too early or too late, replace the valve.

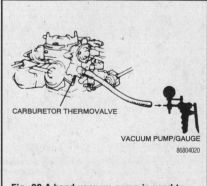

CARBURETOR THERMOVALVE

VACUUM PUMP/GAUGE

86804020

Fig. 20 A hand vacuum pump is used to test the carburetor thermovalve

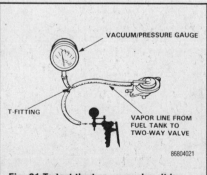

VACUUM/PRESSURE GAUGE

T-FITTING

VAPOR LINE FROM FUEL TANK TO TWO-WAY VALVE

86804021

Fig. 21 To test the two-way valve, it is necessary to use a pump capable of supplying both vacuum and pressure

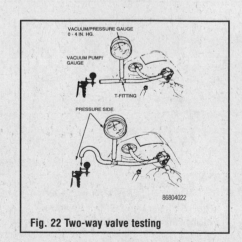

VACUUM/PRESSURE GAUGE 0 - 4 IN. HG.

VACUUM PUMP/GAUGE

T-FITTING

PRESSURE SIDE

86804022

Fig. 22 Two-way valve testing

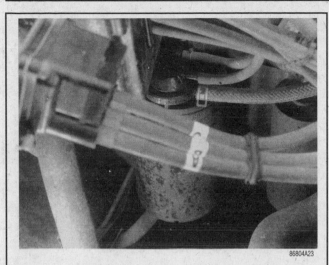

Fig. 23 The charcoal canister is commonly "hidden" near the firewall in the engine compartment

REMOVAL & INSTALLATION

♦ See Figure 23

Removal and installation of the various evaporative emission control system components consists of labeling or marking and unfastening hoses, loosening retaining screws, and removing the part which is to be replaced from its mounting point.

➡**When replacing any EVAP system hoses, always use hoses that are fuel-resistant or are marked EVAP. Use of hose which is not fuel-resistant will lead to premature hose failure.**

Exhaust Gas Recirculation (EGR) System

OPERATION

Carbureted Engines

♦ See Figure 24

On carbureted engines, the system is regulated by a pair of vacuum operated control valves using a compound ported vacuum strategy. Ported vacuum upstream of the throttle opens valve A, which allows manifold vacuum to open

valve B. As B opens, some of the ported vacuum is bled off to the carburetor venturi, causing A to begin closing and the EGR valve to open. Eventually a balance is reached that is dependent upon a manifold vacuum and ported vacuum. This ties EGR valve opening to throttle valve opening and, therefore, to engine load. When the engine is cold or the vehicle is not moving, the purge cut-off solenoid valve for the evaporative emission control system turns off the vacuum to valve B, preventing the venturi vacuum from reaching the EGR valve. The system is far easier to test than to understand. Except for the cut-off solenoid valve, the system is entirely mechanical. Any malfunctions are due to vacuum hose leakage/misrouting or EGR control valve failure.

Fuel Injected Engines

♦ See Figure 25

On fuel injected engines, the system is modulated by controlling the amount of engine vacuum to the valve diaphragm. The ECU modulates the position of the control solenoid valve in order to regulate the EGR valve lift according to an internal program. Upstream of the control solenoid valve, the Constant Volume Control (CVC) valve provides a constant supply of vacuum. This allows precise EGR control under all manifold vacuum conditions. An air chamber inline between the CVC and control solenoid acts as an expansion chamber to dampen any vacuum pulses. The control solenoid valve, CVC and air chamber are in the control box on the firewall.

TESTING

Carbureted Engines

1. With the engine cold, connect a vacuum gauge to the EGR valve vacuum hose and run the engine at about 3000 rpm. There should be no vacuum. If there is, test the evaporative emission control system.
2. Allow the engine to reach normal operating temperature (radiator fan will run).
3. Remove the control box lid on the firewall.
4. Remove the top hose from the purge cut-off solenoid valve and cap the valve. Check the vacuum to the EGR valve hose under the following conditions:
   • At idle—no vacuum.
   • At 3000 rpm—2–6 in. Hg (51–152 mm Hg) of vacuum.
   • At 3000 rpm with venturi hose No. 11 blocked—less than 2 in. Hg (51 mm Hg) of vacuum.
   • Rapid acceleration—2–6 in. Hg (51–150 mm Hg) of vacuum.
   • Deceleration—no vacuum.
5. To test the EGR valve, plug the vacuum hose and connect a hand vacuum pump to the valve. Draw a vacuum of about 6 in. Hg (150 mm Hg) with the engine at idle. The engine should stall (or run very rough) and the vacuum should remain steady, indicating the diaphragm is good. If the engine did not stall or run rough, either the valve is not opening or the passageway is blocked.

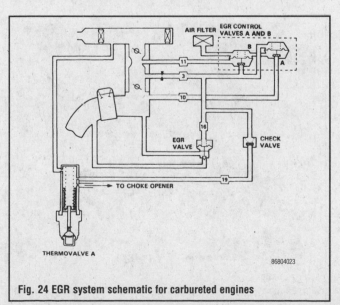

Fig. 24 EGR system schematic for carbureted engines

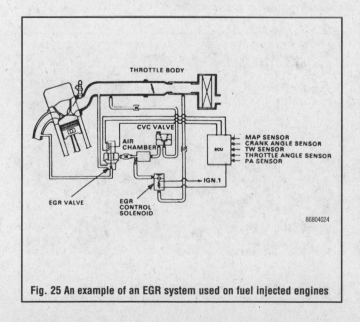

Fig. 25 An example of an EGR system used on fuel injected engines

Fuel Injected Engines

1. First check that all vacuum lines and electrical connections are in good condition.

2. Disconnect the vacuum supply hose to the EGR valve and connect a hand vacuum pump to the valve.

3. Start the engine and allow it to reach normal operating temperature.

4. With the engine at idle, draw a vacuum on the EGR valve. The engine should stall (or run very rough) and the valve should hold vacuum. If not, replace the EGR valve.

5. Connect a vacuum gauge to the vacuum hose from the control solenoid valve; there should be no vacuum at idle. If there is vacuum to the EGR valve at idle, check the wiring for the control solenoid. One wire should have 12 volts anytime the engine is running. The ground wire goes to the ECU, which modulates the control solenoid opening by controlling the ground circuit. Turn the ignition switch **OFF** and use a digital ohmmeter to see if the wire between the ECU and control solenoid is shorted to ground. If the wiring is OK, the ECU is getting an incorrect input signal or the ECU is faulty.

6. The vacuum going to the control solenoid valve should be about 8 in. Hg (200 mm Hg) at idle. Connect a vacuum gauge to the hose coming from the air chamber. If the vacuum is not correct, read the vacuum at the CVC valve outlet. Full manifold vacuum should be available at the CVC inlet. If the air chamber or CVC valve is are not functioning properly, the units must be replaced.

REMOVAL & INSTALLATION

▶ **See Figures 26, 27, 28 and 29**

EGR components are generally simple to work on and easy to access. The air cleaner assembly may need to be removed on some models. Always label each vacuum hose before removing it—they must be reinstalled in the correct position.

EGR valves are held in place by two nuts. The nuts can be difficult to remove due to corrosion. Once the EGR valve is off the engine, clean the studs and the nuts of any rust or debris. Always replace the gasket any time the valve is removed. Tighten the nuts to 16 ft. lbs. (22 Nm).

Most of the other valves and solenoids are made of plastic. Be very careful during removal not to break or crack the ports; you have NO chance of gluing a broken fitting. Remember that the plastic has been in a hostile environment (consisting of heat and vibration); which makes fittings brittle and less resistant to abuse or accidental impact.

Thermostatic Air Cleaner

OPERATION

The thermostatic air cleaner is a temperature-regulated device which improves engine warm up characteristics and helps to minimize carburetor

Fig. 27 An extension is helpful for reaching the nuts securing the EGR valve

Fig. 28 When removing the EGR valve, make sure no debris falls into the intake manifold opening

Fig. 26 Disconnect the vacuum hose from the EGR valve

Fig. 29 Always replace the gasket anytime the EGR valve is removed

icing. The air cleaner assembly is equipped with a vacuum operated air control door at the inlet and a bi-metal air bleed valve inside the air cleaner. When the air control door is open, fresh air is heated by flowing over the exhaust manifold, then taken up a hose and into the air cleaner.

TESTING

The air bleed valve is closed when the air cleaner temperature is less than 77°F (25°C), allowing manifold vacuum to open the air control door and admit heated air to the carburetors. If there is vacuum to the intake air control door above that temperature, the air bleed valve is faulty and should be replaced.

Apply vacuum to the air control door diaphragm. If the diaphragm does not hold vacuum, it must be replaced. Also, make certain the hot air tube is connected to the bottom of the intake duct and to the exhaust manifold shield at the other end. Quite often, the hose gets overlooked when the air cleaner is removed. This could cause cold driveability problems.

CONTROL DOOR DIAPHRAGM REPLACEMENT

▶ **See Figures 30 and 31**

To remove the air control door diaphragm, simply disconnect the vacuum hose, then twist and remove the diaphragm from the air cleaner.

Fig. 30 Disconnect the vacuum hose from the diaphragm . . .

Fig. 31 . . . then simply twist and remove the diaphragm from the air cleaner inlet

Catalytic Converter

INSPECTION

▶ **See Figure 32**

The catalytic converter is a totally passive device, in that there are no actuators or sensors. Contrary to popular opinion of the late 1970's, it has no adverse influence on the operation of the engine, unless it has melted and causes high exhaust backpressure. If this is suspected, the catalyst can be removed for inspection. By looking into the catalyst inlet, it should be possible to see through almost all of the passages in the honey comb pattern ceramic blocks. If there is any melting which may cause high back pressure, it will be quite obvious. On some vehicles, the catalyst is mounted directly to the exhaust manifold, on others it is farther down stream. On all vehicles, the catalytic converter is before the muffler.

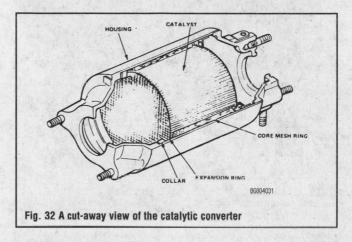

Fig. 32 A cut-away view of the catalytic converter

REMOVAL & INSTALLATION

Please refer to the exhaust system removal and installation procedures found in Section 3.

Oxygen Sensor

OPERATION

The oxygen sensor is mounted in the exhaust manifold or pipe. It is used to sense oxygen concentration in the exhaust gas. If the air/fuel ratio is leaner than the stoichiometric (ideal) ratio, the exhaust gas contains more oxygen. If the air/fuel ratio is richer than the stoichiometric ratio, the exhaust gas contains more fuel.

The oxygen sensor produces a low voltage electrical signal based upon the amount of oxygen found in the exhaust flow. This signal is sent to the ECU and is used in the computation of output control signals. Using this signal, the ECU can control the air/fuel mixture entering the engine, bringing the mixture closer to the ideal ratio of 14.7:1. When the air/fuel mixture is maintained at 14.7:1, efficiency is highest and emissions are lowest.

TESTING

1. Start the engine and bring it to normal operating temperature, then run the engine above 1200 rpm for two minutes.
2. Backprobe with a high impedance averaging voltmeter (set to the DC voltage scale) between the oxygen sensor (02S) and battery ground.
3. Verify that the 02S voltage fluctuates rapidly between 0.40–0.60 volts.
4. If the 02S voltage is stabilized at the middle of the specified range (approximately 0.45–0.55 volts) or if the 02S voltage fluctuates very slowly between the specified range (02S signal crosses 0.5 volts less than 5 times in ten seconds), the 02S may be faulty.

5. If the 02S voltage stabilizes at either end of the specified range, the ECM is probably not able to compensate for a mechanical problem such as a vacuum leak or a faulty pressure regulator. These types of mechanical problems will cause the 02S to sense a constant lean or constant rich mixture. The mechanical problem will first have to be repaired and then the 02S test repeated.

6. Pull a vacuum hose located after the throttle plate. Voltage should drop to approximately 0.12 volts (while still fluctuating rapidly). This tests the ability of the 02S to detect a lean mixture condition. Reattach the vacuum hose.

7. Richen the mixture using a propane enrichment tool. Voltage should rise to approximately 0.90 volts (while still fluctuating rapidly). This tests the ability of the 02S to detect a rich mixture condition.

8. If the 02S voltage is above or below the specified range, the 02S and/or the 02S wiring may be faulty. Check the wiring for any breaks, repair as necessary and repeat the test.

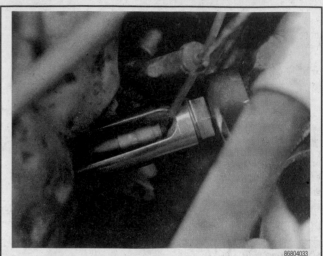

Fig. 34 A special socket is used to remove the oxygen sensor. Note the slot cut into the side of the socket

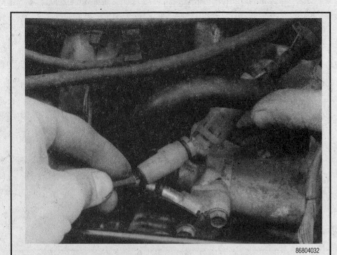

Fig. 33 Be careful not to break the retaining tab when disconnecting the oxygen sensor

REMOVAL & INSTALLATION

♦ See Figures 33 and 34

The sensor(s) may be removed by unscrewing the unit from the manifold or exhaust pipe. Make absolutely certain that the exhaust system is cold to avoid serious burns.

Disengage the wiring connector near the sensor. Use a special oxygen sensor socket to remove and install the unit. These sockets have a slot in the side to prevent damage to the wiring; they are also sized to be an exact fit on the sensor. Keep the socket and driver straight so the sensor is not bent or broken.

When installing the sensor, take great care to keep all compounds and petroleum products off the sensor's tip; its operation will be impaired by pollutants. Install the sensor and tighten it to 33 ft. lbs. (45 Nm). Reconnect the sensor wiring.

ELECTRONIC ENGINE CONTROLS

Carbureted Fuel System

GENERAL INFORMATION

On these vehicles, the engine management system is considered part of the emission control system. The major components include the carburetor(s), feedback control system, the air injection system, a throttle control system and the EGR system. The system consists of sensors and switches that feed information to the Electronic Control Unit (ECU), which will then operate several solenoid valves to maintain the ideal air/fuel ratio under all conditions.

As useful as the tests found in this section are, the first step in repair or service to engine management systems is still to gain as much information as possible about the problem; when and under what conditions it occurs. At highway speed? At idle only? Only under heavy load or hard acceleration? Wet weather? Defining the problem will eliminate many systems from consideration and possibly point to the affected system. Before diving into an extended electrical diagnosis, take the time to review the basics. Check every vacuum line for cracks or leaks. Check every electrical connector for corrosion or loose pins. Quite often, simply unplugging and reconnecting a connector will break up corrosion on the pins and restore the circuit. Watch out for poor grounds, particularly if the car has experienced major bodywork.

COMPONENT TESTING

Air Injection System

The purpose of this system is to supply oxygen to the exhaust stream at a point in the exhaust manifold that is hot enough to burn off some of the hydro-carbon emissions. The main component is an air suction valve. The valve is spring loaded to stay closed, with engine vacuum supplied to a diaphragm that reduces the spring pressure and allows the reeds to open. The ECU regulates the engine vacuum to the diaphragm by operating a solenoid valve.

1. With the engine at normal operating temperature and at idle, remove the air cleaner and listen for a bubbling sound at the air suction port. There should be no sound at idle, meaning the air suction valve is closed.

2. If the noise is heard at the air suction port, disconnect the vacuum hose at the air suction valve and connect a vacuum gauge to the hose. There should be no vacuum. If there is vacuum and the noise stops, the problem is in the control system. If there is no vacuum and the bubbling sound is still there, the air suction valve is defective and must be replaced.

3. To test the valve, draw a vacuum at the air suction valve diaphragm and listen for a bubbling sound at the air suction port. If no sound is heard, the air suction valve or diaphragm is faulty.

Throttle Control System

♦ See Figure 35

The purpose of this system is to help prevent an overly rich air/fuel mixture when the throttle closes at high rpm, such as during shifting or deceleration. At idle, high manifold vacuum is applied to the throttle controller to keep the throttle open to the idle position. When the throttle is opened for increased power, the manifold vacuum decreases and the stored vacuum in the throttle controller leaks away through the check valve. When the throttle pedal is released, the increased manifold vacuum causes the throttle controller to slowly close the throttle to the idle position.

1. With the engine at operating temperature and at idle, disconnect the vacuum hose to the throttle controller. The idle rpm should increase to 2200 rpm

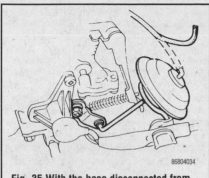

Fig. 35 With the hose disconnected from the throttle controller, the idle speed should change

Fig. 36 The idle boost controller can be tested using a hand vacuum pump

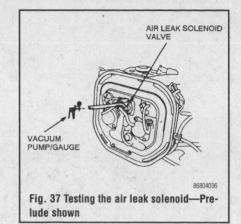

Fig. 37 Testing the air leak solenoid—Prelude shown

on manual transaxles or 1900 rpm with automatic transaxles (in Neutral). If the speed is incorrect, adjust it by bending the tab.

2. If the rpm did not change, check the vacuum at the hose. If there is vacuum, the throttle controller is faulty. If there is no vacuum, there is a vacuum leak or a misrouted hose.

Idle Boost Control

♦ See Figure 36

When the air conditioner is turned on, the solenoid valve is activated to allow manifold vacuum into the idle boost throttle controller. This device pulls the throttle open only enough to maintain the specified idle speed, not increase it. The throttle opening can be adjusted with a screw on top of the unit.

1. With the engine at normal operating temperature and all accessories off, make sure idle speed is 800 rpm on manual transaxle models or 750 rpm with on automatics. If it is incorrect, do not adjust idle speed yet.

2. Remove the vacuum hose from the top of the idle boost controller and attach a vacuum gauge. There should be no vacuum. Turn the air conditioner on; there should be vacuum. When the hose is reconnected to the boost controller, idle speed should return to specification.

3. If there is vacuum to the boost controller when the air conditioner is off, unplug the connector to the idle boost solenoid valve on the firewall. If the vacuum is still there, the solenoid valve is faulty.

4. If there is no vacuum with the air conditioner on, check for 12 volts at the solenoid valve connector. If there is voltage, the solenoid valve is faulty. If there is no voltage at the red wire, look for 12 volts at ECU terminal A 8 with the air conditioner on. If the voltage is there, the wiring is faulty. If there is no voltage and the air conditioner works, the ECU is faulty.

5. If the idle boost controller functions, but needs adjustment, run the engine at idle and disconnect the vacuum hose from the solenoid valve. Attach a hand vacuum pump to the boost controller.

6. Draw a vacuum on the controller. The idle should rise to about 1200 rpm. Remove the cap from the adjusting screw on top of the controller and turn the adjuster as necessary.

Air Leak Solenoid Valve

♦ See Figure 37

During normal operation, a small amount of air is leaked into the primary jets of the carburetors to control the mixture and promote fuel atomization. When starting or under full power, the air leak solenoid valve is closed to provide a slightly richer air/fuel mixture. On Preludes, the valve is mounted inside the air cleaner between the carburetors. The ECU looks at ignition, transmission/clutch, and vacuum switch positions, vehicle speed, coolant/intake air temperatures and the MAP sensor when making the decision to operate this valve.

1. Remove the air cleaner and connect a hand vacuum pump to the valve. With the engine cold and at idle, pull a vacuum; it should hold at about 4 in. Hg (102 mm Hg) of vacuum. If it does, allow the engine to warm up to normal operating temperature.

2. At normal operating temperature and the inlet air temperature at least 158°F or 70°C (when measured at the TA sensor in the intake manifold), the valve should not hold vacuum. If it does hold vacuum and there is no voltage to

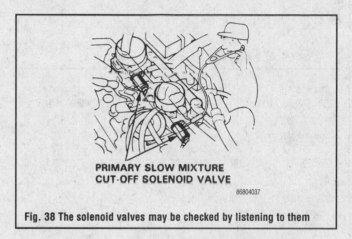

PRIMARY SLOW MIXTURE CUT-OFF SOLENOID VALVE

Fig. 38 The solenoid valves may be checked by listening to them

the solenoid at the green wire, the solenoid or air bleed valve inside the solenoid is faulty.

3. If there is voltage to the solenoid at idle, the ECU is faulty.

Primary Slow Mixture Cut-Off Solenoid Valve

♦ See Figure 38

There is one of these valves in each carburetor, used to cut-off the fuel flow in the idle circuit. They are energized when the ignition is **ON**, and de-energized during deceleration or when the ignition is **OFF**.

1. Turn the ignition **ON** and unplug the black/yellow wire at each valve one at a time. By making and breaking the connection, it should be possible to hear the valve click. If either valve sticks open, the engine will probably run-on after the ignition is turned **OFF**.

Vacuum Piston Control System

♦ See Figure 39

The variable venturi size is achieved by moving a piston up and down inside the venturi. The piston is manifold vacuum actuated. A storage chamber ensures that vacuum is still available at wide open throttle. Since manifold vacuum is used to operate the piston, venturi size is proportional for all throttle openings. A solenoid valve operated by the ECU is used to shut off the vacuum and let the pistons fall during deceleration.

1. Disconnect the vacuum hose from the top of the carburetor, connect a hand vacuum pump to the piston and draw a vacuum. It should leak down slowly as the piston falls.

2. Start the engine. With the engine idling at normal operating temperature, the piston should not hold vacuum. There is an internal passage from the top of the piston to the intake manifold which pulls the vacuum off faster when the engine is running.

3. Disconnect hose No. 28 (refer to the vacuum diagrams in this section) from the air cleaner to the piston control solenoid valve and connect a vacuum gauge. At idle there should be vacuum. Run the engine at about 3000 rpm and

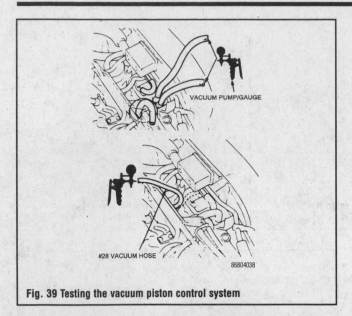

VACUUM PUMP/GAUGE

#28 VACUUM HOSE

86804038

Fig. 39 Testing the vacuum piston control system

allow the throttle to snap closed. The vacuum should drop almost completely for a moment. The solenoid valve is operated by the ECU during deceleration through the yellow (positive) wire and the black (negative) wire.

Power Valve

At the bottom of the carburetor is a valve which opens to allow more fuel into the main jet passage. The valve is vacuum actuated by a 2-way solenoid valve, energized by the ECU during hard acceleration.

1. Start the engine and warm it to normal operating temperature. Disconnect vacuum hose No. 14 (refer to the vacuum diagrams in this section) from the pipe assembly and connect a vacuum gauge. There should be vacuum, indicating the 2-way valve is activated and preventing vacuum from reaching the power valve.

2. If there is no vacuum, check for a vacuum leak. Make sure the solenoid valve is receiving 12 volts between the green/yellow wire and the black wire when the engine is at idle.

3. If no voltage is reaching the solenoid valve, check the green/yellow wire that comes from the ECU. If there is no short or open circuit, the ECU is not receiving the proper sensor inputs or the ECU is faulty.

Automatic Choke

The choke is vacuum actuated by the choke opener and is dependent on coolant temperature. A thermowax valve controls coolant flow through the carburetor heating passages. As the coolant heats up, flow to the carburetor heat passages is decreased and vacuum to the choke opener becomes available. The choke opener is a pull-off diaphragm connected to the choke linkage. Failure of this system can cause hard cold start conditions.

1. With the engine cold, disconnect the vacuum hose from the choke opener and connect a hand vacuum pump with a gauge. Disable the ignition system so the engine will not start and turn the ignition switch to **START**. There should be no vacuum, indicating the solenoid valve is activated.

2. Disconnect the hose from the manifold and draw a vacuum on the opener through the hose. It should stabilize at about 4–8 in. Hg (102–203 mm Hg) of vacuum and the opener should pull the linkage.

Programmed Fuel Injection (PGM-FI) System— 1985–89 Models

GENERAL INFORMATION

In order to get proper amount of fuel into the cylinders at the correct instant, the control system must perform various separate functions. The Electronic Control Unit (ECU), which is the heart of the PGM-FI system, uses an eight-bit microcomputer and consists of a Central Processing Unit (CPU), memory data,

and Input/Output (I/O) ports. Basic data stored in the memory is modified by the signals sent from the various sensors to provide the correct air/fuel mixture for all engine needs.

As useful as the tests found in this section are, the first step in repair or service to engine management systems is still to gain as much information as possible about the problem; when and under what conditions it occurs. At highway speed? At idle only? Only under heavy load or hard acceleration? Wet weather? Defining the problem will eliminate many systems from consideration and possibly point to the affected system. Before diving into an extended electrical diagnosis, take the time to review the basics. Check every vacuum line for cracks or leaks. Check every electrical connector for corrosion or loose pins. Quite often, simply unplugging and reconnecting a connector will break up corrosion on the pins and restore the circuit. Watch out for poor grounds, particularly if the car has experienced major bodywork.

SERVICE PRECAUTIONS

- Do not operate the fuel pump when the fuel lines and tank are empty, or when the fuel pump has been removed from the tank.
- Do not reuse fuel hose clamps.
- The washer(s) below any fuel system bolt (banjo fittings, service bolt, fuel filter, etc.) must be replaced whenever the bolt is loosened. Do not reuse the washers; a high-pressure fuel leak may result.
- Make sure all ECU harness connectors are fastened securely. A poor connection can cause a high voltage surge and result in damage to integrated circuits.
- Keep all ECU parts and harnesses dry during service. Protect the ECU and all solid-state components from rough handling or extremes of temperature.
- Before attempting to remove any parts, turn the ignition switch **OFF** and disconnect the battery ground cable.
- Always use a 12 volt battery as a power source, never a booster or high-voltage charging unit.
- Do not disconnect the battery cables with the engine running.
- Do not unplug any wiring connector with the engine running or the ignition **ON**, unless specifically instructed to do so.
- Do not depress the accelerator pedal when starting.
- Do not rev up the engine immediately after starting or just prior to shutdown.
- Do not apply battery power directly to injectors.
- Whenever possible, use a flashlight or a shatter-proof drop light. The bulbs used in standard drop lights may shatter on impact, creating a spark which may ignite fuel vapors.
- Keep all open flame and smoking material out of the area.
- Use a shop cloth or similar to catch fuel when opening the fuel system.
- Relieve fuel system pressure before servicing.
- Always use eye or full-face protection when working around fuel lines, fittings or components.
- Always keep a dry chemical (class B-C) fire extinguisher near the area.

COMPONENT TESTING

Manifold Air Pressure (MAP) Sensor

▶ See Figure 40

This sensor converts manifold air pressure readings into electrical voltage signals and sends them to the ECU. This information is used along with signals from the crank angle sensor to compute the basic injector duration.

1. Disconnect the vacuum hose between the MAP sensor and throttle body; plug the opening in throttle body. Connect a vacuum hand pump to the open end of vacuum tube.

2. Disconnect the negative battery cable.

3. Unplug the wire harness from the control unit. Connect system checker harness (07999–PD6000A or equivalent) between the control unit and the wire harness connector.

4. Connect the negative battery cable.

5. Turn the ignition switch **ON**. Connect a digital voltmeter positive probe to terminal C 11 of the system checker harness and the negative probe to terminal C 14. Measure the voltage between the two terminals. The voltmeter should indicate 0.5 volts at 4 in. Hg (100 mm Hg) of vacuum and 4.5 volts at 45 in. Hg (1200 mm Hg).

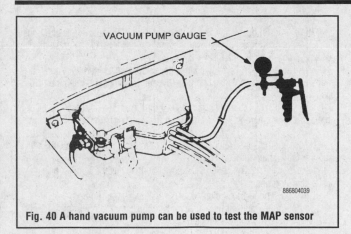

VACUUM PUMP GAUGE

886804039

Fig. 40 A hand vacuum pump can be used to test the MAP sensor

6. If the voltage is incorrect, check the vacuum hose for leakage and check the wires between the control unit and sensor for open or short circuits. Replace the sensor if wires are OK.

Atmospheric Pressure (PA) Sensor

Like the MAP sensor, this sensor converts atmospheric pressures into voltage signals. The ECU modifies the basic injector duration to compensate for changes in the atmospheric pressure.

1. Disconnect the negative battery cable.
2. Unplug the wire harness connector from the control unit. Connect system checker harness (07999–PD6000A or equivalent) between the control unit and the wire harness connector.
3. Connect the negative battery cable.
4. Turn the ignition switch **ON**. Connect a digital voltmeter positive probe to terminal C 9 of system checker harness and the negative probe to terminal C 12. Measure the voltage between the two terminals. Voltmeter should indicate between 2.76–2.96 volts.
5. If the voltage is outside this range, check for open or short circuits between the ECU and PA sensor. Replace the PA sensor if the wires are OK.

Idle Mixture Adjuster (IMA) Sensor

▶ See Figure 41

This sensor is located in vacuum control box No. 1. The primary objective of this unit is to maintain the correct air/fuel ratio at idle. It is used on the 1985 Accord only.

1. Open the No. 1 control box lid and remove the rivets attaching the IMA sensor.
2. Unplug the IMA sensor connector.
3. Measure the resistance between the brown and green wire terminals of IMA sensor while turning the adjuster. Resistance should be between 0.25–6.2k ohm.
4. Replace the IMA sensor if resistance readings are out of range.

Coolant Temperature (TW) Sensor

▶ See Figure 42

This sensor is a thermistor and is used to measure differences in the coolant temperature. The basic injector duration is partially based on the signals sent from this sensor through the ECU. The resistance of the thermistor decreases with a rise in coolant temperature.

1. Unplug the connector from the sensor, then remove the sensor from the thermostat housing.
2. To test the sensor, suspend it in cold water and heat the water slowly. Measure resistance between the terminals. Resistance values are as follows:
- 0.98–1.34k ohms at 95°F (40°C)
- 0.22–0.35k ohms at 176°F (80°C)

3. Replace the sensor if resistance is outside the specified range. Tighten it to 20 ft. lbs. (28 Nm).

Intake Air Temperature (TA) Sensor

▶ See Figure 42

This device is a thermistor and is placed in the intake manifold or air inlet boot. It acts much like the coolant temperature sensor, but has a reduced thermal capacity for quicker response.

1. Unplug the connector from the sensor, then remove the sensor from the intake manifold or air inlet boot.
2. To test the sensor, suspend it in cold water and heat the water slowly. Measure resistance between the terminals. Resistance values are as follows:
- 1985 Accord—0.98–1.34k ohms at 95°F (40°C)
- 1985 Accord—0.22–0.35k ohms at 176°F (80°C)
- 1986–89 Accord and Prelude—0.98–1.34k ohms at 104°F (40°C)
- 1986–89 Accord and Prelude—0.22–0.35k ohm at 176°F (80°C)

3. Replace the sensor if resistance is outside the specified range.

Cylinder (CYL) Sensor

The CYL sensor is used to detect the position of No. 1 cylinder; the signal is used to trigger the sequential fuel injection.

1985–89 ACCORD AND 1985–87 PRELUDE

1. Unplug the connector of the crank angle/cylinder sensors on the distributor.
2. Measure resistance between the orange and white terminals of the sensor. Resistance should be 650–850 ohms.
3. Measure the resistance between both terminals of the sensor and crank angle sensor housing. Resistance should 100k (100,000) ohms or more.

1988–89 PRELUDE

1. Unplug the connector from the cylinder sensor (next to the distributor).
2. Measure the resistance between the two terminals of the sensor. Resistance should be between 700–1000 ohms.
3. Check for continuity between the two sensor terminals and ground. If continuity exists, replace the sensor.

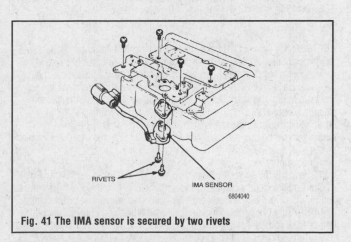

RIVETS

IMA SENSOR

6804040

Fig. 41 The IMA sensor is secured by two rivets

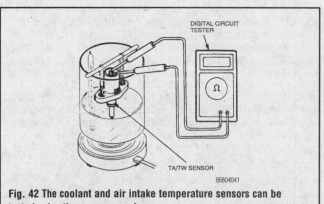

DIGITAL CIRCUIT TESTER

Ω

TA/TW SENSOR

86804041

Fig. 42 The coolant and air intake temperature sensors can be tested using the same procedure

Crank Angle (TDC/CRANK) Sensors

The CRANK or crankshaft angle sensor signal is used to determine the fuel injection and ignition timing. It is also used to generate the engine speed signal. The TDC sensor signal is used to determine ignition timing during start-up or when the CRANK signal is abnormal. The TDC and CRANK sensors are incorporated in one unit.

1985–89 ACCORD AND 1985–87 PRELUDE

1. Unplug the connector of the crank angle/cylinder sensors on the distributor.
2. Measure resistance between the orange/blue and white/blue terminals of the sensor. Resistance should be 650–850 ohms.
3. Measure the resistance between both terminals of the sensor and crank angle sensor housing. Resistance should 100k (100,000) ohms or more.

1988–1989 PRELUDE

1. Unplug the connector of the crank angle sensor on the distributor.
2. Measure resistance between the two top terminals of the sensor connector (located under the locking tab). Resistance should be 700–1000 ohms.
3. Check for continuity between both of the top two terminals of the sensor and ground. If continuity exists, replace the sensor.

Throttle Angle Sensor

This sensor is a potentiometer which translates the position of the throttle plate to an electrical signal. The signal is near 0 volts at idle and increases to just under 5 volts at wide open throttle. The sensor is mounted to the side of the throttle body.

➡**Do not adjust throttle valve stop screw; it is preset at factory.**

1. Unplug the connector of the throttle angle sensor.
2. On 1985 Accords, measure the resistance between the yellow and green wire terminals at the sensor. Resistance should be between 3.2–7.2k (3200–7200) ohms.
3. On 1986–89 Accords and Preludes, measure the resistance between the yellow/white and green/white wire terminals at sensor. Resistance should be between 4–6k (4000–6000) ohms.
4. If the resistance is not as specified, replace the sensor.

Programmed Fuel Injection (PGM-FI) System— 1990–95 Models

GENERAL INFORMATION

The Programmed Fuel Injection (PGM–FI) System is a fully electronic microprocessor based engine management system. The Electronic Control Unit (ECU) is given responsibility for control of injector timing and duration, intake air control, ignition timing, cold start enrichment, fuel pump control, fuel cut-off, A/C compressor operation, alternator control as well as EGR function and canister purge cycles.

Troubleshooting is generally based on symptom diagnosis and stored fault codes, if any. Testing requires the use of the diagnostic charts in conjunction with the Honda test harness (pin-out box) and a digital volt/ohmmeter. On the 1995 Accord V-6, a scan tool is also needed to extract the trouble codes.

As useful as the tests found in this section are, the first step in repair or service to engine management systems is still to gain as much information as possible about the problem; when and under what conditions it occurs. At highway speed? At idle only? Only under heavy load or hard acceleration? Wet weather? Defining the problem will eliminate many systems from consideration and possibly point to the affected system. Before diving into an extended electrical diagnosis, take the time to review the basics. Check every vacuum line for cracks or leaks. Check every electrical connector for corrosion or loose pins. Quite often, simply unplugging and reconnecting a connector will break up corrosion on the pins and restore the circuit. Watch out for poor grounds, particularly if the car has experienced major bodywork.

SERVICE PRECAUTIONS

• Do not operate the fuel pump when the fuel lines and tank are empty, or when the fuel pump has been removed from the tank.

• Do not reuse fuel hose clamps.
• The washer(s) below any fuel system bolt (banjo fittings, service bolt, fuel filter, etc.) must be replaced whenever the bolt is loosened. Do not reuse the washers; a high-pressure fuel leak may result.
• Make sure all ECU harness connectors are fastened securely. A poor connection can cause a high voltage surge and result in damage to integrated circuits.
• Keep all ECU parts and harnesses dry during service. Protect the ECU and all solid-state components from rough handling or extremes of temperature.
• Before attempting to remove any parts, turn the ignition switch **OFF** and disconnect the battery ground cable.
• Always use a 12 volt battery as a power source, never a booster or high-voltage charging unit.
• Do not disconnect the battery cables with the engine running.
• Do not unplug any wiring connector with the engine running or the ignition **ON**, unless specifically instructed to do so.
• Do not depress the accelerator pedal when starting.
• Do not rev up the engine immediately after starting or just prior to shutdown.
• Do not apply battery power directly to injectors.
• Whenever possible, use a flashlight or a shatter-proof drop light. The bulbs used in standard drop lights may shatter on impact, creating a spark which may ignite fuel vapors.
• Keep all open flame and smoking material out of the area.
• Use a shop cloth or similar to catch fuel when opening the fuel system.
• Relieve fuel system pressure before servicing.
• Always use eye or full-face protection when working around fuel lines, fittings or components.
• Always keep a dry chemical (class B-C) fire extinguisher near the area.

COMPONENT DESCRIPTION

Electronic Control Unit (ECU)

Functions of the ECU include:
• Starting Control—The fuel system must vary the air/fuel ratio to suit different operating requirements. For example, the mixture must be rich for starting. Data stored in the unit's memory also contains the injector duration values to be triggered by signals from the starter switch, engine speed and coolant temperature sensors, thereby providing extra fuel needed for starting.
• Injector Control—The ECU regulates the injector durations at various engine speeds and loads by precisely controlling the amount of time the injectors are open.
• Electronic Air Control—The ECU regulates the EACV to maintain correct idle speed based on engine and accessories demand.
• Ignition Timing Control—The ECU regulates the basic ignition timing based on engine load, engine rpm, vehicle speed and coolant temperature.
• Fuel Pump Control—When the engine is not running but the ignition is **ON**, electric current to the fuel pump is cut-off
• Fuel Cut-Off Control—During deceleration with the throttle valve nearly closed, electric current to the injectors is cut-off at engine speeds of approximately 1300–1500 rpm, contributing to improved fuel economy. Fuel cut-off also takes place when engine speed exceeds the red-line or safe operation rpm limit.
• Fail Safe—If the ECU notes the loss of or an out-of-range sensor signal, the computer will ignore the faulty signal and substitute a fixed value in its place. This value may not necessarily be correct for the immediate driving situation, but will allow the engine to operate. For example, many ECU decisions are based on the engine coolant temperature. Should the coolant temperature sensor (TW sensor) signal be lost just after a cold start, the ECU will substitute the default value. This substitution value is based on an engine at normal temperature so vehicle performance may be affected until fully warmed up.
• Back-up System—The ECU also tests itself while operating. If an abnormality occurs within the ECU, the system switches to a back-up circuit independent of the computing system. This system substitutes fixed values for all inputs and controls the injectors accordingly. Vehicle performance is reduced to minimal driveability. The back-up function serves as a lifeboat to prevent the vehicle from being stranded in the event of ECU failure.
• Self-Diagnosis—When an abnormality occurs, the ECU triggers the check

engine lamp and stores a failure code in erasable memory. The ECU will display the code any time the ignition is turned **ON**.

CRANK, TDC and CYL Sensors

The CRANK or crankshaft angle sensor signal is used to determine the fuel injection and ignition timing. It is also used to generate the engine speed signal. The TDC sensor signal is used to determine ignition timing during start-up or when the CRANK signal is abnormal. The CYL sensor is used to detect the position of No. 1 cylinder; the signal is used to trigger the sequential fuel injection.

These sensors are contained within the distributor. The signals are generated by the rotation of toothed wheels passing through pick-up coils. In some cases, the CYL sensor is incorporated with the other two. The function of these components does not change, but if any single sensor is defective, the entire distributor must be replaced as an assembly.

Manifold Air Pressure (MAP) Sensor

This sensor converts manifold air pressure readings into electrical voltage signals and sends them to the ECU. This information is used along with signals from the crank angle sensor to compute the basic injector duration.

Coolant Temperature (TW) Sensor

This sensor uses a temperature-dependent resistor (thermistor) to measure differences in the coolant temperature. The basic injector duration is partially based on the signals sent from this sensor through the ECU. The resistance of the thermistor decreases with a rise in coolant temperature.

Intake Air Temperature (TA) Sensor

This device is also a thermistor and is placed in the intake manifold. It acts much like the coolant temperature sensor, but with a reduced thermal capacity for quicker response. The injector duration determined by the ECU is altered for different operating conditions by the signals sent from this sensor.

Throttle Angle Sensor

This sensor is a potentiometer which translates the position of the throttle plate to an electrical signal. The signal is near zero at idle and increases to just under 5 volts at wide-open throttle. The sensor is mounted to the side of the throttle body.

Oxygen Sensor

The oxygen sensor detects the oxygen content in the exhaust gas and sends an electrical signal to the ECU. The ECU then uses this signal to control fuel injector duration, maintaining the stoichiometric air/fuel ratio of 14.7:1. The sensor is located either in the exhaust manifold or in the exhaust piping ahead of the catalytic converter. Some models use 2 sensors.

Oxygen sensors only become efficient when operating at the proper temperature. Some models use a heated oxygen sensor. The heater stabilizes the sensor's output and allows the sensor to heat quicker after the engine as been started.

EGR Valve Lift Sensor

The ECU regulates the function of the EGR valve through the EGR control solenoid. The lift sensor translates the movement of the EGR shaft into an electric signal which is sent back to the ECU. The control unit compares this signal to pre-programmed values for optimum function. The sensor is located on the EGR valve.

Atmospheric Pressure (PA) Sensor

This sensor converts atmospheric pressures into voltage signals and sends them to the ECU. The signals then modify the basic injector duration to compensate for changes in the atmospheric pressure.

The PA sensor is located inside the passenger compartment of the vehicle, usually next to the ECU. On some models, it is contained within the ECU.

Vehicle Speed Sensor (VSS)

The signal from the vehicle speed sensor is used by the ECU as well as the cruise control and automatic transaxle control units.

Accords and Preludes use an external sensor mounted on top of the power steering speed sensor in the engine compartment. The power steering speed sensor is gear-driven and controls the steering boost in relation to the speed of the vehicle. An electric pulser unit is mounted on top of this unit and is coupled to it by a small shaft. The motion from the lower unit is transferred to the upper unit; the resultant electrical signal is sent to the appropriate control units.

Starter Signal

The **START** position on the ignition switch causes a signal to be sent to the ECU. During cranking, the ECU will increase the amount of fuel injected according to the signals received from the engine temperature sensors.

Alternator FR Signal

The ECU receives a signal from the alternator to control the system charging.

Air Conditioning Signal

The load on the engine increases when the compressor is engaged; the ECU must increase the idle as necessary. In some cases, the ECU will limit A/C operation, cutting it off through the A/C control relay in cases of wide-open throttle or preventing it from engaging in cold engine conditions. If the vehicle has a separate control unit for the air conditioning, the two controllers exchange information regarding system status.

Automatic Transaxle Shift Position Signal

This signal is sent to the ECU through the neutral safety switch. The control unit will not allow the engine to start if the shift selector is not in NEUTRAL or PARK.

Power Steering Fluid Pressure Switch

When the power steering fluid pressure exceeds a predetermined level, the ECU is signaled by a pressure operated switch. If the idle is below a predetermined rpm, as during a parking maneuver, the control unit will increase the idle speed of the engine to compensate for the additional load.

Electric Load Detector (ELD)

This sensor is located in the underhood fuse and relay box. It detects the presence of moderate to large electrical current in the system and sends a signal to the ECU.

The ECU will control the idle speed to compensate for the additional load of headlights, rear defroster, heater fan or similar heavy electrical loads.

The ELD unit is integral with the fuse box in which it is mounted; should the sensor fail, the fuse box assembly must be replaced.

TROUBLE CODES

System Diagnosis

READING CODES

When the "Check Engine" warning light on the dashboard comes on and stays on, it indicates a problem in the fuel injection/emissions system. Check the ECU for fault codes. On certain models, some codes will not trigger the check engine light; if driveability has suffered, check for stored fault codes.

The most common error when using fault codes is to assume the indicated component has failed rather than checking the entire circuit. The presence of a trouble code means simply that the electrical circuit for the named component is not functioning properly. For example, a code for the oxygen sensor circuit does not automatically mean the oxygen sensor has failed. A wire terminal may simply be loose or corroded at the connector. When using diagnostic or fault codes, always remember that the entire circuit including the component must be checked carefully.

Carbureted Models

▶ See Figure 43

Although the 1984–89 Accords and 1984–87 Preludes use a feedback control ECU, the control unit does not have a self-diagnostic capability. If a fault occurs in a circuit, careful diagnosis and testing of the individual components must be used to find the problem. A thorough understanding of electronic systems is required.

Beginning with the 1988 Preludes, the control unit or ECU includes self-diagnostic capabilities similar to those found on fuel injected models. Codes 1 through 9 are indicated by a series of short flashes; two-digit codes use a long flash for the first digit followed by the appropriate number of short flashes. For example, Code 14 would be indicated by 1 long flash followed by 4 short flashes. Codes are separated by a pause between displays. Multiple codes are transmitted in an alternating pattern. For example, a code 3 and 14 would be displayed as 3 short flashes (for Code 3) followed by the separator pause, then 1 long flash and 4 short flashes (for Code 14).

1. The ECU is located on the front floor, about under the passenger's toes. Pull the carpet down; a large protective cover will be seen over the ECU. On the upper edge of the cover is a window or opening, allowing the Light Emitting Diode (LED) to be viewed.

2. Turn the ignition **ON**, but do not start the engine. The LED should begin to flash.

➡ **In the event that a code is encountered which is not on the chart, recount the number of flashes. If the code is truly wrong, it will be necessary to swap the ECU for a known-good unit and recheck. Since this can be expensive, you may wish to bring the car to a reputable repair facility if no other cause of the failure can be found. This may save you the expense of purchasing an unnecessary part.**

3. Once the codes are read, refer to the appropriate troubleshooting chart for testing procedures. Note that some tests will require the Honda test harness. (Use harness No. 07HAZ–PJ7010A and 07HAZ–PH7000A for 1988–89 and 07LAJ–PT30100 for 1990). This is a device which allows safe testing of the electrical circuits without backprobing connectors. It installs between the ECU and the wiring harnesses. This is a specialty item, usually only available from dealers.

1988–90 PRELUDE FAULT CODES PGM-CARB SYSTEM

- CODE 1: Oxygen content
- CODE 2: Vehicle speed pulser
- CODE 3: MAP sensor, electrical signal
- CODE 4: Vacuum switch signal

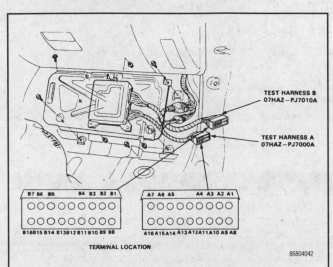

Fig. 43 The test harness allows for safe diagnosis of the electrical circuits without backprobing connectors

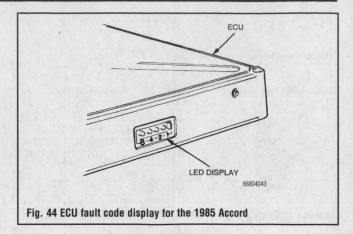

Fig. 44 ECU fault code display for the 1985 Accord

- CODE 5: MAP sensor, vacuum signal
- CODE 6: Coolant temperature
- CODE 7: Clutch switch signal (manual trans.)
- CODE 7: Shift position signal (auto trans.)
- CODE 8: Ignition coil signal
- CODE 10: Intake air temperature
- CODE 14: Electronic Air Control Valve (EACV)

Fuel Injected Models

1985 ACCORD

▶ See Figures 44 and 45

On the 1985 Accord, there are four LEDs. They are part of the ECU, which is located under the passenger's seat, and are numbered 1, 2, 4 and 8 (as counted from right to left). The codes are interpreted by comparing the display on the ECU to the display pattern shown in the chart.

LED Display	Possible Cause	Symptom
○ ○ ○ ○ (Dash Warning Light ON only)	• Loose or poorly connected power line to ECU • Short circuit in combination meter or warning light wire • Faulty ECU	• Engine will not start • No particular symptom shown
○ ○ ○ ● (1)	• Disconnected oxygen sensor coupler • Spark plug mis-fire • Short or open circuit in oxygen sensor circuit • Faulty oxygen sensor	• Idle speed too high • No particular symptom shown
○ ○ ● ○ (2)	• Faulty ECU	• No particular symptom shown or system does not operate
○ ○ ● ● (2 1)	• Disconnected manifold air pressure sensor coupler • Short or open circuit in manifold air pressure sensor wire • Faulty manifold air pressure sensor	• Wet-plug • Frequent engine stalling • Engine fails to pick up speed
○ ● ○ ○ (4)	• Faulty ECU	• No particular symptom shown or system does not operate
○ ● ○ ● (4 1)	• Disconnected manifold air pressure sensor piping	• Engine fails to pick up speed • Wet-plug • Frequent engine stalling
○ ● ● ○ (4 2)	• Disconnected coolant temperature sensor coupler • Open circuit in coolant temperature sensor wire • Faulty coolant temperature sensor (thermostat housing)	• High idle speed during warm-up • High idle speed • Hard starting at low temp
○ ● ● ● (4 2 1)	• Disconnected throttle angle sensor coupler • Open or short circuit in throttle angle sensor wire • Faulty throttle angle sensor	• Poor engine response to open throttle rapidly • High idle speed • Engine does not rev up when cold
● ○ ○ ○ (8)	• Short or open circuit in crank angle sensor wire • Crank angle sensor wire interfering with high tension cord • Crank angle sensor at fault	• Engine does not rev up • High idle speed • Erratic idling
● ○ ○ ● (8)	• Same as above	• Same as above
● ○ ● ○ (8 2)	• Disconnected intake air temperature sensor • Open circuit in intake air temperature sensor wire • Faulty intake air temperature sensor	• High idle speed • Erratic idling when very cold
● ○ ● ● (8 2 1)	• Disconnected idle mixture adjuster sensor coupler • Shorted or disconnected idle mixture adjuster sensor wire • Faulty idle mixture adjuster sensor	• No particular symptom shown • High idle speed
● ● ○ ○ (8 4)	• Disconnected EGR control system coupler • Shorted or disconnected EGR control wire • Faulty EGR control system	• Frequent engine stalling • Erratic or unstable running at low speed • No particular symptom shown
● ● ○ ● (8 4 1)	• Disconnected atmospheric pressure sensor coupler • Shorted or disconnected atmospheric pressure sensor wire • Faulty atmospheric pressure sensor	• Poor acceleration at high altitude • Hard starting at high altitude when cold
● ● ● ○ (8 4 2)	• Faulty ECU	• No particular symptom shown or system does not operate at all
● ● ● ● (8 4 2 1)	• Same as above	• Same as above

Fig. 45 Display code chart for the 1985 Accord

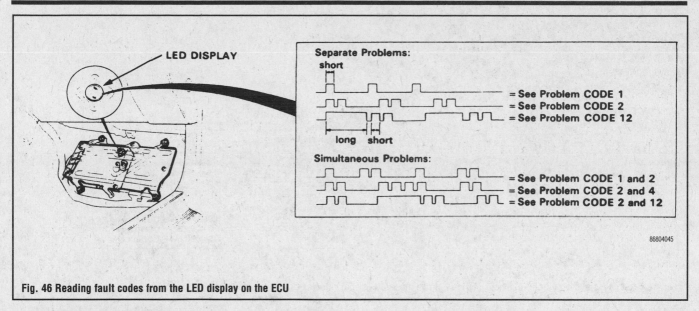

Fig. 46 Reading fault codes from the LED display on the ECU

1. Access the ECU.
2. Turn the ignition switch **ON**; the LEDs will display any stored codes in a pattern.

➡ **In the event that a code is encountered which is not on the chart, recount the number of flashes. If the code is truly wrong, it will be necessary to swap the ECU for a known-good unit and recheck. Since this can be expensive, you may wish to bring the car to a reputable repair facility if no other cause of the failure can be found. This may save you the expense of purchasing an unnecessary part.**

3. If no codes are displayed but a driveablity problem exits, testing of the individual components of the system is necessary to find the problem.

1986–89 ACCORD AND 1985–91 PRELUDE

♦ **See Figures 46, 47 and 48**

On 1986–89 Accord and 1985–91 Prelude models, there is only one LED display. The LED will blink to indicate the trouble code. The ECU is located under the driver's seat on the Accord. On 1985–87 Preludes, it is in the left side trim panel beside the rear seat. On 1988–91 Preludes, it is located under the carpet on the right front passenger footwell.

Codes 1 through 9 are indicated by a series of short flashes; two-digit codes use a long flash for the first digit followed by the appropriate number of short flashes. For example, Code 14 would be indicated by 1 long flash followed by 4 short flashes. Codes are separated by a pause between displays. Multiple codes are transmitted in an alternating pattern. For example, a code 3 and 14 would be displayed as 3 short flashes (for Code 3) followed by the separator pause, then 1 long flash and 4 short flashes (for Code 14).

1. Access the ECU.
2. Turn the ignition switch **ON**; the LED will display any stored codes by rhythmic flashing.

➡ **In the event that a code is encountered which is not on the chart, recount the number of flashes. If the code is truly wrong, it will be necessary to swap the ECU for a known-good unit and recheck. Since this can be expensive, you may wish to bring the car to a reputable repair facility if no other cause of the failure can be found. This may save you the expense of purchasing an unnecessary part.**

3. If no codes are displayed but a driveablity problem exits, testing of the individual components of the system is necessary to find the problem.

SELF-DIAGNOSIS INDICATOR BLINKS	SYSTEM INDICATED
0	ECU
1	OXYGEN CONTENT A
2	OXYGEN CONTENT B
3	MANIFOLD ABSOLUTE PRESSURE
5	
4	CRANK ANGLE
6	COOLANT TEMPERATURE
7	THROTTLE ANGLE
8	TDC POSITION
9	No.1 CYLINDER POSITION
10	INTAKE AIR TEMPERATURE
12	EXHAUST GAS RECIRCULATION SYSTEM
13	ATMOSPHERIC PRESSURE
14	ELECTRONIC IDLE CONTROL
15	IGNITION OUTPUT SIGNAL
16	FUEL INJECTOR
17	VEHICLE SPEED SENSOR

Fig. 47 Fault code chart for 1986–89 Accord and 1985–89 Prelude

SELF-DIAGNOSIS INDICATOR BLINKS	SYSTEM INDICATED
0	ECU
1	OXYGEN CONTENT A*, OXYGEN CONTENT**
2*	OXYGEN CONTENT B
3	MANIFOLD ABSOLUTE PRESSURE
5	
4	CRANK ANGLE
6	COOLANT TEMPERATURE
7	THROTTLE ANGLE
8	TDC POSITION
9	No.1 CYLINDER POSITION
10	INTAKE AIR TEMPERATURE
12	EXHAUST GAS RECIRCULATION SYSTEM
13	ATMOSPHERIC PRESSURE
14	ELECTRONIC AIR CONTROL
15	IGNITION OUTPUT SIGNAL
16	FUEL INJECTOR
17	VEHICLE SPEED SENSOR
41**	OXYGEN SENSOR HEATER
43**	FUEL SUPPLY SYSTEM

Fig. 48 Fault code chart for 1990–91 Prelude. The single asterisk applies to 2.0L engines only; a double asterisk pertains only to the 2.1L engine

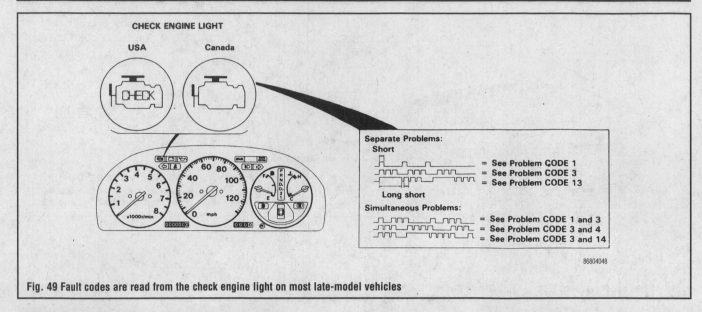

Fig. 49 Fault codes are read from the check engine light on most late-model vehicles

1990–95 FOUR CYLINDER ACCORD AND 1992–95 PRELUDE

▶ See Figures 49 thru 54

On 1990–95 Accord (except V-6) and 1992–95 Prelude, the codes are read from the check engine light after the two-wire service connector has been jumpered. On Accords, the service connector is under the dash on the passenger side. On Preludes, it is located behind the center console. Codes 1 through 9 are indicated by a series of short flashes; two-digit codes use a long flash for the first digit followed by the appropriate number of short flashes. For example, Code 14 would be indicated by 1 long flash followed by 4 short flashes. Codes are separated by a pause between displays. Multiple codes are transmitted in an alternating pattern. For example, a code 3 and 14 would be displayed as 3 short flashes (for Code 3) followed by the separator pause, then 1 long flash and 4 short flashes (for Code 14).

1. Use a jumper wire to connect the two terminals of the service connector together.

2. Turn the ignition switch **ON**; the check engine light will display any stored codes by rhythmic flashing.

➡In the event that a code is encountered which is not on the chart, re-count the number of flashes. If the code is truly wrong, it will be necessary to swap the ECU for a known-good unit and recheck. Since this can be expensive, you may wish to bring the car to a reputable repair facil-

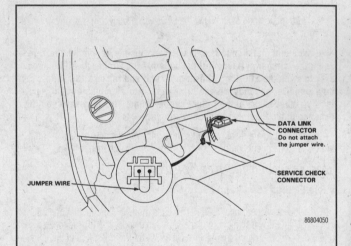

Fig. 51 The service connector on Preludes is located behind the center console

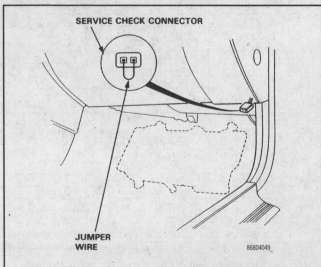

Fig. 50 On Accords, the service connector is located under the dash on the passenger side

SELF-DIAGNOSIS INDICATOR BLINKS	SYSTEM INDICATED
0	ECU
1	OXYGEN CONTENT
3	MANIFOLD ABSOLUTE PRESSURE
5	
4	CRANK ANGLE
6	COOLANT TEMPERATURE
7	THROTTLE ANGLE
8	TDC POSITION
9	No.1 CYLINDER POSITION
10	INTAKE AIR TEMPERATURE
12	EXHAUST GAS RECIRCULATION SYSTEM
13	ATMOSPHERIC PRESSURE
14	ELECTRONIC AIR CONTROL
15	IGNITION OUTPUT SIGNAL
16	FUEL INJECTOR
17	VEHICLE SPEED SENSOR
20	ELECTRIC LOAD DETECTOR
30	A/T FI SIGNAL A
31	A/T FI SIGNAL B
41	OXYGEN SENSOR HEATER
43	FUEL SUPPLY SYSTEM

Fig. 52 Fault code chart for 1990–93 Accords

DIAGNOSTIC TROUBLE CODE (DTC)	SYSTEM INDICATED
0	ENGINE CONTROL MODULE (ECM)
1	HEATED OXYGEN SENSOR (HO2S)
3	MANIFOLD ABSOLUTE PRESSURE (MAP) SENSOR
4	CRANKSHAFT POSITION (CKP) SENSOR
6	ENGINE COOLANT TEMPERATURE (ECT) SENSOR
7	THROTTLE POSITION (TP) SENSOR
8	TOP DEAD CENTER POSITION (TDC) SENSOR
9	No. 1 CYLINDER POSITION (CYP) SENSOR
10	INTAKE AIR TEMPERATURE (IAT) SENSOR
12	EXHAUST GAS RECIRCULATION (EGR) VALVE LIFT SENSOR
13	BAROMETRIC PRESSURE (BARO) SENSOR
14	IDLE AIR CONTROL (IAC) VALVE
15	IGNITION OUTPUT SIGNAL
16	FUEL INJECTOR
17	VEHICLE SPEED SENSOR (VSS)
20	ELECTRICAL LOAD DETECTOR (ELD)
21	VARIABLE VALVE TIMING & VALVE LIFT ELECTRONIC CONTROL (VTEC) SOLENOID VALVE*
22	VARIABLE VALVE TIMING & VALVE LIFT ELECTRONIC CONTROL (VTEC) PRESSURE SWITCH*
30	A/T FI SIGNAL A
31	A/T FI SIGNAL B
41	HEATED OXYGEN SENSOR (HO2S) HEATER
43	FUEL SUPPLY SYSTEM

*: F22B1 engine

86804052

Fig. 53 Fault code chart for 1994–95 Accords (four cylinder)

DIAGONOSTIC TROUBLE CODE (DTC)	SYSTEM INDICATED
0	ENGINE CONTROL MODULE (ECM)
1	HEATED OXYGEN SENSOR (HO2S)
3 5	MANIFOLD ABSOLUTE PRESSURE (MAP) SENSOR
4	CRANKSHAFT POSITION (CKP) SENSOR
6	ENGINE COOLANT TEMPERATURE (ECT) SENSOR
7	THROTTLE POSITION (TPI) SENSOR
8	TOP DEAD CENTER POSITION (TDC) SENSOR
9	No. 1 CYLINDER POSITION (CYP) SENSOR
10	INTAKE AIR TEMPERATURE (IAT) SENSOR
12	EXHAUST GAS RECIRCULATION (EGR) VALVE LIFT SENSOR
13	BAROMETRIC PRESSURE (BARO) SENSOR
14	IDLE AIR CONTROL (IAC) VALVE
15	IGNITION OUTPUT SIGNAL
16	FUEL INJECTOR
17	VEHICLE SPEED SENSOR (VSS)
20	ELECTRICAL LOAD DETECTOR (ELD)
21	VARIABLE VALVE TIMING & VALVE LIFT ELECTRONIC CONTROL (VTEC) SOLENOID VALVE**
22	VARIABLE VALVE TIMING & VALVE LIFT ELECTRONIC CONTROL (VTEC) PRESSURE SWITCH**
23	KNOCK SENSOR (KS)*
30	A/T FI Signal A
31	A/T FI Signal B
41	HEATED OXYGEN SENSOR (HO2S) HEATER
43	FUEL SUPPLY SYSTEM

*: Except F22A1 engine(S)
**: H22A1 engine (USA: Si VTEC/Canada: SR-V)

86804053

Fig. 54 Fault code chart for 1992–95 Preludes

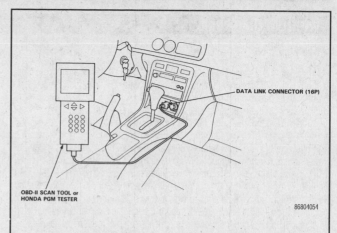

DATA LINK CONNECTOR (16P)

OBD-II SCAN TOOL or
HONDA PGM TESTER

86804054

Fig. 55 On 1995 Accords equipped with the V-6 engine, fault codes can only be read using an OBD-II compliant scan tool or Honda's PGM tester. Note that the service connector is located behind the ashtray in the center console

ity if no other cause of the failure can be found. This may save you the expense of purchasing an unnecessary part.

3. If no codes are displayed but a driveablity problem exits, testing of the system individual components is necessary to find the problem.

1995 ACCORD V-6

♦ See Figure 55

On the 1995 Accord V-6, the fault codes can only be read using an OBD-II compliant scan tool or Honda's PGM tester. Follow the instructions supplied by the scan tool manufacturer. The service connector for the scan tool is located behind the ashtray in the center console.

CLEARING CODES

✴✴ WARNING

Before disconnecting power from the ECU, ALWAYS make sure the ignition switch is in the OFF position. Failure to do so may result in a voltage spike damaging the ECU. This can be a very expensive component to replace.

Stored codes are erased from memory by disconnecting power to the ECU for at least 30 seconds. Disconnecting the negative battery cable will clear the memory of the ECU, as well as other solid-state equipment such as the radio. Keep a record of the station pre-sets and any applicable security codes. The ECU may also be cleared by pulling the appropriate fuse from the underhood fuse and relay box. This may be the BACK-UP, CLOCK or CLOCK/RADIO fuse.

VACUUM DIAGRAMS

▶ **See Figure 56**

The engine and emission control system covered by this manual operate on a combination of vacuum and electrical signals; they are extremely prone to malfunctions due to improper vacuum connections. If a component does not receive vacuum at the correct time, it cannot function when needed. When working under the hood, pay close attention to the routing and placement of every hose.

Following is a listing of vacuum diagrams for most of the engine and emissions package combinations covered by this manual. Because vacuum circuits will vary based on various engine and vehicle options, always refer first to the vehicle emission control information label, if present. Should the label be missing, or should vehicle be equipped with a different engine from the car's original equipment, refer to the diagrams below for the same or similar configuration.

If you wish to obtain a replacement emissions label, most manufacturers make these labels available for purchase. The labels can usually be ordered from a local dealer.

86804445

Fig. 56 The vacuum hoses are usually numbered for easy identification

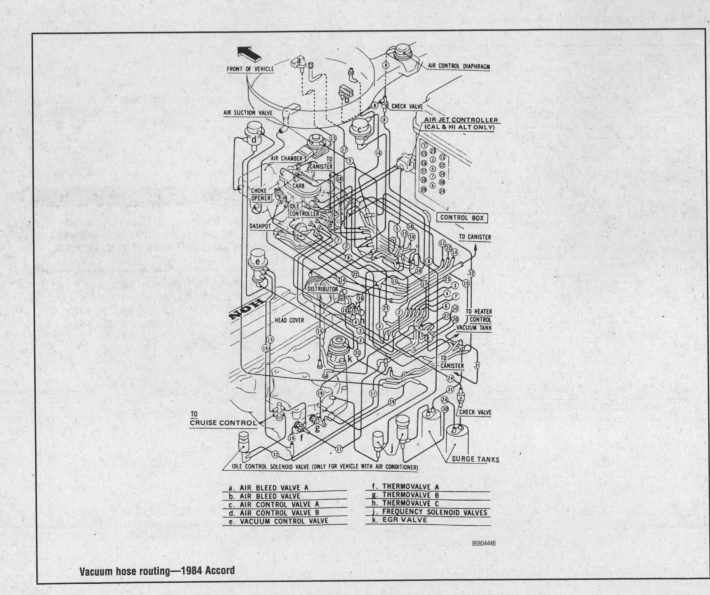

a. AIR BLEED VALVE A	f. THERMOVALVE A
b. AIR BLEED VALVE	g. THERMOVALVE B
c. AIR CONTROL VALVE A	h. THERMOVALVE C
d. AIR CONTROL VALVE B	j. FREQUENCY SOLENOID VALVES
e. VACUUM CONTROL VALVE	k. EGR VALVE

86804446

Vacuum hose routing—1984 Accord

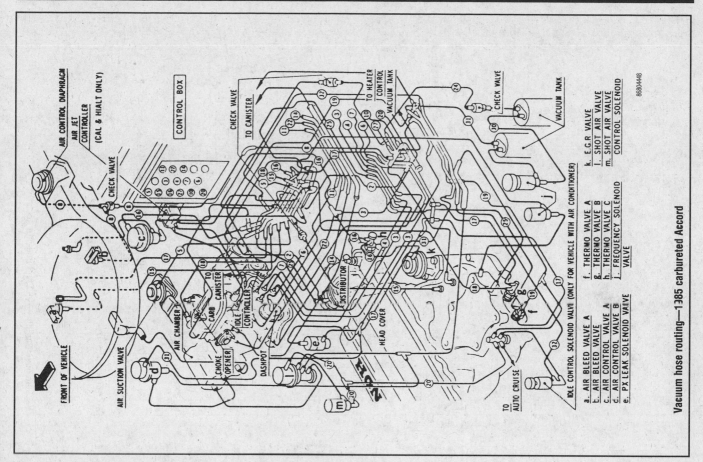

Vacuum hose routing—1385 carbureted Accord

a. AIR BLEED VALVE A
b. AIR BLEED VALVE B
c. AIR CONTROL VALVE B
d. AIR CONTROL VALVE C
e. PX LEAK SOLENOID VALVE
f. THERMO VALVE A
g. THERMO VALVE B
h. THERMO VALVE C
j. FREQUENCY SOLENOID VALVE
k. E.G.R VALVE
l. SHOT AIR VALVE
m. SHOT AIR VALVE CONTROL SOLENOID

IDLE CONTROL SOLENOID VALVE (ONLY FOR VEHICLE WITH AIR CONDITIONER)

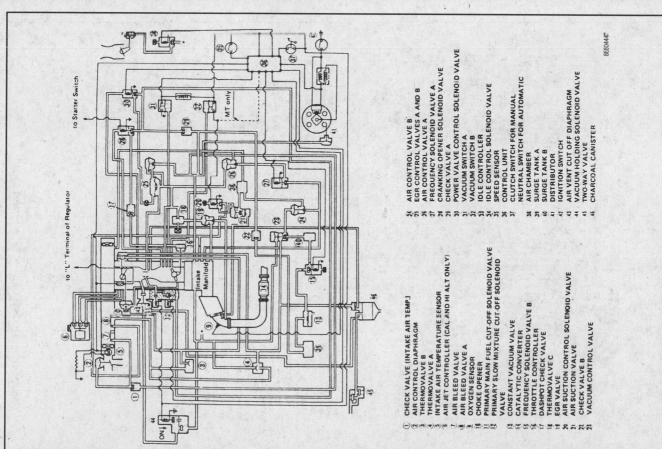

Emission component schematic—1984 Accord

1. CHECK VALVE (INTAKE AIR TEMP.)
2. AIR CONTROL DIAPHRAGM
3. THERMOVALVE B
4. THERMOVALVE A
5. INTAKE AIR TEMPERATURE SENSOR
6. AIR JET CONTROLLER (CAL AND HI ALT ONLY)
7. AIR BLEED VALVE A
8. AIR BLEED VALVE B
9. OXYGEN SENSOR
10. CHOKE OPENER
11. PRIMARY MAIN FUEL CUT-OFF SOLENOID VALVE
12. PRIMARY SLOW MIXTURE CUT-OFF SOLENOID VALVE
13. CONSTANT VACUUM VALVE
14. CATALYTIC CONVERTER
15. FREQUENCY SOLENOID VALVE B
16. THROTTLE CONTROLLER
17. DASHPOT CHECK VALVE
18. THERMOVALVE C
19. EGR VALVE
20. AIR SUCTION CONTROL SOLENOID VALVE
21. AIR SUCTION VALVE
22. CHECK VALVE B
23. VACUUM CONTROL VALVE

24. AIR CONTROL VALVE B
25. EGR CONTROL VALVES A AND B
26. AIR CONTROL VALVE A
27. FREQUENCY SOLENOID VALVE A
28. CRANKING OPENER SOLENOID VALVE
29. CHECK VALVE A
30. POWER VALVE CONTROL SOLENOID VALVE
31. VACUUM SWITCH A
32. VACUUM SWITCH B
33. IDLE CONTROLLER
34. IDLE CONTROL SOLENOID VALVE
35. SPEED SENSOR
36. CONTROL UNIT
37. CLUTCH SWITCH FOR MANUAL NEUTRAL SWITCH FOR AUTOMATIC
38. AIR CHAMBER
39. SURGE TANK A
40. SURGE TANK B
41. DISTRIBUTOR
42. IGNITION SWITCH
43. AIR VENT CUT OFF DIAPHRAGM
44. VACUUM HOLDING SOLENOID VALVE
45. TWO-WAY VALVE
46. CHARCOAL CANISTER

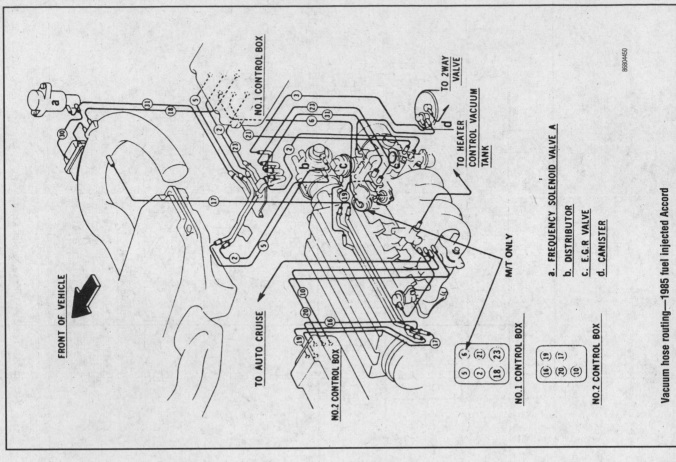

86804450

a. FREQUENCY SOLENOID VALVE A
b. DISTRIBUTOR
c. E.G.R VALVE
d. CANISTER

Vacuum hose routing—1985 fuel injected Accord

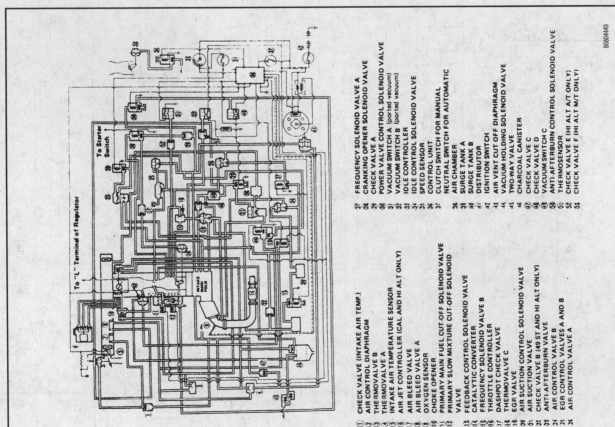

86804449

27 FREQUENCY SOLENOID VALVE A
28 CRANKING OPENER SOLENOID VALVE
29 CHECK VALVE A
30 POWER VALVE CONTROL SOLENOID VALVE
31 VACUUM SWITCH A (ported vacuum)
32 VACUUM SWITCH B (ported vacuum)
33 IDLE CONTROLLER
34 IDLE CONTROL SOLENOID VALVE
35 SPEED SENSOR
36 CONTROL UNIT
37 CLUTCH SWITCH FOR MANUAL
   NEUTRAL SWITCH FOR AUTOMATIC
38 AIR CHAMBER
39 SURGE TANK A
40 SURGE TANK B
41 DISTRIBUTOR
42 IGNITION SWITCH
43 AIR VENT CUT OFF DIAPHRAGM
44 VACUUM HOLDING SOLENOID VALVE
45 TWO-WAY VALVE
46 CHARCOAL CANISTER
47 CHECK VALVE C
48 CHECK VALVE D
49 VACUUM SWITCH C
50 ANTI-AFTERBURN CONTROL SOLENOID VALVE
51 THERMOSENSOR
52 CHECK VALVE E (HI ALT ONLY)
53 CHECK VALVE F (HI ALT M/T ONLY)

① CHECK VALVE (INTAKE AIR TEMP.)
② AIR CONTROL DIAPHRAGM
③ THERMOVALVE B
④ THERMOVALVE A
⑤ INTAKE AIR TEMPERATURE SENSOR
⑥ AIR JET CONTROLLER (CAL AND HI ALT ONLY)
⑦ AIR BLEED VALVE B
⑧ AIR BLEED VALVE A
⑨ OXYGEN SENSOR
10 CHOKE OPENER
11 PRIMARY MAIN FUEL CUT-OFF SOLENOID VALVE
12 PRIMARY SLOW MIXTURE CUT-OFF SOLENOID
   VALVE
13 FEEDBACK CONTROL SOLENOID VALVE
14 CATALYTIC CONVERTER
15 FREQUENCY SOLENOID VALVE B
16 THROTTLE CONTROLLER
17 DASHPOT CHECK VALVE
18 THERMOVALVE C
19 EGR VALVE
20 AIR SUCTION CONTROL SOLENOID VALVE
21 AIR SUCTION VALVE
22 ANTI-AFTERBURN VALVE
23 CHECK VALVE B (49 ST AND HI ALT ONLY)
24 AIR CONTROL VALVE B
25 EGR CONTROL VALVES A AND B
26 AIR CONTROL VALVE A

Emission component schematic—1985 carbureted Accord

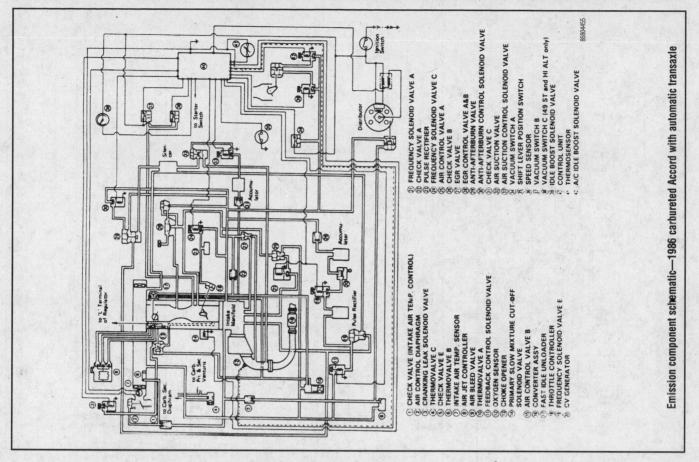

8804455

① CHECK VALVE (INTAKE AIR TEMP. CONTROL)
② AIR CONTROL DIAPHRAGM
③ CRANKING LEAK SOLENOID VALVE
④ THERMOVALVE C
⑤ CHECK VALVE E
⑥ THERMOVALVE B
⑦ INTAKE AIR TEMP. SENSOR
⑧ AIR JET CONTROLLER
⑨ AIR BLEED VALVE
⑩ THERMOVALVE A
⑪ FEEDBACK CONTROL SOLENOID VALVE
⑫ OXYGEN SENSOR
⑬ CHOKE OPENER
⑭ PRIMARY SLOW MIXTURE CUT-OFF
   SOLENOID VALVE
⑮ AIR CONTROL VALVE B
⑯ CONVERTER ASSY
⑰ FAST IDLE UNLOADER
⑱ THROTTLE CONTROLLER
⑲ FREQUENCY SOLENOID VALVE E
⑳ CV GENERATOR

㉑ FREQUENCY SOLENOID VALVE A
㉒ CHECK VALVE A
㉓ PULSE RECTIFIER
㉔ FREQUENCY SOLENOID VALVE C
㉕ AIR CONTROL VALVE A
㉖ CHECK VALVE B
㉗ EGR VALVE
㉘ EGR CONTROL VALVE A&B
㉙ ANTI-AFTERBURN VALVE
㉚ ANTI-AFTERBURN CONTROL SOLENOID VALVE
㉛ CHECK VALVE C
㉜ AIR SUCTION VALVE
㉝ AIR SUCTION CONTROL SOLENOID VALVE
㉞ SHIFT LEVER POSITION SWITCH
㉟ SPEED SENSOR
㊱ VACUUM SWITCH B
㊲ VACUUM SWITCH C (49 ST and HI ALT only)
㊳ IDLE BOOST SOLENOID VALVE
㊴ CONTROL UNIT
㊵ THERMOSENSOR
㊶ A/C IDLE BOOST SOLENOID VALVE

Emission component schematic—1986 carbureted Accord with automatic transaxle

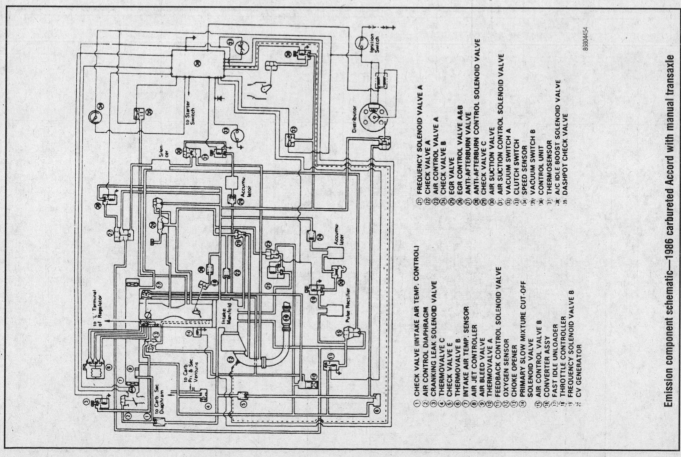

8804454

① CHECK VALVE (INTAKE AIR TEMP. CONTROL)
② AIR CONTROL DIAPHRAGM
③ CRANKING LEAK SOLENOID VALVE
④ THERMOVALVE C
⑤ CHECK VALVE E
⑥ THERMOVALVE B
⑦ INTAKE AIR TEMP. SENSOR
⑧ AIR JET CONTROLLER
⑨ AIR BLEED VALVE
⑩ THERMOVALVE A
⑪ FEEDBACK CONTROL SOLENOID VALVE
⑫ OXYGEN SENSOR
⑬ CHOKE OPENER
⑭ PRIMARY SLOW MIXTURE CUT-OFF
   SOLENOID VALVE
⑮ AIR CONTROL VALVE B
⑯ CONVERTER ASSY
⑰ FAST IDLE UNLOADER
⑱ THROTTLE CONTROLLER
⑲ FREQUENCY SOLENOID VALVE B
⑳ CV GENERATOR

㉑ FREQUENCY SOLENOID VALVE A
㉒ CHECK VALVE A
㉓ AIR CONTROL VALVE A
㉔ CHECK VALVE B
㉕ EGR VALVE
㉖ EGR CONTROL VALVE A&B
㉗ ANTI-AFTERBURN VALVE
㉘ ANTI-AFTERBURN CONTROL SOLENOID VALVE
㉙ CHECK VALVE C
㉚ AIR SUCTION VALVE
㉛ AIR SUCTION CONTROL SOLENOID VALVE
㉜ CLUTCH SWITCH
㉝ SPEED SENSOR
㉞ VACUUM SWITCH B
㉟ CONTROL UNIT
㊱ THERMOSENSOR
㊲ A/C IDLE BOOST SOLENOID VALVE
㊳ DASHPOT CHECK VALVE

Emission component schematic—1986 carbureted Accord with manual transaxle

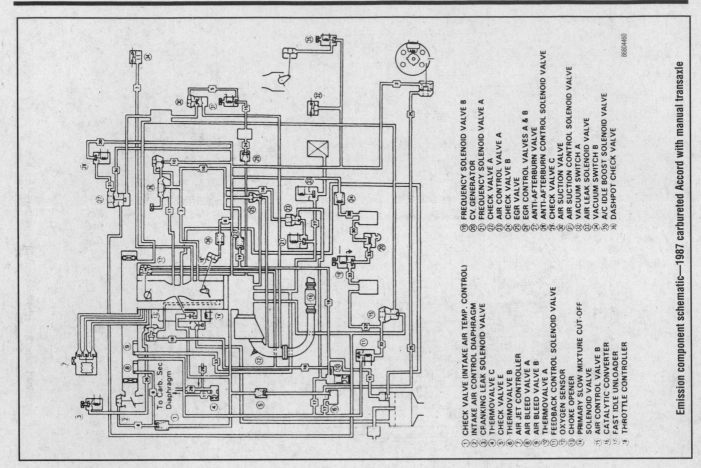

① CHECK VALVE (INTAKE AIR TEMP. CONTROL)
② INTAKE AIR CONTROL DIAPHRAGM
③ CRANKING LEAK SOLENOID VALVE
④ THERMOVALVE C
⑤ CHECK VALVE E
⑥ THERMOVALVE B
⑦ AIR JET CONTROLLER
⑧ AIR BLEED VALVE A
⑨ AIR BLEED VALVE B
⑩ THERMOVALVE A
⑪ FEEDBACK CONTROL SOLENOID VALVE
⑫ OXYGEN SENSOR
⑬ CHOKE OPENER
⑭ PRIMARY SLOW MIXTURE CUT-OFF SOLENOID VALVE
⑮ AIR CONTROL VALVE B
⑯ CATALYTIC CONVERTER
⑰ FAST IDLE UNLOADER
⑱ THROTTLE CONTROLLER
⑲ FREQUENCY SOLENOID VALVE B
⑳ CV GENERATOR
㉑ FREQUENCY SOLENOID VALVE A
㉒ CHECK VALVE A
㉓ AIR CONTROL VALVE A
㉔ CHECK VALVE B
㉕ EGR CONTROL VALVES A & B
㉖ ANTI-AFTERBURN VALVE
㉗ ANTI-AFTERBURN CONTROL SOLENOID VALVE
㉘ CHECK VALVE C
㉙ AIR SUCTION VALVE
㉚ AIR SUCTION CONTROL SOLENOID VALVE
㉛ VACUUM SWITCH A
㉜ AIR LEAK SOLENOID VALVE
㉝ VACUUM SWITCH B
㉞ A/C IDLE BOOST SOLENOID VALVE
㉟ DASHPOT CHECK VALVE

Emission component schematic—1987 carbureted Accord with manual transaxle

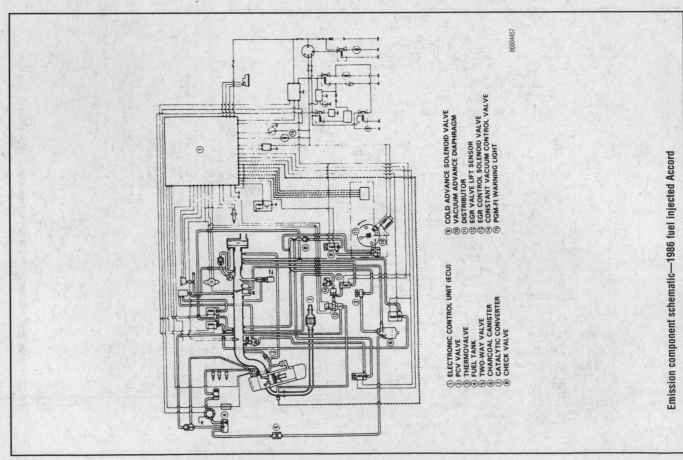

① ELECTRONIC CONTROL UNIT (ECU)
② PCV VALVE
③ THERMOVALVE
④ TWO-WAY VALVE
⑤ CHARCOAL CANISTER
⑥ FUEL TANK
⑦ CATALYTIC CONVERTER
⑧ CHECK VALVE
⑨ COLD ADVANCE SOLENOID VALVE
⑩ VACUUM ADVANCE DIAPHRAGM
⑪ DISTRIBUTOR
⑫ EGR VALVE LIFT SENSOR
⑬ EGR CONTROL SOLENOID VALVE
⑭ CONSTANT VACUUM CONTROL VALVE
⑮ PGM-FI WARNING LIGHT

Emission component schematic—1986 fuel injected Accord

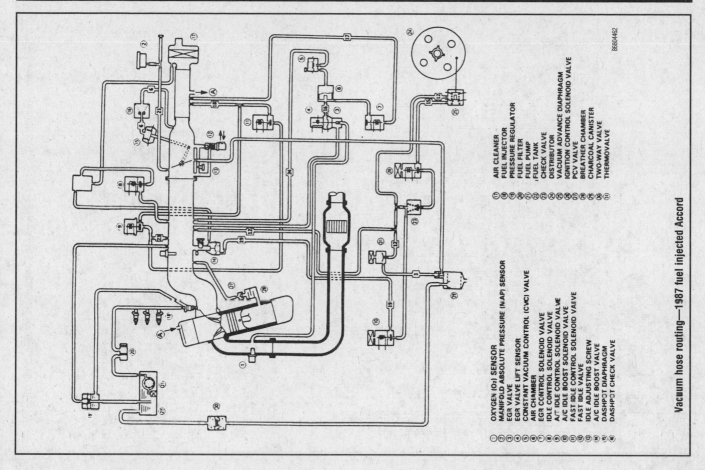

① OXYGEN (O₂) SENSOR
② MANIFOLD ABSOLUTE PRESSURE (MAP) SENSOR
③ EGR VALVE
④ EGR VALVE LIFT SENSOR
⑤ CONSTANT VACUUM CONTROL (CVC) VALVE
⑥ AIR CHAMBER
⑦ EGR CONTROL SOLENOID VALVE
⑧ IDLE CONTROL SOLENOID VALVE
⑨ A/T IDLE CONTROL SOLENOID VALVE
⑩ A/C IDLE BOOST SOLENOID VALVE
⑪ FAST IDLE CONTROL SOLENOID VALVE
⑫ FAST IDLE VALVE
⑬ IDLE ADJUSTING SCREW
⑭ A/C IDLE BOOST VALVE
⑮ DASHPOT DIAPHRAGM
⑯ DASHPOT CHECK VALVE

⑰ AIR CLEANER
⑱ FUEL INJECTOR
⑲ PRESSURE REGULATOR
⑳ FUEL FILTER
㉑ FUEL PUMP
㉒ FUEL TANK
㉓ CHECK VALVE
㉔ VACUUM ADVANCE DIAPHRAGM
㉕ DISTRIBUTOR
㉖ IGNITION CONTROL SOLENOID VALVE
㉗ PCV VALVE
㉘ BREATHER CHAMBER
㉙ CHARCOAL CANISTER
㉚ TWO-WAY VALVE
㉛ THERMOVALVE

Vacuum hose routing—1987 fuel injected Accord

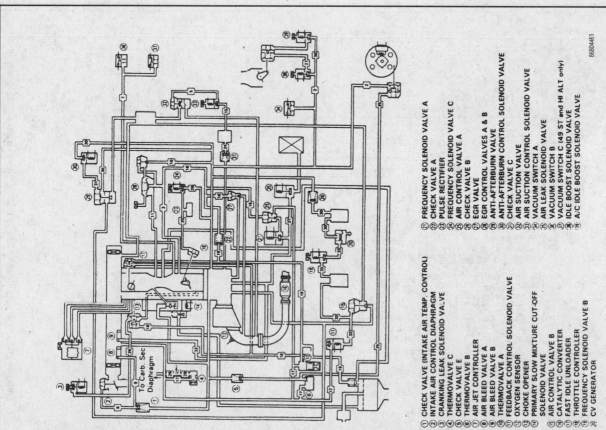

① CHECK VALVE (INTAKE AIR TEMP. CONTROL)
② INTAKE AIR CONTROL DIAPHRAGM
③ CRANKING LEAK SOLENOID VALVE
④ THERMOVALVE C
⑤ CHECK VALVE E
⑥ THERMOVALVE B
⑦ AIR JET CONTROLLER
⑧ AIR BLEED VALVE A
⑨ AIR BLEED VALVE B
⑩ THERMOVALVE A
⑪ FEEDBACK CONTROL SOLENOID VALVE
⑫ OXYGEN SENSOR
⑬ CHOKE OPENER
⑭ PRIMARY SLOW MIXTURE CUT-OFF
   SOLENOID VALVE
⑮ AIR CONTROL VALVE B
⑯ CATALYTIC CONVERTER
⑰ FAST IDLE UNLOADER
⑱ THROTTLE CONTROLLER
⑲ FREQUENCY SOLENOID VALVE B
⑳ CV GENERATOR

㉑ FREQUENCY SOLENOID VALVE A
㉒ CHECK VALVE A
㉓ PULSE RECTIFIER
㉔ FREQUENCY SOLENOID VALVE C
㉕ AIR CONTROL VALVE A
㉖ CHECK VALVE B
㉗ EGR VALVE
㉘ EGR CONTROL VALVES A & B
㉙ ANTI-AFTERBURN VALVE
㉚ ANTI-AFTERBURN CONTROL SOLENOID VALVE
㉛ CHECK VALVE C
㉜ AIR SUCTION VALVE
㉝ AIR SUCTION CONTROL SOLENOID VALVE
㉞ VACUUM SWITCH A
㉟ AIR LEAK SOLENOID VALVE
㊱ VACUUM SWITCH B
㊲ VACUUM SWITCH C (49 ST and HI ALT only)
㊳ IDLE BOOST SOLENOID VALVE
㊴ A/C IDLE BOOST SOLENOID VALVE

Emission component schematic—1987 carbureted Accord with automatic transaxle

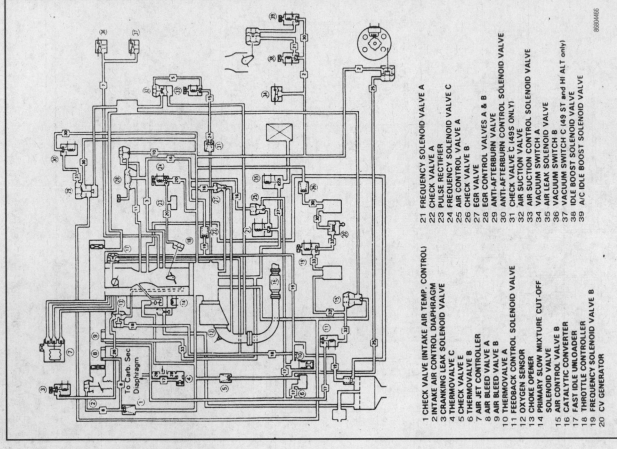

1 CHECK VALVE (INTAKE AIR TEMP. CONTROL)
2 INTAKE AIR CONTROL DIAPHRAGM
3 CRANKING LEAK SOLENOID VALVE
4 THERMOVALVE C
5 CHECK VALVE E
6 THERMOVALVE B
7 AIR JET CONTROLLER
8 AIR BLEED VALVE A
9 AIR BLEED VALVE B
10 THERMOVALVE A
11 FEEDBACK CONTROL SOLENOID VALVE
12 OXYGEN SENSOR
13 CHOKE OPENER
14 PRIMARY SLOW MIXTURE CUT-OFF
   SOLENOID VALVE
15 AIR CONTROL VALVE B
16 CATALYTIC CONVERTER
17 FAST IDLE UNLOADER
18 THROTTLE CONTROLLER
19 FREQUENCY SOLENOID VALVE B
20 CV GENERATOR

21 FREQUENCY SOLENOID VALVE A
22 CHECK VALVE A
23 PULSE RECTIFIER
24 FREQUENCY SOLENOID VALVE C
25 AIR CONTROL VALVE A
26 CHECK VALVE B
27 EGR VALVE
28 EGR CONTROL VALVES A & B
29 ANTI-AFTERBURN VALVE
30 ANTI-AFTERBURN CONTROL SOLENOID VALVE
31 CHECK VALVE C (49S ONLY)
32 AIR SUCTION VALVE
33 AIR SUCTION CONTROL SOLENOID VALVE
34 VACUUM SWITCH A
35 AIR LEAK SOLENOID VALVE
36 VACUUM SWITCH B
37 VACUUM SWITCH C (49 ST and HI ALT only)
38 IDLE BOOST SOLENOID VALVE
39 A/C IDLE BOOST SOLENOID VALVE

Emission component schematic—1988 carbureted Accord with automatic transaxle

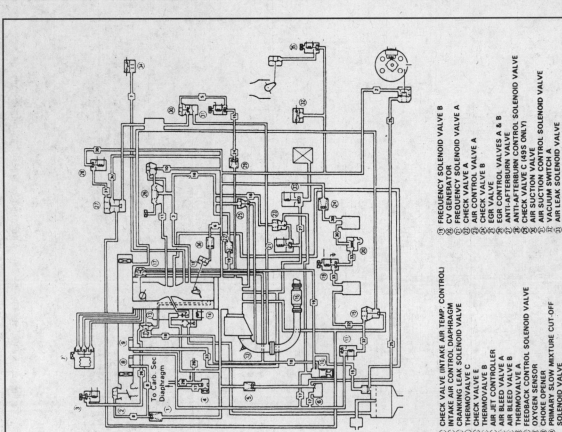

1 CHECK VALVE (INTAKE AIR TEMP. CONTROL)
2 INTAKE AIR CONTROL DIAPHRAGM
3 CRANKING LEAK SOLENOID VALVE
4 THERMOVALVE C
5 CHECK VALVE E
6 THERMOVALVE B
7 AIR JET CONTROLLER
8 AIR BLEED VALVE A
9 AIR BLEED VALVE B
10 THERMOVALVE A
11 FEEDBACK CONTROL SOLENOID VALVE
12 OXYGEN SENSOR
13 CHOKE OPENER
14 PRIMARY SLOW MIXTURE CUT-OFF
   SOLENOID VALVE
15 AIR CONTROL VALVE B
16 CATALYTIC CONVERTER
17 FAST IDLE UNLOADER
18 THROTTLE CONTROLLER
19 FREQUENCY SOLENOID VALVE B
20 CV GENERATOR
21 FREQUENCY SOLENOID VALVE A
22 FREQUENCY SOLENOID VALVE C
23 AIR CONTROL VALVE A
24 CHECK VALVE B
25 EGR VALVE
26 EGR CONTROL VALVES A & B
27 ANTI-AFTERBURN VALVE
28 ANTI-AFTERBURN CONTROL SOLENOID VALVE
29 CHECK VALVE C (49S ONLY)
30 AIR SUCTION VALVE
31 AIR SUCTION CONTROL SOLENOID VALVE
32 VACUUM SWITCH A
33 AIR LEAK SOLENOID VALVE
34 VACUUM SWITCH B
35 A/C IDLE BOOST SOLENOID VALVE
36 DASHPOT CHECK VALVE

Emission component schematic—1988 carbureted Accord with manual transaxle

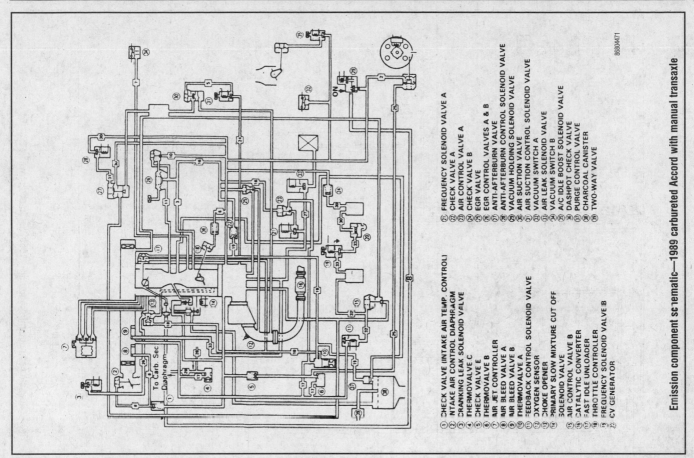

86804471

Emission component schematic—1989 carbureted Accord with manual transaxle

① CHECK VALVE (INTAKE AIR TEMP. CONTROL)
② INTAKE AIR CONTROL DIAPHRAGM
③ CRANKING LEAK SOLENOID VALVE
④ THERMOVALVE C
⑤ CHECK VALVE E
⑥ THERMOVALVE B
⑦ EGR JET CONTROLLER
⑧ AIR BLEED VALVE A
⑨ AIR BLEED VALVE B
⑩ THERMOVALVE A
⑪ FEEDBACK CONTROL SOLENOID VALVE
⑫ OXYGEN SENSOR
⑬ PRIMARY SLOW MIXTURE CUT OFF SOLENOID VALVE
⑭ CHOKE OPENER
⑮ AIR CONTROL VALVE B
⑯ CATALYTIC CONVERTER
⑰ FAST IDLE UNLOADER
⑱ THROTTLE CONTROLLER
⑲ FREQUENCY SOLENOID VALVE B
⑳ CV GENERATOR
㉑ FREQUENCY SOLENOID VALVE A
㉒ CHECK VALVE A
㉓ AIR CONTROL VALVE A
㉔ CHECK VALVE B
㉕ EGR VALVE
㉖ EGR CONTROL VALVES A & B
㉗ ANTI-AFTERBURN VALVE
㉘ VACUUM CONTROL SOLENOID VALVE
㉙ VACUUM HOLDING SOLENOID VALVE
㉚ AIR SUCTION VALVE
㉛ AIR SUCTION CONTROL SOLENOID VALVE
㉜ VACUUM SWITCH A
㉝ AIR LEAK SOLENOID VALVE
㉞ VACUUM SWITCH B
㉟ A/C IDLE BOOST SOLENOID VALVE
㊱ DASHPOT CHECK VALVE
㊲ PURGE CONTROL VALVE
㊳ CHARCOAL CANISTER
㊴ TWO-WAY VALVE

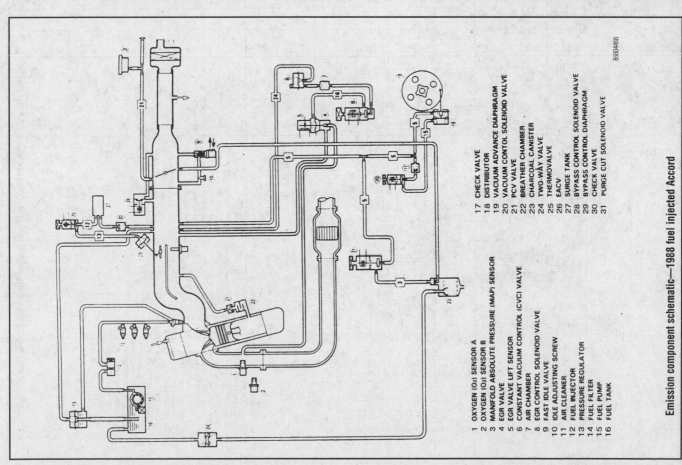

86804468

Emission component schematic—1988 fuel injected Accord

1 OXYGEN (O₂) SENSOR A
2 OXYGEN (O₂) SENSOR B
3 MANIFOLD ABSOLUTE PRESSURE (MAP) SENSOR
4 EGR VALVE
5 EGR VALVE LIFT SENSOR
6 CONSTANT VACUUM CONTROL (CVC) VALVE
7 AIR CHAMBER
8 EGR CONTROL SOLENOID VALVE
9 FAST IDLE VALVE
10 IDLE ADJUSTING SCREW
11 AIR CLEANER
12 FUEL INJECTOR
13 PRESSURE REGULATOR
14 FUEL FILTER
15 FUEL PUMP
16 FUEL TANK
17 CHECK VALVE
18 DISTRIBUTOR
19 VACUUM ADVANCE DIAPHRAGM
20 VACUUM CONTROL SOLENOID VALVE
21 PCV VALVE
22 BREATHER CHAMBER
23 CHARCOAL CANISTER
24 TWO-WAY VALVE
25 THERMOVALVE
26 EACV
27 SURGE TANK
28 BYPASS CONTROL SOLENOID VALVE
29 BYPASS CONTROL DIAPHRAGM
30 CHECK VALVE
31 PURGE CUT SOLENOID VALVE

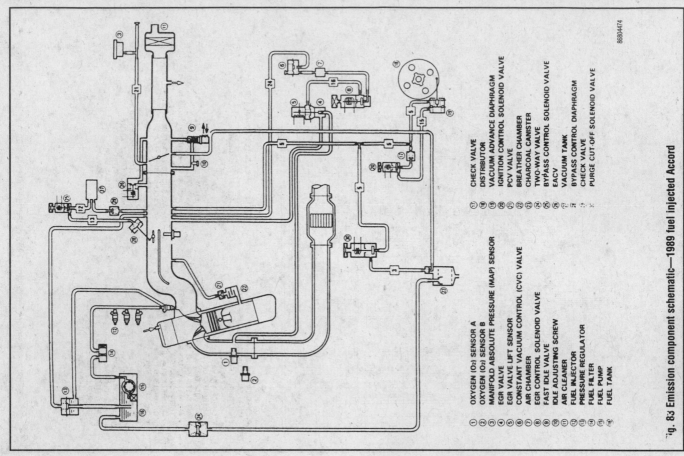

Fig. 83 Emission component schematic—1989 fuel injected Accord

① OXYGEN (O₂) SENSOR A
② OXYGEN (O₂) SENSOR B
③ MANIFOLD ABSOLUTE PRESSURE (MAP) SENSOR
④ EGR VALVE
⑤ EGR VALVE LIFT SENSOR
⑥ CONSTANT VACUUM CONTROL (CVC) VALVE
⑦ AIR CHAMBER
⑧ EGR CONTROL SOLENOID VALVE
⑨ FAST IDLE VALVE
⑩ IDLE ADJUSTING SCREW
⑪ AIR CLEANER
⑫ PRESSURE REGULATOR
⑬ FUEL FILTER
⑭ FUEL PUMP
⑮ FUEL TANK
⑯ CHECK VALVE
⑰ DISTRIBUTOR
⑱ VACUUM ADVANCE DIAPHRAGM
⑲ IGNITION CONTROL SOLENOID VALVE
⑳ PCV VALVE
㉑ BREATHER CHAMBER
㉒ CHARCOAL CANISTER
㉓ TWO-WAY VALVE
㉔ BYPASS CONTROL SOLENOID VALVE
㉕ EACV
㉖ VACUUM TANK
㉗ BYPASS CONTROL DIAPHRAGM
㉘ CHECK VALVE
㉙ PURGE CUT-OFF SOLENOID VALVE

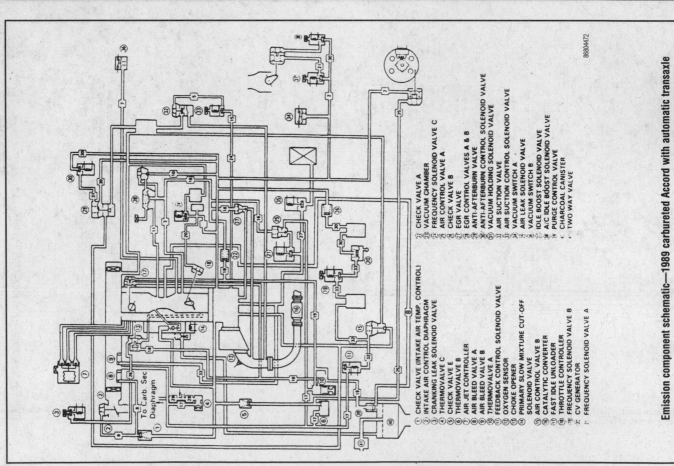

Emission component schematic—1989 carbureted Accord with automatic transaxle

① CHECK VALVE (INTAKE AIR TEMP. CONTROL)
② INTAKE AIR CONTROL DIAPHRAGM
③ CRANKING LEAK SOLENOID VALVE
④ THERMOVALVE C
⑤ CHECK VALVE
⑥ THERMOVALVE B
⑦ AIR JET CONTROLLER
⑧ AIR BLEED VALVE A
⑨ AIR BLEED VALVE B
⑩ THERMOVALVE A
⑪ FEEDBACK CONTROL SOLENOID VALVE
⑫ OXYGEN SENSOR
⑬ CHOKE OPENER
⑭ PRIMARY SLOW MIXTURE CUT-OFF
⑮ SOLENOID VALVE
⑯ AIR CONTROL VALVE B
⑰ CATALYTIC CONVERTER
⑱ FAST IDLE UNLOADER
⑲ THROTTLE CONTROLLER
⑳ FREQUENCY SOLENOID VALVE B
㉑ CV GENERATOR
㉒ FREQUENCY SOLENOID VALVE A
㉓ CHECK VALVE A
㉔ VACUUM CHAMBER
㉕ FREQUENCY SOLENOID VALVE C
㉖ AIR CONTROL VALVE A
㉗ CHECK VALVE B
㉘ EGR VALVE
㉙ EGR CONTROL VALVES A & B
㉚ ANTI-AFTERBURN VALVE
㉛ ANTI-AFTERBURN CONTROL SOLENOID VALVE
㉜ VACUUM HOLDING SOLENOID VALVE
㉝ AIR SUCTION VALVE
㉞ AIR SUCTION CONTROL SOLENOID VALVE
㉟ VACUUM SWITCH A
㊱ AIR LEAK SOLENOID VALVE
㊲ VACUUM SWITCH B
㊳ IDLE BOOST SOLENOID VALVE
㊴ A/C IDLE BOOST SOLENOID VALVE
㊵ PURGE CONTROL VALVE
㊶ CHARCOAL CANISTER
㊷ TWO WAY VALVE

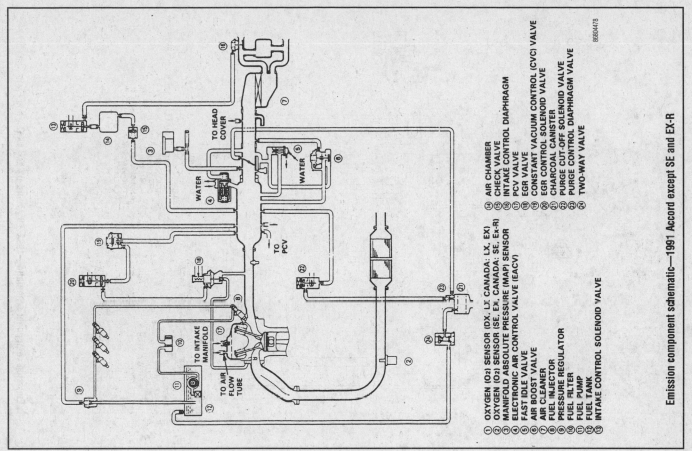

86804478

Emission component schematic—1991 Accord except SE and EX-R

① OXYGEN (O₂) SENSOR (DX, LX CANADA: LX, EX)
② OXYGEN (O₂) SENSOR (SE, EX, CANADA: SE, EX-R)
③ MANIFOLD ABSOLUTE PRESSURE (MAP) SENSOR
④ ELECTRONIC AIR CONTROL VALVE (EACV)
⑤ FAST IDLE VALVE
⑥ AIR BOOST VALVE
⑦ AIR CLEANER
⑧ FUEL INJECTOR
⑨ PRESSURE REGULATOR
⑩ FUEL FILTER
⑪ FUEL PUMP
⑫ FUEL TANK
⑬ INTAKE CONTROL SOLENOID VALVE
⑭ AIR CHAMBER
⑮ CHECK VALVE
⑯ INTAKE CONTROL DIAPHRAGM
⑰ PCV VALVE
⑱ EGR VALVE
⑲ CONSTANT VACUUM CONTROL (CVC) VALVE
⑳ EGR CONTROL SOLENOID VALVE
㉑ CHARCOAL CANISTER
㉒ PURGE CUT-OFF SOLENOID VALVE
㉓ PURGE CONTROL DIAPHRAGM VALVE
㉔ TWO-WAY VALVE

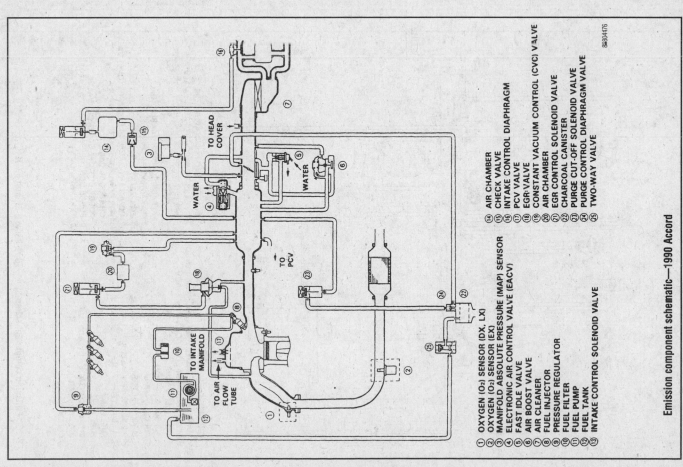

86804476

Emission component schematic—1990 Accord

① OXYGEN (O₂) SENSOR (DX, LX)
② OXYGEN (O₂) SENSOR (EX)
③ MANIFOLD ABSOLUTE PRESSURE (MAP) SENSOR
④ ELECTRONIC AIR CONTROL VALVE (EACV)
⑤ FAST IDLE VALVE
⑥ AIR BOOST VALVE
⑦ AIR CLEANER
⑧ FUEL INJECTOR
⑨ PRESSURE REGULATOR
⑩ FUEL FILTER
⑪ FUEL PUMP
⑫ FUEL TANK
⑬ INTAKE CONTROL SOLENOID VALVE
⑭ AIR CHAMBER
⑮ CHECK VALVE
⑯ INTAKE CONTROL DIAPHRAGM
⑰ PCV VALVE
⑱ EGR VALVE
⑲ CONSTANT VACUUM CONTROL (CVC) VALVE
⑳ AIR CHAMBER
㉑ EGR CONTROL SOLENOID VALVE
㉒ CHARCOAL CANISTER
㉓ PURGE CUT-OFF SOLENOID VALVE
㉔ PURGE CONTROL DIAPHRAGM VALVE
㉕ TWO-WAY VALVE

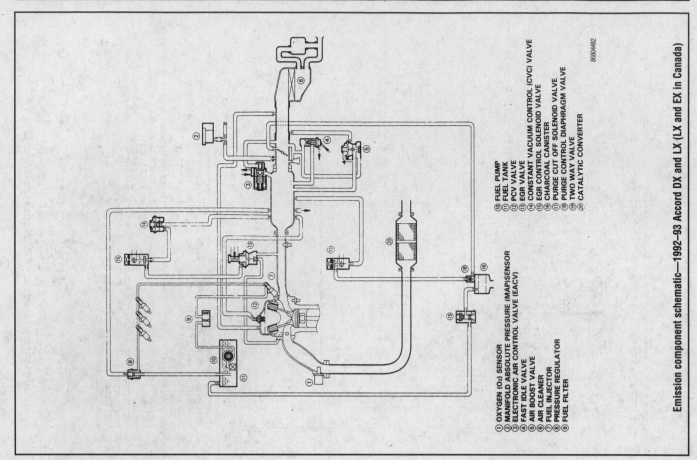

① OXYGEN (O₂) SENSOR
② MANIFOLD ABSOLUTE PRESSURE (MAP) SENSOR
③ ELECTRONIC AIR CONTROL VALVE (EACV)
④ FAST IDLE VALVE
⑤ AIR BOOST VALVE
⑥ AIR CLEANER
⑦ FUEL INJECTOR
⑧ PRESSURE REGULATOR
⑨ FUEL FILTER

⑩ FUEL PUMP
⑪ FUEL TANK
⑫ PCV VALVE
⑬ EGR VALVE
⑭ CONSTANT VACUUM CONTROL (CVC) VALVE
⑮ EGR CONTROL SOLENOID VALVE
⑯ CHARCOAL CANISTER
⑰ PURGE CUT OFF SOLENOID VALVE
⑱ PURGE CONTROL DIAPHRAGM VALVE
⑲ TWO WAY VALVE
⑳ CATALYTIC CONVERTER

Emission component schematic—1992–93 Accord DX and LX (LX and EX in Canada)

86804482

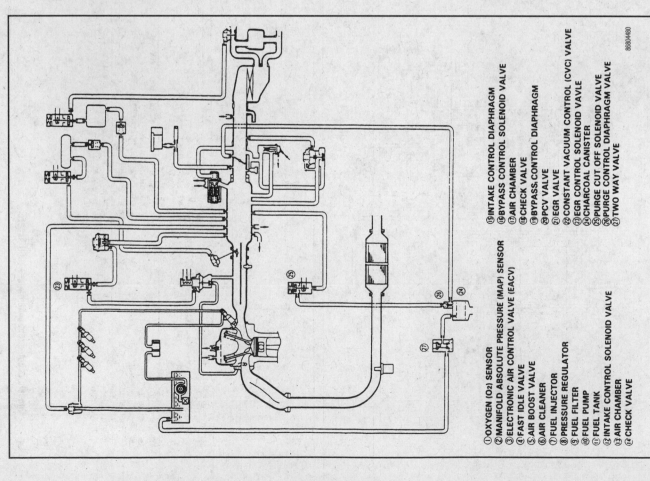

① OXYGEN (O₂) SENSOR
② MANIFOLD ABSOLUTE PRESSURE (MAP) SENSOR
③ ELECTRONIC AIR CONTROL VALVE (EACV)
④ FAST IDLE VALVE
⑤ AIR BOOST VALVE
⑥ AIR CLEANER
⑦ FUEL INJECTOR
⑧ PRESSURE REGULATOR
⑨ FUEL FILTER
⑩ FUEL PUMP
⑪ FUEL TANK
⑫ INTAKE CONTROL SOLENOID VALVE
⑬ AIR CHAMBER
⑭ CHECK VALVE

⑮ INTAKE CONTROL DIAPHRAGM
⑯ BYPASS CONTROL SOLENOID VALVE
⑰ AIR CHAMBER
⑱ CHECK VALVE
⑲ BYPASS, CONTROL DIAPHRAGM
⑳ PCV VALVE
㉑ EGR VALVE
㉒ CONSTANT VACUUM CONTROL (CVC) VALVE
㉓ EGR CONTROL SOLENOID VALVE
㉔ CHARCOAL CANISTER
㉕ PURGE CUT OFF SOLENOID VALVE
㉖ PURGE CONTROL DIAPHRAGM VALVE
㉗ TWO WAY VALVE

Emission component schematic—1991 Accord SE and EX-R

86804480

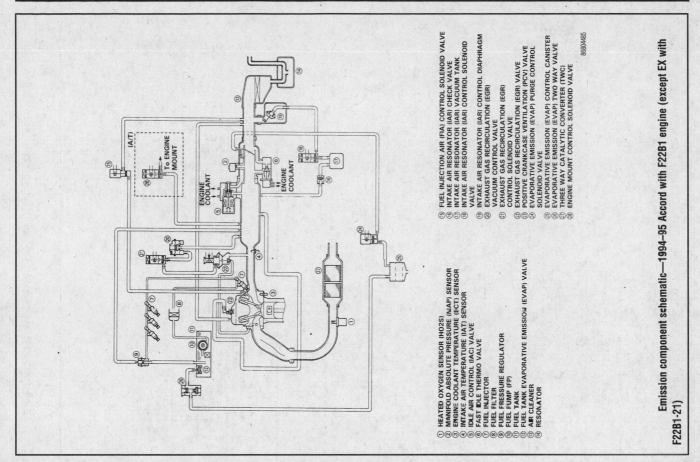

① HEATED OXYGEN SENSOR (HO2S)
② MANIFOLD ABSOLUTE PRESSURE (MAP) SENSOR
③ ENGINE COOLANT TEMPERATURE (ECT) SENSOR
④ INTAKE AIR TEMPERATURE (IAT) SENSOR
⑤ IDLE AIR CONTROL (IAC) VALVE
⑥ FAST IDLE THERMO VALVE
⑦ FUEL INJECTOR
⑧ FUEL FILTER
⑨ FUEL PRESSURE REGULATOR
⑩ FUEL PUMP (FP)
⑪ FUEL TANK
⑫ FUEL TANK EVAPORATIVE EMISSION (EVAP) VALVE
⑬ AIR CLEANER
⑭ RESONATOR

⑮ FUEL INJECTION AIR (FIA) CONTROL SOLENOID VALVE
⑯ INTAKE AIR RESONATOR (IARI) CHECK VALVE
⑰ INTAKE AIR RESONATOR (IARI) VACUUM TANK
⑱ INTAKE AIR RESONATOR (IARI) CONTROL SOLENOID VALVE
⑲ INTAKE AIR RESONATOR (IARI) CONTROL DIAPHRAGM
⑳ EXHAUST GAS RECIRCULATION (EGR)
㉑ VACUUM CONTROL VALVE
㉒ EXHAUST GAS RECIRCULATION (EGR) CONTROL SOLENOID VALVE
㉓ EXHAUST GAS RECIRCULATION (EGR) VALVE
㉔ POSITIVE CRANKCASE VENTILATION (PCV) VALVE
㉕ EVAPORATIVE EMISSION (EVAP) PURGE CONTROL SOLENOID VALVE
㉖ EVAPORATIVE EMISSION (EVAP) CONTROL CANISTER
㉗ EVAPORATIVE EMISSION (EVAP) TWO WAY VALVE
㉘ THREE WAY CATALYTIC CONVERTER (TWC)
㉙ ENGINE MOUNT CONTROL SOLENOID VALVE

86804485

Emission component schematic—1994–95 Accord with F22B1 engine (except EX with F22B1-21)

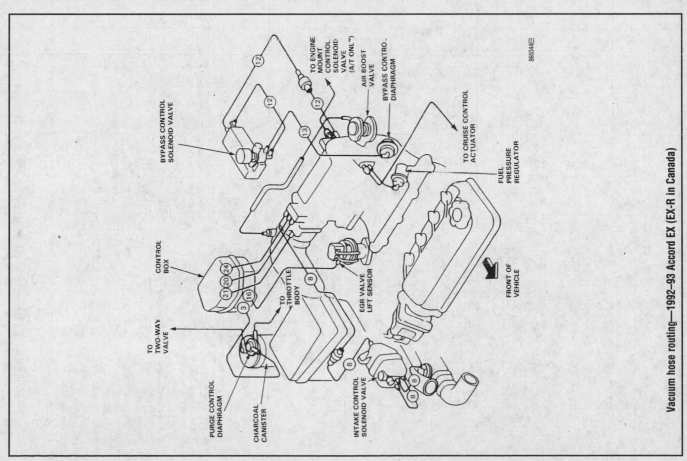

86804044

Vacuum hose routing—1992–93 Accord EX (EX-R in Canada)

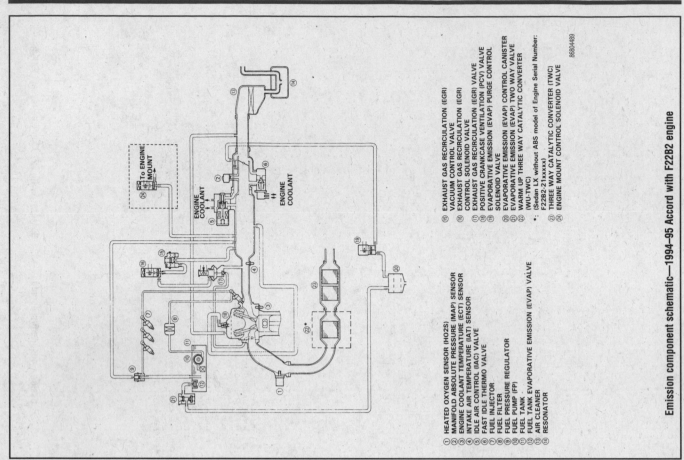

86804489

Emission component schematic—1994–95 Accord with F22B2 engine

① HEATED OXYGEN SENSOR (HO2S)
② MANIFOLD ABSOLUTE PRESSURE (MAP) SENSOR
③ ENGINE COOLANT TEMPERATURE (ECT) SENSOR
④ INTAKE AIR TEMPERATURE (IAT) SENSOR
⑤ IDLE AIR CONTROL (IAC) VALVE
⑥ FAST IDLE THERMO VALVE
⑦ FUEL INJECTOR
⑧ FUEL FILTER
⑨ FUEL PRESSURE REGULATOR
⑩ FUEL PUMP (FP)
⑪ FUEL TANK
⑫ FUEL TANK EVAPORATIVE EMISSION (EVAP) VALVE
⑬ AIR CLEANER
⑭ RESONATOR

⑮ EXHAUST GAS RECIRCULATION (EGR) VACUUM CONTROL VALVE
⑯ EXHAUST GAS RECIRCULATION (EGR) CONTROL SOLENOID VALVE
⑰ EXHAUST GAS RECIRCULATION (EGR) VALVE
⑱ POSITIVE CRANKCASE VENTILATION (PCV) VALVE
⑲ EVAPORATIVE EMISSION (EVAP) PURGE CONTROL SOLENOID VALVE
⑳ EVAPORATIVE EMISSION (EVAP) CONTROL CANISTER
㉑ EVAPORATIVE EMISSION (EVAP) TWO WAY VALVE
㉒ WARM UP THREE WAY CATALYTIC CONVERTER (WU-TWC)
    * (Sedan LX without ABS model of Engine Serial Number: F22B2-21xxxxx)
㉓ THREE WAY CATALYTIC CONVERTER (TWC)
㉔ ENGINE MOUNT CONTROL SOLENOID VALVE

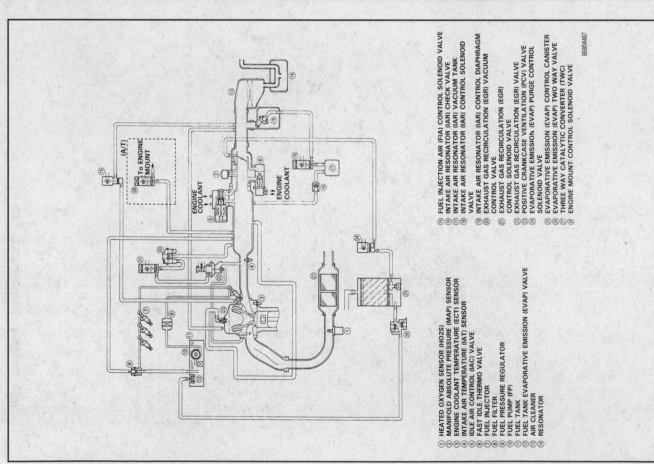

86804487

Emission component schematic—1994–95 Accord EX with F22B1-21 engine

① HEATED OXYGEN SENSOR (HO2S)
② MANIFOLD ABSOLUTE PRESSURE (MAP) SENSOR
③ ENGINE COOLANT TEMPERATURE (ECT) SENSOR
④ INTAKE AIR TEMPERATURE (IAT) SENSOR
⑤ IDLE AIR CONTROL (IAC) VALVE
⑥ FAST IDLE THERMO VALVE
⑦ FUEL INJECTOR
⑧ FUEL FILTER
⑨ FUEL PRESSURE REGULATOR
⑩ FUEL PUMP (FP)
⑪ FUEL TANK
⑫ FUEL TANK EVAPORATIVE EMISSION (EVAP) VALVE
⑬ AIR CLEANER
⑭ RESONATOR

⑮ FUEL INJECTION AIR (FIA) CONTROL SOLENOID VALVE
⑯ INTAKE AIR RESONATOR (IAR) CHECK VALVE
⑰ INTAKE AIR RESONATOR (IAR) VACUUM TANK
⑱ INTAKE AIR RESONATOR (IAR) CONTROL SOLENOID VALVE
⑲ INTAKE AIR RESONATOR (IAR) CONTROL DIAPHRAGM
⑳ EXHAUST GAS RECIRCULATION (EGR) VACUUM CONTROL VALVE
㉑ EXHAUST GAS RECIRCULATION (EGR) CONTROL SOLENOID VALVE
㉒ EXHAUST GAS RECIRCULATION (EGR) VALVE
㉓ POSITIVE CRANKCASE VENTILATION (PCV) VALVE
㉔ EVAPORATIVE EMISSION (EVAP) PURGE CONTROL SOLENOID VALVE
㉕ EVAPORATIVE EMISSION (EVAP) CONTROL CANISTER
㉖ EVAPORATIVE EMISSION (EVAP) TWO WAY VALVE
㉗ THREE WAY CATALYTIC CONVERTER (TWC)
㉘ ENGINE MOUNT CONTROL SOLENOID VALVE

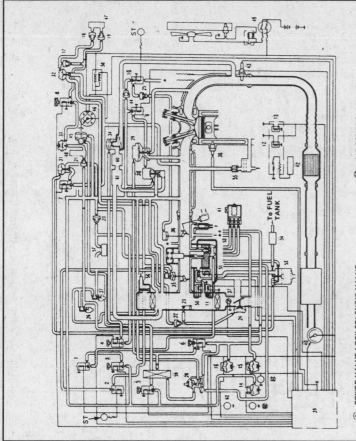

8680493

① POWER VALVE LOCK SOLENOID VALVE
② CRANKING LEAK SOLENOID VALVE
③ POWER VALVE CONTROL SOLENOID VALVE
④ AIR SUCTION CONTROL SOLENOID VALVE
⑤ VACUUM CONTROL SOLENOID VALVE
⑥ EGR CONTROL SOLENOID VALVE A
⑦ FREQUENCY SOLENOID VALVE A
⑧ FREQUENCY SOLENOID VALVE B
⑨ ANTI-AFTERBURN CONTROL SOLENOID VALVE
⑩ CRANKING OPENER SOLENOID VALVE
⑪ MAIN AIR JET CONTROL SOLENOID VALVE
⑫ RIGHT PRIMARY SLOW MIXTURE CUT-OFF
　 SOLENOID VALVE
⑬ LEFT PRIMARY SLOW MIXTURE CUT-OFF
　 SOLENOID VALVE
⑭ VACUUM SWITCH A
⑮ VACUUM SWITCH B
⑯ VACUUM SWITCH C
⑰ CHECK VALVE A
⑱ CHECK VALVE B
⑲ CHECK VALVE C
⑳ CHECK VALVE F
㉑ CHECK VALVE E
㉒ CHECK VALVE (INTAKE AIR TEMP.)
㉓ AIR BLEED VALVE
㉔ INTAKE AIR CONTROL DIAPHRAGM
㉕ DASHPOT CHECK VALVE
㉖ THERMOVALVE B
㉗ THERMOVALVE A
㉘ EGR CONTROL VALVES A & B
㉙ EGR VALVE
㉚ ANTI-AFTERBURN VALVE
㉛ AIR CONTROL VALVE A

㉜ AIR CONTROL VALVE B
㉝ CONSTANT VACUUM VALVE
㉞ AIR SUCTION VALVE
㉟ CHOKE OPENER
㊱ THROTTLE CONTROLLER
㊲ INTAKE AIR TEMPERATURE SWITCH
㊳ THERMOSENSOR
㊴ CONTROL UNIT
㊵ SPEED SENSOR
㊶ AIR JET CONTROLLER
㊷ CATALYTIC CONVERTER
㊸ OXYGEN SENSOR
㊹ CHECK VALVE D
㊺ DISTRIBUTOR VACUUM ADVANCE
㊻ DISTRIBUTOR
㊼ SURGE TANK A
㊽ SURGE TANK B
㊾ IGNITION SWITCH
㊿ INNER VENT SOLENOID VALVE
⑤① AIR VENT CUT-OFF SOLENOID VALVE
⑤② POWER VALVE
⑤③ CANISTER
⑤④ TWO-WAY VALVE
⑤⑤ BLOW-BY FILTER
⑤⑥ PCV VALVE
⑤⑦ VACUUM TANK
⑤⑧ IGNITION COIL
⑤⑨ AIR FILTER
⑥⓪ AIR CHAMBER A
⑥① AIR CHAMBER B
⑥② AUXILIARY COIL

Emission component schematic—1984–85 carbureted Prelude

86804491

① FRONT HEATED OXYGEN SENSOR (HO2S) (SENSOR 1)
② REAR HEATED OXYGEN SENSOR (HO2S) (SENSOR 2)
③ MANIFOLD ABSOLUTE PRESSURE (MAP) SENSOR
④ ENGINE COOLANT TEMPERATURE (ECT) SENSOR
⑤ INTAKE AIR TEMPERATURE (IAT) SENSOR
⑥ IDLE AIR CONTROL (IAC) VALVE
⑦ FAST IDLE THERMO VALVE
⑧ FUEL INJECTOR
⑨ FUEL FILTER
⑩ FUEL PRESSURE REGULATOR
⑪ FUEL PULSATION DAMPER
⑫ FUEL PUMP (FP)
⑬ FUEL TANK
⑭ FUEL TANK EVAPORATIVE EMISSION (EVAP) VALVE
⑮ AIR CLEANER
⑯ RESONATOR
⑰ CRANK POSITION (CKP) SENSOR
⑱ TOP DEAD CENTER/CYLINDER POSITION (TDC/CYP)
　 SENSOR

⑲ INTAKE AIR BYPASS (IAB) CHECK VALVE
⑳ INTAKE AIR BYPASS (IAB) VACUUM TANK
㉑ INTAKE AIR BYPASS (IAB) CONTROL SOLENOID VALVE
㉒ INTAKE AIR BYPASS (IAB) CONTROL DIAPHRAGM
㉓ EXHAUST GAS RECIRCULATION (EGR)
　 VACUUM CONTROL VALVE
㉔ EXHAUST GAS RECIRCULATION (EGR)
　 CONTROL SOLENOID VALVE
㉕ EXHAUST GAS RECIRCULATION (EGR) VALVE
㉖ POSITIVE CRANKCASE VENTILATION (PCV) VALVE
㉗ EVAPORATIVE EMISSION (EVAP) PURGE FLOW SWITCH
㉘ EVAPORATIVE EMISSION (EVAP) CONTROL CANISTER
㉙ EVAPORATIVE EMISSION (EVAP) PURGE CONTROL
　 SOLENOID VALVE
㉚ EVAPORATIVE EMISSION (EVAP) TWO WAY VALVE
㉛ THREE WAY CATALYTIC CONVERTER (TWC)
㉜ ENGINE MOUNT CONTROL SOLENOID VALVE

To CRUISE CONTROL

ENGINE COOLANT

To ENGINE MOUNT

ENGINE COOLANT

Emission component schematic—1995 Accord V-6

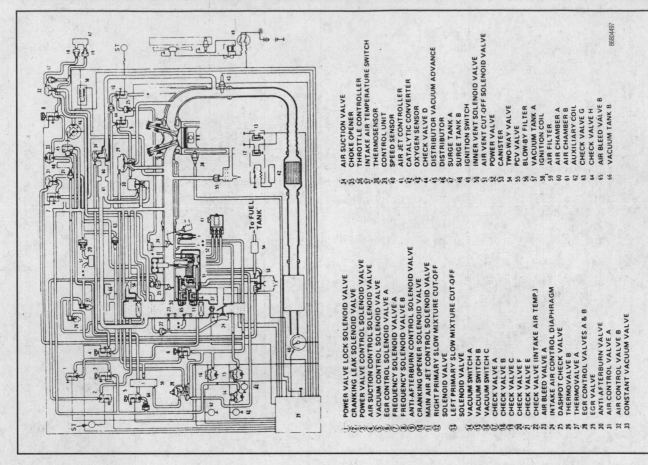

1. POWER VALVE LOCK SOLENOID VALVE
2. CRANKING LEAK SOLENOID VALVE
3. POWER VALVE CONTROL SOLENOID VALVE
4. AIR SUCTION CONTROL SOLENOID VALVE
5. VACUUM CONTROL SOLENOID VALVE
6. EGR CONTROL SOLENOID VALVE A
7. FREQUENCY SOLENOID VALVE A
8. FREQUENCY SOLENOID VALVE B
9. ANTI-AFTERBURN CONTROL SOLENOID VALVE
10. CRANKING OPENER SOLENOID VALVE
11. MAIN AIR JET CONTROL SOLENOID VALVE
12. RIGHT PRIMARY SLOW MIXTURE CUT-OFF SOLENOID VALVE
13. LEFT PRIMARY SLOW MIXTURE CUT-OFF SOLENOID VALVE
14. VACUUM SWITCH A
15. VACUUM SWITCH B
16. VACUUM SWITCH C
17. CHECK VALVE A
18. CHECK VALVE B
19. CHECK VALVE C
20. CHECK VALVE F
21. CHECK VALVE (INTAKE AIR TEMP.)
22. AIR BLEED VALVE A
23. INTAKE AIR CONTROL DIAPHRAGM
24. DASHPOT CHECK VALVE
25. THERMOVALVE B
26. THERMOVALVE A
27. EGR CONTROL VALVES A & B
28. EGR VALVE
29. ANTI-AFTERBURN VALVE
30. AIR CONTROL VALVE A
31. AIR CONTROL VALVE B
32. CONSTANT VACUUM VALVE

34. AIR SUCTION VALVE
35. CHOKE OPENER
36. THROTTLE CONTROLLER
37. INTAKE AIR TEMPERATURE SWITCH
38. THERMOSENSOR
39. CONTROL UNIT
40. SPEED SENSOR
41. AIR JET CONTROLLER
42. CATALYTIC CONVERTER
43. OXYGEN SENSOR
44. CHECK VALVE D
45. DISTRIBUTOR VACUUM ADVANCE
46. DISTRIBUTOR
47. SURGE TANK A
48. SURGE TANK B
49. IGNITION SWITCH
50. INNER VENT SOLENOID VALVE
51. AIR VENT CUT-OFF SOLENOID VALVE
52. POWER VALVE
53. CANISTER
54. TWO-WAY VALVE
55. PCV VALVE
56. BLOW-BY FILTER
57. VACUUM TANK A
58. IGNITION COIL
59. AIR FILTER
60. AIR CHAMBER A
61. AIR CHAMBER B
62. AUXILIARY COIL
63. CHECK VALVE G
64. CHECK VALVE H
65. AIR BLEED VALVE B
66. VACUUM TANK B

Emission component schematic—1986 carbureted Prelude

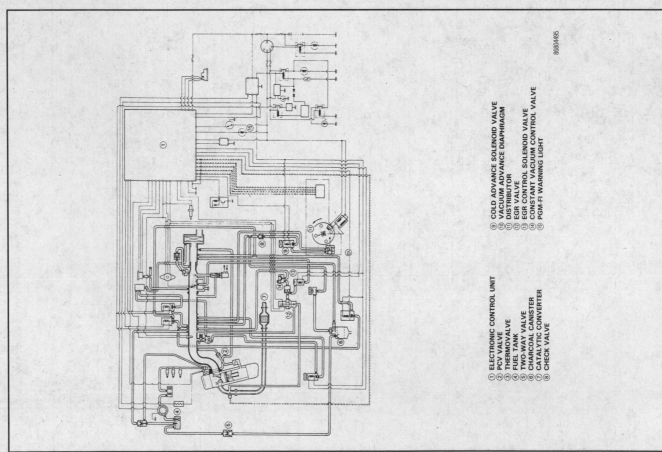

1. ELECTRONIC CONTROL UNIT
2. PCV VALVE
3. THERMOVALVE
4. FUEL TANK
5. TWO-WAY VALVE
6. CHARCOAL CANISTER
7. CATALYTIC CONVERTER
8. CHECK VALVE

9. COLD ADVANCE SOLENOID VALVE
10. VACUUM ADVANCE DIAPHRAGM
11. DISTRIBUTOR
12. EGR VALVE
13. EGR CONTROL SOLENOID VALVE
14. CONSTANT VACUUM CONTROL VALVE
15. PGM-FI WARNING LIGHT

Emission component schematic—1985 fuel injected Prelude

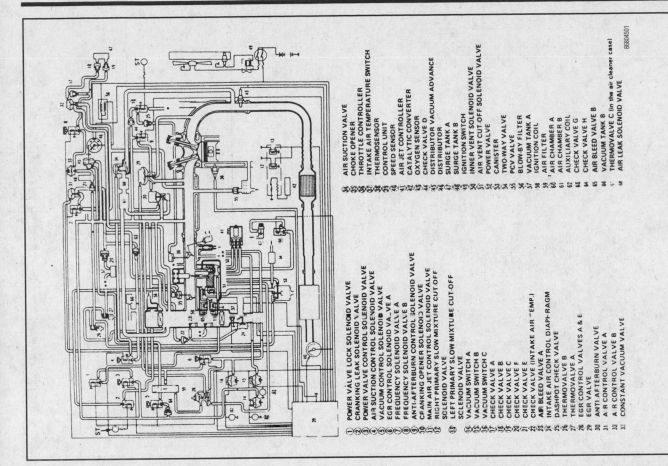

36 AIR SUCTION VALVE
37 CHOKE OPENER
38 THROTTLE CONTROLLER
39 INTAKE AIR TEMPERATURE SWITCH
40 THERMOSENSOR
41 CONTROL UNIT
42 SPEED SENSOR
43 AIR JET CONTROLLER
44 CATALYTIC CONVERTER
45 OXYGEN SENSOR
46 CHECK VALVE D
47 DISTRIBUTOR VACUUM ADVANCE
48 DISTRIBUTOR
49 SURGE TANK A
50 SURGE TANK B
51 IGNITION SWITCH
52 INNER VENT SOLENOID VALVE
53 AIR VENT CUT-OFF SOLENOID VALVE
54 POWER VALVE
55 CANISTER
56 TWO-WAY VALVE
57 PCV VALVE
58 BLOW-BY FILTER
59 VACUUM TANK A
60 IGNITION COIL
61 AIR FILTER
62 AIR CHAMBER A
63 AIR CHAMBER B
64 AUXILIARY COIL
65 CHECK VALVE G
66 CHECK VALVE H
67 AIR BLEED VALVE B
68 VACUUM TANK B
69 THERMOVALVE C (in the air cleaner case)
70 AIR LEAK SOLENOID VALVE

1 POWER VALVE LOCK SOLENOID VALVE
2 CRANKING LEAK SOLENOID VALVE
3 POWER VALVE CONTROL SOLENOID VALVE
4 AIR SUCTION CONTROL SOLENOID VALVE
5 VACUUM CONTROL SOLENOID VALVE
6 EGR CONTROL SOLENOID VALVE A
7 FREQUENCY SOLENOID VALVE A
8 FREQUENCY SOLENOID VALVE B
9 ANTI-AFTERBURN CONTROL SOLENOID VALVE
10 CRANKING OPENER SOLENOID VALVE
11 MAIN AIR JET CONTROL SOLENOID VALVE
12 RIGHT PRIMARY SLOW MIXTURE CUT-OFF SOLENOID VALVE
13 LEFT PRIMARY SLOW MIXTURE CUT-OFF SOLENOID VALVE
14 VACUUM SWITCH A
15 VACUUM SWITCH B
16 VACUUM SWITCH C
17 CHECK VALVE A
18 CHECK VALVE B
19 CHECK VALVE E
20 CHECK VALVE F
21 CHECK VALVE (INTAKE AIR "EMP.)
22 AIR BLEED VALVE A
23 INTAKE AIR CONTROL DIAPHRAGM
24 DASHPOT CHECK VALVE
25 THERMOVALVE A
26 THERMOVALVE B
27 EGR CONTROL VALVES A & E
28 EGR VALVE
29 ANTI-AFTERBURN VALVE
30 A R CONTROL VALVE A
31 A R CONTROL VALVE B
32 CONSTANT VACUUM VALVE

86804501

Emission component schematic—1987 carbureted Prelude

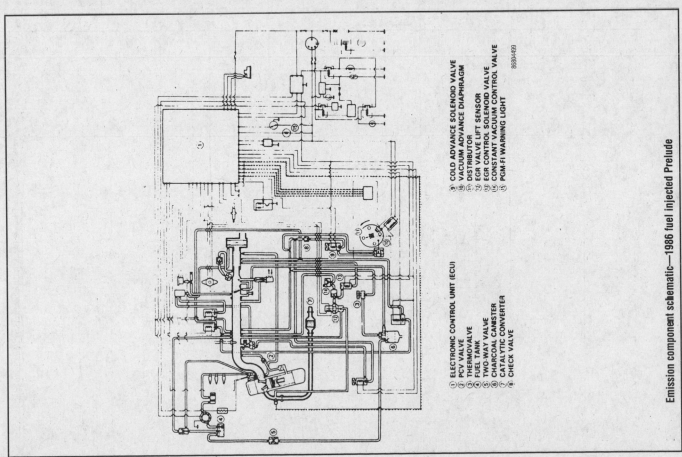

9 COLD ADVANCE SOLENOID VALVE
10 VACUUM ADVANCE DIAPHRAGM
11 DISTRIBUTOR
12 EGR VALVE LIFT SENSOR
13 EGR CONTROL SOLENOID VALVE
14 CONSTANT VACUUM CONTROL VALVE
15 PGM-FI WARNING LIGHT

1 ELECTRONIC CONTROL UNIT (ECU)
2 PCV VALVE
3 THERMOVALVE
4 FUEL TANK
5 TWO-WAY VALVE
6 CHARCOAL CANISTER
7 CATALYTIC CONVERTER
8 CHECK VALVE

86804499

Emission component schematic—1986 fuel injected Prelude

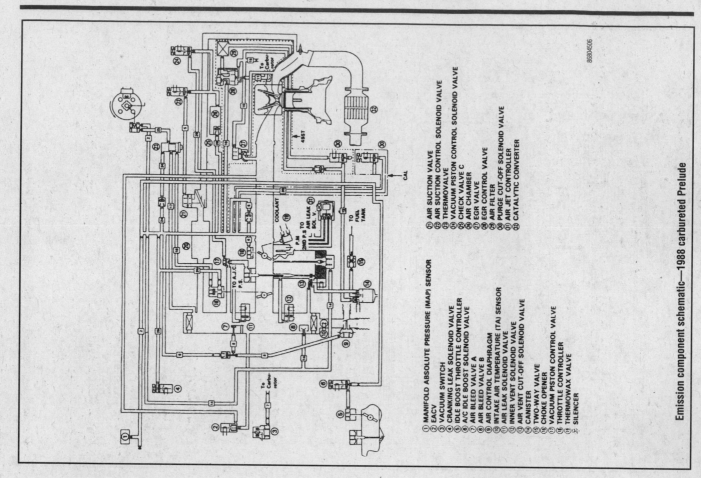

1 MANIFOLD ABSOLUTE PRESSURE (MAP) SENSOR
2 EACV
3 VACUUM SWITCH
4 CRANKING LEAK SOLENOID VALVE
5 IDLE BOOST THROTTLE CONTROLLER
6 A/C IDLE BOOST SOLENOID VALVE
7 AIR BLEED VALVE A
8 AIR BLEED VALVE B
9 AIR CONTROL DIAPHRAGM
10 INTAKE AIR TEMPERATURE (TA) SENSOR
11 AIR LEAK SOLENOID VALVE
12 INNER VENT SOLENOID VALVE
13 AIR VENT CUT-OFF SOLENOID VALVE
14 CANISTER
15 TWO-WAY VALVE
16 CHOKE OPENER
17 VACUUM PISTON CONTROL VALVE
18 THROTTLE CONTROLLER
19 THERMOWAX VALVE
20 SILENCER

21 AIR SUCTION VALVE
22 AIR SUCTION CONTROL SOLENOID VALVE
23 THERMOVALVE
24 VACUUM PISTON CONTROL SOLENOID VALVE
25 CHECK VALVE C
26 AIR CHAMBER
27 EGR VALVE
28 AIR FILTER
29 EGR CONTROL VALVE
30 PURGE CUT-OFF SOLENOID VALVE
31 AIR JET CONTROLLER
32 CATALYTIC CONVERTER

Emission component schematic—1988 carbureted Prelude

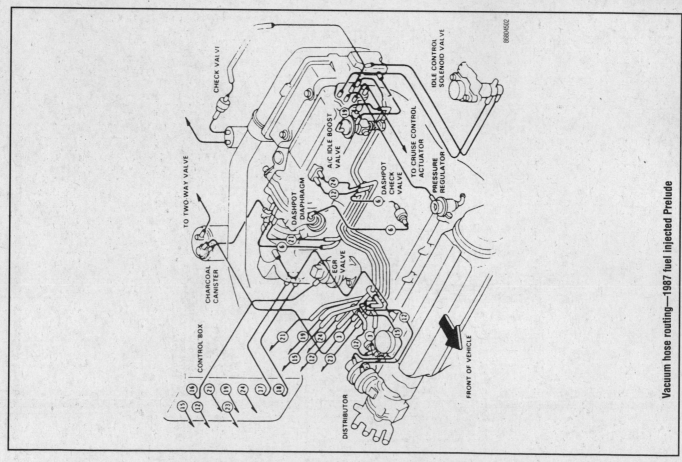

Vacuum hose routing—1987 fuel injected Prelude

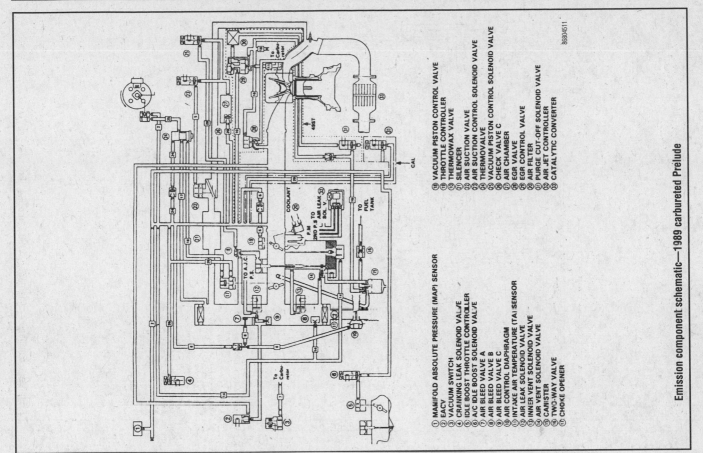

86804511

1. MANIFOLD ABSOLUTE PRESSURE (MAP) SENSOR
2. EACV
3. VACUUM SWITCH
4. CRANKING LEAK SOLENOID VALVE
5. IDLE BOOST THROTTLE CONTROLLER
6. A/C IDLE BOOST SOLENOID VALVE
7. AIR BLEED VALVE A
8. AIR BLEED VALVE B
9. AIR BLEED VALVE C
10. AIR CONTROL DIAPHRAGM
11. INTAKE AIR TEMPERATURE (TA) SENSOR
12. AIR LEAK SOLENOID VALVE
13. INNER VENT SOLENOID VALVE
14. AIR VENT SOLENOID VALVE
15. CANISTER
16. TWO-WAY VALVE
17. CHOKE OPENER

18. VACUUM PISTON CONTROL VALVE
19. THROTTLE CONTROLLER
20. THERMOWAX VALVE
21. SILENCER
22. AIR SUCTION VALVE
23. AIR SUCTION CONTROL SOLENOID VALVE
24. THERMOVALVE
25. VACUUM PISTON CONTROL SOLENOID VALVE
26. CHECK VALVE C
27. AIR CHAMBER
28. EGR VALVE
29. EGR CONTROL VALVE
30. AIR FILTER
31. PURGE CUT-OFF SOLENOID VALVE
32. AIR JET CONTROLLER
33. CATALYTIC CONVERTER

Emission component schematic—1989 carbureted Prelude

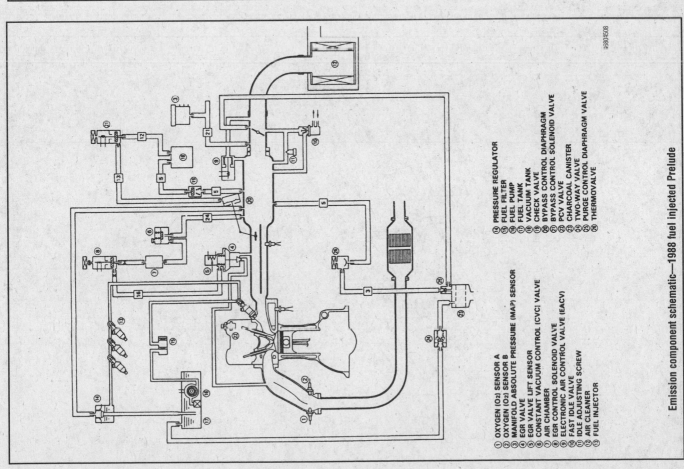

86804508

1. OXYGEN (O2) SENSOR A
2. OXYGEN (O2) SENSOR B
3. MANIFOLD ABSOLUTE PRESSURE (MAP) SENSOR
4. EGR VALVE
5. EGR VALVE LIFT SENSOR
6. CONSTANT VACUUM CONTROL (CVC) VALVE
7. AIR CHAMBER
8. EGR CONTROL SOLENOID VALVE
9. ELECTRONIC AIR CONTROL VALVE (EACV)
10. FAST IDLE VALVE
11. IDLE ADJUSTING SCREW
12. AIR CLEANER
13. FUEL INJECTOR

14. PRESSURE REGULATOR
15. FUEL FILTER
16. FUEL PUMP
17. FUEL TANK
18. VACUUM TANK
19. CHECK VALVE
20. BYPASS CONTROL DIAPHRAGM
21. BYPASS CONTROL SOLENOID VALVE
22. PCV VALVE
23. CHARCOAL CANISTER
24. TWO-WAY VALVE
25. PURGE CONTROL DIAPHRAGM VALVE
26. THERMOVALVE

Emission component schematic—1988 fuel injected Prelude

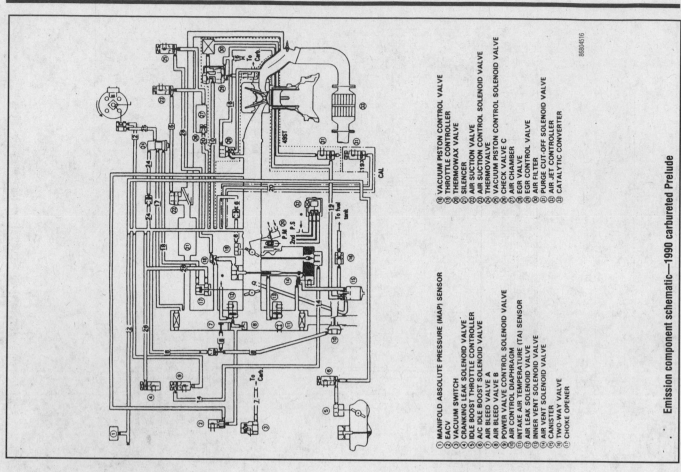

① MANIFOLD ABSOLUTE PRESSURE (MAP) SENSOR
② EACV
③ VACUUM SWITCH
④ CRANKING LEAK SOLENOID VALVE
⑤ IDLE BOOST THROTTLE CONTROLLER
⑥ A/C IDLE BOOST SOLENOID VALVE
⑦ AIR BLEED VALVE A
⑧ AIR BLEED VALVE B
⑨ POWER VALVE CONTROL SOLENOID VALVE
⑩ AIR CONTROL DIAPHRAGM
⑪ INTAKE AIR TEMPERATURE (TA) SENSOR
⑫ AIR LEAK SOLENOID VALVE
⑬ INNER VENT SOLENOID VALVE
⑭ AIR VENT SOLENOID VALVE
⑮ CANISTER
⑯ TWO-WAY VALVE
⑰ CHOKE OPENER

⑱ VACUUM PISTON CONTROL VALVE
⑲ THROTTLE CONTROLLER
⑳ THERMOWAX VALVE
㉑ SILENCER
㉒ AIR SUCTION VALVE
㉓ AIR SUCTION CONTROL SOLENOID VALVE
㉔ THERMOVALVE
㉕ VACUUM PISTON CONTROL SOLENOID VALVE
㉖ CHECK VALVE C
㉗ AIR CHAMBER
㉘ EGR VALVE
㉙ EGR CONTROL VALVE
㉚ AIR FILTER
㉛ PURGE CUT-OFF SOLENOID VALVE
㉜ AIR JET CONTROLLER
㉝ CATALYTIC CONVERTER

Emission component schematic—1990 carbureted Prelude

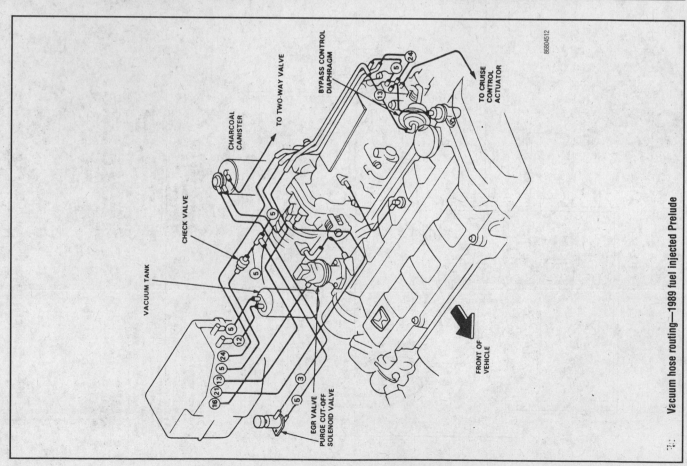

Vacuum hose routing—1989 fuel injected Prelude

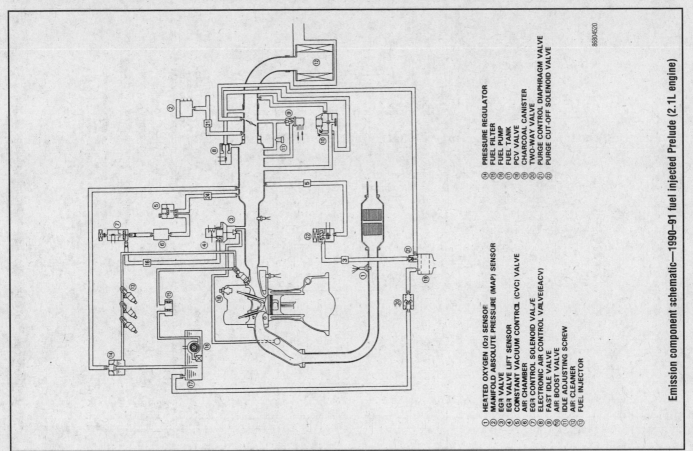

① HEATED OXYGEN (O₂) SENSOR
② MANIFOLD ABSOLUTE PRESSURE (MAP) SENSOR
③ EGR VALVE
④ EGR VALVE LIFT SENSOR
⑤ CONSTANT VACUUM CONTROL (CVC) VALVE
⑥ AIR CHAMBER
⑦ EGR CONTROL SOLENOID VALVE
⑧ ELECTRONIC AIR CONTROL VALVE(EACV)
⑨ FAST IDLE VALVE
⑩ AIR BOOST VALVE
⑪ IDLE ADJUSTING SCREW
⑫ AIR CLEANER
⑬ FUEL INJECTOR

⑭ PRESSURE REGULATOR
⑮ FUEL FILTER
⑯ FUEL PUMP
⑰ FUEL TANK
⑱ PCV VALVE
⑲ CHARCOAL CANISTER
⑳ TWO-WAY VALVE
㉑ PURGE CONTROL DIAPHRAGM VALVE
㉒ PURGE CUT-OFF SOLENOID VALVE

Emission component schematic—1990–91 fuel injected Prelude (2.1L engine)

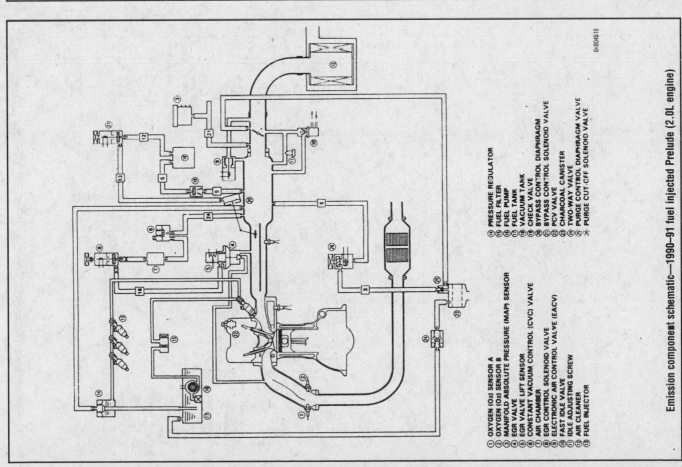

① OXYGEN (O₂) SENSOR A
② OXYGEN (O₂) SENSOR B
③ MANIFOLD ABSOLUTE PRESSURE (MAP) SENSOR
④ EGR VALVE
⑤ EGR VALVE LIFT SENSOR
⑥ CONSTANT VACUUM CONTROL (CVC) VALVE
⑦ AIR CHAMBER
⑧ EGR CONTROL SOLENOID VALVE
⑨ ELECTRONIC AIR CONTROL VALVE (EACV)
⑩ FAST IDLE VALVE
⑪ IDLE ADJUSTING SCREW
⑫ AIR CLEANER
⑬ FUEL INJECTOR

⑭ PRESSURE REGULATOR
⑮ FUEL FILTER
⑯ FUEL PUMP
⑰ FUEL TANK
⑱ VACUUM TANK
⑲ CHECK VALVE
⑳ BYPASS CONTROL DIAPHRAGM
㉑ BYPASS CONTROL SOLENOID VALVE
㉒ PCV VALVE
㉓ CHARCOAL CANISTER
㉔ TWO-WAY VALVE
㉕ PURGE CONTROL DIAPHRAGM VALVE
㉖ PURGE CUT-OFF SOLENOID VALVE

Emission component schematic—1990–91 fuel injected Prelude (2.0L engine)

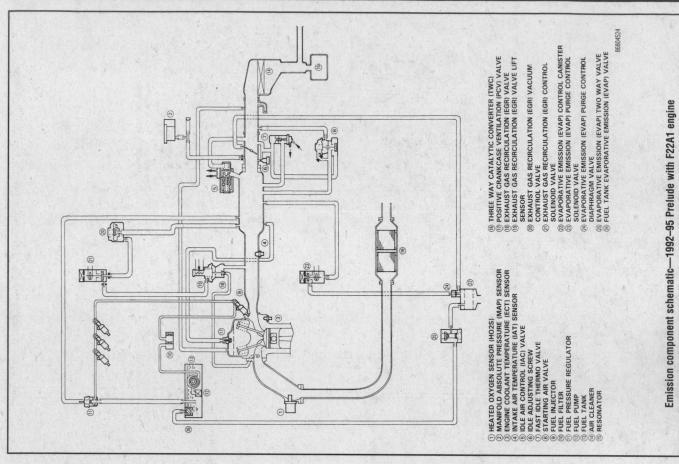

86804524

① HEATED OXYGEN SENSOR (HO2S)
② MANIFOLD ABSOLUTE PRESSURE (MAP) SENSOR
③ ENGINE COOLANT TEMPERATURE (ECT) SENSOR
④ INTAKE AIR TEMPERATURE (IAT) SENSOR
⑤ IDLE AIR CONTROL (IAC) VALVE
⑥ IDLE ADJUSTING SCREW
⑦ FAST IDLE THERMO VALVE
⑧ STARTING AIR VALVE
⑨ FUEL INJECTOR
⑩ FUEL FILTER
⑪ FUEL PRESSURE REGULATOR
⑫ FUEL PUMP
⑬ FUEL TANK
⑭ AIR CLEANER
⑮ RESONATOR

⑯ THREE WAY CATALYTIC CONVERTER (TWC)
⑰ POSITIVE CRANKCASE VENTILATION (PCV) VALVE
⑱ EXHAUST GAS RECIRCULATION (EGR) VALVE
⑲ EXHAUST GAS RECIRCULATION (EGR) VALVE LIFT SENSOR
⑳ EXHAUST GAS RECIRCULATION (EGR) VACUUM CONTROL VALVE
㉑ EXHAUST GAS RECIRCULATION (EGR) CONTROL SOLENOID VALVE
㉒ EVAPORATIVE EMISSION (EVAP) CONTROL CANISTER
㉓ EVAPORATIVE EMISSION (EVAP) PURGE CONTROL SOLENOID VALVE
㉔ EVAPORATIVE EMISSION (EVAP) PURGE CONTROL DIAPHRAGM VALVE
㉕ EVAPORATIVE EMISSION (EVAP) TWO WAY VALVE
㉖ FUEL TANK EVAPORATIVE EMISSION (EVAP) VALVE

Emission component schematic—1992–95 Prelude with F22A1 engine

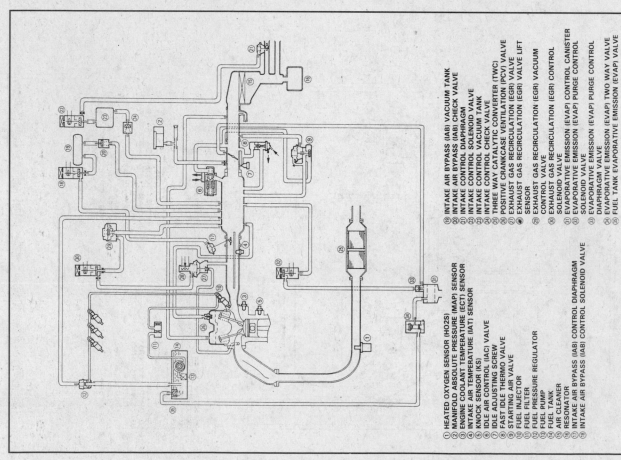

86804523

① HEATED OXYGEN SENSOR (HO2S)
② MANIFOLD ABSOLUTE PRESSURE (MAP) SENSOR
③ ENGINE COOLANT TEMPERATURE (ECT) SENSOR
④ INTAKE AIR TEMPERATURE (IAT) SENSOR
⑤ KNOCK SENSOR (KS)
⑥ IDLE AIR CONTROL (IAC) VALVE
⑦ IDLE ADJUSTING SCREW
⑧ FAST IDLE THERMO VALVE
⑨ STARTING AIR VALVE
⑩ FUEL INJECTOR
⑪ FUEL FILTER
⑫ FUEL PRESSURE REGULATOR
⑬ FUEL PUMP
⑭ FUEL TANK
⑮ AIR CLEANER
⑯ RESONATOR
⑰ INTAKE AIR BYPASS (IAB) CONTROL DIAPHRAGM
⑱ INTAKE AIR BYPASS (IAB) CONTROL SOLENOID VALVE

⑲ INTAKE AIR BYPASS (IAB) VACUUM TANK
⑳ INTAKE AIR BYPASS (IAB) CHECK VALVE
㉑ INTAKE CONTROL DIAPHRAGM
㉒ INTAKE CONTROL SOLENOID VALVE
㉓ INTAKE CONTROL VACUUM TANK
㉔ INTAKE CONTROL CHECK VALVE
㉕ THREE WAY CATALYTIC CONVERTER (TWC)
㉖ POSITIVE CRANKCASE VENTILATION (PCV) VALVE
㉗ EXHAUST GAS RECIRCULATION (EGR) VALVE
㉘ EXHAUST GAS RECIRCULATION (EGR) VALVE LIFT SENSOR
㉙ EXHAUST GAS RECIRCULATION (EGR) VACUUM CONTROL VALVE
㉚ EXHAUST GAS RECIRCULATION (EGR) CONTROL SOLENOID VALVE
㉛ EVAPORATIVE EMISSION (EVAP) CONTROL CANISTER
㉜ EVAPORATIVE EMISSION (EVAP) PURGE CONTROL SOLENOID VALVE
㉝ EVAPORATIVE EMISSION (EVAP) PURGE CONTROL DIAPHRAGM VALVE
㉞ EVAPORATIVE EMISSION (EVAP) TWO WAY VALVE
㉟ FUEL TANK EVAPORATIVE EMISSION (EVAP) VALVE

Emission component schematic—1992–95 Prelude with H23A1 and H22A1 engines

5

FUEL SYSTEM

BASIC FUEL SYSTEM DIAGNOSIS

When there is a problem starting or driving a vehicle, two of the most important checks involve the ignition and the fuel systems. The questions most mechanics attempt to answer first, "is there adequate spark?" and "is there adequate fuel?" will often lead to solving most basic problems. For ignition system diagnosis and testing, please refer to Section 2 of this manual. If the ignition system checks out (there is spark), then you must determine if fuel system is operating properly (is there fuel?).

CARBURETED FUEL SYSTEM

Electric Fuel Pump

The carbureted Accords and Preludes covered in this manual use an electric fuel pump located either near or inside the fuel tank. The 1984–85 Accords and 1984–87 Preludes use an external fuel pump mounted under the car just forward of the left rear wheel. Later models use an electric fuel pump mounted inside the fuel tank.

REMOVAL & INSTALLATION

✳✳ CAUTION

Gasoline vapors are explosive. Remove components slowly and contain spillage. Observe "no smoking/no open flame" precautions. Have a Class B-C (dry powder) fire extinguisher within arm's reach at all times.

Externally Mounted Fuel Pump

▶ **See Figures 1 and 2**

1. Disconnect the negative battery cable.
2. Remove the gas filler cap to relieve any excess pressure in the system.
3. Loosen the lug nuts of the left rear wheel.
4. Elevate the rear of the car and support it safely on properly placed stands. Remove the left rear wheel.
5. Use a pair of suitable fuel line clamps to pinch shut the fuel hoses leading to and from the pump.
6. Label the fuel lines, then loosen the hose clamps. Slide the clamps back; twist the hoses while removing them.
7. Disconnect the positive lead wire and ground wire from the pump.
8. Remove the fuel pump retaining bolts, taking care not to lose the spacers and bolt collars.
9. Remove the fuel pump and its protective cover as a unit.

➡**The pump cannot be disassembled and must be replaced if defective.**

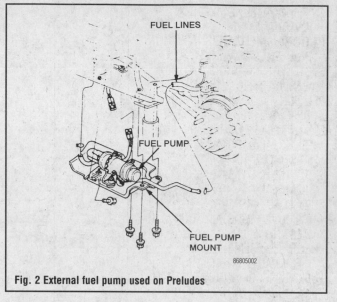

Fig. 2 External fuel pump used on Preludes

To install:

10. Install the fuel pump and cover. Make certain the mounting collars and insulators are in the proper location. Tighten the mounting bolts to 7 ft. lbs. (10 Nm).
11. Engage the wiring to the fuel pump.
12. Connect the fuel hoses, making certain the lines are correctly placed and the clamps are secure. When in doubt, use new clamps; they are cheap insurance against leaks. Remove the fuel line clamps.
13. Install the left rear wheel. Lower the car to the ground.
14. Install the fuel filler cap. Connect the negative battery cable.
15. Turn the ignition **ON** for 3 seconds, listening for the fuel pump operation. Switch the ignition **OFF**, then **ON** again. This will build pressure within the fuel lines.
16. Start the engine. It may crank for several seconds until the lines are completely filled.

In-Tank Fuel Pumps

▶ **See Figure 3**

1. Disconnect the negative battery cable.
2. Lift or reposition the carpet in the luggage area. Remove the left access cover in the floor.
3. Unplug the electrical connector at the pump unit.
4. Label and disconnect the fuel lines.
5. Carefully remove the retaining nuts securing the pump. When all are removed, lift the pump up and out of the tank.

➡**The pump may require some manipulation to remove.**

To install:

6. Install the pump, making certain it is correctly seated and not wedged or jammed. Install the retaining nuts, tightening them evenly and alternately to 4 ft. lbs. (6 Nm).
7. Connect the fuel lines. Make certain the clamps are secure; use new ones if necessary.
8. Engage the wiring to the fuel pump.
9. Install the access cover and seal or gasket, if used.
10. Reposition the carpeting in the luggage compartment.

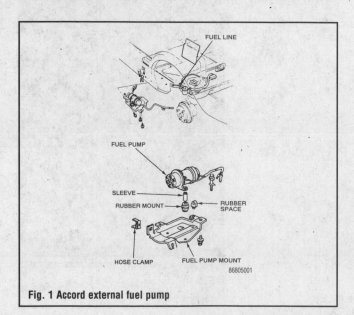

Fig. 1 Accord external fuel pump

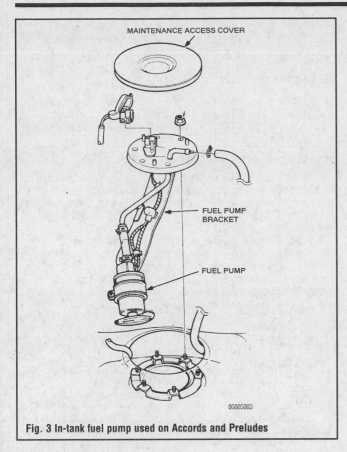

MAINTENANCE ACCESS COVER

FUEL PUMP BRACKET

FUEL PUMP

0G005003

Fig. 3 In-tank fuel pump used on Accords and Preludes

11. Connect the negative battery cable.

12. Start the engine; it may crank longer than normal until fuel pressure is established.

TESTING

▶ **See Figures 4 and 5**

➡ **Always check the fuel filter for clogging and/or the fuel lines for crimping or blockage before testing the fuel pump. A fuel pressure gauge and a graduated quart container are required for these procedures.**

Externally Mounted Fuel Pumps

1. Turn the ignition **OFF**. Remove the screws securing the underdash fuse box to its mount. Remove the fuel cut-off relay from the back of the fuse block and turn the block so you can see the relay mount.

2. Use a jumper wire to connect the two left-most terminals of the relay mount. On Preludes, these terminals are for the Black/Yellow wires. On the Accord, they are designated Terminals 1 and 2.

---

3. Disconnect the fuel line at the fuel filter in the engine compartment. Connect a pressure gauge to the fuel line.

4. Turn the ignition key **ON** until pressure on the gauge stabilizes, then turn the key **OFF**.

5. Pressure should be between 2.4–3.1 psi (16.7–21.6 kPa) for Accords and 2–3 psi (13.6–20 kPa) for Preludes. If the pressure shown is below minimum, the pump must be replaced. If pressure is at least minimum, continue with the test.

6. Remove the pressure gauge from the fuel line; hold the line in the quart container. Have an assistant turn the ignition switch **ON** for 60 seconds, then turn it **OFF**.

7. Fuel flow in 60 seconds must be at least 17 oz. (500 cc) for Accord or 23 oz. (680 cc) for Prelude.

8. If fuel pump volume is below specification, the pump must be replaced.

9. Remove the jumper wire at the fuse block. Reinstall the fuel cut-off relay. Reinstall the fuse block on its mount.

In-Tank Fuel Pumps

1. Turn the ignition **OFF**.

2. On the Accord, remove the screws securing the underdash fuse box to its mount. Remove the fuel cut-off relay from the back of the fuse block and turn the block so you can see the relay mount. Use a jumper wire to connect the two left most terminals of the relay mount (terminal 1 to terminal 2).

3. On Preludes, remove the dashboard under cover; remove the fuel cut-off relay from the fuse block. Use a jumper wire to connect the top 2 terminals (terminals 1 and 2) of the relay mount.

4. Disconnect the fuel line at the fuel filter in the engine compartment. Connect a pressure gauge to the fuel line.

5. Turn the ignition key **ON** until pressure on the gauge stabilizes, then turn the key **OFF**.

6. Pressure should be between 2.6–3.3 psi (18–22.7 kPa). It the pressure shown is below minimum, the pump must be replaced. If pressure is at least minimum, continue with the test.

7. Remove the pressure gauge from the fuel line; hold the line in a quart container. Have an assistant turn the ignition switch **ON** for 60 seconds, then shut it **OFF**.

8. Fuel flow in 60 seconds must be at least 25.7 oz. (760 cc).

9. If fuel pump volume is below specification, the pump must be replaced.

10. Remove the jumper wire at the fuse block. Reinstall the fuel cut-off relay. Reinstall the fuse block on its mount.

Carburetor

ADJUSTMENTS

Throttle Cable

▶ **See Figure 6**

1. The throttle cable should operate smoothly with no binding. If the cable is kinked or binding, replace it.

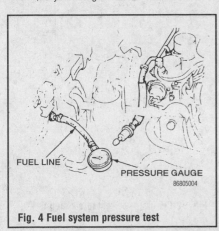

FUEL LINE

PRESSURE GAUGE

86805004

Fig. 4 Fuel system pressure test

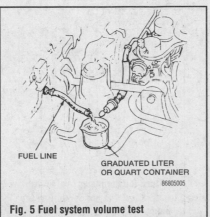
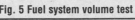

FUEL LINE

GRADUATED LITER OR QUART CONTAINER

86805005

Fig. 5 Fuel system volume test

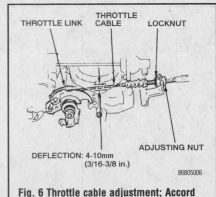

THROTTLE LINK   THROTTLE CABLE   LOCKNUT

ADJUSTING NUT

DEFLECTION: 4-10mm (3/16-3/8 in.)

86805006

Fig. 6 Throttle cable adjustment; Accord shown

2. Check the cable free play at the linkage. The cable should be loose enough to deflect ³⁄₁₆–³⁄₈ in. (4–10mm) between the locknut and the bell crank.

3. If the deflection is not correct, loosen the locknut. Turn the adjusting nut to tighten or loosen the cable as necessary. Once properly set, tighten the locknut.

4. Check the throttle plate while an assistant holds the accelerator pedal to the floor. The throttle should be fully open (the throttle plate should be vertical). Check carefully to see that the throttle plate is opening fully, but is not going "over center" (passing the vertical position and sitting at an angle.) Additionally, the throttle plate must close quickly and smoothly when the accelerator pedal is released.

Choke and Linkage

▶ See Figure 7

1. Remove the air cleaner.

2. Depress the accelerator to the floor and release it smoothly to set the choke plate(s). The plate(s) should close completely if the engine temperature is below 82°F (28°C). Above this temperature the plate(s) will not close totally, but should close to within ⅛ in. (3.175mm).

3. If choke does not close completely, check carefully for signs of dirt or binding in the linkage. Spray the linkage with carburetor cleaner and recheck.

4. If the choke still will not operate properly, remove the choke cover and inspect the linkage for freedom of motion. When reassembling, make certain the index marks align on the carburetor body and choke cover.

5. If the choke still will not operate correctly, replace the choke cover.

Fast Idle

ACCORD

1. Start the engine and allow it to reach normal operating temperature.

2. With the engine off, connect a tachometer.

3. Disconnect and plug the inner vacuum hose from the fast idle unloader.

4. Engage the fast idle cam by opening and closing the throttle fully while holding the choke blade closed.

5. Restart the engine. Fast idle should be between 2000–3000 rpm.

6. If necessary, adjust the engine speed by turning the fast idle adjusting screw.

1984–87 PRELUDE

▶ See Figures 8, 9 and 10

1. Start the engine and allow it to reach normal operating temperature.

2. With the engine off, connect a tachometer.

3. Remove the E-clip and flat washer from the thermowax linkage, then slide the linkage out until it is clear of the fast idle cam.

➡ Be careful not to bend the linkage.

4. Hold the throttle open and turn the fast idle cam counterclockwise until the fast idle lever is positioned as shown in the illustration.

5. Without opening the throttle, start the engine. Fast idle speed should be between 1250–2250 rpm for manual transaxles or 1200–2200 rpm for automatic transaxles.

6. Adjust, if necessary, by turning the fast idle adjusting screw.

7. Stop the engine and reconnect the termowax linkage.

8. Start the engine and check that the fast idle speed decreases as the engine temperature increases. If the fast idle speed does not drop, spray the linkage with carburetor cleaner. If the speed still does not drop, check for stuck or damaged linkage components. Replace as necessary.

1988–90 PRELUDE

▶ See Figures 11, 12, 13 and 14

1. Start the engine and allow it to reach normal operating temperature.

2. With the engine off, connect a tachometer.

3. Disconnect both coolant hoses from the thermowax valve and cap the ends of the hoses.

4. Flush the thermowax valve with cold water. Check the temperature of the water being used to flush the valve.

5. Start the engine and check the engine speed. Compare it to the graph.

6. If necessary, adjust by turning the fast idle adjusting screw.

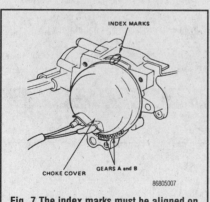

Fig. 7 The index marks must be aligned on the choke cover and housing

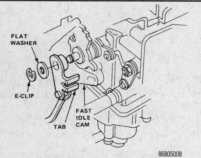

Fig. 8 Remove the E-clip and flat washer from the thermowax linkage, then slide the linkage out until it is clear of the fast idle cam

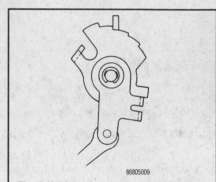

Fig. 9 Hold the throttle open and turn the fast idle cam counterclockwise until the fast idle lever is positioned as shown

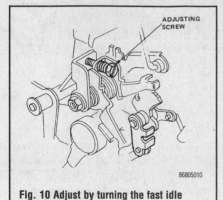

Fig. 10 Adjust by turning the fast idle adjusting screw

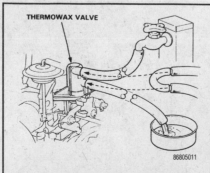

Fig. 11 Flush the thermowax valve with cold water. Check the temperature of the water being used to flush the valve

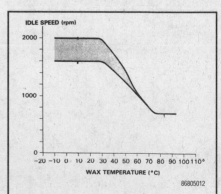

Fig. 12 Compare the fast idle speed to the graph . . .

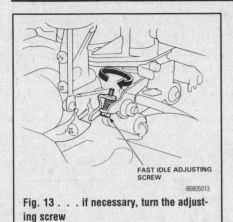

Fig. 13 . . . if necessary, turn the adjusting screw

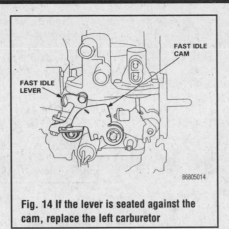

Fig. 14 If the lever is seated against the cam, replace the left carburetor

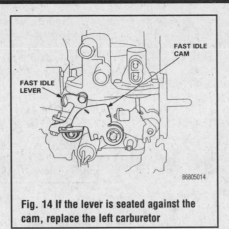

Fig. 15 Check the fuel level in the inspection window

➡If it is not possible to bring the fast idle speed within specification, it may be necessary to replace the left carburetor.

7. Stop the engine and connect both coolant hoses.
8. Start the engine and allow it to reach normal operating temperature. Check the position of the fast idle lever. If the lever is seated against the cam, replace the left carburetor.

Float Level

ACCORD

▸ See Figures 15 and 16

With the vehicle on level ground and at normal operating temperature, check the primary and secondary fuel level inspection windows on the side of the carburetor. Snap the throttle from idle to 3000 rpm several times, then allow the engine to idle. If the fuel level is not touching the indicator, adjust it by turning the screws which are located in recessed bosses above the inspection windows.

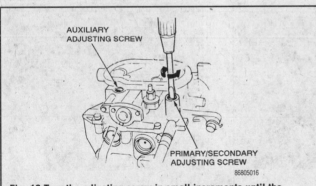

Fig. 16 Turn the adjusting screw in small increments until the proper level is reached

➡Do not turn the adjusting screws more than ⅛ turn every 15 seconds.

When the correct fuel level is achieved in the window(s), put a dab of paint on the adjusting screws to lock their position.

PRELUDE

▸ See Figure 17

With the carburetors and float chambers removed, hold the assembly so that the float chamber surface is inclined about 30 degrees from vertical. Use a float level gauge (Honda tool 07401–0010000 or equivalent) to measure the level with the float tip lightly contacting the needle valve. Correct measurement is 0.56–0.64 in. (14.2–16.2mm). Adjust the floats as needed.

Synchronization

Prelude dual carburetors must operate in synchronization to provide the same amount of air through each carburetor. The carburetors are synchronized at assembly and generally do not require resetting through the life of the car. However, if the carburetors have been removed and disassembled, they must be resynchronized.

1984–87 PRELUDE

▸ See Figures 18 and 19

1. Remove the air cleaner cover and filter.
2. Remove the air intake screens and air intake flanges.
3. Install synchronization adapters (Honda tool 07504–SB00000 or equivalent) to each carburetor intake; tighten the nuts only to 42 inch lbs. (5 Nm).
4. Connect a tachometer and start the engine. Allow the engine to warm up fully until the cooling fans come on at least once.
5. Use a carburetor synchronization tool to measure the flow rate through both adapters. If the flow rates are identical, shut the engine off, remove the adapters and reassemble the air cleaner. The test is complete.
6. If the air flow rates are not identical, loosen the adjusting screw lock nut and adjust as needed. The adjusting screw only affects the right carburetor, so

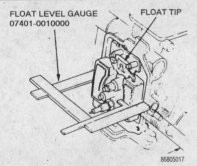

Fig. 17 Checking the float level on Preludes requires the removal of the carburetors and float chambers

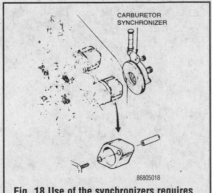

Fig. 18 Use of the synchronizers requires the use of adaptors

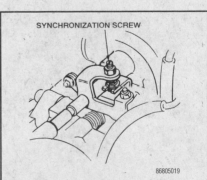

Fig. 19 The synchronization screw is located on the throttle linkage—1984–87 models

use the value from the left one as the baseline. Turn the adjusting screw clockwise to decrease airflow; counterclockwise to increase airflow. If the airflow cannot be balanced, inspect for air leaks around the carburetor or carbon build-up on the throttle plate.

7. Tighten the adjusting screw locknut. Recheck the flow rates.

8. Shut the engine off. Remove the synchronizer and adapters. Install the air intake flanges and screens.

9. Reassemble the air filter and cover.

1988–90 PRELUDE

▶ **See Figures 20 and 21**

1. Disconnect the red braided hose (marked PURGE) from the charcoal canister. Connect a vacuum gauge to the hose.

2. Connect a tachometer and start the engine. Allow the engine to run until it reaches normal operating temperature; the cooling fan should cycle on at least once.

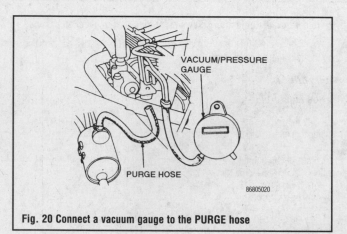

Fig. 20 Connect a vacuum gauge to the PURGE hose

3. Turn the idle speed adjusting screw until the engine speed is 3000 rpm. Note the reading on the gauge.

4. While the engine speed is at 3000 rpm, pinch the smooth red vacuum hose under the choke housing and note the change, if any, in the gauge reading.

5. If there was no change on the gauge, the carburetors are properly synchronized.

6. If the reading changed when the hose was pinched, adjust the synchronization screw until the readings are the same.

7. Remove the vacuum gauge and connect the PURGE hose to the canister. Remove the tachometer.

8. Reset the idle speed.

REMOVAL & INSTALLATION

Accord

▶ **See Figures 22 thru 29**

1. Disconnect the negative battery cable.

2. Remove the air cleaner cover.

3. Disconnect the fresh air and hot air hoses from the air cleaner.

4. Disconnect the vacuum lines from the air cleaner and mark their positions for proper reassembly. Disconnect the breather hose from the valve cover.

5. Remove the air cleaner mounting nuts and the air cleaner.

6. Disconnect the vacuum lines and electrical connectors from the carburetor and mark their positions for proper reassembly.

7. Disconnect the throttle cable. Disconnect the throttle control cable (automatic transaxles) and/or cruise control cable if so equipped.

8. Disconnect and plug the fuel lines.

9. Remove the carburetor mounting nuts. Lift the carburetor off the mounting studs.

10. If equipped, remove the electrically heated Early Fuel Evaporation (EFE) insulator.

11. Plug the holes in the intake manifold with rags or a paper towel. Remove any old gasket material.

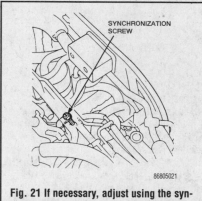

Fig. 21 If necessary, adjust using the synchronization screw—1988–90 models

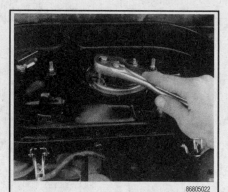

Fig. 22 Remove the air cleaner mounting nuts . . .

Fig. 23 . . . then remove the air cleaner from the engine

Fig. 24 On most models, the vacuum hoses are labeled from the factory

Fig. 25 Loosen the locknut, then disconnect the throttle cable from the linkage

Fig. 26 An extension is useful for removing the mounting nuts

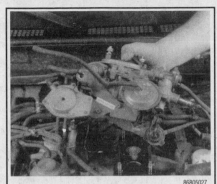

Fig. 27 Lift the carburetor off the mounting studs

Fig. 28 If equipped, remove the electrically heated Early Fuel Evaporation (EFE) insulator

Fig. 29 Plug the holes in the intake manifold with rags or a paper towel. Remove any old gasket material

To install:

12. Remove the rags or paper towels from the intake manifold.
13. Position the EFE insulator on the intake manifold.
14. Reinstall the carburetor on the insulator. Take care to keep debris from falling onto the EFE screen. Tighten the carburetor mounting nuts to 17 ft. lbs. (24 Nm).
15. Connect the fuel lines and secure the clamps.
16. Connect the cruise control and/or throttle control cables if they were removed. Connect and adjust the throttle cable.
17. Reinstall the vacuum lines to their correct ports. Double check the installation.
18. Engage the electrical connectors.
19. Install the air cleaner. Connect the fresh and hot air hoses. Connect the breather hose(s) and vacuum lines to the air cleaner as necessary.
20. Connect the negative battery cable. Start the engine and perform any carburetor adjustments as necessary.

Prelude

▶ See Figure 30

1. Disconnect the negative battery cable.
2. Disconnect the fresh air intake duct and the hot air intake hose from the air cleaner.
3. Disconnect the vacuum hose to the hot air intake control diaphragm.
4. Remove the air cleaner cover and the filter element.
5. Disconnect the breather hose from the valve cover.
6. Carefully label and disconnect the vacuum hoses at the base of the air cleaner.
7. Unplug the electrical connectors at the top of the air cleaner base.
8. Remove the 10mm nuts under the air cleaner base.
9. Remove the 4 nuts, air screens and their flanges.
10. Remove the air cleaner base.
11. Carefully label, then disconnect, the vacuum hose connections running to the carburetor assembly.
12. Disconnect the throttle cable.
13. Disconnect the vacuum hoses at the vacuum tube manifold.
14. Drain the coolant and remove the coolant hoses at the thermowax valve.
15. Disconnect the vent hose running from the charcoal canister to the air vent cut-off solenoid.
16. Disconnect the canister purge hose at the vacuum manifold.
17. Unplug the carburetor wiring and the connector to the choke heater.
18. Remove the main fuel hose from the right side of the vacuum manifold.
19. Loosen the insulator bands and remove the carburetors as a unit with the vacuum manifold attached.

To install:

20. Place the carburetors in position. Make certain they are fully seated and tight in the insulators. Install the retaining bands.
21. Engage the carburetor wiring and the connector to the choke heater.
22. Install the main fuel hose to the right side of the vacuum manifold.
23. Connect the charcoal canister purge hose at the vacuum manifold.
24. Connect the charcoal canister vent hose.

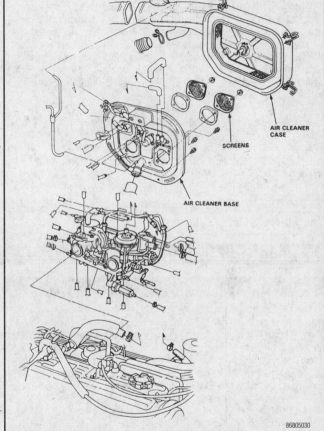

Fig. 30 Carefully label and disconnect the vacuum hoses; they are easily confused

25. Connect the coolant hoses at the thermowax valve.
26. Connect the vacuum hoses to the vacuum manifold.
27. Install the throttle cable.
28. Connect the vacuum lines at the carburetor.
29. Install the air cleaner base.
30. Install the air screens and flanges.
31. Install the 10mm bolts under the air cleaner base.
32. Attach the connectors at the top of the air cleaner base.
33. Connect the vacuum hoses to the air cleaner base.
34. Connect the breather hose to the valve cover.
35. Install the air cleaner housing, filter element and cover. Connect the vacuum hoses and air ducting.

OVERHAUL

➡ **Specific directions and specifications for carburetor overhaul are usually contained in the rebuilding kit.**

Efficient carburetion depends greatly on careful cleaning and inspection during overhaul since dirt, gum, water, or varnish in or on the carburetor parts are often responsible for poor performance.

Overhaul your carburetor in a clean, dust-free area. Carefully disassemble the carburetor, referring often to the exploded views. Keep all similar and look-alike parts segregated during disassembly and cleaning to avoid accidental interchange during assembly. Make a note of all jet sizes.

When the carburetor is disassembled, wash all parts (except diaphragms, electric choke units, pump plunger, and any other plastic or rubber parts) in clean carburetor solvent. Do not leave parts in the solvent any longer than is necessary to sufficiently loosen the deposits. Excessive cleaning may remove the special finish from the float bowl and choke valve bodies, leaving these parts unfit for service. Rinse all parts in clean solvent and blow them dry with compressed air or allow them to air dry. Wipe clean all plastic and plastic parts with a clean, lint-free cloth.

Blow out all passages and jets with compressed air and be sure that there are no restrictions or blockages. Never use wire or similar tools to clean jets, fuel passages, or air bleeds. Clean all jets and valves separately to avoid accidental interchange.

Check all parts for wear or damage. If wear or damage is found, replace the defective parts. Especially check the following:

1. Check the float needle and seat for wear. If wear is found, replace the complete assembly.
2. Check the float hinge pin for wear and the float(s) for dents or distortion. Replace the float if fuel has leaked into it.

3. Check the throttle and choke shaft bores for wear or an out-of-round condition. Damage or wear to the throttle arm, shaft, or shaft bore will often require replacement of the throttle body. These parts require a close tolerance of fit. Wear may allow air leakage, which could adversely affect starting and idling.
4. Inspect the idle mixture adjusting needles for burrs or grooves. Any such condition requires replacement of the needle, since you will not be able to obtain a satisfactory idle.
5. Check the bowl cover for warped surfaces with a straightedge.
6. After the carburetor is assembled, check the choke valve for freedom of operation.

Carburetor overhaul kits are recommended for each overhaul. These kits contain all gaskets and new parts to replace those that deteriorate most rapidly. Failure to replace all parts supplied with the kit (especially gaskets) can result in poor performance later.

Some carburetor manufacturers supply overhaul kits of three basic types: minor repair, major repair and gasket kits. Basically, they contain the following:

Minor Repair Kits
- All gaskets
- Float needle valve
- All diaphragms
- Spring for the pump diaphragm

Major Repair Kits
- All jets and gaskets
- All diaphragms
- Float needle valve
- Pump ball valve
- Float
- Some cover hold-down screws and washers

Gasket kits contain all gaskets.

After cleaning and checking all components, reassemble the carburetor, using new parts and referring to the exploded view supplied in the kit. When reassembling, make sure that all screws and jets are tight in their seats, but do not overtighten, as the tips will be distorted. Tighten all screws gradually, in rotation. Always use new gaskets. Be sure to adjust the float level when reassembling.

PROGRAMMED FUEL INJECTION (PGM-FI)

System Description

The PGM-FI system precisely controls fuel injection to match engine requirements, reducing emissions and increasing driveability. The electric fuel pump supplies fuel to the pressure regulator. The fuel injectors are electric solenoid valves which open and close according to signals received from the Electronic Control Unit (ECU).

The ECU receives input from various sensors to determine engine operating conditions. This allows the ECU to determine the correct amount of fuel to be injected by it's preset program.

SERVICE PRECAUTIONS

- Do not operate the fuel pump when the fuel lines and tank are empty.
- Do not operate the fuel pump when removed from the fuel tank.
- Do not reuse fuel hose clamps.
- The washer(s) below any fuel system bolt (banjo fittings, service bolt, fuel filter, etc.) must be replaced whenever the bolt is loosened. Do not reuse the washers; a high-pressure fuel leak may result.
- Make sure all ECU harness connectors are fastened securely. A poor connection can cause a high voltage surge and result in damage to integrated circuits.
- Keep all ECU parts and harnesses dry during service. Protect the ECU and all solid-state components from rough handling or extremes of temperature.
- Before attempting to remove any parts, turn the ignition switch **OFF** and disconnect the battery ground cable.
- Always use a 12 volt battery as a power source, never a booster or high-voltage charging unit.
- Do not disconnect the battery cables with the engine running.
- Do not unplug any wiring connector with the engine running or the ignition **ON**, unless specifically instructed to do so.

- Do not depress the accelerator pedal when starting.
- Do not rev up the engine immediately after starting or just prior to shut-down.
- Do not apply battery power directly to injectors.
- Whenever possible, use a flashlight instead of a drop light.
- Keep all open flame and smoking material out of the area.
- Use a shop cloth or similar to catch fuel when opening the fuel system.
- Relieve fuel system pressure before servicing.
- Always use eye or full-face protection when working around fuel lines, fittings or components.
- Always keep a dry chemical (class B-C) fire extinguisher near the area.

Relieving Fuel System Pressure

1. Disconnect the negative battery cable.
2. Remove the fuel filler cap.
3. On 1985–89 Accords, 1985–91 Preludes and the 1995 V-6 Accord, the pressure release point is at the top of the fuel filter. On other models, the pressure release point is on the fuel rail. Look at the banjo bolt on the fuel filter or rail, as applicable. On top of this bolt is a smaller bolt; this is called the service bolt. Use an open end wrench to hold the banjo bolt and fit a 6mm closed (box end) wrench to the service bolt.

➡On some models, the service bolt may be covered by a plastic cap, remove this first.

4. Place a cloth over the service bolt. Slowly loosen the service bolt one full turn. Fuel will escape the system into the cloth, releasing the system pressure. The cloth is now a flammable item; handle it carefully and dispose of it properly.

5. When the fuel system service is completed, install the service bolt using new washers and tighten to 9 ft. lbs. (12 Nm).

Electric Fuel Pump

REMOVAL & INSTALLATION

✳✳ CAUTION

Gasoline vapors are explosive. Remove components slowly and contain spillage. Observe "no smoking/no open flame" precautions. Have a Class B-C (dry powder) fire extinguisher within arm's reach at all times.

1985 Accord and 1985–87 Prelude

▶ See Figure 31

1. Disconnect the negative battery cable.
2. Relieve the fuel system pressure.
3. Loosen the lug nuts of the left rear wheel.
4. Elevate the rear of the car, supporting it safely on stands.
5. Remove the left rear wheel.
6. Remove the fuel pump cover.
7. Remove the 3 bolts securing the fuel pump with its mount.
8. Detach the electrical connectors.
9. Disconnect the clamped fuel hose from the pump.
10. Disconnect the flared fuel line fitting from the hose.
11. Remove the clamp, then remove the fuel pump from its mount.
12. Disconnect the fuel hose and silencer chamber from the pump.

➡The fuel pump is not repairable and should not be disassembled.

To install:

13. Install the fuel hose and silencer chamber onto the front of the pump with new washers. Tighten it to 20 ft. lbs. (28 Nm).
14. Install the fuel pump onto its mount.
15. Clean the sealing surface of the flared fuel line and connect it to the hose. Tighten the flare nut to 27 ft. lbs. (38 Nm).
16. Reconnect the wiring and the remaining fuel hose (use a new clamp if necessary.)
17. Install the pump. Tighten the mounting bolts until snug.

18. Connect the negative battery cable.
19. Have an assistant turn the ignition switch **ON** (without starting the engine); check the fuel line connections for any leakage. Cycle the ignition switch **OFF/ON** 2 or 3 more times to build pressure. The fuel line connections must be totally dry; no leakage is allowable.
20. Install the fuel pump cover and rear wheel.

1986–89 Accord and 1988–95 Prelude

▶ See Figure 32

1. Disconnect the negative battery cable.
2. Lift or reposition the carpet in the luggage area. Remove the access cover in the floor.
3. Unplug the electrical connector at the pump unit.
4. Label and disconnect the fuel lines.
5. Carefully remove the retaining nuts securing the pump. When all are removed, lift the pump up and out of the tank.

➡The pump may require some manipulation to remove.

To install:

6. Reinstall the pump, making certain it is correctly seated and not wedged or jammed. Install the retaining nuts, tightening them evenly and alternately to 48 inch lbs. (6 Nm).
7. Install the fuel lines. Make certain the clamps are secure; use new ones if necessary. If a fuel line is equipped with a banjo bolt fitting, use new washers and tighten the bolt to 20 ft. lbs. (28 Nm).
8. Connect the wiring.
9. Connect the negative battery cable, then start the engine. Check for any leaks.
10. Install the access cover and seal or gasket, if used.
11. Reposition the carpeting in the luggage compartment.

1990–95 Accord

▶ See Figure 32

1. Disconnect the negative battery cable.
2. Relieve the fuel system pressure.

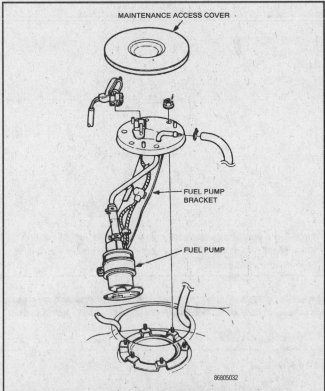

Fig. 32 Internal fuel pump used on Accords and Preludes. On 1990–95 Accords, it is necessary to remove the fuel tank first

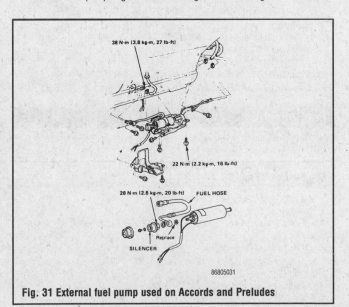

Fig. 31 External fuel pump used on Accords and Preludes

3. Remove the fuel tank (refer to the procedure outlined later in this section).

4. Remove the fuel pump mounting bolts, then remove the fuel pump assembly from the tank.

To install:

5. Reinstall the pump, making certain it is correctly seated and not wedged or jammed. Install the retaining nuts, tightening them evenly and alternately to 48 inch lbs. (6 Nm).

6. Reinstall the fuel tank.

TESTING

▶ **See Figure 33**

1. Relieve the fuel system pressure.
2. Remove the service bolt.
3. Attach a fuel pressure gauge to the banjo bolt.
4. Disconnect the vacuum hose from the pressure regulator, then plug the hose end.
5. Start the engine and let it idle.
6. Record the pressure reading on the gauge and compare it to the following specifications:
   - 1985–86 Prelude and 1985–87 Accord—33–39 psi (235–275 kPa)
   - 1987–90 Prelude and 1988–91 Accord (except 1991 SE and Canada EX-R)—36–41 psi (250–279 kPa)
   - 1991 Accord SE and Canada EX-R—38–48 psi (265–314 kPa)
   - 1991–95 Prelude (except VTEC)—37–44 psi (255–304 kPa)
   - 1992–95 Prelude VTEC—33–40 psi (230–280 kPa)
   - 1992–93 Accord—40–47 psi (274–323 kPa)
   - 1994–95 Accord (except V-6)—38–46 psi (265–314 kPa)
   - 1995 Accord V-6—44–51 psi (304–353 kPa)
7. If the pressure is higher than specified, inspect for a pinched or clogged fuel return hose/line or faulty fuel pressure regulator. If the pressure is lower than specified, inspect for a clogged fuel filter, faulty pressure regulator or leaks in the fuel hose/line.
8. Wrap a shop rag around the fuel pressure gauge fitting, then slowly loosen it to release the system pressure. Remove the pressure gauge.
9. Install the service bolt using new washers and tighten to 9 ft. lbs. (12 Nm).

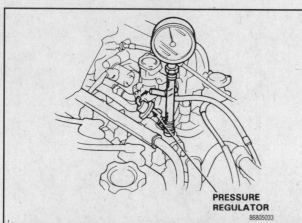

PRESSURE REGULATOR

86805033

Fig. 33 The pressure gauge may be attached to the fuel rail or fuel filter, depending on the model and year. Note the pressure regulator hose is disconnected

Throttle Body

REMOVAL & INSTALLATION

▶ **See Figure 34**

1. Disconnect the negative battery cable.
2. Disconnect the air intake tube from the throttle body.
3. Drain the cooling system, at least to a level below the throttle body.

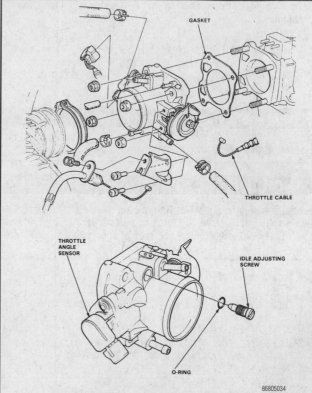

GASKET

THROTTLE CABLE

THROTTLE ANGLE SENSOR

IDLE ADJUSTING SCREW

O-RING

86805034

Fig. 34 The throttle body is attached to the intake manifold inlet. Always use a new gasket anytime the throttle body is removed— 1990–93 Accord shown (others are similar)

4. Disconnect the coolant hoses running to the throttle body.
5. Label and disconnect the vacuum hoses from the throttle body.
6. Unplug the wiring connector(s) from the throttle body.
7. Label and disconnect the throttle control and/or accelerator cable. Do not kink the cable.
8. Remove the nuts securing the throttle body to the intake chamber or plenum. Loosen each nut 1–2 turns at a time to release the pressure evenly.
9. Remove the throttle body assembly. Remove and discard the gasket.

To install:

10. Install a new gasket on the plenum; install the throttle body onto the studs. Note that the gasket is usually not symmetric; there is only one correct position for it.
11. Install the retaining nuts. Tighten them evenly and alternately to 16 ft. lbs. (22 Nm).
12. Install the throttle control and/or accelerator cables.
13. Connect the vacuum hoses and wiring.
14. Connect the coolant hoses.
15. Refill the cooling system.
16. Connect the air intake ducts.

Fuel Injectors

REMOVAL & INSTALLATION

▶ **See Figures 35 and 36**

1. Disconnect the negative battery cable.
2. Relieve the fuel system pressure.
3. Remove the fuel rail assembly (refer to the procedure outlined later in this section).
4. Carefully pull the injectors from the intake manifold.
5. Discard the seal rings, cushion rings and O-rings.

To install:

6. Slide new cushion rings onto the injectors.
7. Coat new O-rings with clean engine oil and put them on the injectors.

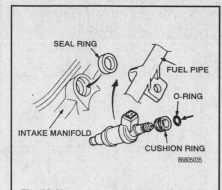

Fig. 35 Always use new cushion rings, seal rings and O-rings

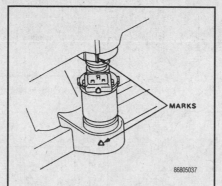

Fig. 36 Be sure to align the center line on the injector with the mark on the fuel rail

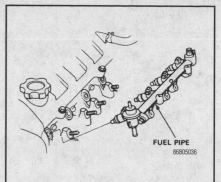

Fig. 37 The fuel rail and injectors are installed as an assembly

8. Insert the injectors into the fuel rail. Be sure to align the center line on the injector with the mark on the fuel rail.

9. Coat new seal rings with clean engine oil and insert them into the intake manifold.

10. Install the fuel rail assembly.

TESTING

The simplest way to test the injectors is to listen to them with the engine running. Use a stethoscope-type tool to touch each injector while the engine is idling. You should hear a distinct clicking as each injector opens and closes.

Additionally, the resistance of the injector can be easily checked. Disconnect the negative battery cable and unplug the electrical connector from the injector to be tested. Use an ohmmeter to check the resistance across the terminals of the injector. Correct resistance is approximately 1.5–2.5 ohms at 68°F (20°C); slight variations are acceptable due to temperature conditions.

Bench testing of the injectors can only be done using expensive special equipment. Generally this equipment can be found at a dealership and sometimes at a well-equipped machine or performance shop. There is no provision for field testing the injectors by the owner/mechanic. DO NOT attempt to test the injector by removing it from the engine and making it spray into a jar.

Never attempt to check a removed injector by hooking it directly to the battery. The injector runs on a lower voltage and the 12 volts from the battery will destroy it internally.

Fuel Rail Assembly

REMOVAL & INSTALLATION

▶ See Figure 37

1. Disconnect the negative battery cable.
2. Relieve the fuel system pressure.
3. Remove any components which may interfere with the fuel rail assembly removal.
4. Unplug the electrical connector of each injector.
5. Disconnect the vacuum hose and fuel return hose from the pressure regulator.

➡ Place a rag or shop towel over hose and tube before disconnecting.

6. Disconnect the fuel line from the rail assembly.
7. Remove the nuts/bolts securing the fuel rail. Take note of any ground cables which may be attached at these points.
8. Remove the fuel rail assembly from the engine.
9. Remove the injectors.

To install:

10. Install the fuel injectors into the fuel rail assembly (refer to the procedure outlined previously in this section).

11. Install the injectors and fuel rail as an assembly into the intake manifold. Tighten the retaining nuts/bolts to 9 ft. lbs. (12 Nm). Be sure to reinstall any ground cables which may have been attached at these points.

12. Connect the fuel line to the rail assembly. Be sure to use new sealing washers.

13. Connect the vacuum hose and fuel return hose to the pressure regulator.

14. Engage the electrical connectors to the injectors.

15. Turn the ignition switch **ON** but do not operate starter. After fuel pump runs for approximately two seconds, fuel pressure in fuel line will rise. Repeat this two or three times, then check for any fuel leakage.

Fuel Pressure Regulator

REMOVAL & INSTALLATION

Except Accord V-6

▶ See Figure 38

1. Disconnect the negative battery cable.
2. Place a cloth or rag under the regulator to contain any escaping fuel.
3. Relieve the fuel system pressure.
4. Disconnect the vacuum hose from the regulator.
5. Disconnect the fuel line from the regulator; plug the line to prevent spillage or the entry of dirt.
6. Remove the 2 retaining bolts and remove the regulator.
7. Remove the O-ring from the regulator and discard it.

To install:

8. Install a new O-ring on the regulator; coat the ring lightly with a thin coat of clean, fresh engine oil.

9. Install the regulator, making sure the O-ring is not distorted or damaged. Tighten the retaining bolts to 9 ft. lbs. (12 Nm).

10. Connect the fuel and vacuum lines.

11. Start the engine and check for leaks.

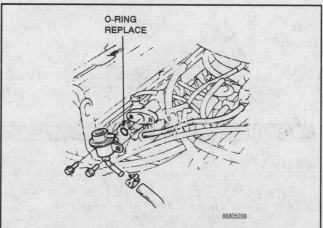

Fig. 38 Always use a new O-ring when replacing the pressure regulator

Accord V-6

♦ See Figure 39

1. Disconnect the negative battery cable.
2. Remove the intake manifold cover.
3. Relieve the fuel system pressure.
4. Place a cloth or rag under the regulator to contain any escaping fuel.
5. Disconnect the vacuum hose from the regulator.
6. Disconnect the fuel line from the regulator; plug the line to prevent spillage or the entry of dirt.
7. Loosen the locking nut, then unthread the regulator from the fuel rail.
8. Discard the O-ring.

To install:

9. Install the regulator in the fuel rail with a new O-ring. Turn it by hand until it stops.
10. Turn the regulator counterclockwise until it is correctly positioned. Refer to the illustration.
11. Tighten the locking nut to 22 ft. lbs. (29 Nm).
12. Connect the fuel return line and the vacuum hose.
13. Start then engine and check for leaks. Install the intake manifold cover.

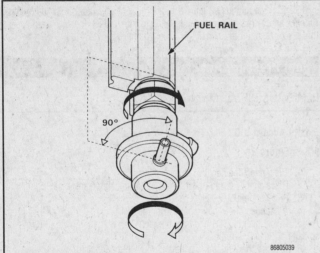

Fig. 39 Turn the regulator counterclockwise until it is correctly positioned

Throttle Position/Angle Sensor

REMOVAL & INSTALLATION

♦ See Figure 34

The throttle position sensor is mounted on the side of the throttle body and is connected to the throttle shaft.

1. Disconnect the negative battery cable.
2. If necessary, remove the throttle body for access.
3. The sensor may be removed by unscrewing the retaining bolts.
4. Reinstall in the reverse order of removal. Make certain the sensor is correctly mated with the throttle body shaft.

Injector Resistor

REMOVAL & INSTALLATION

The injector resistor is located in the engine compartment on the left fender apron (near the strut tower) or on the left side of the firewall.

1. Disconnect the negative battery cable.
2. Unplug the wiring connector of the resistor.
3. Remove or disconnect any wiring harness clamps or retainers secured on the resistor harness.

4. Remove the retaining nuts/bolts securing the resistor, then remove it from the vehicle.
5. Reinstall in the reverse order of removal.

TESTING

♦ See Figures 40, 41, 42, 43 and 44

1. With the ignition **OFF**, unplug the harness connector from the injector resistor.

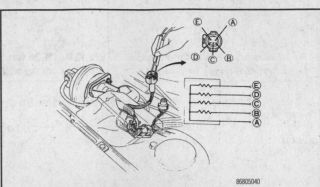

Fig. 40 1985 Accord terminal identification. Terminal A is the power terminal

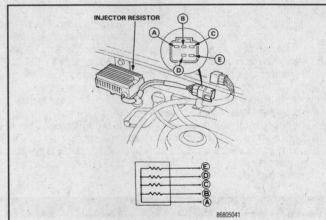

Fig. 41 1985–95 Prelude terminal identification. Terminal A is the power terminal

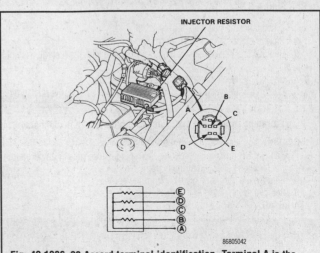

Fig. 42 1986–93 Accord terminal identification. Terminal A is the power terminal

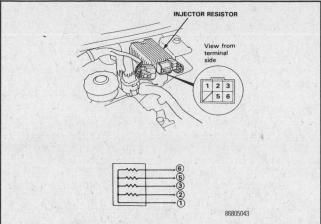

Fig. 43 1994–95 Accord terminal identification. Terminal 1 is the power terminal

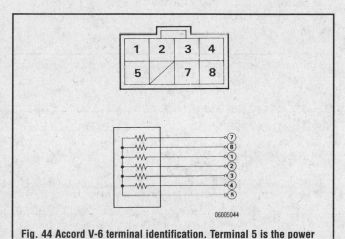

Fig. 44 Accord V-6 terminal identification. Terminal 5 is the power terminal

2. Measure the resistance between each of the resistor terminals and the power terminal of the connector. Refer to the illustrations to determine which is the power terminal.

3. Correct resistance between the power terminal and each other resistor terminal is 5–7 ohms. If any circuit is out of range, the resistor must be replaced.

Manifold Absolute Pressure (MAP) Sensor

REMOVAL & INSTALLATION

On 1985–93 Accords and 1985–91 Preludes, the MAP sensor is located within the emission control box on the firewall. On 1994–95 Accords, the sen-

sor is mounted on the throttle body. On 1992–95 Preludes, the sensor is mounted on the firewall (near the throttle position sensor).

1. Disconnect the negative battery cable.
2. If applicable, access the sensor by removing the control box lid.
3. Unplug the wire harness connector to the sensor, then disconnect the vacuum hose. Remove the sensor from its mount.
4. When reinstalling, handle the unit carefully. Install it securely in the mounting, then attach the vacuum hose and wiring connector. If applicable, install the control box lid.

Intake Air Temperature Sensor

REMOVAL & INSTALLATION

The sensor is located on the intake manifold or air plenum.
1. Disconnect the negative battery cable.
2. Unplug the wiring connector and loosen the mounting screws, then remove the sensor.
3. Install in the reverse order of removal.

Coolant Temperature Sensor

REMOVAL & INSTALLATION

The coolant temperature sensor can be found threaded either into the cylinder head or the coolant crossover passage.
1. Disconnect the negative battery cable.
2. Drain the cooling system to a level at least below the sensor.
3. Using the appropriate sized wrench or socket, remove the sensor.
4. To install, first lightly coat the threads of the sensor with a non-hardening sealer, then tighten the sensor until snug.
5. Refill the cooling system.

Electronic Air Control Valve (EACV)

REMOVAL & INSTALLATION

This valve is located at the side of the intake chamber or plenum, downstream of the throttle body.
1. Disconnect the negative battery cable.
2. Unplug the wiring connector at the valve.
3. Label and disconnect the vacuum hoses from the unit.
4. Remove the mounting bolts and remove the valve. Remove and discard the O-rings from the ports.
To install:
5. Install new O-rings and make certain they are properly seated.
6. Install the valve and the retaining bolts. The pintle or control valve for the EACV must seat correctly in its port. Tighten the EACV bolts to 16 ft. lbs. (22 Nm)
7. Connect the vacuum hoses to the valve; make certain each hose is connected to the proper port. Engage the electrical connector.

FUEL TANK

Tank Assembly

Although draining the tank is part of each procedure, it is unlikely that you can safely store large amounts of fuel during the repair. For this reason, the tank should be as empty as possible before removal is begun. The remaining few gallons must be drained and stored in approved fuel containers. The containers must be tightly capped.

✳ CAUTION

Fuel and its vapors are extremely explosive. Take great care to eliminate all sources of heat, flame and sparks from the work area

before beginning. This must include shutting off heaters or furnaces and shutting off electric motors in machinery, fans, etc. Keep a dry powder (Class B-C) fire extinguisher within arm's reach at all times.

REMOVAL & INSTALLATION

1984–89 Accord and 1984–85 Prelude

◊ See Figures 45 and 46

1. Disconnect the negative battery cable.
2. Relieve the fuel system pressure.

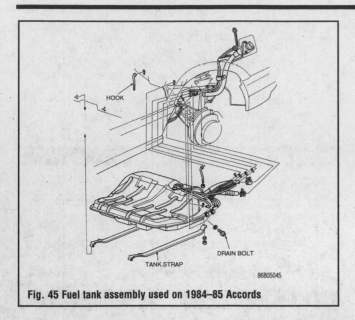

Fig. 45 Fuel tank assembly used on 1984–85 Accords

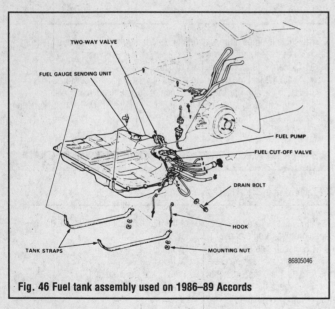

Fig. 46 Fuel tank assembly used on 1986–89 Accords

3. Block the front wheels. Elevate the rear of the car and support it safely on stands.

4. Remove the drain bolt from the tank and drain the remaining fuel into an approved fuel container.

5. Unplug the sending unit connectors.

6. Label and disconnect the hoses from the pipes mounted to the body (over the suspension control arm). Slide the hose clamps back on the hose, then twist the hose while pulling it off the fitting.

7. Use a floor jack and a broad piece of wood under the tank. Adjust the position as necessary to allow the tank to be evenly supported.

8. Remove the nuts securing the tank straps; let the straps fall free.

9. Lower the jack and remove the tank from under the vehicle.

To install:

10. Place the tank on the jack and position it under the car. Lift the tank into position.

11. Install the tank straps and tighten the retaining nuts to 16 ft. lbs. (22 Nm). Make certain the opposite ends of the straps are still firmly mounted in their slots

12. Connect the hoses and engage the wiring connectors.

13. Install the drain bolt in the tank; tighten it to 36 ft. lbs. (50 Nm).

14. Lower the vehicle to the ground.

15. Refill the tank with fuel.

16. When starting, the engine may crank longer than usual due to lack of fuel in the lines.

1986–95 Prelude

♦ **See Figures 47, 48 and 49**

1. Disconnect the negative battery cable.

2. Relieve the fuel system pressure.

3. Block the front wheels. Elevate the rear of the car and support it safely on stands.

4. Remove the drain bolt from the tank and drain the remaining fuel into an approved fuel container.

5. On 1986–87 vehicles, unplug the sending unit connectors.

6. On 1988–95 vehicles, lift the carpet in the luggage area. Remove both access panels. Unplug the wiring to the fuel pump and fuel sender. Disconnect the fuel lines.

7. On 1986–87 Preludes, remove the muffler.

8. Label and disconnect the hoses. Slide the hose clamps back on the hose, then twist the hose while pulling it off the fitting.

9. Use a floor jack and a broad piece of wood under the tank. Adjust the position as necessary to allow the tank to be evenly supported.

10. Remove the nuts securing the tank straps and free them.

11. Lower the jack and remove the tank.

To install:

12. Place the tank on the jack and position it under the car. Lift the tank into position.

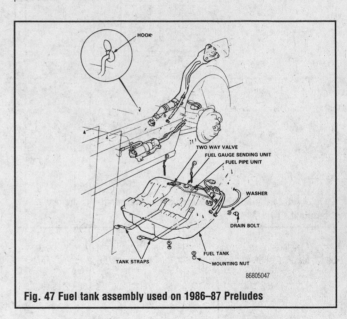

Fig. 47 Fuel tank assembly used on 1986–87 Preludes

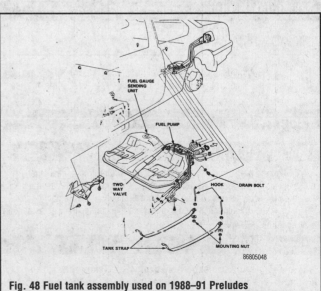

Fig. 48 Fuel tank assembly used on 1988–91 Preludes

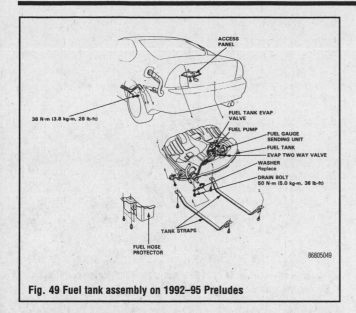

Fig. 49 Fuel tank assembly on 1992–95 Preludes

13. Install the tank straps and tighten the retaining nuts to 16 ft. lbs. (22 Nm). Make certain the opposite ends of the straps are still firmly mounted in their slots.

14. Connect the hoses and engage the wiring connectors. Reinstall the access covers if they were removed. Reposition the carpeting in the cargo area as needed.

15. If removed, install the muffler (use new nuts and gaskets).

16. Install the drain bolt in the tank; tighten it to 36 ft. lbs. (50 Nm).

17. Lower the vehicle to the ground. Refill the tank with fuel.

18. When starting, the engine may crank longer than usual due to lack of fuel in the lines.

1990–95 Accord

♦ See Figures 50 and 51

1. Block the front wheels. Elevate the rear of the car and support it safely on stands.

2. Remove the drain bolt from the tank and drain the remaining fuel into an approved fuel container.

3. Remove the cover from the fuel hoses on the side of the tank.

4. Label and disconnect the hoses. Slide the clamps back, then twist and pull the hoses off the fittings.

5. Use a floor jack and a broad piece of wood under the tank. Adjust the position as necessary to allow the tank to be evenly supported.

6. Remove the nuts holding the tank straps; let the straps fall free.

7. Lower the jack and remove the tank from under the vehicle. The tank may be stuck by the undercoating on the body; use a piece of wood to gently pry it loose.

To install:

8. Place the tank on the jack and position it under the car. Lift the tank into position.

9. Install the tank straps and tighten the retaining nuts to 27 ft. lbs. (38 Nm).

10. Connect the hoses and wiring connectors. Tighten the threaded fuel line fitting to 26 ft. lbs. (37 Nm).

11. Install the cover for the fuel lines.

12. Install the drain bolt in the tank with a new washer; tighten it to 36 ft. lbs. (50 Nm).

13. Lower the vehicle to the ground.

14. Reuse the fuel drained from the tank unless it is heavily polluted with rust, water, etc. Use a funnel at the fuel filler and pour the fuel slowly.

15. When starting, the engine may crank longer than usual due to lack of fuel in the lines.

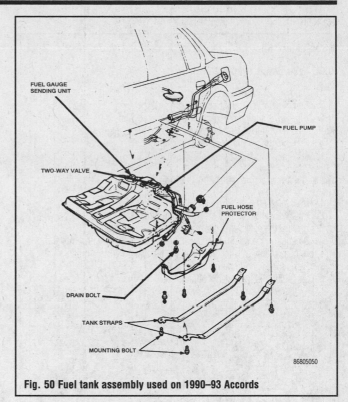

Fig. 50 Fuel tank assembly used on 1990–93 Accords

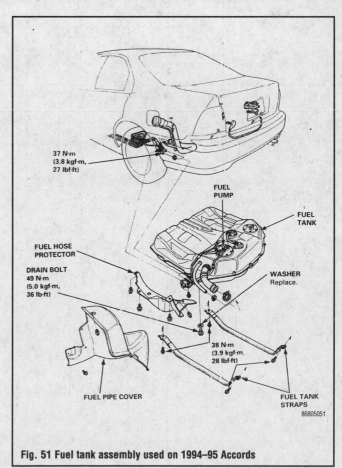

Fig. 51 Fuel tank assembly used on 1994–95 Accords

SENDING UNIT REPLACEMENT

▶ **See Figure 52**

1985 Accord and 1985–87 Prelude

1. Disconnect the negative battery cable.
2. Remove the fuel tank from the vehicle.
3. Disengage the retaining collar using a fuel sending unit removal tool.
This tool is available at Honda dealers and many auto parts stores.
4. Remove the sending unit from the vehicle.
5. Installation is the reverse of removal.

1986–95 Accord and 1988–95 Prelude

1. Disconnect the negative battery cable.
2. Remove the access panels in the luggage area.
3. Unplug the electrical connector from the sending unit.
4. Disengage the retaining collar using a fuel sending unit removal tool.
This tool is available at Honda dealers and many auto parts stores.
5. Remove the sending unit from the vehicle.
6. Installation is the reverse of removal.

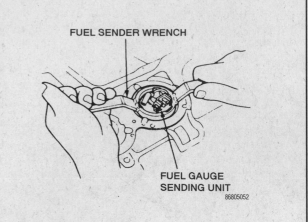

Fig. 52 A special tool is used to disengage the retaining collar of the sending unit

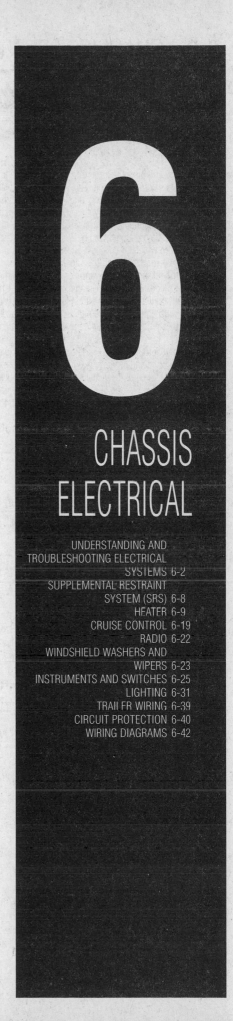

6

CHASSIS ELECTRICAL

UNDERSTANDING AND TROUBLESHOOTING ELECTRICAL SYSTEMS

Basic Electrical Theory

▶ See Figure 1

For any 12 volt, negative ground, electrical system to operate, the electricity must travel in a complete circuit. This simply means that current (power) from the positive (+) terminal of the battery must eventually return to the negative (-) terminal of the battery. Along the way, this current will travel through wires, fuses, switches and components. If, for any reason, the flow of current through the circuit is interrupted, the component fed by that circuit will cease to function properly.

Perhaps the easiest way to visualize a circuit is to think of connecting a light bulb (with two wires attached to it) to the battery—one wire attached to the negative (-) terminal of the battery and the other wire to the positive (+) terminal. With the two wires touching the battery terminals, the circuit would be complete and the light bulb would illuminate. Electricity would follow a path from the battery to the bulb and back to the battery. It's easy to see that with longer wires on our light bulb, it could be mounted anywhere. Further, one wire could be fitted with a switch so that the light could be turned on and off.

The normal automotive circuit differs from this simple example in two ways. First, instead of having a return wire from the bulb to the battery, the current travels through the frame of the vehicle. Since the negative (-) battery cable is attached to the frame (made of electrically conductive metal), the frame of the vehicle can serve as a ground wire to complete the circuit. Secondly, most automotive circuits contain multiple components which receive power from a single circuit. This lessens the amount of wire needed to power components on the vehicle.

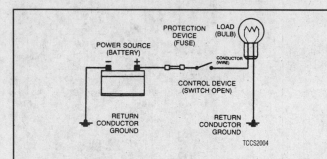

Fig. 1 This example illustrates a simple circuit. When the switch is closed, power from the positive (+) battery terminal flows through the fuse and the switch, and then to the light bulb. The light illuminates and the circuit is completed through the ground wire back to the negative (-) battery terminal. In reality, the two ground points shown in the illustration are attached to the metal frame of the vehicle, which completes the circuit back to the battery

HOW DOES ELECTRICITY WORK: THE WATER ANALOGY

Electricity is the flow of electrons—the subatomic particles that constitute the outer shell of an atom. Electrons spin in an orbit around the center core of an atom. The center core is comprised of protons (positive charge) and neutrons (neutral charge). Electrons have a negative charge and balance out the positive charge of the protons. When an outside force causes the number of electrons to unbalance the charge of the protons, the electrons will split off the atom and look for another atom to balance out. If this imbalance is kept up, electrons will continue to move and an electrical flow will exist.

Many people have been taught electrical theory using an analogy with water. In a comparison with water flowing through a pipe, the electrons would be the water and the wire is the pipe.

The flow of electricity can be measured much like the flow of water through a pipe. The unit of measurement used is amperes, frequently abbreviated as amps (a). You can compare amperage to the volume of water flowing through a pipe. When connected to a circuit, an ammeter will measure the actual amount of current flowing through the circuit. When relatively few electrons flow through a circuit, the amperage is low. When many electrons flow, the amperage is high.

Water pressure is measured in units such as pounds per square inch (psi);

The electrical pressure is measured in units called volts (v). When a voltmeter is connected to a circuit, it is measuring the electrical pressure.

The actual flow of electricity depends not only on voltage and amperage, but also on the resistance of the circuit. The higher the resistance, the higher the force necessary to push the current through the circuit. The standard unit for measuring resistance is an ohm. Resistance in a circuit varies depending on the amount and type of components used in the circuit. The main factors which determine resistance are:

• Material—some materials have more resistance than others. Those with high resistance are said to be insulators. Rubber materials (or rubber-like plastics) are some of the most common insulators used in vehicles as they have a very high resistance to electricity. Very low resistance materials are said to be conductors. Copper wire is among the best conductors. Silver is actually a superior conductor to copper and is used in some relay contacts, but its high cost prohibits its use as common wiring. Most automotive wiring is made of copper.

• Size—the larger the wire size being used, the less resistance the wire will have. This is why components which use large amounts of electricity usually have large wires supplying current to them.

• Length—for a given thickness of wire, the longer the wire, the greater the resistance. The shorter the wire, the less the resistance. When determining the proper wire for a circuit, both size and length must be considered to design a circuit that can handle the current needs of the component.

• Temperature—with many materials, the higher the temperature, the greater the resistance (positive temperature coefficient). Some materials exhibit the opposite trait of lower resistance with higher temperatures (negative temperature coefficient). These principles are used in many of the sensors on the engine.

OHM'S LAW

There is a direct relationship between current, voltage and resistance. The relationship between current, voltage and resistance can be summed up by a statement known as Ohm's law.

Voltage (E) is equal to amperage (I) times resistance (R): $E = I \times R$
Other forms of the formula are $R = E/I$ and $I = E/R$

In each of these formulas, E is the voltage in volts, I is the current in amps and R is the resistance in ohms. The basic point to remember is that as the resistance of a circuit goes up, the amount of current that flows in the circuit will go down, if voltage remains the same.

The amount of work that the electricity can perform is expressed as power. The unit of power is the watt (w). The relationship between power, voltage and current is expressed as:

Power (w) is equal to amperage (I) times voltage (E): $W = I \times E$

This is only true for direct current (DC) circuits; The alternating current formula is a tad different, but since the electrical circuits in most vehicles are DC type, we need not get into AC circuit theory.

Electrical Components

POWER SOURCE

Power is supplied to the vehicle by two devices: The battery and the alternator. The battery supplies electrical power during starting or during periods when the current demand of the vehicle's electrical system exceeds the output capacity of the alternator. The alternator supplies electrical current when the engine is running. Just not does the alternator supply the current needs of the vehicle, but it recharges the battery.

The Battery

In most modern vehicles, the battery is a lead/acid electrochemical device consisting of six 2 volt subsections (cells) connected in series, so that the unit is capable of producing approximately 12 volts of electrical pressure. Each subsection consists of a series of positive and negative plates held a short distance apart in a solution of sulfuric acid and water.

The two types of plates are of dissimilar metals. This sets up a chemical reaction, and it is this reaction which produces current flow from the battery when its positive and negative terminals are connected to an electrical load.

The power removed from the battery is replaced by the alternator, restoring the battery to its original chemical state.

The Alternator

On some vehicles there isn't an alternator, but a generator. The difference is that an alternator supplies alternating current which is then changed to direct current for use on the vehicle, while a generator produces direct current. Alternators tend to be more efficient and that is why they are used.

Alternators and generators are devices that consist of coils of wires wound together making big electromagnets. One group of coils spins within another set and the interaction of the magnetic fields causes a current to flow. This current is then drawn off the coils and fed into the vehicles electrical system.

GROUND

Two types of grounds are used in automotive electric circuits. Direct ground components are grounded to the frame through their mounting points. All other components use some sort of ground wire which is attached to the frame or chassis of the vehicle. The electrical current runs through the chassis of the vehicle and returns to the battery through the ground (-) cable; if you look, you'll see that the battery ground cable connects between the battery and the frame or chassis of the vehicle.

➡It should be noted that a good percentage of electrical problems can be traced to bad grounds.

PROTECTIVE DEVICES

▶ **See Figure 2**

It is possible for large surges of current to pass through the electrical system of your vehicle. If this surge of current were to reach the load in the circuit, the

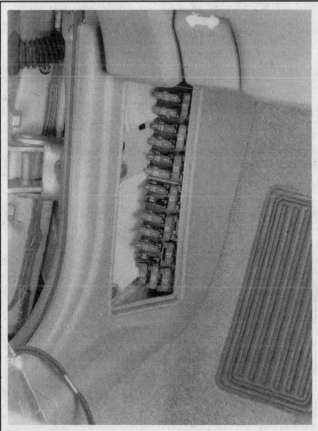

Fig. 2 Most vehicles use one or more fuse panels. This one is located on the driver's side kick panel

surge could burn it out or severely damage it. It can also overload the wiring, causing the harness to get hot and melt the insulation. To prevent this, fuses, circuit breakers and/or fusible links are connected into the supply wires of the electrical system. These items are nothing more than a built-in weak spot in the system. When an abnormal amount of current flows through the system, these protective devices work as follows to protect the circuit:

• Fuse—when an excessive electrical current passes through a fuse, the fuse "blows" (the conductor melts) and opens the circuit, preventing the passage of current.

• Circuit Breaker—a circuit breaker is basically a self-repairing fuse. It will open the circuit in the same fashion as a fuse, but when the surge subsides, the circuit breaker can be reset and does not need replacement.

• Fusible Link—a fusible link (fuse link or main link) is a short length of special, high temperature insulated wire that acts as a fuse. When an excessive electrical current passes through a fusible link, the thin gauge wire inside the link melts, creating an intentional open to protect the circuit. To repair the circuit, the link must be replaced. Some newer type fusible links are housed in plug-in modules, which are simply replaced like a fuse, while older type fusible links must be cut and spliced if they melt. Since this link is very early in the electrical path, it's the first place to look if nothing on the vehicle works, yet the battery seems to be charged and is properly connected.

✳ CAUTION

Always replace fuses, circuit breakers and fusible links with identically rated components. Under no circumstances should a component of higher or lower amperage rating be substituted.

SWITCHES & RELAYS

▶ **See Figures 3 and 4**

Switches are used in electrical circuits to control the passage of current. The most common use is to open and close circuits between the battery and the various electric devices in the system. Switches are rated according to the amount of amperage they can handle. If a sufficient amperage rated switch is not used in a circuit, the switch could overload and cause damage.

Some electrical components which require a large amount of current to operate use a special switch called a relay. Since these circuits carry a large amount of current, the thickness of the wire in the circuit is also greater. If this large wire were connected from the load to the control switch, the switch would have to carry the high amperage load and the fairing or dash would be twice as large to accommodate the increased size of the wiring harness. To prevent these problems, a relay is used.

Relays are composed of a coil and a set of contacts. When the coil has a current passed though it, a magnetic field is formed and this field causes the contacts to move together, completing the circuit. Most relays are normally open, prevent-

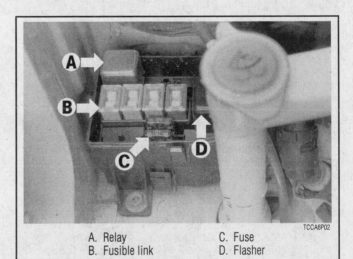

A. Relay   C. Fuse
B. Fusible link   D. Flasher

Fig. 3 The underhood fuse and relay panel usually contains fuses, relays, flashers and fusible links

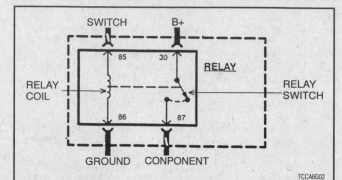

Fig. 4 Relays are composed of a coil and a switch. These two components are linked together so that when one operates, the other operates at the same time. The large wires in the circuit are connected from the battery to one side of the relay switch (B+) and from the opposite side of the relay switch to the load (component). Smaller wires are connected from the relay coil to the control switch for the circuit and from the opposite side of the relay coil to ground

ing current from passing through the circuit, but they can take any electrical form depending on the job they are intended to do. Relays can be considered "remote control switches." They allow a smaller current to operate devices that require higher amperages. When a small current operates the coil, a larger current is allowed to pass by the contacts. Some common circuits which may use relays are the horn, headlights, starter, electric fuel pump and other high draw circuits.

LOAD

Every electrical circuit must include a "load" (something to use the electricity coming from the source). Without this load, the battery would attempt to deliver its entire power supply from one pole to another. This is called a "short circuit." All this electricity would take a short cut to ground and cause a great amount of damage to other components in the circuit by developing a tremendous amount of heat. This condition could develop sufficient heat to melt the insulation on all the surrounding wires and reduce a multiple wire cable to a lump of plastic and copper.

WIRING & HARNESSES

The average vehicle contains meters and meters of wiring, with hundreds of individual connections. To protect the many wires from damage and to keep them from becoming a confusing tangle, they are organized into bundles, enclosed in plastic or taped together and called wiring harnesses. Different harnesses serve different parts of the vehicle. Individual wires are color coded to help trace them through a harness where sections are hidden from view.

Automotive wiring or circuit conductors can be either single strand wire, multi-strand wire or printed circuitry. Single strand wire has a solid metal core and is usually used inside such components as alternators, motors, relays and other devices. Multi-strand wire has a core made of many small strands of wire twisted together into a single conductor. Most of the wiring in an automotive electrical system is made up of multi-strand wire, either as a single conductor or grouped together in a harness. All wiring is color coded on the insulator, either as a solid color or as a colored wire with an identification stripe. A printed circuit is a thin film of copper or other conductor that is printed on an insulator backing. Occasionally, a printed circuit is sandwiched between two sheets of plastic for more protection and flexibility. A complete printed circuit, consisting of conductors, insulating material and connectors for lamps or other components is called a printed circuit board. Printed circuitry is used in place of individual wires or harnesses in places where space is limited, such as behind instrument panels.

Since automotive electrical systems are very sensitive to changes in resistance, the selection of properly sized wires is critical when systems are repaired. A loose or corroded connection or a replacement wire that is too small for the circuit will add extra resistance and an additional voltage drop to the circuit.

The wire gauge number is an expression of the cross-section area of the conductor. Vehicles from countries that use the metric system will typically describe the wire size as its cross-sectional area in square millimeters. In this method, the larger the wire, the greater the number. Another common system for

expressing wire size is the American Wire Gauge (AWG) system. As gauge number increases, area decreases and the wire becomes smaller. An 18 gauge wire is smaller than a 4 gauge wire. A wire with a higher gauge number will carry less current than a wire with a lower gauge number. Gauge wire size refers to the size of the strands of the conductor, not the size of the complete wire with insulator. It is possible, therefore, to have two wires of the same gauge with different diameters because one may have thicker insulation than the other.

It is essential to understand how a circuit works before trying to figure out why it doesn't. An electrical schematic shows the electrical current paths when a circuit is operating properly. Schematics break the entire electrical system down into individual circuits. In a schematic, usually no attempt is made to represent wiring and components as they physically appear on the vehicle; switches and other components are shown as simply as possible. Face views of harness connectors show the cavity or terminal locations in all multi-pin connectors to help locate test points.

CONNECTORS

▶ **See Figures 5 and 6**

Three types of connectors are commonly used in automotive applications—weatherproof, molded and hard shell.

• Weatherproof—these connectors are most commonly used where the connector is exposed to the elements. Terminals are protected against moisture and dirt by sealing rings which provide a weathertight seal. All repairs require the use of a special terminal and the tool required to service it. Unlike standard blade type terminals, these weatherproof terminals cannot be straightened once they are bent. Make certain that the connectors are properly seated and all of the sealing rings are in place when connecting leads.

Fig. 5 Hard shell (left) and weatherproof (right) connectors have replaceable terminals

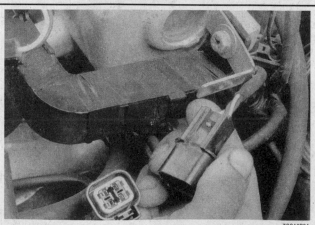

Fig. 6 Weatherproof connectors are most commonly used in the engine compartment or where the connector is exposed to the elements

• Molded—these connectors require complete replacement of the connector if found to be defective. This means splicing a new connector assembly into the harness. All splices should be soldered to insure proper contact. Use care when probing the connections or replacing terminals in them, as it is possible to create a short circuit between opposite terminals. If this happens to the wrong terminal pair, it is possible to damage certain components. Always use jumper wires between connectors for circuit checking and NEVER probe through weatherproof seals.

• Hard Shell—unlike molded connectors, the terminal contacts in hard-shell connectors can be replaced. Replacement usually involves the use of a special terminal removal tool that depresses the locking tangs (barbs) on the connector terminal and allows the connector to be removed from the rear of the shell. The connector shell should be replaced if it shows any evidence of burning, melting, cracks, or breaks. Replace individual terminals that are burnt, corroded, distorted or loose.

Test Equipment

Pinpointing the exact cause of trouble In an electrical circuit is most times accomplished by the use of special test equipment. The following describes different types of commonly used test equipment and briefly explains how to use them in diagnosis. In addition to the information covered below, the tool manufacturer's instructions booklet (provided with the tester) should be read and clearly understood before attempting any test procedures.

JUMPER WIRES

❋ CAUTION

Never use jumper wires made from a thinner gauge wire than the circuit being tested. If the jumper wire Is of too small a gauge, it may overheat and possibly melt. Never use jumpers to bypass high resistance loads in a circuit. Bypassing resistances, in effect, creates a short circuit. This may, in turn, cause damage and fire. Jumper wires should only be used to bypass lengths of wire or to simulate switches.

Jumper wires are simple, yet extremely valuable, pieces of test equipment. They are basically test wires which are used to bypass sections of a circuit. Although jumper wires can be purchased, they are usually fabricated from lengths of standard automotive wire and whatever type of connector (alligator clip, spade connector or pin connector) that is required for the particular application being tested. In cramped, hard-to-reach areas, it is advisable to have insulated boots over the jumper wire terminals in order to prevent accidental grounding. It is also advisable to include a standard automotive fuse in any jumper wire. This is commonly referred to as a "fused jumper". By inserting an in-line fuse holder between a set of test leads, a fused jumper wire can be used for bypassing open circuits. Use a 5 amp fuse to provide protection against voltage spikes.

Jumper wires are used primarily to locate open electrical circuits, on either the ground (-) side of the circuit or on the power (+) side. If an electrical component fails to operate, connect the jumper wire between the component and a good ground. If the component operates only with the jumper installed, the ground circuit is open. If the ground circuit is good, but the component does not operate, the circuit between the power feed and component may be open. By moving the jumper wire successively back from the component toward the power source, you can isolate the area of the circuit where the open is located. When the component stops functioning, or the power is cut off, the open is in the segment of wire between the jumper and the point previously tested.

You can sometimes connect the jumper wire directly from the battery to the "hot" terminal of the component, but first make sure the component uses 12 volts in operation. Some electrical components, such as fuel injectors or sensors, are designed to operate on about 4 to 5 volts, and running 12 volts directly to these components will cause damage.

TEST LIGHTS

♦ See Figure 7

The test light is used to check circuits and components while electrical current is flowing through them. It is used for voltage and ground tests. To use a

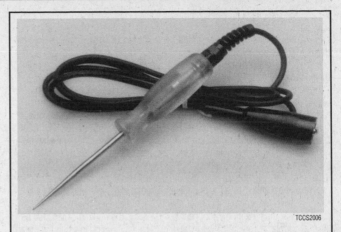

TCCS2006

Fig. 7 A 12 volt test light is used to detect the presence of voltage in a circuit

12 volt test light, connect the ground clip to a good ground and probe wherever necessary with the pick. The test light will illuminate when voltage is detected. This does not necessarily mean that 12 volts (or any particular amount of voltage) is present; it only means that some voltage is present. It is advisable before using the test light to touch its ground clip and probe across the battery posts or terminals to make sure the light is operating properly.

❋ WARNING

Do not use a test light to probe electronic ignition, spark plug or coil wires. Never use a pick-type test light to probe wiring on computer controlled systems unless specifically instructed to do so. Any wire insulation that is pierced by the test light probe should be taped and sealed with silicone after testing.

Like the jumper wire, the 12 volt test light is used to isolate opens in circuits. But, whereas the jumper wire is used to bypass the open to operate the load, the 12 volt test light is used to locate the presence of voltage in a circuit. If the test light illuminates, there is power up to that point in the circuit; if the test light does not illuminate, there is an open circuit (no power). Move the test light in successive steps back toward the power source until the light in the handle illuminates. The open is between the probe and a point which was previously probed.

The self-powered test light is similar in design to the 12 volt test light, but contains a 1.5 volt penlight battery in the handle. It is most often used in place of a multimeter to check for open or short circuits when power is isolated from the circuit (continuity test).

The battery in a self-powered test light does not provide much current. A weak battery may not provide enough power to illuminate the test light even when a complete circuit is made (especially if there is high resistance in the circuit). Always make sure that the test battery is strong. To check the battery, briefly touch the ground clip to the probe; if the light glows brightly, the battery is strong enough for testing.

➡**A self-powered test light should not be used on any computer controlled system or component. The small amount of electricity transmitted by the test light is enough to damage many electronic automotive components.**

MULTIMETERS

Multimeters are an extremely useful tool for troubleshooting electrical problems. They can be purchased in either analog or digital form and have a price range to suit any budget. A multimeter is a voltmeter, ammeter and ohmmeter (along with other features) combined into one instrument. It is often used when testing solid state circuits because of its high input impedance (usually 10 megaohms or more). A brief description of the multimeter main test functions follows:

• Voltmeter—the voltmeter is used to measure voltage at any point in a circuit, or to measure the voltage drop across any part of a circuit. Voltmeters usually have various scales and a selector switch to allow the reading of different voltage ranges. The voltmeter has a positive and a negative lead. To avoid damage to the meter, always connect the negative lead to the negative (-) side of the circuit (to ground or nearest the ground side of the circuit) and connect the positive lead to the positive (+) side of the circuit (to the power source or the nearest power source). Note that the negative voltmeter lead will always be black and that the positive voltmeter will always be some color other than black (usually red).

• Ohmmeter—the ohmmeter is designed to read resistance (measured in ohms) in a circuit or component. Most ohmmeters will have a selector switch which permits the measurement of different ranges of resistance (usually the selector switch allows the multiplication of the meter reading by 10, 100, 1,000 and 10,000). Some ohmmeters are "auto-ranging" which means the meter itself will determine which scale to use. Since the meters are powered by an internal battery, the ohmmeter can be used like a self-powered test light. When the ohmmeter is connected, current from the ohmmeter flows through the circuit or component being tested. Since the ohmmeter's internal resistance and voltage are known values, the amount of current flow through the meter depends on the resistance of the circuit or component being tested. The ohmmeter can also be used to perform a continuity test for suspected open circuits. In using the meter for making continuity checks, do not be concerned with the actual resistance readings. Zero resistance, or any ohm reading, indicates continuity in the circuit. Infinite resistance indicates an opening in the circuit. A high resistance reading where there should be none indicates a problem in the circuit. Checks for short circuits are made in the same manner as checks for open circuits, except that the circuit must be isolated from both power and normal ground. Infinite resistance indicates no continuity, while zero resistance indicates a dead short.

✷✷ WARNING

Never use an ohmmeter to check the resistance of a component or wire while there is voltage applied to the circuit.

• Ammeter—an ammeter measures the amount of current flowing through a circuit in units called amperes or amps. At normal operating voltage, most circuits have a characteristic amount of amperes, called "current draw" which can be measured using an ammeter. By referring to a specified current draw rating, then measuring the amperes and comparing the two values, one can determine what is happening within the circuit to aid in diagnosis. An open circuit, for example, will not allow any current to flow, so the ammeter reading will be zero. A damaged component or circuit will have an increased current draw, so the reading will be high. The ammeter is always connected in series with the circuit being tested. All of the current that normally flows through the circuit must also flow through the ammeter; if there is any other path for the current to follow, the ammeter reading will not be accurate. The ammeter itself has very little resistance to current flow and, therefore, will not affect the circuit, but it will measure current draw only when the circuit is closed and electricity is flowing. Excessive current draw can blow fuses and drain the battery, while a reduced current draw can cause motors to run slowly, lights to dim and other components to not operate properly.

Troubleshooting Electrical Systems

When diagnosing a specific problem, organized troubleshooting is a must. The complexity of a modern automotive vehicle demands that you approach any problem in a logical, organized manner. There are certain troubleshooting techniques, however, which are standard:

• Establish when the problem occurs. Does the problem appear only under certain conditions? Were there any noises, odors or other unusual symptoms? Isolate the problem area. To do this, make some simple tests and observations, then eliminate the systems that are working properly. Check for obvious problems, such as broken wires and loose or dirty connections. Always check the obvious before assuming something complicated is the cause.

• Test for problems systematically to determine the cause once the problem area is isolated. Are all the components functioning properly? Is there power going to electrical switches and motors. Performing careful, systematic checks will often turn up most causes on the first inspection, without wasting time checking components that have little or no relationship to the problem.

• Test all repairs after the work is done to make sure that the problem is fixed. Some causes can be traced to more than one component, so a careful verification of repair work is important in order to pick up additional malfunctions that may cause a problem to reappear or a different problem to arise. A blown fuse, for example, is a simple problem that may require more than another fuse to repair. If you don't look for a problem that caused a fuse to blow, a shorted wire (for example) may go undetected.

Experience has shown that most problems tend to be the result of a fairly simple and obvious cause, such as loose or corroded connectors, bad grounds or damaged wire insulation which causes a short. This makes careful visual inspection of components during testing essential to quick and accurate troubleshooting.

Testing

OPEN CIRCUITS

▸ **See Figure 8**

This test already assumes the existence of an open in the circuit and it is used to help locate the open portion.

1. Isolate the circuit from power and ground.
2. Connect the self-powered test light or ohmmeter ground clip to the ground side of the circuit and probe sections of the circuit sequentially.
3. If the light is out or there is infinite resistance, the open is between the probe and the circuit ground.
4. If the light is on or the meter shows continuity, the open is between the probe and the end of the circuit toward the power source.

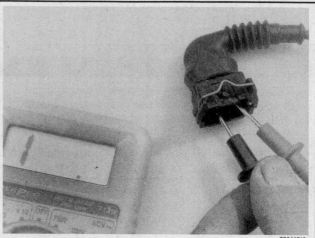

TCCA6P10

Fig. 8 The infinite reading on this multimeter indicates that the circuit is open

SHORT CIRCUITS

➥**Never use a self-powered test light to perform checks for opens or shorts when power is applied to the circuit under test. The test light can be damaged by outside power.**

1. Isolate the circuit from power and ground.
2. Connect the self-powered test light or ohmmeter ground clip to a good ground and probe any easy-to-reach point in the circuit.
3. If the light comes on or there is continuity, there is a short somewhere in the circuit.
4. To isolate the short, probe a test point at either end of the isolated circuit (the light should be on or the meter should indicate continuity).
5. Leave the test light probe engaged and sequentially open connectors or switches, remove parts, etc. until the light goes out or continuity is broken.
6. When the light goes out, the short is between the last two circuit components which were opened.

VOLTAGE

This test determines voltage available from the battery and should be the first step in any electrical troubleshooting procedure after visual inspection. Many electrical problems, especially on computer controlled systems, can be caused by a low state of charge in the battery. Excessive corrosion at the battery cable terminals can cause poor contact that will prevent proper charging and full battery current flow.

1. Set the voltmeter selector switch to the 20V position.

2. Connect the multimeter negative lead to the battery's negative (-) post or terminal and the positive lead to the battery's positive (+) post or terminal.

3. Turn the ignition switch **ON** to provide a load.

4. A well charged battery should register over 12 volts. If the meter reads below 11.5 volts, the battery power may be insufficient to operate the electrical system properly.

VOLTAGE DROP

▶ **See Figure 9**

When current flows through a load, the voltage beyond the load drops. This voltage drop is due to the resistance created by the load and also by small resistances created by corrosion at the connectors and damaged insulation on the wires. The maximum allowable voltage drop under load is critical, especially if there is more than one load in the circuit, since all voltage drops are cumulative.

1. Set the voltmeter selector switch to the 20 volt position.

2. Connect the multimeter negative lead to a good ground.

3. Operate the circuit and check the voltage prior to the first component (load).

4. There should be little or no voltage drop in the circuit prior to the first component. If a voltage drop exists, the wire or connectors in the circuit are suspect.

5. While operating the first component in the circuit, probe the ground side of the component with the positive meter lead and observe the voltage readings. A small voltage drop should be noticed. This voltage drop is caused by the resistance of the component.

6. Repeat the test for each component (load) down the circuit.

7. If a large voltage drop is noticed, the preceding component, wire or connector is suspect.

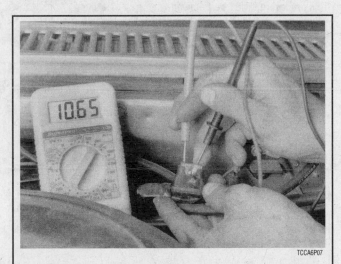

Fig. 9 This voltage drop test revealed high resistance (low voltage) in the circuit

RESISTANCE

▶ **See Figures 10 and 11**

✳✳ WARNING

Never use an ohmmeter with power applied to the circuit. The ohmmeter is designed to operate on its own power supply. The normal 12 volt electrical system voltage could damage the meter!

1. Isolate the circuit from the vehicle's power source.

2. Ensure that the ignition key is **OFF** when disconnecting any components or the battery.

3. Where necessary, also isolate at least one side of the circuit to be checked, in order to avoid reading parallel resistances. Parallel circuit resistances will always give a lower reading than the actual resistance of either of the branches.

4. Connect the meter leads to both sides of the circuit (wire or component) and read the actual measured ohms on the meter scale. Make sure the selector switch is set to the proper ohm scale for the circuit being tested, to avoid misreading the ohmmeter test value.

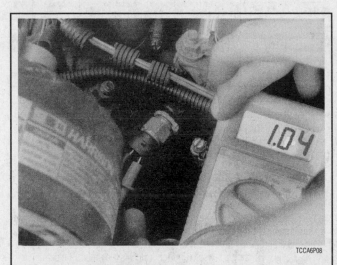

Fig. 10 Checking the resistance of a coolant temperature sensor with an ohmmeter. Reading is 1.04 kilohms

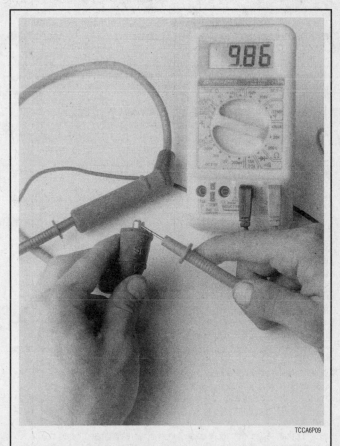

Fig. 11 Spark plug wires can be checked for excessive resistance using an ohmmeter

Wire and Connector Repair

Almost anyone can replace damaged wires, as long as the proper tools and parts are available. Wire and terminals are available to fit almost any need. Even the specialized weatherproof, molded and hard shell connectors are now available from aftermarket suppliers.

Be sure the ends of all the wires are fitted with the proper terminal hardware and connectors. Wrapping a wire around a stud is never a permanent solution and will only cause trouble later. Replace wires one at a time to avoid confusion. Always route wires exactly the same as the factory.

➡**If connector repair is necessary, only attempt it if you have the proper tools. Weatherproof and hard shell connectors require special tools to release the pins inside the connector. Attempting to repair these connectors with conventional hand tools will damage them.**

SUPPLEMENTAL RESTRAINT SYSTEM (SRS)

General Information

SYSTEM OPERATION

Certain models covered in this manual are equipped with a Supplemental Restraint System (SRS), commonly referred to as an air bag. The bag itself is stored within the hub of the steering wheel; the sensors and control module are behind the dashboard. Some models are equipped with dual air bags; one air bag is stored in the steering wheel and the other in the passenger's side of the dashboard, above the glove box. The air bag system is designed to aid in restraining the driver (and passenger on dual air bag models) during a frontal collision; the system supplements (assists) the seat belt system. An air bag system is ineffective if seat belts are not worn.

The air bag is a fabric bag or balloon with an explosive inflator unit attached. The system employs impact sensors and a safing sensor as well as an inflator circuit and control module. A back-up power system is connected in parallel with the battery. No single sensor can trigger SRS deployment. The safing sensor, and at least one of the impact sensors must engage together for at least 0.002 seconds. This "agreement" of the sensors is required to help prevent accidental deployment.

When the control unit receives these signals, power is supplied to the inflator circuit, either from the battery or back-up system. A small heater causes a chemical reaction in the igniter; the non-toxic gas from the chemical mixture expands very rapidly (in milliseconds), filling the bag and forcing it through the cover pad. Since all this is happening very rapidly, the expanding bag should reach the occupant before he/she reaches the steering wheel/dashboard during a frontal collision. The chemical reaction is complete by the time the air bag is fully inflated; as the occupant hits the bag, the gas is allowed to escape slowly through vents in the back of the bag.

The control unit contains a self-diagnostic circuit. When the ignition switch is turned **ON**, the SRS dash warning lamp should light for about 6 seconds, then go out. If the light does not come on, does not go out or comes on when driving, the system must be diagnosed and repaired by a Honda dealer or reputable shop. The system is NOT repairable at home.

SYSTEM PRECAUTIONS

✳✳ CAUTION

While the SRS is fully capable of operating trouble-free for years, its presence poses a great hazard during repair. Unintentional inflation can cause severe injury and/or property damage. For that reason ALL of the following items must be fully observed during any repair or procedure in or around the steering column or dashboard. Proper safety precautions MUST be observed at all times.

- Do not attempt to repair or alter any part of the SRS. If the system needs repair or diagnosis, take the car to a Honda dealer or reputable service facility.
- Before making repairs to the steering wheel, column or dashboard, the system must be disarmed by installing the shorting connector.
- All SRS-related wiring and connectors are identified by yellow outer insulation. NEVER attempt to test these circuits or use them to power other components.
- Disconnect both battery cables and wait at least three minutes before working on the vehicle.

- Once the steering wheel pad is removed, store it face up in a clean area. If stored face down, accidental detonation could launch it.
- Keep the steering wheel pad in a clean, dry location. Contact with acid, water or heavy metals (copper, lead, mercury) can cause accidental discharge. Storage temperature must not exceed 200°F (93°C).
- Do not replace the original steering wheel with any other type; do not interchange SRS parts between vehicles.
- Never attempt to modify, splice or repair any SRS-related wire or cable. Do not disconnect the SRS wiring during repairs; always follow the proper disarming procedure first.
- The system must be inspected by a Honda dealer 10 years after the date of manufacture as shown on the certification plate. Note that this "build date" will be earlier than your actual purchase date.
- The system must be checked after ANY frontal accident, even if the system did NOT deploy.

DISARMING THE SYSTEM

▶ **See Figures 12 and 13**

✳✳ CAUTION

This procedure MUST be followed whenever working on or near SRS components and when otherwise noted. The shorting connector must be installed whenever the air bag is disconnected from the harness. If equipped with dual air bags, always disarm the passenger's air bag as well.

1. Disconnect the negative battery cable, then the positive cable from the battery. Wait at least three minutes before proceeding.
2. Remove the maintenance lid below the air bag on the steering wheel; it is secured by two screws. Remove the red shorting connector stored inside the lid.
3. Disengage the connector between the air bag and the cable reel in the

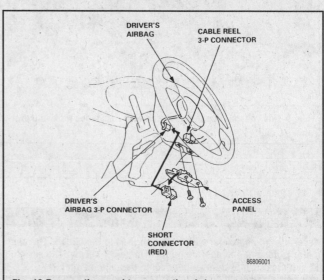

Fig. 12 Remove the panel to access the air bag connector

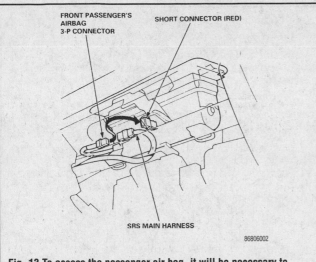

Fig. 13 To access the passenger air bag, it will be necessary to remove the glove box

steering wheel. The connector can be reached through the opening provided by removing the maintenance lid. Install the shorting connector into the air bag side of the wiring connector.

4. To disarm the passenger's side air bag, first remove the glove box. Now disengage the connector between the SRS main harness and the air bag. Install the red shorting connector into the air bag side of the connector.

5. DON'T forget to enable the system after the repairs are finished.

ENABLING THE SYSTEM

1. Remove the shorting connector from the air bag, then engage the air bag and cable reel (driver's side) or SRS main harness (passenger side) connectors.

2. Reinstall the maintenance lid and glove box (as applicable).

3. Reconnect the battery cables, positive cable first.

4. Turn the ignition switch **ON**, the SRS dash warning lamp should light for about 6 seconds, then go out. If the light does not come on, does not go out or comes on when driving, the system must be diagnosed and repaired by a Honda dealer or reputable shop.

HEATER

Blower Motor

REMOVAL & INSTALLATION

1984–89 Accord and 1984–87 Prelude

▶ See Figure 14

1. Disconnect the negative battery cable.
2. Remove the glove box.
3. Remove the duct between the blower and heater box.
4. Unplug the wiring connector and the vacuum hose from the blower.
5. Remove the three mounting bolts and remove the blower assembly.
6. Install in reverse order, tightening the mounting bolts to 7 ft. lbs. (10 Nm). Make certain the blower mating surfaces are tightly sealed. Install the blower duct; make certain there is no leakage at its joints.

1990–93 Accord

▶ See Figures 15, 16 and 17

1. Disconnect the negative battery cable. If so equipped, disable the Supplemental Restraint System (SRS).
2. Remove the glove box.
3. Remove the glove box frame (lower support)
4. If not equipped with air conditioning:

a. Remove the three screws and remove the heater duct.
b. Remove the blower mounting nuts. Unplug the wiring from the blower motor, resistor and recirculation control motor, then remove the blower assembly.

5. If equipped with air conditioning:

a. Lift the carpet in the passenger compartment. Remove the side cover (kick panel).
b. Remove the control unit bracket nuts; unplug the five connectors and remove the control unit bracket.
c. Remove the retaining band, then remove the blower lower covers. Do not break the tabs on the lower covers.
d. Remove the retaining nuts and remove the blower assembly.

To install:

6. Install the blower unit and tighten the retaining nuts.
7. On air conditioned vehicles:

a. Install the lower covers and the retaining band.
b. Install the control unit bracket and carefully engage the wiring connectors to their proper location.
c. Install the kick panel and reposition the carpet.

8. Connect the wiring to the blower assembly. For non-air conditioned vehicles, install the air duct and tighten the screws.

9. Install the glove box frame and install the glove box. Note that some of trim on the frame is held with 2-sided tape; replace the tape when reassembling as necessary.

10. If applicable, enable the SRS.
11. Connect the negative battery cable.

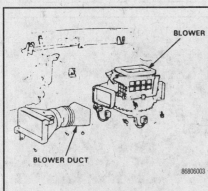

Fig. 14 The blower motor assembly is secured to the right side of the dashboard

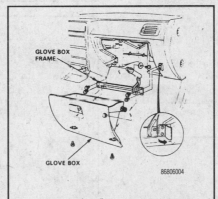

Fig. 15 Remove the glove box and frame

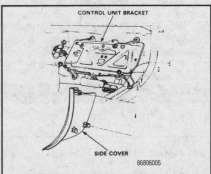

Fig. 16 Air conditioned models require the removal of the control unit. Handle it carefully

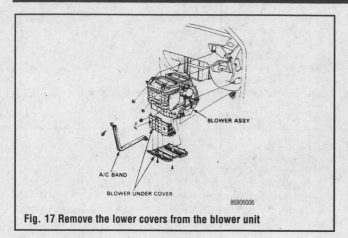

Fig. 17 Remove the lower covers from the blower unit

1988–91 Prelude

▶ See Figure 18

1. Disconnect the negative battery cable.
2. Remove the glove box and frame (lower support).
3. Remove the 4 screws and remove the heater duct.
4. Remove the 3 mounting bolts.
5. Unplug the wiring connectors from the blower motor, resistor and recirculation controller. Remove the blower motor assembly.
6. Reinstall in reverse order. Make certain the blower mating surfaces are tightly sealed.

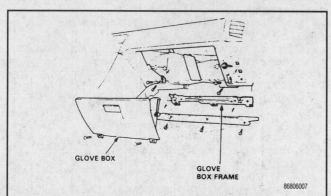

Fig. 18 The glove box and frame are secured by several small screws

1994–95 Accord and 1992–95 Prelude

▶ See Figure 19

1. Disconnect the battery cables and disable the Supplemental Restraint System (SRS).
2. Unplug any electrical connections on the blower motor.
3. Remove the screws securing the blower motor, then remove it from the vehicle.
4. Installation is the reverse of removal. Be sure to enable the SRS.

Heater Core

REMOVAL & INSTALLATION

▶ See Figures 20 and 21

1984–85 Accord and 1984–87 Prelude

▶ See Figures 22 and 23

1. Disconnect the negative battery cable.
2. Drain the coolant from the radiator.

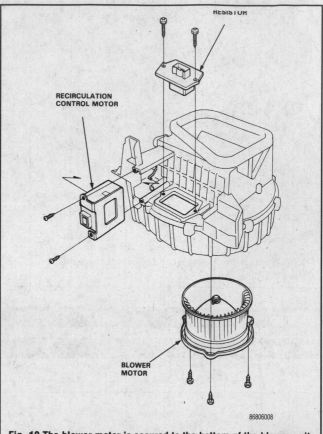

Fig. 19 The blower motor is secured to the bottom of the blower unit

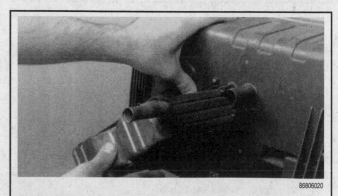

Fig. 20 The heater core is secured to the unit by clamps

Fig. 21 After the clamps are removed, the core can be extracted from the unit

3. From under the dash, remove the heater pipe cover and clamp.
4. Remove the heater core retaining plate.
5. Place a drip pan under the heater pipe connections.
6. Pull out the cotter pin of the joint hose clamp and separate the heater pipes. Some coolant will run out, be sure to have the drip pan in place.

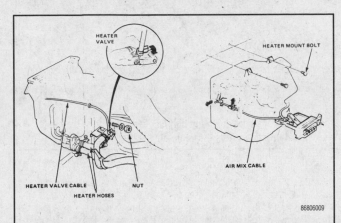

Fig. 22 Heater assembly used on 1984–85 Accords. Note the heater valve is located on the side of the assembly

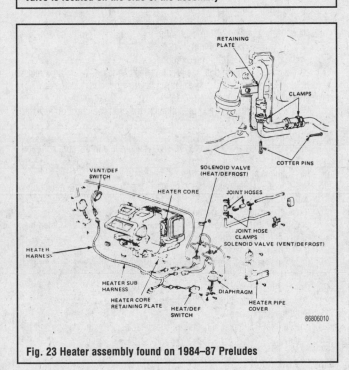

Fig. 23 Heater assembly found on 1984–87 Preludes

7. Pull the heater core from the heater housing.

To install:

8. Slide the heater core into the housing.
9. Connect the heater pipes. Use new clamps if necessary.
10. Install the heater core retaining plate. Tighten the screws until snug.
11. Install the heater pipe cover and clamp.
12. Fill the cooling system.
13. Start the engine. Turn the heater on and check for leaks.

1986–89 Accord

♦ **See Figures 24 and 25**

1. Disconnect the negative battery cable.
2. Drain coolant from the radiator. Put a drain pan underneath the hose connections at the firewall. Note the hose locations, then disconnect the two hoses.
3. Disconnect the heater valve cable from the valve. Remove the two lower heater mounting nuts.
4. On push button type heaters, disconnect the cool vent cable at the heater. On lever type heaters, disconnect the function cable and the air mix cable from the heater.
5. Remove the dashboard.
6. Remove the heater ducts.
7. On pushbutton type heaters, disconnect the air mix cable from the heater and the wiring harness from the connector.
8. Remove the bolts, then pull the heater assembly away from its mounts.
9. Remove the screws securing the heater core, then slide the core out of the heater assembly.

To install:

10. Install the heater core into the heater assembly. Tighten the screws securing the heater core until snug.
11. Position the heater assembly on its mounts, then tighten the retaining bolts.
12. On pushbutton type heaters, connect the air mix cable and engage the wiring harness connector.
13. Install the heater ducts.
14. Install the dashboard.
15. On push button type heaters, connect the cool vent cable at the heater. On lever type heaters, connect the function cable and the air mix cable to the heater.
16. Install the two lower heater mounting nuts.
17. Connect the heater valve cable to the valve. Connect the hoses to the heater core; use new clamps as necessary.
18. Refill the cooling system. Start the engine and check for leaks.

1990–93 Accord

♦ **See Figure 26**

1. Disconnect the negative battery cable. If so equipped, disable the Supplemental Restraint System (SRS).
2. Drain the engine coolant.
3. Label and disconnect the heater hoses at the firewall. Be prepared to contain spilled coolant from the hoses and fittings.

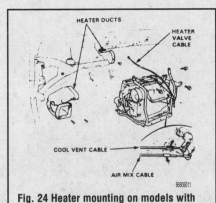

Fig. 24 Heater mounting on models with pushbutton controls

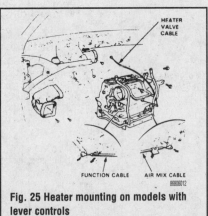

Fig. 25 Heater mounting on models with lever controls

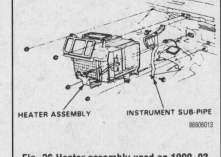

Fig. 26 Heater assembly used on 1990–93 Accords

4. Disconnect the heater valve control cable from the valve.
5. Remove the dashboard.
6. Remove the dashboard support pipe.
7. Remove the 4 mounting bolts, then remove the heater assembly.
8. Remove the heater core cover and the clamp securing the heater core.
9. Remove the core from the heater assembly.

To install:

10. Slide the core into the heater assembly.
11. Install the heater core clamp and cover.
12. Position the heater assembly in the vehicle and secure it with the mounting bolts.
13. Install the dashboard support pipe.
14. Install the dashboard.
15. Connect the heater control valve cable to the valve.
16. Connect the heater hoses at the firewall.
17. Refill the engine coolant.
18. If applicable, enable the SRS.
19. Connect the negative battery cable. Start the engine and check for leaks.

1994–95 Accord

▶ **See Figures 27 and 28**

1. Disconnect the battery cables, then disable the Supplemental Restraint System (SRS).

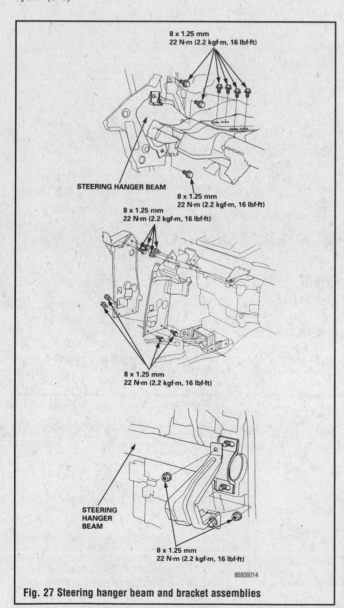

8 x 1.25 mm
22 N·m (2.2 kgf·m, 16 lbf·ft)

STEERING HANGER BEAM

8 x 1.25 mm
22 N·m (2.2 kgf·m, 16 lbf·ft)

8 x 1.25 mm
22 N·m (2.2 kgf·m, 16 lbf·ft)

8 x 1.25 mm
22 N·m (2.2 kgf·m, 16 lbf·ft)

STEERING HANGER BEAM

8 x 1.25 mm
22 N·m (2.2 kgf·m, 16 lbf·ft)

86806014

Fig. 27 Steering hanger beam and bracket assemblies

6 x 1.0 mm
9.8 N·m (1.0 kgf·m, 7.2 lbf·ft)

86806015

Fig. 28 After the final mounting bolt has been removed, the heater unit can be removed from the vehicle

2. Drain the engine coolant.
3. Label and disconnect the heater hoses at the firewall. Be prepared to contain spilled coolant from the hoses and fittings.
4. Disconnect the heater valve control cable from the valve.
5. Remove the two heater unit mounting nuts from inside the engine compartment.
6. Remove the dashboard.
7. Remove the mounting nuts and bolts securing the steering hanger beam and brackets, then remove the beam and brackets from the vehicle.
8. Remove the heater duct (on cars without air conditioning) or the evaporator case (cars with air conditioning).
9. Unplug the mode control motor connector.
10. Remove the mounting bolt, then remove the heater unit from the vehicle.
11. Remove the clips and screws securing the vent/defroster duct, then remove the duct.
12. Remove the heater core and pipe clamps, then remove the core from the unit.

To install:

13. Position the heater core in the unit, then secure it with the core and pipe clamps.
14. Install the vent/defroster duct on the heater unit.
15. Position the heater unit in the vehicle, then secure it with the mounting bolt. Engage the mode control motor connector.
16. Install the heater duct or evaporator case as applicable.
17. Install the steering hanger beam and brackets in the vehicle. Tighten the nuts/bolts to 16 ft. lbs. (22 Nm).
18. Install the dashboard.
19. Install the two heater unit mounting nuts in the engine compartment. Tighten them to 16 ft. lbs. (22 Nm).
20. Connect the heater control valve cable to the valve.
21. Connect the heater hoses at the firewall.
22. Refill the engine coolant.
23. Enable the SRS, then connect the battery cables. Start the engine and check for leaks.

1988–91 Prelude

▶ **See Figure 29**

1. Disconnect the negative battery cable.
2. Drain the engine coolant.
3. Label and disconnect the heater hoses at the firewall.
4. Disconnect the heater valve cable from the heater valve.
5. Remove the dashboard.
6. Remove the heater duct.
7. Remove the lower mounting nuts holding the heater.
8. Remove the steering column bracket.
9. Remove the two remaining mounting bolts holding the heater. Disconnect the wiring from the function control motor. Remove the heater assembly.
10. Remove the integrated control unit and bracket from the case.
11. Remove the 2 screws, bracket, retaining plate and the heater core cover.
12. Remove the heater core cover, setting plate and clamp.
13. Carefully pull the heater core from the housing.

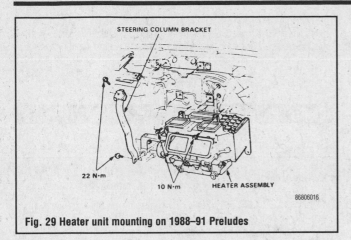

Fig. 29 Heater unit mounting on 1988–91 Preludes

To install:

14. Install the heater core into the case. Install the setting plate and the clamp.

15. Install the core cover, set plate and bracket.

16. Install the integrated control unit and bracket.

17. Fit the heater assembly into the vehicle. Apply a sealant around the grommets.

18. Install the upper two mounting bolts, tightening them to 7 ft. lbs. (10 Nm).

19. Install the steering column bracket.

20. Install the lower mounting nuts, tightening them to 16 ft. lbs. (22 Nm).

21. Install the heater duct.

22. Install the dashboard.

23. Connect the hoses at the firewall fittings. Use new clamps. Make certain the hoses are on their correct fittings.

24. Connect the heater valve cable.

25. Refill the coolant. Start the engine and check for leaks.

1992–95 Prelude

♦ **See Figures 30 and 31**

1. Disconnect the battery cables, then disable the Supplemental Restraint System (SRS).

2. Drain the engine coolant.

3. Label and disconnect the heater hoses at the firewall. Be prepared to contain spilled coolant from the hoses and fittings.

4. Disconnect the heater valve control cable from the valve.

5. Remove the two heater unit mounting nuts from inside the engine compartment.

6. Remove the dashboard.

7. Remove the heater duct (on cars without air conditioning) or the evaporator case (cars with air conditioning).

8. Remove the mounting bolts, then remove the heater unit from the vehicle.

9. Remove the screws securing the vent/defroster duct, then remove the duct.

10. Remove the heater core and pipe clamps, then remove the core from the unit.

To install:

11. Position the heater core in the unit, then secure it with the core and pipe clamps.

12. Install the vent/defroster duct on the heater unit.

13. Position the heater unit in the vehicle, then secure it with the mounting bolts.

14. Install the heater duct or evaporator case as applicable.

15. Install the dashboard.

16. Install the two heater unit mounting nuts in the engine compartment. Tighten them to 16 ft. lbs. (22 Nm).

17. Connect the heater control valve cable to the valve.

18. Connect the heater hoses at the firewall.

19. Refill the engine coolant.

20. Enable the SRS, then connect the battery cables. Start the engine and check for leaks.

Heater Control Valve

REMOVAL & INSTALLATION

♦ **See Figures 22 and 32**

The heater control valve for 1984–85 Accords is mounted at the side of the heater case in the car. All others are at the firewall in the engine compartment. When removing or installing the valve, take care not to damage or kink the control cable.

1. Drain the coolant.

2. Disconnect the heater valve cable from the valve.

3. Place a drain pan under the valve, particularly on Accords with the valve inside the car. Loosen and remove the hose clamps at the valve. Disconnect the hoses from the valve.

4. If the valve is held by a retaining screw or bolt, remove it. Remove the valve.

To install:

5. Fit the valve into position. Install the hoses with new clamps and secure the retaining bolt.

6. Refill the cooling system.

7. Adjust the control cables.

Control Cables

REMOVAL & INSTALLATION

♦ **See Figure 33**

1. Disconnect the negative battery cable.

2. Remove the control panel from the dashboard.

3. Remove the small clamp securing the appropriate cable to the control panel assembly. Detach the cable from the control panel lever. Remove the con-

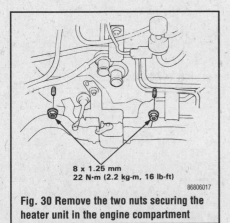

Fig. 30 Remove the two nuts securing the heater unit in the engine compartment

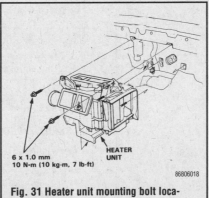

Fig. 31 Heater unit mounting bolt locations

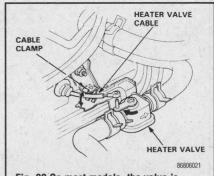

Fig. 32 On most models, the valve is located at the firewall in the engine compartment

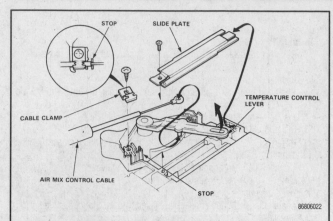

Fig. 33 On some models it may be necessary to remove the slide plate to gain additional clearance

trol lever slide plate if additional clearance is needed; it is usually secured by a single screw.

4. Installation is the reverse of removal; make sure the cables are properly routed and are not kinked. Adjust the cable(s).

ADJUSTMENT

▶ **See Figures 34 and 35**

The control cables on all models are adjusted using the same basic procedure. First, detach the heater valve cable at the heater unit and at the heater control valve by carefully pulling them from their clamps. Set the temperature control lever to the COLD position. Gently slide the temperature control cable outer sleeve back enough to take up any slack, but not enough to make the con-

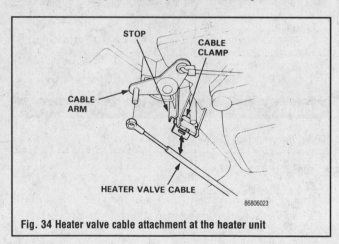

Fig. 34 Heater valve cable attachment at the heater unit

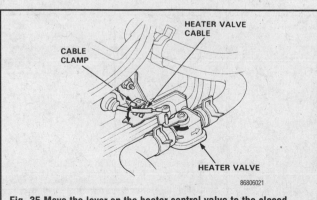

Fig. 35 Move the lever on the heater control valve to the closed position

trol lever move. Snap the cable into its clamp. Now, move the lever on the heater control valve to the closed position, then gently slide the heater valve cable outer sleeve back enough to take up any slack, but not enough to make the control lever move. Snap the cable into its clamp.

Start the engine and allow it to reach normal operating temperature. Check for proper operation of the cables. Readjust, if necessary.

Control Panel

REMOVAL & INSTALLATION

1984–85 Accord

▶ **See Figure 36**

1. Disconnect the negative battery cable.
2. Remove the temperature slider and fan control knobs.
3. Remove the control panel cover.
4. Remove the upper steering column support bracket, then lower the steering column.
5. Remove the center console and remove the radio.
6. Remove the screws from the front of the control panel. Loosen the panel by pushing it into the dash a little bit.
7. Disconnect the temperature control cable from the heater unit.
8. Disconnect the hot water control cable from the valve.
9. Disconnect the wiring to the blower switch and remove the unit under the dash.
10. The control assembly may be disassembled into individual parts after removal.
To install:
11. Assemble the components if they were separated. Install the assembly from the back of the dash, setting it in place.
12. Connect the switch wiring. Make certain it is routed out of the way of the installation.
13. Connect and adjust the air and water control cables.
14. Install the front retaining screws.
15. Install the console and radio.
16. Reposition and secure the steering column.
17. Install the heater control cover panel; install the control knobs.
18. Connect the negative battery cable.

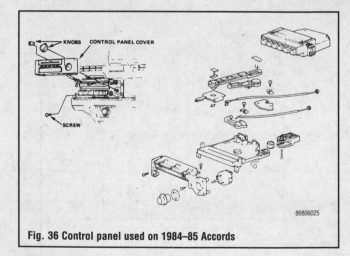

Fig. 36 Control panel used on 1984–85 Accords

1986–89 Accord

PUSHBUTTON CONTROLS

▶ **See Figures 37 and 38**

1. Disconnect the negative battery cable.
2. Remove the knobs from the temperature and fan controls.
3. Remove the heater control panel cover.
4. Remove the instrument cluster visor.

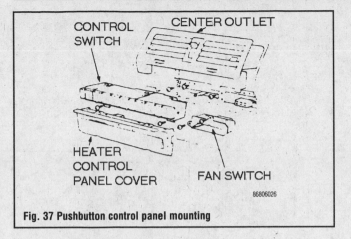

Fig. 37 Pushbutton control panel mounting

5. Remove the center air outlet.
6. Remove the 4 screws holding the pushbutton unit and slide it outward gently. Disconnect the switch wires.
7. The blower fan switch may be removed individually if desired. Remove its mounting bolts and remove the switch.
8. If the temperature control lever is to be removed, remove the radio first. Disconnect the air mix cable at the heater box (not at the lever) and remove the assembly.

To install:

9. Assemble and install the individual components (fan switch or temperature control cable) if they were removed.
10. Connect the wiring harness and install the pushbutton controller. Install and tighten the retaining screws.
11. Install the center air outlet.
12. Install the instrument visor.
13. Install the control panel cover; install the control knobs.

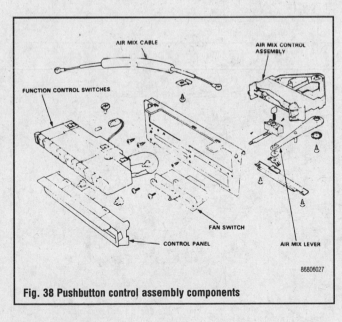

Fig. 38 Pushbutton control assembly components

LEVER CONTROLS

♦ See Figures 39 and 40

1. Disconnect the negative battery cable.
2. Remove the knobs from the control levers.
3. Remove the control panel cover.
4. Remove the radio.
5. At this point, the temperature/function levers, the recirculation switch or the fan control switch may be removed individually.
6. If the main lever assembly is to be removed, remove the six retaining

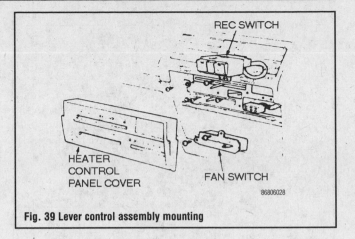

Fig. 39 Lever control assembly mounting

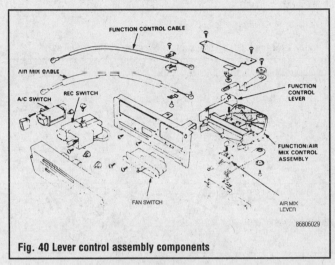

Fig. 40 Lever control assembly components

screws. Disconnect the temperature control cable and the function cable at the heater. Disconnect the wiring and remove the control unit.
7. If the fan switch or recirculation controller is to be removed, remove the retaining screws and unplug the wiring connector.

To install:

8. Place the fan switch or recirculation connector in position, connect the wiring and secure the retaining screws.
9. Fit the control panel into place and route the cables to the heater.
10. Connect the cables to their proper fittings at the heater.
11. Install the retaining screws holding the control panel.
12. Install the radio.
13. Install the control panel cover and install the knobs on the levers.

1990–93 Accord

♦ See Figures 41, 42, 43 and 44

1. Disconnect the negative battery cable. If so equipped, disable the Supplemental Restraint System (SRS).
2. Remove the ashtray. Remove the center console.
3. Remove the coin box, air vents and ashtray lighting bracket.
4. Remove the dashboard switches on the left and right of the steering wheel.
5. Remove the radio/tape player. Note that there are concealed screws at the back or bottom of the radio unit.
6. Lower the steering wheel to its lowest position. Remove the dash visor. This is a large, one-piece assembly which includes the center dash trim.
7. Disconnect the control cables at the heater assembly.
8. Remove the four screws and gently pull the control panel forward.
9. Unplug the wiring connectors and remove the control panel.
10. If the fan switch or other individual components are to be replaced, the appropriate control knobs must be removed before disassembly.

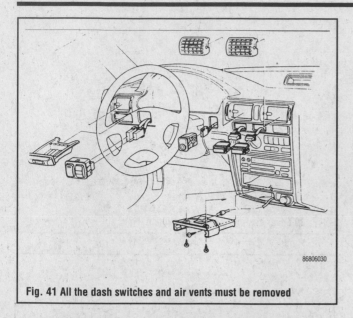

Fig. 41 All the dash switches and air vents must be removed

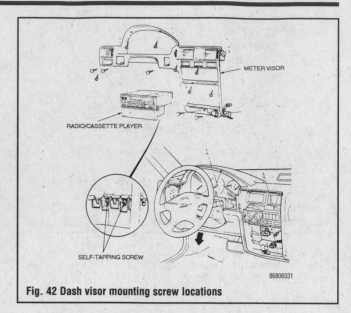

Fig. 42 Dash visor mounting screw locations

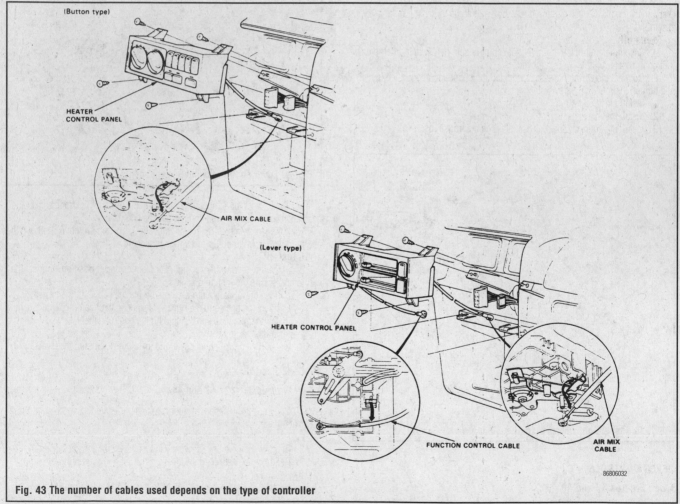

Fig. 43 The number of cables used depends on the type of controller

To install:

11. Assemble the individual components if they were removed.
12. Insert the panel into the dash and route the cables to the heater box.
13. Engage the wiring connectors, making certain the harness is out of the way.
14. Connect the cables at the heater assembly. Install the 4 retaining screws holding the control panel.

15. Install the dash visor. Make sure it is correctly positioned and that each retaining screw is in place.
16. Install the radio/tape player.
17. Install and connect the dash switches, air vents and ashtray bracket. Install the coin box.
18. Install the console; install the ashtray.

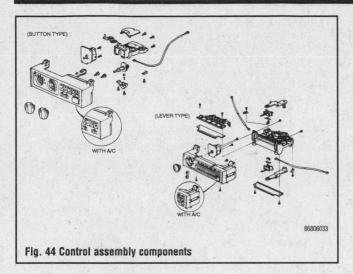

Fig. 44 Control assembly components

19. If applicable, enable the SRS.
20. Connect the negative battery cable.

1994–95 Accord

▶ **See Figures 45, 46 and 47**

1. Disconnect the battery cables, then disable the Supplemental Restraint System (SRS).
2. Disconnect the temperature control cable from the heater unit.
3. Remove the radio and the glove box.
4. Remove the dashboard switches on the left and right of the steering wheel.
5. Remove the six screws securing the instrument panel.
6. Carefully pull the panel out until the electrical connectors for the control panel and blower switch can be reached. Unplug the connectors, then remove the panel assembly from the vehicle.
7. Remove the screws securing the control panel to the instrument panel.
8. If necessary, the blower switch can be removed from the control panel after its knob and retaining screws have been removed.

To install:

9. If applicable, install the blower switch to the control panel.
10. Install the control panel onto the instrument panel.

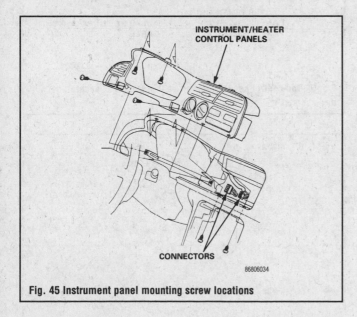

Fig. 45 Instrument panel mounting screw locations

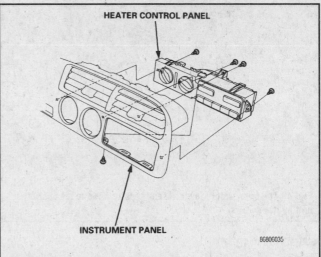

Fig. 46 Remove the screws securing the control panel to the instrument panel

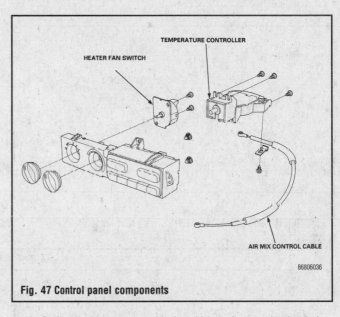

Fig. 47 Control panel components

11. Position the instrument panel in the vehicle, and engage the electrical connectors.
12. Install the screws securing the instrument panel.
13. Install the dashboard switches into the instrument panel.
14. Install the radio and glove box.
15. Connect the temperature control cable to the heater unit.
16. Enable the SRS, then connect the battery cables.

1984–87 Prelude

▶ **See Figure 48**

1. Disconnect the negative battery cable.
2. Disconnect the heater control harness.
3. Remove the temperature control/dash outlet assembly by removing the four screws. Remove the lower screws first.
4. If necessary, the temperature lever assembly can be removed from the control unit by removing the two screws from the bottom.
5. Remove the 4 screws securing the control unit to the dash outlet, then remove the unit.
6. Install in the reverse order of removal.

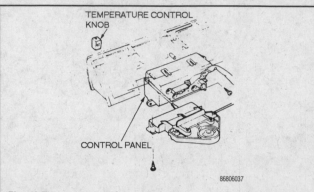

Fig. 48 The temperature lever assembly is secured to the control unit by two screws

1988–91 Prelude

▶ See Figures 49 and 50

1. Disconnect the negative battery cable.
2. Remove the center console.

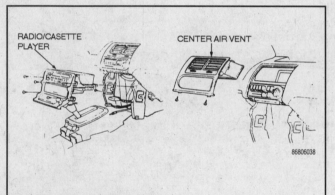

Fig. 49 It is necessary to remove the radio first on 1988–91 Pre-ludes

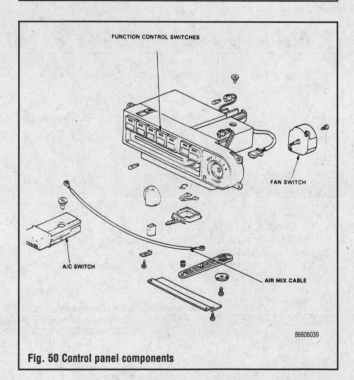

Fig. 50 Control panel components

3. Remove the radio.
4. Remove the two screws at the bottom of the center air vent and remove the air vent assembly.
5. Disconnect the temperature cable at the heater assembly.
6. Remove the 4 screws securing the control assembly; pull the controller forward gently. Unplug the wiring connectors and remove the control unit.
7. If the blower switch is to be replaced, remove the control knob and remove the switch from the control assembly.

To install:

8. Reinstall any components removed from the control assembly.
9. Install the control assembly and tighten the retaining screws.
10. Connect the temperature cable at the heater unit.
11. Install the center air vent.
12. Install the radio.
13. Install the center console.

1992–95 Prelude

▶ See Figures 51 and 52

1. Disconnect the battery cables, then disable the Supplemental Restraint System (SRS).
2. Remove the front console.

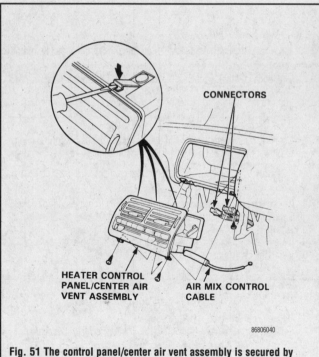

Fig. 51 The control panel/center air vent assembly is secured by three screws

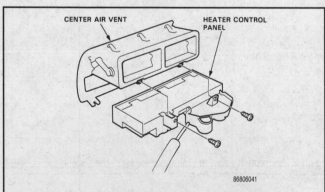

Fig. 52 The control panel can be removed from the center air vent assembly

3. Remove the radio.

4. Disconnect the temperature control cable from the heater unit.

5. Remove the three screws securing the control panel/center air vent assembly. Disengage the lock tabs with a small prytool and pull the assembly out of the dash enough to unplug the electrical connectors.

6. Remove the two screws securing the control panel to the center air vent.

7. If necessary, remove the screws securing the blower switch, then remove it from the control panel.

To install:

8. If applicable, install the blower switch on the control panel.

9. Install the control unit to the center air vent.

10. Engage the electrical connectors, then install the center air vent/control unit assembly into the dash.

11. Connect the temperature control cable to the heater unit.

12. Install the radio and front console.

13. Enable the SRS, then connect the battery cables.

Blower Switch

REMOVAL & INSTALLATION

On most models, the blower switch can be replaced after the control panel is removed. Unplug the electrical connector, then remove the retaining screws or release its retaining clips. Remove the knob from the switch, then remove the switch from the control panel. On models without a replaceable switch, the entire control panel will need to be replaced.

Air Conditioning Components

REMOVAL & INSTALLATION

Repair or service of air conditioning components is not covered by this manual, because of the risk of personal injury or death, and because of the legal ramifications of servicing these components without the proper EPA certification and experience. Cost, personal injury or death, environmental damage, and legal considerations (such as the fact that it is a federal crime to vent refrigerant into the atmosphere), dictate that the A/C components on your vehicle should be serviced only by a Motor Vehicle Air Conditioning (MVAC) trained, and EPA certified automotive technician.

➡**If your vehicle's A/C system uses R-12 refrigerant and is in need of recharging, the A/C system can be converted over to R-134a refrigerant (less environmentally harmful and expensive). Refer to Section 1 for additional information on R-12 to R-134a conversions, and for additional considerations dealing with your vehicle's A/C system.**

CRUISE CONTROL

Main Switch

REMOVAL & INSTALLATION

1984–85 Accord and 1984–87 Prelude

The main switch is easily removed from the dash. Disconnect the wiring behind the dash, then remove the switch. It may be necessary to use a blunt, non-marring tool to pop the switch free. Don't use a screwdriver and be careful not to damage the surrounding area.

1986–89 Accord

To remove the main switch, first remove the fusebox door. Reach behind the dash with your fingers and push the switch outward. Unplug the wiring connector.

1988–91 Prelude

1. Disconnect the negative battery cable.

2. Remove the headlight retractor and fog light switch from the dash. Remove the dashlight brightness controller from the dash.

3. Behind each of these switches is a retaining screw holding the instrument panel face plate. Remove these screws and the three screws at the top of the clear plastic lens.

4. Carefully remove the face plate. Disconnect the wiring from the cruise control and sunroof switch (if equipped) when access is gained.

5. The cruise control and sunroof control switch is held to the panel by two screws fitted from the back of the face plate. Remove the screws and remove the switch assembly.

6. Reassemble in reverse order, taking care not to crack or damage the face plate. Install the switches and connect the wiring harnesses. Check the operation of each switch after reassembly.

1990–95 Accord and 1992–95 Prelude

The cruise control/sunroof switch (if equipped) assembly may be removed by carefully prying the switch housing from the dash. If necessary, use a blunt, non-marring tool to pry with. Don't use a screwdriver and be careful not to damage the dash.

Set/Resume Switches

REMOVAL & INSTALLATION

Models Without Supplemental Restraint System

▶ **See Figure 53**

1. Disconnect the negative battery cable.

2. Remove the steering wheel. Please refer to Section 8 for the procedure.

3. Separate the back cover from the steering wheel by removing the retaining screws.

4. Remove the screws securing the cruise control switch, then remove the switch from the steering wheel.

5. Installation is the reverse of removal.

Models With Supplemental Restraint System

▶ **See Figure 54**

1. Disconnect the battery cables, then disable the Supplemental Restraint System (SRS).

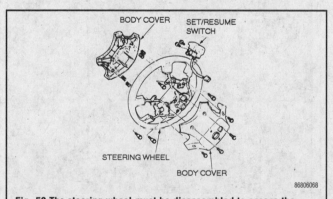

Fig. 53 The steering wheel must be disassembled to access the switches

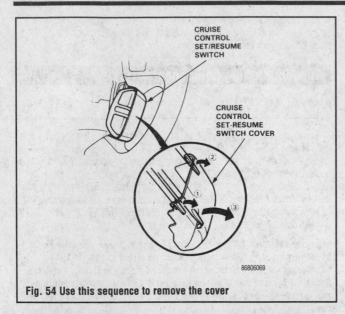

Fig. 54 Use this sequence to remove the cover

2. Carefully remove the switch cover by prying between the cover and switch using the sequence shown in the illustration.

3. Remove the screws securing the switch assembly to the steering wheel, then pull the switch assembly from the wheel.

4. Installation is the reverse of removal. Be sure to enable the SRS.

Brake Lamp Switch/Clutch Switch

REMOVAL & INSTALLATION

▶ **See Figure 55**

These switches provide electrical signals to the control unit to interrupt cruise control when either pedal is used. The switches are located at the respective pedals, at the top of the pedal shaft. The brake switch also operates the brake lights.

To remove either switch, unplug the wiring connector, loosen the locknut and remove the switch. When reinstalling, adjust the switch with the locknut so that the switch engages within the first ½ in. (13mm) of pedal motion. If the switch is set with no slack or free-play in its motion, a healthy bump in the road may interrupt the cruise control operation.

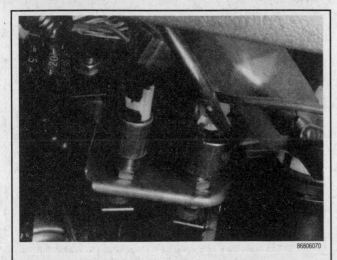

Fig. 55 The switches are located at the respective pedals, at the top of the pedal shaft

Control Unit

REMOVAL & INSTALLATION

▶ **See Figure 56**

1984–85 Accord

The control unit is located behind the dash, near the back of the instrument cluster.

1. Disconnect the negative battery cable.

2. From under the dash, remove the screws securing the bracket and carefully lower the assembly. If access to the screws is not possible from under the dash, remove the instrument cluster.

3. Unplug the wire harness from the cruise control unit, then remove the unit from the bracket.

4. Installation is the reverse of removal.

1984–87 Prelude

The control unit is located inside the right rear side trim panel.

1. Disconnect the negative battery cable.

2. Remove the right rear side trim panel.

3. Remove the screws securing the control unit to the bracket. Unplug the wiring and remove the control unit from the vehicle.

4. Installation is the reverse of removal.

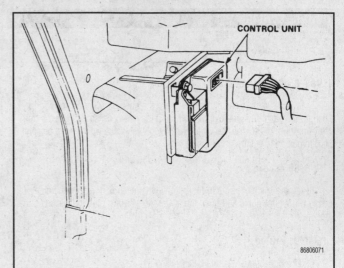

Fig. 56 The control unit is usually secured to a bracket behind the dash

1986–89 Accord

The control unit is secured under the top left side of the dashboard.

1. Disconnect the negative battery cable.

2. Lower the fuse box from under the dash after removing its retaining screws.

3. From under the dash, unplug its connector and remove the fasteners securing the unit. If needed, additional access may be gained by removing the instrument cluster. Remove the unit from the vehicle.

4. Installation is the reverse of removal.

1988–91 Prelude and 1990–95 Accord

The control unit is mounted in the lower left side of the dashboard, next to the steering column.

1. Disconnect the negative battery cable. If so equipped, disable the Supplemental Restraint System (SRS).

2. Remove the left lower dash panel or knee bolster.

3. Unplug the connector from the control unit.

4. Remove the bolts securing the bracket, then remove the assembly from the vehicle.

5. Installation is the reverse of removal. If applicable, be sure to enable the SRS.

1992–95 Prelude

1. Disconnect the battery cables, then disable the Supplemental Restraint System (SRS).
2. Remove the instrument cluster.
3. Unplug the connector from the control unit.
4. Remove the bolts securing the bracket, then remove the assembly from the vehicle.
5. Installation is the reverse of removal. Be sure to enable the SRS.

Actuator and Cable

REMOVAL & INSTALLATION

▶ **See Figures 57 and 58**

1984–85 Accord and 1984–87 Prelude

1. Pull back the rubber boot on the cable and loosen the locknut.
2. Disconnect the cable end from the actuator rod.
3. Disconnect the actuator cable from the center arm on the actuator.
4. Turn the grommet 90 degrees in the firewall and remove the cable.

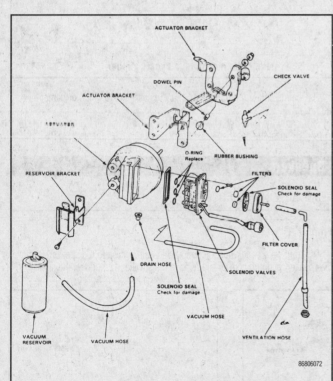

Fig. 57 Common actuator components used on Accords and Preludes

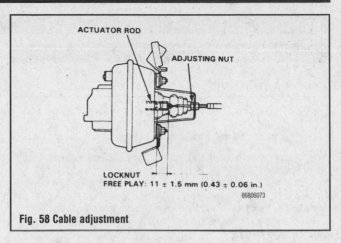

Fig. 58 Cable adjustment

5. Unplug the wire connector and vacuum hose.
6. Remove the retaining bolts and remove the actuator.
7. The solenoid valve assembly may be unbolted from the actuator if desired.

To install:

8. Install the solenoid assembly if it was removed. Install the actuator and retaining bolts.
9. Connect the wiring connector and vacuum hose(s).
10. Install the cable. Connect it to the actuator bracket.
11. Connect the cable to the actuator and adjust the cable. There should be less than ½ in. (13mm) of free-play in the cable. Tighten the locknut.

1986–95 Accord and 1988–95 Prelude

1. Disconnect the negative battery cable. If so equipped, disable the Supplemental Restraint System (SRS).
2. Pull back the rubber boot on the cable and loosen the locknut. Disconnect the cable from the bracket.
3. Disconnect the cable end from the actuator rod.
4. Unplug the connector and disconnect the vacuum hose from the check valve. Free the ventilation hose from the grommet.
5. Remove the mounting bolts and remove the actuator with the bracket and vacuum tank.
6. If necessary, disconnect the cable end from the linkage over the accelerator pedal, then turn the grommet in the firewall 90 degrees and remove the cable.
7. The solenoid valves may be removed from the actuator if desired.

To install:

8. Install the solenoid assembly if it was removed. Install the actuator and vacuum tank.
9. Connect the vacuum hose to the check valve. Fit the vent hose through the grommet and install the wire harness connector.
10. Connect the cable end to the actuator rod. Connect the cable to the accelerator if it was removed.
11. Check that the actuator cable moves smoothly with no binding.
12. Connect the negative battery cable. If applicable, enable the SRS.
13. Start the engine. Measure the amount of movement of the actuator rod until the cable pulls on the accelerator linkage. (The engine speed will begin to increase). Correct free-play is 0.43 in. (11mm).
14. Loosen the locknut and turn the adjusting nut as required to correct cable free-play.
15. Retighten the locknut, then recheck the free-play.
16. Test drive the vehicle to check the operation of the cruise control system.

RADIO

Radio/Tape Player

REMOVAL & INSTALLATION

Accord

▶ See Figures 59, 60 and 61

1. Disconnect the negative battery cable. If so equipped, disable the Supplemental Restraint System (SRS).
2. Remove the floor console and the front console panel. On 1984–85 cars, if access to the back of the radio may be gained through other means, such as removing the "pocket" from the console, the console need not be removed.
3. Remove the ashtray and ashtray holder.
4. On 1986–89 cars:
   a. Remove the coin box, air vents and ashtray lighting bracket.
   b. Remove the dashboard switches on the left and right of the steering wheel.
   c. Lower the steering wheel to its lowest position. Remove the dash visor. This is a large, one-piece assembly which includes the center dash trim. It's plastic; don't break it.
5. Remove the two screws holding the radio at the rear of the unit.
6. Carefully push the unit out the front of the dash. When access is gained, disconnect the multi-pin connector and the antenna cable from the unit. Remove the unit.
7. Reinstall in the reverse order. Take great care not to damage the dash trim and instrument visor. Make certain the connectors are firmly and squarely installed. If applicable, be sure to enable the SRS.

Prelude

▶ See Figure 62

1. Disconnect the negative battery cable. If so equipped, disable the Supplemental Restraint System (SRS).
2. Remove the console.
3. Remove the screws securing the center instrument panel. Remove the panel with the switches and radio attached. Use care; the panel is easily damaged.
4. When access is gained, disconnect the multi-pin connector to the radio and any other applicable connectors.
5. With the dash panel and radio unit clear of the dash, remove the two retaining screws holding the radio.

To install:

6. Reinstall the radio and secure the mounting bolts.
7. Connect the wiring, making sure connectors are firmly and squarely seated.

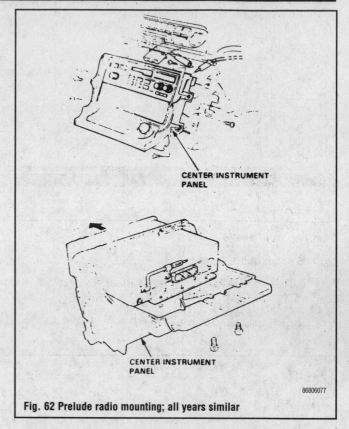

CENTER INSTRUMENT PANEL

CENTER INSTRUMENT PANEL

Fig. 62 Prelude radio mounting; all years similar

8. Fit the entire unit into the dash, taking care not to pinch or damage wiring.
9. Install the front console.
10. Connect the negative battery cable. If applicable, enable the SRS.

Speakers

REMOVAL & INSTALLATION

Front

The front door panel must be removed to gain access to the speaker. Remove the speaker retaining screws and remove the speaker; disconnect the speaker

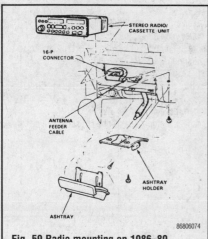

STEREO RADIO/ CASSETTE UNIT

16-P CONNECTOR

ANTENNA FEEDER CABLE

ASHTRAY HOLDER

ASHTRAY

Fig. 59 Radio mounting on 1986–89 Accords

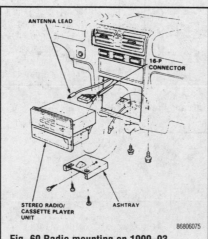

ANTENNA LEAD

16-P CONNECTOR

STEREO RADIO/ CASSETTE PLAYER UNIT

ASHTRAY

Fig. 60 Radio mounting on 1990–93 Accords

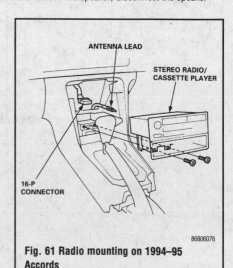

ANTENNA LEAD

STEREO RADIO/ CASSETTE PLAYER

16-P CONNECTOR

Fig. 61 Radio mounting on 1994–95 Accords

wiring. Most of the front speakers are set into a plastic sleeve or protector in the door. This protects the speaker from water and moisture in the door. Make sure the shield is in place when reinstalling the speakers.

Rear

ACCORD

On Accord hatchbacks, remove the speaker grille or cover. Some are press-fit in place, others are held by plastic retaining pins. Look carefully before prying. Once the speaker is exposed, remove the retaining screws and remove the speaker. On 1984–85 Accord sedans, remove the speaker cover. Carefully lift or remove the rear shelf to gain access to the speaker; remove the retaining screws and the speaker. The 1986–89 sedans, remove the speaker grille, then remove the screws securing the speaker. On 1990–95 Accord sedans, three speaker

retaining nuts must be removed from the trunk side. While in there, disconnect the wiring. Then remove the speaker grille and remove the speaker.

All the rear speakers sit in some type of support or frame. This provides both a firm mount and isolates the speaker from its surroundings, preventing distortion. Make sure the frame is present when reinstalling the speaker.

PRELUDE

On 1984–91 Preludes, remove the speaker grille, then remove the screws securing the radio. On 1992–95 models, three speaker retaining nuts must be removed from inside the trunk. While in there, disconnect the wiring, then remove the grille and speaker.

All the rear speakers sit in some type of support or frame. This provides both a firm mount and isolates the speaker from its surroundings, preventing distortion. Make sure the frame is present when reinstalling the speaker.

WINDSHIELD WASHERS AND WIPERS

Blade and Arm

REMOVAL & INSTALLATION

♦ **See Figures 63 and 64**

1. To remove the wiper blades (front or rear), lift up on the spring release tab on the wiper blade-to-wiper arm connector.
2. Pull the blade assembly off the wiper arm.
3. To replace a wiper arm, unscrew the acorn nut which secures it to the pivot and carefully pull the arm upward and off the pivot. Install the arm by reversing this procedure. Make certain the wiper arm is reinstalled in the correct position; if not correctly aligned, the blade will slap the bodywork at the top or bottom of its stroke.

➡**If one wiper arm does not move when turned on or only moves a little bit, check the retaining nut at the bottom of the arm. The extra effort of**

moving snow or wet leaves off the glass can cause the nut to come loose; the pivot will then move without moving the arm.

Windshield Wiper Motor and Linkage

REMOVAL & INSTALLATION

♦ **See Figures 65, 66, 67 and 68**

1. Disconnect the negative battery cable.
2. Remove the cap nuts and remove the wiper arms.
3. Remove the air grille or cowl. Use care not to mar the finish. The panels are held by plastic clips; the heads look like screws. Remove the plastic liner or seal below the cowl.
4. If the motor has a protective cover, remove it.
5. Unplug the wiring connector to the wiper motor.

86806078

Fig. 63 Remove the nut securing the wiper arm . . .

86806079

Fig. 64 . . . then lift the arm off the pivot

86806080

Fig. 65 Remove the clips securing the cowl, then remove it from the vehicle

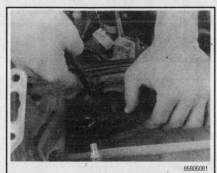
86806081

Fig. 66 On early model Accords and Preludes, the linkage is pried off the drive arm

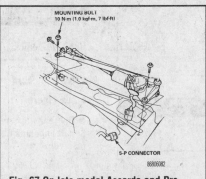
86806082

Fig. 67 On late model Accords and Preludes, remove the entire linkage assembly. . .

86806083

Fig. 68 . . . then unbolt the motor from the linkage

6. On 1984–89 Accords and 1984–91 Preludes, pry the wiper linkage rod off the motor drive arm. The joint is a ball-and-socket type, but can be very stiff to remove.

7. On 1990–95 Accords and 1992–95 Preludes, remove the bolts securing the linkage/motor assembly, then remove the assembly from the vehicle. Remove the center nut and washer to disconnect the motor shaft from the linkage.

8. Remove the mounting bolts and remove the motor.

9. If the linkage is to be removed on 1984–89 Accords and 1984–91 Preludes, disconnect the rods from the wiper pivots. Joints are ball-and-socket and may be carefully pried apart. The pivots are bolted to the firewall and may be unbolted for replacement.

10. Reassemble in reverse order. Make certain the linkage is firmly connected to the motor. Tighten the mounting bolts to 7 ft. lbs. (10 Nm). Tighten the center nut on 1990–95 Accords and 1992–95 Preludes to 13 ft. lbs. (18 Nm). When reinstalling the wiper arms, allow about 1 in. (25mm) of clearance between the base of the windshield and the blade. If the wipers are too far out of position they may slap either the bottom molding or pillar trim when operating.

Rear Wiper Motor

REMOVAL & INSTALLATION

▶ **See Figure 69**

1. Disconnect the negative battery cable.
2. Remove the tonneau (luggage cover) if equipped and remove the inner trim panel from the hatch lid.
3. Remove the wiper arm from the outside of the hatch lid. Remove the caps, washers and shaft nut from the wiper arm shaft.
4. Unplug the wiring from the wiper motor.
5. Remove the mounting bolts and remove the motor.
6. Reassemble in reverse order. Make certain the linkage is firmly connected to the motor. Tighten the mounting bolts to 7 ft. lbs. (10 Nm). When reinstalling the wiper arm, allow about 1 in. (25mm) of clearance between the base of the glass and the blade. If the wiper is too far out of position it may slap the bottom molding or pillar trim when operating.

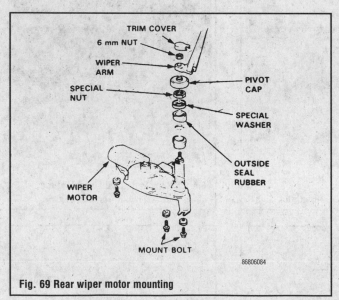

Fig. 69 Rear wiper motor mounting

Wiper Controller/Relay

REMOVAL & INSTALLATION

▶ **See Figures 70 and 71**

The 1984–89 Accord and 1984–87 Prelude wiper system operates through a wiper relay. On Accords, it is located on the underdash fuse box. On Preludes it is located under the dash, just to the right of the steering column. The relay

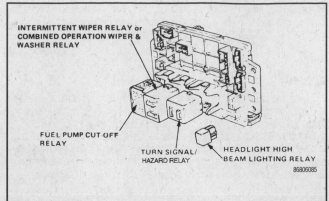

Fig. 70 Early models use a wiper control relay

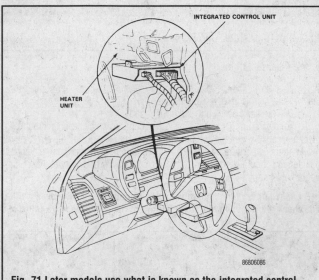

Fig. 71 Later models use what is known as the integrated control unit

controls the intermittent wiper function, cycling the wipers approximately every 5–6 seconds. The relay is removed by unplugging it from the fuseblock.

On 1990 and later Accords, as well as 1988 and later Preludes, the task is assigned to the integrated control unit. On the Accord, this large, multi-function unit is mounted above the left kick panel. On Prelude, it is located under the dash, between the accelerator pedal and the heater box. The integrated control unit oversees operation of the intermittent wipers as well as other circuits requiring a time sense (seat belt buzzers, key chimes, entry lights, etc.). Additionally, a separate intermittent wiper relay is found under the Accord relay box in the right rear corner of the engine compartment.

Windshield Washer Reservoir and Pump

REMOVAL & INSTALLATION

1984–85 Accord

▶ **See Figure 72**

➡**The rear washer for hatchback models works from the front reservoir. Separate pumps for the front and rear circuits are located on the washer reservoir.**

1. Disconnect and remove the battery.
2. Disconnect the washer hose(s) from the pump(s).
3. Unplug the wiring connector.
4. Remove the retaining bolts. Remove the washer reservoir with the motor(s) attached.

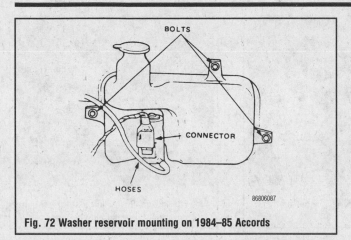

Fig. 72 Washer reservoir mounting on 1984–85 Accords

5. Remove the motor from the reservoir.
6. Reassemble in reverse order.

1986–95 Accord and 1984–95 Prelude

1. Disconnect the negative battery cable.
2. To gain access to the reservoir, either remove the front bumper or engine under cover.
3. Disconnect the filler tube.
4. Unplug the electrical connector and remove the hose(s) from the pump(s).
5. Remove the washer tank with the motor(s) attached by lowering it out of the car.
6. Remove the motor from the reservoir. On Preludes, the motor is held by a retaining clamp.
7. Reassemble in reverse order. Make certain the motor is firmly seated on the reservoir and all clamps and seals are in place. Don't forget to connect the wiring and hoses. Take care to align the bumper properly.

INSTRUMENTS AND SWITCHES

Instrument Cluster

REMOVAL & INSTALLATION

1984–85 Accord

▶ See Figure 73

1. Disconnect the negative battery cable.
2. Remove the steering wheel.
3. Remove the three screws at the top of the bezel (surround or trim piece). Use a spray lubricant such as silicone or vinyl protectant to lubricate the area between the bezel and the dashboard. The panel is a tight fit.
4. Remove the trim panel from the dash. A prytool may be used at the bottom, but great care must be taken not to crack the plastic.
5. When the panel is loose in the dash, remove the 4 screws securing the gauge assembly. Pull the gauge assembly forward just enough to allow access to the wires and speedometer cable.
6. Disconnect the speedometer cable and the electrical harnesses. Do not pull on the wires when disconnecting the harnesses. Remove the gauge assembly.
7. Individual instruments may be removed from the cluster after it is removed from the car. Avoid damage to any terminals or the printed circuit board.
   To install:
8. Install the gauge cluster; connect the wiring and speedometer cable before it is fully in place. Install the retaining screws.
9. Re-lubricate the area contacted by the bezel. Install the bezel, making certain it is evenly placed with no gaps or bends.

10. Install the retaining screws.
11. Install the steering wheel.

1986–89 Accord

▶ See Figures 74, 75, 76, 77 and 78

1. Disconnect the negative battery cable.
2. Lower the steering wheel to its lowest position.
3. Remove each switch from the lower dashboard. The switches may be removed by gently prying up on the bottom edge to release them. Use care to avoid damage to the surrounding area. Once loose, pull the switch straight out and disconnect the wiring.
4. On top of the instrument visor, remove the small access lid. Remove the two screws below the lid.
5. Remove the 4 lower screws (in the ports occupied by the switches). Remove the instrument visor.
6. Remove the 4 screws holding the gauge cluster. Pull it forward just enough to gain access to the wiring and speedometer cable.
7. Disconnect the wiring harness and the speedometer cable. Remove the gauge assembly.
8. Individual instruments may be removed from the cluster after it is removed from the car. Avoid damage to any terminals or the printed circuit board.
   To install:
9. Install the gauge cluster; connect the wiring and speedometer cable before it is fully in place. Install the retaining screws.
10. Install the panel, making sure it is squarely set and properly seated. Install the retaining screws at the top and the bottom.
11. Install the upper lid.
12. Connect the wiring to each switch. Reinstall the switches, making sure they are firmly seated in place.

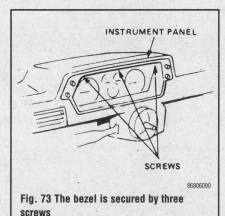

Fig. 73 The bezel is secured by three screws

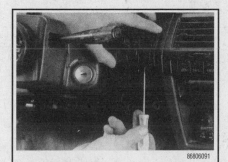

Fig. 74 The switches may be carefully pried from the dash. Although the steering wheel has been removed for clarity, removal is not necessary

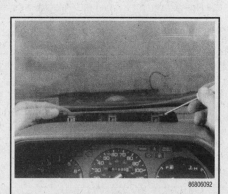

Fig. 75 Remove the small lid on the visor to access the two retaining screws

Fig. 76 After the retaining screws are removed, the visor can be removed from the gauge cluster

Fig. 77 Remove the screws securing the gauge cluster

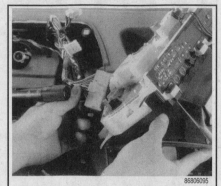

Fig. 78 Pull the cluster out just far enough to access the electrical connections

1990–95 Accord

▶ See Figures 79, 80 and 81

1. Disconnect the negative battery cable. If so equipped, disable the Supplemental Restraint System (SRS).
2. Lower the steering wheel to its lowest position.
3. Remove the center console.
4. Remove the ashtray and ashtray holder.
5. Remove the radio/tape player.
6. Remove the coin box, switches and dash light controller from the instrument panel.

7. On models through 1993, remove the side and center air vents.
8. Remove the mounting screws securing the instrument panel. This is a large, formed piece of plastic—don't crack it.
9. Lay a protective piece of cloth over the steering wheel pad.
10. Remove the four screws holding the instrument cluster. Pull the cluster forward enough to allow access to the wiring connectors.
11. Disconnect the wiring harnesses and remove the instrument cluster.
12. Individual instruments may be removed from the cluster after it is removed from the car. Avoid damage to any terminals or the printed circuit board.

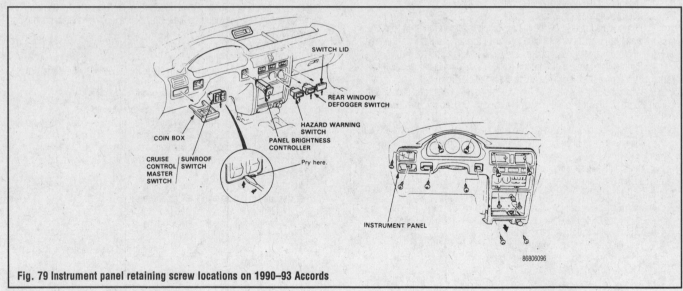

Fig. 79 Instrument panel retaining screw locations on 1990–93 Accords

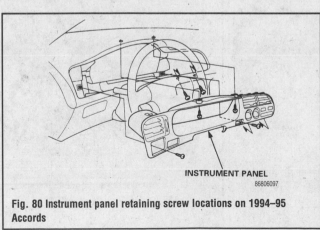

Fig. 80 Instrument panel retaining screw locations on 1994–95 Accords

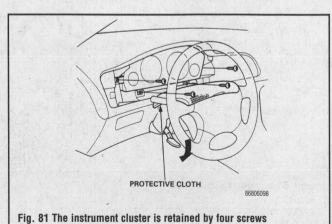

Fig. 81 The instrument cluster is retained by four screws

To install:

13. Install the gauge cluster; connect the wiring before it is fully in place. Install the retaining screws.

14. Install the instrument panel. Make sure it is correctly placed. Install the retaining screws.

15. If applicable, install the air vents.

16. Install the coin box, switches and dash light controller.

17. Install the radio, ashtray holder and ashtray.

18. Install the console.

19. If applicable, enable the SRS.

20. Connect the negative battery cable.

1984–87 Prelude

1. Disconnect the negative battery cable.

2. Lower the steering wheel.

3. Remove the lower dash panel.

4. Remove the four screws securing the instrument panel. Gently pull the panel away from the dash. Reach behind it and unplug the wiring connectors to the switches.

5. Remove the panel.

6. Remove the two screws holding the gauge assembly. They are reached from under the dash and thread upwards.

7. Lift the gauge assembly; disconnect the wiring and the speedometer cable.

8. Remove the gauge assembly.

9. Individual instruments may be removed from the cluster after it is removed from the car. Avoid damage to any terminals or the printed circuit board.

To install:

10. Install the gauge cluster; connect the wiring and speedometer cable before it is fully in place. Install the retaining screws.

11. With the instrument panel loosely in place, connect the wiring to each switch or control.

12. Install the panel, making sure it is properly seated. Install the retaining screws.

13. Install the lower dash panel and reposition the steering wheel if necessary.

1988–91 Prelude

▶ See Figure 82

1. Disconnect the negative battery cable.

2. Lower the steering wheel to its lowest position.

3. Remove the dash light brightness controller and remove the headlight/foglight switch assembly.

4. Remove the five screws securing the instrument panel. Pull the panel away from the dash until the wires and connectors can be reached and disconnected.

5. Remove the four screws holding the gauge assembly and pull the assembly outward a bit. Unplug the wiring connectors without pulling on the wiring.

6. Remove the gauge assembly.

7. Individual instruments may be removed from the cluster after it is removed from the car. Avoid damage to any terminals or the printed circuit board.

To install:

8. Install the gauge cluster; connect the wiring before it is fully in place. Install the retaining screws. Be careful not to pinch any wiring during installation.

9. Install the panel and the five screws.

10. Install the dash light controller and the lighting switches.

1992–95 Prelude

▶ See Figures 83, 84, 85 and 86

1. Disconnect the battery cables, then disable the Supplemental Restraint System (SRS).

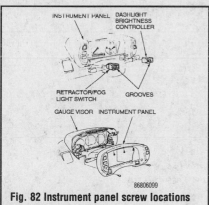

Fig. 82 Instrument panel screw locations on 1988–91 Preludes

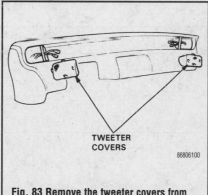

Fig. 83 Remove the tweeter covers from the dashboard

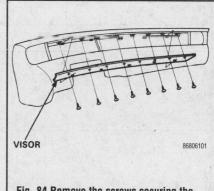

Fig. 84 Remove the screws securing the instrument panel visor

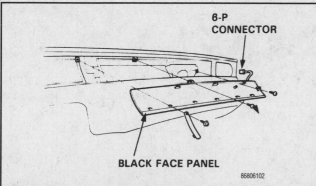

Fig. 85 Remove the screws and black face panel, then unplug the connector from the clock reset switch

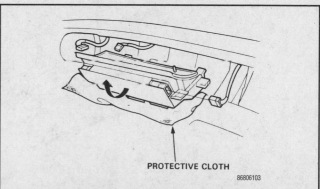

Fig. 86 Remove the screws securing the gauge assembly, then pull it out slightly and unplug the connectors

2. Remove the tweeter covers from the dashboard.

3. Remove the screws securing the instrument panel visor.

4. Remove the screws and black face panel, then unplug the connector from the clock reset switch.

5. Place a protective piece of cloth over the dashboard.

6. Remove the screws securing the gauge assembly, then pull it out slightly and unplug the connectors.

7. Individual instruments may be removed from the cluster after it is removed from the car. Avoid damage to any terminals or the printed circuit board.

To install:

8. Position the cluster on the dash and engage the wiring. Install the retaining screws.

9. Connect the wiring for the clock reset switch and install the black face panel.

10. Install the dash visor and tweeter covers.

11. Enable the SRS, then connect the battery cables.

Speedometer, Tachometer and Gauges

REMOVAL & INSTALLATION

▶ **See Figure 87**

Once the instrument cluster has been removed, the speedometer, tachometer and gauges can usually be replaced using the same basic procedure. In most cases, removal of the gauges involves disassembling the printed circuit board and front lens from the meter. The gauges are normally secured by a series of small screws or bolts. Be careful not to damage the indicator needles and gauge faces when disassembling the meter.

Speedometer Cable

REMOVAL & INSTALLATION

➡**This procedure only applies to 1984–89 Accords and 1984–91 Preludes. Later models use an electronic speedometer that receives pulses from a vehicle speed sensor.**

1. Disconnect the negative battery cable.

2. Remove the instrument cluster and disconnect the cable at the speedometer. On some models it may be possible to disconnect the cable by reaching under the dash. Some connectors screw onto the back of the speedometer; others are held by plastic clips.

3. Disconnect the other end of the speedometer cable at the transaxle housing and pull the cable from its jacket at the transmission end. If you are replacing the cable because it is broken, don't forget to remove both pieces of broken cable.

4. Lubricate the new cable with graphite speedometer cable lubricant and feed it into the cable jacket from the lower end.

5. Connect the cable to the transaxle, then to the speedometer. Note that both ends of the cable are square; the ends must fit properly in the fittings.

6. Install the instrument cluster.

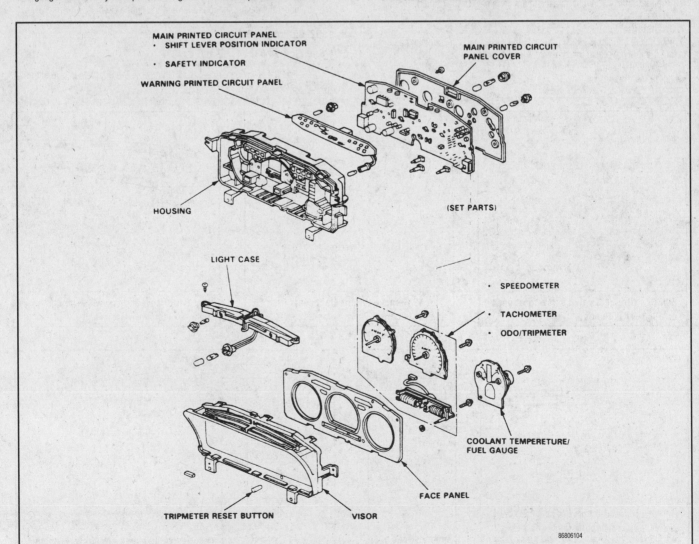

MAIN PRINTED CIRCUIT PANEL
• SHIFT LEVER POSITION INDICATOR
• SAFETY INDICATOR
WARNING PRINTED CIRCUIT PANEL
MAIN PRINTED CIRCUIT PANEL COVER
HOUSING
(SET PARTS)
LIGHT CASE
• SPEEDOMETER
• TACHOMETER
• ODO/TRIPMETER
COOLANT TEMPERATURE/ FUEL GAUGE
FACE PANEL
TRIPMETER RESET BUTTON
VISOR

86806104

Fig. 87 The gauge cluster can be disassembled to replace individual components

Vehicle Speed Sensor

REMOVAL & INSTALLATION

▶ **See Figure 88**

➡This procedure applies to 1990–95 Accords and 1992–95 Preludes only. These models are equipped with an electronic speedometer that uses the pulses generated by the speed sensor to determine vehicle speed.

1. Disconnect the negative battery cable.
2. Unplug the electrical connector from the speed sensor.
3. Remove the three bolts securing the speed sensor to the transaxle.
4. Remove the sensor from the transaxle. Be careful not to lose the drive link; it is a very small part.
5. Installation is the reverse of removal. Tighten the bolts until snug.

Printed Circuit Board

REMOVAL & INSTALLATION

▶ **See Figure 87**

The printed circuit board is attached to the back of the instrument cluster. It is usually secured by a series of screws/nuts and by the bulb sockets. These sockets are normally removed by first twisting, then pulling them from the meter. Do not force any components as they are easily damaged.

Combination Switch

REMOVAL & INSTALLATION

In some cases, the headlight/turn signal and wiper switches are not individually replaceable. If either switch fails (or the lever breaks off), the entire combination switch must be replaced. In general, later models may have replaceable switches.

1984–87 Prelude and 1984–89 Accord

▶ **See Figure 89**

1. Disconnect the negative battery cable.
2. Remove the steering wheel.
3. Remove the upper and lower column covers.
4. If equipped with cruise control, disconnect and remove the slip ring assembly.

5. Remove the turn signal canceling sleeve. This is a small fitting on the steering shaft inside the combination switch.
6. Unplug the wiring harness connectors for the combination switch.
7. On Prelude, remove the screws securing the slip ring guard and remove the guard.
8. Remove the screws securing the combination switch. Carefully remove the switch from the steering shaft.

➡Check the switch closely; some versions have a removable wiper switch assembly held by retaining screws. Replacement cost for the single switch is much lower than for the entire assembly.

To install:
9. Install the wiper switch if it was removed.
10. Install the combination switch on the steering shaft and route the wiring harnesses properly.
11. Install the retaining screws and connect the harness connectors.
12. Install the cancel sleeve and install the slip ring guard.
13. Install the upper and lower column covers.
14. Install the steering wheel.
15. Connect the negative battery cable.

1988–91 Prelude

▶ **See Figure 90**

1. Disconnect the negative battery cable.
2. Remove the steering wheel.
3. Unplug the wiring connector for the switch to be removed. The lighting switch involves a 14-pin connector at the main harness and an 8-pin connector at the fusebox. The wiper switch requires disconnecting the 10-pin connector at the fusebox.
4. Remove the lower dashboard panel.
5. Remove the upper and lower covers from the steering column.
6. Remove the two screws securing either the headlight or wiper switch to the housing and slide the switch outward. Be advised these mounting screws are tight; use a screwdriver of the correct size to avoid damaging the screw heads.
7. Installation is the reverse of removal. Make certain all wiring connections are tight and the harnesses are secured in place.

1990–95 Accord and 1992–95 Prelude

▶ **See Figure 91**.

1. Disconnect the negative battery cable. If so equipped, disable the Supplemental Restraint System (SRS).
2. Remove the dashboard lower cover and knee bolster.
3. Remove the upper and lower column covers.
4. Remove the two screws securing either the headlight or wiper switch to the housing and slide the switch outward. Be advised these mounting screws

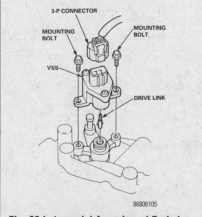

3-P CONNECTOR
MOUNTING BOLT
MOUNTING BOLT
VSS
DRIVE LINK

86806105

Fig. 88 Late model Accords and Preludes use an electronic speedometer that uses the pulses generated by the speed sensor to determine vehicle speed

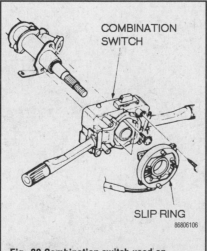

COMBINATION SWITCH
SLIP RING
86806106

Fig. 89 Combination switch used on 1984–87 Preludes and 1984–89 Accords

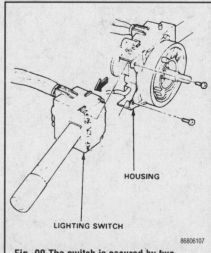

HOUSING
LIGHTING SWITCH
86806107

Fig. 90 The switch is secured by two screws

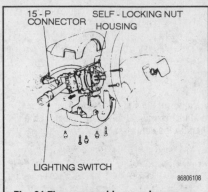

Fig. 91 The upper and lower column covers must be removed to access the switch

Fig. 92 Carefully pull the clock bezel from the dash

Fig. 93 Be careful not to break the locktab on the connector when unplugging it

are tight; use a screwdriver of the correct size to avoid damaging the screw heads. Remove the steering wheel if additional access to the screws is needed.

5. Unplug the wiring connector.
6. Installation is the reverse of removal. Make certain all wiring connections are tight and the harnesses are secured in place. If applicable, be sure to enable the SRS.

Clock

REMOVAL & INSTALLATION

Dashboard Mounted

▶ See Figures 92 and 93

1. Disconnect the negative battery cable.
2. Carefully pull the clock bezel from the dash.
3. Remove the screws securing the clock to the dash.
4. Pull the clock out slightly and unplug the electrical connector.
5. Installation is the reverse of removal.

Front Console Mounted

▶ See Figure 94

1. Disconnect the negative battery cable.
2. Remove the rear console.
3. Remove the screws securing the front console cover and pull the assembly out slightly.
4. Unplug the electrical connectors on the back of the panel.

![Front console clock diagram]

Fig. 94 The clock is secured to the console panel by two screws

5. Remove the screws securing the clock, then remove it from the panel.
6. Installation is the reverse of removal.

Ignition Switch

REMOVAL & INSTALLATION

1984–93 Accord and 1984–95 Prelude

▶ See Figure 95

1. Disconnect the negative battery cable. If so equipped, disable the Supplemental Restraint System (SRS).
2. On 1988–91 Preludes and 1990–93 Accords, remove the steering wheel.
3. On 1992–95 Preludes, remove the dashboard lower cover/knee bolster and left kick panel.
4. Remove the steering column covers.
5. Unplug the ignition switch connector.
6. Insert the key and turn it to the **0** position.
7. If present, remove the tape on the switch wires.
8. On 1992–95 Preludes remove the screw securing the switch cover, then remove the cover.
9. Remove the two screws securing the switch, then remove the switch.

To install:

10. Make certain the recess of the switch aligns with the tab of the lock housing. Insert the switch and install the retaining screws.
11. If applicable, install the switch cover and retape the wires.
12. Remove the key.
13. Connect the wiring harness to the ignition switch.
14. Reinstall the steering column covers.
15. Install the steering wheel or any other applicable trim panels.
16. If applicable, enable the SRS.
17. Connect the negative battery cable.

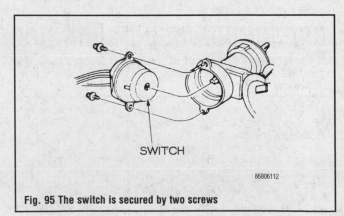

Fig. 95 The switch is secured by two screws

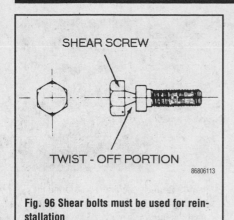

Fig. 96 Shear bolts must be used for reinstallation

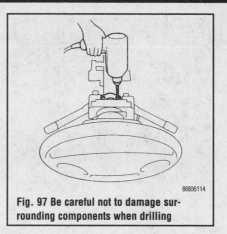

Fig. 97 Be careful not to damage surrounding components when drilling

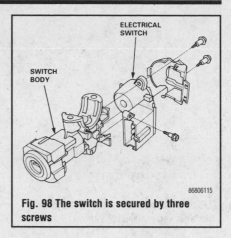

Fig. 98 The switch is secured by three screws

1994–95 Accord

▶ **See Figures 96, 97 and 98**

➡ Do not attempt to remove the ignition switch assembly if you do not have replacement bolts available. These special bolts have break-away heads which shear off when tightened. This is an "anti-theft" measure used to prevent easy removal of the bolts.

1. Disconnect the negative battery cable and disable the SRS system.
2. Remove the dashboard lower cover/knee bolster.
3. Remove the steering column covers.
4. Unplug the ignition switch connector.
5. Remove the two nuts and two bolts securing the steering column, carefully lower the column assembly.
6. Use a center punch to mark each of the two shear bolt heads securing the ignition switch assembly to the steering column. Use a 3/16 in. (5mm) drill bit to drill off the heads. Take care not to damage the switch when drilling.

7. Remove the bolts. Remove the clamp and remove the ignition switch assembly.
8. Remove the three screws securing the switch and remove the switch.

To install:

9. Make certain the recess of the switch aligns with the tab of the lock housing. Insert the switch and install the retaining screws.
10. Position the switch assembly on the steering column. Install the new shear bolts; tighten them finger-tight.
11. Use a wrench or socket of the correct size. Tighten the shear bolts until the heads break off.
12. Raise the column and install the nuts/bolts. Tighten the nuts to 10 ft. lbs. (13 Nm) and the bolts to 16 ft. lbs. 22 Nm).
13. Connect the ignition switch wiring harness.
14. Install the column covers.
15. Install the dashboard lower cover/knee bolster.
16. Connect the negative battery cable.

LIGHTING

Headlights

There are two general styles of headlamps, the sealed beam and replaceable bulb type. The sealed beam is by far the most common and includes almost all of the circular and rectangular lamps found on vehicles built through the 1980s. The sealed beam is so named because it includes the lamp (filament), the reflector and the lens in one sealed unit. Sealed beams are available in several sizes and shapes. All Honda vehicles covered in this book except the 1990–95 Accord and 1992–95 Prelude use sealed beam headlights. These latest Accords and Preludes use replaceable bulbs in fixed housings.

REMOVAL & INSTALLATION

Sealed Beams

▶ **See Figures 99 thru 104**

※ **CAUTION**

Most headlight retaining rings and trim bezels have very sharp edges. Wear gloves. Never pry or push on a headlamp; it can shatter suddenly.

1. On cars with pop-up or retracting headlamps, turn the ignition switch **OFF**. Operate the retractor switch on the dash to bring the headlight doors up. The headlights should be off when the doors are up.
2. Remove the headlight bezel (trim). On 1984–85 Accord, the trim involves the one piece lamp surround and corner molding.
3. The sealed beam is held in place by a retainer and either 2 or 4 small screws. Identify these screws before applying any tools. Do not confuse the small retaining screws with the larger aiming screws. There will be two aiming screws or adjustors for each lamp. (One adjustor controls the up/down motion and the other controls the left/right motion.) Identify the adjustors and avoid

them during removal. If they are not disturbed, the new headlamp should be in identical aim to the old one.
4. Using a small screwdriver (preferably magnetic) and a pair of needle-nose pliers if necessary, remove the small screws in the headlamp retainer.

➡ A good kitchen or household magnet placed on the shank of the screwdriver will provide enough grip to hold the screw during removal.

5. Remove the retainer and the headlamp may be gently pulled free from its mounts. Detach the connector from the back of the sealed beam unit and remove the unit from the car.

To install:

6. Place the new headlamp in position and connect the wiring harness. Remember to install the rubber boot on the back of the new lamp. Also, make sure the headlight is right-side up.
7. Have an assistant turn on the headlights and check the new lamp for proper function, checking both high and low beams before final assembly.

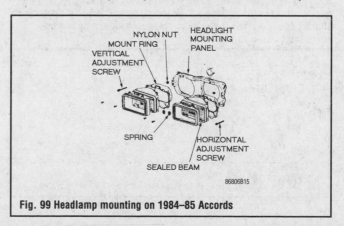

Fig. 99 Headlamp mounting on 1984–85 Accords

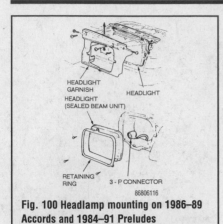

Fig. 100 Headlamp mounting on 1986–89 Accords and 1984–91 Preludes

Fig. 101 Remove the screws securing the headlight bezel

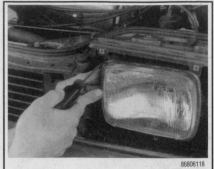

Fig. 102 Remove the screws securing the retaining ring. Be sure not to disturb the adjusting screws

Fig. 103 Remove the retaining ring . . .

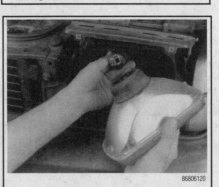

Fig. 104 . . . then unplug the connector from the back of the lamp. Be sure to transfer the rubber boot to the new lamp

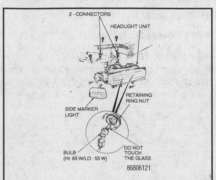

Fig. 105 Late model Accords and preludes are equipped with replaceable bulb head-lamps

8. Install the retainer and the small screws that secure it.
9. Reinstall the headlight trim.

Replaceable Bulb

▶ See Figure 105

1. Disconnect the negative battery cable.
2. Raise and prop the hood.
3. Remove any components necessary to access the lamp.
4. Unplug the connector from the back of the lamp. The connector may be very tight and require wiggling to loosen; support the lamp while with your other hand while wiggling the connector loose.
5. Turn the retaining ring counterclockwise, then pull the bulb from the lamp housing.
   To install:

✳✳ WARNING

Hold the new bulb by the base; do not touch the glass part with fingers or gloves. The grease left on the glass will form hot spots and shorten the life of the bulb. If the glass is accidentally touched, clean the glass with alcohol.

6. Install the new bulb. Make certain all three guide tabs fit into their correct slots. Turn the ring clockwise to lock it in place.
7. Engage the wiring connector firmly.
8. Connect the negative battery cable and turn the headlights on. Check both high and low beam function.
9. Reinstall any components removed for lamp access.

AIMING

▶ See Figures 106 and 107

The head lamps should be aimed using a special alignment tool, however this procedure may be used for temporary adjustment. Local regula-tions may vary regarding head lamp aiming, consult with your local authori-ties.

1. Verify the tires are at their proper inflation pressure. Clean the head lamp lenses and make sure there are no heavy loads in the trunk. The gas tank should be filled.
2. Position the vehicle on a level surface facing a flat wall 25 ft. (7.7 m) away.
3. Measure and record the distance from the floor to the center of the head lamp. Place a strip of tape across the wall at this same height.
4. Place strips of tape on the wall, perpendicular to the first measurement, indicating the vehicle centerline and the centerline of both head lamps.
5. Rock the vehicle side-to-side a few times to allow the suspension to stabilize.
6. Turn the lights on, adjust the head lamps to achieve a high intensity pattern in the areas shown in the illustrations.

Signal, Marker and Interior Lamps

REMOVAL & INSTALLATION

▶ See Figures 108 thru 122

✳✳ WARNING

Any light bulb gets hot when operating. If you're removing a good bulb to test or work on the circuit, either wear gloves or disconnect the circuit and allow the lamp to cool before removal.

The lens or lighting assembly is generally removed to allow access to the bulb. Removable external lenses usually have a rubber gasket around them to keep dust and water out of the housing; the gasket must be present and in good condition at reinstallation.

Newer cars use many sealed lamp units, the lens is not separately removable for bulb access. These sealed units are much more efficient at eliminating dust and water from the housing; bulb access is from the rear of the unit. In this case, the assembly must be removed from its mount. In some cases, the mount-

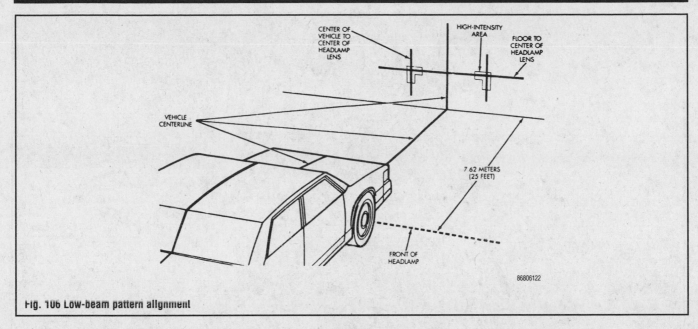

Fig. 106 Low-beam pattern alignment

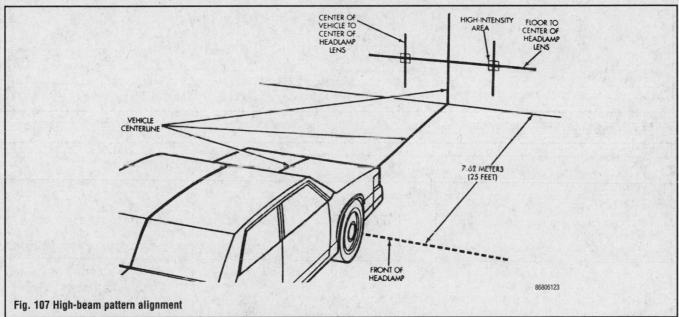

Fig. 107 High-beam pattern alignment

Fig. 108 Some bulbs can be removed by simply pulling them out

ing screws are visible and in other situations, the lamp is on a bracket which secures the lamp.

Whenever an assembly is to be removed, study the situation carefully; other trim pieces may need to be removed to expose retaining screws. Always beware of any hidden screws.

For the rear lamps, front marker lamps and some front turn signals, the socket and bulb is removed from the lens with a counterclockwise turn. Once the socket is removed from the lens, the bulb is removed either with a half-twist motion or, on smaller bulbs, by pulling it straight out. Use care and wear gloves; bulbs can break easily.

When installing new lamps, note that the socket for some turn signal bulbs have two different length guide grooves; the lamp only fits correctly one way. It is possible to do it wrong, but it requires a lot of force. If you find that you're pushing on the bulb with no result during installation, you've probably got it backwards.

Smaller interior lenses usually fit in place with plastic clips and must be pried or popped out of place. A small, flat, plastic tool is ideal for this job; if other tools are used, care must be taken not to break the lens or the clip.

The lamps used on Honda vehicles are all US standard and may be purchased at most auto parts stores or at the dealer. Because of the variety of lamps used on any vehicle, take the old one with you when shopping for the replacement.

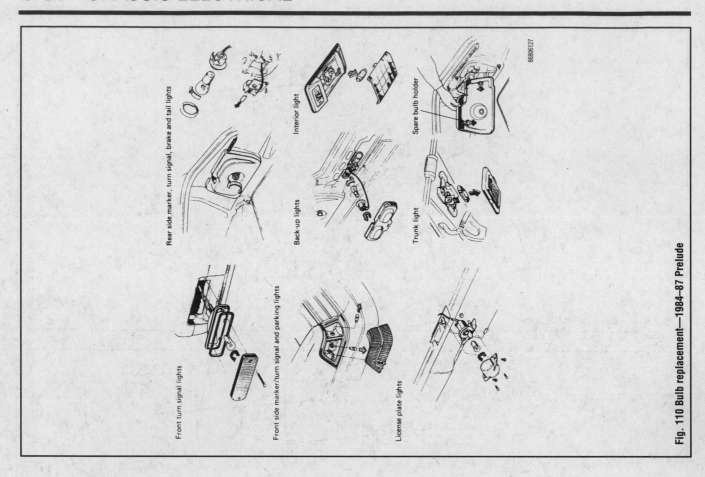

Fig. 110 Bulb replacement—1984–87 Prelude

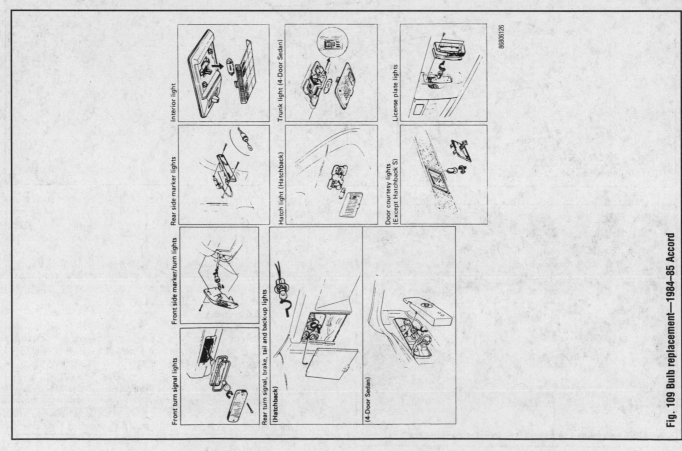

Fig. 109 Bulb replacement—1984–85 Accord

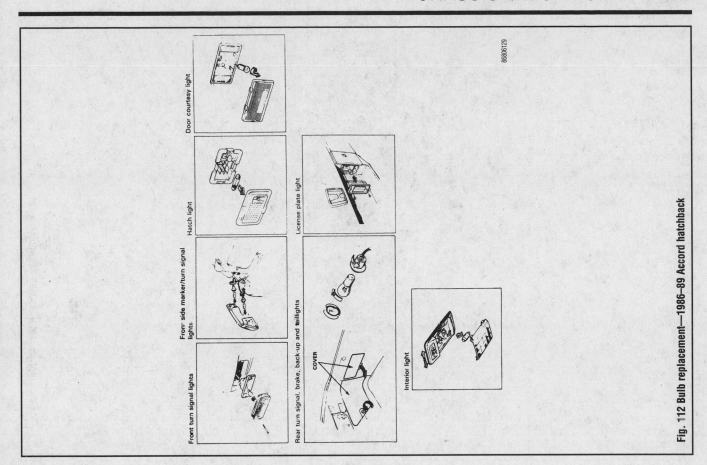

Fig. 112 Bulb replacement—1986–89 Accord hatchback

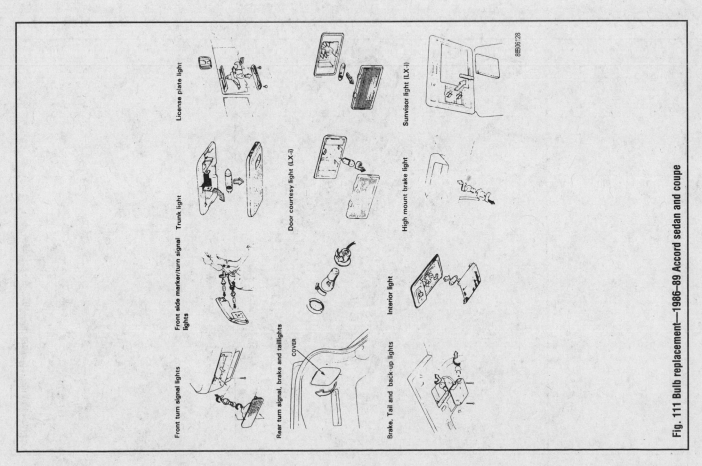

Fig. 111 Bulb replacement—1986–89 Accord sedan and coupe

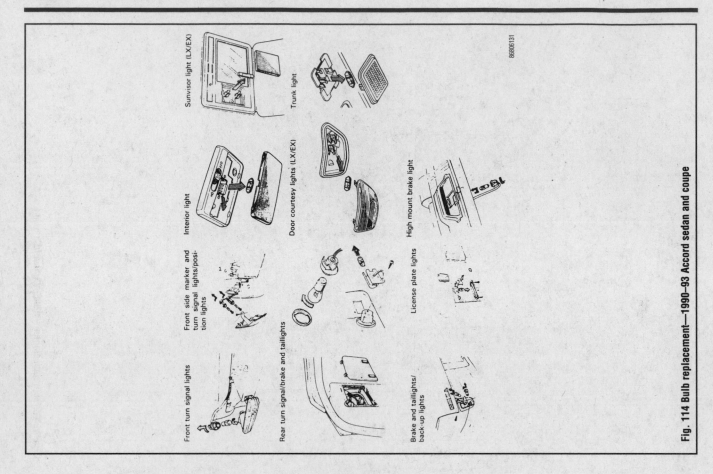

Fig. 114 Bulb replacement—1990–93 Accord sedan and coupe

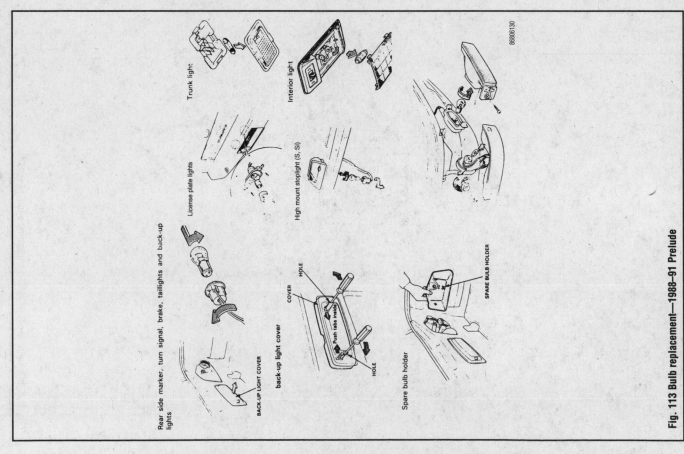

Fig. 113 Bulb replacement—1988–91 Prelude

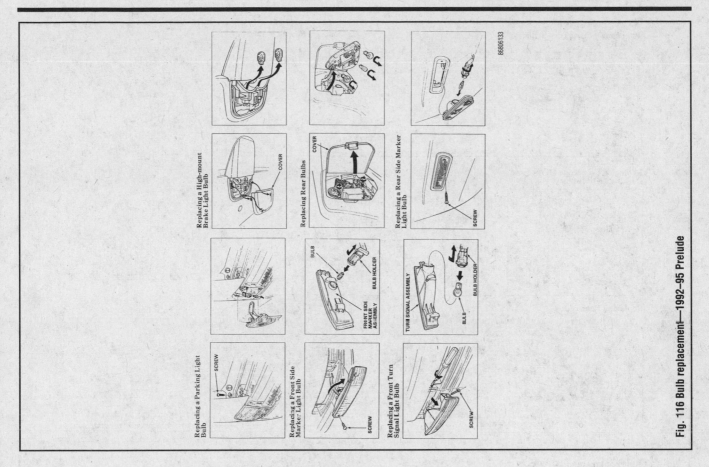

Fig. 116 Bulb replacement—1992–95 Prelude

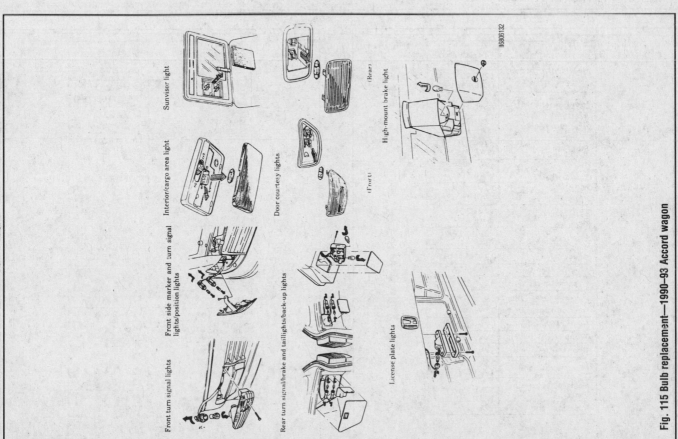

Fig. 115 Bulb replacement—1990–93 Accord wagon

Replacing a Front Turn Signal
Light Bulb

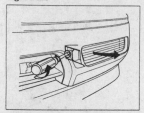

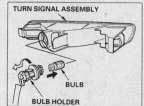

Replacing a Rear Side Marker
Light Bulb

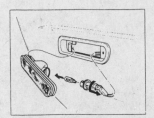

Replacing Front Side Marker and
Parking Light Bulbs

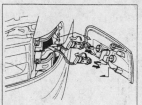

Replacing a High-mount Brake
Light Bulb

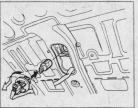

CEILING LIGHT

Replacing Rear Bulbs

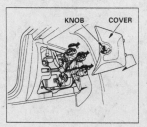

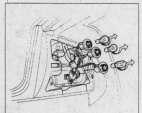

Replacing a Rear License Bulb

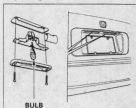

Replacing a Trunk Light Bulb

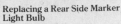

86806134

Fig. 117 Bulb replacement—1994–95 Accord

Lights

Headlights	Low	12V–35/35 W (SAE 4656)
	High	12V–50W (SAE 4651)
Front turn signal		12V–32/3 CP (SAE 1157)
Rear turn signal		12V–32 CP (SAE 1156)
Stop/Tail lights		12V–32/3 CP (SAE 1157)
Side marker lights	Front	12V–2 CP (SAE 194)
	Rear	12V–2 CP (SAE 194)
Back-up lights		12V–32 CP (SAE 1156)
License lights		12V–4 CP (SAE 67)
Gauge lights		12V–3.4/1.2W
Indicator lights		12V–1.2W
Warning lights		12V–1.2W
Glove box light		12V–3.4W
Interior lights		12V–8W
Vanity Mirror light		12V–1.8W
Trunk or Hatch light		12V–5W
Door courtesy lights		12V–3.4W
Illumination lights		12V–1.2/ 1.4/1.5W
Heater illumination lights		12V–1.4W
Fuse box light		12V–2W

86806135

Fig. 118 Light bulb application—1984–85 Accord

Lights

Headlights	High/ Low	12V–65/35 W (2BI)
Front turn signal		12 V–32/3 CP (SAE 1156/194)
Rear turn signal		12 V–32 CP (SAE 1156)
Stop/Tail lights		12 V–32/3 CP (SAE 1157)
Stop light (Rear shelf)		12 V–32 CP (SAE 1156)
Side marker lights	Front	12V–3 CP (SAE 194)
	Rear	12V–3 CP (SAE 194)
Back-up lights		12 V–32 CP (SAE 1156)
License lights		12 V–4 CP (SAE 67)
Interior light		12V–8 W
Trunk light		12V–3.4 W
Glove box light		12V–3.4 W
Illumination lights		12V–1.4 W 12V–1.2 W
Gauge illumination lights		12V–1.4 W 12V–3.4 W
Indicator and warning lights		12V–1.4 W 12V–1.2 W

86806136

Fig. 119 Light bulb application—1984–87 Prelude

Lights		
Headlight	Low/ High	12V – 35/65W (SAE H6052)
Front turn signal		12V – 32CP (SAE 1156)
Rear turn signal		12V – 32CP (SAE 1156)
Stop/Tail lights		12V – 32/2CP (SAE 2057)
High mount brake light		12V – 32CP (SAE 1156)
Interior lights		12V – 8W
Trunk light		12V – 3.4W
Door courtesy lights		12V – 3.4W
Side marker lights	Front	12V – 5W
	Rear	12V – 3CP (SAE 168)
Back-up lights		12V – 32CP (SAE 1156)
License plate lights		12V – 8W
Sunvisor light (LX-i only)		12V – 2W

86806137

Fig. 120 Light bulb application—1986–89 Accord

Lights		
Headlight	High/ Low	12V – 65/35W (2BI)
Front turn signal		12V – 45CP (SAE 3497)
Rear turn signal		12V – 32CP (SAE 1156)
Stop/Taillights		12V – 32/2CP (SAE 1156/194)
Side marker lights	Front	12V – 3CP (SAE 194)
	Rear	12V – 3CP (SAE 194)
Back-up lights		12V – 32CP (SAE 1156)
License lights		12V – 4CP (SAE 67)
Interior light		12V – 8W
Trunk light		12V – 3.4W

86806138

Fig. 121 Light bulb application—1988–91 Prelude

Lights	
Headlights	12V – 65/55W
Front turn signal lights	12V – 45CP (SAE 3497)
Front position lights	12V – 5W (6CP) (SAE 3652)
Rear turn signal lights	12V – 45CP
Stop/Taillights	12V – 43/3CP
Side marker lights Front	12V – 5W
Rear	12V – 43/3CP
Back-up lights	12V – 32CP (SAE 1156)
High-mount brake lamp	12V – 45CP (SAE 3497)
License plate lights	12V – 8W (4CP)
Interior light	12V – 8W
Cargo area light	12V – 3.4W
Vanity mirror light	12V – 1.8W
Door courtesy lights	12V – 3.4W

86806139

Fig. 122 Light bulb application—1990–95 Accord and 1992–95 Prelude

TRAILER WIRING

Wiring the car for towing is fairly easy. There are a number of good wiring kits available and these should be used, rather than trying to design your own.

All trailers will need brake lights and turn signals as well as tail lights and side marker lights. Most states require extra marker lights for overwide trailers. Also, most states have recently required back-up lights for trailers, and most trailer manufacturers have been building trailers with back up lights for several years.

Additionally, some Class I, most Class II and just about all Class III trailers will have electric brakes. Add to this number an accessories wire, to operate trailer internal equipment or to charge the trailer's battery, and you can have as many as seven wires in the harness.

Determine the equipment on your trailer and buy the wiring kit necessary. The kit will contain all the wires needed, plus a plug adapter set which included the female plug, mounted on the bumper or hitch, and the male plug, wired into, or plugged into the trailer harness.

When installing the kit, follow the manufacturer's instructions. The color coding of the wires is usually standard throughout the industry. One point to note: some domestic vehicles, and most imported vehicles, have separate turn signals. On most domestic vehicles, the brake lights and rear turn signals operate with the same bulb. For those vehicles with separate turn signals, you can purchase an isolation unit so that the brake lights won't blink whenever the turn signals are operated, or, you can go to your local electronics supply house and buy four diodes to wire in series with the brake and turn signal bulbs. Diodes will isolate the brake and turn signals. The choice is yours. The isolation units are simple and quick to install, but far more expensive than the diodes. The diodes, however, require more work to install properly, since they require the cutting of each bulb's wire and soldering in place of the diode.

One, final point, the best kits are those with a spring loaded cover on the vehicle mounted socket. This cover prevent dirt and moisture from corroding the terminals. Never let the vehicle socket hang loosely; always mount it securely to the bumper or hitch.

CIRCUIT PROTECTION

Fuses

REPLACEMENT

▶ See Figures 123, 124 and 125

The fuse block is located below the left side of the instrument panel on all vehicles. Additional fuses are found on the underhood relay board. The radio or audio unit is protected by an additional fuse in the body of the unit. In the event that anything electrical isn't working, the fuse should be the first item checked. Generally, the in-car fusebox holds fuses for the cabin circuits such as wipers, cigarette lighter, rear defogger, etc. The underhood fusebox generally contains fuses and relays for engine and major electrical systems such as air conditioning, headlights (left and right separately), fuel injection components, etc.

Each fuse location is labeled on the fuseblock, identifying its primary circuit, but designations such as BACKUP, CCON or IG 1 may not tell you what you need to know. A fuse can control more than one circuit, so check related circuits as well. This sharing of fuses is necessary to conserve space and wiring.

The underdash or underhood fusebox contains a fuse puller which can be used to grip and remove the fuse. The fuse cannot be checked while in the fuse-

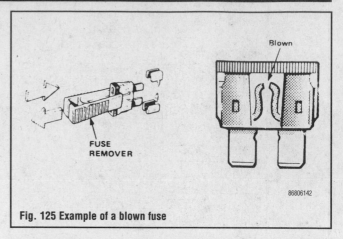

Fig. 125 Example of a blown fuse

block; it must be removed. View the fuse from the side, looking for a broken element in the center.

✳✳ WARNING

Do not use fuses of a higher amperage than recommended. Major component damage and even fire may result.

Fusible Links

REPLACEMENT

▶ See Figures 126, 127 and 128

The fusible links serve as main circuit protection for certain high amperage circuits. The Honda fusible or main links are located at the in the underhood fuse and relay box. On earlier models, these are large strips of conductive metal held by bolts between two terminals. The thickness and length of the material determines the amperage rating of the link. To replace one of these, disconnect the negative battery cable, unscrew the failed one and install the new one.

On later cars, the main links appear about the same size as the fuses; they are square cases with a small window on top. Close examination will reveal the amperage rating, usually 50 or 80 amps. Remove these links as you would a fuse after loosening their retaining screws.

If the link failed, it was due to a high amperage load passing through the circuit; find the cause or the new link will fail again.

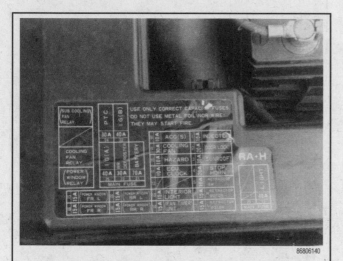

Fig. 123 The label on the lid of the fuse block indicates the fuse application, position and amperage rating

Fig. 124 There is also a fuse block located below the left side of the instrument panel

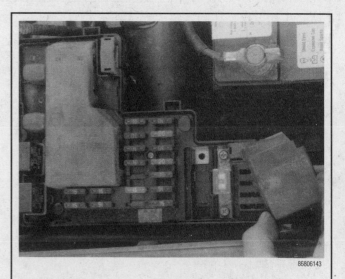

Fig. 126 The fusible links are located under protective covers

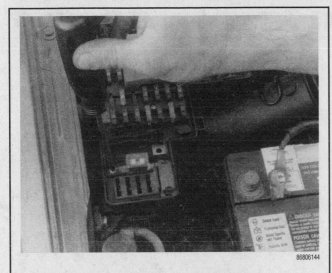

Fig. 127 Remove the screws securing the fusible link . . .

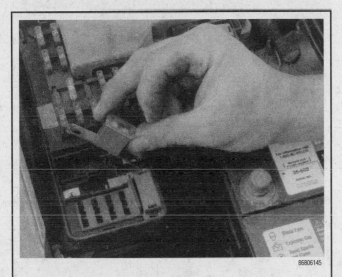

Fig. 128 . . . then pull it out of its port

Relays

As vehicles rely more and more on electronic systems and electrically operated options, the number of relays grows steadily. Many relays are located in logical positions on the relay and fuse board under the dash or in the engine compartment. However, some relays may be located near the component they control.

Relays can be removed by pulling them from their socket.

Communication and "Add-on" Electrical Equipment

The electrical system in your car is designed to perform under reasonable operating conditions without interference between components. Before any additional electrical equipment is installed, it is recommended that you consult your Honda dealer or a reputable repair facility familiar with the vehicle and its systems.

If the vehicle is equipped with mobile radio equipment (CB, HAM, Business radio and/or mobile telephone) it may have an effect upon the operation of the electric fuel injection and other engine systems. Radio frequency interference (RFI) from the communications system can be picked up by the car's wiring harnesses and conducted into the computer, giving it the wrong messages at the wrong time. Although well-shielded against RFI, the controller should be further protected through the following steps:

1. Install the antenna as far as possible from the any computer. Since the ECM is located in the passenger compartment, the antenna should be mounted at the rear of the car.

2. Keep the antenna wiring a minimum of 8 in. (203mm) away from any wiring running to the computer and from the computer itself. NEVER wind the antenna wire around any other wiring.

3. Mount the equipment as far from the computer as possible. Be very careful during installation not to drill through any wires or short a wire harness with a mounting screw.

4. Insure that the electrical feed wire(s) to the equipment are properly and tightly connected. Loose connectors can cause interference.

5. Make certain that the equipment is properly grounded to the car. Poor grounding can damage expensive equipment.

6. Make sure the antenna is "trimmed" or adjusted for optimum function.

WIRING DIAGRAMS

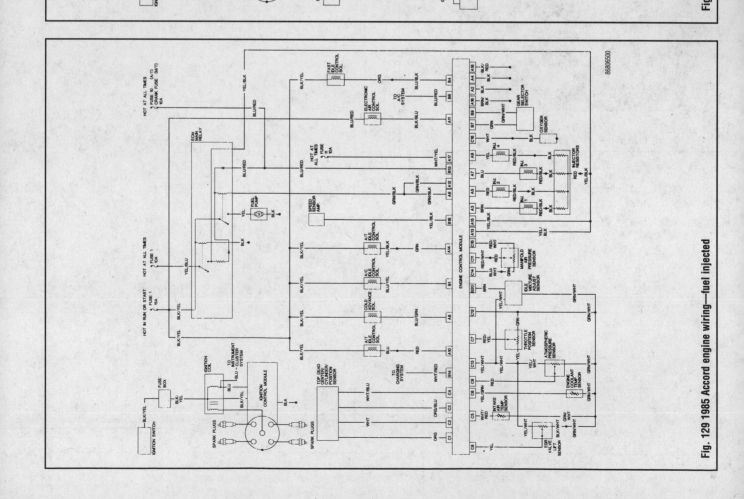

Fig. 130 1984-85 Accord engine wiring—carbureted

Fig. 129 1985 Accord engine wiring—fuel injected

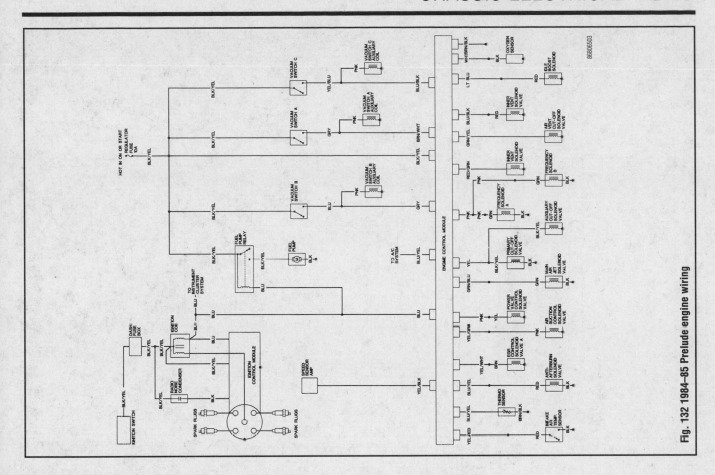

Fig. 132 1984–85 Prelude engine wiring

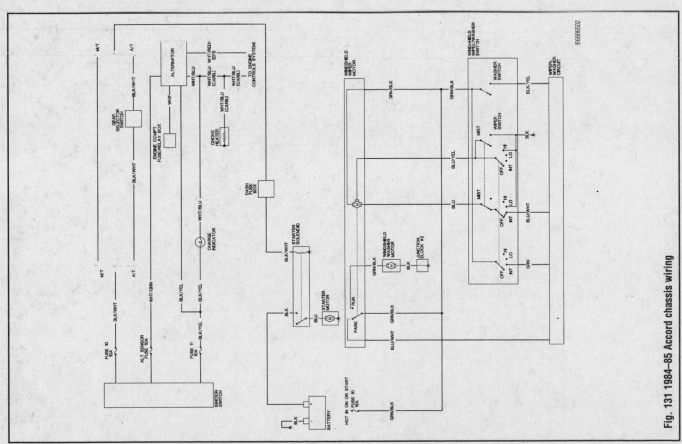

Fig. 131 1984–85 Accord chassis wiring

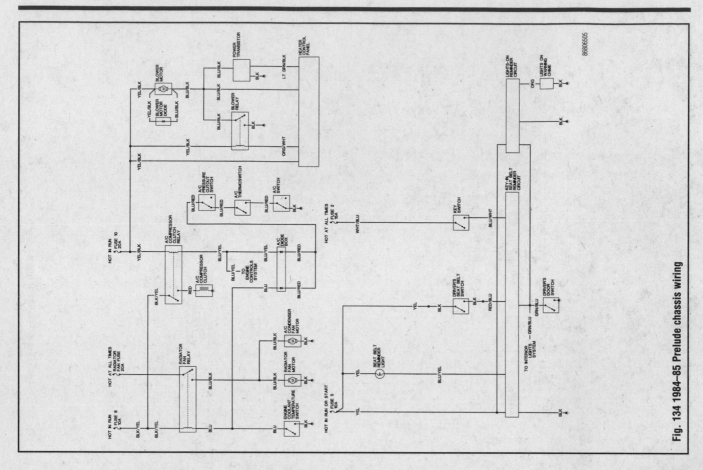

Fig. 134 1984–85 Prelude chassis wiring

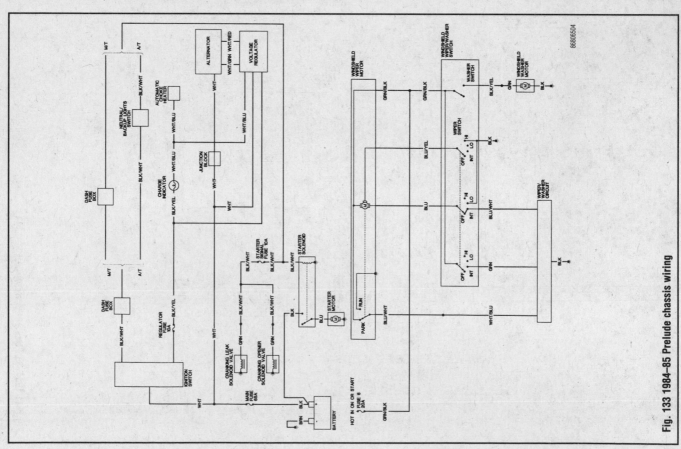

Fig. 133 1984–85 Prelude chassis wiring

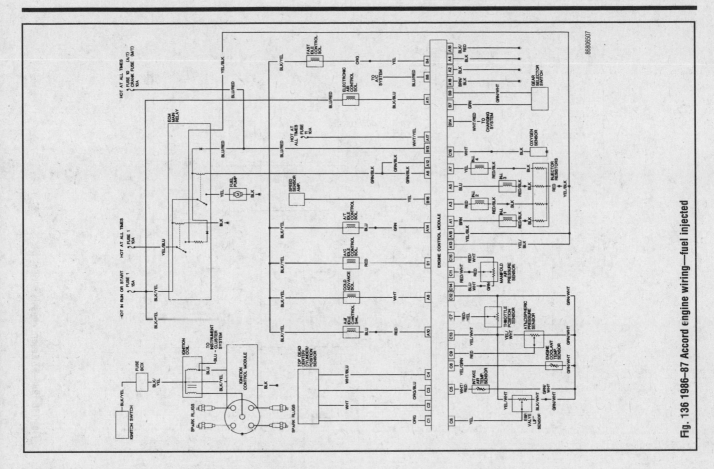

Fig. 136 1986-87 Accord engine wiring—fuel injected

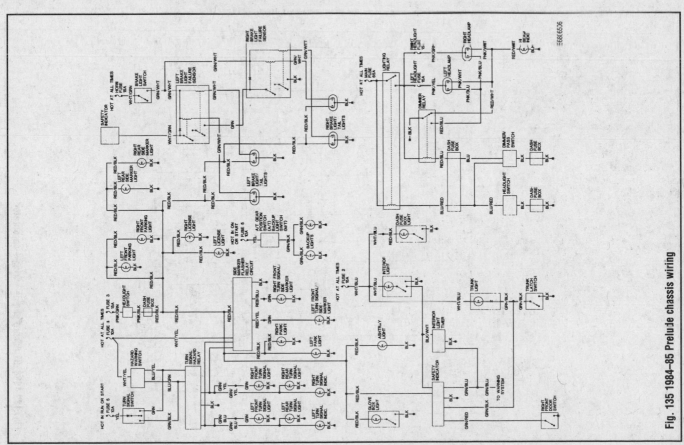

Fig. 135 1984-85 Prelude chassis wiring

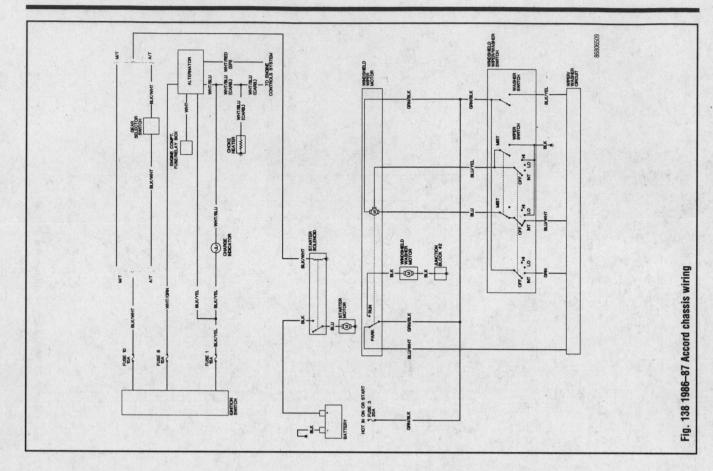

Fig. 138 1986-87 Accord chassis wiring

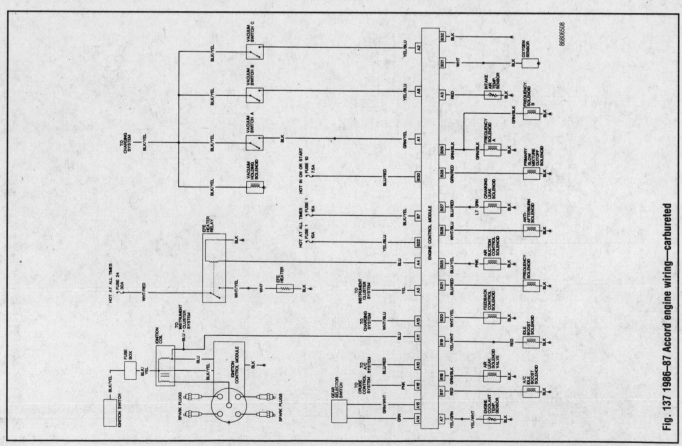

Fig. 137 1986-87 Accord engine wiring—carbureted

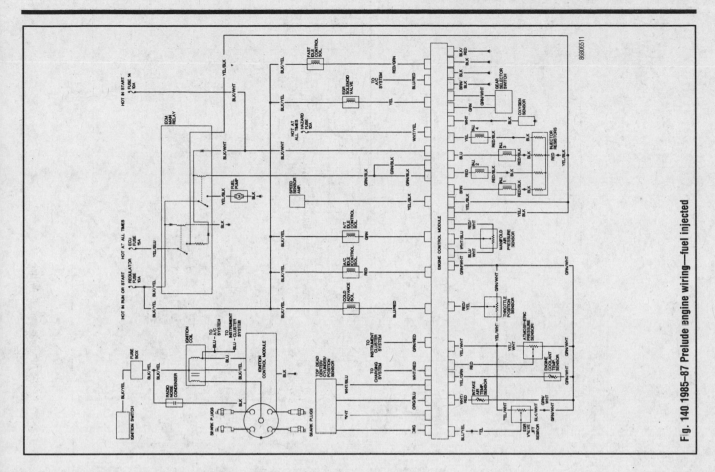

Fig. 140 1985-87 Prelude engine wiring—fuel injected

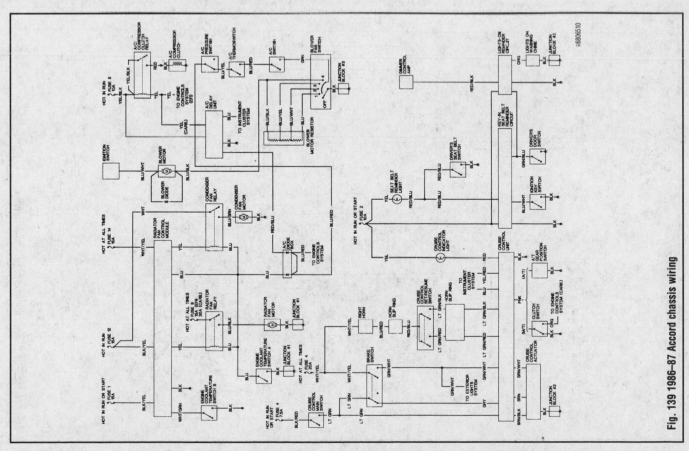

Fig. 139 1986-87 Accord chassis wiring

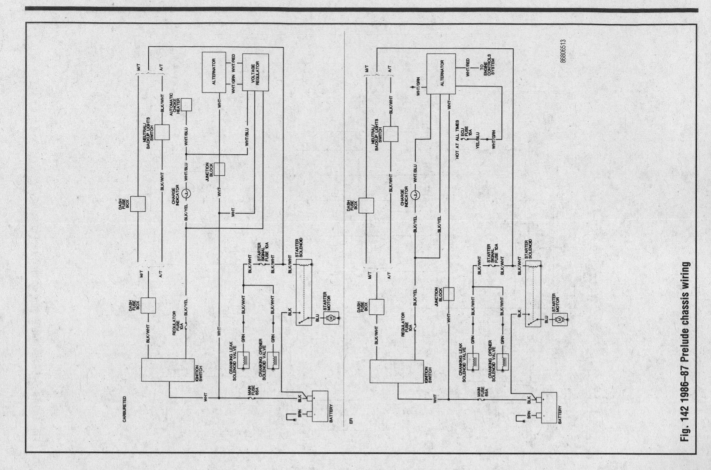

Fig. 142 1986–87 Prelude chassis wiring

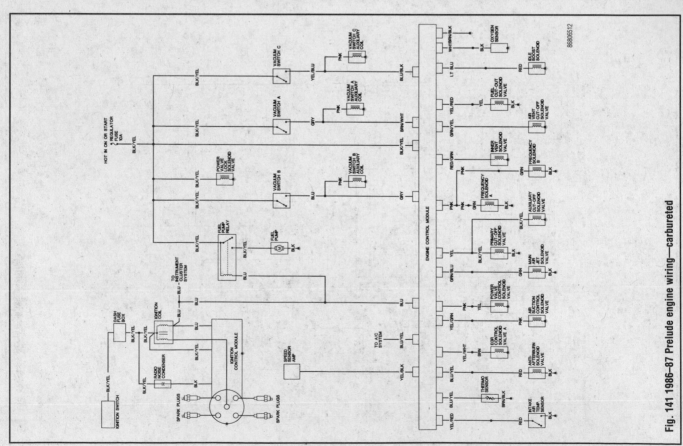

Fig. 141 1986–87 Prelude engine wiring—carbureted

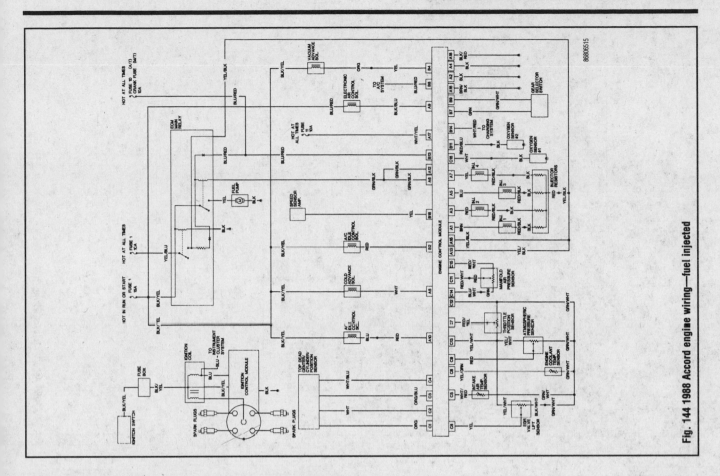

Fig. 144 1988 Accord engine wiring—fuel injected

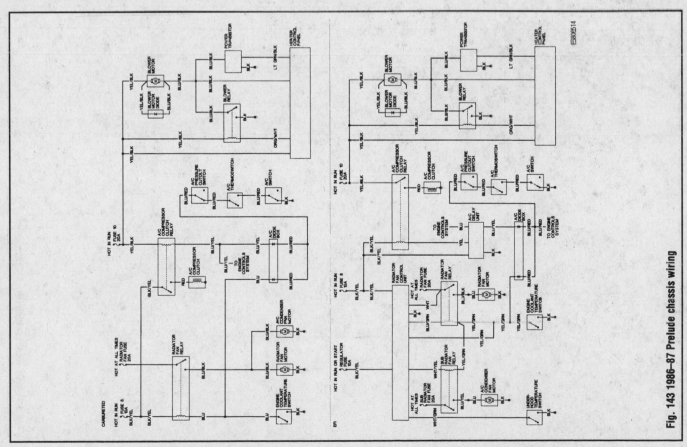

Fig. 143 1986-87 Prelude chassis wiring

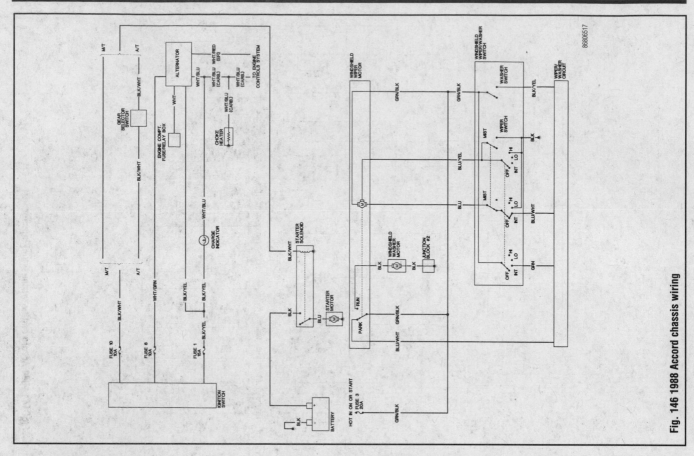

Fig. 146 1988 Accord chassis wiring

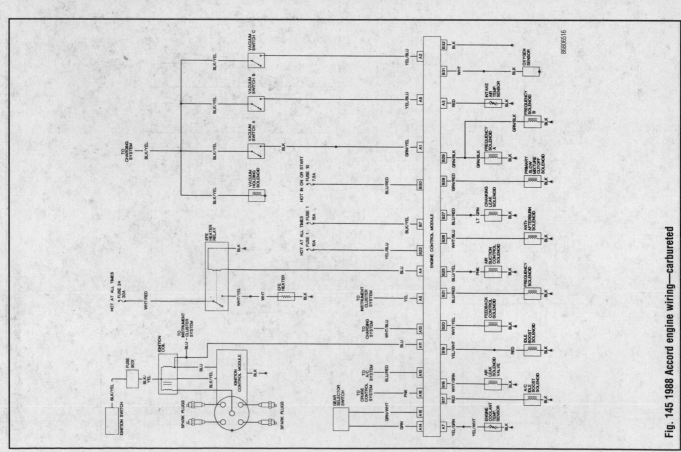

Fig. 145 1988 Accord engine wiring—carbureted

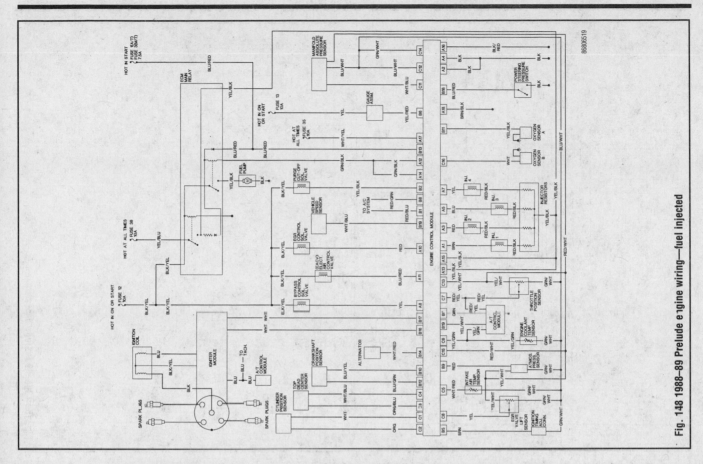

Fig. 148 1988-89 Prelude engine wiring—fuel injected

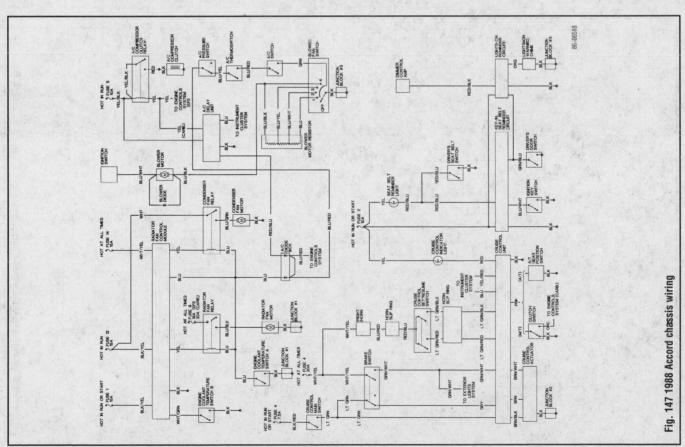

Fig. 147 1988 Accord chassis wiring

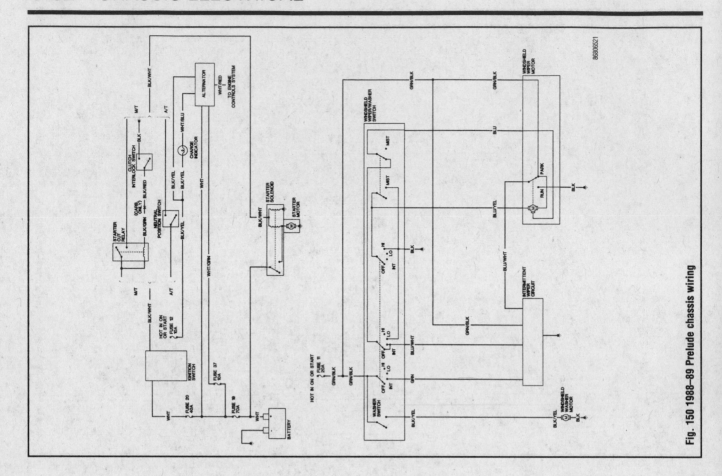

Fig. 150 1988–89 Prelude chassis wiring

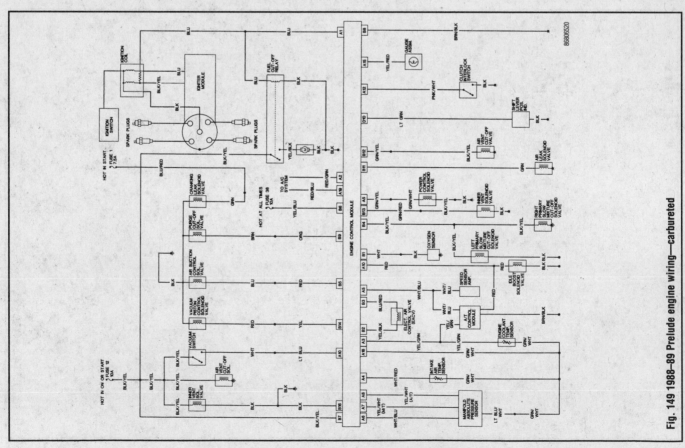

Fig. 149 1988–89 Prelude engine wiring—carbureted

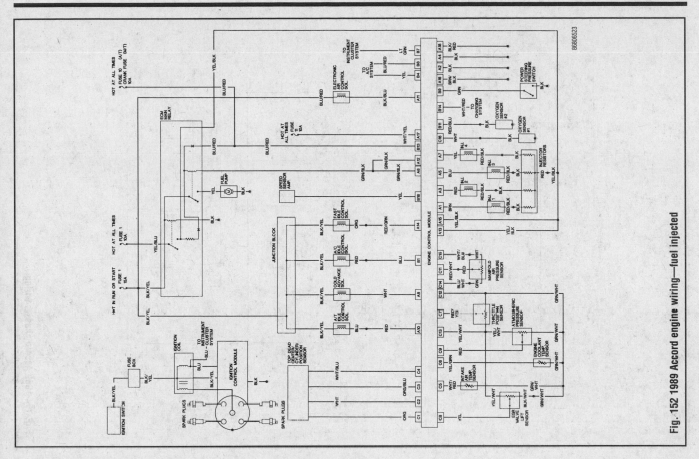

Fig. 152 1989 Accord engine wiring—fuel injected

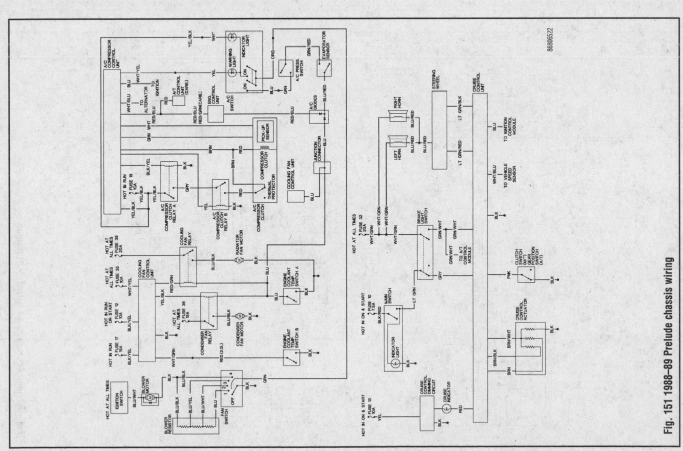

Fig. 151 1988-89 Prelude chassis wiring

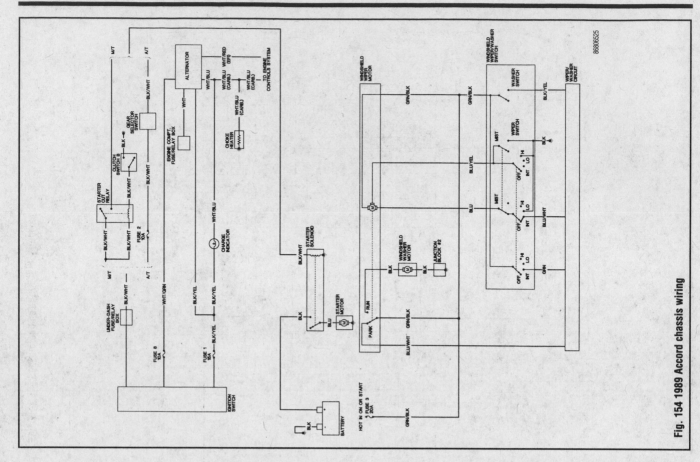

Fig. 154 1989 Accord chassis wiring

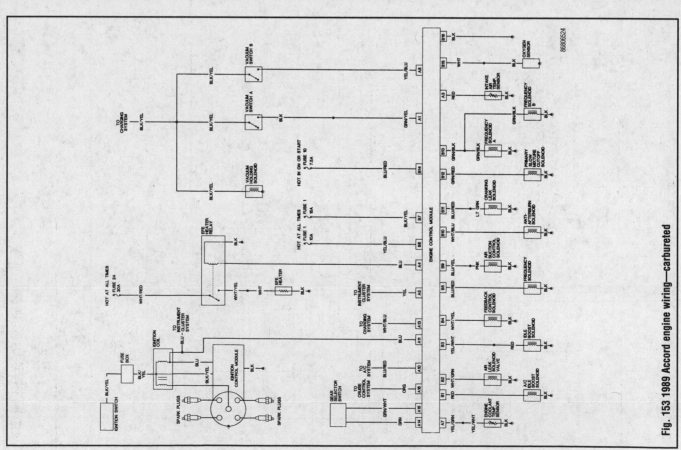

Fig. 153 1989 Accord engine wiring—carbureted

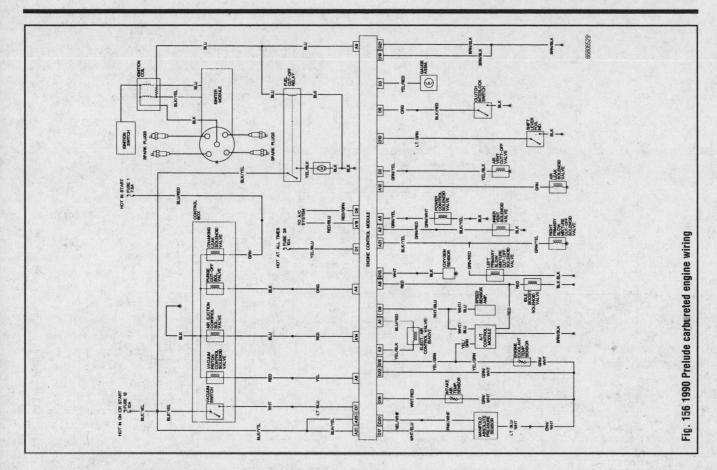

Fig. 156 1990 Prelude carbureted engine wiring

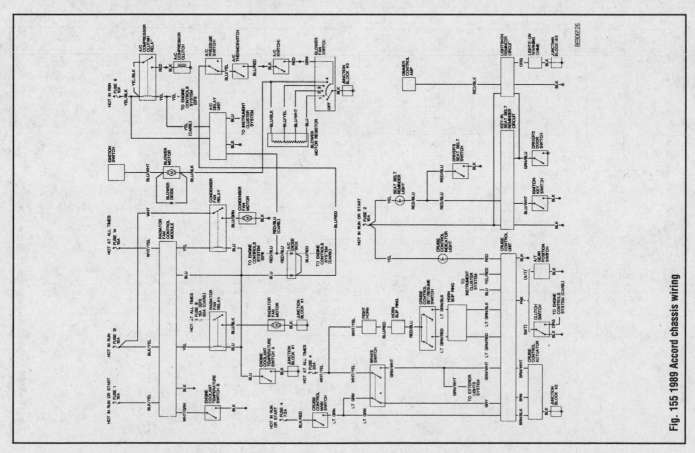

Fig. 155 1989 Accord chassis wiring

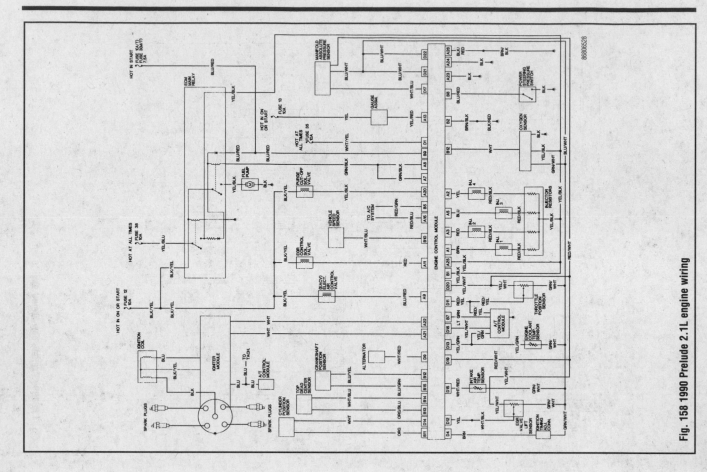

Fig. 158 1990 Prelude 2.1L engine wiring

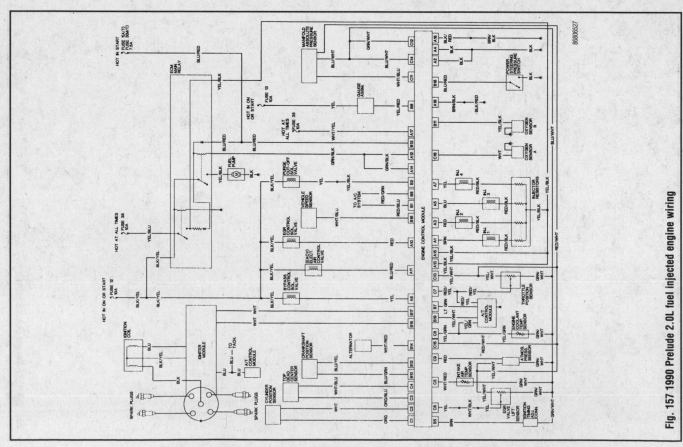

Fig. 157 1990 Prelude 2.0L fuel injected engine wiring

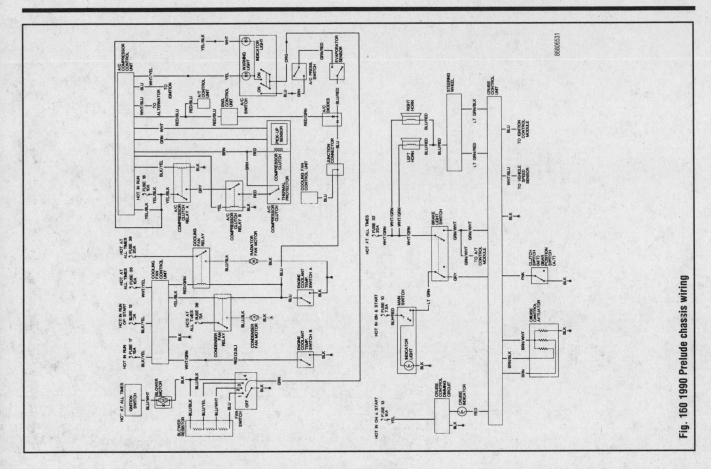

Fig. 160 1990 Prelude chassis wiring

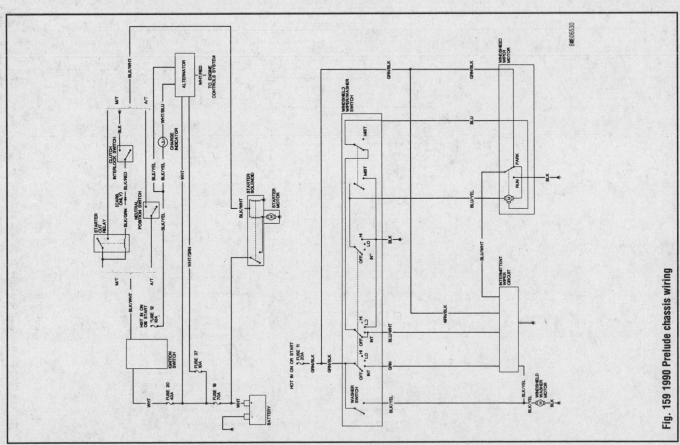

Fig. 159 1990 Prelude chassis wiring

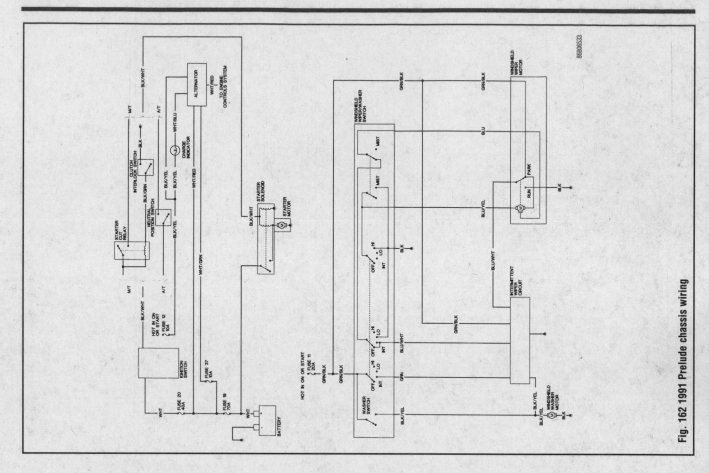

Fig. 162 1991 Prelude chassis wiring

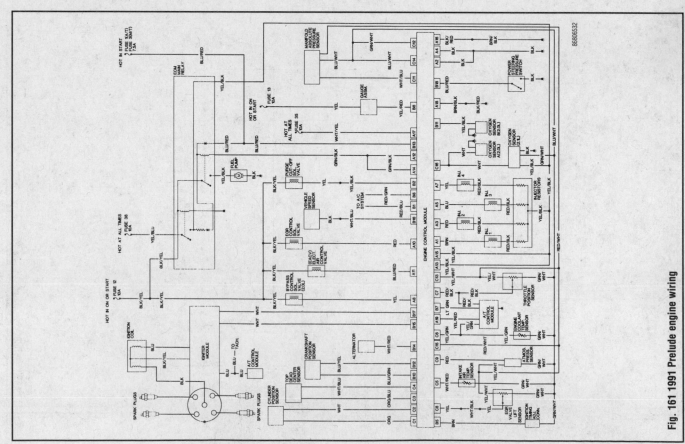

Fig. 161 1991 Prelude engine wiring

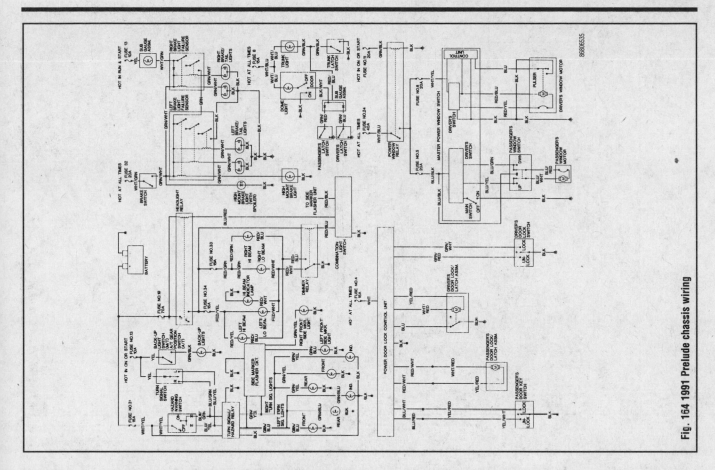

Fig. 164 1991 Prelude chassis wiring

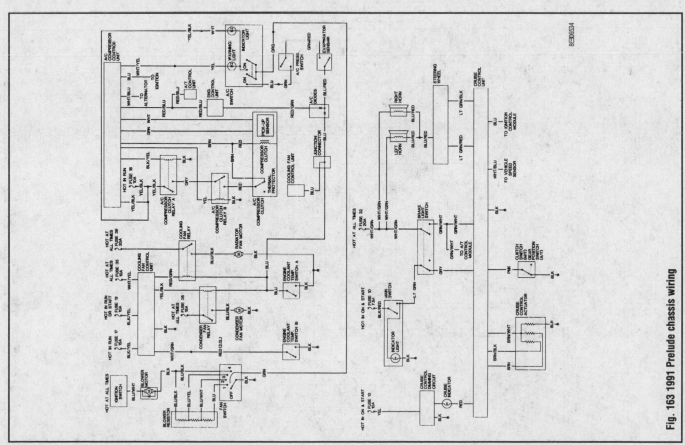

Fig. 163 1991 Prelude chassis wiring

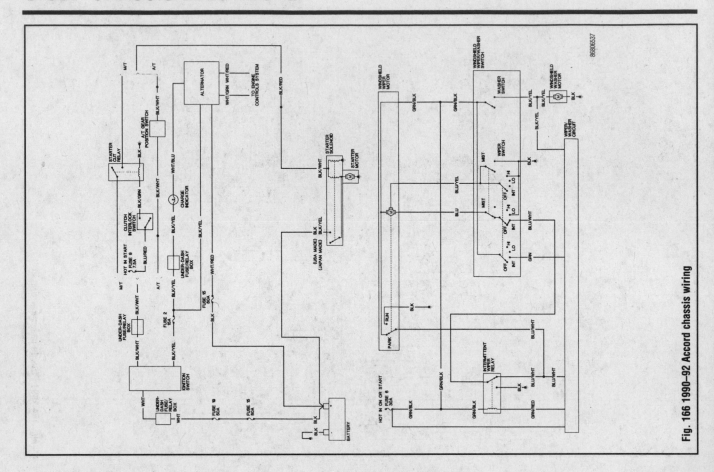

Fig. 166 1990–92 Accord chassis wiring

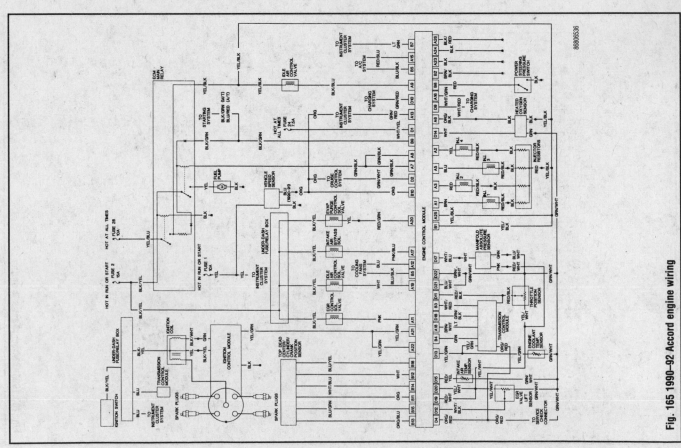

Fig. 165 1990–92 Accord engine wiring

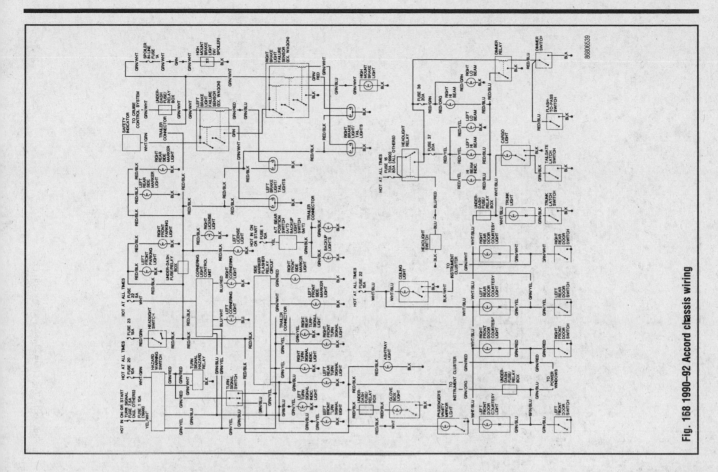

Fig. 168 1990–92 Accord chassis wiring

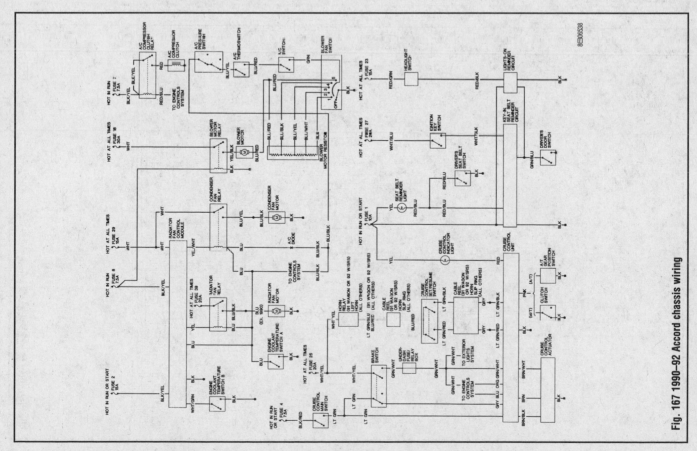

Fig. 167 1990–92 Accord chassis wiring

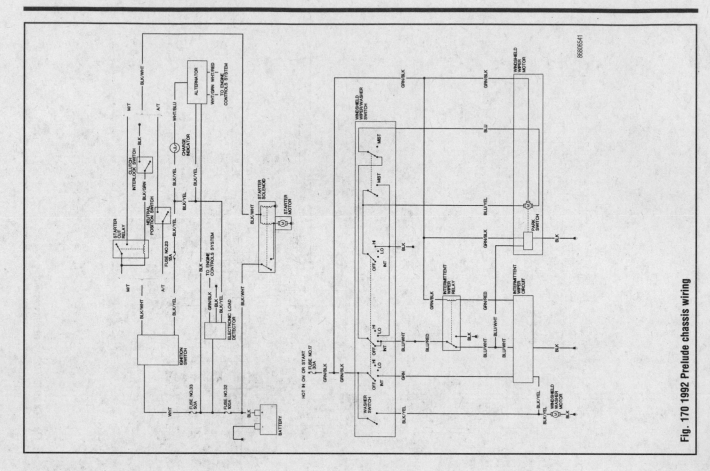

Fig. 170 1992 Prelude chassis wiring

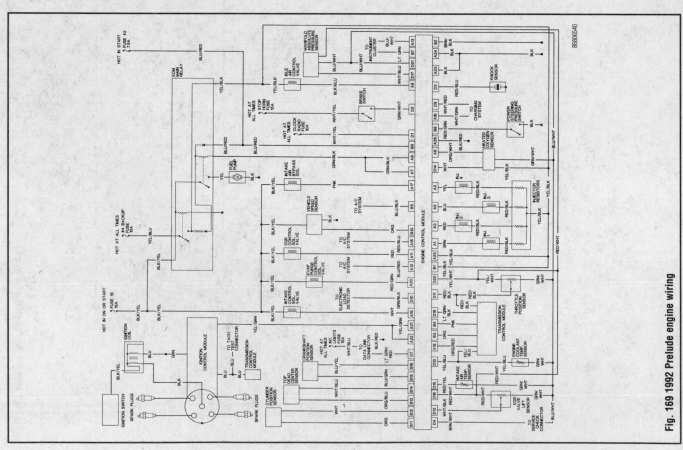

Fig. 169 1992 Prelude engine wiring

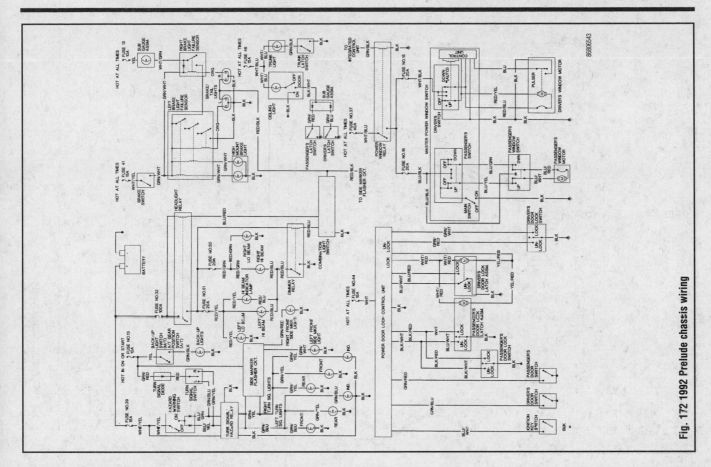

Fig. 172 1992 Prelude chassis wiring

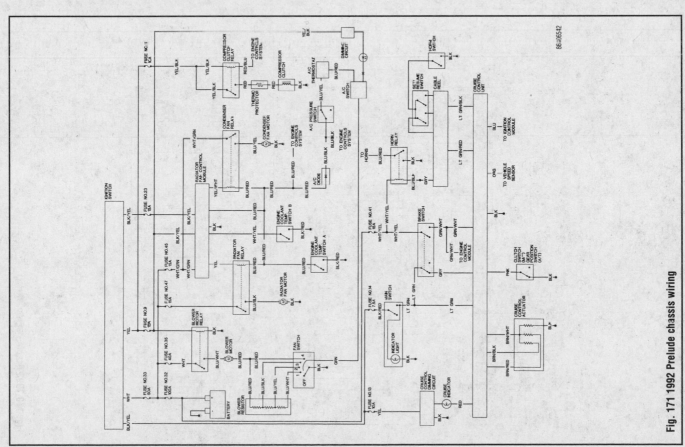

Fig. 171 1992 Prelude chassis wiring

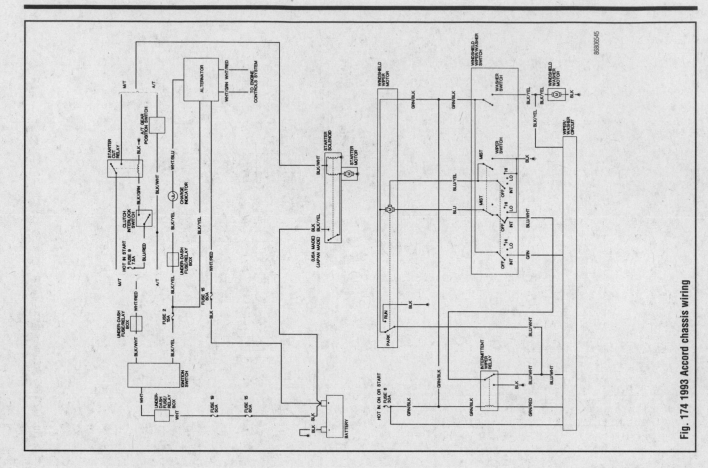

Fig. 174 1993 Accord chassis wiring

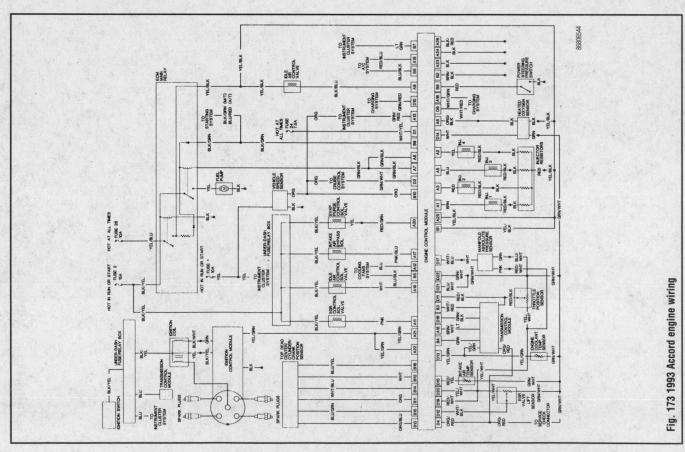

Fig. 173 1993 Accord engine wiring

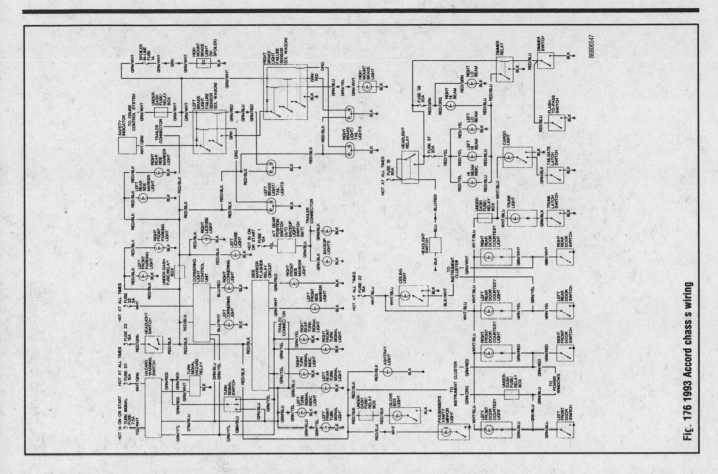

Fig. 176 1993 Accord chassis wiring

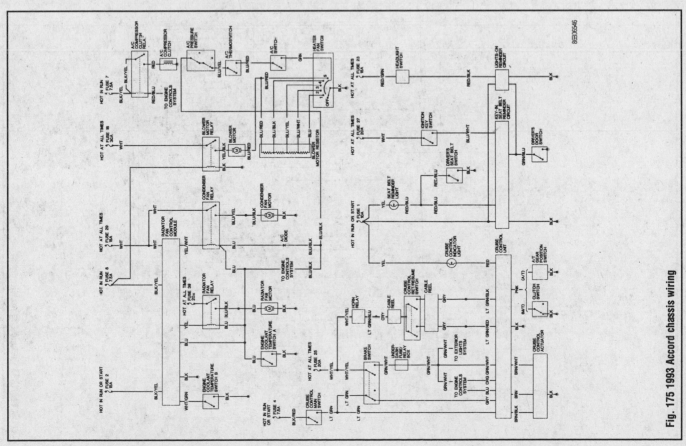

Fig. 175 1993 Accord chassis wiring

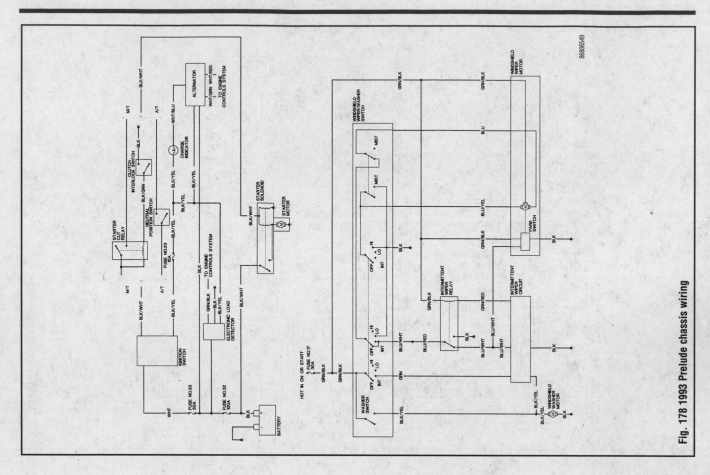

Fig. 178 1993 Prelude chassis wiring

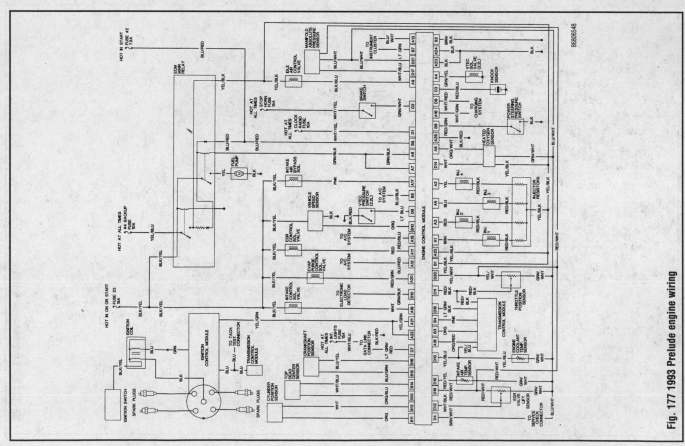

Fig. 177 1993 Prelude engine wiring

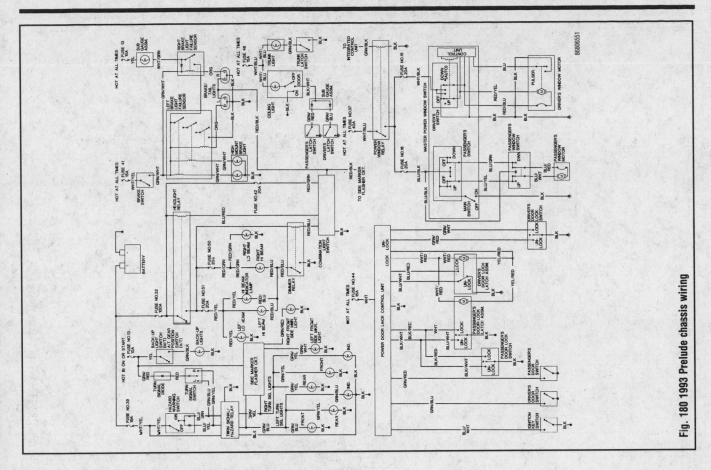

Fig. 180 1993 Prelude chassis wiring

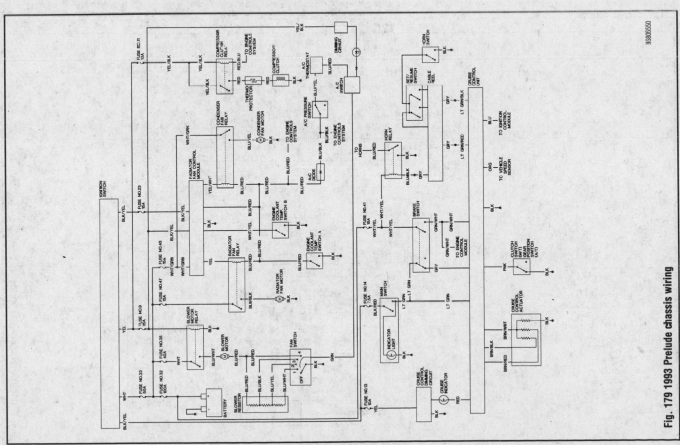

Fig. 179 1993 Prelude chassis wiring

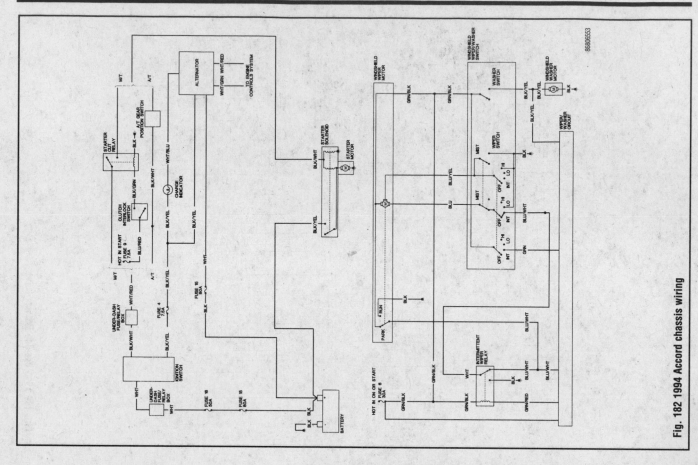

Fig. 182 1994 Accord chassis wiring

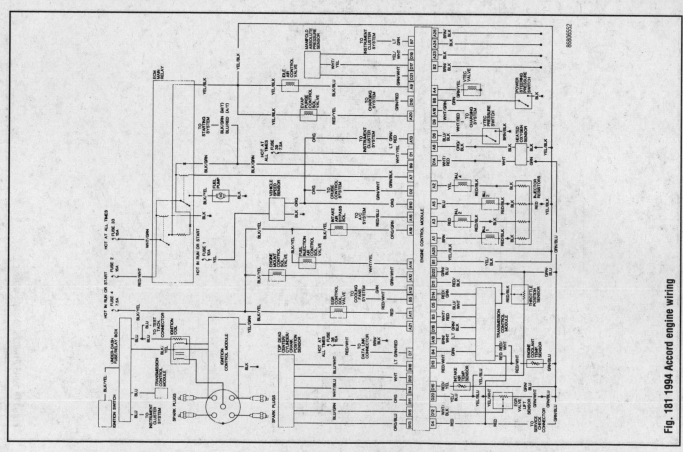

Fig. 181 1994 Accord engine wiring

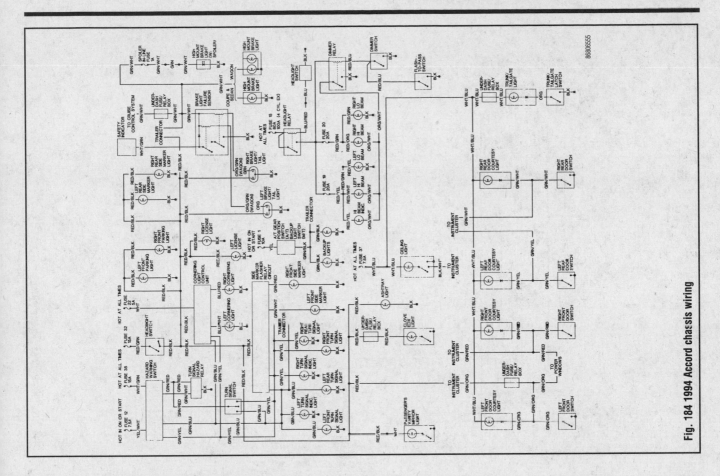

Fig. 184 1994 Accord chassis wiring

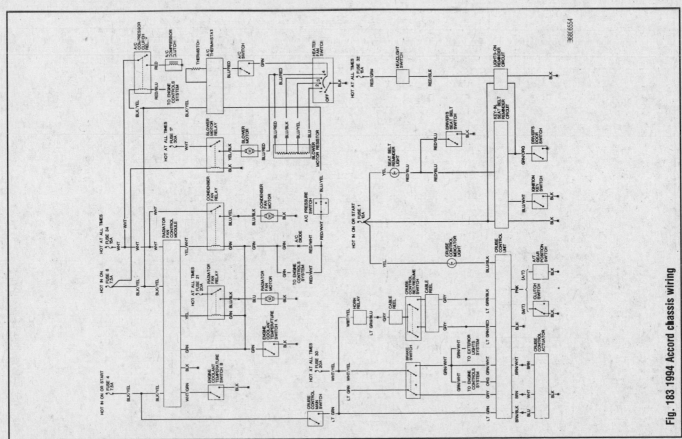

Fig. 183 1994 Accord chassis wiring

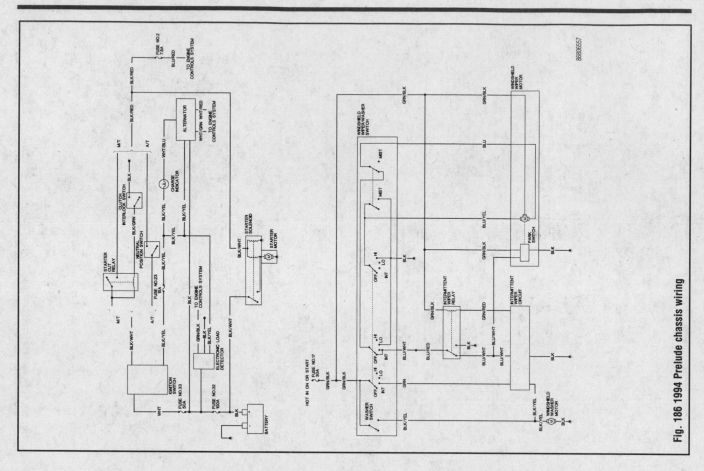

Fig. 186 1994 Prelude chassis wiring

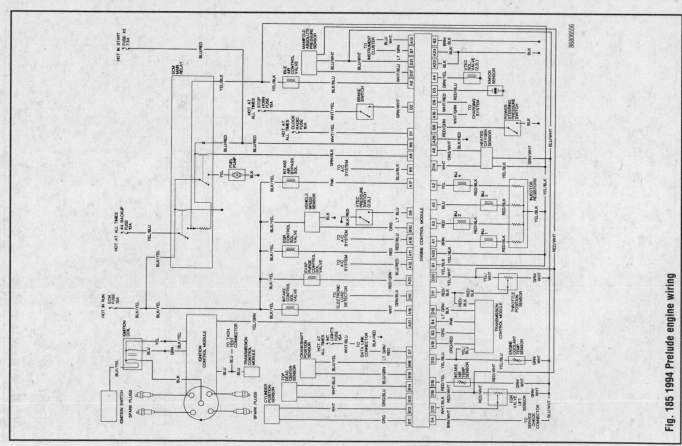

Fig. 185 1994 Prelude engine wiring

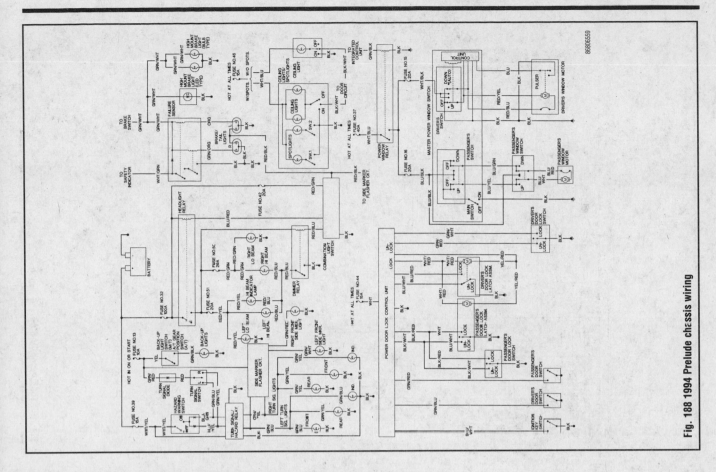

Fig. 188 1994 Prelude chassis wiring

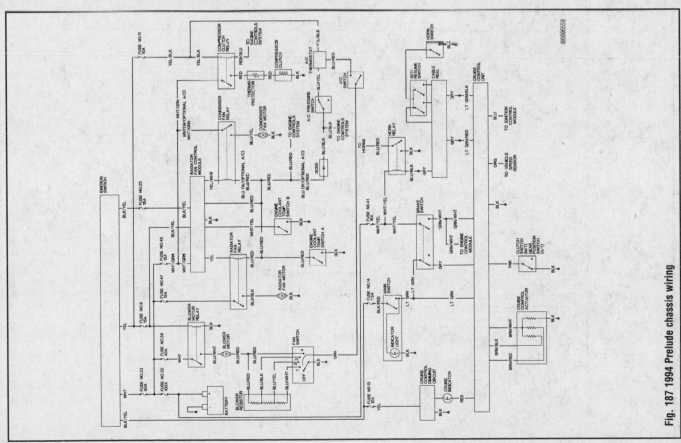

Fig. 187 1994 Prelude chassis wiring

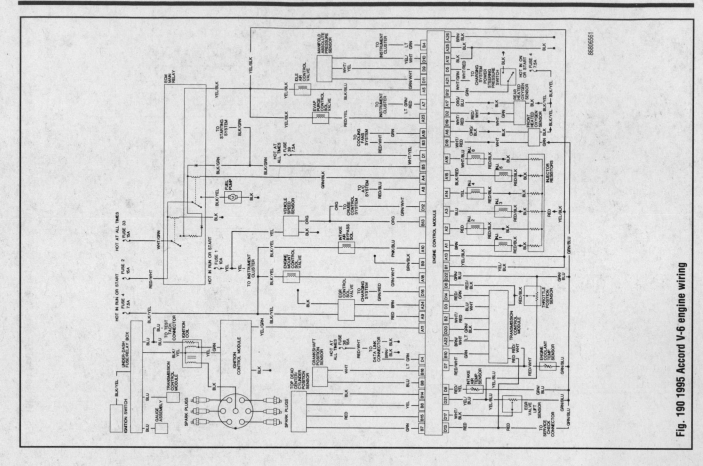

Fig. 190 1995 Accord V-6 engine wiring

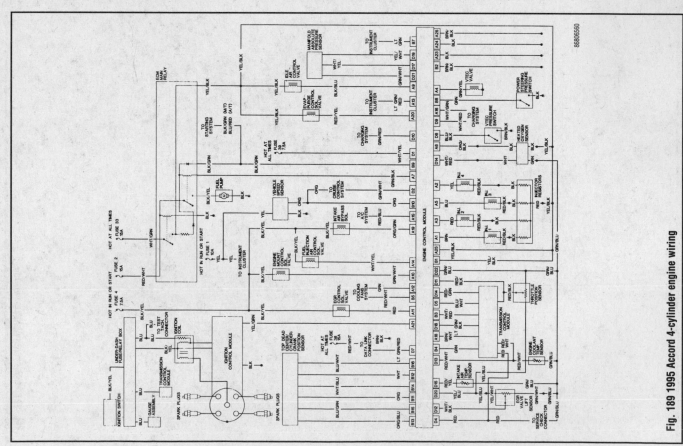

Fig. 189 1995 Accord 4-cylinder engine wiring

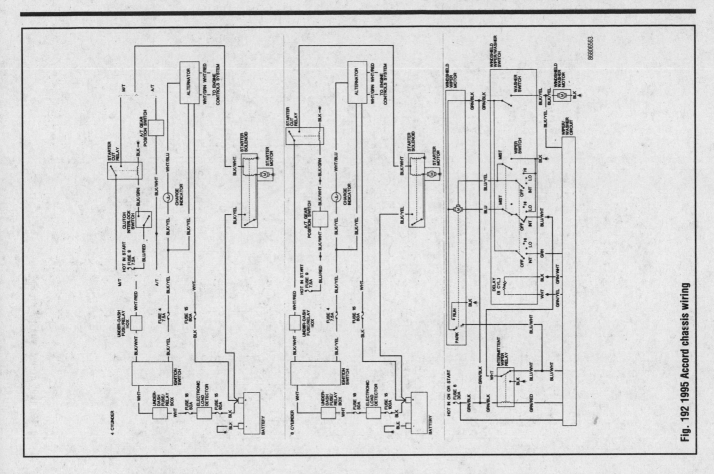

Fig. 192 1995 Accord chassis wiring

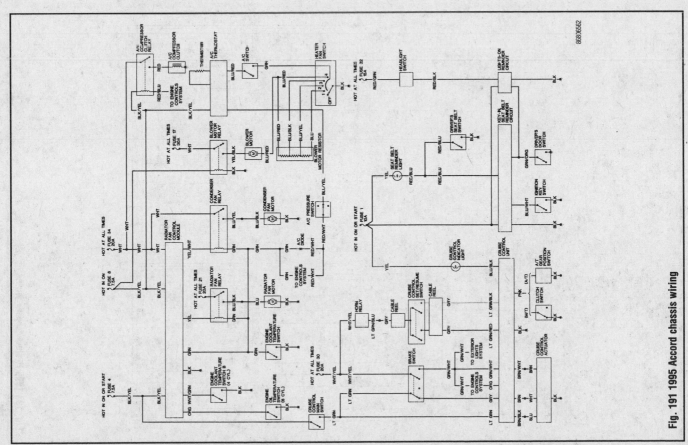

Fig. 191 1995 Accord chassis wiring

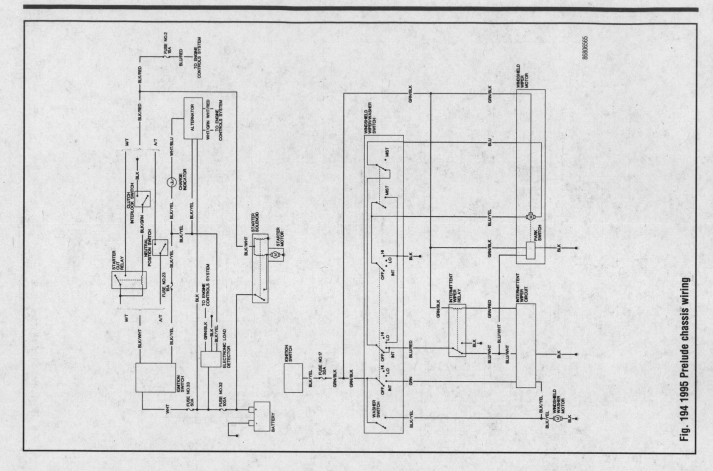

Fig. 194 1995 Prelude chassis wiring

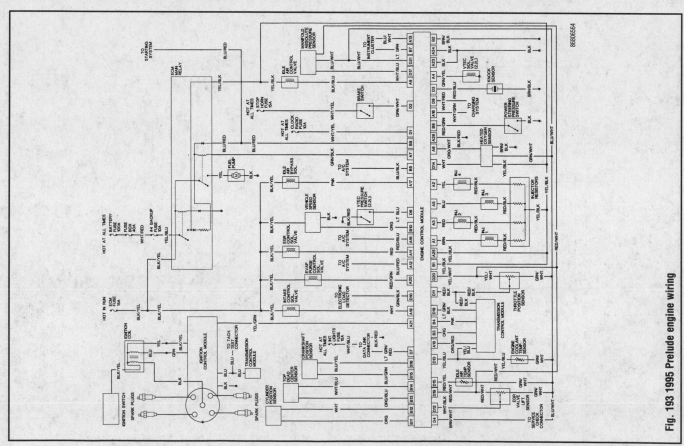

Fig. 193 1995 Prelude engine wiring

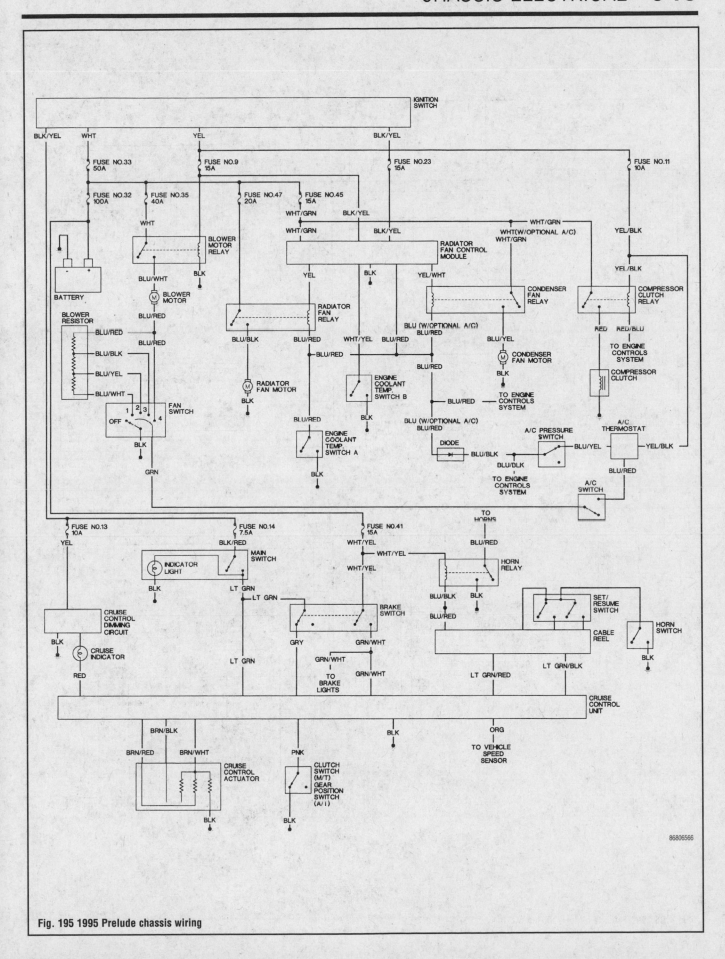

Fig. 195 1995 Prelude chassis wiring

86806566

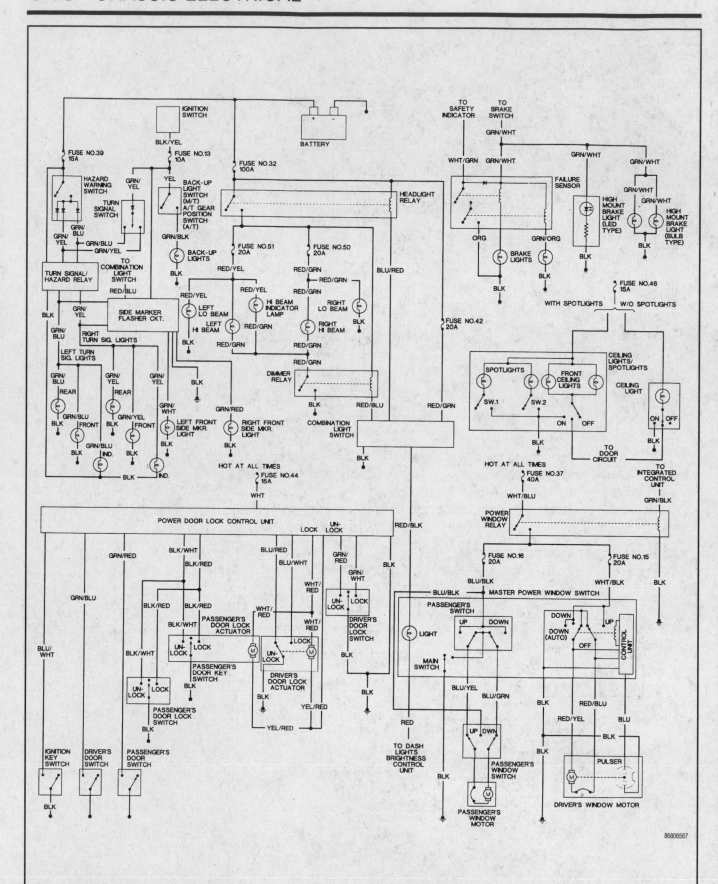

Fig. 196 1995 Prelude chassis wiring

86806567

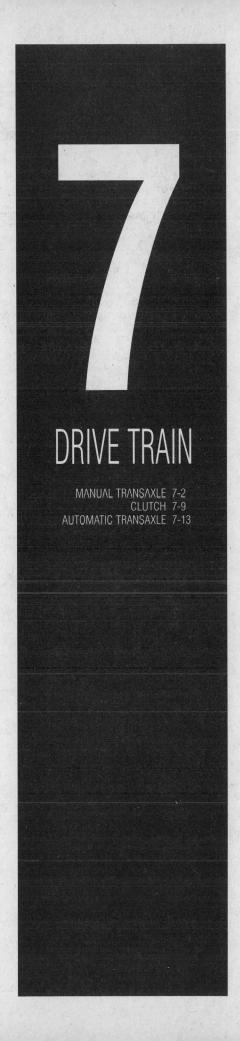

7

DRIVE TRAIN

MANUAL TRANSAXLE

Identification

▶ See Figure 1

The transaxle number, stamped on the case, indicates the family and running serial number for the transaxle. In general, transaxles are not interchangeable between model families.

Transaxles are selected by the manufacturer to fit the engine performance characteristics of the car with consideration to other variables such as area of sale, emission class, vehicle loading, brakes, etc. Even if a replacement unit physically fit into a dissimilar car, the performance of the transaxle would be a poor match to the present engine; driveability, fuel economy and emissions would suffer.

If you're considering replacing the transaxle rather than repairing a failure, stick to the same transaxle group; that is, if the old unit's trans number was A2Q5, then that is also what the replacement unit must be. Transaxle identification numbers begin with the following groups:

- 1984–85 Accord, California, 49 State and Hi Alt: GS
- 1984–85 Accord, Low Altitude (49 State only): GY
- 1984–85 Prelude, All: GM
- 1986–87 Accord, Fuel injected: A2Q5
- 1986–87 Accord, Carbureted: A2Q6
- 1986–87 Prelude, Fuel injected: A2K5
- 1986–87 Prelude, Carbureted: A1B5
- 1988 Accord, Fuel injected: E2Q5
- 1988 Accord, Carbureted: E2Q6
- 1988 Prelude, Fuel injected: D2J5
- 1988 Prelude, Carbureted: D2J4
- 1989 Accord, Fuel injected: E2R5
- 1989 Accord, Carbureted: E2R6
- 1989 Prelude, Fuel injected: D2J3
- 1989 Prelude, Carbureted: D2M4
- 1990–91 Accord, All: H2A5
- 1990–91 Prelude, All: D2A4
- 1992 Accord, All: H2U4
- 1992–95 Prelude, VTEC: M2F4
- 1992–95 Prelude, 2.2L: M2L5
- 1992–95 Prelude, 2.3L: M2S4
- 1993 Accord, wagon: H2U4
- 1993 Accord, DX and LX: H2A5
- 1993 Accord, EX and SE: H2U5
- 1994–95 Accord, VTEC: P2U5
- 1994–95 Accord, 2.2L: P2A5

Adjustments

SHIFTER LINKAGE

On 1984–89 Accords and 1984–87 Preludes, the rods running between the shift lever and the transaxle are not adjustable. Trouble or stiffness in the mechanism is repaired by cleaning, lubrication or the replacement of worn bushings, seals, etc.

Later cars use a set of two cables rather than fixed-length rods to transfer the motion of the shifter. The cables are adjustable, but the need for adjustment is rare. The cables rarely go out of adjustment; altering their settings should only be considered in cases of collision repair or cable replacement. Even if the transaxle is removed, the cables may be disconnected without altering their settings.

1990–95 Accord

▶ See Figures 2 and 3

➡ **The select cable is on the driver's side of the shifter; the shift cable is on the right side of the shift lever.**

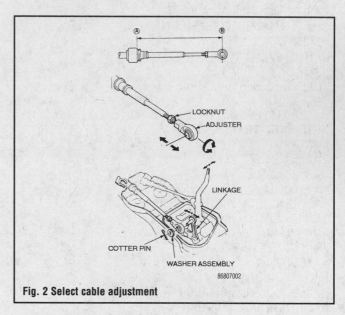

Fig. 2 Select cable adjustment

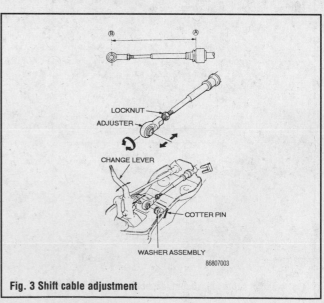

Fig. 3 Shift cable adjustment

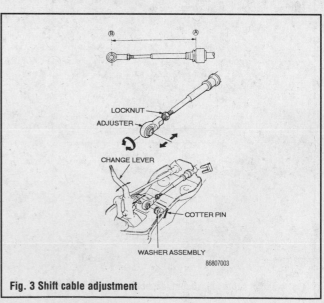

Transmission Number (Manual)

Transmission Number (Automatic)

86807001

Fig. 1 Transaxle serial number locations

1. Firmly set the parking brake, block the wheels and place the shifter in Neutral.

2. Remove the console.

3. At the select cable, measure the distance from the center of the mounting eye (at the shift lever) to the face just behind the locking clip (horseshoe clip). Correct distance should be 8.37–8.4 in. (212.5–213.5mm).

4. At the shift cable, measure the same interval. Correct distance is 6.86–6.90 in. (174.3–175.3mm).

5. If either cable is out of adjustment, remove the cotter pin holding the cable to the shifter, remove the plastic washer (take note of its correct position) and disconnect the cable from the shifter.

6. Loosen the locknut and turn the adjuster until the correct dimension is achieved. Measure the distance carefully each time and turn the adjuster in small increments.

7. Once the measurement is correct, tighten the locknut firmly.

8. Install the cable to the shift lever. Install the plastic washer and install a new cotter pin.

9. Check the operation of the gearshift lever. Reinstall the console.

1988–95 Prelude

♦ See Figures 4 and 5

➡The select cable is on the right side of the shift lever; the gearshift cable is closest to the driver.

1. Firmly set the parking brake, block the wheels and place the shifter in Neutral.

2. Remove the console.

3. With the transaxle in Neutral, inspect the select cable adjustment. The groove in the lever bracket must align with the index mark or notch on the cable housing. The mark is between the adjusting sleeve and the connection to the shifter.

4. If the marks do not align, loosen the two locknuts on the adjuster sleeve and turn the adjuster as necessary.

5. When the marks align, tighten the locknuts on the adjuster. Inspect the threads projecting out of the adjuster; no more than 0.4 in. (10mm) of threads must be exposed.

6. Check the operation of the shifter.

7. Inspect the adjustment of the gearshift cable. Place the shift lever in 4th gear.

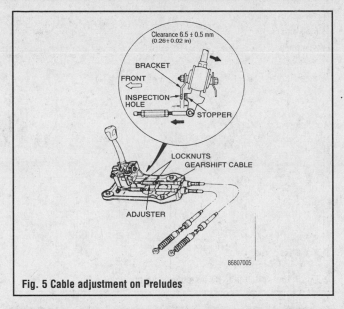

Fig. 5 Cable adjustment on Preludes

8. Measure the clearance between the lever bracket and the front edge of the stopper while pushing the lever forward. There is an inspection hole in the front of the bracket for using an insertable measuring tool. Clearance must be 0.24–0.28 in. (6.0–7.0mm).

9. If the clearance is incorrect, loosen the two locknuts on the adjuster sleeve and turn the adjuster as necessary.

10. When the correct clearance is gained, tighten the locknuts on the adjuster. Inspect the threads projecting out of the adjuster; no more than 0.4 in. (10mm) of threads must be exposed.

11. Check the operation of the shifter. Reinstall the console.

Back-up Light Switch

REMOVAL & INSTALLATION

♦ See Figures 6 and 7

The reverse light switch is externally mounted on the transaxle case. To remove it, place the shifter in Neutral. Elevate and safely support the car. Unplug the wiring connectors. Remove the switch and washer by unscrewing it from the case.

Once removed, the switch may be easily tested with an ohmmeter. Connect one probe to each switch lead. In the normal position, there should be no continuity. With the tip or plunger of the switch pressed in, the switch should show continuity.

When installing, ALWAYS replace the washer between the switch and the case. It not only guards against oil leaks, but also sets the reach of the switch inside the transaxle. Install the switch and tighten it to 18 ft. lbs. (25 Nm). Connect the wiring and lower the vehicle to the ground.

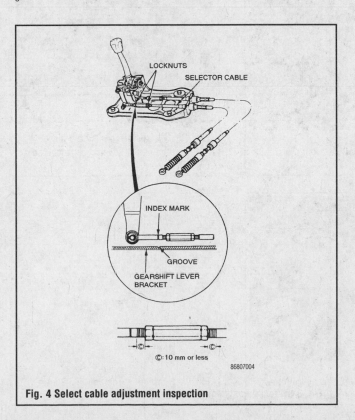

Fig. 4 Select cable adjustment inspection

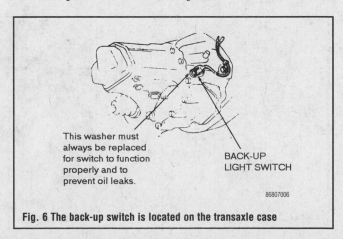

Fig. 6 The back-up switch is located on the transaxle case

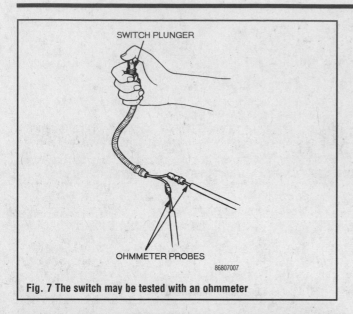

Fig. 7 The switch may be tested with an ohmmeter

Transaxle

REMOVAL & INSTALLATION

1984–89 Accord and 1984–87 Prelude

▸ See Figures 8 thru 13

➡All wires and hoses should be labeled at the time of removal. The amount of time saved during reassembly makes the extra effort well worthwhile.

1. Disconnect the battery ground cable at the battery and the transaxle case. Unlock the steering column; place the transaxle in Neutral.
2. Disconnect the following cables and wires:
   a. Clutch cable at the release arm.
   b. Back-up light switch wires.
   c. TCS (Transmission Controlled Spark) switch wires.
   d. Wire from the starter solenoid.
3. Release the engine sub-wiring harness from the clamp at the clutch housing. Remove the upper two transaxle mounting bolts.
4. Raise the front of the car and support it securely with safety stands. Double check the stand placement and security. Drain the transaxle.
5. Remove the front wheels. Place a suitable transaxle jack into position under the transaxle.
6. Disconnect the speedometer cable.

➡When removing the speedometer cable from the transaxle, it is not necessary to remove the entire cable holder. Remove the end boot (gear holder seal), the cable retaining clip and then pull the cable out of the holder. In no way should you disturb the holder, unless it is absolutely necessary.

7. Disconnect the shift lever torque rod from the clutch housing. Remove the bolt from the shift rod clevis.
8. Disconnect the tie rod ball joints and remove them using a ball joint remover.
9. Remove the lower arm ball joint bolt from the right side lower control arm, then use a puller to disconnect the ball joint from the knuckle. Remove the damper fork bolt.
10. Disconnect the driveshafts from the transaxle. Move the axles out of the way but do not let them hang; support them with string or wire. Remove the right side radius rod.
11. Remove the damper bracket from the transaxle. Remove the clutch housing bolts from the front transaxle mount.
12. Remove the clutch housing bolts from the rear transaxle mounting bracket. Remove the clutch cover.

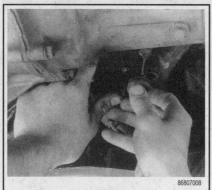

Fig. 8 Disconnect the clutch cable from the release arm

Fig. 9 Remove the bolt securing the shift rod clevis . . .

Fig. 10 . . . and disconnect the torque rod from the clutch housing by removing the bolt

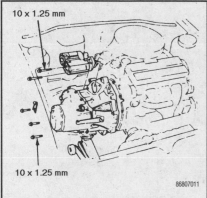

Fig. 11 Transaxle mounting bolt locations

Fig. 12 Pull the transaxle away from the engine block and lower the transaxle jack

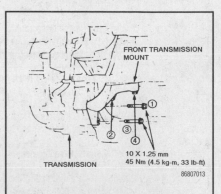

Fig. 13 Tighten the front mount bolts in this sequence

13. Remove the starter mounting bolts and remove the starter assembly through the chassis. Remove the transaxle mounting bolts.

14. Pull the transaxle away from the engine block to clear the two 14mm dowel pins and lower the transaxle jack.

✳ WARNING

Do not allow the transaxle to hang on the input shaft. Once removal begins, remove it completely from the engine.

To install:

15. Place the transaxle on the jack. Clean and grease the release bearing sliding surface.

16. Check that the two dowel pins are present in the bell housing.

17. Raise the unit enough to align the pins with the matching holes in the block.

18. Move the transaxle toward the engine and install the mainshaft into the clutch disc splines. If the left suspension was left in place, install new spring clips on both axles and carefully insert the left axle into the differential while installing the transaxle.

19. Push and wiggle the transaxle until it fits flush with the engine flange.

20. Tighten the bolts until the bell housing is seated against the engine block.

21. Loosely install the bolts for the front transaxle mount, then tighten them in sequence to 33 ft. lbs. (45 Nm).

22. Install the rear transaxle mount, tightening the bolts to 33 ft. lbs. (45 Nm).

23. Install the upper torque arm and its brackets. Tighten the bracket mounting bolts to 47 ft. lbs. (65 Nm) and the through-bolts to 54 ft. lbs. (75 Nm).

24. Carefully remove the transaxle jack.

25. Install the starter.

26. Install the driveshaft(s) if not previously done.

27. Install the lower arm ball joints, tie rod ball joints and damper fork bolts.

28. Connect the shift rod linkage.

29. Connect the shift linkage.

30. Connect the shift lever torque rod to the clutch housing. Tighten the 8mm bolt to 16 ft. lbs. (22 Nm).

31. Install the front wheels.

32. Double check that the transaxle drain plug is present and tightened.

33. The car may be lowered to the ground for the final steps.

34. Install the clutch cable at the release arm.

35. Coat a new O-ring with clean oil and install it on the speedometer gear holder. Install the holder in the transaxle and secure the hold-down tab and bolt.

36. Install the engine sub-wire harness in the clamp at the bell housing.

37. Connect the engine compartment wiring for the starter, starter solenoid and back-up light switch.

38. Fill the transaxle with the proper amount of lubricant.

39. Check the transaxle and clutch for smooth operation.

1988–95 Prelude

1. Disconnect the battery ground cable at the battery and the transaxle case. If so equipped, disable the Supplemental Restraint System (SRS), as described in Section 6.

2. Unlock the steering column; place the transaxle in Neutral.

3. Disconnect the following wires:
   a. Back-up light switch wires.
   b. Black/white wire from the starter solenoid.

4. On the fuel injected models, remove the air cleaner assembly.

5. Remove the power steering speed sensor from the transaxle without removing the power steering hose.

6. Remove the shift cable and the select cable from the top cover of the transaxle. Remove the mounting bolt from the cable stay. Be sure not to bend or kink the cable more than necessary. Remove both cables and the stay together.

7. Remove the upper transaxle mounting bracket. Remove the four transaxle-to-block attachment bolts that must be removed from the engine compartment.

8. Raise and support the vehicle safely. Remove both front wheels and remove the splash shield.

9. Drain the transaxle oil into a drain pan. Remove the clutch slave cylinder. The cylinder may be moved out of the way without disconnecting the hose.

10. Remove the center beam. Remove the right radius rod completely. Remove the right and left drive shafts.

11. Remove the engine stiffener. Remove the clutch cover. Support the transaxle with a transaxle jack.

12. Remove the three lower bolts from the rear engine mounting bracket. Loosen but do not remove the top bolt. This bolt will support the weight of the engine.

13. Remove the two remaining engine-to-transaxle mounting bolts.

14. With the transaxle on the jack, disengage the input shaft from the clutch disc and lower the transaxle out of the vehicle.

✳ WARNING

Do not allow the transaxle to hang on the input shaft. Once removal begins, remove it completely from the engine.

To install:

15. Place the transaxle on the jack. Clean and grease the release bearing sliding surface.

16. Check that the two dowel pins are present in the bell housing.

17. Raise the unit enough to align the pins with the matching holes in the block.

18. Install and tighten the transaxle mount bolt on the engine side to 47 ft. lbs. (65 Nm).

19. Install and tighten the transaxle bolts on the transaxle side to 47 ft. lbs. (65 Nm).

20. Install the transaxle mounting bracket; tighten the 3 bolts to 28 ft. lbs. (39 Nm). Tighten the horizontal bolt to 54 ft. lbs. (75 Nm).

21. Install the transaxle mounting bolts to the rear engine mounting bracket and tighten them to 54 ft. lbs. (75 Nm).

22. Install the engine stiffener. Tighten the bolts in sequence to 28 ft. lbs. (39 Nm).

23. Attach the intermediate shaft.

24. Install the driveshafts.

25. Install the center beam. Tighten the nuts to 37 ft. lbs. (51 Nm).

26. Attach the clutch slave cylinder; tighten the mounting bolts to 16 ft. lbs. (22 Nm).

27. Install the shift and select cables to the transaxle.

28. Connect the reverse lamp wiring.

29. Install the right and left front damper forks.

30. Install the speed sensor assembly.

31. Install the air cleaner case if it was removed.

32. Connect the starter ground and battery wires.

33. If applicable, enable the SRS as described in Section 6.

34. Connect the positive cable at the battery.

35. Install the front wheels.

36. Refill the transaxle with the proper amount of lubricant.

37. Check the shifter and clutch for smooth operation. Make adjustments as necessary.

1990–95 Accord

♦ See Figures 14 thru 21

1. Disconnect the battery cables and remove the battery. If so equipped, disable the Supplemental Restraint System (SRS), as described in Section 6.

2. Raise and safely support the vehicle.

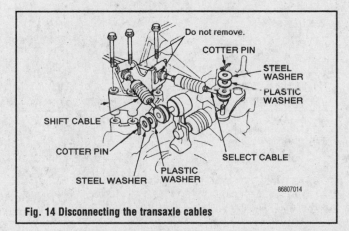

Fig. 14 Disconnecting the transaxle cables

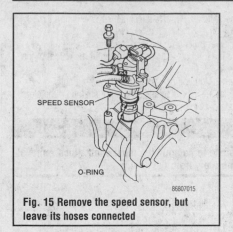

SPEED SENSOR

O-RING

86807015

Fig. 15 Remove the speed sensor, but leave its hoses connected

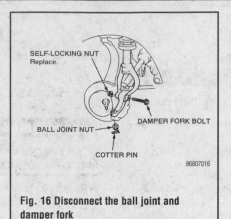

SELF-LOCKING NUT
Replace.

DAMPER FORK BOLT

BALL JOINT NUT

COTTER PIN

86807016

Fig. 16 Disconnect the ball joint and damper fork

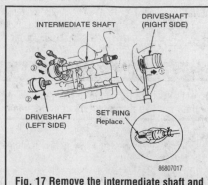

INTERMEDIATE SHAFT

DRIVESHAFT (RIGHT SIDE)

DRIVESHAFT (LEFT SIDE)

SET RING
Replace.

86807017

Fig. 17 Remove the intermediate shaft and protect the splined ends by covering them with plastic

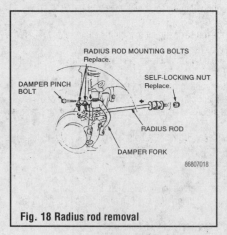

RADIUS ROD MOUNTING BOLTS
Replace.

DAMPER PINCH BOLT

SELF-LOCKING NUT
Replace.

RADIUS ROD

DAMPER FORK

86807018

Fig. 18 Radius rod removal

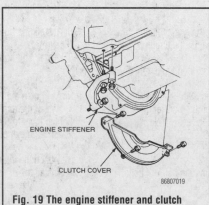

ENGINE STIFFENER

CLUTCH COVER

86807019

Fig. 19 The engine stiffener and clutch cover are secured by bolts

REAR ENGINE MOUNT BRACKET

BRACKET MOUNTING BOLTS

TRANSMISSION HOUSING MOUNTING BOLTS (ENGINE SIDE)

STAY

REAR ENGINE MOUNT BRACKET

86807020

Fig. 20 Removing the rear engine support and transaxle bolts

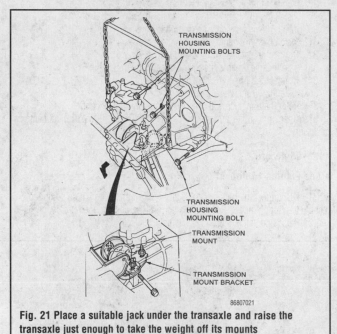

TRANSMISSION HOUSING MOUNTING BOLTS

TRANSMISSION HOUSING MOUNTING BOLT

TRANSMISSION MOUNT

TRANSMISSION MOUNT BRACKET

86807021

Fig. 21 Place a suitable jack under the transaxle and raise the transaxle just enough to take the weight off its mounts

3. Remove the air intake hose and battery base.
4. Disconnect the starter wires and remove the starter.
5. Disconnect the transaxle ground cable and the back-up light switch wire.
6. Remove the cable support and then disconnect the cables from the top housing of the transaxle. Remove both cables and the support together; do not remove the clips holding the cables to the support.
7. Remove the speed sensor, but leave its hoses connected.

8. Remove the front wheels.
9. Remove the engine splash shield and drain the transaxle fluid.
10. Remove the mounting bolts and clutch slave cylinder with the clutch pipe and pushrod.
11. Remove the mounting bolt and clutch hose joint with the clutch pipe and clutch hose.

➡**Do not operate the clutch pedal once the slave cylinder has been removed. Be careful not to bend the pipe.**

12. Remove the center beam and the header pipe.
13. Remove the cotter pins and lower arm ball joint nuts. Separate the ball joints and lower arms.
14. Remove the damper fork bolt.
15. Pry the right and left halfshafts out of the differential and the intermediate shaft. Pull on the inboard joint and remove the right and left halfshafts.
16. Remove the 3 mounting bolts and lower the bearing support.
17. Remove the intermediate shaft from the differential.
18. Remove the right damper pinch bolt, then separate the damper fork and damper. Remove the bolts and nut, then remove the right radius rod.
19. Remove the engine stiffener and the clutch cover.
20. Remove the intake manifold bracket.
21. Remove the rear engine mount bracket support and remove the 3 rear engine mount bracket mounting bolts.
22. Remove the transaxle housing mounting bolt on the engine side. Swing the right halfshaft to the inner fender.
23. Place a suitable jack under the transaxle and raise the transaxle just enough to take the weight off the mounts.
24. Remove the transaxle mount bolt and loosen the mount bracket nuts.
25. Remove the 3 transaxle housing mounting bolts.
26. Remove the transaxle from the vehicle.

To install:
27. Make sure the 4 dowel pins are installed.
28. Raise the transaxle into position.
29. Install the 3 transaxle mounting bolts and tighten to 47 ft. lbs. (65 Nm).

30. Install the transaxle mount and mount bracket. Install the through-bolt and tighten temporarily. Make sure the engine is level and tighten the 3 mount bracket nuts to 40 ft. lbs. (55 Nm). Tighten the through-bolt to 47 ft. lbs. (65 Nm).

31. Install the transaxle housing mounting bolts on the engine side and tighten to 47 ft. lbs. (65 Nm).

32. Install the 3 rear engine bracket mounting bolts and tighten to 40 ft. lbs. (55 Nm).

33. Install the rear engine mount bracket stay. Tighten the mounting bolt to 28 ft. lbs. (39 Nm) and then tighten the mounting nut to 15 ft. lbs. (21 Nm).

34. Install the intake manifold bracket and tighten the bolts to 16 ft. lbs. (22 Nm).

35. Install the clutch cover and tighten the bolts to 9 ft. lbs. (12 Nm).

36. Install the engine stiffener and loosely install the mounting bolts. Tighten the stiffener-to-transaxle case mounting bolt to 28 ft. lbs. (39 Nm), then tighten the 2 stiffener-to-cylinder block mounting bolts to 28 ft. lbs. (39 Nm) beginning with the bolt closest to the transaxle.

37. Install the radius rod. Tighten the radius rod mounting bolts to 76 ft. lbs. (105 Nm) and the radius rod nut to 32 ft. lbs. (44 Nm).

38. Install the damper fork. Tighten the damper pinch bolt to 32 ft. lbs. (44 Nm).

39. Install the intermediate shaft.

40. Install a new snapring on the end of each halfshaft. Install the right and left halfshafts. Turn the right and left steering knuckle fully outward and slide the axle into the differential until the spring clip is felt to engage in the differential side gear.

41. Install the damper fork bolt and ball joint nut to the lower arms. Tighten the nut while holding the damper fork bolt to 40 ft. lbs. (55 Nm). Tighten the ball joint nut to 40 ft. lbs. (55 Nm). Install a new cotter pin.

42. Install the header pipe and center beam. Tighten the center beam bolts to 28 ft. lbs. (39 Nm).

43. Install the clutch hose joint and clutch slave cylinder to the transaxle housing. Tighten the slave cylinder mounting bolts to 16 ft. lbs. (22 Nm).

44. Install the speed sensor. Tighten the mounting bolt to 13 ft. lbs. (18 Nm).

45. Install the shift cable and select cable to the shift arm lever and to the select lever respectively. Tighten the cable bracket mounting bolts to 16 ft. lbs. (22 Nm). Install new cotter pins.

46. Connect the back-up light switch coupler.

47. Install the starter.

48. Install the transaxle ground cable.

49. Install the front wheel and tire assemblies.

50. Fill the transaxle with the proper type and quantity of oil.

51. Lower the vehicle.

52. If applicable, enable the SRS as described in Section 6.

53. Install the battery and connect the battery cables.

54. Start the vehicle and check the transaxle for smooth operation.

Halfshafts

REMOVAL & INSTALLATION

▶ **See Figures 22, 23, 24 and 25**

1. Disconnect the negative battery cable. If so equipped, disable the Supplemental Restraint System (SRS), as described in Section 6.

2. Remove the wheel cover or hubcap from the front wheel and then remove the center cap.

3. Pull out the 4mm cotter pin and loosen but do not remove the spindle nut. Loosen the lugnuts.

4. Raise and safely support the front of the vehicle on jackstands. Double check the stand placement and the security of the support.

5. Remove the wheel lug nuts and the wheel.

6. Pry up the lock tabs and remove the large spindle nut.

7. Drain the transaxle.

8. Using a ball joint separator, remove the lower arm ball joints from the knuckle. Disconnect the tie rods from the steering knuckle.

9. On cars using a lower control arm, disconnect the stabilizer bar retaining bolts and free the bar.

10. On later cars with the "wishbone" suspension, remove the damper fork bolt and the damper pinch bolt.

11. To remove the halfshaft, hold the knuckle and move it outwards while sliding the shaft out of the hub

12. At the inboard or transaxle end, pry the CV-joint out about ½ in. (13mm). Prying the axle outward causes an internal snapring to come out of its locking groove. Pry carefully to avoid damaging the oil seal.

13. Carefully pull the inboard side of the driveshaft out of the differential case.

To install:

14. Replace the snapring on the inboard end of the axle.

15. Install the inner end of the axle to the transaxle. The splined fitting and clip must fit all the way into position; the clip will engage with a noticeable click. Double check it by prying lightly against it; don't pull on the CV-joint to test it.

16. Pull the front hub outward and install the outer end of the halfshaft.

17. Reassemble the suspension and steering ball joints. Use new cotter pins and new self-locking nuts for each fitting. Tighten the individual components as follows:

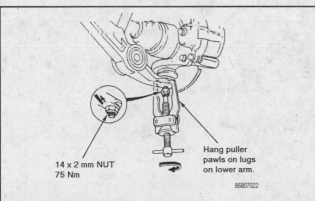

14 x 2 mm NUT
75 Nm

Hang puller pawls on lugs on lower arm.

86807022

Fig. 22 Use a ball joint separator to disconnect the ball joints

86807023

Fig. 23 Hold the knuckle and move it outwards while sliding the shaft out of the hub

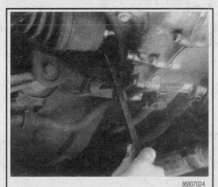

86807024

Fig. 24 Pry the joint out of the differential case . . .

86807025

Fig. 25 . . . then carefully pull the inboard side of the driveshaft out of the differential case

- 1984–85 Accord: Stabilizer bar bolts, 16 ft. lbs. (22 Nm); lower ball joint 40 ft. lbs. (55 Nm); tie rod castle nut, 32 ft. lbs. (44 Nm).
- 1986–95 Accord: Damper pinch bolt, 32 ft. lbs. (44 Nm); damper fork or lower locknut, 47 ft. lbs. (65 Nm); lower ball joint castle nut, 40 ft. lbs. (55 Nm).
- 1984–95 Prelude: Damper pinch bolt, 32 ft. lbs. (44 Nm); damper fork or lower locknut, 47 ft. lbs. (65 Nm).
- 1984–87 and 1990–95 Prelude: Lower ball joint castle nut, 40 ft. lbs. (55 Nm).
- 1988–89 Prelude: Lower ball joint castle nut, 54 ft. lbs. (75 Nm).

18. Install the washer and a new spindle nut. Tighten the nut very snug but do not attempt to achieve final torque with the vehicle elevated.

19. Install the wheel. Lower the vehicle to the ground.

20. Tighten the spindle nut. Correct torque for the spindle nut is:
- 1984–89 Accord: 134 ft. lbs. (185 Nm)
- 1990–93 Accord: 180 ft. lbs. (245 Nm)
- 1984–87 Prelude: 137 ft. lbs. (190 Nm)
- 1988–89 Prelude: 134 ft. lbs. (185 Nm)
- 1994–95 Accord and 1990–95 Prelude: 181 ft. lbs. (250 Nm)

21. Use a drift or punch to deform the ring on the spindle nut into the groove in the axle. This locks the nut in place.

22. Tighten the lug nuts.

23. Refill the transaxle.

24. If applicable, enable the SRS as described in Section 6.

25. Connect the negative battery cable.

CV-JOINT OVERHAUL

♦ **See Figures 26, 27 and 28**

1. Remove the halfshaft.

2. Remove the large retaining band from the inboard boot. Remove the smaller band from the inboard boot and slide the boot off the joint.

3. Carefully remove the stub end of the inboard joint. Check the splines for cracks, wear or damage. Check the inside bore for any sign of wear.

4. Remove and discard the snapring from the end of the halfshaft. This will allow removal of the spider assembly.

5. Mark the rollers, spider and the stub end of the axle so that all parts may be reassembled in the same position. Remove the rollers from the spider.

6. Remove the second snapring from the shaft. Remove the joint boot. If equipped, remove the dynamic damper from the shaft.

7. If the outer joint's boot is to be replaced, remove the boot clamps and slide the boot off the joint, then off the shaft. Hold the outer joint and swivel the end. If the joint is noisy, it must be replaced. The replacement joint will come with a new shaft; the inner joint must be assembled onto the shaft.

8. Clean and inspect all disassembled parts. Any sign of wear requires replacement.

To install:

9. Thoroughly pack the inboard and outboard joints with moly grease. Use only moly grease; other lubricants will not last. Wrap the splines of the shaft in vinyl or electrical tape to protect the boots as they are installed.

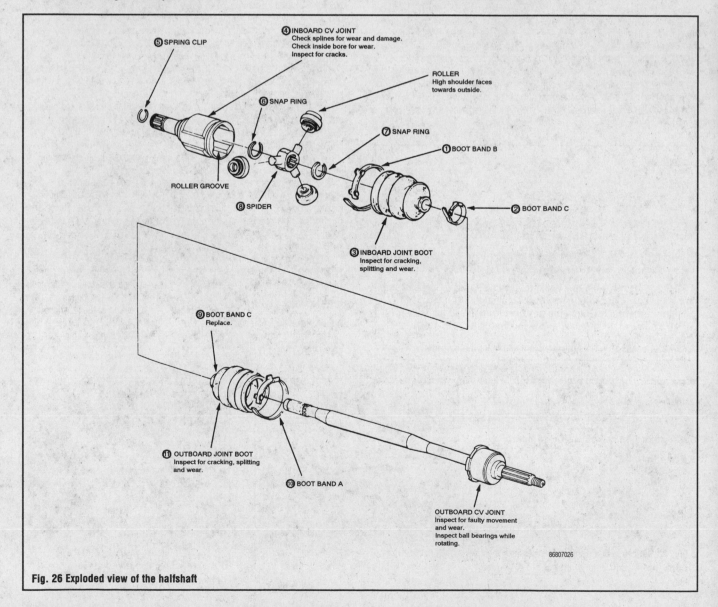

Fig. 26 Exploded view of the halfshaft

86807026

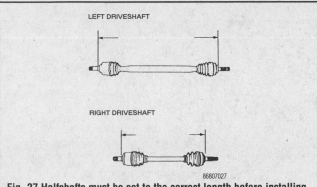

Fig. 27 Halfshafts must be set to the correct length before installing boot bands

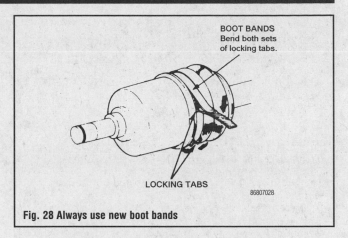

Fig. 28 Always use new boot bands

10. Slide the boot for the outer joint over the shaft and onto the joint. Do not install the bands yet.

11. Slide the inner boot onto the shaft. Install the dynamic damper if it was removed.

12. Install the inboard snapring on the shaft. Install the rollers and bearing races on the spider shafts. Hold the shaft upright, then slide the spider assembly into the inboard shaft joint. Install the outer snapring.

13. Slide the boots over both joints. Position the small end of the boot so that the band will be centered between the locating humps on the shaft. Install the band; bend both sets of locking tabs. Once the band is in place, expand and compress the boots once or twice; allow the boots to return to their normal size and length.

14. Adjust the length of the halfshaft by properly positioning the boots. When the shaft is at the correct length, adjust the boots to halfway between full extension and full compression. Correct shaft lengths are:
- 1984–85 Accord—Right: 19.3–19.5 in. (496–500.5mm). Left, manual trans: 30.3–30.5 in. (779–783.5mm). Left, automatic trans: 30.7–30.8 in. (787–791.5mm).
- 1986–89 Accord—Right: 19.7–19.9 in. (506–510.5mm). Left, manual trans: 31.3–31.5 in. (805–809.5mm). Left, automatic trans: 31.6–31.8 in. (812–816.5mm).
- 1984–87 Prelude, Carbureted—Right: 20.0–20.2 in. (514–518.5mm). Left, manual trans: 31.2–31.4 in. (800–804.5mm). Left, automatic trans: 31.5–31.7 in. (809–813.5mm).

- 1984–87 Prelude, Fuel injected—Right: 19.7–19.9 in. (506–510.5mm). Left, manual trans: 31.3–31.5 in. (805–809.5mm). Left, automatic trans: 31.6–31.8 in. (812–816.5mm).
- 1988–91 Prelude—Left and right shafts: 19.3 in. (496mm).
- 1990–93 Accord, manual trans—Left and right shafts: 18.6–18.8 in. (470.7–483.7mm).
- 1990–93 Accord, automatic trans—Left: 32.6–32.8 in. (836.7–841.7mm). Right: 18.6–18.8 in. (478.7–483.7mm).
- 1994–95 Accord, manual trans—Left and right shafts: 19.1–19.3 in. (486–491mm).
- 1994–95 Accord, automatic trans—Left: 33.3–33.5 in. (845–850mm). Right: 19.1–19.9 in. (486–491mm).
- 1992–95 Prelude—Right: 20.0–20.1 in. (507.9–512.9mm). Left, manual trans: 20.5–20.7 in. (520.9–525.9mm). Left, automatic trans: 33.9–34.1 in. (862.9–867.9mm).

15. Install new boot bands on the large ends of the boots. Be sure to bend both sets of locking tabs. Lightly tap the doubled-over portion of the band(s) to reduce the height. Do NOT hit the boot.

16. Position the dynamic damper so that it is 0.1–1.2 in. (3–7mm) from the CV-boot. Install a new retaining band in the same fashion as the boot bands.

17. Install a new snapring on the inboard end of the joint, then install the halfshaft.

CLUTCH

✳✳ CAUTION

The clutch disc may contain asbestos, which has been determined to be a cancer causing agent. Never clean clutch surfaces with compressed air! Avoid inhaling any dust from the clutch surface! When cleaning the surfaces, use a commercially available brake cleaning fluid.

Adjustments

PEDAL HEIGHT/FREE-PLAY ADJUSTMENT

1984–89 Accord and 1984–87 Prelude

▶ See Figure 29

1. Measure the clutch pedal disengagement height.
2. Measure the clutch pedal free-play.
3. Adjust the clutch pedal free-play by turning the clutch cable adjusting nut, found at the end of the clutch cable housing near the release shaft.
4. Turn the adjusting nut until the clutch pedal free-play is 0.6–1.0 in. (15–25mm).
5. After adjustment, make sure the free-play at the tip of the release arm is 0.12–0.16 in. (5.2–6.4mm).

➡ Too little free-play will lead to clutch slippage and premature wear; excessive play will lead to difficult shifting. Inspect the clutch free-play frequently and adjust as necessary.

1990–95 Accord and 1988–95 Prelude

▶ See Figure 30

The clutch is self-adjusting to compensate for wear. The total clutch pedal free-play is 0.35–0.59 in. (9–15mm). If there is no clearance between the master cylinder piston and pushrod, the release bearing is held against the diaphragm spring of the pressure plate, resulting in clutch slippage.

1. Loosen the locknut on clutch pedal switch A; back off the pedal switch until it no longer touches the clutch pedal. Clutch pedal switch A is the switch that contacts the clutch pedal below the clutch pedal pivot.
2. Loosen the locknut on the clutch master cylinder pushrod and turn the pushrod in or out to get the specified stroke and height at the clutch pedal. The pedal stroke should be 5.3–5.5 in. (135–140mm) on Prelude and 5.6 in. (142mm) on Accord. The pedal height should be 8.1 in. (207mm) on Prelude and 8.27 in. (210mm) on Accord.
3. Tighten the pushrod locknut.
4. Thread in clutch pedal switch A until it contacts the clutch pedal, then turn it in ¼–½ turn further.
5. Tighten the locknut on clutch pedal switch A.

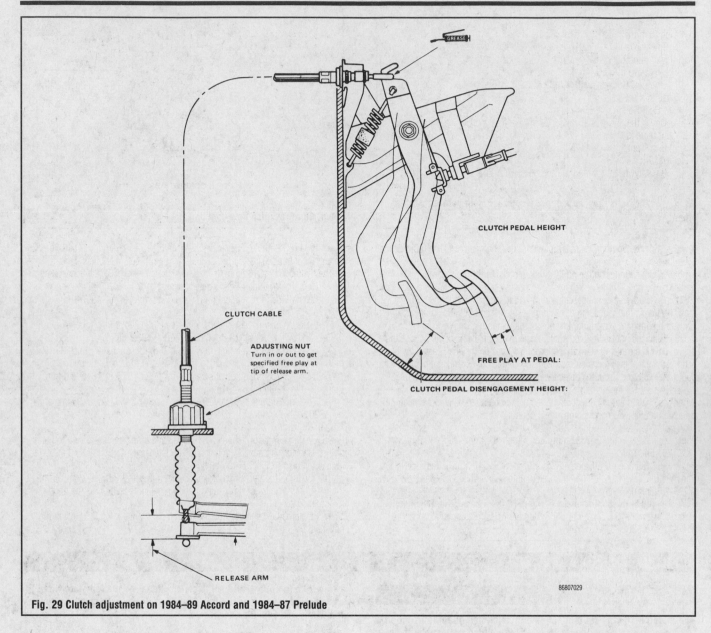

CLUTCH CABLE

ADJUSTING NUT
Turn in or out to get
specified free play at
tip of release arm.

CLUTCH PEDAL HEIGHT

FREE PLAY AT PEDAL:

CLUTCH PEDAL DISENGAGEMENT HEIGHT:

RELEASE ARM

86807029

Fig. 29 Clutch adjustment on 1984–89 Accord and 1984–87 Prelude

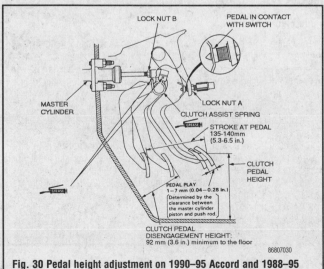

LOCK NUT B

PEDAL IN CONTACT
WITH SWITCH

MASTER
CYLINDER

LOCK NUT A

CLUTCH ASSIST SPRING

STROKE AT PEDAL
135–140mm
(5.3–6.5 in.)

CLUTCH
PEDAL
HEIGHT

PEDAL PLAY
1–7 mm (0.04–0.28 in.)
Determined by the
clearance between
the master cylinder
piston and push rod.

CLUTCH PEDAL
DISENGAGEMENT HEIGHT:
92 mm (3.6 in.) minimum to the floor

86807030

Fig. 30 Pedal height adjustment on 1990–95 Accord and 1988–95 Prelude

Driven Disc and Pressure Plate

REMOVAL & INSTALLATION

▶ See Figures 31, 32, 33, 34 and 35

1. Disconnect the negative battery cable. If so equipped, disable the Supplemental Restraint System (SRS), as described in Section 6.
2. Raise and safely support the vehicle.
3. Remove the transaxle from the vehicle. Matchmark the flywheel and clutch for reassembly.
4. Hold the flywheel ring gear with a tool made for this purpose, remove the retaining bolts and remove the pressure plate and clutch disc. Remove the bolts 2 turns at a time working in a crisscross pattern, to prevent warping the pressure plate.
5. Remove the assembly from the flywheel.
6. At this time, inspect the flywheel for wear, cracks or scoring and replace, as necessary. Resurfacing the flywheel surface is not recommended.
7. If the clutch release bearing is to be replaced, perform the following procedure on all except Prelude and 1990–95 Accord:
   a. Remove the 8mm bolt.
   b. Remove the release shaft and the release bearing assembly.

c. Separate the release fork from the bearing by removing the release fork spring from the holes in the release bearing.

8. To remove the release bearing on Prelude and 1990–95 Accord, perform the following procedure:

a. Remove the boot from the clutch housing.

b. Remove the release fork from the clutch housing by squeezing the release fork set spring.

c. Remove the release bearing from the release fork.

9. Check the release bearing for excessive play by spinning it by hand. Replace if there is excessive play. The bearing is packed with grease; do not wash it in solvent.

To install:

10. If the flywheel was removed, make sure the flywheel and crankshaft mating surfaces are clean. Align the hole in the flywheel with the crankshaft dowel pin and install the flywheel bolts finger-tight. Install the ring gear holder and tighten the flywheel bolts in a crisscross pattern. Tighten the flywheel bolts to 76 ft. lbs. (105 Nm) on Prelude and Accord.

11. Install the clutch disc and pressure plate by aligning the dowels on the flywheel with the dowel holes in the pressure plate. If the same pressure plate is being installed that was removed, align the marks that were made during the removal procedure. Install the pressure plate bolts finger-tight.

12. Insert a clutch disc alignment tool into the splined hole in the clutch disc. These inexpensive tools are available at most auto supply or parts stores. Using the tool assures that the clutch disc and pressure plate are exactly centered. Tighten the pressure plate bolts in a crisscross pattern 2 turns at a time to prevent warping the pressure plate. The final torque should be 19 ft. lbs. (26 Nm).

13. Remove the alignment tool and ring gear holder.

14. If the release bearing was removed, replace it in the reverse order of the removal procedure. Place a light coat of molybdenum disulfide grease on the inside diameter of the bearing prior to installation.

15. Install the transaxle, making sure the mainshaft is properly aligned with the clutch disc splines and the transaxle case is properly aligned with the cylinder block, before tightening the transaxle case bolts.

16. Adjust the clutch pedal free-play.

17. If applicable, enable the SRS as described in Section 6.

18. Connect the negative battery cable.

Clutch Cable

REMOVAL & INSTALLATION

1. Disconnect the negative battery cable.
2. Disconnect the cable end from the brake pedal.
3. Remove the adjuster nut assembly from its mounting.
4. Raise and safely support the vehicle.
5. Disconnect the cable end from the release arm. Remove the cable from the vehicle.
6. Installation is the reverse of the removal procedure. Adjust the cable to specification.

Clutch Master Cylinder

REMOVAL & INSTALLATION

1. Disconnect the negative battery cable. If so equipped, disable the Supplemental Restraint System (SRS), as described in Section 6.
2. At the top of the clutch pedal, remove the cotter pin and pull the pedal pin out of the yoke.
3. Remove the nuts and bolts holding the clutch master cylinder and remove the cylinder from the engine compartment.
4. Disconnect and plug the hydraulic lines from the master cylinder.
5. Installation is the reverse of the removal procedure. Bleed the clutch hydraulic system.

OVERHAUL

Overhaul of the clutch master cylinder is not recommended. In the event that the master cylinder requires replacement, it is recommended to replace both the master cylinder and slave cylinder as a set for added reliability.

Slave Cylinder

REMOVAL & INSTALLATION

1. Disconnect the negative battery cable. If so equipped, disable the Supplemental Restraint System (SRS), as described in Section 6.
2. Disconnect and plug the clutch hose from the slave cylinder.
3. Remove the 2 retaining bolts and remove the slave cylinder.
4. Install in reverse order. Bleed the clutch hydraulic system.

OVERHAUL

Overhaul of the slave cylinder is not recommended. In the event that the cylinder requires replacement, it is recommended to replace both the master cylinder and slave cylinder as a set for added reliability.

SYSTEM BLEEDING

The hydraulic system must be bled whenever the system has been leaking or dismantled. The bleed screw is located on the slave cylinder.

1. Remove the bleed screw dust cap.
2. Attach a clear hose to the bleed screw. Immerse the other end of the hose in a clear jar, half filled with brake fluid.
3. Fill the clutch master cylinder with fresh brake fluid.
4. Open the bleed screw slightly and have an assistant slowly depress the clutch pedal. Close the bleed screw when the pedal reaches the end of its travel. Allow the clutch pedal to return slowly.
5. Repeat until all air bubbles are expelled from the system.
6. Properly dispose of the brake fluid in the jar. Install the dust cap. Refill the master cylinder.

86807034

Fig. 31 Remove the pressure plate and clutch disc as an assembly

86807035

Fig. 32 Insert a clutch disc alignment tool into the splined hole in the disc, then tighten the bolts to specification

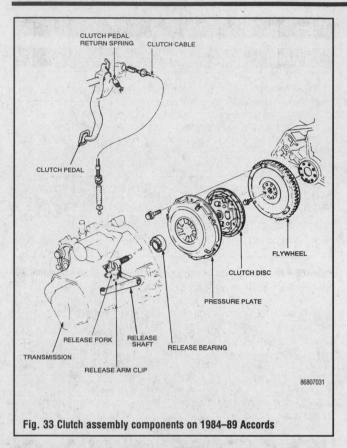

Fig. 33 Clutch assembly components on 1984–89 Accords

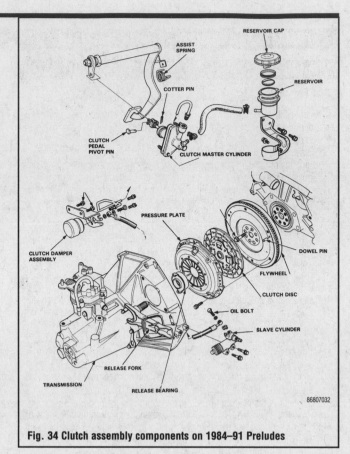

Fig. 34 Clutch assembly components on 1984–91 Preludes

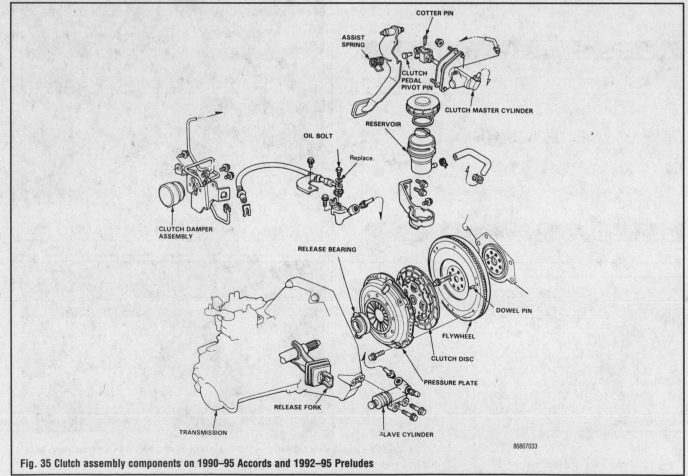

Fig. 35 Clutch assembly components on 1990–95 Accords and 1992–95 Preludes

AUTOMATIC TRANSAXLE

Identification

◆ See Figure 36

The transaxle number, stamped on the case, indicates the family and running serial number for the transaxle. In general, transaxles are not interchangeable between model families.

Transaxles are selected by the manufacturer to fit the engine performance characteristics of the car with consideration to other variables such as area of sale, emission class, vehicle loading, brakes, etc. Even if a replacement unit physically fit into a dissimilar car, the performance of the transaxle would be a poor match to the present engine; driveability, fuel economy and emissions would suffer.

If you're considering replacing the transaxle rather than repairing a failure, stick to the same transaxle group; that is, if the old unit's transaxle number was AOYA, then that is also what the replacement unit must be. Transaxle identification numbers begin with the following groups:

- 1984–85 Accord and 1984–87 Prelude: Carbureted—AS; Fuel Injected—F4
- 1986–89 Accord: F4
- 1988–91 Prelude: K4
- 1990–91 Accord: PX4B
- 1992–95 Prelude: MP1A
- 1992 Accord: APX4
- 1993 Accord: MPXA
- 1994–95 Accord, except V-6: AOYA
- 1994–95 Accord V-6: MPZA

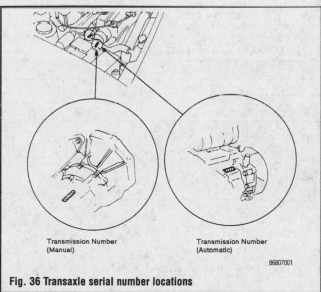

Transmission Number (Manual)

Transmission Number (Automatic)

86807001

Fig. 36 Transaxle serial number locations

Adjustments

SHIFT CABLE

◆ See Figures 37 and 38

1. Start the engine. Shift the transaxle to R, checking that reverse gear engages.
2. Shut the engine off and disconnect the negative battery cable.
3. Remove the console.
4. On 1984–88 Accord, place the selector lever in D. On 1988 Prelude, place the selector lever in R. On 1989 Accord and Prelude, place the selector lever in N or R. On 1990–95 Accord and Prelude, place the selector lever in N. Remove the lock pin from the cable adjuster.
5. Check that the hole in the adjuster is perfectly aligned with the hole in the shift cable.

➡ **There are 2 holes in the end of the shift cable. They are positioned 90 degrees apart to allow cable adjustments in ¼ turn increments.**

6. If not perfectly aligned, loosen the locknut on the shift cable and adjust as required.
7. Tighten the locknut and install the lock pin on the adjuster. If the lock pin feels like it is binding when being installed, the cable is still out of adjustment and must be adjusted again.
8. Connect the negative battery cable, start the engine and check the shift lever in all gears. Install the console.

THROTTLE CONTROL CABLE

Carbureted Engines

1984–88 MODELS

◆ See Figures 39, 40 and 41

1. Start the engine and warm it up to normal operating temperature. The cooling fan must come on at least once.
2. Make sure the throttle cable play, idle speed and automatic choke operation are correct.
3. Turn the engine off and disconnect the negative battery cable.
4. Disconnect the throttle control cable from the control lever.
5. If the vehicle is equipped with a dashpot on the linkage, disconnect the vacuum hose from the dashpot, connect a vacuum pump and apply vacuum. This simulates a normal operating amount of pull by the dashpot, as if the engine were running.
6. Attach a weight of about 3 lbs. (1.36 kg) to the accelerator pedal. Raise the pedal, then release it. This will allow the weight to remove the normal free-play from the throttle cable.
7. Secure the throttle cable with clamps.
8. Place the end of the throttle cable on the shock tower.

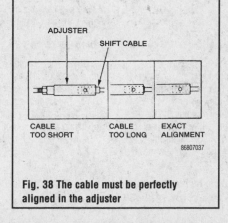

CABLE TOO SHORT

CABLE TOO LONG

EXACT ALIGNMENT

86807037

Fig. 38 The cable must be perfectly aligned in the adjuster

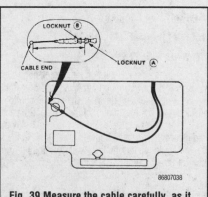

LOCKNUT B

LOCKNUT A

CABLE END

86807038

Fig. 39 Measure the cable carefully, as it must be adjusted precisely

LOCK PIN

SHIFT LEVER (In D₃ or D₄)

LOCK NUT

SHIFT CABLE   ADJUSTER   LOCK NUT

86807036

Fig. 37 Shifter cable and lock pin

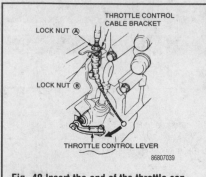

Fig. 40 Insert the end of the throttle control cable into the groove of the throttle control lever

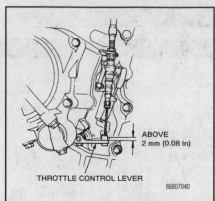

Fig. 41 Check the play at the control lever

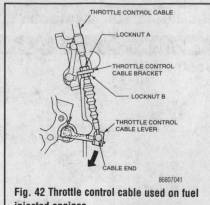

Fig. 42 Throttle control cable used on fuel injected engines

9. Adjust the distance between the throttle control cable end and the locknut closest to the cable housing to 3.366 in. (85.5mm) on all except 1988 Prelude. The distance on 1988 Prelude should be 6.22 in. (158mm).

10. Insert the end of the throttle control cable into the groove of the throttle control lever. Insert the throttle control cable into the bracket and secure with the other locknut. Make sure the cable is not kinked or twisted.

11. Check that the cable moves freely by depressing the accelerator.

12. Remove the weight on the accelerator pedal and push the pedal to make sure there is at least 0.08 in. (2mm) play at the throttle control lever.

13. Connect the negative battery cable and the vacuum hose to the dashpot.

14. Start the engine and check the synchronization between the carburetor and the throttle control cable. The throttle control lever should start to move as the engine speed increases.

15. If the throttle control lever starts to move before the engine speed increases, turn the cable locknut closest to the cable housing counterclockwise and retighten the locknut closest to the cable end.

16. If the throttle control lever moves after the engine speed increases, turn the locknut closest to the cable housing clockwise and retighten the locknut closest to the cable end.

1989–90 MODELS

1. Start the engine and bring it to normal operating temperature. The cooling fan must come on at least once.

2. Make sure the throttle cable free-play and idle speed are correct.

3. On 1990 Prelude, disconnect the vacuum hose from the throttle controller and connect a vacuum pump to the controller and apply vacuum.

4. Apply light thumb pressure to the throttle control lever. Have an assistant depress the accelerator. The lever should move just as the engine speed increases above idle. If not, loosen the nuts on the control cable at the transaxle end and synchronize the control lever to the throttle.

➡The shift/lock-up characteristics can be tailored to the driver's expectations by adjusting the control cable up to 0.11 in. (3mm) shorter than the synchronized point.

Fuel Injected Engines

▸ See Figures 42, 43 and 44

1985–88 MODELS

1. Loosen the locknuts on the throttle control cable.

2. Press down on the throttle control lever until it stops.

3. While pressing down on the throttle control lever, pull on the throttle linkage to check the amount of throttle control cable free-play.

4. Remove all throttle control cable free-play by gradually turning the locknut closest to the cable housing. Keep turning the locknut until no movement can be felt in the throttle link, while continuing to press down on the throttle control lever, pull open the throttle link. The control lever should begin to move at precisely the same time as the link.

➡The adjustment of the throttle control cable is critical for proper operation of the transaxle and lock-up torque converter.

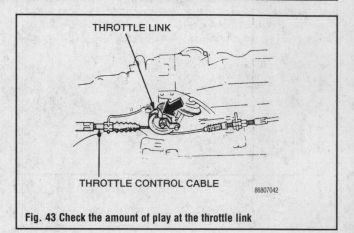

Fig. 43 Check the amount of play at the throttle link

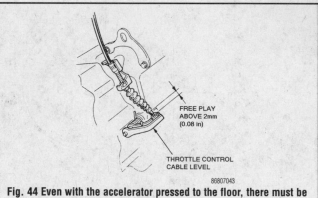

Fig. 44 Even with the accelerator pressed to the floor, there must be play in the lever

5. Have an assistant depress the accelerator to the floor. While depressed, check that there is at least 0.08 in. (2mm) play in the throttle control lever. Check that the cable moves freely by depressing the accelerator.

1989–95 MODELS

1. Start the engine and bring it up to operating temperature. The cooling fan must come on at least once.

2. Make sure the throttle cable free-play and idle speed are correct.

3. On dashpot equipped vehicles, disconnect the vacuum hose from the dashpot, connect a vacuum pump and apply vacuum. This simulates a normal operating amount of pull by the dashpot as if the engine were running.

4. Remove all throttle control cable free-play by gradually turning the locknut.

5. Apply light thumb pressure to the throttle control lever to move the throttle linkage. The lever should move just as the engine speed increases above idle. If not, loosen the nuts on the control cable at the transaxle end and synchronize the control lever to the throttle.

→The shift and lock-up characteristics can be tailored to the driver's expectations by adjusting the control cable up to 0.11 in. (3mm) shorter than the synchronized point.

Back-Up Light Switch/Neutral Safety Switch

REMOVAL & INSTALLATION

▶ See Figure 45

On automatic vehicles, functions of both the reverse lamps and the neutral safety switch are controlled by the shift position switch at the base of the shift selector. This multi-circuit switch also sends signals to the various electronic control units (cruise control, automatic transaxle ECU, etc.), keeping them advised of the selected gear.

To replace the shift position switch, firmly set the parking brake and block the wheels. Place the shift selector in N. Remove the console. The switch is located on the side of the shift selector, held by 2 bolts or nuts. Unplug the wiring connectors, then remove the switch.

When installing the switch, make sure the switch slider is positioned to align with the shifter arm or tab. Install the switch, tighten the retaining nuts or bolts and connect the wiring. Reinstall the console.

After installing the switch, check that the engine starts only in P or N; the starter should not engage with the shifter in any other position. Check also that the back-up lights come on when the selector is placed in R.

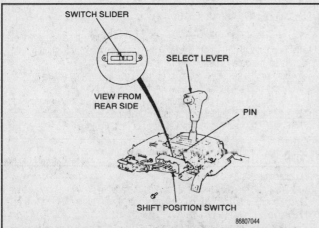

Fig. 45 Reverse lamp and neutral safety switch functions are both controlled by a shift position switch at the base of the shift selector

Transaxle

REMOVAL & INSTALLATION

1984–89 Accord and 1984–87 Prelude

▶ See Figure 46

1. Disconnect the negative battery cable at the battery and the transaxle.
2. Unlock the steering and place the transaxle in Neutral.
3. Disconnect the positive battery cable from the battery, then the starter and disconnect the wire from the starter solenoid.
4. Disconnect and plug the transaxle cooler hoses.
5. Remove the starter and the top transaxle mounting bolt.
6. Raise and safely support the vehicle. Double check the placement and security of the jackstands.
7. Remove the front wheels.
8. Drain the transaxle and reinstall the drain plug with a new washer.
9. Remove the throttle control cable end from the throttle lever, then loosen locknut A and remove the cable from the bracket.
10. Remove the power steering speed sensor complete with speedometer cable and hoses.

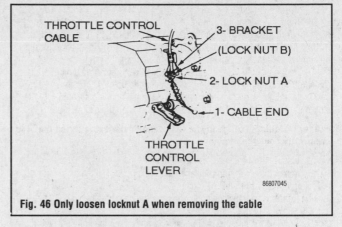

Fig. 46 Only loosen locknut A when removing the cable

11. Remove 2 upper transaxle mounting bolts.
12. Place a suitable transaxle jack securely beneath the transaxle. Attach a hoist to the engine and raise the engine just enough to take the weight of the engine off the mounts.
13. Remove the subframe center beam and splash pan.
14. Remove the ball joint pinch bolt from the right side lower control arm. Use a puller of the proper size to disconnect the ball joint from the knuckle. Remove the damper fork bolt.
15. Turn the right side steering knuckle to its most outboard position. Pry the CV-joint out approximately ½ in. (13mm), then pull the CV-joint out of the transaxle housing.

→Do not pull on the halfshaft or knuckle since this may cause the inboard CV-joint to separate.

16. Remove the transaxle damper bracket located in front of the torque converter cover plate.
17. Remove the torque converter cover plate.
18. Inside the vehicle, remove the center console and shift indicator.
19. Remove the lock pin from the adjuster and shift cable. Remove both bolts and pull the shift cable out of the housing.
20. Unbolt the torque converter assembly from the driveplate by removing the 8 bolts.
21. Remove the 3 rear engine mounting bolts from the transaxle housing. Remove the rear engine mount.
22. Remove two bolts from the front transaxle mount.
23. Remove the lower transaxle mounting bolt.
24. Pull the transaxle away from the engine to clear the two 14mm dowel pins. Pry the left side CV-joint out approximately ½ in. (13mm). Pull the transaxle out and lower the transaxle.

To install:
25. Attach the shift cable to the shift arm with the pin, then secure the cable to the edge of the housing with the cable holder and bolt. Tighten the bolt to 9 ft. lbs. (12 Nm).
26. Make sure the two 14mm dowel pins are installed in the transaxle housing.
27. Install new snaprings on the end of each axle.
28. Raise the transaxle into position, aligning the dowel pins with the holes in the block and the torque converter bolt heads with the holes in the driveplate. Fit the left axle into the differential as the transaxle is raised up to the engine.
29. Install the 2 lower transaxle mounting bolts but do not tighten them at this time.
30. Install the rear engine mounts on the transaxle housing and tighten the bolts to 28 ft. lbs. (39 Nm).
31. Install the front transaxle mount bolts and tighten to 28 ft. lbs. (39 Nm).
32. Attach the torque converter to the driveplate with the eight 12mm bolts. Tighten the bolts in 2 steps to 9 ft. lbs. (12 Nm) in the same pattern.
33. Remove the transaxle jack.
34. Install the torque converter cover plate and tighten the bolts to 9 ft. lbs. (12 Nm).
35. Install the anti-windup rubber on the center beam and tighten the nuts to 40 ft. lbs. (55 Nm). Install the anti-windup bracket on the transaxle housing and tighten the 3 bolts to 22 ft. lbs. (31 Nm).
36. Remove the hoist equipment from the engine.

37. Install the starter.
38. Install the rear torque rod and brackets. Tighten the bracket mounting bolts to 46 ft. lbs. (65 Nm) and the torque rod bolts to 54 ft. lbs. (75 Nm).
39. Turn the right steering knuckle fully outward and slide the axle into the differential until the spring clip engages the differential side gear.
40. Reconnect the ball joint to the knuckle, then tighten the bolt to 40 ft. lbs. (55 Nm). Reinstall the damper fork and tighten the bolt to 32 ft. lbs. (44 Nm).
41. Install the speedometer cable. Align the tab on the cable end with the slot in the holder. Install the clip so the bent leg is on the groove side.

➡**After installing, pull gently on the speedometer cable to see that it is secure. It should be retained in place.**

42. Install the wheels and lower the vehicle.
43. Install the remaining transaxle mounting bolts. Tighten all the transaxle mounting bolts to 33 ft. lbs. (45 Nm).
44. Connect the transaxle cooler hoses and tighten the banjo bolts to 21 ft. lbs. (29 Nm).
45. Connect the positive battery cable to the starter, the solenoid wire to the solenoid, the wire to the water temperature sending unit and the wires to the ignition timing thermosensor.
46. Connect the negative battery cable to the transaxle.
47. Unscrew the dipstick from the top of the transaxle end cover and add 3.2 quarts (3 L) of Dexron®II (or equivalent) ATF through the hole. Reinstall the dipstick.

➡**If the transaxle and torque converter have been disassembled, add a total of 6.3 quarts (6 L).**

48. Install and reconnect the shift cable. Install the console.
49. Connect the negative battery cable, start the engine, set the parking brake and shift the transaxle through all gears 3 times. Allow each gear to engage momentarily before changing. Check for proper shift cable adjustment.
50. Let the engine reach operating temperature with the transaxle in N or P, then turn the engine off and check the fluid level.
51. Install the throttle control cable and adjust.

1988–91 Prelude

1. Disconnect the negative battery cable at the battery and the transaxle.
2. Drain the transaxle fluid and replace the drain plug.
3. Disconnect the wiring for the starter, lock-up control solenoids, shift control solenoids and speed pulser.
4. On fuel injected vehicles, remove the air inlet hose and the air cleaner case.
5. Remove the speed sensor from the transaxle without removing the hoses.
6. Disconnect the throttle control cable at the transaxle bracket.
7. Disconnect the transaxle cooler hoses at the joint pipes and cap the joint pipes.
8. Remove the upper transaxle mounting bracket.
9. Remove the transaxle-to-cylinder block attachment bolts that must be removed from the engine compartment.
10. Raise and safely support the vehicle. Double check placement and security of the jackstands.
11. Remove the front wheels.
12. Remove the splash shield and the center beam.
13. Remove the right radius rod completely.
14. Remove the right and left halfshafts.
15. Remove the engine stiffener and the torque converter cover.
16. Remove the shift cable from the transaxle.
17. Remove the bolts from the driveplate.
18. Support the transaxle with a suitable jack.
19. Remove the lower bolt from the rear engine mounting bracket. Loosen, but do not remove, the top bolt. This bolt will support the weight of the engine.
20. Remove the remaining engine-to-transaxle mounting bolts.
21. Separate the transaxle from the engine block. Disengage the two 14mm dowel pins and lower the transaxle.

To install:

22. Raise the transaxle into position and install the mounting bolts. Tighten the bolts to 47 ft. lbs. (65 Nm).
23. Attach the torque converter to the driveplate with the mounting bolts. Tighten the bolts in 2 steps using a crisscross pattern to 9 ft. lbs. (12 Nm).

24. Install the transaxle to the rear engine mount bracket with the mounting bolts. Tighten the bolts to 55 ft. lbs. (75 Nm).
25. Install the shift cable with the control pin and a new cotter pin.
26. Install the torque converter cover and the cable holder.
27. Install the engine stiffener. The engine stiffener bolts must be tightened to 28 ft. lbs. (39 Nm) in their proper order. First, tighten the uppermost stiffener-to-transaxle housing bolt followed by the remaining stiffener-to-transaxle housing bolt. Next tighten the stiffener-to-cylinder block bolt closest to the transaxle followed by the remaining stiffener-to-cylinder block bolt.
28. Install the halfshafts.
29. Install the center beam and the right and left front damper fork.
30. Install the radius rod on the transaxle side.
31. Install the transaxle mounting bracket and tighten the bolts to 28 ft. lbs. (39 Nm).
32. Attach the lock-up control solenoid valve connector, the shift control solenoid valve coupler and the connector for the speed pulser.
33. Connect the throttle control cable to the throttle control lever.
34. Install the speed sensor assembly and the air cleaner case.
35. Connect the oil cooler hoses; connect the starter and ground cables.
36. Connect the battery cables to the battery.
37. Start the engine, set the parking brake and shift the transaxle through all gears 3 times, pausing in each to allow full engagement. Check for proper control cable adjustment.
38. Let the engine reach operating temperature with the transaxle in N or P, then turn the engine off and check the fluid level.

1990–95 4-Cylinder Accord and 1992–95 Prelude

▶ **See Figures 47, 48, 49 and 50**

1. Disconnect the battery cable and remove the battery. If so equipped, disable the Supplemental Restraint System (SRS), as described in Section 6.
2. Raise and safely support the vehicle.
3. Remove the air intake hose, air cleaner case and battery base.
4. Disconnect the throttle cable from the throttle control lever.
5. Disconnect the transaxle ground cable and the speed sensor connectors.
6. Disconnect the starter cables and remove the starter.
7. Remove the rear mount bracket stay nut first. Remove the bolt, then remove the rear mount bracket stay.
8. Remove the speed sensor, but leave its hoses connected.
9. Disconnect the lock-up control solenoid valve and shift control solenoid valve connectors.
10. Drain the transaxle fluid and reinstall the drain plug with a new washer.
11. Disconnect the transaxle cooler hoses from the joint pipes. Plug the hoses.
12. Remove the center beam.
13. Unplug the oxygen sensor connector.
14. Remove the exhaust header pipe and the splash shield.
15. Remove the cotter pins and lower arm ball joint nuts, then separate the ball joints from the lower arms using a ball joint tool.
16. Pry the right and left halfshafts out of the differential. Pull on the inboard CV-joints and remove the right and left halfshafts.
17. Remove the right damper pinch bolt, then separate the damper fork and damper.
18. Remove the bolts and nut, then remove the right radius rod.
19. Tie plastic bags over the halfshaft ends to protect the machined surfaces.
20. Remove the torque converter cover and control cable holder.
21. Remove the shift control cable by removing the cotter pin, control pin and control lever roller from the control lever.
22. Remove the plug, then remove the driveplate bolts one at a time while rotating the crankshaft pulley.
23. Remove the rear, engine side transaxle housing mounting bolts.
24. Remove the mounting bolts from the rear engine mount bracket.
25. Attach a hoist to the transaxle hoisting brackets; lift the engine slightly with a jack, just enough to take the weight off the mounts.
26. Place a suitable jack under the transaxle and raise the jack just enough to take weight off of the mounts.
27. Remove the transaxle housing mounting bolts and mount bracket nuts.
28. Pull the transaxle away from the engine until it clears the 14mm dowel pins, then lower it on the transaxle jack.

To install:

29. Make sure the two 14mm dowel pins are installed in the torque converter housing.

30. Raise the transaxle into position and install the transaxle housing mounting bolts. Tighten the bolts to 47 ft. lbs. (65 Nm).

31. Install the transaxle-to-transaxle mount bracket and tighten the nuts to 28 ft. lbs. (39 Nm).

32. Remove the transaxle jack.

33. Install the 2 engine side transaxle housing mounting bolts and tighten to 47 ft. lbs. (65 Nm). Install the rear engine mount bracket bolts and tighten to 40 ft. lbs. (55 Nm).

34. Attach the torque converter to the driveplate with 8 bolts. Tighten the bolts in 2 steps using a crisscross pattern to 9 ft. lbs. (12 Nm).

35. Install the shift control cable and control cable holder. Tighten the control cable holder bolts to 13 ft. lbs. (18 Nm).

36. Install the torque converter cover and tighten the bolts to 9 ft. lbs. (12 Nm).

37. Remove the hoist.

38. Install the radius rod. Tighten the mounting bolts to 76 ft. lbs. (105 Nm) and the nut to 32 ft. lbs. (44 Nm).

39. Install the damper fork. Tighten the damper pinch bolt to 32 ft. lbs. (44 Nm).

40. Install a new snapring on the end of each halfshaft.

41. Turn the right steering knuckle fully outward and slide the axle into the differential until the snapring engages the differential side gear. Repeat the procedure on the left side.

42. Install the damper fork bolts and ball joint nuts to the lower arms. Tighten the nut to 40 ft. lbs. (55 Nm) while holding the damper fork bolt. Tighten the ball joint nut to 40 ft. lbs. (55 Nm) and install a new cotter pin.

43. Install the splash shield, the center beam and the exhaust header pipe. Tighten the center beam bolts to 28 ft. lbs. (39 Nm).

44. Connect the oxygen sensor connector.

45. Install the speed sensor and tighten the bolt to 13 ft. lbs. (18 Nm).

46. Install the rear mount bracket stay. Tighten the mounting bolt first, to 28 ft. lbs. (39 Nm) and then tighten the nut to 15 ft. lbs. (21 Nm).

47. Install the starter. Connect the cables to the starter.

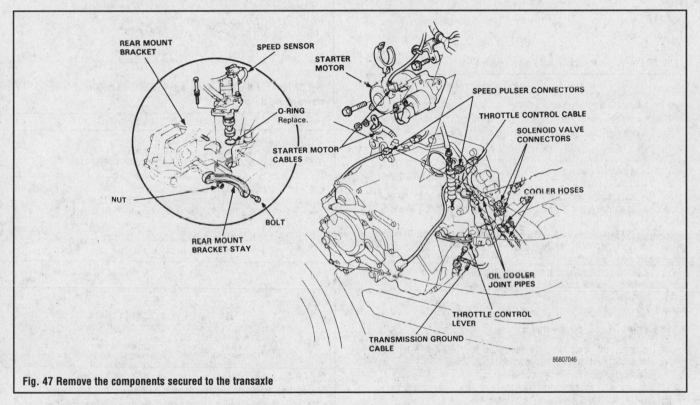

Fig. 47 Remove the components secured to the transaxle

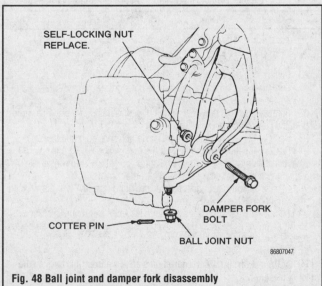

Fig. 48 Ball joint and damper fork disassembly

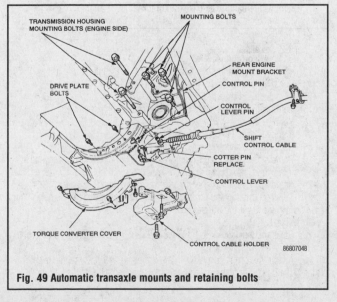

Fig. 49 Automatic transaxle mounts and retaining bolts

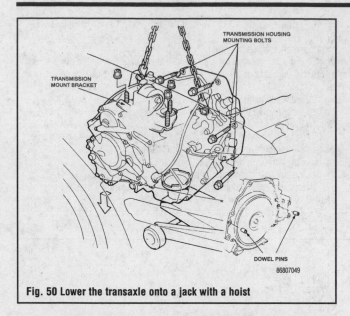

Fig. 50 Lower the transaxle onto a jack with a hoist

48. Connect the lock-up control solenoid valve and shift control solenoid valve connectors.

49. Connect the speed sensor connectors and the transaxle ground cable.

50. Connect the transaxle cooler hoses to the joint pipes.

51. Install the battery base, air cleaner case and air intake hose. Install the battery.

52. Install the wheels, then lower the vehicle.

53. If applicable, enable the SRS as described in Section 6.

54. Connect the battery cables at the battery.

55. Fill the transaxle with the proper type and quantity of fluid. Refer to Section 1.

56. Start the engine, set the parking brake and shift the transaxle through all gears 3 times, pausing momentarily in each gear. Check for proper control cable adjustment.

57. Let the engine reach operating temperature with the transaxle in N or P, then turn the engine off and check the fluid level.

Accord V-6

▶ **See Figures 51, 52, 53, 54 and 55**

1. Disconnect the negative battery cable. If so equipped, disable the Supplemental Restraint System (SRS), as described in Section 6.

2. Raise and safely support the vehicle.

3. Disconnect the support struts from the hood, then prop the hood in a vertical position.

4. Remove the battery, its base and bracket.

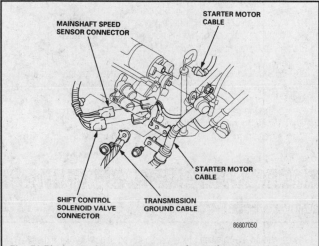

Fig. 51 Disengage the connectors on and near the starter motor

5. Drain the transaxle fluid, then install the plug with a new washer. Tighten to 36 ft. lbs. (49 Nm).

6. Remove the air intake duct.

7. Detach the starter cable from the strut tower brace, then remove the strut brace.

8. Disconnect the transaxle fluid cooler hose and plug the ends.

9. Disconnect the cables from the starter motor, then remove the cables from the clamp.

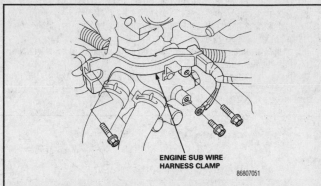

Fig. 52 Remove the bolts securing the engine sub-wire harness clamp above the transaxle

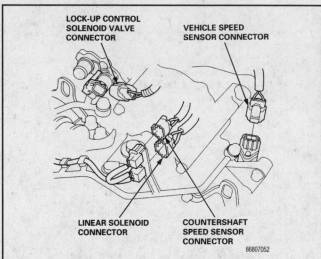

Fig. 53 Unplug the connectors for the lock-up control solenoid valve, countershaft speed sensor, linear solenoid and vehicle speed sensor

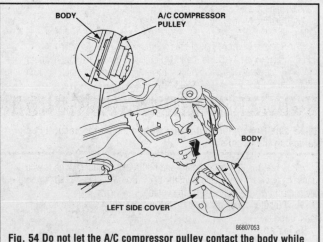

Fig. 54 Do not let the A/C compressor pulley contact the body while tilting the engine

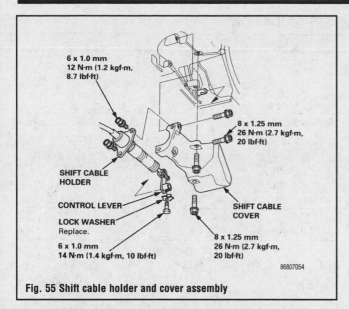

6 x 1.0 mm
12 N·m (1.2 kgf·m,
8.7 lbf·ft)

8 x 1.25 mm
26 N·m (2.7 kgf·m,
20 lbf·ft)

SHIFT CABLE
HOLDER

CONTROL LEVER

LOCK WASHER
Replace.

6 x 1.0 mm
14 N·m (1.4 kgf·m, 10 lbf·ft)

SHIFT CABLE
COVER

8 x 1.25 mm
26 N·m (2.7 kgf·m,
20 lbf·ft)

86807054

Fig. 55 Shift cable holder and cover assembly

10. Disconnect the ground cable from the transaxle.

11. Unplug the connectors from the shift control solenoid valve and main-shaft speed sensor.

12. Remove the bolts securing the engine sub-wire harness clamp above the transaxle.

13. Remove the intake air bypass tank from the transaxle. Do not remove the vacuum hoses.

14. Unplug the connectors for the lock-up control solenoid valve, counter-shaft speed sensor, linear solenoid and vehicle speed sensor.

15. Remove the splash shield from under the engine.

16. Remove the center beam.

17. Remove the cotter pins and castle nut, then separate the damper fork and lower arm.

18. Pry the halfshaft out of the differential and intermediate shaft. Tie plastic bags over the ends to prevent damage to the machined surfaces.

19. Remove the left damper pinch bolt, then separate the damper fork and damper.

20. Remove the bolts and nut securing the left radius rod, then remove the rod.

21. Remove the 3 bolts securing the intermediate shaft, then pull the shaft out of the differential.

22. Remove the shift cable holder bolts and cover.

23. Remove the lockbolt securing the control lever, then remove the shift cable with the control lever.

24. Remove the torque converter cover, then remove the 8 drive plate bolts one at a time while rotating the crankshaft pulley.

25. Place a jack under the engine and support it. Attach a hoist to the transaxle and raise it slightly to take the weight off the mounts.

26. Remove the rear mount stiffener. Remove the nut and bolt from the rear mount.

27. Remove the front mount bracket, then remove the front mount.

28. Remove the transaxle mounting bolts. Remove the transaxle mount.

29. Remove the rear mount bolts, then remove the rear mount bracket from the mount.

✳✳ WARNING

Make sure the engine and transaxle are supported securely before removing these bolts.

30. Lower the transaxle slightly and tilt the engine just enough for the transaxle to clear the left side from the body. Do not let the A/C compressor pulley contact the body while tilting the engine.

31. Pull the transaxle away from the engine until it clears the dowel pins, then lower it.

To install:

32. Position the transaxle under the vehicle and attach a hoist to the transaxle.

33. Tilt the engine and lift the transaxle to a level that will allow assembly.

34. Attach the transaxle to the engine, then install the transaxle housing mounting bolts. Tighten them to 47 ft. lbs. (64 Nm).

35. Place the rear mount bracket between the transaxle and the engine, then install the bracket to the mount.

36. Install new rear mount bolts to the transaxle through the rear mount bracket. Tighten them to 40 ft. lbs. (54 Nm).

37. Install the remaining transaxle mounting bolts. Tighten them to 47 ft. lbs. (64 Nm).

38. Install a new nut and bolt loosely in the rear mount while raising the transaxle and engine.

39. Install the front mount and bracket to the transaxle, then install the nut loosely in the front mount.

40. Install the transaxle mount. Tighten the bolt loosely and tighten the nuts to 28 ft. lbs. (38 Nm). Now tighten the bolt to 47 ft. lbs. (64 Nm).

41. Tighten the nuts and bolts that were loosely installed to 40 ft. lbs. (54 Nm).

42. Install the rear mount stiffener and tighten the bolts to 28 ft. lbs. (38 Nm).

43. Remove the jack supporting the engine and the hoist from the transaxle.

44. Attach the drive plate to the torque converter. Tighten the bolts in 2 steps using a crisscross pattern to 9 ft. lbs. (12 Nm).

45. Install the torque converter cover and tighten to 9 ft. lbs. (12 Nm).

46. Tighten the crankshaft pulley bolt. Refer to Section 3.

47. Install the control lever with the shift cable on the control shaft. Tighten the bolts to 9 ft. lbs. (12 Nm).

48. Install the lockbolt on the control lever with a new washer. Tighten to 10 ft. lbs. (14 Nm) and bend the locktab.

49. Install the shift cable cover. Tighten the bolts to 20 ft. lbs. (26 Nm).

50. Install the intermediate shaft and tighten the mounting bolts to 16 ft. lbs. (22 Nm).

51. Install the left radius rod and damper fork. Tighten the damper pinch bolt to 32 ft. lbs. (43 Nm). Tighten the rod bolts to 76 ft. lbs. (103 Nm) and the nut to 32 ft. lbs. (43 Nm).

52. Install new snaprings on the ends of the halfshafts. Install the halfshafts.

53. Connect the damper fork to the lower arm, then install the ball joint on the lower arm. Use new cotter pins with the castle nuts. Tighten the damper nut to 47 ft. lbs. (64 Nm) and the ball joint nut to 43 ft. lbs. (59 Nm).

54. Install the center beam and tighten the bolts to 37 ft. lbs. (50 Nm).

55. Install the splash shield. Tighten the bolts to 7 ft. lbs. (10 Nm).

56. Install the intake air bypass tank on the transaxle. Tighten the bolts to 9 ft. lbs. (12 Nm).

57. Install the engine sub-wire harness clamp, tightening the bolts to 9 ft. lbs. (12 Nm).

58. Engage the electrical connections and connect the cables to the starter. Connect the ground cable to the transaxle.

59. Connect the transaxle cooler lines.

60. Install the strut tower brace and connect the starter cable to it. Tighten the bolts to 16 ft. lbs. (22 Nm).

61. Install the air intake duct.

62. Install the battery base and bracket. Tighten the bolts to 16 ft. lbs. (22 Nm).

63. If applicable, enable the SRS as described in Section 6.

64. Install the battery. Connect the support struts to the hood.

65. Fill the transaxle with the proper type and quantity of fluid. Refer to Section 1.

66. Start the engine, set the parking brake and shift the transaxle through all gears 3 times, pausing momentarily in each gear. Check for proper control cable adjustment.

67. Let the engine reach operating temperature with the transaxle in N or P, then turn the engine off and check the fluid level.

68. Loosen the front an rear mount nuts, then retighten them to 40 ft. lbs. (54 Nm).

Halfshafts

REMOVAL & INSTALLATION

Please refer to the halfshaft procedures outlined under Manual Transaxles, earlier in this section.

TORQUE SPECIFICATIONS

Component	US	Metric
Manual transaxle		
Mounting bolts		
1984-89 Accord and 1984-87 Prelude	33 ft. lbs.	45 Nm
1990-95 Accord and 1988-95 Prelude	47 ft. lbs.	65 Nm
Halfshafts		
Spindle nut		
1984-89 Accord and 1988-89 Prelude	134 ft. lbs.	185 Nm
1984-87 Prelude	137 ft. lbs.	190 Nm
1990-93 Accord	180 ft. lbs.	245 Nm
1994-95 Accord and 1990-95 Prelude	181 ft. lbs.	250 Nm
Clutch		
Pressure plate mounting bolts	19 ft. lbs.	26 Nm
Automatic transaxle		
Mounting bolts		
1984-89 Accord and 1984-87 Prelude	28 ft. lbs.	39 Nm
1988-91 Prelude	55 ft. lbs.	75 Nm
1990-95 Accord and 1992-95 Prelude	47 ft. lbs.	65 Nm

86807900

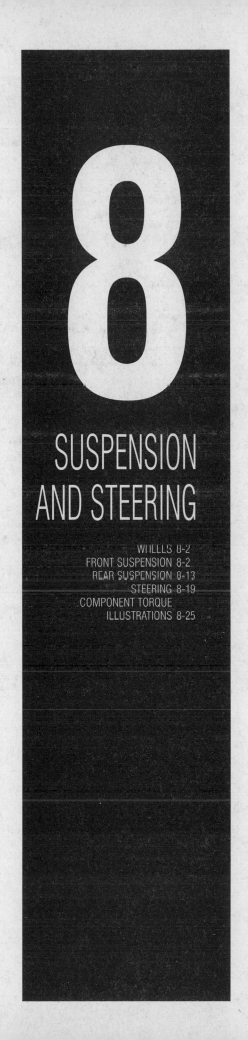

8

SUSPENSION
AND STEERING

WHEELS

Tire and Wheel Assembly

REMOVAL & INSTALLATION

1. If using a lug wrench, loosen the lug nuts slightly, in a crisscross pattern, before raising the vehicle..
2. Raise the vehicle and safely support it with jackstands.
3. Remove the lug nuts in a crisscross pattern, then pull the wheel assembly from the vehicle.
   To install:
4. Install the wheel, then thread the lug nuts onto the studs. Tighten the nuts until snug.

5. Lower the vehicle, then torque the nuts to 80 ft. lbs. (110 Nm) using a crisscross pattern.

INSPECTION

Before installing the wheels, check for any cracks or enlarged bolt holes. Remove any corrosion on the mounting surfaces with a wire brush. Installation of the wheels without a good metal–to–metal contact can cause wheel nuts to loosen. Recheck the wheel nut torque after 1000 miles (1610 km) of driving.

FRONT SUSPENSION

✳✳ CAUTION

Exercise great caution when working with the front suspension. Coil springs and other suspension components are under extreme tension and could cause severe injury if released improperly. Never remove the nut on the top of the strut piston without using the proper spring compressor tool.

MacPherson Strut/Damper

REMOVAL & INSTALLATION

✳✳ CAUTION

The use of a coil spring compressor is required for this procedure. A spring compressor must be used to retain the spring before removing it from the strut. Failure to use this tool can result component damage as well as serious or even fatal injury.

1984–85 Accord

▶ See Figure 1

1. Disconnect the negative battery cable.
2. Raise and safely support the front of the vehicle. Make sure the stands are correctly placed.

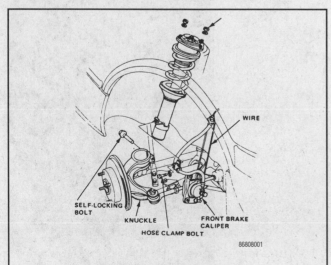

Fig. 1 Strut mounting used on 1984–85 Accords

3. Remove the front wheels.
4. Disconnect the brake hose clamp from the strut.
5. Remove the brake caliper mounting bolts, then remove the caliper. Use string or stiff wire to hang the caliper out of the way. Do not disconnect the brake hose from the caliper.
6. Disconnect the stabilizer bar from the lower control arm.
7. Remove the pinchbolt at the bottom of the strut. Place a jack or other support under the control arm. Use a plastic or rubber-faced hammer to tap the knuckle downward and off the strut; do not allow the disc and knuckle assembly to fall when it comes loose.
8. In the engine compartment, remove the rubber cap and the 3 nuts from the upper shock mount.

✳✳ CAUTION

DO NOT remove the center or shaft nut from the top of the shock absorber.

9. Remove the strut assembly from the vehicle.
   To install:
10. Place the strut into position at the top mounting point. Make certain the tab on the base of the strut is aligned with the slot in the strut fork. Install and finger-tighten the nuts.
11. With the strut correctly aligned at the bottom and top, place a jack under the lower control arm. Raise the jack until the car BARELY lifts from the stand; this will force the strut into the knuckle.
12. Install and tighten the self-locking pinchbolt to 47 ft. lbs. (65 Nm).
13. Tighten the three upper mounting nuts to 28 ft. lbs. (39 Nm). Install the rubber cap at the top mount.
14. Install the stabilizer rod and tighten the bolts to 16 ft. lbs. (22 Nm).
15. Install the brake caliper. Install the brake line clip to the strut; tighten it only to 7 ft. lbs. (10 Nm).
16. Install the front wheels and lower the car to the ground.

1986–95 Accord and 1984–95 Prelude

▶ See Figures 2, 3, 4, 5 and 6

1. Disconnect the negative battery cable. If equipped with an air bag, properly disable the Supplemental Restraint System (SRS), as detailed in Section 6 of this manual.
2. Raise and support the front of the vehicle on jackstands. Remove the front wheels.
3. Disconnect the brake line bracket from the strut. Remove the damper fork pinchbolt.
4. Separate the fork from the damper.
5. Remove the three nuts from the shock tower in the engine compartment. Remove the damper assembly.

✳✳ CAUTION

DO NOT remove the center or shaft nut from the top of the damper.

Fig. 2 Remove the bolt securing the brake line bracket

Fig. 3 Remove the damper fork pinchbolt . . .

Fig. 4 . . . then separate the fork from the damper

Fig. 5 Remove the three nuts securing the damper to the shock tower . . .

Fig. 6 . . . then lower the damper assembly from the vehicle

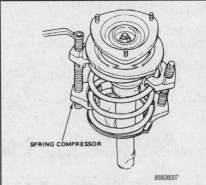

Fig. 7 A spring compressor must be used when disassembling the strut

To install:

6. Install the damper fork over the driveshaft and lower arm. Install the damper into the fork so that the strut tab matches the slot in the fork. Align the three upper bolts with the holes in the shock tower.

7. Install the bolts and nuts finger-tight, but make sure all are present and reasonably snug.

8. With the damper correctly aligned at the bottom and top, place a jack under the lower control arm. Raise the jack until the car BARELY lifts from the stand; this will force the damper into the fork.

9. Tighten the lower fork bolt to 47 ft. lbs. (65 Nm).

10. Tighten the pinchbolt to 32 ft. lbs. (44 Nm). Do not tighten the upper mount nuts yet.

11. Install the brake hose clamp to the strut.

12. Install the front wheels. Lower the vehicle to the ground.

13. With the weight of the car on the suspension, tighten the upper mount nuts to 28 ft. lbs. (39 Nm).

14. Properly enable the SRS system, if equipped, and connect the negative battery cable.

OVERHAUL

▶ See Figures 7, 8, 9 and 10

1. Remove the strut/damper assembly from the vehicle.

2. Install a spring compressor on the spring. These tools are usually available at auto parts suppliers. There are many different types; follow the manufacturer's instructions carefully. Tighten the compressor just enough to take the tension off the top spring seat.

3. With the spring compressed, remove the center or seat nut. Use a hex wrench to keep the shaft from turning while the nut is being removed.

4. Remove the upper mount. Carefully remove the seals, spacers and bearing (on 1984–85 Accords) at the top of the damper; keep them in order for proper reassembly. Remove the compressed spring.

5. If the spring is to be replaced, release tension on the arms of the com-

Fig. 8 Use a hex wrench to keep the shaft from turning while the nut is being removed

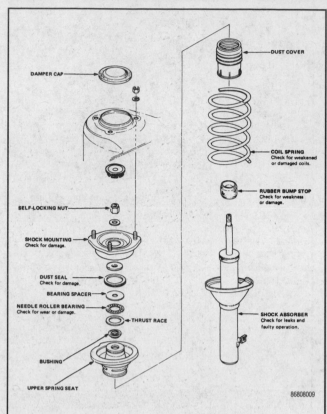

Fig. 9 Damper assembly and components used on 1984–85 Accords

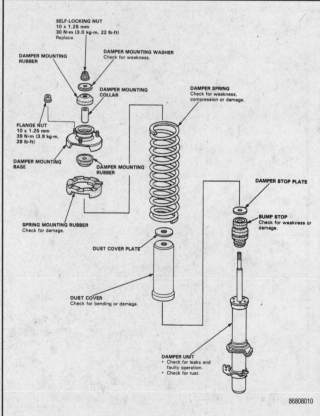

Fig. 10 Damper assembly and components used on 1986–95 Accords and Preludes

pressor slowly. Remove the tool when the spring is at normal length with no tension on the compressor.

6. By hand, check the shock absorber for smooth operation through the full range of travel. Check it also for smoothness during short strokes of 2–4 in. (51–102mm). Replace the unit if any sign of binding or uneven travel is felt.

To assemble:

7. Hold the strut assembly upright. If a vise is used, pad the jaws to avoid damage to the strut/damper assembly.

8. Install the rubber bump stop on the shaft.

9. Compress the spring and install it onto the shock. Make certain the bottom coil is exactly aligned in the bottom seat. Install the shaft dust cover.

10. Install the upper spring seat, spacers, bearing (on 1984–85 Accords), seal and mount. On 1984–85 Accords, coat both sides of the needle bearing with grease before installing it. Make certain the upper spring seat is aligned with upper coil of the spring.

11. Install a new upper shaft nut. Tighten it to 33 ft. lbs. (45 Nm) on 1984–85 Accords and 22 ft. lbs. (30 Nm) on all other models.

12. Slowly release the spring compressor, making sure the released spring fits into the upper mount correctly.

13. Install the strut/damper assembly in the vehicle.

Upper Ball Joint

Only the Prelude upper ball joints through 1991 are replaceable. The 1984–85 Accord has no upper control arm and therefore, no joint. On 1986–91 Accords and 1992–95 Preludes, the ball joint is permanently installed to the upper arm; it is not removable. If the joint fails or becomes loose, the upper arm assembly must be replaced.

INSPECTION

♦ **See Figure 11**

1. Raise and safely support the vehicle.
2. Remove the front wheel.
3. Grasp the steering knuckle and move it back and forth.
4. If any play is detected at the ball joint, replace the upper ball joint or control arm as applicable.

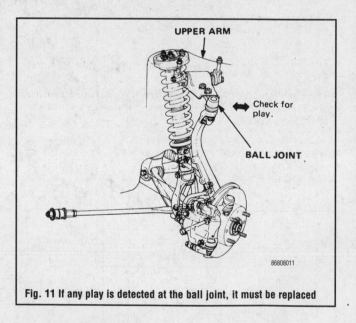

Fig. 11 If any play is detected at the ball joint, it must be replaced

REMOVAL & INSTALLATION

♦ **See Figure 12**

This procedures applies to 1984–91 Preludes only.
1. Disconnect the negative battery cable.
2. Raise and safely support the vehicle.

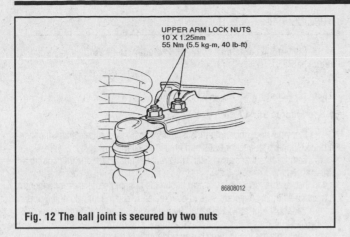

Fig. 12 The ball joint is secured by two nuts

3. Remove the front wheel.
4. Remove the cotter pin and castle nut from the upper ball joint.
5. Using a ball joint separator, remove the upper ball joint from the steering knuckle.
6. Remove the 2 retaining nuts/bolts securing the ball joint assembly to the upper control arm. Remove the ball joint.
7. Installation is the reverse of the removal procedure. Tighten the ball joint retaining nuts to 40 ft. lbs. (55 Nm). Tighten the ball joint castle nut to 32 ft. lbs. (44 Nm). Install a new cotter pin.
8. Have the front wheel alignment checked at a reputable service facility.

Lower Ball Joint

INSPECTION

1. Raise and support the front of the vehicle on jackstands.
2. Clamp a dial indicator onto the lower control arm and place the indicator tip on the steering knuckle, near the ball joint.
3. Place a prybar between the lower control arm and the steering knuckle.
4. Work the ball joint back and forth to check for looseness. If the movement exceeds 0.02 in. (0.5mm), replace the ball joint.

REMOVAL & INSTALLATION

▶ See Figures 13, 14 and 15

➡ **Lower ball joints on 1984–85 Accords and 1992–95 Preludes are integral with the control arm. If the joint becomes loose, the lower control arm must be replaced.**

This procedure is performed after the removal of the steering knuckle and requires the use of the following special tools or their equivalent:
• Ball joint removal/installation tool No. 07965–SB00100 for Accords through 1990 and Preludes through 1991

• Ball joint removal/installation tool No. 07HAF–SF10110 for 1990–95 Accords
• Ball joint removal base tool 07965–SB00200 for 1985–87 Preludes
• Ball joint removal base tool 07965–SB00300 for 1986–89 Accords and 1988–91 Preludes
• Ball joint removal base tool 07HAF–SF10130 for 1990–95 Accords
• A large vise
• Boot clip guide tool No. 07974–SA50700 or 07GAG–SD40700

1. Disconnect the negative battery cable. If equipped with an air bag, properly disable the Supplemental Restraint System (SRS), as detailed in 2. Remove the knuckle/hub assembly with the joint attached. Pry the snapring off and remove the boot.
3. Pry the snapring out of the groove in the ball joint.
4. Using the ball joint removal tool with the large end facing out, tighten the ball joint nut.
5. Position the removal base tool on the ball joint and set the assembly in a large vise. Press the ball joint out of the steering knuckle.

To install:

6. Position the new ball joint into the hole of the steering knuckle.
7. Install the ball joint installer tool with the small end facing out.
8. Position the installation base tool on the ball joint and set the assembly in a large vise. Press the ball joint into the steering knuckle.
9. Seat the snapring in the groove of the ball joint.
10. Adjust the boot clip guide tool with the adjusting bolt until the end of the tool aligns with the groove on the boot. Slide the clip over the tool and into position.
11. Install the knuckle and hub assembly.
12. Properly enable the SRS system, if equipped, and connect the negative battery cable.

Stabilizer Bar/Sway Bar

REMOVAL & INSTALLATION

1. Disconnect the negative battery cable. If equipped with an air bag, properly disable the Supplemental Restraint System (SRS), as detailed in Section 6 of this manual.
2. Raise and safely support the vehicle.
3. Remove the front wheels.
4. Disconnect the sway bar ends from both lower control arms.
5. Remove the bolts retaining the sway bar bushing brackets.
6. Remove the sway bar.

➡ **Examine the rubber bushings very carefully for any splits or deformation. Clean the inner and outer surfaces of the bushings before installation.**

7. Installation is the reverse of the removal procedure. Make certain the bushings are properly seated in their brackets. Tighten the brackets to 12 ft. lbs. (16 Nm) and the end mounts or link bolts to 16 ft. lbs. (22 Nm).
8. Properly enable the SRS system, if equipped, and connect the negative battery cable.

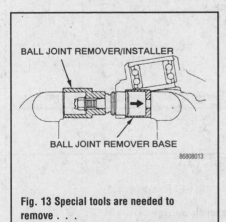

Fig. 13 Special tools are needed to remove . . .

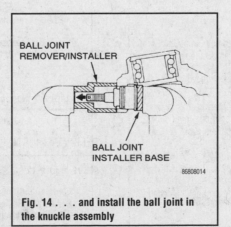

Fig. 14 . . . and install the ball joint in the knuckle assembly

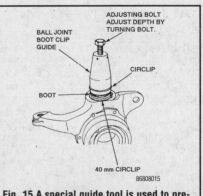

Fig. 15 A special guide tool is used to prevent damage to the boot while installing

Radius Rod/Compression Rod

The radius rod, bolted between the lower arm and the body or subframe, keeps the control arm in place against the forces of acceleration and braking. The rear or trailing end of the rod is mounted in bushings to allow just a bit of motion in the system. If the bushings wear or fail, the front suspension may be pulled out of position. Noise, tire wear and impaired handling may result from worn or faulty bushings. If the rod is visibly bent, as from someone elevating the car with a jack under the rod, the rod must be replaced.

REMOVAL & INSTALLATION

1. Disconnect the negative battery cable. If equipped with an air bag, properly disable the Supplemental Restraint System (SRS), as detailed in Section 6 of this manual.
2. Elevate and safely support the front of the car.
3. Remove the wheel.
4. Loosen the nut at the rear of the radius rod. Remove the nut, washers, bushing, etc. Keep them in the correct order for reinstallation.
5. Remove the bolts securing the rod to the control arm. Remove the rod.

To install:
6. Inspect the bushings carefully for wear or deformation. Replace them if any damage is found.
7. Fit the rod into place and install the bolts at the control arm. Tighten the bolts to 40 ft. lbs. (55 Nm) on Accords through 1989 and Preludes through 1991. On 1990–95 Accords and 1992–95 Preludes, tighten the bolts to 76 ft. lbs. (105 Nm).
8. Install the bushings, washers and spacers on the rod. Install a new locking nut. On all except 1992–95 Preludes, tighten the end nut to 33 ft. lbs. (44 Nm). On 1992–95 Preludes, tighten the nut to 40 ft. lbs. (55 Nm).
9. Install the wheels and lower the vehicle.
10. Properly enable the SRS system, if equipped, and connect the negative battery cable.

Upper Control Arm

REMOVAL & INSTALLATION

1986–89 Accord and 1984–91 Prelude

1. Disconnect the negative battery cable.
2. Raise and support the vehicle safely.
3. Remove the front wheels. Support the lower control arm assembly with a jack.
4. Remove the nuts, upper control arm bolts and upper control anchor bolts. Remove the upper ball joint using a ball joint separator tool.

To install:
5. Install the upper arm, tightening the Accord flange bolts to 54 ft. lbs. (73 Nm) or the Prelude bolts to 61 ft. lbs. (83 Nm).
6. Connect the upper ball joint. Tighten the nut to 32 ft. lbs. (44 Nm).
7. Install the wheel and lower the car.

1990–95 Accord and 1992–95 Prelude

1. Disconnect the negative battery cable. If equipped with an air bag, properly disable the Supplemental Restraint System (SRS), as detailed in Section 6 of this manual.
2. Raise and support the vehicle safely.
3. Remove the front wheels. Support the lower control arm assembly with a jack.
4. Remove the nuts, upper control arm bolts and upper control anchor bolts. Remove the upper ball joint using a ball joint separator tool.

To install:
5. Install the upper arm, tightening the flange nuts to 47 ft. lbs. (65 Nm).
6. Connect the upper ball joint. Tighten the nut to 32 ft. lbs. (44 Nm).
7. Install the wheel and lower the car.
8. Properly enable the SRS system, if equipped, and connect the negative battery cable.

BUSHING REPLACEMENT

➡ On 1994–95 Accords and 1992–95 Preludes, the bushings are not replaceable.

1986–89 Accord and 1984–91 Prelude

◆ See Figures 16, 17 and 18

1. Place the upper control arm assembly into a vise; remove the nut, upper arm bolt, upper arm anchor bolts and housing seals.
2. Remove the upper arm collar. Drive out the upper arm bushings using a drift.
3. Replace the upper control arm bushings, bushing seals and upper control arm collar with new ones. Be sure to coat the ends and the insides of the upper control arm bushings and the sealing lips of the upper control arm bushing with grease.
4. Apply sealant to the threads and underside of the bolt head and nut. Install the upper arm bolt and tighten the nut to 40 ft. lbs. (55 Nm).

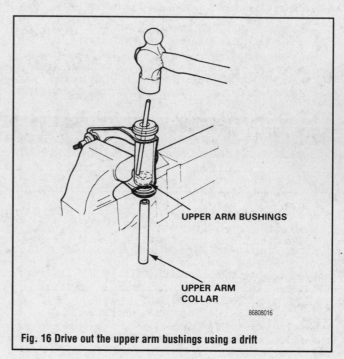

Fig. 16 Drive out the upper arm bushings using a drift

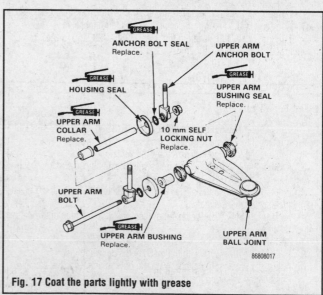

Fig. 17 Coat the parts lightly with grease

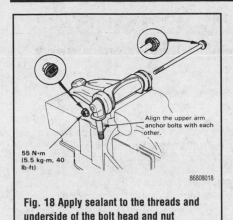

Fig. 18 Apply sealant to the threads and underside of the bolt head and nut

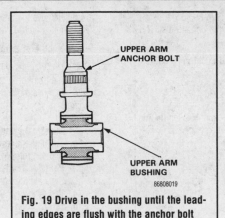

Fig. 19 Drive in the bushing until the leading edges are flush with the anchor bolt

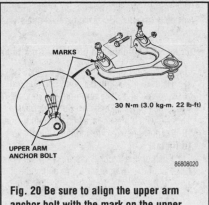

Fig. 20 Be sure to align the upper arm anchor bolt with the mark on the upper

1990–93 Accord

♦ See Figures 19 and 20

1. Place the upper control arm assembly into a holding fixture
2. Remove the though-bolts securing the upper arm anchor bolts.

To install:

3. Drive the new upper arm bushing into the upper arm anchor bolts. Drive in the bushing until the leading edges are flush with the anchor bolt.
4. Install the upper arm anchor bolts, then tighten the nuts to 22 ft. lbs. (30 Nm). Be sure to align the upper arm anchor bolt with the mark on the upper arm.

Lower Control Arms

REMOVAL & INSTALLATION

1. Disconnect the negative battery cable. If equipped with an air bag, properly disable the Supplemental Restraint System (SRS), as detailed in Section 6 of this manual.
2. Raise the vehicle and support it safely. Remove the front wheels.
3. Properly support the hub and knuckle assembly with a jack. Use a ball joint separator to disconnect the lower arm ball joint. Be careful not to damage the seal.
4. Remove the stabilizer bar retaining bolts.
5. Remove the bolt securing the damper fork to the control arm.
6. Remove the lower arm pivot bolt.
7. Remove the lower arm. Check the bushings carefully for wear or deterioration. Replace the bushings if any wear is found. Even if the bushings are not replaced, clean the centers and the bolt shafts.
8. Install in reverse order. Tighten the lower control arm to chassis bolt to 40 ft. lbs. (55 Nm).
9. Properly enable the SRS system, if equipped, and connect the negative battery cable.

BUSHING REPLACEMENT

♦ See Figure 21

This procedure requires the use of tool 07NAD-SS00100 or an equivalent bushing removal tool and a hydraulic press.

1. Remove the lower control arm from the vehicle.
2. Position the lower arm on the press with the machined surface facing down.
3. Adjust the driver so it matches the inner diameter of the bushing hole. Tighten the socket bolt securely.
4. Position the driver on the bushing, then push the bushing out of the arm using the press.

To install:

5. Position the lower arm with the machined side facing up.
6. Adjust the driver so it matches with the outer diameter of the bushing.
7. Position the driver on the bushing, then push the bushing (using the

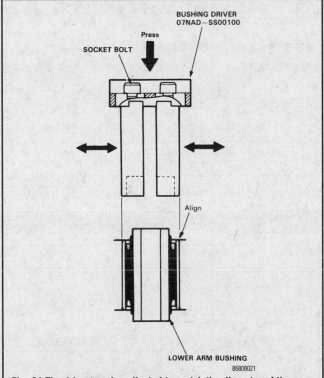

Fig. 21 The driver can be adjusted to match the diameter of the bushing or bushing hole as needed

press) into the arm until the edge of the bushing is flush with the machined surface of the arm.

8. Install the lower control arm.

Steering Knuckle

REMOVAL & INSTALLATION

1984–85 Accord

1. Disconnect the negative battery cable.
2. Pry the lock tab away from the spindle, then loosen the nut. Loosen the lug nuts slightly.
3. Raise the front of the car and support it with jackstands. Remove the front wheel and spindle nut.
4. Remove the bolts retaining the brake caliper and separate the caliper from the knuckle. Do not let the caliper hang by the brake hose but support it with a length of wire.

5. Remove the disc brake rotor retaining screws. Screw two 8 x 1.25 x 12mm bolts into the disc brake removal holes, and turn the bolts to push the rotor away from the hub.

➡**Turn each bolt only two turns at a time to prevent cocking the disc.**

6. Disconnect the tie rod from the knuckle.
7. Remove lower arm ball joint bolt and nut.
8. Separate the lower arm from the knuckle.
9. Loosen the lockbolt which retains the strut in the knuckle. Tap the top of the knuckle with a plastic-faced hammer and slide it off the shock.
10. Remove the knuckle and hub from the driveshaft.

To install:

11. Position the knuckle assembly on the vehicle.
12. Install the lower control arm bolt and nut. Install the lockbolt securing the strut to the knuckle. Tighten the control arm bolt to 40 ft. lbs. (55 Nm) and the lockbolt to 47 ft. lbs. (65 Nm).
13. Connect the tie rod to the knuckle.
14. Install the brake disc and caliper.
15. Install a new spindle nut on the end of the driveshaft. Tighten the spindle nut snug. When the vehicle is on its wheels on the ground, tighten the spindle nut to 137 ft. lbs. (190 Nm) and stake the nut into the groove.

1986–89 Accord and 1984–95 Prelude

▶ **See Figure 22**

1. Disconnect the negative battery cable. If equipped with an air bag, properly disable the Supplemental Restraint System (SRS), as detailed in Section 6 of this manual.
2. Pry the spindle nut stake away from the spindle and loosen the nut.
3. Raise and safely support the vehicle.
4. Remove the wheel and the spindle nut.
5. Remove the caliper mounting bolts and the caliper. Support the caliper out of the way with a length of wire. Do not let the caliper hang from the brake hose.

6. Remove the 6mm brake disc retaining screws. Screw two 8 x 1.25 x 12mm bolts into the disc to push it away from the hub.

➡**Turn each bolt 2 turns at a time to prevent cocking the brake disc.**

7. On Preludes with anti-lock brakes, remove the bolts securing the wheel sensor and position it aside.
8. Remove the cotter pin from the tie rod castle nut, then remove the nut. Separate the tie rod ball joint using a ball joint remover, then lift the tie rod out of the knuckle.
9. Remove the cotter pin and remove the lower arm ball joint nut and bolt.
10. Separate the lower arm from the knuckle.
11. Remove the two bolts securing the upper ball joint shield.
12. Pry off the cotter pin and remove the upper ball joint nut.
13. Separate the upper ball joint and knuckle.
14. Remove the knuckle and hub by sliding them off the halfshaft.

To install:

15. Install the knuckle/hub assembly on the vehicle. Thread a new nut onto the spindle until it is just snug.
16. Tighten the upper ball joint nut and tie rod end nut to 32 ft. lbs. (44 Nm). Install new cotter pins. Tighten the lower ball joint nut to 40 ft. lbs. (55 Nm) and install a new cotter pin.
17. Install the wheel speed sensor (if equipped). Tighten the bolts to 16 ft. lbs. (22 Nm).
18. Install the brake disc and caliper.
19. Install the wheel.
20. With all vehicle resting on the ground, tighten the spindle nut to 134 ft. lbs. (185 Nm) except on 1990–95 Preludes, where it is tightened to 180 ft. lbs. (250 Nm).
21. Properly enable the SRS system, if equipped, and connect the negative battery cable.

1990–95 Accord

▶ **See Figure 23**

1. Disconnect the negative battery cable. If equipped with an air bag, properly disable the Supplemental Restraint System (SRS), as detailed in Section 6 of this manual.

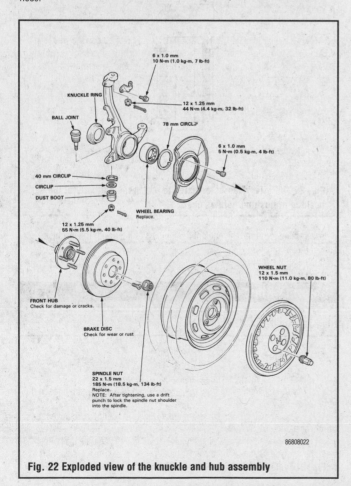

Fig. 22 Exploded view of the knuckle and hub assembly

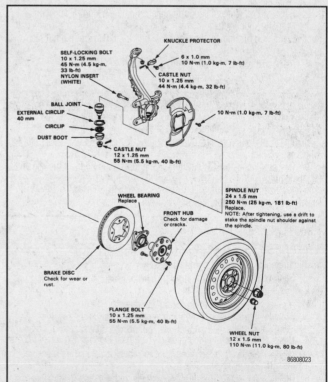

Fig. 23 Exploded view of the knuckle and hub assembly used on 1990–95 Accords

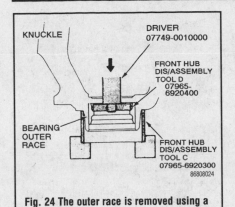

Fig. 24 The outer race is removed using a hydraulic press

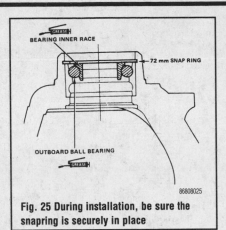

Fig. 25 During installation, be sure the snapring is securely in place

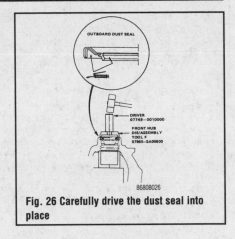

Fig. 26 Carefully drive the dust seal into place

2. Pry the spindle nut stake away from the spindle, then loosen the nut.

3. Raise and safely support the vehicle.

4. Remove the wheel and the spindle nut.

5. Remove the caliper mounting bolts and the caliper. Support the caliper out of the way with a length of wire. Do not let the caliper hang from the brake hose.

6. Remove the cotter pin from the tie rod castle nut, then remove the nut. Separate the tie rod ball joint using a ball joint remover, then lift the tie rod out of the knuckle.

7. Separate the ball joint and lower arm using a puller with the pawls applied to the lower arm.

8. Remove the cotter pin and the upper ball joint nut. Separate the upper ball joint.

9. Remove the knuckle assembly by pulling it off the halfshaft.

To install:

10. Install the knuckle/hub assembly on the vehicle. Tighten the upper ball joint nut and the tie rod nut to 32 ft. lbs. (44 Nm) and install new cotter pins. Tighten the lower ball joint nut to 40 ft. lbs. (55 Nm) and install a new cotter pin.

11. Thread a new nut onto the spindle until it is snug.

12. Install the caliper and wheel.

13. With the vehicle resting on the ground, tighten the spindle nut to 180 ft. lbs. (250 Nm). After tightening, use a drift to stake the spindle nut shoulder against the spindle.

14. Properly enable the SRS system, if equipped, and connect the negative battery cable.

Front Hub and Bearing

REMOVAL & INSTALLATION

The use special tools or their equivalent is required for these procedures. A hydraulic press, correct diameter drivers and supports are required for disassembly of the hub and bearing. If necessary, take the knuckle assembly to a machine shop or dealership to have the bearings replaced.

1984–85 Accord

▶ See Figures 24, 25, 26 and 27

1. Remove the knuckle assembly from the vehicle.

2. Press the hub from the knuckle using the proper sized drivers and a hydraulic press.

3. Remove the bolts securing the splash guard.

4. Remove the snapring, then remove the outer bearing.

5. Turn the knuckle over and remove the inboard dust seal, bearing and inner race.

6. Press the bearing outer race out of the knuckle using the proper sized driver and a hydraulic press.

7. Remove the outboard bearing inner race from the hub using a bearing puller.

8. Remove the outboard dust seal from the hub.

➡ Whenever the wheel bearings are removed, they must be replaced with a new set of bearings and outer dust seal. They cannot be reused.

9. Clean any old grease from the driveshafts and spindles on the car.

10. Clean any old grease from the hub and knuckle and thoroughly dry and wipe clean all components.

To install:

11. When fitting new bearings, you must pack them with wheel bearing grease. To do this:

   a. Place a glob of grease in your left palm.

   b. Holding one of the bearings in your right hand, drag the face of the bearing heavily through the grease. This must be done to work as much grease as possible through the ball bearings and the cage.

   c. Turn the bearing and continue to pull it through the grease until the grease is thoroughly packed between the bearing balls and the cage, all around the bearing. You'll be able to see grease emerging from the clean side of the bearing if the lubricant is going all the way through. Repeat this operation until all of the bearings are completely packed with grease.

➡ This messy job can be made much easier with the use of a bearing packer. This handy tool fits tightly over the bearing; grease is injected with a grease-gun. If this system is used, make very certain that the grease is evenly distributed and the bearing is completely packed.

12. Press the bearing outer race into the knuckle using the tools used above, plus an installation base. Do not exceed 2.5 tons of pressure with the press.

13. Install the outboard ball bearing and its inner race in the knuckle.

14. Install the snapring. Pack grease in the groove around the sealing lip of the outboard grease dust seal.

15. Drive the outboard grease seal into the knuckle, using a seal driver and mallet, until it is flush with the knuckle surface.

16. Install the splash guard, then turn the knuckle upside down and install the inboard ball bearing and its inner race.

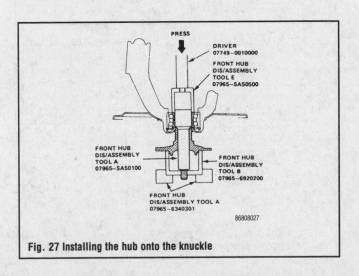

Fig. 27 Installing the hub onto the knuckle

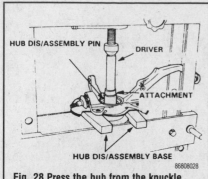

Fig. 28 Press the hub from the knuckle using a driver of the proper diameter (be sure to support the knuckle)

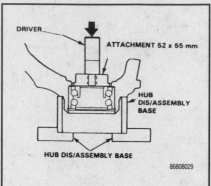

Fig. 29 Support the knuckle, then press the bearing out

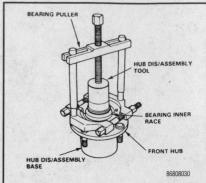

Fig. 30 A puller is required to remove the outer bearing race

17. Pack grease in the groove around the sealing lip of the inboard dust seal.

18. Drive the dust seal into the knuckle using a seal driver.

19. Place the hub in the press holder; set the knuckle in position on the press and apply downward pressure. Do not exceed 2 tons of pressure during installation.

20. Install the knuckle assembly on the vehicle.

1986–89 Accord and 1984–95 Prelude

♦ See Figures 28, 29, 30, 31 and 32

1. Remove the knuckle assembly from the vehicle.
2. Remove the splash guard screws from the knuckle.
3. Position the knuckle/hub assembly in a hydraulic press. Press the hub from the knuckle using a driver of the proper diameter. Be sure to support the knuckle when pressing the hub off.

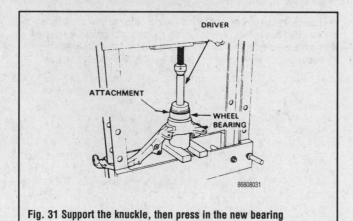

Fig. 31 Support the knuckle, then press in the new bearing

➡The bearing must be replaced with a new one after removal. It cannot be reused.

4. Remove the splash guard and snapring from the knuckle.
5. Press the wheel bearing out of the knuckle while supporting the knuckle.
6. Remove the outboard bearing inner race from the hub using a bearing puller.

To install:

7. Clean the knuckle and hub thoroughly.
8. Press a new wheel bearing into the knuckle using a driver while supporting the knuckle.
9. Install the snapring.
10. Install the splash shield tightening the screws until snug.
11. Press the knuckle onto the hub using a proper sized driver and hydraulic press.
12. Install a new seal on the knuckle.
13. Install the knuckle assembly on the vehicle.

1990–95 Accord

♦ See Figures 33, 34, 35, 36 and 37

1. Remove the knuckle assembly from the vehicle.
2. Remove the four bolts and remove the knuckle from the hub unit.
3. Remove the splash guard from the knuckle.
4. Remove the four bolts and separate the hub unit from the brake disc.
5. Position the hub unit on a hydraulic press. Support the wheel bearing assembly and press the hub out of the assembly.
6. Remove the outboard bearing inner race from the hub using a bearing puller.

➡The wheel bearing must be replaced with a new one after removal.

To install:

7. Clean the knuckle and hub thoroughly.
8. Position the hub in a hydraulic press. Press a new wheel bearing into the hub using a driver of the proper diameter.

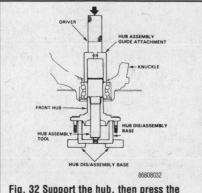

Fig. 32 Support the hub, then press the knuckle onto the hub

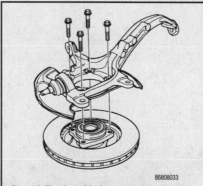

Fig. 33 The knuckle is secured to the hub by four bolts

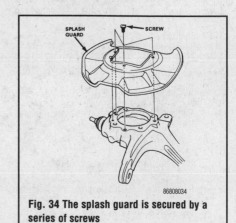

Fig. 34 The splash guard is secured by a series of screws

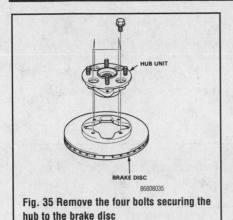

Fig. 35 Remove the four bolts securing the hub to the brake disc

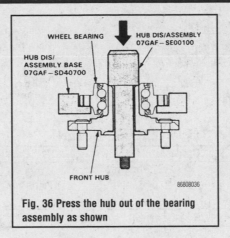

Fig. 36 Press the hub out of the bearing assembly as shown

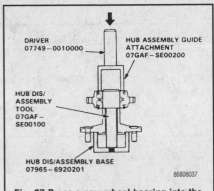

Fig. 37 Press a new wheel bearing into the hub using a driver of the proper diameter

9. Install the hub on the brake disc and tighten the bolts to 40 ft. lbs. (55 Nm).
10. Install the splash guard. Tighten the bolts until just snug.
11. Install the knuckle on the hub; tighten the bolts to 33 ft. lbs. (45 Nm).
12. Install the knuckle assembly on the vehicle.

Front Wheel Alignment

▶ **See Figure 38**

Alignment of the front wheels is essential if your car is to go, stop and turn as designed. Alignment can be altered by collision, overloading, poor repair or bent components.

If you are diagnosing bizarre handling and/or poor road manners, the first place to look is the tires. Although the tires may wear as a result of an alignment problem, worn or poorly inflated tires can make you chase alignment problems which don't exist.

Once you have eliminated all other causes, unload everything from the trunk except the spare tire, set the tire pressures to the correct level and take the car to a reputable alignment facility. Since the alignment settings are measured in very small increments, it is almost impossible for the home mechanic to accurately determine the settings. The explanations that follow will help you understand the three dimensions of alignment: caster, camber and toe.

CASTER

Caster is the tilting of the steering axis either forward or backward from the vertical, when viewed from the side of the vehicle. A backward tilt is said to be positive and a forward tilt is said to be negative. Changes in caster affect the straight line tendency of the vehicle and the "return to center" of the steering after a turn. If the camber is radically different between the left and right wheels (such as after hitting a major pothole), the car will exhibit a nasty pull to one side.

CAMBER

Camber is the tilting of the wheels from the vertical (leaning in or out) when viewed from the front of the vehicle. When the wheels tilt outward at the top, the camber is said to be positive. When the wheels tilt inward at the top the camber is said to be negative. The amount of tilt is measured in degrees from the vertical. This measurement is called camber angle.

Camber affects the position of the tire on the road surface during vertical suspension movement and cornering. Changes in camber affect the handling and ride qualities of the car as well as tire wear. Many tire wear patterns indicate camber-related problems from misalignment, overloading or poor driving habits.

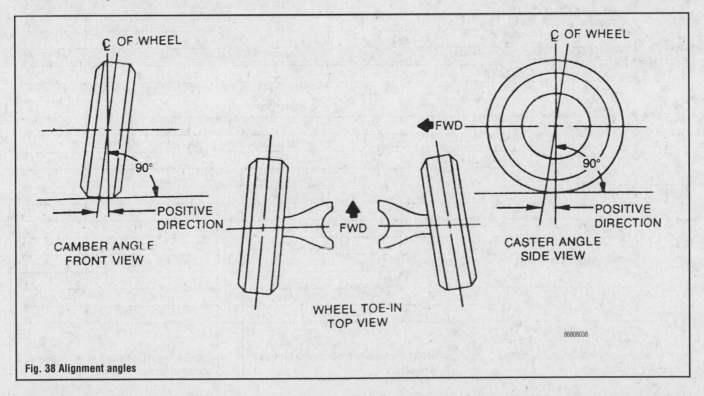

Fig. 38 Alignment angles

TOE

Toe is the turning in or out (parallelism) of the wheels. The actual amount of toe setting is normally only a fraction of an inch. The purpose of toe-in (or out) specification is to ensure parallel rolling of the wheels. Toe-in also serves to off-set the small deflections of the steering support system which occur when the vehicle is rolling forward.

Changing the toe setting will radically affect the overall "feel" of the steering, the behavior of the car under braking, tire wear and even fuel economy. Excessive toe (in or out) causes excessive drag or scrubbing on the tires.

Toe is adjustable on all Hondas. It is generally measured in decimal inches or degrees. It is adjusted by loosening the locknut on each tie-rod end and turning the rod until the correct reading is achieved. The rods, left and right, must remain equal in length during all adjustments.

WHEEL ALIGNMENT

Year	Model		Caster Range (deg.)	Caster Preferred Setting (deg.)	Camber Range (deg.)	Camber Preferred Setting (deg.)	Toe-in (in.)	Steering Axis Inclination (deg.)
1984	Accord		1/2P-2 1/2P	1 1/2P	1N-1P	0	0	12 1/2
	Prelude		1N-1P	0	1N-1P	0	0	6 13/16
1985	Accord		1/2P-2 1/2P	1 1/2P	1N-1P	0	0	12 1/2
	Prelude		1N-1P	0	1N-1P	0	0	6 13/16
1986	Accord		1N-1P	0	1N-1P	0	0	6 13/16
	Prelude		1N-1P	0	1N-1P	0	0	6 13/16
1987	Accord		1N-1P	0	1N-1P	0	0	6 13/16
	Prelude		1N-1P	0	1N-1P	0	0	6 13/16
1988	Accord		1/2N-1 1/2P	1/2P	1N-1P	0	0	6 13/16
	Prelude		1 3/16P-2 13/16P	2 3/8P	1N-1P	0	0	6 13/16
1989	Accord		1/2N-1 1/2P	1/2P	1N-1P	0	0	-
	Prelude		1 13/16P-2 13/16P	2 3/8P	1N-1P	0	0	-
1990	Accord		2P-4P	3P	1N-1P	0	0	-
	Prelude		1 13/16P-2 13/16P	2 3/8 P	1N-1P	0	0	-
1991	Accord		2P-4P	3P	1N-1P	0	0	-
	Prelude		1 13/16P-2 13/16P	2/3/8P	1N-1P	0	0	-
1992	Accord		2P-4P	3P	1N-1P	9/16P	0	-
	Prelude		113/16P-2 13/16P	2 3/8P	1N-1P	0	0	-
1993	Accord	F	2P-4P	3P	1N-1P	0	0	-
		R	-	-	1N-0	0.50N	0	-
	Prelude (2WS)	F	1.67P-3.67P	2.67P	1N-1P	0	0	-
		R	-	-	1.75N-0.25P	0.75N	0.08	-
	Prelude (4WS)	F	1.67P-3.67P	2.67P	1N-1P	0	0	-
		R	-	-	1.25N-0.25N	0.75N	0.08	-
1994	Accord	F	2P-4P	3P	1N-1P	0	0	-
		R	-	-	0.92N-0.08P	0.42P	0.08	-
	Prelude 2WS	F	1.67P-3.67P	2.67P	1N-1P	0	0	-
		R	-	-	1.75N-0.25P	0.75N	0.08	-
	Prelude 4WS	F	1.67P-3.67P	2.67P	1N-1P	0	0	-
		R	-	-	1.25N-0.25N	0.75N	0.08	-
1995	Accord	F	2P-4P	3P	1N-1P	0	0	-
		R	-	-	1N-0	0.50N	0.08	-
	Accord V-6	F	2P-4P	3P	1N-1P	0	0	-
		R	-	-	0.92N-0.08P	0.42N	0.08	-
	Prelude 2WS	F	1.67P-3.67P	2.67P	1N-1P	0	0	-
		R	-	-	1.75N-0.25P	0.75N	0.08	-
	Prelude 4WS	F	1.67P-3.67P	2.67P	1N-1P	0	0	-
		R	-	-	1.25N-0.25N	0.75N	0.08	-

P- Positive
N- Negative

86808900

REAR SUSPENSION

MacPherson Strut/Damper

REMOVAL & INSTALLATION

❋❋ CAUTION

Exercise great caution when working with the rear suspension. Coil springs and other suspension components are under extreme tension and could cause severe injury if released improperly. Never remove the nut on the top of the strut piston without using the proper spring compressor tool.

1984–85 Accord

▶ **See Figures 39 and 40**

1. Disconnect the negative battery cable and loosen the lug nuts on the rear wheel(s).
2. Firmly block the front wheels. Elevate and safely support the rear of the car.
3. Remove the rear wheel(s).
4. Disconnect the brake line from the hose. Plug the line and hose immediately to prevent fluid leakage and entry of dirt.
5. Disconnect the stabilizer bar from the lower arm.
6. Remove the brake drum and disconnect the parking brake cable.
7. Remove the bolt securing the strut assembly to the hub carrier.
8. Remove the strut mounting nuts.

❋❋ CAUTION

DO NOT remove the center or shaft nut from the top of the shock absorber.

9. Remove the strut assembly from the vehicle.
To install:
10. Place the strut into position at the top mounting point. Make certain the tab on the base of the strut is aligned with the slot in the strut fork. Install and finger-tighten the nuts.
11. With the strut correctly aligned at the bottom and top, place a jack under the lower control arm. Raise the jack until the car BARELY lifts from the stand; this will force the shock into the knuckle.
12. Install and tighten the pinchbolt to 40 ft. lbs. (55 Nm).

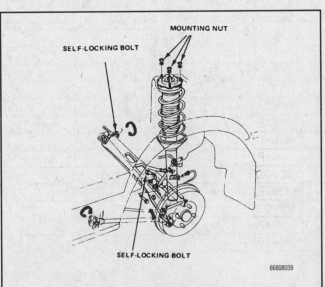

Fig. 39 Rear strut assembly on 1984–85 Accords

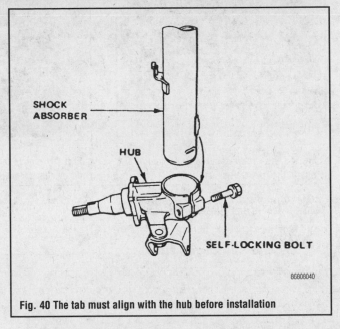

Fig. 40 The tab must align with the hub before installation

13. Tighten the three upper mounting nuts to 16 ft. lbs. (22 Nm). Install the rubber cap at the top mount.
14. Connect the parking brake cable and install the drum.
15. Install the stabilizer bar.
16. Remove the line plugs and connect the brake line to the brake hose.
17. Install the rear wheel; lower the car to the ground.
18. Top up the brake fluid and bleed the rear brakes.

1984–87 Prelude

1. Disconnect the negative battery cable.
2. Firmly block the front wheels and loosen the lug nuts on the rear wheels.
3. Elevate and support the rear of the car. Remove the rear wheels.
4. Remove the clamp securing the rear brake hose.
5. Remove the stabilizer from the lower arm.
6. Loosen the lower arm pivot (inboard) bolt.
7. Loosen the radius rod nut and the bolt securing the hub carrier to the lower arm.
8. Remove the lockbolt securing the bottom of the strut.
9. Remove the three retaining nuts securing the top of the strut. Lower the suspension and remove the strut.

❋❋ CAUTION

DO NOT remove the center or shaft nut from the top of the shock absorber.

To install:
10. Fit the shock into the upper mount; install the upper retaining nuts finger-tight.
11. Place the strut into position on the lower arm. Install the mounting bolt. The tab on the strut must align with the groove in the hub carrier.
12. Place a jack under the lower strut mount. Raise the jack until the weight of the car is on the jack.
13. With the suspension under load, tighten the lower mount bolt to 40 ft. lbs. (55 Nm). Tighten the upper nuts to 16 ft. lbs. (22 Nm).
14. Tighten the radius rod nut to 47 ft. lbs. (65 Nm) and the lower arm pivot bolt to 40 ft. lbs. (55 Nm).
15. Install the stabilizer bar.
16. Install the rear brake hose and secure the line clamp.
17. Install the rear wheel. Lower the vehicle to the ground.

Fig. 41 The strut is secured to the body and to the knuckle assembly

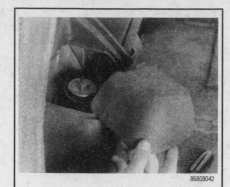

Fig. 42 Remove the screw securing the cover, then remove the cover

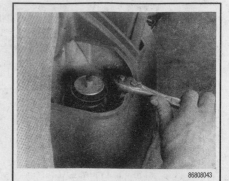

Fig. 43 Remove the strut retaining nuts. Do not loosen the center nut

1986–95 Accord and 1988–95 Prelude

▶ See Figures 41, 42, 43 and 44

1. Disconnect the negative battery cable.
2. Remove the strut upper cover from inside the vehicle and remove the upper strut retaining nuts.
3. Firmly block the front wheels and loosen the lug nuts for the rear wheels.
4. Raise and safely support the rear of the vehicle.
5. Remove the rear wheel.
6. Remove the strut mounting bolt and remove the strut.

✴✴ CAUTION

DO NOT remove the center or shaft nut from the top of the shock absorber.

To install:

7. Fit the shock into the upper mount; install the upper retaining nuts finger-tight.
8. Place the strut into position on the lower arm. Install the mounting bolt.
9. Place a jack under the lower strut mount. Raise the jack until the weight of the car is on the jack.
10. With the suspension under load, tighten the lower mount bolt to 40 ft. lbs. (55 Nm) on Accords or 47 ft. lbs. (65 Nm) on Preludes. Tighten the upper nuts to 28 ft. lbs. (39 Nm).
11. Install the rear wheel. Lower the vehicle to the ground.
12. Connect the negative battery cable.

OVERHAUL

▶ See Figures 45, 46, 47, 48 and 49

1. Remove the strut assembly from the vehicle.
2. Install a spring compressor on the spring. These tools are usually available at auto parts suppliers. There are many different types; follow the manufacturer's instructions carefully. Tighten the compressor just enough to take the spring tension off the top spring seat.
3. With the spring compressed, remove the center nut. Use a hex wrench to keep the shaft from turning while the nut is removed.
4. Remove the upper mount. Carefully remove the seals, spacers, bearing or bushings at the top of the shock; keep them in order for proper reassembly. Remove the compressed spring.
5. If the spring is to be replaced, release tension on the arms of the compressor slowly. Remove the tool when the spring is at normal length with no tension on the compressor.
6. By hand, check the shock absorber for smooth operation through the full range of travel. Check it also for smoothness during short strokes of 2–4 in. (51–102mm). Replace the unit if any sign of binding or uneven travel is felt.

To assemble:

7. Hold the strut assembly upright. If a vise is used, pad the jaws to avoid damage.
8. Install the rubber bump stop on the shaft.
9. Compress the spring and install it onto the shock. Make certain the bottom coil is exactly aligned in the bottom seat. Install the shaft dust cover.
10. Install the upper seat, bushings, collar, seals and mount base.
11. Install a new upper shaft nut. Tighten it to 33 ft. lbs. (45 Nm) on 1984–85 Accords. On 1984–87 Preludes tighten it to 40 ft. lbs. (55 Nm). On

Fig. 44 Remove the bolt securing the strut to the knuckle, then remove it from the vehicle

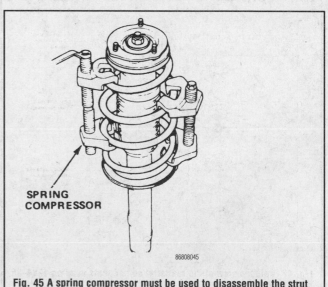

SPRING COMPRESSOR

Fig. 45 A spring compressor must be used to disassemble the strut

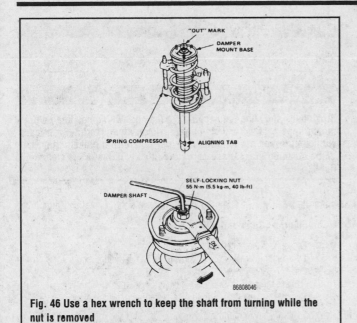

Fig. 46 Use a hex wrench to keep the shaft from turning while the nut is removed

1986–89 Accords tighten it to 16 ft. lbs. (22 Nm) and on 1990–95 Accords and 1988–95 Preludes, tighten it to 22 ft. lbs. (30 Nm).

12. Slowly release the spring compressor, making sure the released spring fits into the upper mount correctly.

13. Install the strut assembly in the vehicle.

Control Arms/Links

REMOVAL & INSTALLATION

Trailing Arm

1. Disconnect the negative battery cable.
2. Loosen the lug nuts for the rear wheels.

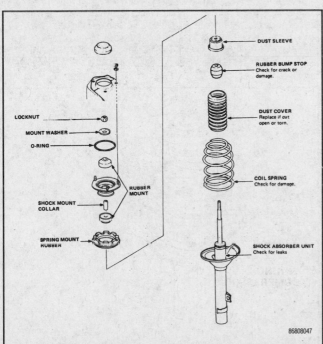

Fig. 47 Exploded view of the rear strut components used on 1984–85 Accords

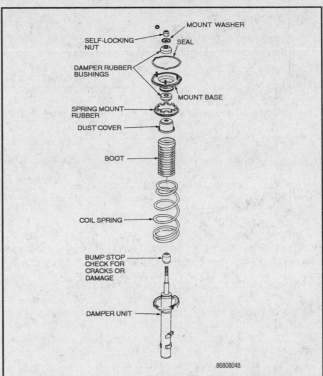

Fig. 48 Exploded view of the rear strut components used on 1984–87 Preludes

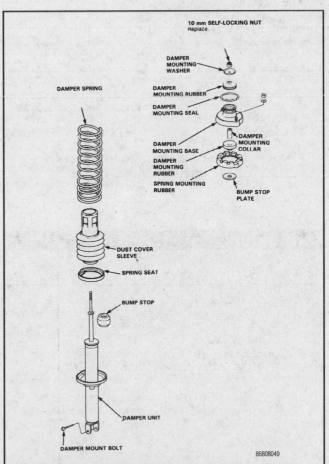

Fig. 49 Exploded view of the strut components used on 1988–95 Preludes and 1986–95 Accords

3. Raise and safely support the vehicle.
4. Remove the rear wheels.
5. Support the lower control arm using a jack.
6. Remove the nuts/bolts securing the trailing arm to the knuckle.
7. Remove the pivot bolt, then remove the trailing arm.
8. Install in reverse order. When installing, make certain the passages in the bushings and the bolts are clean and lightly lubricated. Install the nuts and bolts finger-tight, but do not apply final torque until the vehicle is on the ground. Refer to the component torque illustrations at the end of this section to determine the proper specification.
9. Connect the negative battery cable.

Upper Control Arm

1. Disconnect the negative battery cable.
2. Loosen the lug nuts for the rear wheels.
3. Raise and safely support the vehicle.
4. Remove the rear wheels.
5. Support the lower control arm with a jack.
6. Remove the cotter pin and castle nut from the upper ball joint. Use a ball joint separator to remove the ball joint from the knuckle.
7. Remove the upper control arm mounting bolts and the upper control arm.
8. Position the upper arm on the vehicle and install the mounting bolts. Refer to the component torque illustrations at the end of this section for the proper specification.
9. Connect the ball joint. Install and tighten the nut to 32 ft. lbs. (44 Nm), then install a new cotter pin.
10. Install the wheel; lower the car to the ground.
11. Connect the negative battery cable.

Lower Control Arm

1. Disconnect the negative battery cable.
2. Loosen the lug nuts for the rear wheels.
3. Raise and safely support the vehicle.
4. Remove the rear wheels.
5. If applicable, disconnect the sway bar from the lower control arm.
6. If applicable, remove the bolts securing the trailing arm to the lower control arm.
7. On some models, a ball joint connects the arm to the knuckle. If so, remove the cotter pin and castle nut from the ball joint, then separate the ball joint from the knuckle.
8. Remove the remaining lower arm mounting bolts and remove the lower control arm.
9. Install in reverse order. Refer to the component torque illustrations at the end of this section for the proper specification. Any nut/bolts connected to rubber mounts or bushings should not be fully torqued until the vehicle is on the ground.
10. Connect the negative battery cable.

Sway Bar

REMOVAL & INSTALLATION

1. Disconnect the negative battery cable.
2. Loosen the lug nuts on the rear wheels.
3. Raise and safely support the vehicle.
4. Remove the rear wheels.
5. Disconnect the sway bar ends.
6. Remove the bolts retaining the sway bar bushing brackets.
7. Remove the sway bar.

➡**Examine the rubber bushings very carefully for any splits or deformation. Clean the inner and outer surfaces of the bushings before installation.**

8. Installation is the reverse of the removal procedure. Make certain the bushings are properly seated in their brackets. Tighten the bolts according to the value listed in the component torque illustrations at the end of this section.
9. Connect the negative battery cable.

Rear Wheel Bearings

REPLACEMENT

❋❋ CAUTION

Brake pads and shoes may contain asbestos, which has been determined to be a cancer causing agent. Never clean the brake surfaces with compressed air. Avoid inhaling any dust from brake surfaces. When cleaning brakes, use commercially available brake cleaning fluids.

1984–85 Accord and 1984–87 Prelude

▶ **See Figures 50, 51 and 52**

1. Disconnect the negative battery cable.
2. Loosen the rear lug nuts slightly. Raise the car and support safely on jackstands.
3. Release the parking brake. Remove the rear wheels.
4. Remove the rear bearing hub cap, cotter pin and pin holder.
5. If equipped with disc brakes, remove the caliper.
6. Remove the spindle nut, then pull the hub and drum/disc off the spindle.
7. Drive the outboard inboard bearing races out of the hub using a brass drift. Punch in a crisscross pattern to avoid cocking the bearing race in the bore.
8. Clean the bearing seats thoroughly.
9. Drive the inboard bearing race into the hub, using a bearing driver.
10. Turn the hub over and drive the outboard bearing race in the same way.
11. Check to see that the bearing races are seated properly and not cocked.
12. When fitting new bearings, you must pack them with wheel bearing grease. To do this, place a glob of grease in your left palm. Holding one of the bearings in your right hand, drag the face of the bearing heavily through the grease. This must be done to work as much grease as possible through the bearings and the cage. Turn the bearing and continue to pull it through the grease until the grease is thoroughly packed between the bearings and the cage, all around the bearing. You'll be able to see grease emerging from the clean

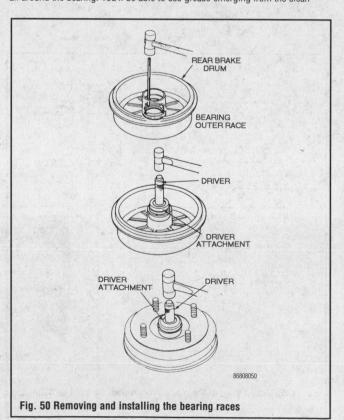

Fig. 50 Removing and installing the bearing races

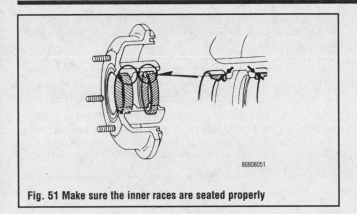

Fig. 51 Make sure the inner races are seated properly

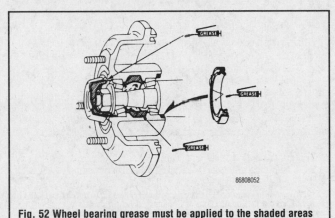

Fig. 52 Wheel bearing grease must be applied to the shaded areas

side of the bearing if the lubricant is going all the way through. Repeat this operation until all of the bearings are completely packed with grease.

13. Pack the inside of the hub with a moderate amount of grease. Do not overload the hub with grease.

14. Apply a small amount of grease to the spindle and to the lip of the inner seal before installing.

15. Place the inboard bearings into the hub.

16. Apply grease to the hub seal, and carefully tap into place. Tap in a criss-cross pattern to avoid cocking the seal in the bore.

17. Slip the drum/disc over the spindle, then insert the outboard bearing, hub, washer, and spindle nut.

18. Tighten the spindle nut to 18 ft. lbs. (24 Nm). Rotate the drum/disc 2–3 turns by hand, then retighten the spindle nut to 18 ft. lbs. (24 Nm). Repeat until the spindle nut holds the proper torque after the disc or drum is rotated.

19. Loosen the spindle nut until it just breaks free

20. Retorque the spindle nut to 4 ft. lbs. (6 Nm).

21. Set the pin holder so the slots will be as close as possible to the hole in the spindle.

22. Tighten the spindle nut just enough to align the slot and hole, then secure it with a new cotter pin.

1986–95 Accord and 1992–95 Prelude

▶ **See Figures 53, 54 and 55**

➡The rear wheel bearings on these models are part of a sealed hub unit. If replacement of the bearings is necessary, the entire hub unit must be replaced.

1. Disconnect the negative battery cable.
2. Loosen the rear lug nuts and the spindle nut. Raise the vehicle and support it safely.
3. Release the parking brake and remove the rear wheel.
4. If equipped with disc brakes, remove the caliper.
5. Remove the brake disc/drum.
6. Remove the spindle nut cap.
7. Remove the stake on the spindle nut.
8. Remove the spindle nut and pull the hub unit off of the spindle.
9. Install in reverse order of removal. Thread a new nut onto the spindle and tighten until just snug. With the vehicle on the ground, torque the spindle nut to 134 ft. lbs. (185 Nm), then stake the nut.
10. Connect the negative battery cable.

1988–91 Prelude

▶ **See Figures 56 thru 61**

The use special tools or their equivalent is required for these procedures. A hydraulic press, correct diameter drivers and supports are required for disassembly of the hub and bearing. If necessary, take the knuckle assembly to a machine shop or dealership to have the bearings replaced.

1. Disconnect the negative battery cable.
2. Loosen the rear lug nuts slightly. Raise the vehicle and support it safely.
3. Release the parking brake. Remove the rear wheel.
4. Remove the bolts retaining the brake caliper and separate the caliper from the knuckle. Do not let the caliper hang by the brake hose; support it with a length of wire.
5. Remove the two 6mm screws from the brake disc. Tighten two 8 x 12mm bolts into the holes of the brake disc, then remove the brake disc from the rear hub.
6. Remove the cotter pin from the lower control arm on 2-wheel steering vehicles, or the tie rod on 4-wheel steering vehicles. Remove the castle nut.
7. Separate the tie rod ball joint using a ball joint removal tool.
8. Remove the cotter pin and the lower arm ball joint nut.
9. Separate the ball joint and lower arm using a puller.
10. Remove the cotter pin and castle nut. Separate the upper ball joint using a ball joint removal tool. Remove the knuckle assembly from the vehicle.
11. Remove the rear hub spindle nut from the rear hub.
12. Remove the splash guard mounting bolts.
13. Using a hydraulic press, separate the hub from the knuckle.

➡Set the rear hub in a base securely so the knuckle will not tilt the assembly in the press. Hold onto the hub to keep it from falling after it is pressed out.

Fig. 53 Remove the spindle nut cap using a hammer and small chisel

Fig. 54 Remove the stake on the spindle nut before attempting to remove the nut

Fig. 55 Remove the spindle nut, then pull the hub unit off of the spindle

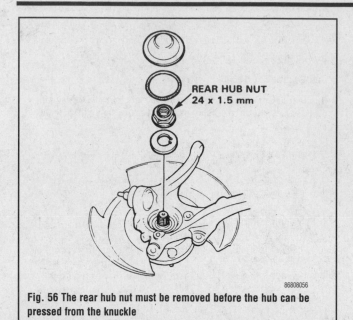

Fig. 56 The rear hub nut must be removed before the hub can be pressed from the knuckle

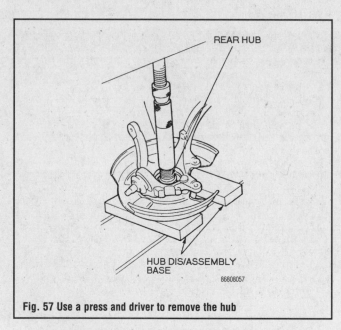

Fig. 57 Use a press and driver to remove the hub

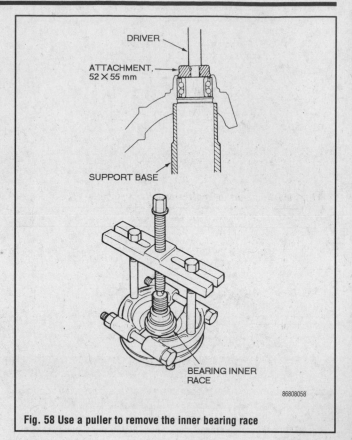

Fig. 58 Use a puller to remove the inner bearing race

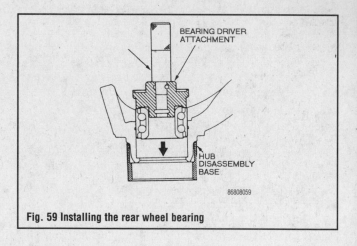

Fig. 59 Installing the rear wheel bearing

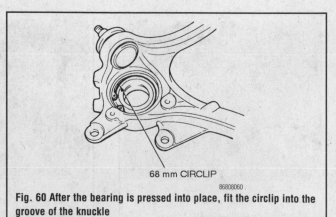

Fig. 60 After the bearing is pressed into place, fit the circlip into the groove of the knuckle

14. Remove the splash guard and circlip from the knuckle.

15. Using a hydraulic press and proper sized driver, press the wheel bearing out of the knuckle.

16. Remove the bearing inner race using a bearing remover.

To install:

17. Position the rear wheel bearing on the knuckle and apply downward pressure with a hydraulic press.

18. After the bearing is pressed into place, fit the circlip into the groove of the knuckle.

19. Install the splash guard. Place the hub in position, and apply downward pressure with a hydraulic press. Install the rear hub nut and torque the spindle nut to 180 ft. lbs. (250 Nm).

20. Install the knuckle assembly onto the vehicle, then loosely install all nuts and bolts. Tighten the lower ball joint nut to 40 ft. lbs. (55 Nm). On vehicles with 4-wheel steering, tighten the tie rod end joint to 32 ft. lbs. (44 Nm). Install a new cotter pin.

21. When everything is assembled, lower the vehicle and tighten the rubber bushing nuts and bolts with the weight of the vehicle on the wheels. Tighten the upper bushing nut to 32 ft. lbs. (44 Nm) and the lower bushing bolt to 40 ft. lbs. (55 Nm).

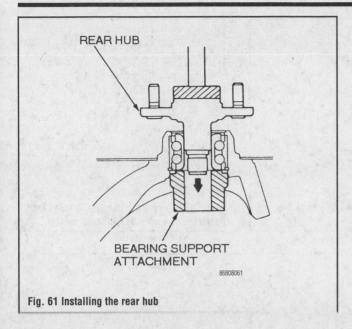

Fig. 61 Installing the rear hub

Rear Wheel Alignment

♦ See Figure 38

All the models covered by this guide have rear suspension systems on which bent or damaged components can cause unusual tire wear and/or handling problems. The alignment dimensions of caster, camber and toe are applicable to the rear wheels as well as the front. All Accords and Preludes are adjustable for rear toe setting; some models are adjustable for camber.

Rear alignment should be checked periodically by a reputable alignment facility. Preludes with 4WS require rear alignment with every front wheel alignment.

Checking the alignment of the rear wheels can be a quick, low-cost diagnostic tool when investigating rear tire wear. Discovering a bent component and replacing it can save the cost and aggravation of replacing two tires, only to have them wear prematurely.

➡**Vehicles equipped with 4-wheel steering require the use of a rear steering center locking pin tool during alignment. This is a special purpose tool, unlikely to be found in the aftermarket. It must be installed any time the rear steering gearbox or the center shaft is removed.**

Additionally, check the alignment any time the rear wheels or suspension undergoes a heavy impact. Suspension components are reasonably strong in their normal working dimensions but a world-class pothole or off-road excursion can force them over the limit.

STEERING

Steering Wheel

REMOVAL & INSTALLATION

Without SRS (Air Bag)

♦ See Figures 62, 63 and 64

1. Disconnect the negative battery cable.
2. Remove the steering wheel nut cover.
3. Make certain the steering wheel is set approximately straight-ahead. Lock the ignition and remove the key.
4. Use a fine-tipped marker or similar to make an alignment mark on the wheel and shaft. Remove the steering wheel retaining nut. Be sure to counter-hold the wheel with your hand; do not let the full force of the wrench push on the steering lock.
5. Remove the steering wheel by rocking it from side-to-side, while pulling up steadily by hand. Do not use excessive force. If the wheel will not slide off the shaft, it will be necessary to use a steering wheel puller.
6. Unplug the necessary electrical connections.
7. Install in reverse order. Be sure to tighten the steering wheel nut to 36 ft. lbs (50 Nm).

With SRS (Air Bag)

♦ See Figures 65, 66, 67 and 68

1. Disconnect the negative battery cable. Properly disable the Supplemental Restraint System (SRS), as detailed in Section 6 of this manual.
2. Remove the small plastic covers on both sides behind the steering wheel. Remove the two (one on each side) Torx® bolts using a T30 bit. Remove the air bag assembly.

✳✳ CAUTION

Store the air bag in a safe area with the bag portion facing upwards. This will prevent launching of the air bag assembly in case of accidental deployment.

3. Unplug the connectors from the horn and cruise control SET/RESUME switches.
4. Make certain the steering wheel is set approximately straight-ahead. Lock the ignition and remove the key.
5. Use a fine-tipped marker or similar to make an alignment mark on the wheel and shaft. Remove the steering wheel retaining nut/bolt. Be sure to counter-hold the wheel with your hand; do not let the full force of the wrench push on the steering lock.

Fig. 62 A small prybar can be used to remove the steering wheel nut cover

Fig. 63 Hold the steering wheel while removing the nut

Fig. 64 The steering wheel should pull off the shaft

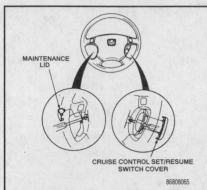

Fig. 65 Remove the small plastic covers on both sides behind the steering wheel

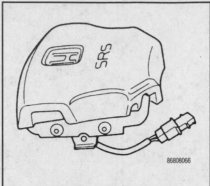

Fig. 66 Always store the air bag facing upwards

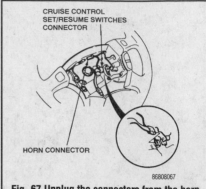

Fig. 67 Unplug the connectors from the horn and cruise control SET/RESUME switches

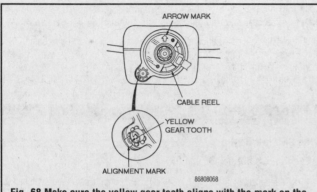

Fig. 68 Make sure the yellow gear tooth aligns with the mark on the cover and the arrow on the cable reel points straight up

6. Remove the steering wheel by rocking it from side-to-side, while pulling up steadily by hand. If the wheel will not slide off the shaft, it will be necessary to use a steering wheel puller.

To install:

7. Center the cable reel:
   a. Rotate the cable reel clockwise until it stops.
   b. Rotate it counterclockwise approximately 2 turns until the yellow gear tooth aligns with the mark on the cover AND the arrow on the cable reel points straight up.

8. Install the steering wheel. Make certain the wheel shaft engages the cable reel. Tighten the nut to 36 ft. lbs. (50 Nm).

9. Insert the cruise control SET/RESUME connector and the air bag connector into the steering wheel clips. Check that they are firmly seated.

10. Engage the horn connector.

11. Install the air bag assembly with new Torx® bolts. Tighten them to 7 ft. lbs. (10 Nm).

12. Install the connector on the maintenance lid and install the lid.

13. Enable the SRS system and connect the battery cable. Turn the ignition switch **ON**; check for proper operation of the SRS dash warning lamp. Confirm proper operation of the horn and cruise control buttons. Turn the steering wheel counterclockwise; check that the yellow tooth still aligns with the mark.

Steering Column

REMOVAL & INSTALLATION

▶ **See Figures 69, 70, 71 and 72**

1. Disconnect the negative battery cable. If equipped with an air bag, properly disable the Supplemental Restraint System (SRS), as detailed in Section 6 of this manual.

2. Remove the steering wheel.

3. Remove the lower cover panel. Remove the driver's knee bolster, if equipped.

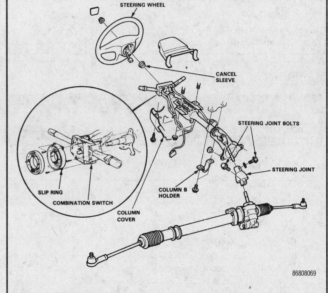

Fig. 69 Steering column used on Preludes through 1991

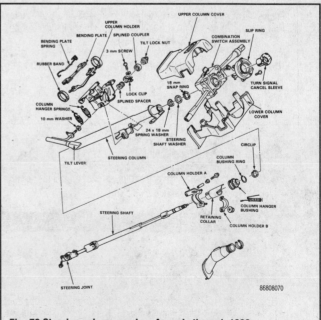

Fig. 70 Steering column used on Accords through 1989

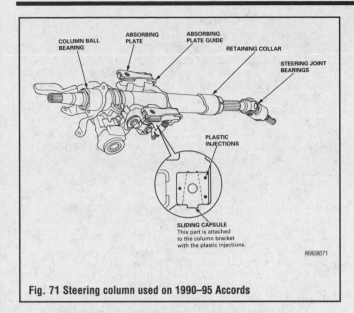

Fig. 71 Steering column used on 1990–95 Accords

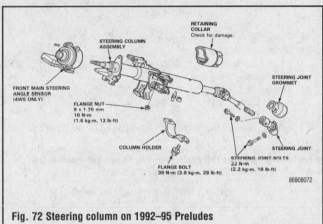

Fig. 72 Steering column on 1992–95 Preludes

4. Remove the upper and lower column covers.

5. Disconnect the wire couplers from the combination switch. Remove the turn signal canceling sleeve and the combination switch.

6. Remove the steering joint cover and remove the steering joint bolt(s).

7. Disconnect each wire coupler from the fuse box under the left side of the dashboard.

8. Remove the steering column retaining brackets.

9. Remove the nuts attaching the bending plate guide and bending plate (part of the tilt-wheel assembly), then remove the steering column assembly.

To install:

10. Fit the column into place and secure the bracket, bending plate and guide. Torque the nuts to 16 ft. lbs. (22 Nm).

11. Install the steering joint bolts and torque to 16 ft. lbs. (22 Nm).

12. Connect the wiring at the fuse box.

13. Install the switches and connect the wiring.

14. Install the knee bolster and steering wheel.

15. Properly enable the SRS system, if equipped, and connect the negative battery cable.

Manual Steering Rack

REMOVAL & INSTALLATION

▶ **See Figure 73**

1. Disconnect the negative battery cable. If equipped with an air bag, properly disable the Supplemental Restraint System (SRS), as detailed in Section 6 of this manual.

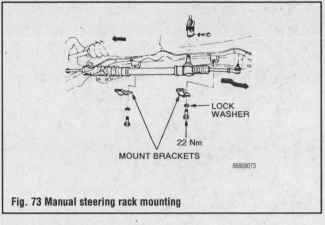

Fig. 73 Manual steering rack mounting

2. Raise and safely support the front end of the car on jackstands. Double check the placement and security of the stands.

3. Remove the cover panel and steering joint cover at the firewall. Unbolt and separate the steering shaft at the coupling.

4. Remove the front wheels.

5. Remove the cotter pins and unscrew the castle nuts on the tie rod ends. Using a ball joint separator, disconnect the tie rod ends. After the joints are separated, lift the tie rod ends out of the steering knuckles.

6. Remove the center beam.

7. On cars with manual transaxles, disconnect the shift rod and extension from the clutch housing.

8. On cars with automatic transaxles, remove the shift cable guide from the floor and pull the shift cable down by hand.

9. Remove the nuts connecting the exhaust header pipe to the exhaust pipe and remove the exhaust pipe bracket. Move the exhaust pipe out of the way; support it with a length of wire.

10. Push the rack all the way to the right (simulating a left turn) and remove the gearbox brackets. Slide the tie rod ends all the way to the right.

11. Drop the gearbox far enough to permit the end of the pinion shaft to come out of the hole in the frame channel, then rotate it forward until the shaft is pointing rearward.

12. Slide the gearbox to the right until the left tie rod clears the exhaust pipe, then drop it down and out of the car to the left.

To install:

13. Set the rack with the arms simulating a left turn. Install the rack by reversing the removal manipulation. Rotate the rack so that the pinion shaft fits into its hole in the frame channel.

14. Once in place and centered, install the mount brackets; tighten the bolts to 16 ft. lbs. (22 Nm).

15. Reconnect the exhaust pipe and install the brackets. Tighten the pipe nuts to 40 ft. lbs. (55 Nm) and the bracket nuts to 16 ft. lbs. (22 Nm).

16. Reconnect the transaxle controls, either the shift rod or shift cable guide.

17. Install the center beam. Make certain the insulator is centered with its mount on the transaxle. It may be necessary to loosen the center beam bolt and insulator nuts to adjust the position. Tighten the center beam bolts to 36 ft. lbs. (50 Nm).

18. Connect the tie-rod ball joints, install the castle nut and fit a new cotter pin.

19. Inside the car, connect the steering shaft connector to the pinion shaft. Tighten the bottom bolt to 22 ft. lbs. (30 Nm).

20. Install the front wheels and lower the car to the ground.

21. Properly enable the SRS system, if equipped, and connect the negative battery cable.

22. Have the alignment (toe) setting checked at a reputable alignment facility.

ADJUSTMENT

▶ **See Figure 74**

This procedure adjusts steering effort only. A steering gearbox locknut wrench such as Honda tool 07916–SA50001, or its equivalent, is required.

1. Raise the front wheels and place them in a straight-ahead position. Using a spring scale, turn the steering wheel and check the steering force; it should be

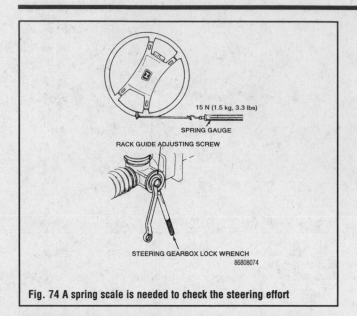

Fig. 74 A spring scale is needed to check the steering effort

no more than 3.3 lbs. If steering force exceeds this amount, adjust by performing the following steps.

2. Make sure that the rack is well lubricated.

3. Loosen the rack guide adjusting locknut.

4. Tighten the adjusting screw just to the point where the screw bottoms.

5. Back off the adjusting screw 45 degrees and hold it in that position while tightening the locknut.

6. Recheck the play, then, move the wheels lock-to-lock, to make sure that the rack moves freely.

7. Check the steering force, readjust as necessary.

Power Steering Rack

REMOVAL & INSTALLATION

▶ **See Figures 75, 76 and 77**

1. Raise the vehicle and support it safely.

2. Remove the steering shaft joint cover and disconnect the steering shaft at the coupling.

3. Drain the power steering fluid by disconnecting the gearbox return hose at the reservoir. Plug the reservoir port and place the end of the hose in a container. Start the engine, running it while turning the steering wheel lock-to-lock. When the fluid stops draining, switch the engine off immediately. Remove the plug and reinstall the hose.

4. Disconnect the negative battery cable. If equipped with an air bag, properly disable the Supplemental Restraint System (SRS), as detailed in Section 6 of this manual.

5. Remove the gearbox shield.

6. Remove the front wheels.

7. Remove the castle nuts securing the tie rods to the knuckles. Using a ball joint separator, disconnect the tie rods from the knuckles.

8. If equipped with a manual transaxle, remove the shift extension from the transaxle case. Disconnect the gear shift rod from the transaxle case by removing the 8mm bolt.

9. If equipped with an automatic transaxle, remove the control cable clamp.

10. Remove the center beam.

11. On Preludes through 1991 with 4-Wheel Steering (4WS), separate the joint guard cap and the joint guard. Remove the joint bolt from the driven pinion side. Remove the joint bolt from the center steering shaft side, then slide the joint back to disconnect it from the driven pinion.

12. Remove the exhaust header pipe.

13. Label and disconnect the hydraulic lines at the steering control unit. The 4 nuts are of three different sizes, 12 mm, 14mm and 17mm; use flare-nut wrenches.

14. On Preludes, remove the mounting bolts and lower the front sway bar.

15. Shift the tie rods so they are simulating a left turn.

16. Remove the gearbox mounting bolts.

17. Slide the gearbox right until the left tie rod clears the bottom of the rear beam. Remove the gearbox.

To install:

18. Position the gear box in the vehicle and torque the clamp bolts to 16 ft. lbs. (22 Nm) on 1986–89 Accord and 29 ft. lbs. (40 Nm) on all others.

19. On Preludes, install the sway bar.

20. Connect the hydraulic lines and the exhaust pipe.

21. Connect the shift linkage.

22. Connect the tie rod ends to the steering knuckles. Tighten the nuts to 32 ft. lbs. (44 Nm) and install a new cotter pin.

23. Connect the steering shaft coupling and tighten to 22 ft. lbs. (30 Nm).

24. Fill the reservoir with fluid. Do not fill the reservoir above the FULL mark.

25. Properly enable the SRS system, if equipped, and connect the negative battery cable.

➡**Remember that your Honda uses only Honda power steering fluid. Substitution of other fluids may damage the system**

26. Bleed the air from the system. After refilling the reservoir, start the engine and run it at fast idle while turning the steering wheel lock-to-lock several times. Check the fluid level and top it as necessary.

ADJUSTMENT

A steering gearbox locknut wrench such as Honda tool 07916-SA50001, or its equivalent, is required.

Accord

▶ **See Figure 78**

1. Raise and safely support the vehicle.

2. Remove the steering gear splash shield, if equipped.

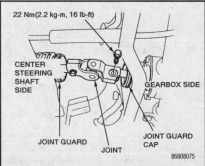

Fig. 75 On Preludes through 1991 with 4WS, disconnect the rear steering shaft at the front joint

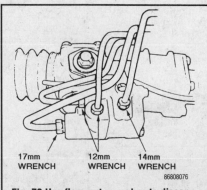

Fig. 76 Use flare-nut wrenches to disconnect the lines

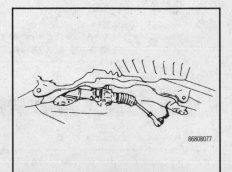

Fig. 77 Slide the gearbox to the right until the left tie rod clears the bottom of the rear beam, then remove the assembly

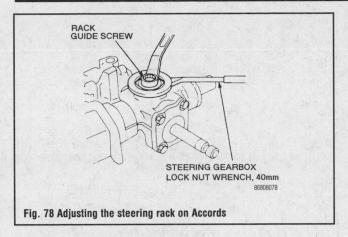

Fig. 78 Adjusting the steering rack on Accords

3. Loosen the rack guide adjusting locknut.
4. Tighten the adjusting screw until it compresses the spring and seats against the guide, then loosen it. Retorque it to 35 inch lbs. (4 Nm), then back it off about 25 degrees on 1986–89 Accords or about 35 degrees on 1990–95 Accords.
5. Hold it in that position while tightening the locknut to 10 ft. lbs. (25 Nm).
6. Move the wheel lock-to-lock to make sure the rack moves freely.
7. Lower the vehicle.

Prelude

1. Raise and safely support the vehicle.
2. Loosen the rack guide adjusting locknut.
3. Tighten the adjusting screw until it compresses the spring and seats against the guide, then loosen it. Retorque it to 24 inch lbs. (3 Nm), then back it off 20–30 degrees on models through 1990 or 15–25 degrees on 1990–95 vehicles. On 2-wheel steering vehicles, retighten the screw to 24 inch lbs. (3 Nm), then tighten the locknut to 18 ft. lbs. (25 Nm). On 4WS cars, back the adjuster off about 30–40 degrees, retighten it to 24 inch lbs. (3 Nm) and secure the locknut.
4. Move the steering wheel lock-to-lock to make sure the rack moves freely.
5. Lower the vehicle.

4-Wheel Steering (4WS) System

PRECAUTIONS

- Once removed, handle the rear steering gearbox with extreme care.
- Do not twist or apply any torque to the offset (input) shaft.
- Do not strike or apply force to the stroke rod.
- Do not attempt to disassemble or repair the gearbox. Do not loosen any of the external locknuts.

REMOVAL & INSTALLATION

Use of the rear steering center locking pin tool is required for these procedures. This is a special purpose tool, unlikely to be found in the aftermarket. It must be installed any time the rear steering gearbox or the center shaft is removed. It must also be used during rear wheel alignment.

Preludes Through 1991

▶ See Figures 79, 80, 81 and 82

1. Disconnect the negative battery cable.
2. Raise and safely support the rear of the car. Double check the jackstands for correct placement and stability.
3. Remove the rear wheels.
4. Remove the cotter pins from the tie-rod joints. Loosen the castle nuts. Separate the joint from the steering knuckle with a ball joint separator, then disconnect the tie-rod.
5. At the center shaft connection to the rear steering gearbox, slide the joint guard toward the front of the car. Remove the steering yoke bolt.

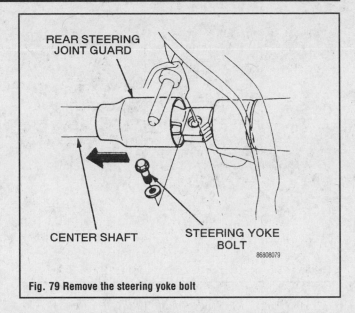

Fig. 79 Remove the steering yoke bolt

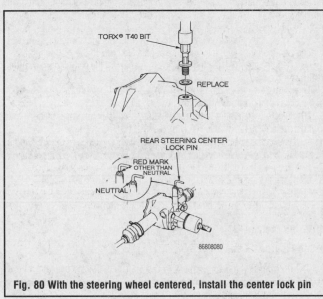

Fig. 80 With the steering wheel centered, install the center lock pin

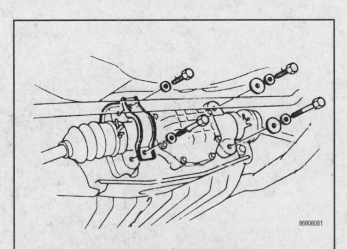

Fig. 81 Remove the bolts, then remove the rear gearbox assembly from the vehicle. Note that the lower bolts are longer than the other two

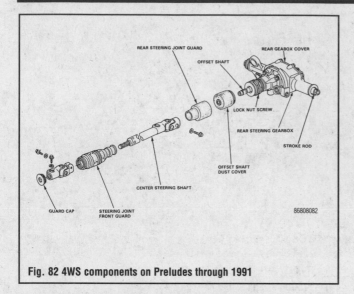

Fig. 82 4WS components on Preludes through 1991

6. Remove the cap bolt from the gearbox. With the steering wheel centered, install the center locking pin. If the steering is centered (and locked), no red will be visible around the shaft of the lock pin. If it is not correctly engaged, the red mark will be seen.

7. Remove the 4 gearbox retaining bolts. Note that the lower bolts are longer than the other two; they must be reinstalled correctly.

8. Remove the rear steering gearbox to the rear of the car, lifting it over the rear beam.

To install:

9. Place the gearbox in position.

10. Install the retaining bolts, making sure each is in its proper place. Tighten the bolts to 29 ft. lbs. (40 Nm).

11. Connect the gearbox shaft to the center shaft. Tighten the yoke bolt to 16 ft. lbs. (22 Nm) and install the joint guard.

12. Remove the center locking pin. Reinstall the cap bolt and washer.

13. Connect the tie-rods to the knuckles. Tighten the castle nuts to 32 ft. lbs. (44 Nm) and install new cotter pins.

14. Install the rear wheels. Lower the car to the ground.

1992–95 Prelude

▶ See Figures 83 and 84

1. Disconnect the negative battery cable.

2. Raise and safely support the rear of the car. Double check the jackstands for correct placement and stability.

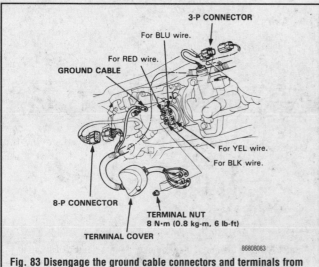

Fig. 83 Disengage the ground cable connectors and terminals from the actuator

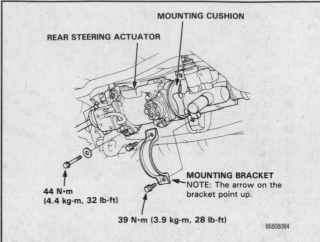

Fig. 84 Remove the four mounting bolts and brackets, then lower the assembly from the vehicle

3. Remove the rear wheels.

4. Remove the cotter pins from the tie-rod joints. Loosen the castle nuts. Separate the joint from the steering knuckle with a ball joint separator, then disconnect the tie-rod.

5. With the steering wheel centered, install the center locking pin tool.

6. Remove the rear steering actuator cover.

7. Disengage the ground cable connectors and terminals from the actuator.

8. Remove the four mounting bolts and brackets, then lower the assembly from the vehicle.

To install:

9. Position the assembly on the vehicle and install the mounting bolts and brackets. Tighten the bracket bolts to 28 ft. lbs. (39 Nm) and the mounting bolts to 32 ft. lbs. (44 Nm).

10. Reconnect the tie rods and tighten the castle nut to 43 ft. lbs. (36 Nm).

11. Engage the electrical connections.

12. Install the terminal cover and actuator cover.

13. Remove the center locking pin tool.

14. Connect the negative battery cable.

15. Start the engine and turn the wheel lock-to-lock. This must be done to reset the rear steering actuator.

Power Steering Pump

REMOVAL & INSTALLATION

▶ See Figure 85

1. Disconnect the negative battery cable. If equipped with an air bag, properly disable the Supplemental Restraint System (SRS), as detailed in Section 6 of this manual.

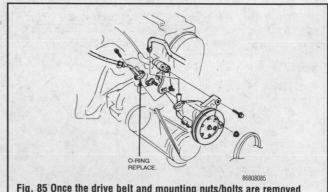

Fig. 85 Once the drive belt and mounting nuts/bolts are removed from the pump, it can be removed from the engine

2. Drain the fluid from the system as follows:

 a. Disconnect the pump return hose from the reservoir and place the end in a large container. Plug the port in the reservoir.

 b. Start the engine and allow it to run at fast idle. Turn the steering wheel from lock-to-lock several times, until fluid stops running from the hose. Shut off the engine immediately; don't run the pump without fluid.

 c. Reattach the hose.

3. Disconnect the inlet and outlet hoses at the pump. Remove the drive belt.

4. Remove the mounting bolts/nuts and remove the pump.

5. Install in reverse order. Adjust the belt tension, fill the reservoir and bleed the air from the system. Tighten the bolts/nuts to the following:

- 1984–85 Accord and Prelude pivot bolt 32 ft. lbs. (45 Nm); adjusting nut 20 ft. lbs. (27 Nm)
- 1986–89 Accord pivot bolt 28 ft. lbs. (39 Nm); adjusting nut 16 ft. lbs. (22 Nm)
- 1986–87 Prelude pivot bolt and mounting nut 28 ft. lbs. (39 Nm)

- 1990–93 Accord through bolt 33 ft. lbs. (45 Nm); mounting nut 16 ft. lbs. (22 Nm)
- 1988–91 Prelude mounting nuts and bolts 35 ft. lbs. (49 Nm)
- 1994–95 Accord mounting nuts 17 ft. lbs. (24 Nm)
- 1992–95 Prelude mounting nuts and bolts 16 ft. lbs. (22 Nm)

6. Properly enable the SRS system, if equipped, and connect the negative battery cable.

SYSTEM BLEEDING

1. Make sure the reservoir is filled to the FULL mark; do not overfill.
2. Start the engine and allow it to idle.
3. Turn the steering wheel from side-to-side several times, lightly contacting the stops.
4. Turn the engine **OFF**.
5. Check the fluid level in the reservoir and add if necessary.

COMPONENT TORQUE ILLUSTRATIONS

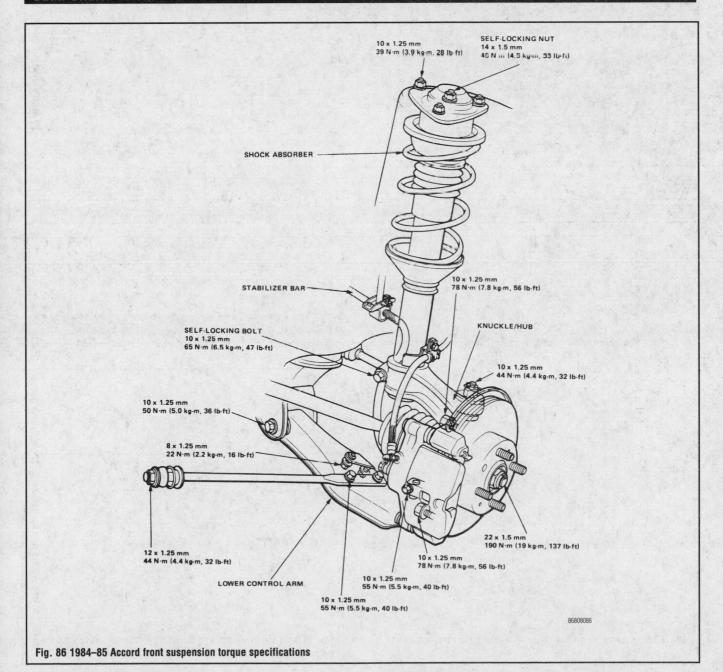

Fig. 86 1984–85 Accord front suspension torque specifications

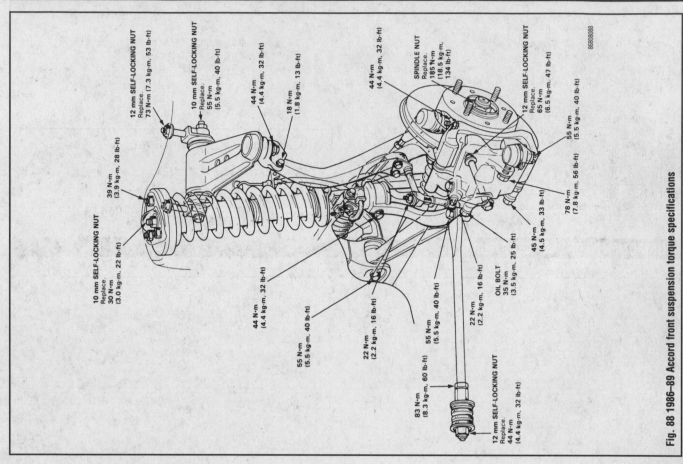

12 mm SELF-LOCKING NUT
Replace.
73 N·m (7.3 kg-m, 53 lb-ft)

10 mm SELF-LOCKING NUT
Replace.
55 N·m
(5.5 kg-m, 40 lb-ft)

44 N·m
(4.4 kg-m, 32 lb-ft)

18 N·m
(1.8 kg-m, 13 lb-ft)

44 N·m
(4.4 kg-m, 32 lb-ft)

SPINDLE NUT
Replace.
185 N·m
(18.5 kg-m, 134 lb-ft)

12 mm SELF-LOCKING NUT
Replace.
65 N·m (6.5 kg-m, 47 lb-ft)

55 N·m
(5.5 kg-m, 40 lb-ft)

78 N·m
(7.8 kg-m, 56 lb-ft)

45 N·m
(4.5 kg-m, 33 lb-ft)

10 mm SELF-LOCKING NUT
Replace.
30 N·m
(3.0 kg-m, 22 lb-ft)

10 mm SELF-LOCKING NUT
39 N·m
(3.9 kg-m, 28 lb-ft)

44 N·m
(4.4 kg-m, 32 lb-ft)

55 N·m
(5.5 kg-m, 40 lb-ft)

22 N·m
(2.2 kg-m, 16 lb-ft)

55 N·m
(5.5 kg-m, 40 lb-ft)

22 N·m
(2.2 kg-m, 16 lb-ft)

OIL BOLT
35 N·m
(3.5 kg-m, 25 lb-ft)

83 N·m
(8.3 kg-m, 60 lb-ft)

12 mm SELF-LOCKING NUT
Replace.
44 N·m
(4.4 kg-m, 32 lb-ft)

Fig. 88 1986–89 Accord front suspension torque specifications

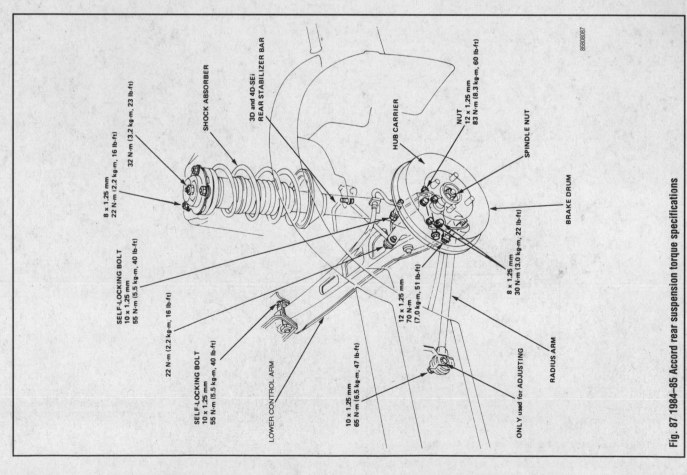

8 x 1.25 mm
22 N·m (2.2 kg-m, 16 lb-ft)

32 N·m (3.2 kg-m, 23 lb-ft)

SHOCK ABSORBER

3D and 4D-SEi
REAR STABILIZER BAR

HUB CARRIER

NUT
12 x 1.25 mm
83 N·m (8.3 kg-m, 60 lb-ft)

SPINDLE NUT

SELF-LOCKING BOLT
10 x 1.25 mm
55 N·m (5.5 kg-m, 40 lb-ft)

22 N·m (2.2 kg-m, 16 lb-ft)

SELF-LOCKING BOLT
10 x 1.25 mm
55 N·m (5.5 kg-m, 40 lb-ft)

LOWER CONTROL ARM

10 x 1.25 mm
65 N·m (6.5 kg-m, 47 lb-ft)

12 x 1.25 mm
70 N·m
(7.0 kg-m, 51 lb-ft)

8 x 1.25 mm
30 N·m (3.0 kg-m, 22 lb-ft)

BRAKE DRUM

ONLY used for ADJUSTING

RADIUS ARM

Fig. 87 1984–85 Accord rear suspension torque specifications

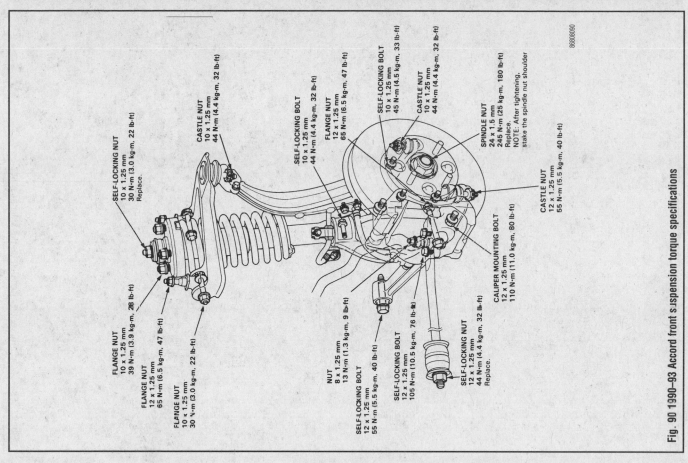

SELF-LOCKING NUT
10 x 1.25 mm
30 N·m (3.0 kg-m, 22 lb-ft)
Replace.

CASTLE NUT
10 x 1.25 mm
44 N·m (4.4 kg-m, 32 lb-ft)

SELF-LOCKING BOLT
10 x 1.25 mm
44 N·m (4.4 kg-m, 32 lb-ft)

FLANGE NUT
12 x 1.25 mm
65 N·m (6.5 kg-m, 47 lb-ft)

SELF-LOCKING BOLT
10 x 1.25 mm
45 N·m (4.5 kg-m, 33 lb-ft)

CASTLE NUT
10 x 1.25 mm
44 N·m (4.4 kg-m, 32 lb-ft)

SPINDLE NUT
24 x 1.5 mm
245 N·m (25 kg-m, 180 lb-ft)
Replace.
NOTE: After tightening,
stake the spindle nut shoulder.

CASTLE NUT
12 x 1.25 mm
55 N·m (5.5 kg-m, 40 lb-ft)

CALIPER MOUNTING BOLT
12 x 1.25 mm
110 N·m (11.0 kg-m, 80 lb-ft)

SELF-LOCKING NUT
12 x 1.25 mm
44 N·m (4.4 kg-m, 32 lb-ft)
Replace.

SELF-LOCKING BOLT
12 x 1.25 mm
105 N·m (10.5 kg-m, 76 lb-ft)

NUT
8 x 1.25 mm
13 N·m (1.3 kg-m, 9 lb-ft)

SELF-LOCKING BOLT
12 x 1.25 mm
55 N·m (5.5 kg-m, 40 lb-ft)

FLANGE NUT
10 x 1.25 mm
30 N·m (3.0 kg-m, 22 lb-ft)

FLANGE NUT
12 x 1.25 mm
65 N·m (6.5 kg-m, 47 lb-ft)

FLANGE NUT
10 x 1.25 mm
39 N·m (3.9 kg-m, 28 lb-ft)

Fig. 90 1990–93 Accord front suspension torque specifications

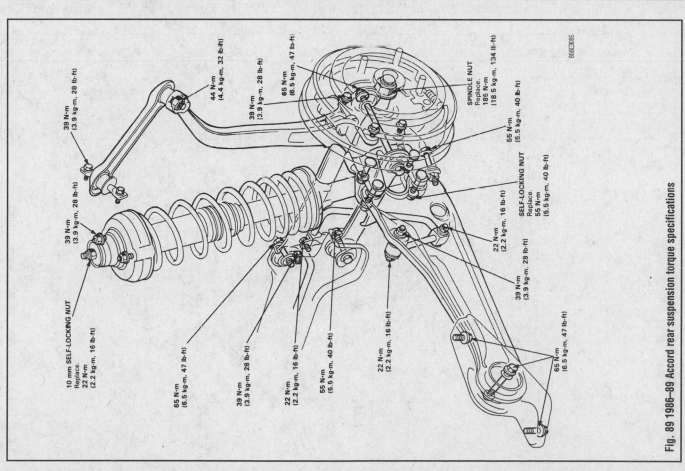

10 mm SELF-LOCKING NUT
Replace.
22 N·m
(2.2 kg-m, 16 lb-ft)

39 N·m
(3.9 kg-m, 28 lb-ft)

39 N·m
(3.9 kg-m, 28 lb-ft)

44 N·m
(4.4 kg-m, 32 lb-ft)

39 N·m (3.9 kg-m, 28 lb-ft)

65 N·m
(6.5 kg-m, 47 lb-ft)

SPINDLE NUT
Replace.
185 N·m
(18.5 kg-m, 134 lb-ft)

55 N·m
(5.5 kg-m, 40 lb-ft)

65 N·m
(6.5 kg-m, 47 lb-ft)

39 N·m
(3.9 kg-m, 28 lb-ft)

22 N·m
(2.2 kg-m, 16 lb-ft)

55 N·m
(5.5 kg-m, 40 lb-ft)

22 N·m
(2.2 kg-m, 16 lb-ft)

SELF-LOCKING NUT
Replace.
55 N·m
(5.5 kg-m, 40 lb-ft)

22 N·m
(2.2 kg-m, 16 lb-ft)

39 N·m
(3.9 kg-m, 28 lb-ft)

65 N·m
(6.5 kg-m, 47 lb-ft)

Fig. 89 1986–89 Accord rear suspension torque specifications

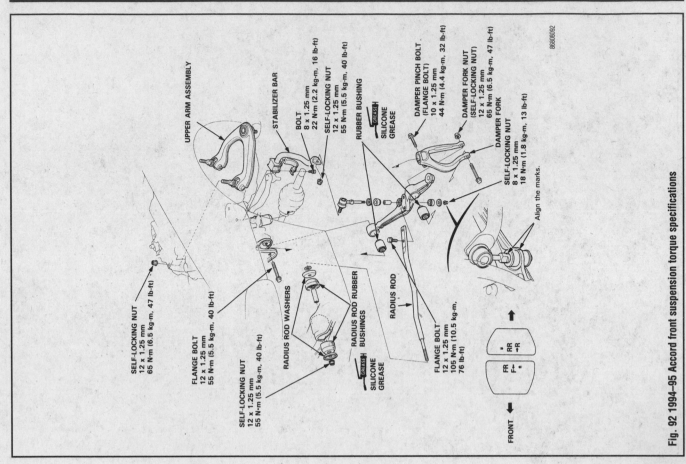

Fig. 92 1994–95 Accord front suspension torque specifications

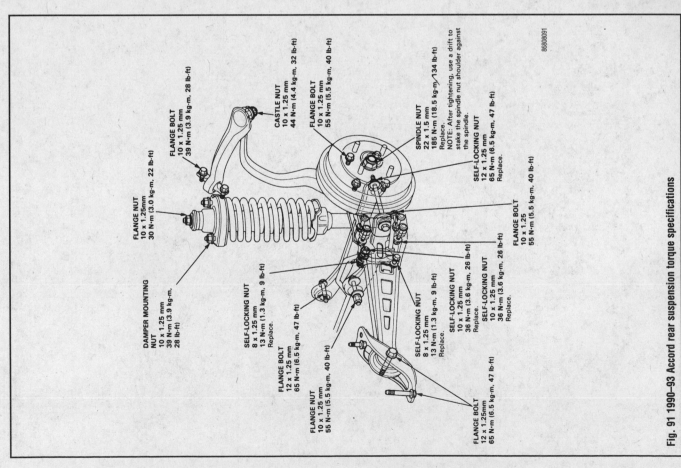

Fig. 91 1990–93 Accord rear suspension torque specifications

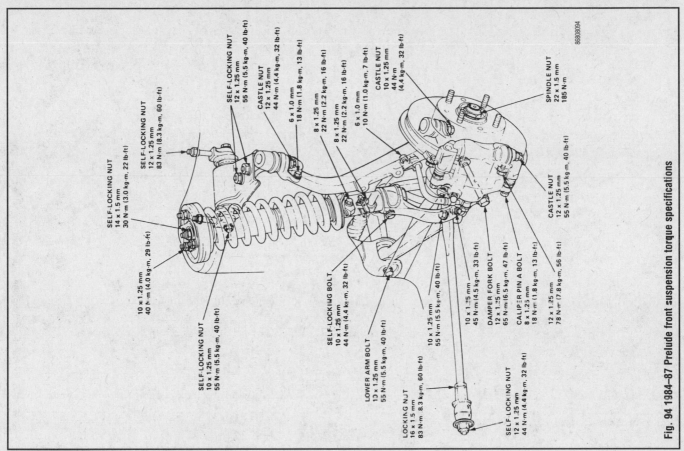

SELF-LOCKING NUT
14 x 1.5
30 N·m (3.0 kg·m, 22 lb-ft)

SELF-LOCKING NUT
12 x 1.25 mm
55 N·m (5.5 kg·m, 40 lb-ft)

SELF-LOCKING NUT
12 x 1.25 mm
83 N·m (8.3 kg·m, 60 lb-ft)

CASTLE NUT
12 x 1.25 mm
44 N·m (4.4 kg·m, 32 lb-ft)

6 x 1.0 mm
18 N·m (1.8 kg·m, 13 lb-ft)

8 x 1.25 mm
22 N·m (2.2 kg·m, 16 lb-ft)

8 x 1.25 mm
22 N·m (2.2 kg·m, 16 lb-ft)

6 x 1.0 mm
10 N·m (1.0 kg·m, 7 lb-ft)

CASTLE NUT
10 x 1.25 mm
44 N·m (4.4 kg·m, 32 lb-ft)

SPINDLE NUT
22 x 1.5 mm
185 N·m

10 x 1.25 mm
40 N·m (4.0 kg·m, 29 lb-ft)

SELF-LOCKING NUT
10 x 1.25 mm
55 N·m (5.5 kg·m, 40 lb-ft)

SELF-LOCKING BOLT
10 x 1.25 mm
44 N·m (4.4 kg·m, 32 lb-ft)

LOWER ARM BOLT
12 x 1.25 mm
55 N·m (5.5 kg·m, 40 lb-ft)

10 x 1.25 mm
45 N·m (4.5 kg·m, 33 lb-ft)

10 x 1.25 mm
55 N·m (5.5 kg·m, 40 lb-ft)

DAMPER FORK BOLT
12 x 1.25 mm
65 N·m (6.5 kg·m, 47 lb-ft)

CALIPER PIN A BOLT
8 x 1.25 mm
18 N·m (1.8 kg·m, 13 lb-ft)

12 x 1.25 mm
78 N·m (7.8 kg·m, 56 lb-ft)

CASTLE NUT
12 x 1.25 mm
55 N·m (5.5 kg·m, 40 lb-ft)

LOCKING NUT
16 x 1.5 mm
83 N·m (8.3 kg·m, 60 lb-ft)

SELF-LOCKING NUT
12 x 1.25 mm
44 N·m (4.4 kg·m, 32 lb-ft)

Fig. 94 1984-87 Prelude front suspension torque specifications

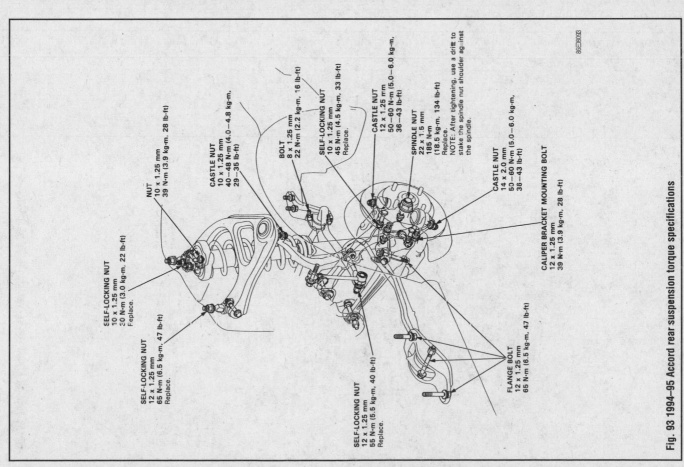

NUT
10 x 1.25 mm
39 N·m (3.9 kg·m, 28 lb-ft)

CASTLE NUT
10 x 1.25 mm
40—48 N·m (4.0—4.8 kg·m,
29—35 lb-ft)

BOLT
8 x 1.25 mm
22 N·m (2.2 kg·m, 16 lb-ft)

SELF-LOCKING NUT
10 x 1.25 mm
45 N·m (4.5 kg·m, 33 lb-ft)
Replace.

CASTLE NUT
12 x 1.25 mm
50—60 N·m (5.0—6.0 kg·m,
36—43 lb-ft)

SPINDLE NUT
22 x 1.5 mm
185 N·m
(18.5 kg·m, 134 lb-ft)
Replace.
NOTE: After tightening, use a drift to
stake the spindle nut shoulder against
the spindle.

CASTLE NUT
14 x 2.0 mm
50—60 N·m (5.0—6.0 kg·m,
36—43 lb-ft)

CALIPER BRACKET MOUNTING BOLT
12 x 1.25 mm
39 N·m (3.9 kg·m, 28 lb-ft)

SELF-LOCKING NUT
10 x 1.25 mm
30 N·m (3.0 kg·m, 22 lb-ft)
Replace.

SELF-LOCKING NUT
12 x 1.25 mm
65 N·m (6.5 kg·m, 47 lb-ft)
Replace.

SELF-LOCKING NUT
12 x 1.25 mm
55 N·m (5.5 kg·m, 40 lb-ft)
Replace.

FLANGE BOLT
12 x 1.25 mm
65 N·m (6.5 kg·m, 47 lb-ft)

Fig. 93 1994-95 Accord rear suspension torque specifications

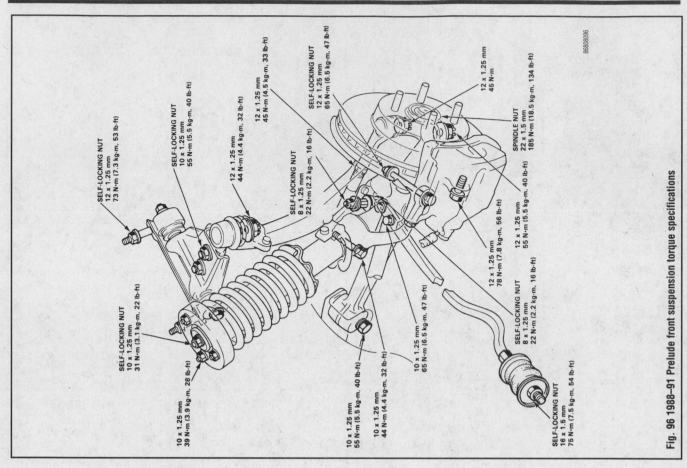

Fig. 96 1988–91 Prelude front suspension torque specifications

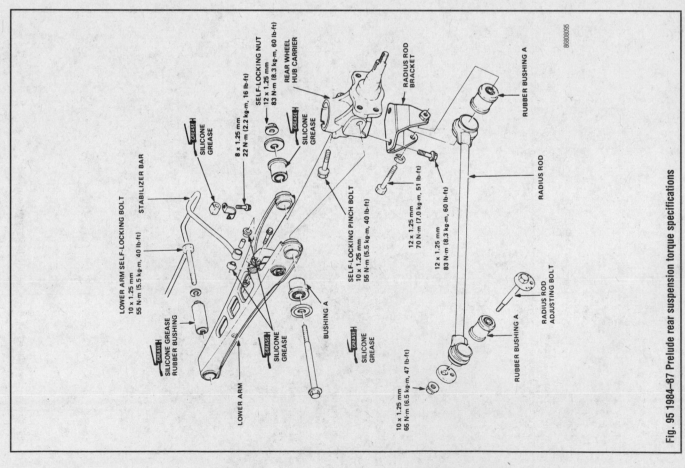

Fig. 95 1984–87 Prelude rear suspension torque specifications

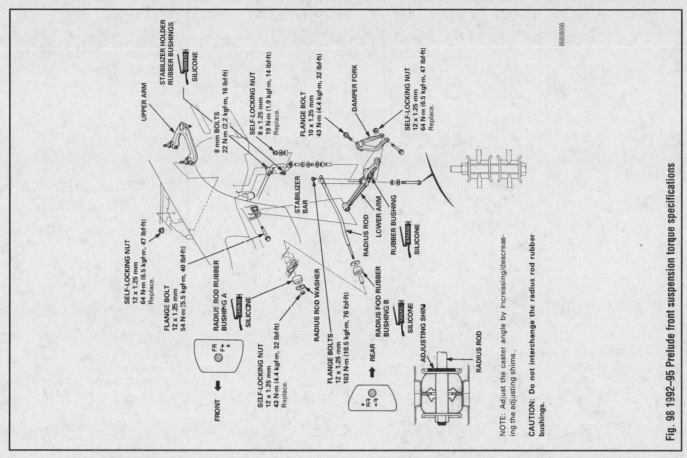

Fig. 98 1992–95 Prelude front suspension torque specifications

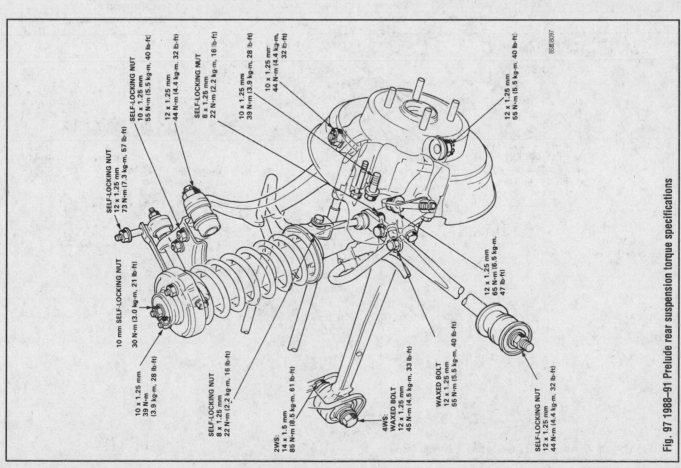

Fig. 97 1988–91 Prelude rear suspension torque specifications

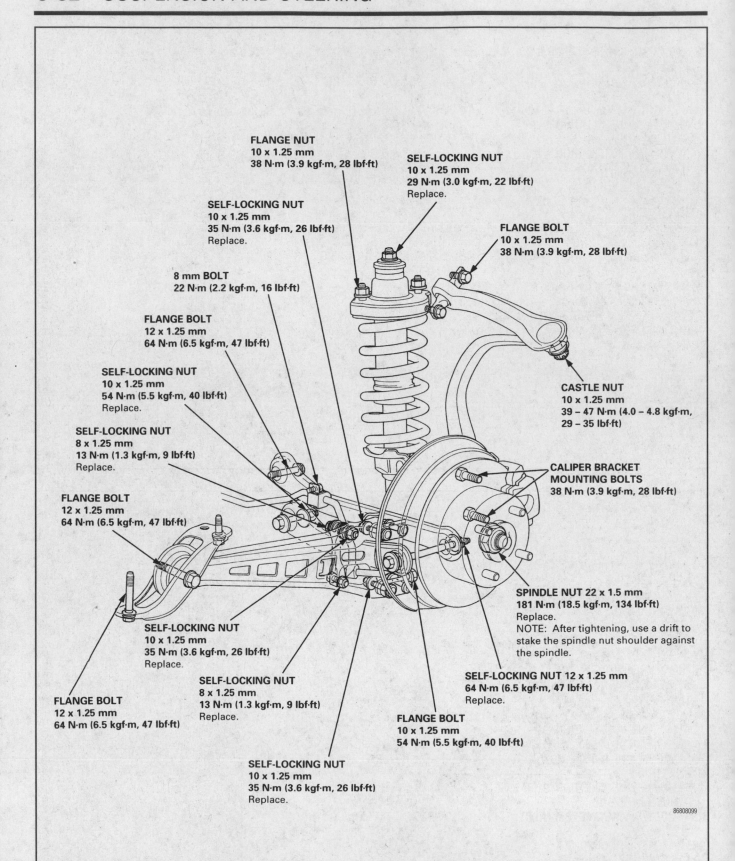

FLANGE NUT
10 x 1.25 mm
38 N·m (3.9 kgf·m, 28 lbf·ft)

SELF-LOCKING NUT
10 x 1.25 mm
29 N·m (3.0 kgf·m, 22 lbf·ft)
Replace.

SELF-LOCKING NUT
10 x 1.25 mm
35 N·m (3.6 kgf·m, 26 lbf·ft)
Replace.

FLANGE BOLT
10 x 1.25 mm
38 N·m (3.9 kgf·m, 28 lbf·ft)

8 mm BOLT
22 N·m (2.2 kgf·m, 16 lbf·ft)

FLANGE BOLT
12 x 1.25 mm
64 N·m (6.5 kgf·m, 47 lbf·ft)

CASTLE NUT
10 x 1.25 mm
39 – 47 N·m (4.0 – 4.8 kgf·m,
29 – 35 lbf·ft)

SELF-LOCKING NUT
10 x 1.25 mm
54 N·m (5.5 kgf·m, 40 lbf·ft)
Replace.

SELF-LOCKING NUT
8 x 1.25 mm
13 N·m (1.3 kgf·m, 9 lbf·ft)
Replace.

**CALIPER BRACKET
MOUNTING BOLTS**
38 N·m (3.9 kgf·m, 28 lbf·ft)

FLANGE BOLT
12 x 1.25 mm
64 N·m (6.5 kgf·m, 47 lbf·ft)

SPINDLE NUT 22 x 1.5 mm
181 N·m (18.5 kgf·m, 134 lbf·ft)
Replace.
NOTE: After tightening, use a drift to
stake the spindle nut shoulder against
the spindle.

SELF-LOCKING NUT 12 x 1.25 mm
64 N·m (6.5 kgf·m, 47 lbf·ft)
Replace.

SELF-LOCKING NUT
10 x 1.25 mm
35 N·m (3.6 kgf·m, 26 lbf·ft)
Replace.

SELF-LOCKING NUT
8 x 1.25 mm
13 N·m (1.3 kgf·m, 9 lbf·ft)
Replace.

FLANGE BOLT
10 x 1.25 mm
54 N·m (5.5 kgf·m, 40 lbf·ft)

FLANGE BOLT
12 x 1.25 mm
64 N·m (6.5 kgf·m, 47 lbf·ft)

SELF-LOCKING NUT
10 x 1.25 mm
35 N·m (3.6 kgf·m, 26 lbf·ft)
Replace.

86808099

Fig. 99 1992–95 Prelude rear suspension torque specifications

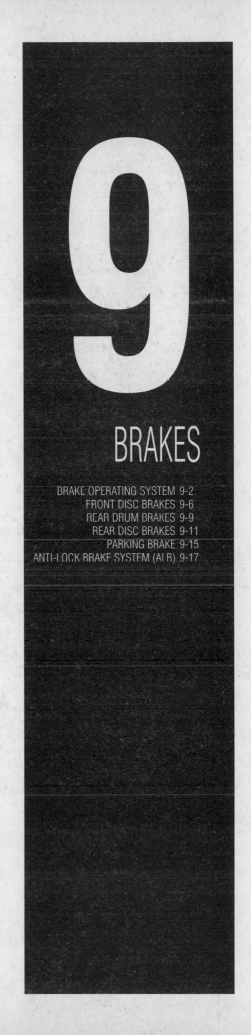

9

BRAKES

BRAKE OPERATING SYSTEM

Adjustments

BRAKE PEDAL HEIGHT

▶ **See Figures 1, 2 and 3**

1. Loosen the brake light switch locknut. Back off the switch until it no longer touches the pedal shaft.

2. Loosen the locknut on the pedal pushrod (at the top of the pedal); turn the pushrod in or out until the correct pedal height is achieved. When measuring the pedal height, do so with the carpets and floor mats removed. Correct pedal height is:
- 1984–85 Accord: 7.36 in. (187mm)
- 1986–89 Accord: 8.07 in. (205mm)
- 1990–95 Accord and 1992–95 Prelude, manual trans: 7.48 in. (190mm)
- 1990–95 Accord and 1992–95 Prelude, auto. trans: 7.68 in. (195mm)
- 1984–87 Prelude: 7.00 in. (176mm)
- 1988–91 Prelude, manual trans: 7.00 in. (176mm)
- 1988–91 Prelude, auto. trans: 7.20 in. (183mm)

3. Firmly tighten the locknut on the pushrod.

4. Screw in the brake light switch until the plunger is fully depressed. (The threaded end should be touching the pad on the pedal arm.) Back the switch off ½ turn and tighten the locknut.

5. Inspect the brake light function; the lights should come on just after the pedal is pressed and go off when the pedal is released.

DRUM BRAKES

1. Loosen the lug nuts on the rear wheels.
2. Raise and safely support the vehicle on jackstands.
3. Remove the rear wheels and drums.
4. Turn the adjuster bolt to force the brake shoes out until the brake drum will not easily go on. Back off the adjuster bolt just enough that the brake drum will go on and turn easily.
5. Install the wheel; lower the vehicle to the ground.
6. Depress the brake pedal several times to set the self-adjusting brake. Adjust the parking brake.

Brake Light Switch

REMOVAL & INSTALLATION

▶ **See Figure 3**

The brake switch operates the brake lights when the brakes are applied. A signal from the switch is also used to disengage the cruise control immediately after braking has begun.

To remove the switch, unplug the wiring connector, loosen the locknut and remove the switch. When reinstalling, adjust the switch with the locknut so that the switch engages within the first ½ in. (13mm) of pedal motion. If the switch is set to trip with no slack or free-play in its motion, a healthy bump in the road may disengage the cruise control and/or flicker the brake lights at the car behind you.

Master Cylinder

REMOVAL & INSTALLATION

▶ **See Figures 4 and 5**

✸✸ WARNING

Brake fluid is extremely damaging to painted, plastic or rubber surfaces. If any fluid is spilled, immediately flush the area with water. Be prepared to plug brake lines and hoses during disassembly. Dirt and moisture MUST be kept out of the system. Perform workbench operations in a clean, well-lit area.

1. If equipped with an air bag, disconnect the negative battery cable and properly disable the Supplemental Restraint System (SRS), as detailed in Section 6 of this manual.

2. Use a syringe or similar tool to remove as much fluid as possible from the fluid reservoir.

3. Label each brake line by its position on the master cylinder. Use flare-nut wrenches to loosen and disconnect the brake lines from the master cylinder. Wipe any spillage immediately to prevent paint damage.

4. Remove the nuts securing the cylinder to the brake booster. Remove the master cylinder.

To install:

5. If the master cylinder has been disassembled or replaced, the pushrod clearance must be checked and adjusted before reinstallation. Refer to the adjustment procedure in this section.

6. Install the master cylinder to the brake booster. Tighten the nuts to 11 ft. lbs. (15 Nm).

7. Reconnect the brake lines. Hand-thread the fittings to avoid stripping the threads; do not move or manipulate the lines to the point of bending or crimping them. Tighten the flare nuts to 11 ft. lbs. (15 Nm).

8. Refill the reservoir with clean, fresh brake fluid. Do not reuse old fluid.

9. Bleed the brake system thoroughly.

10. If equipped, enable the SRS system and connect the negative battery cable.

PUSHROD CLEARANCE ADJUSTMENT

▶ **See Figures 6, 7 and 8**

➡ **The use of special tools or their equivalent is required for this procedure. Rod bolt adjustment gauge, Honda tool 07975–SA50000 or equivalent must be used.**

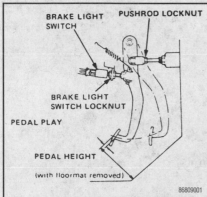

Fig. 1 Measure the pedal height from the contact surface to the bare floor

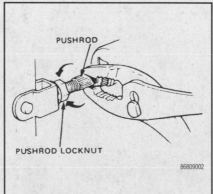

Fig. 2 If necessary to adjust the height, loosen the locknut on the pushrod

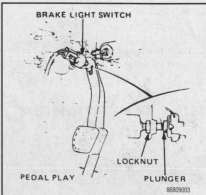

Fig. 3 Make certain the switch is properly adjusted

1. Install the adjustment gauge tool on the end of the master cylinder. Adjust the bolt so the top of the gauge is flush with the end of the master cylinder piston.

2. Without disturbing the adjusting bolt's position, put the gauge upside down on the booster. Install the nuts and tighten them to 11 ft. lbs. (15 Nm).

3. Install a vacuum gauge and T-fitting into the booster vacuum line. Start the engine; have an assistant maintain an engine speed yielding 20 in. Hg on the vacuum gauge.

4. Use a feeler gauge to measure the clearance between the gauge body and the adjusting nut. Correct clearance is 0–0.016 in. (0–0.4mm). If the clearance is incorrect, loosen the star locknut at the back of the booster; turn the adjuster to alter the position. Tighten the locknut securely.

5. Switch the ignition **OFF**.

6. Remove the vacuum gauge. Remove the adjusting gauge tool.

7. Install the master cylinder.

OVERHAUL

1984–89 Models

▶ **See Figures 9 thru 14**

1. With the master cylinder removed and the reservoir drained, remove the outer snapring.

2. Remove the washer, secondary cup and secondary piston bushing from the shaft.

3. Remove the stop bolt. Push in on the secondary piston assembly to take tension off the seal.

4. Remove the secondary and primary piston assemblies.

5. Remove the screw from the secondary piston assembly; remove the spring.

Fig. 4 Use a syringe or similar tool to remove as much fluid as possible from the fluid reservoir

Fig. 5 After its retaining nuts are removed, the master cylinder can be removed from the booster

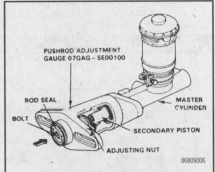

Fig. 6 Adjust the bolt so the top of the gauge is flush with the end of the master cylinder piston

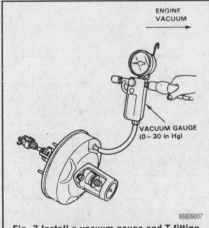

Fig. 7 Install a vacuum gauge and T-fitting into the booster vacuum line

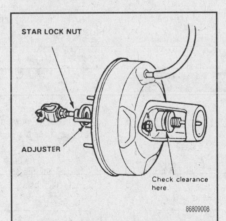

Fig. 8 Use a feeler gauge to measure the clearance between the gauge body and the adjusting nut

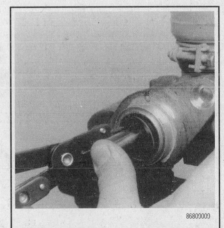

Fig. 9 Push in on the piston assembly and remove the snapring

Fig. 10 Push in on the piston assembly and remove the stop bolt

Fig. 11 Carefully pull the piston assemblies out of the master cylinder bore

Fig. 12 Remove the screw from the secondary piston assembly

6. Clean all parts thoroughly with clean brake fluid only. Any other cleaner may damage components.

To install:

7. Lubricate the new piston assemblies with clean, fresh brake fluid. Install them in the cylinder bore. Installation is easier if the pistons are rotated during insertion.

8. Stand the cylinder on the shaft and press downward on the cylinder; install the stop bolt with a new metal gasket.

9. Invert the cylinder so that the shaft is now up. Press down on the shaft and install the inner snapring.

10. Install the secondary cups, bushing and the outer snapring.

11. Install the seal on the master cylinder mounting flange.

1990–95 Models

Disassembly of the master cylinder is not recommended by the manufacturer. If an internal problem is suspected, the unit must be replaced.

Power Brake Booster

REMOVAL & INSTALLATION

1. If equipped with an air bag, disconnect the negative battery cable and properly disable the Supplemental Restraint System (SRS), as detailed in Section 6 of this manual.

2. Disconnect the vacuum hose at the booster.

3. Remove the master cylinder. Plug the brake lines immediately. Place the master cylinder in a clean, protected location out of the work area.

4. Remove the brake pedal-to-booster link pin and the 4 nuts retaining the booster. The pushrod and nuts are located inside the vehicle under the instrument panel.

5. Remove the booster assembly from the vehicle.

6. To install, reverse the removal procedure. Tighten the 4 retaining bolts to 10 ft. lbs. (14 Nm).

7. Bleed the brake system.

8. If equipped, enable the SRS system and connect the negative battery cable.

Proportioning Valve

REMOVAL & INSTALLATION

The dual brake proportioning valve provides two functions. It distributes pressurized brake fluid from the master cylinder to the diagonal brake circuits (left front/right rear and right front/left rear), as well as reducing fluid pressure to the rear brakes under heavy braking.

The proportioning valves are not repairable and should never be disassembled. They rarely fail, and all other causes of a brake problem should be thoroughly investigated before changing this valve.

The valve is located either on the right fender apron or directly below the master cylinder. To remove the valve, label each brake line as to its correct position on the valve. Carefully remove the lines from the valve and plug the lines immediately. Unbolt the valve from its mount. When reinstalling, mount the valve securely. Hand-thread each brake line into its correct port, then tighten the fittings to 10 ft. lbs. (14 Nm) with a flare-nut wrench. Do not overtighten the line fittings.

Brake Lines and Hoses

Metal lines and rubber brake hoses should be checked frequently for leaks and external damage. Metal lines are particularly prone to crushing and kinking under the car. Any such deformation can restrict the proper flow of fluid and therefore impair braking at the wheels. Rubber hoses should be checked for cracking or scraping; such damage can create a weak spot in the hose and it could fail under pressure.

Any time the lines are removed or disconnected, extreme cleanliness must be observed. Clean all joints and connections before disassembly (use a stiff bristle brush and clean brake fluid); be sure to plug the lines and ports as soon as they are opened. New lines and hoses should be flushed clean with brake fluid before installation to remove any contamination.

REMOVAL & INSTALLATION

1. If equipped with an air bag, disconnect the negative battery cable and properly disable the Supplemental Restraint System (SRS), as detailed in 2. Elevate and safely support the car on jackstands.

3. Remove the wheel(s) as necessary for access.

4. Clean the surrounding area at the joints to be disconnected.

5. Place a catch pan under the joint to be disconnected.

6. Using two wrenches (one to hold the joint and one to turn the fitting), disconnect the hose or line to be replaced.

7. Disconnect the other end of the line or hose, moving the drain pan if necessary. Always use two wrenches if possible.

8. Disconnect any retaining clips or brackets holding the line and remove the line.

9. If the system is to remain open for more time than it takes to swap lines, tape or plug each remaining line and port to keep dirt out and fluid in.

10. Install the new line or hose, starting with the end farthest from the master cylinder. Connect the other end, then confirm that both fittings are correctly threaded and turn smoothly using finger pressure. Make sure the new line will not rub against any other part. Brake lines must be at least ½ in. (13mm) from the steering column and other moving parts. Any protective shielding or insulators must be reinstalled in the original location.

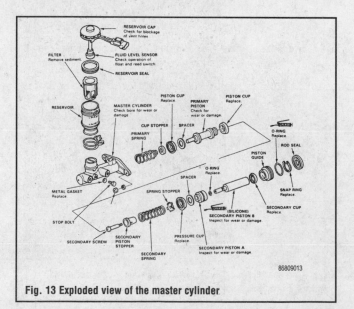

Fig. 13 Exploded view of the master cylinder

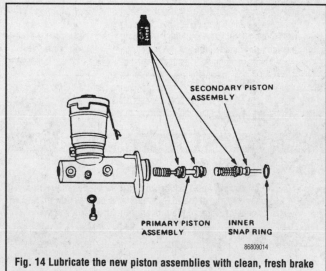

Fig. 14 Lubricate the new piston assemblies with clean, fresh brake fluid

⁎⁎ WARNING

If the new metal line requires bending, do so gently using a pipe bending tool. Do not attempt to bend the tubing by hand; it will kink the pipe and render it useless.

11. Using two wrenches as before, tighten each fitting to 9–12 ft. lbs. (13–17 Nm). Brake hoses connecting to front or rear calipers should be tightened to 25 ft. lbs. (35 Nm). Brake lines connecting to rear wheel cylinders (drum brakes) should be tightened to 14 ft. lbs. (19 Nm).
12. Install any retaining clips or brackets on the lines.
13. Refill the brake reservoir with clean, fresh brake fluid.
14. Bleed the brake system.
15. Install the wheels and lower the car to the ground.
16. If equipped, enable the SRS system and connect the negative battery cable.

BRAKE PIPE FLARING

Flaring steel lines is a skill which needs to be practiced before it should be done on a line which is to be used on a vehicle. A special flaring kit with double flaring adapters is required. It is essential that the flare is formed evenly to prevent any leaks when the brake system is under pressure. Only steel lines, not copper lines, should be used. It is also mandatory that the flare be a double flare. With the supply of parts available today, a pre-flared steel brake line should be available to fit your needs. Due to the high pressures in the brake system and the serious injuries that could occur if the flare should fail, it is strongly advised that pre-flared lines should be installed when repairing the braking system. If a line were to leak brake fluid due to a defective flare, and the leak were to go undetected, brake failure would result.

⁎⁎ WARNING

A double flaring tool must be used, as single flaring tools cannot produce a flare strong enough to hold the necessary pressure.

1. Determine the length of pipe needed. Allow ⅛ in. (3.2 mm) for each flare. Cut using an appropriate tool.
2. Square the end of the tube with a file and chamfer the edges. Remove any burrs.
3. Install the required fittings on the pipe.
4. Install the flaring tool into a vice and install the handle into the operating cam.
5. Loosen the die clamp screw and rotate the locking plate to expose the die carrier.
6. Select the required die set and install in the carrier.
7. Insert the prepared line through the rear of the die and push forward until the line end is flush with the die face.
8. Make sure the rear of both halves of the die are resting against the hexagonal die stops. Then, rotate the locking plate to the fully closed position and clamp the die firmly by tightening the clamp screw.
9. Rotate the punch turret until the appropriate size points toward the open end of the line to be flared.
10. Pull the operating handle against the line resistance in order to create the flare, then return the handle to the original position.
11. Release the clamp screw and rotate the locking plate to the open position.
12. Remove the die set and the line, then separate by gently tapping both halves on the bench. Inspect the flare for proper size and shape.

Bleeding The Brake System

▸ **See Figures 15 and 16**

➡**Vehicles equipped with Anti-Lock Brake Systems (ALB) require separate bleeding procedures if any of the ALB components have been removed or the lines disconnected. Refer to the procedure later in this section.**

It is necessary to bleed the hydraulic system any time the system has been opened or has trapped air within the fluid lines. It may be necessary to bleed the system at all four brakes if air has been introduced through a low fluid level or by disconnecting brake pipes at the master cylinder.

If a line is disconnected at one wheel only, generally only that brake circuit needs bleeding; although bleeding all four wheels is always recommended. If lines are disconnected at any fitting between the master cylinder and the brake, the system served by the disconnected pipe must be bled.

➡**On vehicles with rear drum brakes, misadjusted brake shoes can cause a "long" pedal and reduced braking, giving the illusion of air in the lines. If you're trying to track down such a problem, adjust the rear brakes and test drive the car before bleeding the system.**

1. Fill the master cylinder reservoir to the MAX or FULL line with brake fluid and keep it at least half full throughout the bleeding procedure.
2. It is strongly recommended that whenever bleeding is required, all wheels be bled rather than just one or two. The correct order of bleeding is:
• Prelude: Left front, right front, right front, left rear
• 1984–89 Accord: Left front, right rear, right front, left rear
• 1990–95 Accord: Right rear, left front, left rear, right front
3. At the wheel to be bled, place the correct size box-end or line wrench over the bleeder valve and attach a tight-fitting hose over the bleeder. Allow the tube to hang submerged in a transparent container half full of clean brake fluid. The hose end must remain submerged in the fluid at all times.
4. Have an assistant slowly pump the brake pedal several times slowly and hold it down.
5. Slowly unscrew the bleeder valve (¼–½ turn is usually enough). After the initial rush of air and fluid, tighten the bleeder and have the assistant slowly release the pedal.
6. Repeat until no air bubbles are seen in the hose or container. If air is constantly appearing after repeated bleedings, the system must be examined for the source of the leak or loose fitting. When you are finished with a wheel, tighten the bleeder screw to 5–7 ft. lbs. (7–9 Nm).

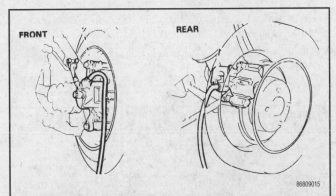

Fig. 15 Examples of bleeding the brakes. Prelude with rear disc brakes shown

Fig. 16 A shatter-proof bottle can help prevent messy accidents. Accord drum brake system shown

7. Periodically check the reservoir on the master cylinder, topping it as needed to maintain the proper level.

8. After bleeding, check the pedal for "sponginess" or vague feel. Repeat the bleeding procedure as necessary to correct. Top off the reservoir level.

9. Test drive the car to check for proper brake function.

FRONT DISC BRAKES

✳✳ CAUTION

Brake pads and shoes may contain asbestos, which has been determined to be a cancer causing agent. Never clean the brake surfaces with compressed air. Avoid inhaling any dust from brake surfaces. When cleaning brakes, use commercially available brake cleaning fluids.

Brake Pads

INSPECTION

▶ **See Figures 17 and 18**

The front brake pads may be inspected without removal. With the front end elevated and safely supported, remove the wheel(s). Unlock the steering column lock and turn the wheel so that the brake caliper is out from under the fender.

View the pads (both inner and outer) through the cut-out in the center of the caliper. Remember to look at the thickness of the pad friction material (the part that actually presses on the disc) rather than the thickness of the backing plate which does not change with wear. Replace the brake pads if the remaining lining is below ³⁄₃₂ in. (2.4mm).

Remember that you are looking at the profile of the pad, not the whole thing. Brake pads can wear on a taper which may not be visible through the window. It is also not possible to check the contact surface for cracking or scoring from this position. This quick check can be helpful only as a reference; detailed inspection requires pad removal.

REMOVAL & INSTALLATION

▶ **See Figures 19, 20, 21, 22 and 23**

✳✳ CAUTION

If the car was recently driven, the brake components will be hot. Wear protective gloves.

1. If equipped with an air bag, disconnect the negative battery cable and properly disable the Supplemental Restraint System (SRS), as detailed in Section 6 of this manual.

2. Loosen the lug nuts, then raise and support the vehicle safely.

3. Remove the wheel.

4. As required, separate the brake hose clamp from the strut or knuckle by removing the retaining bolts.

5. Remove the lower caliper retaining bolt and pivot the caliper upward, off the pads.

6. Remove the pads, shims and pad retainers.

To install:

7. Clean the caliper thoroughly; remove any rust from the lip of the disc or rotor. Check the brake rotor for grooves or cracks. If any heavy scoring is present, the rotor must be replaced.

8. Install the pad retainers. Apply a brake-quiet compound (available at most auto parts strores) to both surfaces of the shims and the back of the disc brake pads. Do not get the compound on the braking surface of the pad.

9. Install the pads and shims. The pad with the wear indicator goes in the inboard position.

Fig. 17 The pads can be viewed through the inspection hole

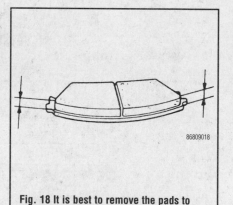

Fig. 18 It is best to remove the pads to check for taper

Fig. 19 Remove the lower caliper retaining bolt . . .

Fig. 20 . . . and pivot the caliper upward, off the pads

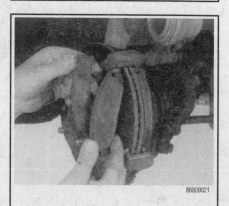

Fig. 21 Remove the pads, shims . . .

Fig. 22 . . . and pad retainers

10. Push in the caliper piston so the caliper will fit over the pads. This is most easily accomplished with a large C-clamp. As the piston is forced back into the caliper, fluid will be forced back into the master cylinder reservoir. It may be necessary to siphon some fluid out to prevent overflowing.

11. Pivot the caliper down into position and tighten the mounting bolt to 33 ft. lbs. (45 Nm).

12. Connect the brake hose to the strut or knuckle, if removed. Install the wheel and lower the vehicle to the ground.

13. Check the master cylinder and add fluid as required, then install the master cylinder cover.

14. Depress the brake pedal several times and make sure that the movement feels normal. The first brake pedal application may result in a very "long" pedal due to the pistons being retracted. Always make several brake applications before starting the vehicle. Bleeding is not usually necessary after pad replacement.

➡**Braking should be moderate for the first 5 miles or so until the new pads seat correctly. The new pads will bed best if put through several moderate heating and cooling cycles. Avoid hard braking until the brakes have experienced several long, slow stops with time to cool in between. Taking the time to properly bed the brakes will yield quieter operation, more efficient stopping and contribute to extended brake life.**

15. If equipped, enable the SRS system and connect the negative battery cable.

Brake Caliper

REMOVAL & INSTALLATION

1. If equipped with an air bag, disconnect the negative battery cable and properly disable the Supplemental Restraint System (SRS), as detailed in Section 6 of this manual.

2. Loosen the lug nuts, then Raise and safely support the vehicle on jackstands.

3. Remove the wheels.

4. Remove the banjo bolt and disconnect the brake hose from the caliper. Plug the hose immediately.

5. Remove the mounting bolt(s) and the caliper.

To install:

6. Position the caliper on the vehicle. Use new gaskets on the banjo bolt and tighten to 25 ft. lbs. (35 Nm).

7. Install the mounting bolt(s). On vehicles that have long pins below the threads of the caliper bolt, tighten the bolt to 54 ft. lbs. (75 Nm). Vehicles with short bolts and no pin beyond the threads should be tightened to 33 ft. lbs. (45 Nm).

8. Bleed the brakes.

9. If equipped, enable the SRS system and connect the negative battery cable.

OVERHAUL

◆ **See Figures 24, 25, 26, 27 and 28**

1. Remove the caliper from the vehicle and drain the remaining brake fluid from it.

2. Remove the piston from the caliper. Resist the temptation to grab it with pliers; you'll score the metal. Follow this procedure instead:

a. Place a narrow wooden block or several rags opposite the piston but within the jaws of the caliper.

b. Apply a limited amount of compressed air (no more than 30 psi or 207 kPa) into the brake line port. Do not place fingers in front of the piston; let it hit the wood stopper on the way out.

3. Remove the piston, boot and seal.

4. Clean the piston and bore with clean brake fluid. Inspect the surfaces very carefully; they must be virtually perfect. Any scoring or rust is grounds for replacement. Very light surface rust may be removed with fine crocus cloth wet with brake fluid, but any pitting requires replacement.

To install:

5. Install a new piston seal into the groove of the cylinder lubricated with brake fluid.

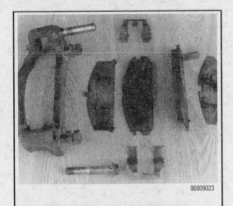

Fig. 23 Front brake pad components

Fig. 24 Do not place your fingers in front of the piston; let it hit the wood stopper

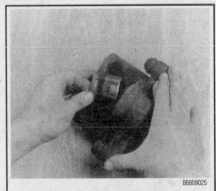

Fig. 25 Withdraw the piston from the bore . . .

Fig. 26 . . . then remove the boot . . .

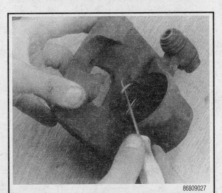

Fig. 27 . . . and seal. A small pick is helpful for removing the seal

Fig. 28 Inspect the parts for any scoring or rust. Always replace the boot and seal

6. Install the boot on the piston.

7. Lubricate the caliper bore and piston with clean brake fluid. Install the piston into the cylinder bore, solid end in first.

8. Make certain the piston boot is fitted into the lip around the caliper bore. Push the piston all the way in so the caliper will reinstall over the brake pads easily.

9. Reinstall the caliper. Fill the reservoir as needed and bleed the brake system.

Brake Disc (Rotor)

REMOVAL & INSTALLATION

Except 1990–95 Accord

▶ See Figures 29, 30 and 31

1. If equipped with an air bag, disconnect the negative battery cable and properly disable the Supplemental Restraint System (SRS), as detailed in Section 6 of this manual.

2. Loosen the lug nuts, then Raise and safely support the vehicle on jackstands.

3. Remove the wheels.

4. Remove the two 6mm screws from the brake disc.

5. Disconnect the caliper from the caliper bracket. Support the caliper out of the way with a length of wire. Do not allow the caliper to hang from the brake hose.

6. Remove the caliper bracket.

7. Remove the brake disc. If the brake disc is difficult to remove, install two 8mm bolts into the threaded holes and tighten them evenly and alternately to prevent cocking the rotor.

8. Installation is the reverse of the removal procedure.

9. If equipped, enable the SRS system and connect the negative battery cable.

1990–95 Accord

▶ See Figures 32 and 33

1. If equipped with an air bag, disconnect the negative battery cable and properly disable the Supplemental Restraint System (SRS), as detailed in Section 6 of this manual.

2. Loosen the lug nuts, then Raise and safely support the vehicle on jackstands.

3. Remove the wheels.

4. Remove the steering knuckle from the vehicle. Please refer to Section 8 for procedures.

5. Remove the 4 bolts retaining the hub unit to the steering knuckle and remove the hub unit.

6. Remove the 4 bolts, then separate the hub unit from the brake rotor.

To install:

7. Assemble the disc to the hub unit and tighten the bolts to 40 ft. lbs. (55 Nm).

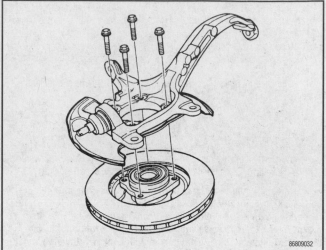

Fig. 32 Remove the 4 bolts retaining the hub unit to the steering knuckle and remove the hub unit/rotor assembly

8. When installing the hub to the knuckle, use new self-locking bolts and tighten them to 33 ft. lbs. (45 Nm).

9. Install the steering knuckle.

10. Lower the vehicle and check for proper brake operation.

11. If equipped, enable the SRS system and connect the negative battery cable.

INSPECTION

▶ See Figures 34 and 35

1. The brake disc develops circular scores during braking due to trapped dust and road grit. Excessive scoring not only contributes to squealing brakes but also shortens the life of the brake pads. However, light scoring of the disc surface, not exceeding 0.015 in. (0.38mm) in depth, will result from normal use and is not detrimental to brake operation. In general, if the scoring is deep enough to catch a fingernail passing over it, it's too deep and requires corrective action.

2. Disc run-out is the movement of the disc from side-to-side; caused by warpage or distortion. Excess run-out causes wobble or pounding in the brake pedal. Position a dial indicator in the middle of the pad wear area and turn the disc, while checking the indicator. If disc run-out exceeds 0.004 in. (0.10mm), replace or refinish the disc.

3. Disc parallelism is the measurement of variations in disc thickness at several locations on the disc circumference. It indicates whether or not the two faces of the disc are true and parallel. To measure parallelism, place a mark on the disc and measure the disc thickness with a micrometer. Repeat this measurement at eight (8) equal increments (about 45 degrees apart) on the circumference of the disc. If any of the measurements vary more than 0.0006 in. (0.015mm), replace the disc.

Fig. 29 Remove the two 6mm screws securing the brake disc

Fig. 30 Remove the bolt and guide pin from the caliper bracket, then remove the bracket

Fig. 31 Remove the brake disc from the caliper assembly

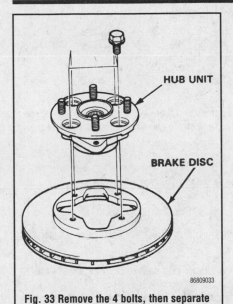

Fig. 33 Remove the 4 bolts, then separate the hub unit from the brake rotor

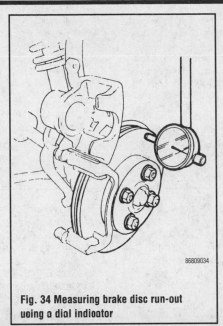

Fig. 34 Measuring brake disc run-out using a dial indicator

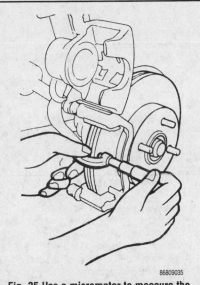

Fig. 35 Use a micrometer to measure the thickness and to check for parallelism

REAR DRUM BRAKES

✳✳ CAUTION

Brake pads and shoes may contain asbestos, which has been determined to be a cancer causing agent. Never clean the brake surfaces with compressed air. Avoid inhaling any dust from brake surfaces. When cleaning brakes, use commercially available brake cleaning fluids.

Brake Drums

REMOVAL & INSTALLATION

1984–85 Accord

1. Disconnect the negative battery cable.
2. Loosen the lug nuts.
3. Block the front wheels securely. Raise and support the rear of the vehicle on jackstands. Remove the rear wheels. Make sure that the parking brake is off.
4. Remove the bearing cap, cotter pin and the castle nut.
5. Pull off the rear brake drum. If the drum is difficult to remove, use a brake drum puller or tap it a few times with a rubber mallet. Make certain to remove it squarely; if cocked to one side, it will jam.
   To install:
6. Make certain the brake shoes are adjusted to allow the drum clearance during installation. Fit the drum into position.
7. Install the outer bearing, washer, and castle nut. Finger-tighten the nut.
8. Adjust the wheel bearing according to the procedure found in Section 8.
9. Install the wheel, then lower the vehicle to the ground. Check for proper brake operation.

Except 1984–85 Accord

▶ **See Figures 36 and 37**

1. Disconnect the negative battery cable.
2. Loosen the lug nuts.
3. Block the front wheels securely. Raise and support the rear of the vehicle on jackstands. Remove the rear wheels. Make sure that the parking brake is off.
4. Pull off the rear brake drum. If the brake drum is difficult to remove, install two 8mm bolts into the threaded holes, then tighten them evenly and alternately to prevent cocking the drum. Make certain to remove it squarely; if cocked to one side, it will jam.

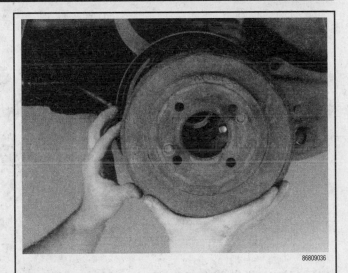

Fig. 36 Pull off the rear drum to remove it

To install:
5. Make certain the brake shoes are adjusted to allow the drum clearance during installation. Fit the drum into position.
6. Install the wheel, then lower the vehicle to the ground. Check for proper brake operation.

INSPECTION

Check the drum for cracks and the inner surface of the shoe for excessive wear and damage. The inner diameter (I.D.) of the drum should be no greater than 0.04 in. (1mm) beyond the new or standard specification. Additionally, the drum should be no more than 0.004 in. (0.10mm) out-of-round.

Brake Shoes

INSPECTION

An inspection hole is provided in the backing plate of each rear wheel which allows the brakes to be checked without removing the drum. Remove the hole plug, then check the lining thickness through the hole. If below minimum, the shoes must be replaced. Always install the plug after inspection making certain it is properly seated and tight.

This method doesn't provide a lot of information about how the brakes are wearing since it only shows one part of one shoe, but is a quick and easy first check. The only way to see the friction faces of the shoes is to remove the brake drums. No generalities can be drawn between the left and right side shoes, so both drums must be removed to perform a proper inspection.

With the drums removed:

1. Liberally spray the entire brake assembly with aerosol brake cleaner. Do not use other solvents, compressed air or a dry brush.

2. Measure the thickness of the friction surface on each shoe at several different locations. If any measurement is below the minimum thickness, replace all the shoes (both sides) as a set.

3. Check the contact surfaces closely for any signs of scoring, cracking, uneven or tapered wear, discoloration or separation from the backing plate. Anything that looks abnormal should be replaced.

4. If the shoes are in otherwise good condition except for glazing (a shiny, hard surface), the glaze may be removed by light sanding with emery cloth. Also, lightly sand the inside of the drum to de-glaze its surface. Do not attempt to rub out grooves or ridges; this is best done with a resurfacing lathe. After sanding the components, wash them thoroughly with aerosol brake cleaner to remove any grit.

REMOVAL & INSTALLATION

▸ **See Figures 38 thru 44**

➡ Although this procedure can be accomplished with common hand tools, there are a variety of specialty brake tools available in retail stores which make the job much easier.

1. If equipped with an air bag, disconnect the negative battery cable and properly disable the Supplemental Restraint System (SRS), as detailed in Section 6 of this manual.

2. Remove the rear wheel and brake drum.

3. Saturate the rear brake assembly with brake cleaning fluid.

4. On 1990 and later Accords, remove the upper return spring from the brake shoe.

➡ **All springs and fittings should be labeled or diagrammed at the time of removal. The amount of time saved during reassembly makes the extra effort well worthwhile.**

5. Remove the tension pins by pushing the retainer spring and turning them.

6. Slightly lower the brake shoe assembly and remove the lower return spring.

7. Remove the brake shoe assembly.

8. Disconnect the parking brake cable from the lever.

9. Remove the upper return spring, self-adjuster lever and self-adjuster spring. Separate the brake shoes.

10. Remove the wave washer, parking brake lever and pivot pin from the brake shoe by removing the C-clip.

To install:

11. Install the parking brake lever and wave washer on the pivot pin and secure with a new C-clip.

➡ **Pinch the C-clip securely to prevent the pivot pin from coming out of the brake shoe.**

12. Connect the parking brake cable to the parking brake lever.

13. Apply grease on each sliding surface of the brake backing plate.

Fig. 37 If the brake drum is difficult to remove, install two 8mm bolts into the threaded holes and tighten them evenly and alternately. This will draw the drum off the rear hub

Fig. 38 Saturate the rear brake assembly with brake cleaning fluid

Fig. 39 Remove the tension pins by pushing the retainer spring and turning them

Fig. 40 Slightly lower the brake shoe assembly and remove the lower return spring. This small spring can be removed using a pair of pliers

Fig. 41 Remove the brake shoe assembly from the backing plate

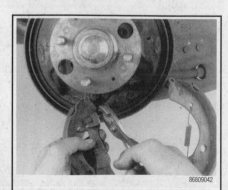
Fig. 42 Carefully slide the spring up the cable with a pair of pliers, then disconnect the cable from the lever

➡️**Do not allow grease to come in contact with the brake linings. Grease will contaminate the linings and reduce stopping ability.**

14. Clean the threaded portions of the clevises of the adjuster bolt. Coat the threads with grease. Turn the adjuster bolt to shorten the clevises.
15. Hook the adjuster spring to the adjuster lever first, then to the brake shoe.
16. Install the adjuster bolt/clevis assembly and the upper return spring.
17. Install the brake shoes to the backing plate.
18. Install the lower return spring, the tension pins and retaining springs.
19. On 1990 and later Accords, connect the upper return spring.
20. Turn the adjuster bolt to force the brake shoes out until the brake drum will not easily go on. Back off the adjuster bolt just enough that the brake drum will go on and turn easily.
21. Install the wheel; lower the vehicle to the ground.
22. If equipped, enable the SRS system and connect the negative battery cable.
23. Depress the brake pedal several times to set the self-adjusting mechanism. Adjust the parking brake.

Wheel Cylinder

When inspecting the cylinders for leakage, just lift the outer lip of the boot and check for fluid. A slight moistness, usually covered with brake dust, is

normal. Any sign of wetness or running fluid is cause for immediate replacement.

REMOVAL & INSTALLATION

▶ **See Figure 45**

1. If equipped with an air bag, disconnect the negative battery cable and properly disable the Supplemental Restraint System (SRS), as detailed in Section 6 of this manual.
2. Remove the brake drum and shoes.
3. Disconnect the brake line from the wheel cylinder. Plug the line.
4. Remove the 2 wheel cylinder retaining nuts on the inboard side of the backing plate; remove the wheel cylinder.

To install:

5. Install the cylinder; tighten the nuts to 6 ft. lbs. (8 Nm).
6. Connect the brake line and tighten the fitting to 11 ft. lbs. (15 Nm).
7. Install the brake shoes and drum.
8. Bleed the brakes.
9. Install the wheel; lower the car to the ground.
10. If equipped, enable the SRS system and connect the negative battery cable.

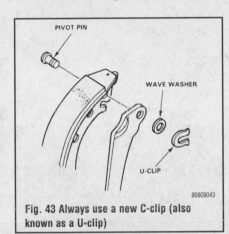

Fig. 43 Always use a new C-clip (also known as a U-clip)

Fig. 44 Use a high temperature grease to lubricate the backing plate

Fig. 45 After the retaining nuts are unscrewed, remove the wheel cylinder from the backing plate

REAR DISC BRAKES

✳ CAUTION

Brake pads and shoes may contain asbestos, which has been determined to be a cancer causing agent. Never clean the brake surfaces with compressed air. Avoid inhaling any dust from brake surfaces. When cleaning brakes, use commercially available brake cleaning fluids.

Brake Pads

REMOVAL & INSTALLATION

▶ **See Figure 46**

1. If equipped with an air bag, disconnect the negative battery cable and properly disable the Supplemental Restraint System (SRS), as detailed in Section 6 of this manual.
2. Loosen the lug nuts, then Raise and safely support the vehicle on jackstands.
3. Remove the rear wheel.
4. Remove the 2 caliper mounting bolts and remove the caliper from the bracket.
5. Remove the pads, shims and pad retainers.

To install:

6. Clean the caliper thoroughly removing any dirt or dust. Check the brake rotor for grooves or cracks; machine or replace, as necessary.
7. Install the pad retainers. Apply a disc brake pad lubricant to both surfaces of the shims and the back of the disc brake pads. Do not get any lubricant on the braking surface of the pad.
8. Install the pads and shims.
9. Use a suitable tool to rotate the caliper piston clockwise into the caliper bore, enough to fit over the brake pads. Lubricate the piston boot with silicone grease to avoid twisting the piston boot.
10. Install the brake caliper, aligning the cut-out in the piston with the tab on the inner pad. Tighten the mounting bolts.
11. Install the wheel. Lower the vehicle.
12. Check the fluid in the master cylinder and add as required. Depress the brake pedal several times to seat the pads.
13. If equipped, enable the SRS system and connect the negative battery cable.

INSPECTION

▶ **See Figure 47**

View the pads (both inner and outer) through the cut-out in the center of the caliper. Remember to look at the thickness of the pad friction material (the part that actually presses on the disc) rather than the thickness of the backing plate

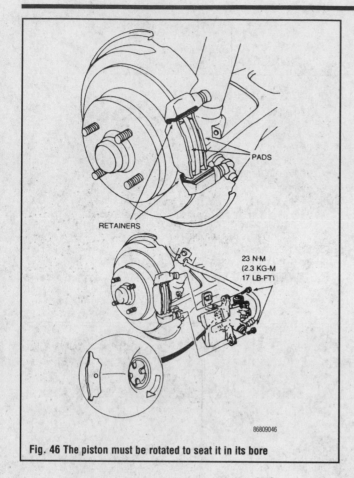

Fig. 46 The piston must be rotated to seat it in its bore

23 N·M
(2.3 KG-M
17 LB-FT)

RETAINERS

PADS

86809046

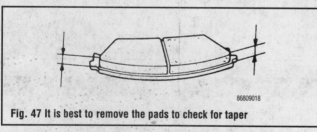

Fig. 47 It is best to remove the pads to check for taper

86809018

which does not change with wear. Replace the brake pads if the remaining lining is below ³⁄₃₂ in. (2.4mm).

Remember that you are looking at the profile of the pad, not the whole thing. Brake pads can wear on a taper which may not be visible through the window. It is also not possible to check the contact surface for cracking or scoring from this position. This quick check can be helpful only as a reference; detailed inspection requires pad removal.

Brake Caliper

REMOVAL & INSTALLATION

1. If equipped with an air bag, disconnect the negative battery cable and properly disable the Supplemental Restraint System (SRS), as detailed in Section 6 of this manual.
2. Loosen the lug nuts, then Raise and safely support the vehicle on jackstands.
3. Remove the rear wheel and tire assembly.
4. Remove the caliper shield.
5. Disconnect the parking brake cable from the lever on the caliper by removing the lock pin.
6. Remove the banjo bolt and disconnect the brake hose from the caliper. Plug the hose immediately.

7. Remove the 2 caliper mounting bolts and the caliper from the bracket.
8. Installation is the reverse of the removal procedure. Use new gaskets on the banjo bolt and tighten it to 25 ft. lbs. (35 Nm).
9. Tighten the caliper bracket bolts to 28 ft. lbs. (39 Nm).
10. Bleed the brake system. Adjust the parking brake if necessary.
11. If equipped, enable the SRS system and connect the negative battery cable.

OVERHAUL

▶ **See Figures 48 thru 54**

➡ **The use of special tools or their equivalent is required for this procedure.**

1. With the caliper removed from the car, remove the pad spring from the inside of the caliper housing.
2. Rotate the piston to remove the piston and boot. Take great care not to damage the components.
3. After removing the circlip, remove the washer, adjusting spring and the nut from the piston.

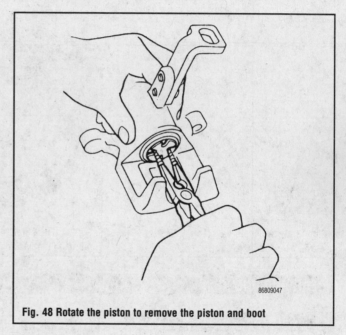

Fig. 48 Rotate the piston to remove the piston and boot

86809047

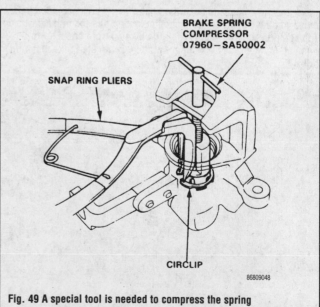

BRAKE SPRING
COMPRESSOR
07960—SA50002

SNAP RING PLIERS

CIRCLIP

86809048

Fig. 49 A special tool is needed to compress the spring

4. Carefully remove the piston seal.

5. Install Honda tool 07960–SA50002 or an equivalent spring compressor between the caliper body and the spring guide.

6. Turn the shaft of the special tool to compress the adjusting spring; remove the circlip with snapring pliers.

7. Once released, remove the spring cover, adjusting spring spacer, bearing and adjusting bolt.

8. Remove the sleeve piston; remove the pin from the cam.

9. Disassemble the return spring, parking nut, spring washer, lever, cam and cam boot.

To install:

10. After cleaning and inspecting all parts for wear or deterioration, pack the needle bearing with grease. Coat a new cam boot with grease and install it into the caliper.

11. Install the cam with the threaded end up.

12. Install the lever, spring washer and parking nut. Tighten the nut to 20 ft. lbs. (28 Nm).

13. Install the return spring.

14. Install the pin into the cam. Install a new O-ring onto the sleeve piston.

15. Install the sleeve piston. The hole in the bottom of the piston must align with the pin in the cam; the two pins on the piston must align with the holes in the caliper.

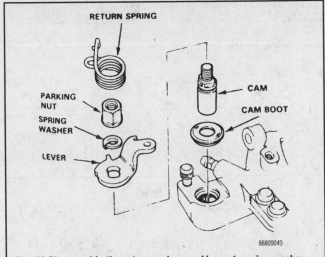

Fig. 50 Disassemble the return spring, parking nut, spring washer, lever, cam and cam boot

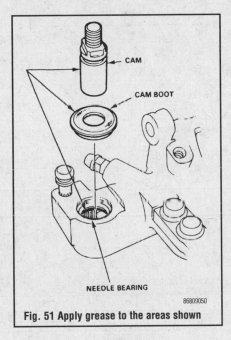

Fig. 51 Apply grease to the areas shown

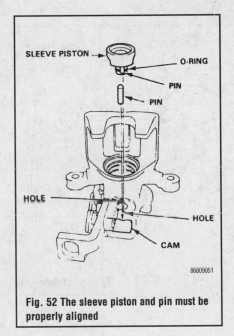

Fig. 52 The sleeve piston and pin must be properly aligned

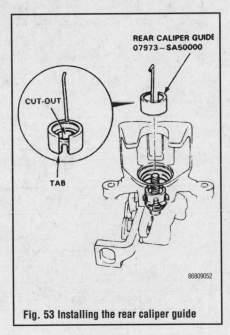

Fig. 53 Installing the rear caliper guide

16. Install a new cup with its groove facing the bearing side of the adjusting bolt.

17. Install the bearing, spacer adjusting spring and spring cover onto the adjusting bolt. Install the bolt into the cylinder bore.

18. Install rear caliper guide tool 07973–SA50000 or an equivalent into the cylinder. The cut-out on the tool must align with the tab on the spring cover.

19. Install the spring compressor (used earlier) and compress the spring until it bottoms. Make sure the caliper guide doesn't bind or hang-up while the spring is being compressed.

20. Remove the caliper guide. Make sure the flared end of the spring cover is below the clip groove.

21. Install the circlip. Make certain it is seated properly before removing the spring compressor.

22. Install the adjusting nut, spring and washer into the piston and secure the assembly by installing the circlip.

23. Coat a new piston seal and boot with silicone grease; install them into the caliper.

24. After coating the outside of the piston with silicone grease, install the piston on the adjusting bolt. Rotate the piston clockwise during installation. Take great care not to damage the piston boot.

25. Install the pad retainer.

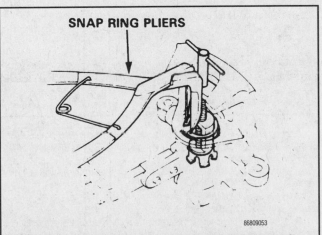

Fig. 54 Make certain the circlip is seated properly before removing the spring compressor

Brake Disc (Rotor)

REMOVAL & INSTALLATION

▶ **See Figures 55 and 56**

1. If equipped with an air bag, disconnect the negative battery cable and properly disable the Supplemental Restraint System (SRS), as detailed in Section 6 of this manual.

2. Loosen the lug nuts, then Raise and safely support the vehicle on jackstands.

3. Remove the rear wheel.

4. Remove the rear brake caliper and mounting bracket.

5. Remove the hub center cap.

6. On 1984–87 Preludes and 1984–85 Accords, remove the cotter pin, holder and spindle nut. On other models, remove the screws securing the rotor to the hub assembly.

To install:

7. On 1984–87 Preludes and 1984–85 Accords, apply a light coat of grease or oil to the spindle nut and the spindle threads. Install the washer and spindle nut. Adjust the wheel bearing; refer to the procedure outlined in Section 8. On other models, secure the disc with its retaining screws.

8. Install the caliper.

9. Install the wheel and lower the vehicle to the ground.

10. If equipped, enable the SRS system and connect the negative battery cable.

INSPECTION

▶ **See Figures 57 and 58**

1. The brake disc develops circular scores during braking due to trapped dust and road grit. Excessive scoring not only contributes to squealing brakes but also shortens the life of the brake pads. However, light scoring of the disc surface, not exceeding 0.38mm in depth, will result from normal use and is not detrimental to brake operation. In general, if the scoring is deep enough to catch a fingernail passing over it, it's too deep and requires corrective action.

2. Disc run-out is the movement of the disc from side-to-side; warpage or distortion. Excess run-out causes wobble or pounding in the brake pedal. Position a dial indicator in the middle of the pad wear area and turn the disc, while checking the indicator. If disc run-out exceeds 0.004 in. (0.10mm), replace or refinish the disc.

3. Disc parallelism is the measurement of variations in disc thickness at several locations on the disc circumference. It indicates whether or not the two faces of the disc are true and parallel. To measure parallelism, place a mark on the disc and measure the disc thickness with a micrometer. Repeat this measurement at eight (8) equal increments (about 45 degrees apart) on the circumference of the disc. If any of the measurements vary more than 0.0006 in. (0.015mm), replace the disc.

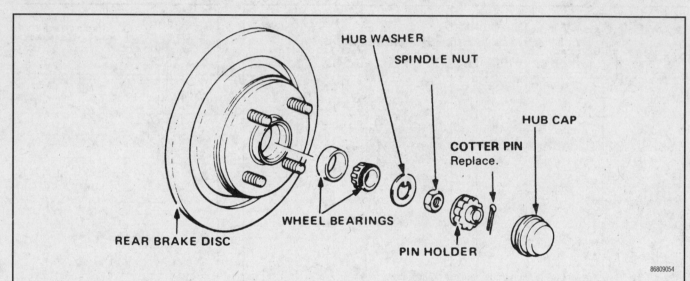

Fig. 55 Rear disc assembly used on 1984–85 Accords and 1984–87 Preludes

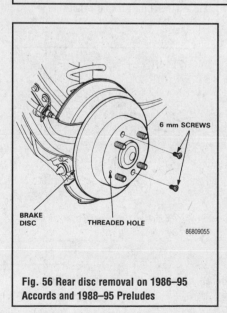

Fig. 56 Rear disc removal on 1986–95 Accords and 1988–95 Preludes

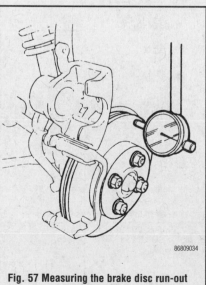

Fig. 57 Measuring the brake disc run-out

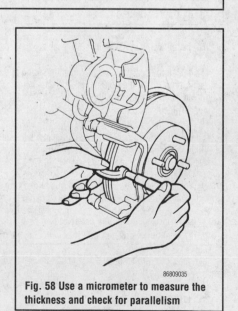

Fig. 58 Use a micrometer to measure the thickness and check for parallelism

PARKING BRAKE

Cables

The parking brake is a mechanical type which applies braking force to the rear wheels through the rear brakes. The cable, attached to the parking brake lever, extends to the equalizer and to both rear brakes. When the lever is pulled, the cable becomes taut, pulling both the parking brake arms fitted to the brake shoes or rear calipers.

REMOVAL & INSTALLATION

▶ **See Figure 59**

1. If equipped with an air bag, disconnect the negative battery cable and properly disable the Supplemental Restraint System (SRS), as detailed in 2. Remove the access cover at the rear of the console. In some cases, removing the console may be necessary for access. Loosen the adjusting nut until the cable ends can be disconnected from the equalizer. With the cables detached, the parking brake lever may be removed, if desired, by removing the mounting bolts holding it to the floor.

2. Remove the access cover at the rear of the console. In some cases, removing the console may be necessary for access. Loosen the adjusting nut until the cable ends can be disconnected from the equalizer. With the cables detached, the parking brake lever may be removed, if desired, by removing the mounting bolts holding it to the floor.

3. Loosen the lug nuts, then Raise and safely support the vehicle on jackstands.

Fig. 59 Use a box-end wrench to depress the retaining tangs, then slide the cable out of the backing plate

4. Remove the rear wheels.

5. On disc brake equipped vehicles, pull out the lock pin, remove the clevis pin and remove the clip.

6. On drum brake equipped vehicles, remove the brake drum and brake shoes. Disconnect the cable from the backing plate.

7. Detach the cables from the cable guides and remove the cables from the vehicle.

To install:

8. Fit the cable loosely into place. Begin reattachment at the rear brake shoes or calipers. Make certain the cable is routed correctly and firmly seated in it mounts.

9. Connect the cable(s) at the lever inside the car.

10. Install the cable bracket retaining bolts. Do not allow the cable to become kinked or bent. Make certain the rubber boots are in place where the cables pass into the cabin.

11. Adjust the cables.

12. Lower the vehicle to the ground and check for proper brake operation.

13. If equipped, enable the SRS system and connect the negative battery cable.

ADJUSTMENT

▶ **See Figures 60, 61, 62, 63 and 64**

➡ **If the rear brakes have been serviced or replaced, start the engine and press the brake pedal several times to adjust the brakes before adjusting the parking brake cable. Incorrectly adjusted rear brakes (disc or drum) will affect the function of the parking brake mechanism.**

1. Raise and safely support the vehicle on jackstands.

2. On rear disc brake equipped vehicles, make sure the lever of the rear brake caliper contacts the brake caliper pin.

3. On drum brake equipped vehicles, make sure the rear brakes are properly adjusted.

4. Pull the parking brake lever up 1 notch.

5. Remove the access cover at the rear of the console or remove the rear seat ashtray. On some models, it may be necessary to remove the center console to gain access to the adjusting nut. Tighten the adjusting nut until the rear wheels drag slightly when turned.

6. Release the parking brake lever and check that the rear wheels do not drag when turned. (Don't confuse a light brushing noise with drag; you'll feel the drag.) Readjust if necessary.

7. With the equalizer properly adjusted, the parking brake should be fully applied when the parking brake lever is pulled up 7–11 clicks on 1984–89 Accord and 1984–91 Prelude or 4–8 clicks on 1990–95 Accords and 1992–95 Preludes.

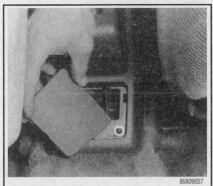

Fig. 60 Remove the access cover at the back of the console

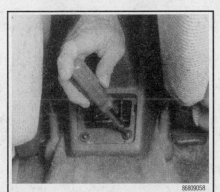

Fig. 61 Remove the screws securing the back of the console and position it aside

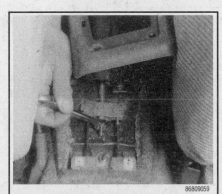

Fig. 62 Adjust the cable as necessary through the adjusting nut

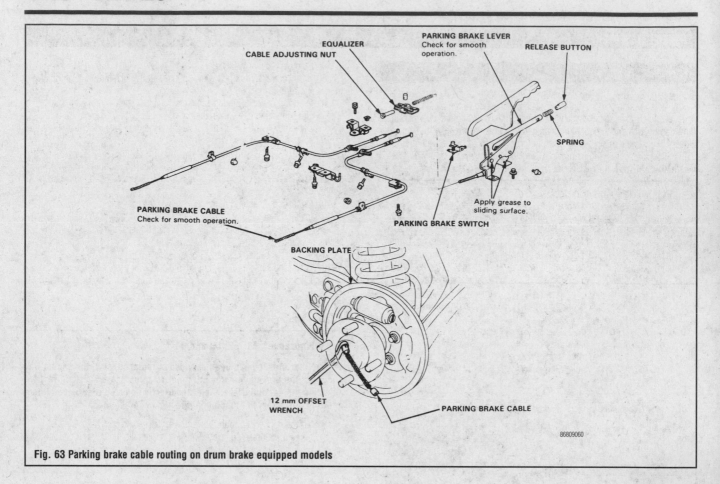

EQUALIZER

CABLE ADJUSTING NUT

PARKING BRAKE LEVER
Check for smooth operation.

RELEASE BUTTON

SPRING

PARKING BRAKE CABLE
Check for smooth operation.

Apply grease to sliding surface.

PARKING BRAKE SWITCH

BACKING PLATE

12 mm OFFSET WRENCH

PARKING BRAKE CABLE

86809060

Fig. 63 Parking brake cable routing on drum brake equipped models

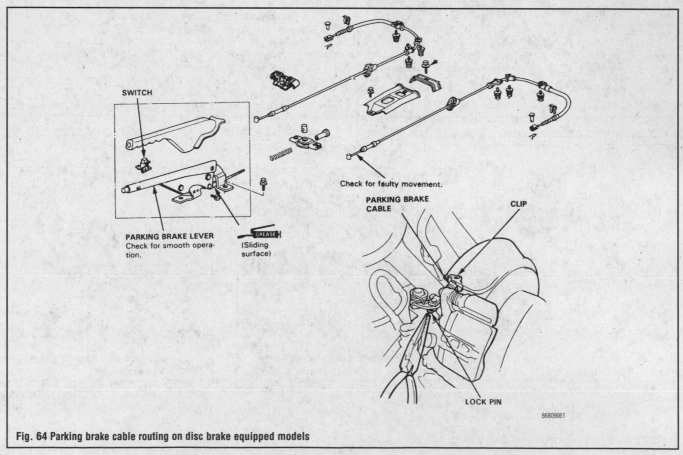

SWITCH

Check for faulty movement.

PARKING BRAKE CABLE

CLIP

PARKING BRAKE LEVER
Check for smooth operation.

GREASE
(Sliding surface)

LOCK PIN

86809061

Fig. 64 Parking brake cable routing on disc brake equipped models

ANTI-LOCK BRAKE SYSTEM (ALB)

System Description

▶ **See Figures 65 and 66**

Anti-Lock Braking (ALB) systems are designed to prevent locked-wheel skidding during hard braking or during braking on slippery surfaces. The front wheels of a vehicle cannot apply steering force if they are locked and sliding; the vehicle will continue in its previous direction of travel. The four wheel anti-lock brake systems found on Honda automobiles hold the wheels just below the point of locking, thereby allowing some steering response and preventing the rear of the vehicle from sliding sideways.

There are conditions for which the ALB system provides no benefit. Hydroplaning is possible when the tires ride on a film of water, losing contact with the paved surface. This renders the vehicle totally uncontrollable until road contact is regained. Extreme steering maneuvers at high speed or cornering beyond the limits of tire adhesion can result in skidding which is independent of

vehicle braking. For this reason, the system is named anti–lock rather than anti–skid. Wheel spin during acceleration on slippery surfaces may also fool the system into entering its fail-safe mode.

SYSTEM OPERATION

Under normal braking conditions, the ALB system functions in the same manner as a standard brake system. The system is a combination of electrical and hydraulic components, working together to control the flow of brake fluid to the wheels when necessary.

The ALB Control Unit is the electronic brain of the system, receiving and interpreting speed signals from the speed sensors. The unit will enter anti-lock mode when it senses impending wheel lock-up at any wheel and immediately controls the brake line pressure(s) to the affected wheel(s). The modulator assembly is separate from the master cylinder and booster. It contains the wheel circuit solenoid valves used to control the brake fluid pressure to each wheel circuit.

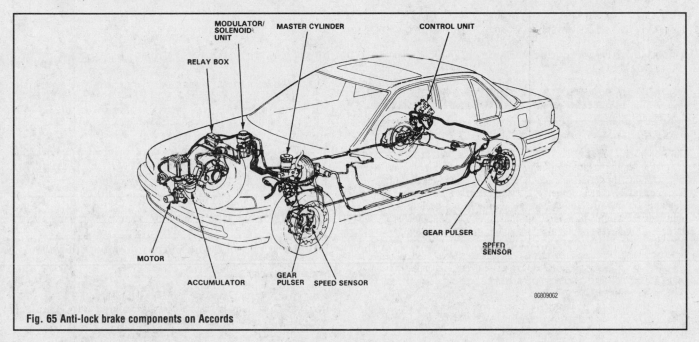

Fig. 65 Anti-lock brake components on Accords

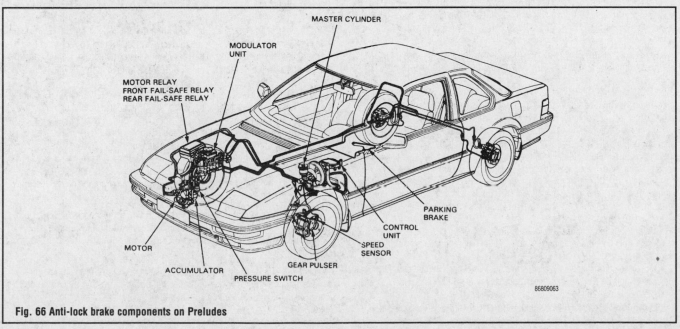

Fig. 66 Anti-lock brake components on Preludes

During anti-lock braking, line pressures are controlled or modulated by the rapid cycling of electronic valves within the modulator. These valves can allow pressures within the system to increase, remain constant or decrease depending on the needs of the moment as registered by the control unit. The front wheels are controlled individually. The rear wheel circuits receive the same pressure control, based on the rear wheel with the greatest locking tendency.

The operator may hear a popping or clicking sound as the pump and/or control valves cycle on and off during anti-lock operation. The sounds are due to normal operation and are not indicative of a system problem. Under most conditions, the sounds are only faintly audible. When ALB is engaged, the operator may notice some pulsation in the brake pedal and/or body of the vehicle during a hard stop; this is also normal operation but can be surprising to a driver who engages ALB for the first time.

Although the ALB system prevents wheel lock–up under hard braking, as brake pressure increases, wheel slip is allowed to increase as well. This slip will result in some tire chirp during ALB operation. The sound should not be interpreted as lock–up but rather as an indication of the system holding the wheel(s) just outside the point of lock–up. Additionally, the final few feet of an ALB–engaged stop may be completed with the wheels locked; the electronic controls do not operate at very low speeds.

When the ignition is **ON** and the vehicle's speed is over 6 mph, the control unit monitors the function of the system. Should a fault be noted, such as loss of signal from a speed sensor or excessive pump running time, the ALB system is immediately de-energized. Normal brake function remains but the anti-lock function is disabled.

Service Precautions

✳✳ CAUTION

The Honda anti-lock brake system contains brake fluid under extremely high pressure within the pump, accumulator and modulator assembly. Do not disconnect or loosen any lines, hoses, fittings or components without properly relieving the system pressure. Use only tool 07HAA–SG00101 or equivalent to relieve pressure. Improper procedures or failure to discharge the system pressure may result in severe personal injury and/or property damage.

• If the vehicle is equipped with an air bag or Supplemental Restraint System (SRS) system, always properly disable the system before commencing work on the ALB system. Air bag wiring and connectors are yellow; do not use electrical test equipment on these circuits.

• Certain components within the ALB system are not intended to be serviced or repaired individually. Only those components with removal and installation procedures should be serviced.

• Do not use rubber hoses or other parts not specifically specified for the ALB system. When using repair kits, replace all parts included in the kit. Partial or incorrect repair may lead to functional problems and require the replacement of other components.

• Lubricate rubber parts with clean, fresh brake fluid to ease assembly. Do not use compressed air to clean parts; damage to rubber components may result.

• Use only brake fluid from an unopened container. Use of suspect or contaminated brake fluid can reduce system performance and/or durability. Never reuse brake fluid recovered during bleeding or pressure release procedures.

• A clean repair area is essential. Perform repairs after components have been thoroughly cleaned; use only denatured alcohol to clean components. Do not allow ALB components to come into contact with any substance containing mineral oil or petroleum based products; this includes used shop rags.

• The control unit is a microprocessor similar to other computer units in the vehicle. Insure that the ignition switch is **OFF** before removing or installing controller harnesses. Avoid static electricity discharge at or near the controller.

• Never disengage any electrical connection with the ignition switch **ON**.

• Avoid touching connector pins with fingers.

• Leave new components and modules in the shipping package until ready to install them.

• To avoid static discharge, always touch a vehicle ground after sliding across a vehicle seat or walking across carpeted or vinyl floors.

• If any arc welding is to be done on the vehicle, the ALB control unit should be disconnected before welding operations begin.

• Never allow welding cables to lie on, near or across any vehicle electrical wiring.

• If the vehicle is to be baked after paint repairs, disconnect and remove the control unit from the vehicle.

System Diagnosis

VISUAL INSPECTION

Before diagnosing an apparent ALB problem, make absolutely certain that the normal braking system is in correct working or der. Many common brake problems (dragging parking brake, seepage, etc.) will affect the ALB system. A visual check of specific system components may reveal problems creating an apparent ALB malfunction. Performing this inspection may reveal a simple failure, thus eliminating extended diagnostic time.

1. Inspect the tire pressures; they must be approximately equal for the system to operate correctly.

2. Inspect the brake fluid level in the reservoirs.

3. Inspect brake lines, hoses, master cylinder assembly and brake calipers for leakage.

4. Visually check brake lines and hoses for excessive wear, heat damage, punctures, contact with other parts, missing clips or holders, blockage or crimping.

5. Check the calipers for rust or corrosion. Check for proper sliding action, if applicable.

6. Check the calipers for freedom of motion during application and release.

7. Inspect the wheel speed sensors for proper mounting and connections.

8. Inspect the sensor wheels for broken teeth or poor mounting.

9. Inspect the wheels and tires on the vehicle. They must be of the same size and type to generate accurate speed signals.

10. Confirm the fault occurrence. Certain driver induced faults, such as not releasing the parking brake fully, spinning the wheels under acceleration, sliding due to excessive cornering speed or driving on extremely rough surfaces will set a fault code and trigger the dash warning light. These induced faults are not system failures but examples of vehicle performance outside the parameters of the control unit.

11. Many system shut–downs are due to loss of sensor signals to or from the controller. The most common cause is not a failed sensor but a loose, corroded or dirty connector. Check harness and component connectors carefully.

Warning Lamp Check

Once the dash warning lamp illuminates, it will remain lit until the code (if any) is cleared. The easiest precheck of the system is simply to turn the ignition switch **ON** and check for the dash warning lamp to come on. Start the engine; if the warning lamp goes off after a few seconds, the system is operative with no faults found by the control unit. If the warning lamp does not extinguish, further diagnostics are required.

If the dash lamp does not come on when the ignition is turned **ON**, check for a failed warning bulb, an open circuit between fuse 13 on Prelude or fuse 1 on Accord and the instrument cluster, an open in the blue/red wire from the instrument cluster to the ALB control unit, or a faulty ground in the attachment of the control unit to the body.

The dash warning lamp may remain on after the engine is started. Common causes are loose or weak connection of the ALB harness to the control unit, faulty Accord ALB B2 fuse or Prelude No. 27 fuse, or an open circuit in the white wire between ALB 2 or 27 fuse and the control unit. The problem may also be caused by an open circuit between Prelude fuse 17 or Accord fuse 8 and the fail-safe relays, or an open/shorted circuit in the yellow/green wire to the fail-safe relays. Additionally, check the white/blue wire between the alternator and the control unit for an open circuit. The blue/red wire from the gauge assembly to the control unit should also be checked for shorted or open conditions.

➡**The dashboard warning lamp will light when there is insufficient battery voltage to the control unit. Once proper voltage is restored, the light will extinguish and the system will work normally.**

The electronic control unit for the ALB system possesses self-diagnostic capabilities similar to the fuel injection system. If a signal is seen to be out of range, either high or low, the controller will note the fault and trigger the ALB dash warning lamp. A fault code is stored in the system memory to identify the faulty signal.

Diagnosis of the system requires Honda's ALB checker, a sophisticated test tool available at dealerships. In the event that the warning lamp on your car stays on during normal operation, check the simple things carefully. The most frequent causes of signal error or loss are not the most difficult to investigate.

If the problem is not solved through your efforts, take the car to your Honda dealer for a system inspection.

Pressure Relief Procedure

▶ See Figure 67

✳✳ CAUTION

The Honda anti-lock brake system contains brake fluid under extremely high pressure within the pump, accumulator and modulator assembly. Do not disconnect or loosen any lines, hoses, fittings or components without properly relieving the system pressure. Use tool 07HAA–SG00101 or equivalent to relieve pressure. Improper procedures or failure to discharge the system pressure may result in severe personal injury and/or property damage.

1. Insure the ignition switch is **OFF**.
2. Using a syringe or similar device, remove all the fluid from the master cylinder reservoir and the modulator reservoir.
3. Remove the red cover from the bleeder port on top of the pump assembly.
4. Install the bleeding tool onto the bleeder. Make certain the reservoir cap on the tool is secured.
5. Using the tool, turn the bleeder about 90 degrees to admit high pressure fluid into the reservoir. As the pressure drops, turn the bleeder open about 1 full turn to completely relieve the system.
6. Retighten the bleeder to 4 ft. lbs. (5.5 Nm) and remove the tool. Discard the captured brake fluid; do not reuse it. Install the red cap on the bleeder port.

Accumulator

REMOVAL & INSTALLATION

▶ See Figures 68 and 69

The modulator, accumulator and power unit must be bled if any of their lines are removed or loosened during repairs or if any component is replaced. Bleed-ing can ONLY be accomplished with Honda's ALB scan tool and the special bleeder T-wrench or their equivalents. DO NOT attempt to use any other procedures or tools to bleed the high pressure components.

Accord

1. If equipped with an air bag, disconnect the negative battery cable and properly disable the Supplemental Restraint System (SRS), as detailed in Section 6 of this manual.
2. Relieve the system pressure using the bleeder T-wrench.
3. Remove the 3 bolts holding the accumulator to the pressure block. Remove the accumulator from the block; check that the O-ring on the neck of the accumulator is not lodged within the pressure block.
To install:
4. Make certain a new O-ring is in place on the neck of the accumulator. Position the accumulator against the pressure block and install the 3 retaining bolts finger-tight.
5. Make certain the accumulator ball is squarely and securely placed against its mount. Tighten the retaining bolts to 7 ft. lbs. (10 Nm).
6. Fill the modulator reservoir to the upper limit. Bleed the high pressure components using the ALB scan tool. Bleed the wheel circuits at each caliper.
7. If equipped, enable the SRS system and connect the negative battery cable.

Prelude

1. If equipped with an air bag, disconnect the negative battery cable and properly disable the Supplemental Restraint System (SRS), as detailed in Section 6 of this manual.
2. Relieve the system pressure using the bleeder T-wrench.
3. Remove the bolt holding the accumulator assembly to the bracket. Remove the accumulator assembly. Do NOT attempt to disassemble the unit.
4. Installation is the reverse of removal.
5. If equipped, enable the SRS system and connect the negative battery cable.

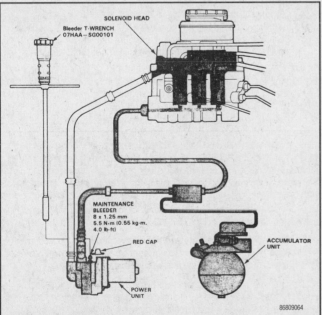

Fig. 67 The shaded areas are under high pressure. Use only the correct tool to relieve the pressure

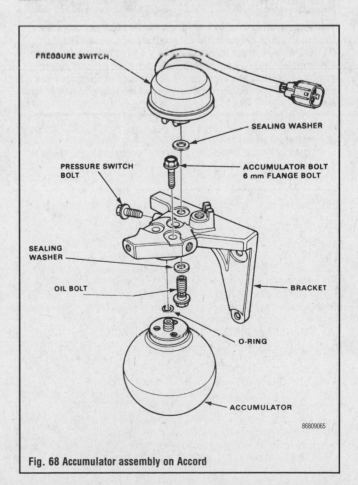

Fig. 68 Accumulator assembly on Accord

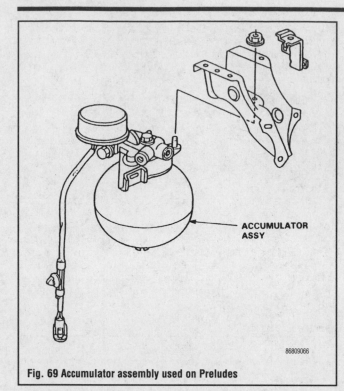

Fig. 69 Accumulator assembly used on Preludes

DISPOSAL

▶ See Figure 70

❋❋ CAUTION

The accumulator contains high-pressure nitrogen gas, even after fluid pressure is relieved. Do not puncture or expose to heat or flame. Do not attempt to disassemble the accumulator. Failure to follow correct safety precautions may cause the accumulator to explode, resulting in severe injury and/or property damage. The accumulator must be correctly relieved of internal pressure before disposal.

1. After removal, secure the neck of the accumulator in a vise; the relief plug should point straight up.
2. Wear goggles or other face and eye protection. The escaping gas, although non-toxic, can carry dust and debris with it.

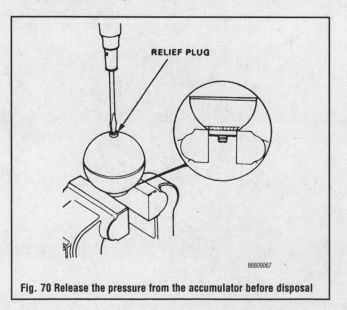

Fig. 70 Release the pressure from the accumulator before disposal

3. Slowly turn the relief plug 3½ turns; wait 3 minutes for all pressurized gas to escape.

➡**Nitrogen is an inert, non-flammable, non-toxic gas. It is safe for release into the atmosphere.**

4. Slowly remove the relief plug completely. Dispose of the accumulator unit.

Electronic Control Unit

REMOVAL & INSTALLATION

▶ See Figure 71

Accord

1. If equipped with an air bag, disconnect the negative battery cable and properly disable the Supplemental Restraint System (SRS), as detailed in Section 6 of this manual.
2. Remove the control unit attaching bolts. Don't lose the nuts behind the stay. Disconnect the bolt holding the ground lug.

➡**Once the bolts are removed, any stored codes are lost.**

3. Remove the control unit and cover. Remove the cover.
4. Carefully unplug the connectors from the control unit.
   To install:
5. Engage the connectors to the unit.
6. Fit the cover into position; install the assembly and tighten the bolts snugly. Install the bolt holding the ground lug.
7. If equipped, enable the SRS system and connect the negative battery cable.
8. Turn the ignition switch **ON** and check for correct ALB system function.

Prelude

1. If equipped with an air bag, disconnect the negative battery cable and properly disable the Supplemental Restraint System (SRS), as detailed in Section 6 of this manual.
2. Remove the cover at the front of the console. The console need not be removed.
3. Remove the 4 mounting bolts holding the control unit.

➡**When the mounting bolts are removed, any fault codes stored in the memory will be lost.**

4. Carefully disconnect the wiring harnesses.
   To install:
5. Connect the wiring harnesses; fit the control unit into place.
6. Install the 4 retaining bolts; tighten them to 7 ft. lbs. (10 Nm).
7. Install the front cover on the console.
8. If equipped, enable the SRS system and connect the negative battery cable.
9. Turn the ignition switch **ON** and check for correct ALB system function.

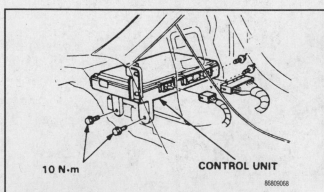

Fig. 71 The control unit is usually secured to the mounting bracket by four bolts

Wheel Speed Sensor

REMOVAL & INSTALLATION

▶ See Figures 72, 73, 74 and 75

✳✳ CAUTION

Vehicles equipped with air bag or Supplemental Restraint Systems (SRS) may have components and wiring in the same area as the front speed sensor wiring harnesses. The air bag system connectors are yellow. Do not use electrical test equipment on these circuits. Do not damage the SRS wiring while working on other wiring or components. Failure to observe correct procedures may cause the air bag system to inflate unexpectedly or render the system totally inoperative.

1. If equipped with an air bag, disconnect the negative battery cable and properly disable the Supplemental Restraint System (SRS), as detailed in Section 6 of this manual.

2. Raise and safely support the vehicle on jackstands as necessary for access.

➡**Access to the Prelude rear sensor and pulser requires removal of the wheel, caliper and brake disc.**

3. Unplug the sensor harness connector.

4. Beginning at the connector end, remove grommets, clips or retainers as necessary to free the harness. Take careful note of the placement and routing of the harness; it must be reinstalled in the exact original position.

5. Remove the bolts holding the speed sensor to its mounting; remove the sensor. If it is stuck in place, gently tap on the side of the mounting flange with a hammer and small punch; do not tap on the sensor.

To install:

6. Place the sensor in position and loosely install the retaining bolts. Route the harness correctly; avoid twisting or crimping the harness by using the white line on the wires as a guide.

7. Once the harness and sensor are correctly but loosely placed, tighten the sensor mounting bolts. Accord front and rear sensor bolts and Prelude front sensor bolts should be tightened to 16 ft. lbs. (22 Nm). Prelude rear sensor bolts are tightened only to 7 ft. lbs. (10 Nm).

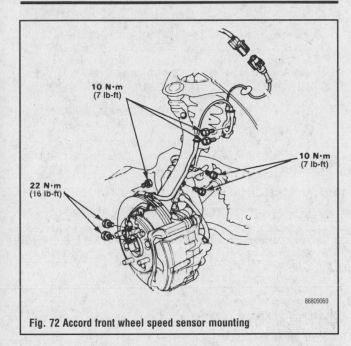

Fig. 72 Accord front wheel speed sensor mounting

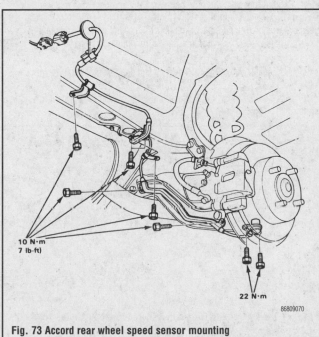

Fig. 73 Accord rear wheel speed sensor mounting

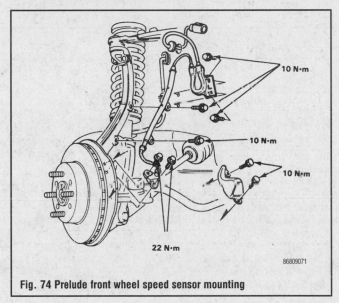

Fig. 74 Prelude front wheel speed sensor mounting

Fig. 75 Prelude rear wheel speed sensor mounting

8. Working from the sensor end to the connector, install each clip, retainer, bracket or grommet holding the sensor harness. The harness must not be twisted. Tighten the bolt(s) securing the brackets to 7 ft. lbs. (10 Nm). If the harness must pass through a body panel, make certain the rubber grommet is correctly and firmly seated.

9. Engage the wiring connector.

10. If equipped, enable the SRS system and connect the negative battery cable.

AIR GAP INSPECTION

▶ **See Figure 76**

The air gap between the tip of the sensor and the pulser is critical to the proper operation of the system. The gap is established by the correct installation of the wheel speed sensor; the gap may be measured for reference but is not adjustable.

Use a non-metallic feeler gauge to measure the gap. Rotate the hub or axle slowly by hand, taking measurements at several locations. The front or rear air gap must be 0.016–0.039 in. (0.4–1.0mm) at every location. If the gap exceeds 0.039 in. (1.0mm) at any location, there is a high probability of a damaged or distorted suspension knuckle.

➡**Access to the Prelude rear sensor and pulser requires removal of the wheel, caliper and brake disc.**

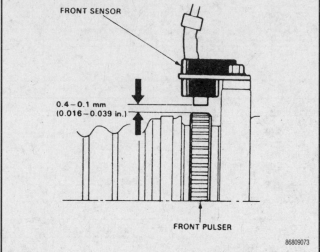

0.4 – 0.1 mm
(0.016 – 0.039 in.)

FRONT SENSOR

FRONT PULSER

86809073

Fig. 76 An incorrect air gap may indicate damaged suspension components

Tone (Exciter) Ring

REMOVAL & INSTALLATION

The pulser wheels are integral with either the front constant velocity joints or the rear hub assembly. If a pulser is damaged or requires replacement, a new joint or hub must be installed. The toothed wheels may be visually inspected for chipped or damaged teeth without removal.

Filling and Bleeding

FILLING THE SYSTEM

The ALB brake system uses 2 brake fluid reservoirs, one on the master cylinder and one on the modulator. Each must be maintained at minimum fluid levels for the system to operate properly.

While relieving the system pressure is not required when adding fluid, the caps of the reservoirs and the surrounding area must be wiped clean of dirt before the cap is removed. The slightest amount of dirt or foreign matter in the fluid may impair the ALB function.

Use only DOT 3 or DOT 4 brake fluid from an unopened container. Do not use other grades or types of brake fluid; never reuse aerated brake fluid which has been bled or removed from the system. Bring the fluid level only to the word MAX or UPPER level on the reservoir. Overfilling the reservoir may cause overflowing during testing or system operation. After filling, install the reservoir cap tightly.

BLEEDING THE SYSTEM

Brake Lines and Calipers

The brake lines and calipers are bled in the usual fashion with no special procedures required. Make certain the master cylinder reservoir is filled before the bleeding is begun and check the level frequently. The system should be bled in the correct sequence; always bleed all 4 calipers. Each bleeder should be tightened to 7 ft. lbs. (9 Nm). The bleeding sequence is:
- Accord — Left rear, right front, right rear and left front
- Prelude — Right rear, left front, left rear and right front.

Bleeding High-Pressure Components

The modulator, accumulator and power unit must be bled if any of their lines are removed or loosened during repairs or if any component is replaced. Bleeding can ONLY be accomplished with Honda's ALB scan tool and the special bleeder T-wrench or their equivalents. DO NOT attempt to use any other procedures or tools to bleed the high pressure components.

BRAKE SPECIFICATIONS
All measurements in inches unless noted

Year	Model		Master Cylinder Bore	Brake Disc Original Thickness	Brake Disc Minimum Thickness	Brake Disc Maximum Runout	Brake Drum Diameter Original Inside Diameter	Brake Drum Diameter Max. Wear Limit	Brake Drum Diameter Maximum Machine Diameter	Minimum Lining Thickness Front	Minimum Lining Thickness Rear
1984	Accord		NA	-	0.670	0.004	7.85	-	-	0.120	0.080
	Prelude	1	NA	-	0.670	0.004	7.85	-	-	0.120	0.080
1985	Accord		NA	-	0.670	0.004	7.85	-	-	0.120	0.080
	Prelude	1	NA	-	0.670	0.004	7.85	-	-	0.120	0.080
1986	Accord		NA	-	0.670	0.004	7.85	-	-	0.120	0.080
	Prelude	1	NA	-	0.670	0.004	7.75	-	-	0.120	0.080
1987	Accord		NA	-	0.670	0.004	7.85	-	-	0.120	0.080
	Prelude	1	NA	-	0.670	0.004	7.85	-	-	0.120	0.060
1988	Accord		NA	-	0.670	0.006	7.85	-	-	0.120	0.080
	Prelude	1	NA	-	0.670	0.004	7.85	-	-	0.120	0.080
1989	Accord		NA	-	0.670	0.006	7.87	-	-	0.120	0.031
	Prelude	1	NA	-	0.670	0.004	7.85	-	-	0.120	0.080
1990	Accord	F	NA	0.91	0.830	0.004	8.661	8.701	8.701	0.063	0.080
		R		0.390	0.320	0.004					
	Prelude	F	NA	0.830	0.750	0.004	-	-	-	0.120	0.080
		R		0.390	0.310	0.004					
1991	Accord	F	NA	0.910	0.830	0.004	8.66	8.701	8.701	0.120	0.080
		R		0.390	0.320	0.004					
	Prelude	F	NA	0.750	0.750	0.004	-	-	-	0.080	0.800
		R		0.310	0.310	0.004					
1992	Accord	F	NA	0.906	0.827	0.004	8.66	8.701	8.701	0.120	0.080
		R		0.390	0.315	0.004					
	Prelude	F	NA	0.906	0.827	0.004	-	-	-	0.080	0.080
		R		0.390	0.320	0.004					
1993	Accord	F	NA	0.910	0.830	0.004	-	-	-	0.060	-
		R		0.390	0.310	0.004	8.66	8.70	8.70	-	0.080
	Prelude	F	NA	0.910	0.830	0.004	-	-	-	0.060	-
		R		0.390	0.320	0.004	-	-	-	-	0.060
1994	Accord	F	NA	0.910	0.830	0.004	-	-	-	0.060	-
		R		0.390	0.310	0.004	8.66	8.70	8.70	-	0.080
	Prelude	F	NA	0.910	0.830	0.004	-	-	-	0.060	-
		R		0.390	0.320	0.004	-	-	-	-	0.060
1995	Accord	F	NA	0.910	0.830	0.004				0.060	-
		R		0.400	0.310	0.004	8.66	8.70	8.70	-	0.080
	Prelude	F	NA	0.910	0.830	0.004	-	-	-	0.060	-
		R		0.390	0.320	0.004	-	-	-	-	0.060

NA: Not available
F=Front
R=Rear
1: Front and rear

86809900

Troubleshooting the Brake System

Problem	Cause	Solution
Low brake pedal (excessive pedal travel required for braking action.)	• Excessive clearance between rear linings and drums caused by inoperative automatic adjusters	• Make 10 to 15 alternate forward and reverse brake stops to adjust brakes. If brake pedal does not come up, repair or replace adjuster parts as necessary.
	• Worn rear brakelining	• Inspect and replace lining if worn beyond minimum thickness specification
	• Bent, distorted brakeshoes, front or rear	• Replace brakeshoes in axle sets
	• Air in hydraulic system	• Remove air from system. Refer to Brake Bleeding.
Low brake pedal (pedal may go to floor with steady pressure applied.)	• Fluid leak in hydraulic system	• Fill master cylinder to fill line; have helper apply brakes and check calipers, wheel cylinders, differential valve tubes, hoses and fittings for leaks. Repair or replace as necessary.
	• Air in hydraulic system	• Remove air from system. Refer to Brake Bleeding.
	• Incorrect or non-recommended brake fluid (fluid evaporates at below normal temp).	• Flush hydraulic system with clean brake fluid. Refill with correct-type fluid.
	• Master cylinder piston seals worn, or master cylinder bore is scored, worn or corroded	• Repair or replace master cylinder
Low brake pedal (pedal goes to floor on first application—o.k. on subsequent applications.)	• Disc brake pads sticking on abutment surfaces of anchor plate. Caused by a build-up of dirt, rust, or corrosion on abutment surfaces	• Clean abutment surfaces
Fading brake pedal (pedal height decreases with steady pressure applied.)	• Fluid leak in hydraulic system	• Fill master cylinder reservoirs to fill mark, have helper apply brakes, check calipers, wheel cylinders, differential valve, tubes, hoses, and fittings for fluid leaks. Repair or replace parts as necessary.
	• Master cylinder piston seals worn, or master cylinder bore is scored, worn or corroded	• Repair or replace master cylinder
Decreasing brake pedal travel (pedal travel required for braking action decreases and may be accompanied by a hard pedal.)	• Caliper or wheel cylinder pistons sticking or seized	• Repair or replace the calipers, or wheel cylinders
	• Master cylinder compensator ports blocked (preventing fluid return to reservoirs) or pistons sticking or seized in master cylinder bore	• Repair or replace the master cylinder
	• Power brake unit binding internally	• Test unit according to the following procedure: (a) Shift transmission into neutral and start engine (b) Increase engine speed to 1500 rpm, close throttle and fully depress brake pedal (c) Slow release brake pedal and stop engine (d) Have helper remove vacuum check valve and hose from power unit. Observe for backward movement of brake pedal. (e) If the pedal moves backward, the power unit has an internal bind—replace power unit

TCCA9C01

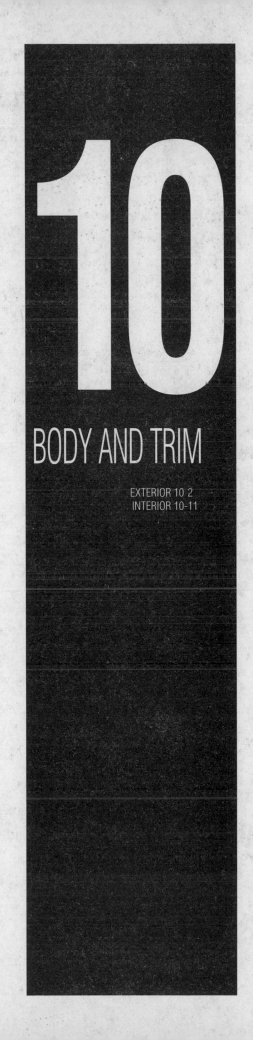

10

BODY AND TRIM

EXTERIOR

Doors

REMOVAL & INSTALLATION

Front and Rear

▶ **See Figure 1**

1. Matchmark the hinge-to-body and hinge-to-door locations. Support the door either on a padded jack or have an assistant hold it for you.
2. Push in on the detent rod and pull out the stopper pin. The rod may also be unbolted from the door.

➡ **Depending on vehicle options, it may be necessary to disconnect various wires running into the door. This will require removal of the door panel.**

3. Remove the lower hinge-to-door bolts.
4. Remove the upper hinge-to-door bolts and lift the door off the hinges.

➡ **The door is heavier than it looks; be prepared**

5. If the hinges are being replaced, remove them from the door pillar.
6. Install the door and hinges with the bolts finger-tight.
7. Adjust the door and tighten the hinge bolts until snug.

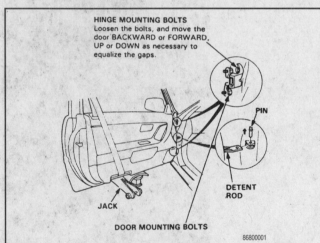

HINGE MOUNTING BOLTS
Loosen the bolts, and move the door BACKWARD or FORWARD, UP or DOWN as necessary to equalize the gaps.

PIN

DETENT ROD

JACK

DOOR MOUNTING BOLTS

86800001

Fig. 1 Support the door either on a padded jack or have an assistant hold it for you

ADJUSTMENT

▶ **See Figures 2 and 3**

When checking door alignment, look carefully at each seam between the door and body. The gap should be even all the way around the door. Pay particular attention to the door seams at the corners farthest from the hinges; this is the area where errors will be most evident. Additionally, the door should pull in against the weatherstrip when latched to seal out wind and water. The contact should be even all the way around and the stripping should be about half compressed.

The position of the door can be adjusted in three dimensions: fore and aft, up and down, in and out. The primary adjusting points are the hinge-to-body bolts. Apply tape to the fender and door edges to protect the paint. Two layers of common masking tape works well. Loosen the bolts just enough to allow the hinge to move in place. With the help of an assistant, position the door and retighten the bolts. Inspect the door seams carefully and repeat the adjustment until correctly aligned.

The in-out adjustment (how far the door "sticks out" from the body) is adjusted by loosening the hinge-to-door bolts. Again, move the door into place, then retighten the bolts. This dimension affects both the amount of "crush" on the weatherstrips and the amount of "bite" on the striker.

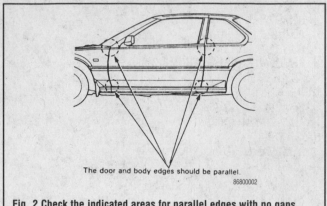

The door and body edges should be parallel.

86800002

Fig. 2 Check the indicated areas for parallel edges with no gaps

STRIKER

86800003

Fig. 3 Adjust the striker if necessary

Further adjustment for closed position and smoothness of latching is made at the striker. This is secured on the door pillar; it is where the latch engages when the door is closed.

Although the striker size and style may vary between models or from front to rear, the method of adjusting it is the same:

1. Loosen the screw(s) securing the striker. These bolts can be very tight; an impact screwdriver is a handy tool to have for this job. Make sure you are using the proper size bit.
2. With the bolts just loose enough to allow the striker to move, hold the outer door handle in the released position and close the door. The striker will move into the correct location to match the door latch. Open the door and tighten the mounting bolts. The striker may be adjusted towards or away from the center of the car, thereby tightening or loosening the door fit. The striker can be moved up and down to compensate for door position, but if the door is correctly mounted at the hinges this should not be necessary.

➡ **Do not attempt to correct height variations (sag) by adjusting the striker.**

3. Additionally, some models may use one or more spacers or shims behind the striker or at the hinges. These shims may be removed or added in combination to adjust the reach of the striker or hinge.
4. After the striker bolts have been tightened, open and close the door several times. Observe the motion of the door as it engages the striker; it should continue its straight-in motion and not deflect up or down as it hits the striker.
5. Check the feel of the latch during opening and closing. It must be smooth and linear, without any trace of grinding or binding during engagement and release.

➡ **It may be necessary to repeat the striker adjustment several times (and possibly re-adjust the hinges) before the correct door to body match is present.**

Hood

REMOVAL & INSTALLATION

▶ **See Figures 4, 5 and 6**

1. Open the hood and support it on the prop rod.
2. Disconnect the washer hose from the hood.
3. Matchmark the hinge position on the hood (use a felt-tipped marker.)
4. Have an assistant secure the hood.
5. Remove the hood-to-hinge bolts and lift the hood with the help of an assistant.

Fig. 4 Disconnect the washer hose from the hood

Fig. 5 Matchmark the hinge position on the hood

Fig. 6 Remove the hood-to-hinge bolts

6. If the hinges are to be removed, matchmark their position and remove the mounting bolts.
7. Installation is the reverse of removal. Loosely install the hood and align the matchmarks. Adjust the position.
8. Connect the washer hose.

ADJUSTMENT

Once the hood is installed, tighten the hood-to-hinge bolts just snug. Close the hood and check the seam alignment.

Loosen the bolts and position the hood as necessary, then snug them and recheck. Continue the process until the hood latches smoothly and aligns evenly at all the seams.

➡ **Do not adjust hood position by moving the latch.**

Shims may be used behind the hinge mounts if necessary. When everything aligns correctly, final-tighten the bolts to 7 ft. lbs. (10 Nm.)

The elevation of the hood at the latch end may be adjusted by turning the rubber stops or cushions. These bumpers have threaded bottoms and move up or down when turned. An annoying hood rattle on bumps may be caused by these cushions being missing or out of adjustment.

Trunk Lid

REMOVAL & INSTALLATION

▶ **See Figure 7**

1. Open the trunk lid.
2. On 1986–91 Accords, unplug the wiring connectors from the latch and lighting units inside the trunk lid. Label or identify each connector to ease reassembly. Tie a long piece of string to the end of the wire harness. Slowly and carefully remove the harness from the trunk lid. Leave the string in place to reroute the harness at reassembly.
3. Have an assistant support the trunk lid. Remove the bolts securing the lid to the hinges. Lift the trunk lid from the vehicle.
4. Installation is the reverse of removal. Tighten the bolts just snug until the position is adjusted.

ADJUSTMENT

Once the trunk lid is installed, tighten the bolts just snug. Close the lid and check the seam alignment.

Loosen the hinge bolts and position the trunk lid as necessary, then snug them and recheck. Continue the process until the lid latches smoothly and aligns evenly at all the seams.

The striker may be adjusted in fashion similar to adjusting a door striker. Shims may be added or removed as necessary. Keep in mind it is usually not necessary to adjust the latch to align the trunk lid. Tighten the mounting bolts to 7 ft. lbs. (10 Nm.)

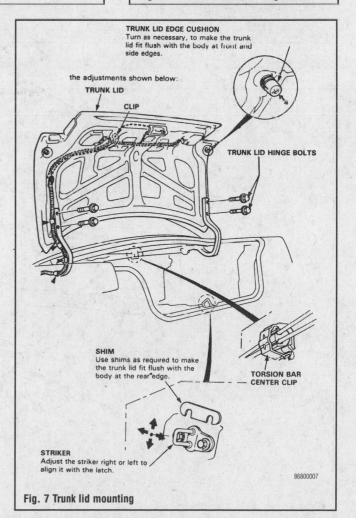

Fig. 7 Trunk lid mounting

Hatch

REMOVAL & INSTALLATION

▶ **See Figure 8**

1. Remove the tailgate trim panel; this is the small shelf on the inside of the lid.

2. Remove the plastic trim at the rear of the headliner.

3. On 1984–85 models, remove the taillight covers. On 1986 and later models, remove the hatch trim panel and side moldings.

4. Disconnect the wire harness in the hatch lid. Label or identify each connector to ease reassembly. Tie a long piece of string to the end of the wire harness. Slowly and carefully remove the harness from the lid. Leave the string in place to reroute the harness at reassembly.

5. Have an assistant secure the hatch. Disconnect the hatch support struts from the lid.

6. Disconnect the washer hose from the lid.

7. Pull the headliner down enough to allow access to the hinge mounting nuts. Make certain the lid is properly supported; remove the mounting nuts. Remove the hatch lid.

To install:

8. Position the lid and install the hinge mounting nuts just snug. Adjust the lid fore-and-aft or left-right at the hinges. Install shims as necessary. Check the latching ease and seam match all the way around. When everything is properly aligned, tighten the mounting nuts to 7 ft. lbs. (10 Nm.)

9. Install the hatch support struts.

10. Install the wiring harness and attach the connectors. Connect the washer hose.

11. Reinstall the trim panels.

12. Reposition the headliner and install the trim at the roof.

13. Install the rear trim panel.

Tailgate

REMOVAL & INSTALLATION

▶ **See Figure 9**

1. Remove the tailgate upper and lower trim panels. The panels are held by both clips and screws.

2. Disconnect the washer hose.

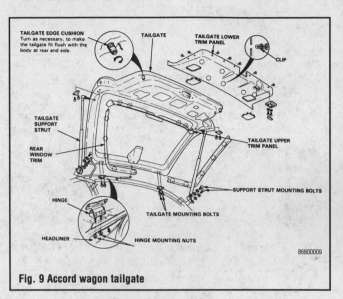

Fig. 9 Accord wagon tailgate

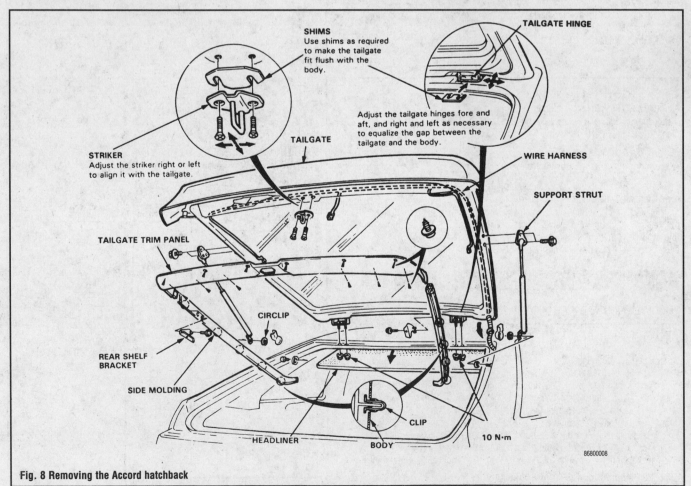

Fig. 8 Removing the Accord hatchback

3. Disconnect the wire harness in the tailgate. Label or identify each connector to ease reassembly. Tie a long piece of string to the end of the wire harness. Slowly and carefully remove the harness from the tailgate. Leave the string in place to reroute the harness at reassembly.

4. Have an assistant secure the tailgate. Disconnect the tailgate support struts from the tailgate.

5. Remove the bolts securing the tailgate to the hinge. Remove the tailgate. Use care not to damage the roof, headliner or tailgate.

➡ **The tailgate is heavy. Be prepared.**

6. If the hinge must be removed, lower the rear of the headliner enough to allow access to the hinge mounting bolts. Remove the bolts and remove the hinge.

To install:

7. Install the hinge if it was removed. Tighten the hinge mounting nuts to 16 ft. lbs. (22 Nm.)

8. Position the tailgate and install the mounting bolts. Tighten them just snug.

9. Install the tailgate support struts.

10. Adjust the position of the hinges and striker as needed to provide matched seams and ease of latching. When the lid is in its final position, tighten the bolts to 7 ft. lbs. (10 Nm.)

11. Install the wiring harness and engage the connectors. Connect the washer hose.

12. Install the upper and lower trim panels.

Bumpers

REMOVAL & INSTALLATION

1984–85 Accord

▶ **See Figure 10**

FRONT

1. Remove the splash guard under the engine.
2. Remove the bumper mount bolts.
3. Slide the bumper forward off the clips securing its corners to the wheel well.
4. Reassemble in reverse order. The bumper must be slid over the end clips at the time of installation. Tighten the bumper bolts to 28 ft. lbs. (39 Nm.)

REAR

1. Remove the 3 screws or clips securing the bumper at each wheel well.
2. Remove the bumper mounting bolts and remove the bumper.
3. Reassemble in reverse order. Tighten the mounting bolts to 28 ft. lbs. (39 Nm.)

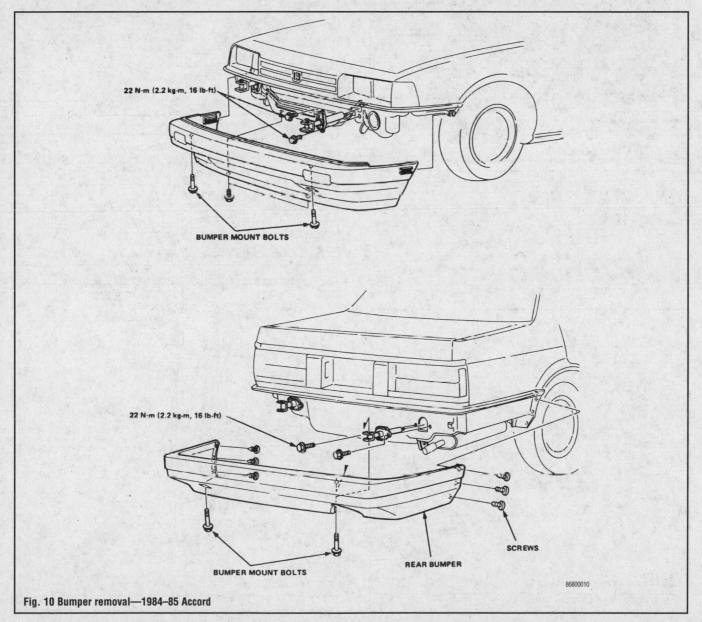

22 N·m (2.2 kg-m, 16 lb-ft)

BUMPER MOUNT BOLTS

22 N·m (2.2 kg-m, 16 lb-ft)

BUMPER MOUNT BOLTS

REAR BUMPER

SCREWS

86800010

Fig. 10 Bumper removal—1984–85 Accord

1986–89 Accord

FRONT

▶ **See Figure 11**

1. Remove the front side and turn signal fixtures and disconnect the wiring.
2. Remove the two rear bumper mount screws at each wheel well.
3. Remove the two lower bumper mount bolts.
4. Remove the four bumper mount bolts; remove the bumper by sliding it forward.
5. Reinstall in reverse order. Tighten all bumper mounting bolts to 16 ft. lbs. (22 Nm.) Reinstall the signal lamp assemblies.

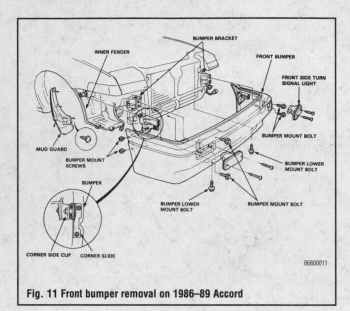

Fig. 11 Front bumper removal on 1986–89 Accord

REAR

▶ **See Figure 12**

1. Remove the 3 screws or clips securing the bumper at each wheel well.
2. Remove the bumper mounting bolts and remove the bumper.
3. Reassemble in reverse order. Tighten the mounting bolts to 28 ft. lbs. (39 Nm.)

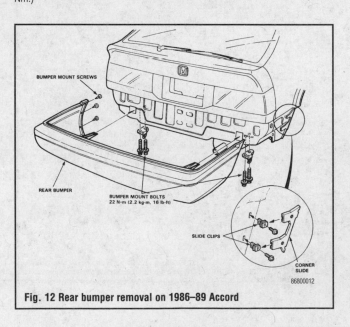

Fig. 12 Rear bumper removal on 1986–89 Accord

1990–95 Accord

FRONT

▶ **See Figures 13 and 14**

1. Disconnect the negative battery cable and disable the SRS system (if equipped.)
2. Open the hood and remove the bumper mounting nuts.
3. Remove the front turn signal assemblies.
4. Remove the screws at each rear edge of the bumper (at the wheels.)
5. Remove the lower bumper mounting clips.
6. Remove the mounting bolts. Lift and remove the bumper by sliding it forward.

To install:

7. Install the bumper by sliding it into place.
8. Loosely install all the mounting bolts; check the position of the bumper on the car, adjusting if necessary.
9. Tighten the mounting nuts and bolts to 18 ft. lbs. (25 Nm.)
10. Reinstall the turn signal assemblies.
11. Connect the battery cable and enable the SRS system.

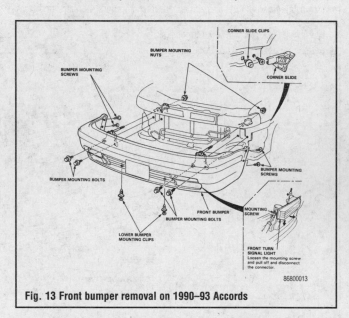

Fig. 13 Front bumper removal on 1990–93 Accords

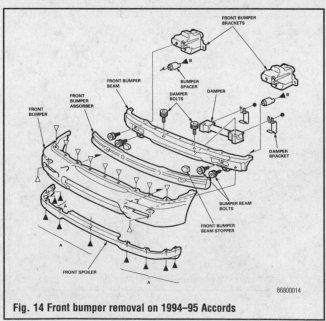

Fig. 14 Front bumper removal on 1994–95 Accords

REAR

♦ See Figures 15 and 16

1. Open the trunk lid. Remove the small round access covers from the trunk liner panels. Remove the upper bumper mounting nuts from the trunk side.

2. Remove the bumper mounting screws at each wheel well.

3. Remove the clips, then remove the protectors from below the trunk floor.

4. Remove the lower bumper mounting nuts. Remove the center clip from under the trunk floor.

5. Remove the bumper by sliding it to the rear of the car.

6. Install in reverse order. Tighten the mounting bolts to 18 ft. lbs. (25 Nm.)

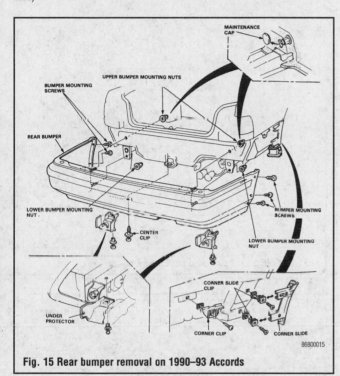

Fig. 15 Rear bumper removal on 1990–93 Accords

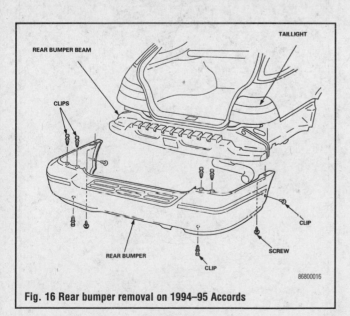

Fig. 16 Rear bumper removal on 1994–95 Accords

1984–85 Prelude

FRONT

♦ See Figure 17

1. Remove the splash guard under the engine.

2. Remove the bumper mount bolts.

3. Slide the bumper forward from the clips securing its corners to the wheel well.

4. Reassemble in reverse order. The bumper must be slid over the end clips at the time of installation. Tighten the bumper bolts to 16 ft. lbs. (22 Nm.)

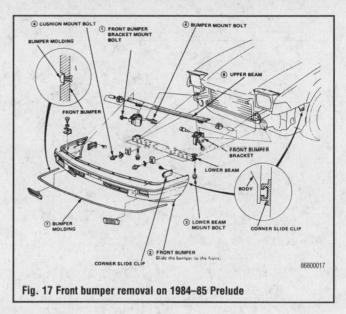

Fig. 17 Front bumper removal on 1984–85 Prelude

REAR

♦ See Figure 18

1. Remove the 3 screws or clips securing the bumper at each wheel well.

2. Remove the bumper mounting bolts and remove the bumper.

3. Reassemble in reverse order. Tighten the mounting bolts to 16 ft. lbs. (22 Nm.)

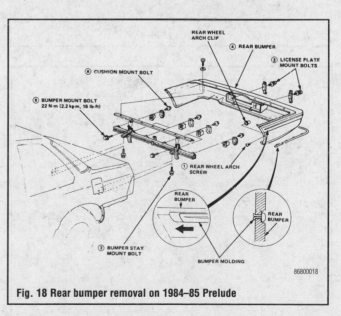

Fig. 18 Rear bumper removal on 1984–85 Prelude

1986–95 Prelude

FRONT

◆ **See Figures 19, 20 and 21**

1. Disconnect the negative battery cable and disable the SRS system (if equipped.)
2. Remove the side marker and turn signal lamps if mounted in the bumper.
3. Remove the fog lamps or the lid if so equipped.
4. Remove the bumper mounting bolts.
5. Remove the bumper by sliding it forward.
6. Reinstall in reverse order. Tighten the mounting bolts to 16 ft. lbs. (22 Nm.)

REAR

◆ **See Figures 22, 23 and 24**

1. Open the trunk lid. Remove the access covers from the trunk liner panels. Remove the upper bumper mounting nuts from inside the trunk.
2. Remove the bumper mounting screws at each wheel well.

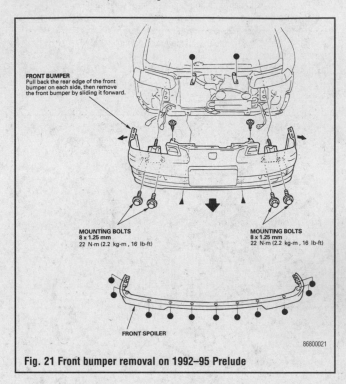

Fig. 21 Front bumper removal on 1992–95 Prelude

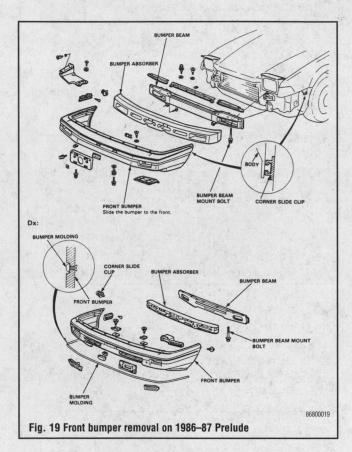

Fig. 19 Front bumper removal on 1986–87 Prelude

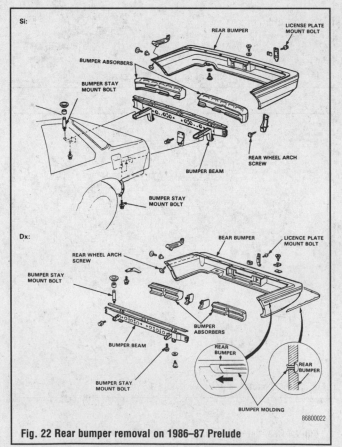

Fig. 22 Rear bumper removal on 1986–87 Prelude

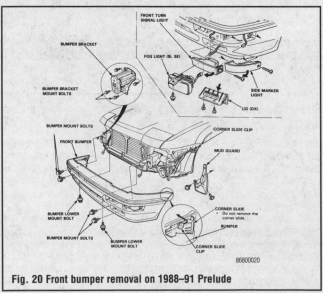

Fig. 20 Front bumper removal on 1988–91 Prelude

3. Remove the clips, then remove the protectors from below the trunk floor.

4. Remove the lower bumper mounting nuts. Remove the center clip from under the trunk floor.

5. Remove the bumper by sliding it to the rear of the car.

6. Install in reverse order. Tighten the mounting bolts to 18 ft. lbs. (25 Nm.)

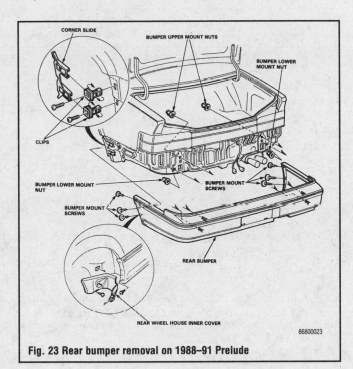

Fig. 23 Rear bumper removal on 1988–91 Prelude

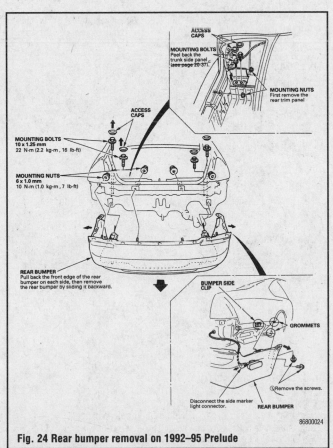

Fig. 24 Rear bumper removal on 1992–95 Prelude

Grille

REMOVAL & INSTALLATION

▶ **See Figure 25**

1984–85 Accord

Remove the five mounting screws, then remove the grille.

1986–89 Accord

Remove the five screws and three nuts. Remove the grille.

1990–93 Accord

1. Remove the five screws securing the top of the grille.
2. Use a thin flat tool to compress and release the lower clips.
3. Remove the grille.
4. When installing, set the clips in place on the grille; install the grille and make certain each clip engages firmly.

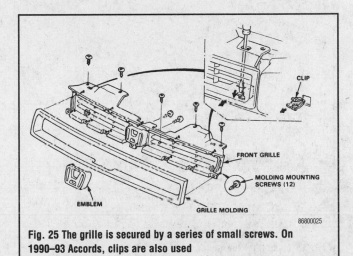

Fig. 25 The grille is secured by a series of small screws. On 1990–93 Accords, clips are also used

1984–91 Prelude

1. Raise the headlights (use the UP/DOWN switch on the dash) and remove the two screws at the side of the grille.
2. Remove the three screws on the front of the grille.
3. Remove the grille.

Outside Mirrors

REMOVAL & INSTALLATION

▶ **See Figures 26 and 27**

Except for 1988–91 Prelude, the mirrors can be removed from the door without disassembling the door liner or other components. On 1988–91 Preludes, the door panel must be removed. Both left and right outside mirrors may be either manual remote (small lever on the inside to adjust the mirror) or electric remote. If the mirror glass is damaged, replacements may be available through your dealer or a reputable glass shop. If the plastic housing is cracked or damaged, the entire mirror unit must be replaced. To remove the mirror:

1. If the mirror is manual remote, check to see if the adjusting handle is retained by a hidden screw, usually under an end cap on the lever. If so, remove the screw and remove the adjusting knob.
2. Remove the triangular inner cover where the mirror mounts to the door. It can be removed with a blunt plastic or wooden tool. Don't use a screwdriver; the plastic may become marred.

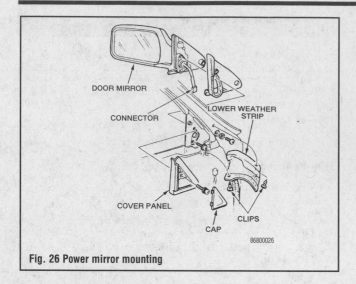

Fig. 26 Power mirror mounting

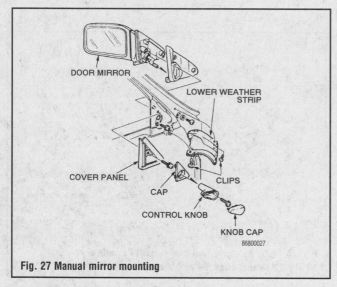

Fig. 27 Manual mirror mounting

3. Depending on the model and style of mirror, there may be concealment plugs under the cover. Remove them. If electric connectors are present, unplug them.

4. Support the mirror housing from the outside and remove the three bolts or nuts securing the mirror to the door. Remove the mirror.

To install:

5. Fit the mirror to the door and install the nuts and bolts to secure it. Connect any wiring. Pay particular attention to the placement and alignment of any gaskets or weatherstrips around the mirror; serious wind noises may result from careless work.

6. Install the cover, pressing it firmly into position. Install the control lever knob if it was removed.

7. If applicable, install the door panel.

Antenna

REMOVAL & INSTALLATION

Front Mounted Manual Antenna

1. Remove the radio and disconnect the antenna cable. On some models it may be possible to disconnect the antenna without removing the radio by reaching under and behind the dash.

2. Remove the two antenna mounting screws on the roof.

3. Tie a long piece of string or mechanic's wire to the end of the antenna cable.

4. Slowly extract the antenna mast and cable from the pillar. An assistant may be helpful in directing the wire through the other harnesses under the dashboard.

5. Remove the antenna cable completely; when the connector is clear of the roof, untie the string or wire leaving it in the pillar.

To install:

6. Attach the pull string or wire to the connector on the antenna cable. Feed the cable down the roof pillar. Have an assistant pull gently on the string to guide it along.

7. As the cable is pulled, fit the mast into the pillar. When properly positioned, install the retaining screws. The screws must be clean and tight for proper antenna function.

8. Under the dash, route the antenna cable to the radio. Make certain the cable is routed out of the way of feet, pedals, steering column motion or other hazards.

9. Connect the antenna to the radio and install the radio.

Front Mounted Power Antenna

MAST AND CABLE

The power antenna uses a plastic drive cable to raise and lower the mast. The cable is driven by the electric motor. There is a separate antenna cable running from the mast to the radio. During repairs, take care not to damage the cable or wiring.

1. Turn the ignition switch **ON** and fully extend the antenna. Turn the ignition **OFF**.

2. If necessary for additional access, remove the 2 bolts securing the fusebox and lower the fusebox.

3. Remove the clip that secures the antenna cable to the sheath.

4. Remove the mounting nut and remove the antenna from its bracket.

5. While lightly pulling the drive cable, operate the antenna motor until the drive cable is forced out.

6. If the antenna and drive cable are to be replaced, tie a long string or wire to the cable end before pulling it out of the pillar. Leave the string in the pillar when the mast is removed.

To install:

7. Extend the antenna and tie the string to the cable end and sheath. Pull the string through the pillar until it can be reached at the bottom.

8. Remove the string and slide the sheath up enough to expose several inches of the drive cable.

9. Insert the drive cable into the motor. Operate the motor to pull the drive cable into the motor housing.

10. When the cable is retracted, attach the cable sheath to the motor and install the clip.

11. If applicable, install the fusebox.

ANTENNA MOTOR

1. Disconnect the negative battery cable.
2. Unplug the wiring connector from the motor. Disconnect the antenna lead.
3. Remove the mounting nuts, then remove the motor.
4. Reinstall in reverse order of removal.

Rear Mounted Power Antenna

MAST AND CABLE

1. The mast can be replaced without removing the motor. Remove the special antenna nut, spacer and bushing at the base of the mast. Honda tool 07JAA–001000A or equivalent is recommended for turning the special nut.

2. Turn the ignition switch **ON** and operate the antenna, either by the switch or by turning the radio on.

3. Allow the motor to expel the mast and cable from the bodywork. Pull up gently to assist the cable. Do not let the mast fall and damage the body or paint of the car.

To install:

4. Install the new drive cable into the housing; the teeth of the cable must face the rear of the car. When the cable is fed into the housing, check that the teeth are engaged on the motor gear by gently moving the cable up and down; you should be able to feel the engagement.

5. Operate the antenna by using the switch or turning the radio **OFF**. The motor will rewind, drawing the cable and mast into the housing. If the motor runs but does not engage the cable, the teeth are not engaged. Reset the motor to the up position. Twist the cable a small amount until the teeth are felt to engage, then use the motor to rewind the cable.

6. Install the bushing, spacer and tighten the antenna nut.

7. Operate the antenna several times, making sure the mast extends and retracts fully.

ANTENNA MOTOR

1. Disconnect the negative battery cable.
2. Remove the trunk side panel.
3. Unplug the wiring connector from the motor. Disconnect the antenna lead.
4. Remove the special nut, using Honda tool 07JAA–001000A or equivalent, then remove the two mounting nuts.
5. Reinstall in reverse order. Tighten the special nut before tightening the two mounting nuts. Connect the wiring harness and antenna lead.

Power Sunroof

REMOVAL & INSTALLATION

▶ See Figures 28, 29 and 30

➥Many vehicles have had aftermarket electric sunroofs installed by dealers or owners. These procedures are only for factory-installed Honda sunroof assemblies.

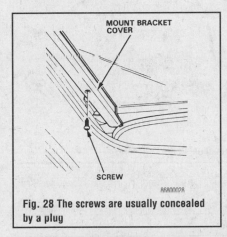

Fig. 28 The screws are usually concealed by a plug

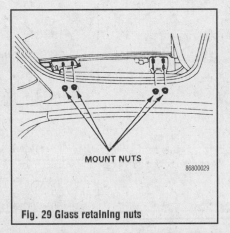

Fig. 29 Glass retaining nuts

1. Slide the sun shield all the way back.
2. Carefully pry out the plug from each bracket cover. Remove the screw and slide each cover off to the rear.
3. Close the glass roof completely.
4. Remove the nuts from the front and rear mounts on both sides.
5. Lift the front of the glass upward, then pull forward to remove it.
6. Remove the sun shade from the tracks. On some models, remove the six guide rail mounting nuts, then spread the rails to remove the shade. The shade may be bent slightly to ease removal.

To install:

7. Reinstall the shade; position the tracks correctly and install the rail nuts if they were removed.
8. Install the glass. Place the rear edge in at an angle and lower the front edge into position.
9. Install the nuts
10. Install the covers, retaining screws and plugs.

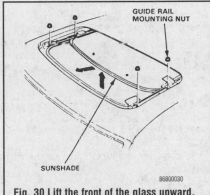

Fig. 30 Lift the front of the glass upward, then pull forward to remove it

INTERIOR

Instrument Panel/Dashboard

REMOVAL & INSTALLATION

➥The dashboard removal procedures require removal of the steering wheel and/or instrument cluster before beginning these procedures. Please refer to the appropriate sections. All wires and hoses should be labeled at the time of removal. The amount of time saved during reassembly makes the extra effort well worthwhile.

1984–85 Accord

▶ See Figure 31

1. Disconnect the negative battery cable.
2. Remove the left side lower dash panel and the fuse box cover. Take careful note of the screw installation positions; what appears to be a screw hole in the panel is the sound outlet for the seat belt buzzer.
3. Lower the steering column.
4. Disconnect the instrument panel wire harness from the fusebox, the side wiring harness, the interior lighting harness, brake light harness and the engine harness.
5. Remove the heater control panel.
6. Remove the heater control bracket.
7. Remove the dashboard center access panel.
8. Remove the ashtray.
9. Remove the nine dash mounting bolts. Don't forget the two bolts at the sides of the dash; they are concealed by plastic caps.
10. With an assistant, lift the dash to release the center guide pin; support the dash evenly and remove it from the car.

To install:

11. Fit the dash into position, making sure the guide pin is engaged.
12. Install the nine bolts and tighten them just snug. Check the position of the dash in all dimensions and adjust as necessary. When properly positioned, tighten the mounting bolts.
13. Install the ash tray and center access panel.
14. Install the heater control bracket and the heater controls.

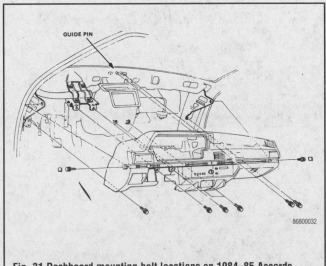

Fig. 31 Dashboard mounting bolt locations on 1984–85 Accords

15. Engage the wiring connectors. Make certain all harnesses are routed and secured properly.
16. Raise the steering column.
17. Install the fuse box cover and install the lower dash panel.

1986–89 Accord

▶ **See Figure 32**

1. Disconnect the negative battery cable.
2. Remove the lower dash panel.
3. Remove the steering column cover(s).
4. Remove the turn signal cancel sleeve and the combination switch.
5. Remove the ashtray holder.
6. Disconnect the wire harnesses at the fusebox area. Label the connectors for ease of reassembly.
7. Remove the hood release handle, but do not disconnect the cable.
8. Disconnect the cables at the center outlet of the heater duct. Disconnect the antenna cable at the radio.
9. Remove the dash mounting bolts.
10. With an assistant, lift the dash to release the center guide pin; support the dash evenly and remove it from the car.

To install:
11. Fit the dash into position, making sure the guide pin is engaged.
12. Install the bolts and tighten them just snug. Check the position of the dash in all dimensions and adjust as necessary. When properly positioned, tighten the mounting bolts. Double check for pinched wires or interference with heater control cables.
13. Connect the antenna cable.
14. Connect the cables at the center heater outlet.
15. Install the hood release handle.
16. Engage the wiring connectors at the fusebox.
17. Install the ashtray holder.
18. Install the combination switch, cancel sleeve and the steering column cover(s).
19. Install the dash lower panel.

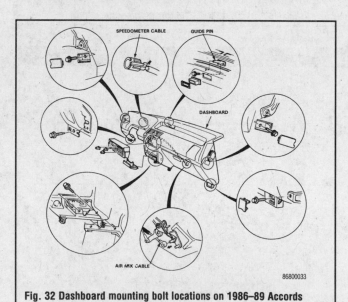

Fig. 32 Dashboard mounting bolt locations on 1986–89 Accords

1990–93 Accord

▶ **See Figure 33**

1. Disconnect the negative battery cable and disable the SRS system (if equipped.)
2. Slide the seats back all the way.
3. Remove the console.
4. Remove the knee bolster and lower panel.
5. Remove the steering column. Observe all precautions for SRS systems.

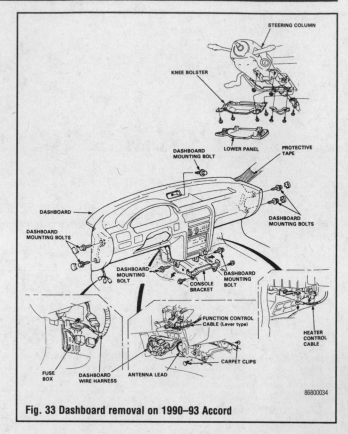

Fig. 33 Dashboard removal on 1990–93 Accord

6. Disconnect the dash wiring harness from the individual connectors and the fusebox.
7. Remove the clips securing the carpet and disconnect the antenna lead.
8. Disconnect the heater control cable and function control cable.
9. Remove the caps on the side panels of the dashboard.
10. Remove the clock.
11. Remove the seven mounting bolts.
12. With an assistant, lift the dashboard and remove it from the vehicle.

To install:
13. Fit the dash into position, making sure the guide pin is engaged.
14. Install the bolts and tighten them just snug. Check the position of the dash in all dimensions and adjust as necessary. When properly positioned, tighten the mounting bolts. Double check for pinched wires or interference with heater control cables.
15. Install the clock. Install the caps on the side panels.
16. Connect the heater control and function cables.
17. Connect the antenna lead, then reposition and secure the carpet.
18. Connect the dash harness to the individual connectors and the fusebox.
19. Install the steering column.
20. Install the knee bolster and lower panel.
21. Connect the negative battery cable and enable the SRS system.

1994–95 Accord

▶ **See Figure 34**

1. Disconnect the negative battery cable and disable the SRS system.
2. Remove the console.
3. Remove the dashboard lower covers.
4. Remove the screws securing the glove box, then remove it from the vehicle.
5. Lower the steering column.
6. Unplug the dashboard wire harness connectors and detach the harness clips. Label the connectors for ease of assembly.
7. Disconnect the air mix control cable.
8. Disconnect the recirculation control motor and resistor connectors.
9. Remove the side defogger outlets on each side of the dash. These can be removed from the dash using a small prytool.
10. Remove the bolts securing the dashboard.

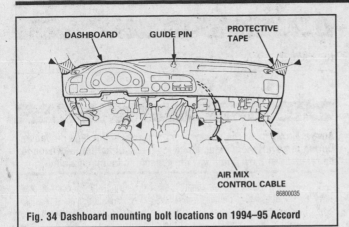

Fig. 34 Dashboard mounting bolt locations on 1994–95 Accord

11. Remove the nuts securing the air bag assembly, and remove it from the dashboard. Carefully store the air bag in a safe area with the pad side facing upwards.

12. With an assistant, lift the dashboard and remove it from the vehicle.

To install:

13. Fit the dash into position, making sure the guide pin is engaged.

14. Fit the air bag in the dashboard. Use new mounting nuts to secure the air bag; tighten them to 7 ft. lbs. (10 Nm.)

15. Tighten the bolts securing the dashboard until snug.

16. Install the side defogger outlets.

17. Connect the air mix control cable and engage the electrical connections.

18. Raise the steering column.

19. Install the glove box, dashboard lower covers and console.

20. Connect the negative battery cable and enable the SRS system.

1984–87 Prelude

▶ **See Figure 35**

1. Disconnect the negative battery cable.

2. Remove the left side lower trim panel and the fusebox cover. Remove the lower left dash panel by unscrewing the four bolts.

3. Open the glove box. Remove the ashtray.

4. Remove the bolts securing the lower right dash panel (inside the glove box.) Disconnect the wiring for the glove box light, ashtray light, radio and antenna.

5. Remove the panel with the radio still installed.

6. Remove the heater control panel.

7. Remove the cable mounting screws and disconnect the wiring harness to the heater controls.

8. Remove the instrument cluster.

9. Remove the clock.

10. Label and disconnect the instrument harness from the fusebox, side harness, instrument sub-harness, heater, interior light timer and chime.

11. Remove the nine dash mounting bolts. Don't forget the two bolts at the sides of the dash.

12. With an assistant, lift the dash to release the center guide pin; support the dash evenly and remove it from the car.

To install:

13. Fit the dash into position, making sure the guide pin is engaged.

14. Install the nine bolts and tighten them just snug. Check the position of the dash in all dimensions and adjust as necessary. When properly positioned, tighten the mounting bolts.

15. Engage the individual wiring connectors to the instrument wire harness.

16. Install the clock.

17. Install the instrument cluster.

18. Engage the heater control wiring connector; install the heater control panel.

19. Install the right side lower panel and radio.

20. Connect the related wiring circuits at the right side lower panel.

21. Install the ashtray.

22. Install the lower left dash panel. Install the trim panel and fuse box cover.

1988–91 Prelude

▶ **See Figure 36**

1. Disconnect the negative battery cable.

2. Slide the seats all the way back.

3. Remove the lower left dash panel. When the panel is loose, unplug the wiring connector.

4. Remove the front and rear consoles.

5. Unplug the wire harnesses from the connector bracket and the fusebox.

6. Disconnect the speedometer cable.

7. Remove the six screws securing the radio panel, remove the panel and disconnect the wiring and antenna at the radio.

8. Remove the radio assembly.

9. Disconnect the heater control cable.

10. If equipped with automatic transaxle, unplug the shift position switch connectors at the shifter.

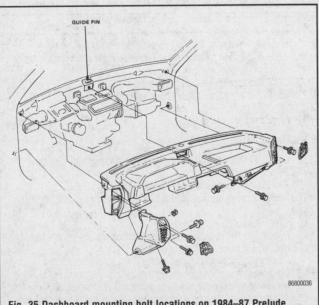

Fig. 35 Dashboard mounting bolt locations on 1984–87 Prelude

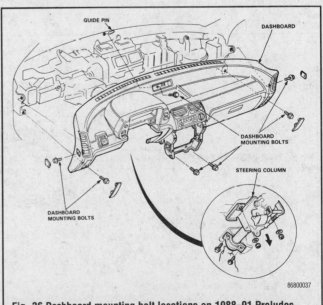

Fig. 36 Dashboard mounting bolt locations on 1988–91 Preludes

11. Disconnect the wiring at the heater control.
12. Remove the clock.
13. Lower the steering column.
14. Remove the dash mounting bolts
15. With an assistant, lift the dash to release the center guide pin; support the dash evenly and remove it from the car.

To install:

16. Fit the dash into position, making sure the guide pin is engaged.
17. Install the nine bolts and tighten them just snug. Check the position of the dash in all dimensions and adjust as necessary. When properly positioned, tighten the mounting bolts.
18. Raise and install the steering column.
19. Install the clock.
20. Connect the wiring to the heater controls.
21. Connect the wiring to the automatic shift selector.
22. Install the heater control cable.
23. Install the radio. Engage the radio wiring and antenna connectors.
24. Install the radio panel.
25. Connect the speedometer cable.
26. Connect the wiring at the fusebox and connector bracket.
27. Install the front and rear consoles.
28. Install the lower dash panel.

1992–95 Prelude

▶ See Figure 37

1. Disconnect the negative battery cable and disable the SRS system.
2. Remove the front seats.
3. Remove the console and glove box.
4. Remove the dashboard lower covers.
5. Lower the steering column.
6. Remove the nuts securing the passenger's air bag bracket and remove the bracket.
7. Unplug the dashboard wire harness connectors and disconnect the heater control cable.
8. Remove the six mounting bolts, then remove the dashboard from the vehicle.

To install:

9. Fit the dash into position, making sure the guide pin is engaged.
10. Install the six mounting bolts and tighten them until snug.
11. Connect the heater control cable and engage the wire harness connectors.
12. Install the nuts securing the air bag bracket; tighten them to 7 ft. lbs. (10 Nm.)
13. Raise the steering column.
14. Install the dashboard lower covers and console.
15. Install the glove box and front seats.

Consoles

REMOVAL & INSTALLATION

▶ See Figure 38

❊❊ CAUTION

Always firmly block the wheels front and rear before this procedure. During removal, the parking brake lever and/or shifter may need to be released or moved to allow the console to be manipulated.

1. Remove the shift knob on manual transaxles. For 1984–85 Accords and 1984–87 Preludes with automatic transaxles, remove the shift selector handle.
2. Remove the rear ash tray, end-cap or lighter as required. Remove the screws securing the console to the rear mount.
3. Remove the side retaining screws and carefully remove the rear console. Unplug any wiring connectors as soon as access is gained. Do the same for the front console.

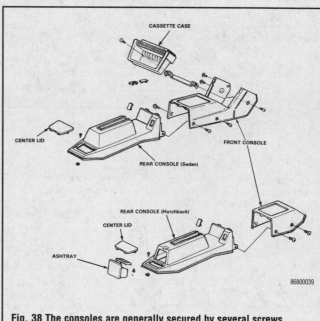

Fig. 38 The consoles are generally secured by several screws

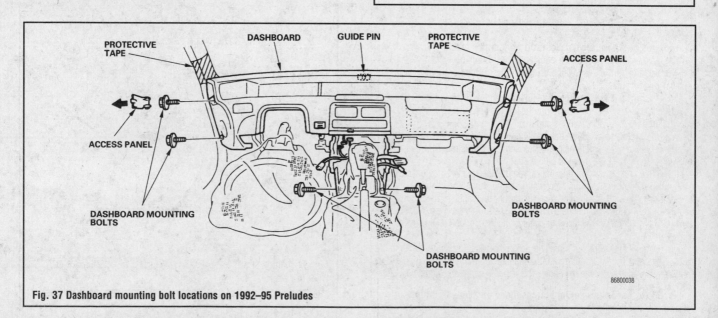

Fig. 37 Dashboard mounting bolt locations on 1992–95 Preludes

4. When installing, fit and secure the front console first. Make certain the brackets did not get bent or moved during other repairs. The console must be properly positioned before tightening the bolts. Install the rear console in the same fashion. Remember to engage the wiring during reassembly.

Door Panels

REMOVAL & INSTALLATION

▶ See Figures 39, 40, 41 and 42

➥This is a general procedure. Depending on vehicle and model, the order of steps may need to be changed slightly.

1. Remove the mirror control knob (if manual remote) and remove the cover from the mirror mount.

2. Remove the screws securing the armrest and remove the armrest. The screws may be concealed behind plastic caps which can be removed with a non-marring tool.

3. Remove the cover for the inside door handle. It is usually secured by a single screw. Remove it, then slide the cover off over the handle.

4. If not equipped with electric windows, remove the window winder handle. This can be tricky, but not difficult. The handle is retained onto the winder axle by a spring clip shaped like the Greek letter Omega. The clip is located between the back of the winder handle and the door pad. It is correctly installed with the legs pointing away from the length of the winder handle. There are three common ways of removing the clip:

9. Once the panel is free, keep it close to the door and look behind it. Disconnect any wiring for switches, lights or speakers which may be attached.

➥Behind the panel is a plastic sheet, taped or glued to the door. This is a water shield and must be intact to prevent water entry into the car. It must be securely attached at its edges and not be ripped or damaged. Small holes or tears can be patched with waterproof tape applied to both sides of the liner.

To install:

10. Connect any applicable wiring harnesses and align the upper edge of the panel along the top of the door. Make sure the left-right alignment is correct; tap the top of the panel into place with the heel of your hand.

11. Make sure the plastic clips align with their holes; secure each retainer into place.

12. Install the armrest and door handle cover. Remember to install any caps or covers over the screws.

13. Install the window winder handle on vehicles with manual windows. Place the spring clip into the slot on the handle. Remember that the legs should point away from the long dimension of the handle. Align the handle and position it over the end of the axle. Use the heel of your hand to give the center of the winder a short, sharp blow. This will cause the winder to move inward and the spring will engage its locking groove. The secret to this trick is to push the winder straight on; if it's crooked, it won't engage and you may end up looking for the spring clip.

14. Install any remaining parts or trim pieces which may have been removed earlier (map pockets, speaker grilles, etc.)

15. Install the cover and the remote mirror handle if they were removed.

Fig. 39 Remove the screws securing the armrest

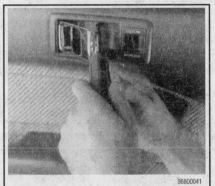

Fig. 40 Remove the screw securing the cover for the inside door handle

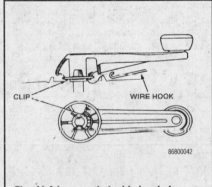

Fig. 41 A homemade tool is handy for removing the window winder clip

a. Use a door handle removal tool. This inexpensive tool can be fitted between the winder and the panel and used to push the spring clip free.

b. Use a rag or piece of cloth and work it back and forth between the winder and door panel. If constant upward tension is kept, the clip will be forced free. Keep watch on the clip as it pops out; it may get lost.

c. Straighten a common paper clip and bend a very small J-hook at the end of it. Work the hook down from the top of the winder and engage the loop of the spring clip. Pull the clip free.

5. In general, power door lock and window switches mounted on the door pad (not the armrest) may remain in place until the pad is removed. Some cannot be removed until the panel is off the door.

6. If the car has manual door locks, remove the lock knob by unscrewing it. If this is not possible at this time, wait until the panel is lifted free.

7. Using a wide, flat-bladed tool, gently pry the panel away from the door. You are releasing plastic inserts from plastic seats. There will be 6 to 12 of them around the door. With care, the plastic inserts can be reused several times.

8. When all the clips are loose, lift up on the panel to release the lip at the top of the door. This may require a bit of manipulation to loosen the panel; do so gently and don't damage the panel. The upper edge (at the window sill) is attached by a series of retaining clips.

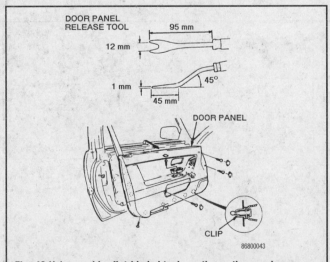

Fig. 42 Using a wide, flat-bladed tool, gently pry the panel away from the door

Headliner

REMOVAL & INSTALLATION

➡**Replacing the headliner requires substantial disassembly of interior trim panels and components. Use great care not to damage or break any of the panels. Pay attention to the placement of screws, clips and washers when reinstalling the panels.**

1984–85 Accord

1. If equipped, remove the sunroof winder handle.
2. Remove the dome light.
3. Remove the inner rear view mirror and both sunvisors.
4. Remove the three grab handles.
5. Disconnect the right and left upper anchors for the seat belts.
6. Remove all the trim surrounding each door opening.
7. Remove the trim from the right and left windshield pillars.
8. Remove the trim from the right and left center pillars.
9. Remove the trim from the upper quarter or sail panels at the rear of the passenger compartment.
10. If equipped, remove the sunroof molding.
11. On hatchbacks, remove the upper tailgate molding.
12. Remove the headliner trim.
13. Remove the headliner from the car carefully, taking care not to damage seats, other interior components or the headliner itself.

To install:

14. Fit the headliner into the car and lift it into position. Secure it in place, making sure all the clips are engaged.
15. Install the headliner trim or hatchback upper molding.
16. Install the sunroof molding.
17. Install the quarter panel trim pieces.
18. Install the center pillar and front pillar trim.
19. Reinstall the trim surrounding each door.
20. Secure the upper seat belt mounting points. Make certain the belts move freely and do not bind or twist.
21. Install the grab handles.
22. Install the sunvisors and mirror.
23. Install the dome light.
24. If applicable, install the sunroof winder handle.

1984–91 Prelude and 1986–89 Accord

▶ **See Figure 43**

1. Remove the sunvisors and grab handles.
2. Remove the rear view mirror and base.

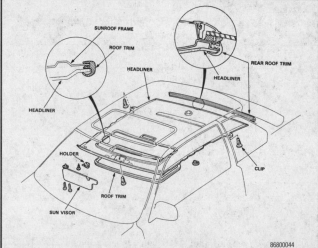

Fig. 43 Headliner assembly used on 1984–91 Prelude; Accord similar

3. If the high-mount rear brake lamp is positioned on the upper edge of the rear window, remove it.
4. Remove the front pillar trim.
5. Remove the dome light.
6. Remove the rear quarter window trim panel from all Preludes and Accord hatchbacks.
7. Remove the rear roof trim.
8. If equipped, remove the sunroof trim.
9. Remove the headliner from the car carefully, taking care not to damage seats, other interior components or the headliner itself.

To install:

10. Fit the headliner into the car and lift it into position. Secure it in place, making sure all the clips are engaged.
11. Install the sunroof trim.
12. Install the rear roof trim.
13. Install the quarter panel trim if it was removed. Make certain the panels align and are secure.
14. Install the dome light.
15. Install the front pillar trim.
16. Install the rear view mirror and base. Install the sun visors.

1990–95 Accord and 1992–95 Prelude

1. Remove the sunvisors.
2. Remove the dome light.
3. Remove the rear view mirror.
4. Carefully remove the front pillar trims.
5. On sedan models, remove the rear pillar trim panels.
6. If equipped, remove the sunroof trim.
7. Remove the grab handles.
8. Remove the rear roof side trim panels.
9. Remove the rear seat.
10. Remove the right front seat.
11. Fully recline the driver's seat.
12. Remove the front and rear clips. Remove the headliner. Do not bend the liner and be careful not to damage any interior components.
13. Remove the headliner through the right door opening.

To install:

14. Carefully fit the headliner into the car through the right door. Lift it into position and secure the front and rear clips.
15. Install the two mounting screws.
16. Install the front right seat and the rear seat.
17. Install the rear roof side trim panels.
18. Install the grab handles.
19. If equipped with sunroof, install the sunroof trim.
20. Install the rear pillar trim if it was removed.
21. install the front pillar trim panels.
22. Install the rear view mirror and dome light.
23. Install the sunvisors.

Door Locks

REMOVAL & INSTALLATION

➡**Removing the door lock will require disconnecting some of the link rods within the door. Many of the clips used to secure the rods are non-reusable and may break when disassembled. Make certain there is a supply of new clips on hand for reassembly.**

Lock In Door Handle

1. Remove the door panel.
2. Carefully remove the inner door liner. Take great care not to rip or damage the plastic.
3. Disconnect or release the clips securing the link rods to both the lock cylinder and the door handle. Depending on the model, it may be easier to disconnect the other end of the rod (at the latch assembly) first.
4. Disconnect any wiring harnesses running to the lock or handle. Generally, these cables have connectors in the line; do not try to disconnect the wiring right at the lock.

5. Remove the retaining nuts or bolts securing the handle assembly to the door and remove the handle. The lock portion can be removed by a competent locksmith. Disassembly by the owner/mechanic is not recommended due to the number of small parts and springs within the lock.

To install:

6. Before reinstalling, the lock assembly must be installed in the door handle and the small lever (arm) attached. Place the handle in the door and secure the mounting nuts and bolts.

7. Connect the wiring, if any, to the handle or lock.

8. Carefully connect the link rods to the handle and lock. Use new clips if necessary. Reconnect the rods to the latch if any were removed.

9. Reinstall the moisture liner. Apply a bead of waterproof sealer to the outer edge if needed and align the sheet carefully.

10. Install the door panel.

Lock In Door

1. Remove the door panel.

2. Carefully remove the inner door liner. Take great care not to rip or damage the plastic.

3. Disconnect or release the clips securing the link rods to both the lock cylinder and the door handle. Depending on the model, it may be easier to disconnect the other end of the rod (at the latch assembly) first.

4. Disconnect any wiring harnesses running to the lock or handle. Generally, these cables have connectors in the line; do not try to disconnect the wiring right at the lock.

5. The lock cylinder is retained by a horseshoe-shaped spring clip. Remove the clip and remove the lock cylinder. The cylinder may be repaired by a competent locksmith. Disassembly by the owner/mechanic is not recommended due to the number of small parts and springs within the lock.

To install:

6. Install the cylinder into the door and fit the horseshoe clip. Make sure the cylinder is firmly held in place.

7. Connect the link rod, using new clips if necessary.

8. Reinstall the moisture liner. Apply a bead of waterproof sealer to the outer edge if needed and align the sheet carefully.

9. Install the door panel.

Door Glass and Regulator

REMOVAL & INSTALLATION

▶ **See Figures 44 thru 49**

1. Remove the door pad and inner moisture barrier.

2. If working on the rear window of a sedan, remove the two upper screws securing the center channel. Remove the two lower bolts (in the door) securing the channel and remove it. On some cars, the two screws are concealed below the weatherstrip.

3. For sedan rear doors, remove the quarter glass. The entire glass and rubber seal may be removed as an assembly from the door.

4. Lower the door glass until the glass mounting bolts are accessible. One will be easily seen in the large access hole in the door; the other will appear in the smaller, round access hole. Remove the bolts.

5. Stand next to the inside of the door. Tilt the door glass and remove it through the slot.

✳✳ WARNING

The glass is easily broken; don't force it while removing. Handle it carefully and store it out of the work area in a protected location.

6. On front doors, remove the bolts securing the front run channel, then remove the channel.

7. Remove the regulator mounting bolts and remove the regulator. On later models, there are additional roller guide bolts to be removed. Mark the roller guide mounting bolts to ease window alignment later.

8. For power windows, remove the motor from the regulator if desired.

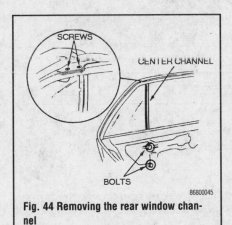

Fig. 44 Removing the rear window channel

Fig. 45 Carefully remove the rear quarter glass

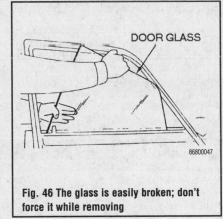

Fig. 46 The glass is easily broken; don't force it while removing

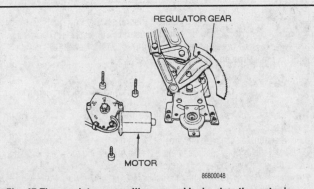

Fig. 47 The regulator gear will move suddenly when the motor is removed. Keep hands well clear

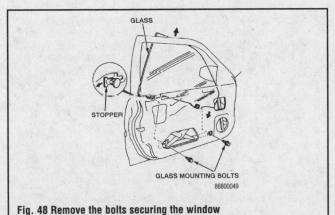

Fig. 48 Remove the bolts securing the window

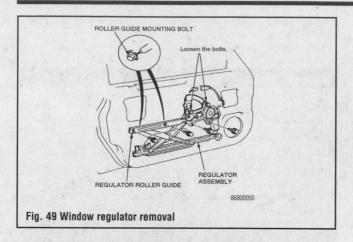

Fig. 49 Window regulator removal

❋❋ CAUTION

The regulator gear will move suddenly when the motor is removed due to action of the large spring. Keep hands well clear.

To install:

9. Inspect the regulator carefully for any sign of damage or binding. Grease all the sliding surfaces of the regulator before installation.

10. If equipped with power windows, compress the regulator gear by hand. When in position, install the motor with the collar and mounting bolt.

11. Check the position of the breather pipe on power window motors; it must be correctly mounted to keep water out of the motor.

12. Install the regulator.

13. Install the front door run channel. Tighten the bolts until just snug.

14. Fit the glass into position inside the door. Set it loosely on the regulator.

15. Adjust the position of the regulator until the glass mounting bolts align with the access holes. On power windows, connect the wiring and operate the window switch briefly to move the regulator.

16. Install the glass mounting bolts and tighten until just snug. Operate the window up and down, checking the placement of the glass and the front run channel. Make adjustments as necessary.

17. Tighten the front run channel bolts and tighten the glass mounting bolts.

18. For sedan rear doors, install the quarter glass and the center channel. Tighten the mounting bolts until snug.

19. Double check the operation of the window in all regards. It should move smoothly and evenly, sealing completely when closed.

20. Reinstall the liner and door panel.

Windshield Glass

REMOVAL & INSTALLATION

If your windshield, or other fixed window, is cracked or chipped, you may decide to replace it with a new one yourself. However, there are two main reasons why replacement windshields and other window glass should be installed only by a professional automotive glass technician: safety and cost.

The most important reason a professional should install automotive glass is for safety. The glass in the vehicle, especially the windshield, is designed with safety in mind in case of a collision. The windshield is specially manufactured from two panes of specially-tempered glass with a thin layer of transparent plastic between them. This construction allows the glass to "give" in the event that a part of your body hits the windshield during the collision, and prevents the glass from shattering, which could cause lacerations, blinding and other harm to passengers of the vehicle. The other fixed windows are designed to be tempered so that if they break during a collision, they shatter in such a way that there are no large pointed glass pieces. The professional automotive glass technician knows how to install the glass in a vehicle so that it will function optimally during a collision. Without the proper experience, knowledge and tools, installing a piece of automotive glass yourself could lead to additional harm if an accident should ever occur.

Cost is also a factor when deciding to install automotive glass yourself. Performing this could cost you much more than a professional may charge for the same job. Since the windshield is designed to break under stress, an often life saving characteristic, windshields tend to break VERY easily when an inexperienced person attempts to install one. Do-it-yourselfers buying two, three or even four windshields from a salvage yard because they have broken them during installation are common stories. Also, since the automotive glass is designed to prevent the outside elements from entering your vehicle, improper installation can lead to water and air leaks. Annoying whining noises at highway speeds from air leaks or inside body panel rusting from water leaks can add to your stress level and subtract from your wallet. After buying two or three windshields, installing them and ending up with a leak that produces a noise while driving and water damage during rainstorms, the cost of having a professional do it correctly the first time may be much more alluring. We here at Chilton, therefore, advise that you have a professional automotive glass technician service any broken glass on your vehicle.

WINDSHIELD CHIP REPAIR

▶ **See Figures 50 and 51**

➡ **Check with your state and local authorities on the laws for state safety inspection. Some states or municipalities may not allow chip repair as a viable option for correcting stone damage to your windshield.**

Although severely cracked or damaged windshields must be replaced, there is something that you can do to prolong or even prevent the need for replace-

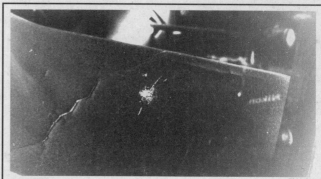

Fig. 50 Small chips on your windshield can be fixed with an aftermarket repair kit, such as the one from Loctite®

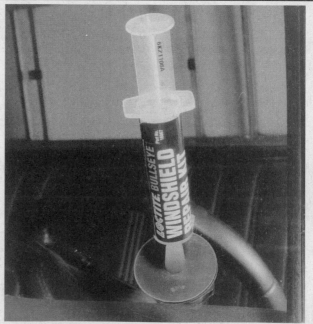

Fig. 51 Most kits use a self-stick applicator and syringe to inject the adhesive into the chip or crack

ment of a chipped windshield. There are many companies which offer windshield chip repair products, such as Loctite's® Bullseye™ windshield repair kit. These kits usually consist of a syringe, pedestal and a sealing adhesive. The syringe is mounted on the pedestal and is used to create a vacuum which pulls the plastic layer against the glass. This helps make the chip transparent. The adhesive is then injected which seals the chip and helps to prevent further stress cracks from developing

➡**Always follow the specific manufacturer's instructions.**

Vent Windows

REMOVAL & INSTALLATION

1984–85 Accord

▶ **See Figures 52 and 53**

1. Release the latch. Remove the latch mount cover and remove the screws.
2. Remove the upper and lower quarter trim panels and remove the quarter trim.
3. Remove the window hinge mounting nuts and remove the window glass.
4. On the window, remove the E-clip securing the latch assembly to the glass. Before removal, take careful note of the placement of the washers and pads; they must be reassembled in the correct sequence.
5. If the window is to be replaced with another piece, remove the nuts and remove the pillar trim.
6. Remove the clips from the pillar trim.
7. Remove the moldings and weatherstrip.
8. Transfer the pillar trim, molding and weatherstrip to the new glass.
To install:
9. Reassemble the latch onto the glass; make certain each washer and pad is in the correct location. Installing the E-clip can be harder than it looks; don't damage the glass. If the clip is not firmly in place, the latch will loosen.

4. On the window, remove the E-clip securing the latch assembly to the glass. Before removal, take careful note of the placement of the washers and pads; they must be reassembled in the correct sequence.
5. If the window is to be replaced with another piece, remove the weather strip and upper molding. Transfer them to the new glass.
To install:
6. Reassemble the latch onto the glass; make certain each washer and pad is in the correct location. Installing the E-clip can be harder than it looks; don't damage the glass. If the clip is not firmly in place, the latch will loosen.
7. Install the assembled window glass to the pillar and tighten the mounting bolts.
8. Install the mounting bolts for the latch assembly.
9. Install the quarter pillar trim panel.
10. Install the cover on the latch mount.

Inside Rear View Mirror

➡**The inside mirrors on all Hondas are designed to break loose under impact. If your mirror has fallen or been knocked off the mount, it can usually be reinstalled without any new parts.**

REMOVAL & INSTALLATION

▶ **See Figure 56**

1. Remove the rubber damper from the shaft of the mirror if one is present.
2. Carefully pry off the plastic cover. On 1988–91 Preludes, press in at the front of the cover to release the clips. Remove the cover.
3. Remove the retaining screws securing the base. On some Preludes, the screws also hold the warning lamp assembly; be prepared to remove and disconnect it.
4. Remove the large cross-point screw securing the mirror to the base.
5. Reassemble in reverse order.

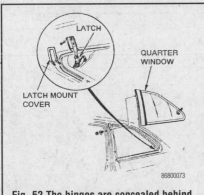

Fig. 52 The hinges are concealed behind the pillar trim

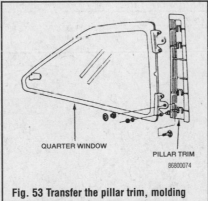

Fig. 53 Transfer the pillar trim, molding and weatherstrip to the new glass

Fig. 54 Remove the screws and remove the outer quarter pillar molding

10. Install the assembled window glass to the pillar and tighten the mounting nuts until snug.
11. Install the mounting bolts for the latch assembly.
12. Install the quarter trim along with the upper and lower trim panels.
13. Install the cover on the latch mount.

1986–89 Accord

▶ **See Figures 54 and 55**

1. Release the latch. Remove the latch mount cover and remove the screws.
2. Remove the screws and remove the outer quarter pillar molding.
3. Remove the window hinge mounting screws and remove the window glass.

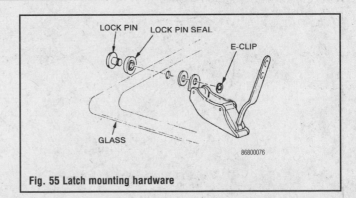

Fig. 55 Latch mounting hardware

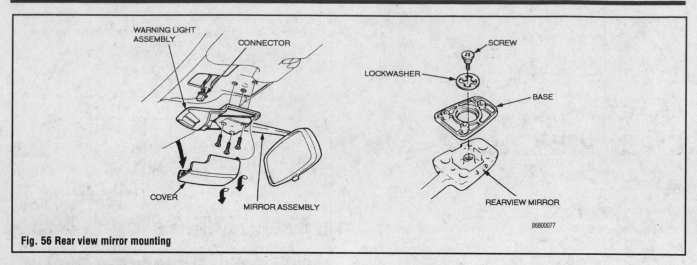

Fig. 56 Rear view mirror mounting

Seats

REMOVAL & INSTALLATION

Front

❋ WARNING

Many electrical components are mounted on the floor under the seats. Do not damage the components during removal or installation of the seat.

1. Slide the seat fully forward. In the rear passenger area, remove the covers from the two seat retaining bolts.

2. Remove the bolts.
3. Slide the seat fully to the rear. Remove the front mounting bolt covers and remove the bolts.
4. Remove the seat.
5. Reinstall in reverse order; tighten the seat rail mounting bolts to 23 ft. lbs. (32 Nm.)

Rear

1984–89 ACCORD

▶ **See Figures 57 and 58**

1. With your hands, press down on the seat cushion where it meets the seat back. Locate the retaining bolt(s.) Some models retain the seat with one bolt in the center; others use two, evenly spaced left and right.
2. Remove the retaining bolts.

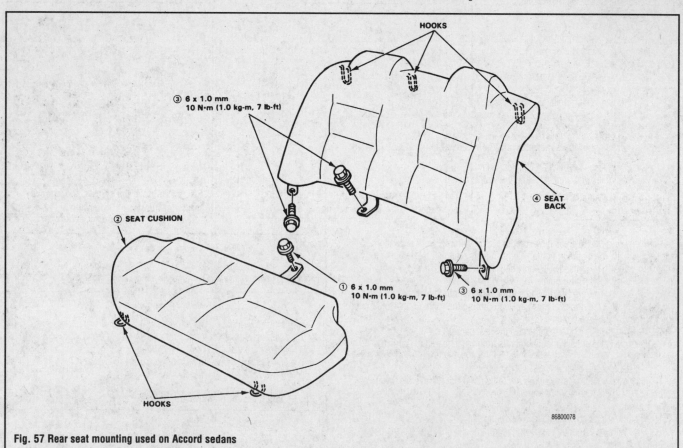

Fig. 57 Rear seat mounting used on Accord sedans

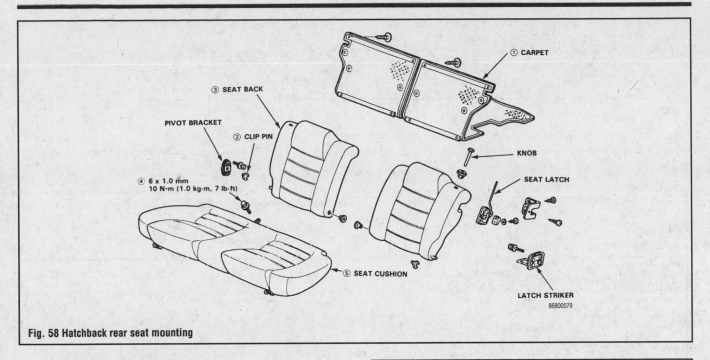

Fig. 58 Hatchback rear seat mounting

3. Lift the back of the seat upwards while rotating it to the front of the car.

4. Disconnect the hooks at the front edge (during the rolling motion) of the seat and remove the seat bottom.

5. On hatchback Accords, remove the carpeting from the seat back.

6. Remove the bolts securing the bottom of the seat back.

7. On 1984–85 Accord sedans, push against the middle of the seat back just below the top edge with one hand while pulling up firmly on the bottom edge with the other hand. This combined motion releases a J-shaped hook securing the seat back at each lower edge.

8. On 1986–89 Accord sedans, wiggle and lift the seat back upwards, releasing the upper hooks.

9. On hatchbacks, remove the clip pin at the outboard lower pivot of each seat. Remove the seat back

To install:

10. Fit the rear seat back into position, making sure all clips and retainers are firmly engaged.

11. Install the retaining bolts; tighten them to 7 ft. lbs. (10 Nm).

12. Install the seat bottom. Start by fitting the front hooks in place, then roll the seat into position.

➡ **Don't forget to route the seat belts into their correct locations.**

13. Install the retaining bolts and tighten them to 7 ft. lbs. (10 Nm).

14. Reinstall the cargo area carpeting if it was removed.

1990–95 ACCORD

▶ **See Figure 59**

1. With your hands, press down on the seat cushion where it meets the seat back. Locate the retaining bolt(s.) Some models retain the seat with one bolt in the center; others use two, evenly spaced left and right.

2. Remove the retaining bolts.

3. Lift the back of the seat upwards while rotating it to the front of the car.

4. Disconnect the hooks at the front edge (during the rolling motion) of the seat and remove the seat bottom.

5. Remove the carpet from the rear of the seat backs.

6. Remove the seat back mounting bolts from the luggage compartment side.

7. Lift out the seat back.

8. If the rear side bolsters or pads are to be removed, remove the lower mounting bolt, then push upward to free the hooks.

To install:

9. Install the side bolsters if they were removed.

10. Install the seat bottom, engaging the front hooks first. Tighten the bolts to 7 ft. lbs. (10 Nm.)

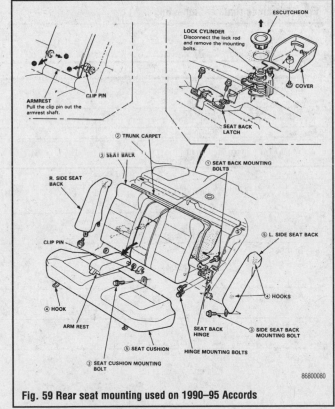

Fig. 59 Rear seat mounting used on 1990–95 Accords

11. Install the seat back.

12. Install the seat back retaining bolts; when they are just snug, check the fit of the seat and its position in the upper latch. Adjust as necessary.

13. Tighten the bolts to 16 ft. lbs. (22 Nm.)

14. Install the rear carpeting to the seat back.

PRELUDE

▶ **See Figure 60**

1. Pull the seat back all the way down. Remove the luggage area carpet from the back of the seat.

2. Remove the clip pin on the left side of the seat back. Slide the seat back to the left (removing it from the right mount) and remove the back.

3. Remove the bolt(s) securing the seat bottom

4. Move the rear of the seat upwards and towards the front; disengage the hooks from the floor holes.

5. Reassemble in reverse order. Tighten the seat mounting bolts to 7 ft. lbs. (10 Nm.)

➡**Don't forget to route the seat belts through the pockets in the seat bottom.**

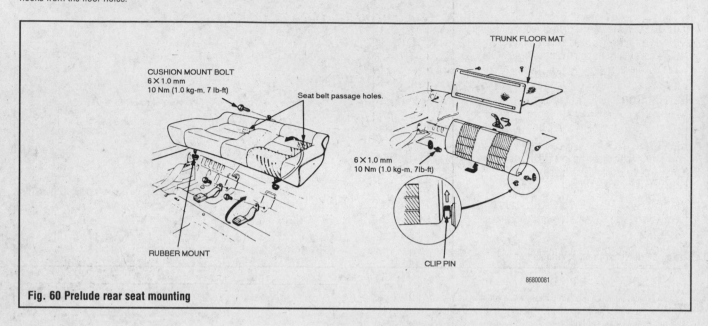

Fig. 60 Prelude rear seat mounting

TORQUE SPECIFICATIONS

Component		US	Metric
Hood			
	Mounting bolts	7 ft. lbs.	10 Nm
Trunk Lid			
	Mounting bolts	7 ft. lbs.	10 Nm
Hatchback			
	Mounting bolts	7 ft. lbs.	10 Nm
Tailgate			
	Mounting bolts	7 ft. lbs.	10 Nm
	Hinge bolts	16 ft. lbs.	22 Nm
Door			
	Mounting bolts	7 ft. lbs.	10 Nm
Bumper			
	Mounting bolts	28 ft. lbs.	39 Nm
	Bracket bolts	16 ft. lbs.	22 Nm
Air Bag			
	Mounting nuts	7 ft. lbs.	10 Nm
Front Seat			
	Mounting bolts		
Rear Seat			
	Seatback		
	Except 1990-95 Accord	7 ft. lbs.	10 Nm
	1990-95 Accord	16 ft. lbs.	22 Nm
	Seatbottom	7 ft. lbs.	10 Nm
Seat Belt			
	Except 1990-95 Accord and 1992-95 Prelude		
	All mounting bolts	23 ft. lbs.	32 Nm
	1990-95 Accord and 1992-95 Prelude		
	Front lap belt	29 ft. lbs.	40 Nm
	Front shoulder belt	25 ft. lbs.	35 Nm
	Rear belts	23 ft. lbs.	32 Nm

86800900

GLOSSARY

AIR/FUEL RATIO: The ratio of air-to-gasoline by weight in the fuel mixture drawn into the engine.

AIR INJECTION: One method of reducing harmful exhaust emissions by injecting air into each of the exhaust ports of an engine. The fresh air entering the hot exhaust manifold causes any remaining fuel to be burned before it can exit the tailpipe.

ALTERNATOR: A device used for converting mechanical energy into electrical energy.

AMMETER: An instrument, calibrated in amperes, used to measure the flow of an electrical current in a circuit. Ammeters are always connected in series with the circuit being tested.

AMPERE: The rate of flow of electrical current present when one volt of electrical pressure is applied against one ohm of electrical resistance.

ANALOG COMPUTER: Any microprocessor that uses similar (analogous) electrical signals to make its calculations.

ARMATURE: A laminated, soft iron core wrapped by a wire that converts electrical energy to mechanical energy as in a motor or relay. When rotated in a magnetic field, it changes mechanical energy into electrical energy as in a generator.

ATMOSPHERIC PRESSURE: The pressure on the Earth's surface caused by the weight of the air in the atmosphere. At sea level, this pressure is 14.7 psi at 32°F (101 kPa at 0°C).

ATOMIZATION: The breaking down of a liquid into a fine mist that can be suspended in air.

AXIAL PLAY: Movement parallel to a shaft or bearing bore.

BACKFIRE: The sudden combustion of gases in the intake or exhaust system that results in a loud explosion.

BACKLASH: The clearance or play between two parts, such as meshed gears.

BACKPRESSURE: Restrictions in the exhaust system that slow the exit of exhaust gases from the combustion chamber.

BAKELITE: A heat resistant, plastic insulator material commonly used in printed circuit boards and transistorized components.

BALL BEARING: A bearing made up of hardened inner and outer races between which hardened steel balls roll.

BALLAST RESISTOR: A resistor in the primary ignition circuit that lowers voltage after the engine is started to reduce wear on ignition components.

BEARING: A friction reducing, supportive device usually located between a stationary part and a moving part.

BIMETAL TEMPERATURE SENSOR: Any sensor or switch made of two dissimilar types of metal that bend when heated or cooled due to the different expansion rates of the alloys. These types of sensors usually function as an on/off switch.

BLOWBY: Combustion gases, composed of water vapor and unburned fuel, that leak past the piston rings into the crankcase during normal engine operation. These gases are removed by the PCV system to prevent the buildup of harmful acids in the crankcase.

BRAKE PAD: A brake shoe and lining assembly used with disc brakes.

BRAKE SHOE: The backing for the brake lining. The term is, however, usually applied to the assembly of the brake backing and lining.

BUSHING: A liner, usually removable, for a bearing; an anti-friction liner used in place of a bearing.

CALIPER: A hydraulically activated device in a disc brake system, which is mounted straddling the brake rotor (disc). The caliper contains at least one piston and two brake pads. Hydraulic pressure on the piston(s) forces the pads against the rotor.

CAMSHAFT: A shaft in the engine on which are the lobes (cams) which operate the valves. The camshaft is driven by the crankshaft, via a belt, chain or gears, at one half the crankshaft speed.

CAPACITOR: A device which stores an electrical charge.

CARBON MONOXIDE (CO): A colorless, odorless gas given off as a normal byproduct of combustion. It is poisonous and extremely dangerous in confined areas, building up slowly to toxic levels without warning if adequate ventilation is not available.

CARBURETOR: A device, usually mounted on the intake manifold of an engine, which mixes the air and fuel in the proper proportion to allow even combustion.

CATALYTIC CONVERTER: A device installed in the exhaust system, like a muffler, that converts harmful byproducts of combustion into carbon dioxide and water vapor by means of a heat-producing chemical reaction.

CENTRIFUGAL ADVANCE: A mechanical method of advancing the spark timing by using flyweights in the distributor that react to centrifugal force generated by the distributor shaft rotation.

CHECK VALVE: Any one-way valve installed to permit the flow of air, fuel or vacuum in one direction only.

CHOKE: A device, usually a moveable valve, placed in the intake path of a carburetor to restrict the flow of air.

CIRCUIT: Any unbroken path through which an electrical current can flow. Also used to describe fuel flow in some instances.

CIRCUIT BREAKER: A switch which protects an electrical circuit from overload by opening the circuit when the current flow exceeds a predetermined level. Some circuit breakers must be reset manually, while most reset automatically.

COIL (IGNITION): A transformer in the ignition circuit which steps up the voltage provided to the spark plugs.

COMBINATION MANIFOLD: An assembly which includes both the intake and exhaust manifolds in one casting.

COMBINATION VALVE: A device used in some fuel systems that routes fuel vapors to a charcoal storage canister instead of venting them into the atmosphere. The valve relieves fuel tank pressure and allows fresh air into the tank as the fuel level drops to prevent a vapor lock situation.

COMPRESSION RATIO: The comparison of the total volume of the cylinder and combustion chamber with the piston at BDC and the piston at TDC.

CONDENSER: 1. An electrical device which acts to store an electrical charge, preventing voltage surges. 2. A radiator-like device in the air conditioning system in which refrigerant gas condenses into a liquid, giving off heat.

CONDUCTOR: Any material through which an electrical current can be transmitted easily.

CONTINUITY: Continuous or complete circuit. Can be checked with an ohmmeter.

COUNTERSHAFT: An intermediate shaft which is rotated by a mainshaft and transmits, in turn, that rotation to a working part.

CRANKCASE: The lower part of an engine in which the crankshaft and related parts operate.

CRANKSHAFT: The main driving shaft of an engine which receives reciprocating motion from the pistons and converts it to rotary motion.

CYLINDER: In an engine, the round hole in the engine block in which the piston(s) ride.

CYLINDER BLOCK: The main structural member of an engine in which is found the cylinders, crankshaft and other principal parts.

CYLINDER HEAD: The detachable portion of the engine, usually fastened to the top of the cylinder block and containing all or most of the combustion chambers. On overhead valve engines, it contains the valves and their operating parts. On overhead cam engines, it contains the camshaft as well.

DEAD CENTER: The extreme top or bottom of the piston stroke.

DETONATION: An unwanted explosion of the air/fuel mixture in the combustion chamber caused by excess heat and compression, advanced timing, or an overly lean mixture. Also referred to as "ping".

DIAPHRAGM: A thin, flexible wall separating two cavities, such as in a vacuum advance unit.

DIESELING: A condition in which hot spots in the combustion chamber cause the engine to run on after the key is turned off.

DIFFERENTIAL: A geared assembly which allows the transmission of motion between drive axles, giving one axle the ability to turn faster than the other.

DIODE: An electrical device that will allow current to flow in one direction only.

DISC BRAKE: A hydraulic braking assembly consisting of a brake disc, or rotor, mounted on an axle, and a caliper assembly containing, usually two brake pads which are activated by hydraulic pressure. The pads are forced against the sides of the disc, creating friction which slows the vehicle.

DISTRIBUTOR: A mechanically driven device on an engine which is responsible for electrically firing the spark plug at a predetermined point of the piston stroke.

DOWEL PIN: A pin, inserted in mating holes in two different parts allowing those parts to maintain a fixed relationship.

DRUM BRAKE: A braking system which consists of two brake shoes and one or two wheel cylinders, mounted on a fixed backing plate, and a brake drum, mounted on an axle, which revolves around the assembly.

DWELL: The rate, measured in degrees of shaft rotation, at which an electrical circuit cycles on and off.

ELECTRONIC CONTROL UNIT (ECU): Ignition module, module, amplifier or igniter. See Module for definition.

ELECTRONIC IGNITION: A system in which the timing and firing of the spark plugs is controlled by an electronic control unit, usually called a module. These systems have no points or condenser.

END-PLAY: The measured amount of axial movement in a shaft.

ENGINE: A device that converts heat into mechanical energy.

EXHAUST MANIFOLD: A set of cast passages or pipes which conduct exhaust gases from the engine.

FEELER GAUGE: A blade, usually metal, or precisely predetermined thickness, used to measure the clearance between two parts.

FIRING ORDER: The order in which combustion occurs in the cylinders of an engine. Also the order in which spark is distributed to the plugs by the distributor.

FLOODING: The presence of too much fuel in the intake manifold and combustion chamber which prevents the air/fuel mixture from firing, thereby causing a no-start situation.

FLYWHEEL: A disc shaped part bolted to the rear end of the crankshaft. Around the outer perimeter is affixed the ring gear. The starter drive engages the ring gear, turning the flywheel, which rotates the crankshaft, imparting the initial starting motion to the engine.

FOOT POUND (ft. lbs. or sometimes, ft.lb.): The amount of energy or work needed to raise an item weighing one pound, a distance of one foot.

FUSE: A protective device in a circuit which prevents circuit overload by breaking the circuit when a specific amperage is present. The device is constructed around a strip or wire of a lower amperage rating than the circuit it is designed to protect. When an amperage higher than that stamped on the fuse is present in the circuit, the strip or wire melts, opening the circuit.

GEAR RATIO: The ratio between the number of teeth on meshing gears.

GENERATOR: A device which converts mechanical energy into electrical energy.

HEAT RANGE: The measure of a spark plug's ability to dissipate heat from its firing end. The higher the heat range, the hotter the plug fires.

HUB: The center part of a wheel or gear.

HYDROCARBON (HC): Any chemical compound made up of hydrogen and carbon. A major pollutant formed by the engine as a byproduct of combustion.

HYDROMETER: An instrument used to measure the specific gravity of a solution.

INCH POUND (inch lbs.; sometimes in.lb. or in. lbs.): One twelfth of a foot pound.

INDUCTION: A means of transferring electrical energy in the form of a magnetic field. Principle used in the ignition coil to increase voltage.

INJECTOR: A device which receives metered fuel under relatively low pressure and is activated to inject the fuel into the engine under relatively high pressure at a predetermined time.

INPUT SHAFT: The shaft to which torque is applied, usually carrying the driving gear or gears.

INTAKE MANIFOLD: A casting of passages or pipes used to conduct air or a fuel/air mixture to the cylinders.

JOURNAL: The bearing surface within which a shaft operates.

KEY: A small block usually fitted in a notch between a shaft and a hub to prevent slippage of the two parts.

MANIFOLD: A casting of passages or set of pipes which connect the cylinders to an inlet or outlet source.

MANIFOLD VACUUM: Low pressure in an engine intake manifold formed just below the throttle plates. Manifold vacuum is highest at idle and drops under acceleration.

MASTER CYLINDER: The primary fluid pressurizing device in a hydraulic system. In automotive use, it is found in brake and hydraulic clutch systems and is pedal activated, either directly or, in a power brake system, through the power booster.

MODULE: Electronic control unit, amplifier or igniter of solid state or integrated design which controls the current flow in the ignition primary circuit based on input from the pick-up coil. When the module opens the primary circuit, high secondary voltage is induced in the coil.

NEEDLE BEARING: A bearing which consists of a number (usually a large number) of long, thin rollers.

OHM: (Ω) The unit used to measure the resistance of conductor-to-electrical flow. One ohm is the amount of resistance that limits current flow to one ampere in a circuit with one volt of pressure.

OHMMETER: An instrument used for measuring the resistance, in ohms, in an electrical circuit.

OUTPUT SHAFT: The shaft which transmits torque from a device, such as a transmission.

OVERDRIVE: A gear assembly which produces more shaft revolutions than that transmitted to it.

OVERHEAD CAMSHAFT (OHC): An engine configuration in which the camshaft is mounted on top of the cylinder head and operates the valve either directly or by means of rocker arms.

OVERHEAD VALVE (OHV): An engine configuration in which all of the valves are located in the cylinder head and the camshaft is located in the cylinder block. The camshaft operates the valves via lifters and pushrods.

OXIDES OF NITROGEN (NOx): Chemical compounds of nitrogen produced as a byproduct of combustion. They combine with hydrocarbons to produce smog.

OXYGEN SENSOR: Use with the feedback system to sense the presence of oxygen in the exhaust gas and signal the computer which can reference the voltage signal to an air/fuel ratio.

PINION: The smaller of two meshing gears.

PISTON RING: An open-ended ring with fits into a groove on the outer diameter of the piston. Its chief function is to form a seal between the piston and cylinder wall. Most automotive pistons have three rings: two for compression sealing; one for oil sealing.

PRELOAD: A predetermined load placed on a bearing during assembly or by adjustment.

PRIMARY CIRCUIT: the low voltage side of the ignition system which consists of the ignition switch, ballast resistor or resistance wire, bypass, coil, electronic control unit and pick-up coil as well as the connecting wires and harnesses.

PRESS FIT: The mating of two parts under pressure, due to the inner diameter of one being smaller than the outer diameter of the other, or vice versa; an interference fit.

RACE: The surface on the inner or outer ring of a bearing on which the balls, needles or rollers move.

REGULATOR: A device which maintains the amperage and/or voltage levels of a circuit at predetermined values.

RELAY: A switch which automatically opens and/or closes a circuit.

RESISTANCE: The opposition to the flow of current through a circuit or electrical device, and is measured in ohms. Resistance is equal to the voltage divided by the amperage.

RESISTOR: A device, usually made of wire, which offers a preset amount of resistance in an electrical circuit.

RING GEAR: The name given to a ring-shaped gear attached to a differential case, or affixed to a flywheel or as part of a planetary gear set.

ROLLER BEARING: A bearing made up of hardened inner and outer races between which hardened steel rollers move.

ROTOR: 1. The disc-shaped part of a disc brake assembly, upon which the brake pads bear; also called, brake disc. 2. The device mounted atop the distributor shaft, which passes current to the distributor cap tower contacts.

SECONDARY CIRCUIT: The high voltage side of the ignition system, usually above 20,000 volts. The secondary includes the ignition coil, coil wire, distributor cap and rotor, spark plug wires and spark plugs.

SENDING UNIT: A mechanical, electrical, hydraulic or electro-magnetic device which transmits information to a gauge.

SENSOR: Any device designed to measure engine operating conditions or ambient pressures and temperatures. Usually electronic in nature and designed to send a voltage signal to an on-board computer, some sensors may operate as a simple on/off switch or they may provide a variable voltage signal (like a potentiometer) as conditions or measured parameters change.

SHIM: Spacers of precise, predetermined thickness used between parts to establish a proper working relationship.

SLAVE CYLINDER: In automotive use, a device in the hydraulic clutch system which is activated by hydraulic force, disengaging the clutch.

SOLENOID: A coil used to produce a magnetic field, the effect of which is to produce work.

SPARK PLUG: A device screwed into the combustion chamber of a spark ignition engine. The basic construction is a conductive core inside of a ceramic insulator, mounted in an outer conductive base. An electrical charge from the spark plug wire travels along the conductive core and jumps a preset air gap to a grounding point or points at the end of the conductive base. The resultant spark ignites the fuel/air mixture in the combustion chamber.

SPLINES: Ridges machined or cast onto the outer diameter of a shaft or inner diameter of a bore to enable parts to mate without rotation.

TACHOMETER: A device used to measure the rotary speed of an engine, shaft, gear, etc., usually in rotations per minute.

THERMOSTAT: A valve, located in the cooling system of an engine, which is closed when cold and opens gradually in response to engine heating, controlling the temperature of the coolant and rate of coolant flow.

TOP DEAD CENTER (TDC): The point at which the piston reaches the top of its travel on the compression stroke.

TORQUE: The twisting force applied to an object.

TORQUE CONVERTER: A turbine used to transmit power from a driving member to a driven member via hydraulic action, providing changes in drive ratio and torque. In automotive use, it links the driveplate at the rear of the engine to the automatic transmission.

TRANSDUCER: A device used to change a force into an electrical signal.

TRANSISTOR: A semi-conductor component which can be actuated by a small voltage to perform an electrical switching function.

TUNE-UP: A regular maintenance function, usually associated with the replacement and adjustment of parts and components in the electrical and fuel systems of a vehicle for the purpose of attaining optimum performance.

TURBOCHARGER: An exhaust driven pump which compresses intake air and forces it into the combustion chambers at higher than atmospheric pressures. The increased air pressure allows more fuel to be burned and results in increased horsepower being produced.

VACUUM ADVANCE: A device which advances the ignition timing in response to increased engine vacuum.

VACUUM GAUGE: An instrument used to measure the presence of vacuum in a chamber.

VALVE: A device which control the pressure, direction of flow or rate of flow of a liquid or gas.

VALVE CLEARANCE: The measured gap between the end of the valve stem and the rocker arm, cam lobe or follower that activates the valve.

VISCOSITY: The rating of a liquid's internal resistance to flow.

VOLTMETER: An instrument used for measuring electrical force in units called volts. Voltmeters are always connected parallel with the circuit being tested.

WHEEL CYLINDER: Found in the automotive drum brake assembly, it is a device, actuated by hydraulic pressure, which, through internal pistons, pushes the brake shoes outward against the drums.

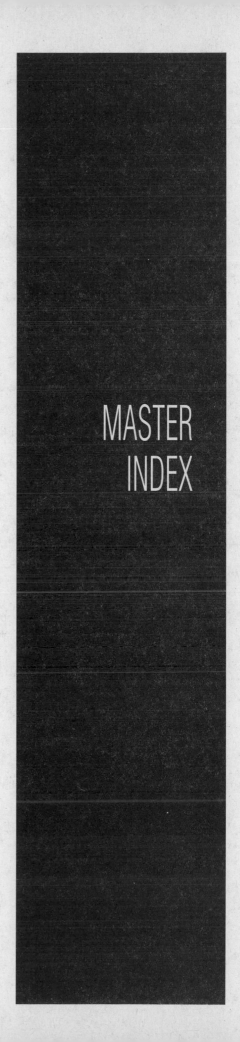

MASTER INDEX